Books by Frances Parkinson Keyes

ALL FLAGS FLYING

THE HERITAGE   DINNER AT ANTOINE'S

I, THE KING   CAME A CAVALIER

THE EXPLORER   ONCE ON ESPLANADE

TONGUES OF FIRE   THE RIVER ROAD

THREE WAYS OF LOVE   ALSO THE HILLS

THE RESTLESS LADY AND   CRESCENT CARNIVAL
OTHER STORIES   ALL THAT GLITTERS

A TREASURY OF FAVORITE POEMS   THE GRACE OF GUADALUPE

MADAME CASTEL'S LODGER   FIELDING'S FOLLY

THE ROSE AND THE LILY   THE SUBLIME SHEPHERDESS (Revised
   and reissued as)

THE CHESS PLAYERS

ROSES IN DECEMBER   BERNADETTE OF LOURDES

THE THIRD MYSTIC OF AVILA   ALONG A LITTLE WAY

FRANCES PARKINSON KEYES'   THE GREAT TRADITION
CHRISTMAS GIFT   PARTS UNKNOWN

MOTHER CABRINI: *Missionary to the*   CAPITAL KALEIDOSCOPE
World

WRITTEN IN HEAVEN (Revised and
STATION WAGON IN SPAIN   reissued as)

VICTORINE   THERESE: *Saint of a Little Way*

THE LAND OF STONES AND SAINTS   HONOR BRIGHT

BLUE CAMELLIA   THE HAPPY WANDERER

ST. ANNE: *Grandmother of*   SENATOR MARLOWE'S DAUGHTER
Our Saviour   THE SAFE BRIDGE

THE FRANCES PARKINSON KEYES   LADY BLANCHE FARM
COOKBOOK

SILVER SEAS AND GOLDEN CITIES

THE ROYAL BOX   QUEEN ANNE'S LACE

STEAMBOAT GOTHIC   LETTERS FROM A SENATOR'S WIFE

JOY STREET   THE CAREER OF DAVID NOBLE

THE COST OF A BEST SELLER   THE OLD GRAY HOMESTEAD

ALL THIS IS LOUISIANA

All Flags Flying

ALL FLAGS FLYING

Reminiscences of

FRANCES PARKINSON KEYES

McGraw-Hill Book Company

NEW YORK   ST. LOUIS   SAN FRANCISCO

DÜSSELDORF   MEXICO   TORONTO

Library of Congress Catalog Card Number: 70-38971

First Edition

07-034456-6

"Letters From a Senator's Wife" reprinted with the permission of *Good Housekeeping* Magazine.

Acknowledgments

THE ASSISTANCE of the following is gratefully acknowledged: Mr. Jules Abels for permission to quote from his book, *In the Time of Silent Cal;* Miss Katherine Andrews, Research Assistant to the Hon. Norris Cotton; Mrs. Charles Greer and the Hon. Robert Woodward, all of Washington, D.C.; Mrs. Richard B. Cobb, Miss Mary Hale and Mrs. Harry Wells of Newbury, Vermont; Mrs. George W. Davis of New Orleans; Mrs. Robert Edge and Mrs. Rene Mathey of Littleton, New Hampshire; Mrs. John M. Enochs of Lorton, Virginia; Mrs. Earl Greer of South Burlington, Vermont; Mrs. Emmet C. Gudger of Lake Mc-Donald, Montana; Mr. Kenneth Hale of North Attleboro, Massachusetts; Mrs. Hubert R. Harmon of San Antonio; Mrs. J. J. Hayes and Mrs. Raymond Worthen of St. Johnsbury, Vermont; Mrs. Jerry James of Rio de Janeiro; Mr. Herbert A. Kenney, Miss Virginia Wing and Miss Constance Worcester of Boston; Mrs. Edwin Graham Kintner of Bethesda, Maryland; Mrs. Roger I. Lee of Brookline, Massachusetts; Miss Nichola Malim of London, England; Mr. Liam Miller and Miss Maire Miller of Dublin, Ireland; Miss Sally M. Moffitt, Reference Assistant of the Alerman Library, University of Virginia; Mr. William I. Nichols of Paris, France; Frank J. Sulloway, Esq., of Concord, New Hampshire; Mrs. Rexford Tuttle of Scranton, Pennsylvania; and Mr. Linwood H. Warwick of Charlottesville, Virginia.

Some there be who have no memorial, and these we thank also, trusting they will forgive us for not mentioning their names, not because their help was not appreciated, but because we have no adequate record concerning them.

Permission of *Good Housekeeping* to use and quote from material in Mrs. Keyes's articles is gratefully acknowledged. The high standards of the magazine and kindness of its editor, William Frederick Bigelow, and other members of its staff are remembered vividly by the Keyes family.

For devotion above and beyond the call of duty, not merely in helping with the book but in all they have done for Mrs. Keyes in her life itself, recognition goes to Geraldine Elizabeth Bullock and Carroll Dan Fuller.

HWK

Foreword

FALSTAFF, pretending to be King Henry IV addressing Prince Hal, says: "That thou art my son, I have partly thy mother's word, partly my own opinion, but chiefly a villainous trick of thine eye and a foolish hanging of thy nether lip that doth warrant me." [1] Here are rather more of my mother's words than I might have desired. Few children are privileged to read such complete accounts of their conception. If any member of the Union Boat Club happens upon this book, I am likely to be reminded of some portions of the text. This is the last foreword of the first edition of a book by Frances Parkinson Keyes, and she cannot write it. She died July 3, 1970, leaving this book unfinished, but already too long for a normal volume. However, my brothers and I agreed that although some editorial cuts were necessary to reduce the total number of words to achieve a volume of publishable size, we could not fairly make any changes not required by normal cutting procedures or factual corrections. Mother is not here to defend her work and her opinions, and we have not substituted ours.

In a subtle way, Mother emerges as the heroine. She deserves the role. Nevertheless, some others she mentions appear to us to have lost some of the stature we think they deserve. We remember our mother's mother as the truly gracious hostess so often depicted in Frances Parkinson Keyes's fiction, so genuinely interested in other people that she gladly and truly entertained them. We remember our father's mother and the other senior members of the Keyes family as much more kind than one might gather from their conduct to the bride who invaded their stronghold.

---

[1] Henry IV, Part I, Act II, Scene IV, line 444

Above all, we think our father's fifty-year tenure of public office deserves recognition for what it was; a faithful and modest lifetime of genuine service to a constituency which fortunately appreciated him. Perhaps because he had been a fine oarsman and successful coach, he took a sporting view of politics. One summer when we were dreading the possibility of opposition which would mean further demands on our depleted treasury, I brought home a copy of the Manchester *Union* bearing the banner headline: "BLANDIN TO RUN AGAINST KEYES." I put it on top of his mail. He sat at his desk, glanced at the paper, opened his letters, and walked out doors without comment. At lunch, he remarked as usual on the weather—vital to the Farm, but not to the campaign. I could stand the suspense no longer.

"Dad," I said, "what about the piece in the paper that says Blandin is going to run?"

"Blandin?" he answered. "Blandin? Good friend of mine."

"But, Dad, he's running against you."

"Well, he can if he wants to. I don't own the office. That's the way the country's run."

As we recall the incident, his refusal to remove Spaulding or Moses as an opponent (p. 114) was active rather than passive and represented again a clear decision based on sportsmanship, even if, as Mother says, he wasn't thinking in terms of horses. He spent about eighteen years in Washington contributing more than his share of all kinds of beneficial legislation, much of it nonpartisan, and stuck to his convictions in matters he considered vital principles. Every flyer in the Navy in World War II was indirectly indebted to him, and there are bridges, parks and buildings in Washington which will long stand as memorials to him and those with whom he worked.

With these additions, we are content to let Mother speak for herself, as she could do with or without preparation, and in a manner which puzzled many a critic and captured many a hearer and reader. It is indeed likely, as one critic suggested, that a hundred other women could have written "Letters From a Senator's Wife," but nobody else did. It is well known that many do not use their gifts or seize their opportunities. As a member of a great orchestra once said of its supposedly great conductor: "He is a good musician, but he is lazy". Mother was not lazy —indeed there were times when we wished she were. Given a formal education which ceased at the secondary school level and confronted by a series of physical handicaps, she met a monthly deadline for readable articles in *Good Housekeeping* for many years, and thereafter brought her total output of all kinds of books to 50—this being the 51st.

Here for all to see are the telltale elements of an emotional life resulting from deprivation of a father's love and the frustrations of a male environment thrust upon the only daughter of a mother who was herself an only child. But here also one can glimpse a human being who made people understandable to each other and a mother who bridged the generation gap so successfully that we did not know it was there.

HENRY W. KEYES

Contents

Part One

Harry Keyes's Wife at Home
in the North Country

Chapter 1

As I look back over the years of which I have definite memories—
now nearly fourscore I realize that a pattern of existence seemingly as stable as it was smooth has been subject to sudden changes,
some sad, some gay, but all significant.

The first of these, though I was not aware of it then, took place at
The Oxbow, my mother's home near Newbury, Vermont, on the day of
my wedding to Harry Keyes. When I said good-bye to my Boston
bridesmaids—Marion Burdett, Helen Cutler, Marian and Grace Edmands—I knew that in a sense I was also saying good-bye to the Boston
which had been my winter home through my schooldays. But Helen,
who had been with me at Miss Winsor's School there, would soon be
marrying, too, and going to Chicago to live, so our days together would
have been over shortly in any case, and the rest had gone to different
schools. My other bridesmaids, Betty Chamberlain and Mary Kittredge,
I would continue to see frequently, since Betty lived in Newbury and
Mary often visited her aunt, who would be my next-door neighbor in
Haverhill, New Hampshire, just across the Connecticut River, where
my husband and I would be living. And it was unthinkable that distance
could ever separate me from my maid of honor Elizabeth Sweetser, for
she had meant more to me throughout my teens than almost anyone else
in the world. As she helped me shed my lace and tulle and orange blossoms and put on serviceable tweed, I was still happily close to her.
Really, I thought, marriage would not make much difference. I joined
my bridegroom at the head of the stairs and we went quickly down
them and sped through the front door of The Oxbow to our horse-
drawn bridal carriage, one of those light, open, four-wheeled vehicles
with rubber tires we then called runabouts.

(3)

Since I had carried a prayer book in church, I had no bouquet to throw and we were not delayed by clamor as to who should catch it and the general atmosphere was one of good cheer and affection as more confetti than rice was tossed in our direction as we ran. I had been horrified by tales of horseplay instigated by the Canadian cousins at other Keyes weddings and my earnest hope that there should be none at mine was fortunately fulfilled. A coachman had been standing guard by the runabout, so there had been no opportunity to attach noisy or conspicuous objects to it; and when Harry took the reins, we drove away with little more furor than if we had been starting for an afternoon's outing.

Actually we were going less than fifteen miles—only as far as the camp Harry had built himself. To ensure its complete privacy, he had bought all the land on one side of Lake Tarleton and had declined to permit the construction of a road leading to any part of this property. It could be approached only by a trail he had blazed through the woods or in the rowboat he kept moored on the opposite shore. He had made this woodland and lakeside retreat extremely attractive, for he had great talent along those lines. A few years earlier he had given a housewarming and included my mother and me among a score of guests. After that, he had frequently put the camp at my disposal for the entertainment of my house guests, and Elizabeth Sweetser, my bridesmaids and various other friends had stayed there with me several times, and on such occasions Harry had gone there as a visitor. At other times he had again been the host, but the groups invited had tended to grow smaller and eventually had dwindled to myself with my mother as chaperone. I had spent many happy days there, and now I was to have nearly three weeks at this camp—with no chaperone. Harry had offered me a wedding journey, but I knew there was no money to spare for one; and I also knew that the only kind of journey he really enjoyed was a hunting trip in the wilds of New Brunswick or some such place, and personally I could not imagine anything worse. Finally, I had been traveling abroad the greater part of a year and had come home feeling glad to be at my journey's end. When I asked Harry what he would think of spending our honeymoon quietly at the camp instead of in traveling, his enthusiastic response had betrayed his relief, and I had made the suggestion with no sense of deprivation or regret, but with a sense of pleasurable accord. I was going to a place I had always enjoyed, and my companion was a man I loved, with whom my friendship had long been happy and harmonious before it led to an engagement beset with difficulties, which had gradually been surmounted. My departure from The Oxbow seemed like the logical sequence to everything that had happened before. It was not until afterward that I recognized it as the first of the sudden and significant changes in an apparently fixed pattern.

I must acknowledge that the gently born girl of that era was apt to be very inadequately prepared for marriage, especially in a family of "comfortable circumstances." It was very seldom that the servant problem complicated a design for gracious living, and the *jeune fille de la maison* was not expected, and often not even allowed, to have a share in the household working schedule. Even if the family finances permitted the employment of only a general maid, it was taken for granted that this overburdened domestic should be able and willing to turn her hand to anything and everything. Though a carefully nurtured adolescent might make her own bed, do a little light dusting, arrange the flowers and sew a fine seam, she rarely strayed into the kitchen, except to make fudge on the maid's afternoon off (there were no *days* off then!), when practically everything had been left in readiness for the evening meal. The idea that a young lady was responsible for much more active participation in running a home seldom occurred to her until she was faced with the fact.

But it was not only in the domestic arts that the gently born girl of my generation was often ill prepared for marriage. She did not study biology, and the physiology textbooks which allegedly dealt with "the functions and vital processes of living organisms and their parts and organs" completely omitted the subject of sex in both text and illustrations. The word "sex" was never used, at least to my knowledge, in general conversation, and the taboo extended to related words. I had even been cautioned that bulls should not be mentioned. Reading material was carefully screened, and the most daring publishers of the day—for fear of landing in court—would not have ventured to print many things which are today accepted without qualm or question. Suitors were also carefully screened, and those who met with parental approval were still subject to an amount of supervision which seems almost incredible now. Until the week before my marriage, when the house became so full of guests that she felt there was safety in numbers, my mother always sat in the dining room at The Oxbow while I received my fiancé in the connecting library. She did not even consider the more comfortable parlor, because, though it also connected with the library, this was by a short passage with a door at either end instead of through only a single door! "A little talk" was supposed to be in order shortly before the ceremony, but the bride's mother was often so embarrassed at the idea of this that she said nothing enlightening or postponed the talk so long that there was no time for it after all. I assume that where consorts of kings and great noblemen were involved, the bride must have been warned that the sheets on her nuptial bed would be inspected the morning after the wedding in order to furnish proof, first, that she was a virgin when she retired and, second, that the marriage had been consummated. But such knowledge was far from general. Besides, many mothers felt very strongly that prenuptial revelations about the marriage relationship would sully a young girl's innocence and make her less desirable to "the right man." He, of course, took it for granted that she would be a virgin and would have felt justified in breaking the engagement at a suspicion that he might be mistaken, unless—as rarely happened—he himself was to blame; in this case, if he had any claims to being a gentleman, he usually felt duty bound to marry her, but quite free to reproach her after their marriage.

But in the eyes of most women, a mother's responsibility ended at the altar. She wanted to see her daughter suitably married, and by suitably she meant to a man with a good education, a good social position, a reasonably good reputation for sobriety and continence, and an ample income. If the applicant fulfilled these requirements, she did not want to risk doing anything that would jeopardize the match. The result of this reasoning was that a young girl's initiation into the full experience of love became a tremendous responsibility for the bridegroom, and if he failed in sensitivity, wisdom and understanding, a marriage might well be wrecked at the very outset.

My own shortcomings, both practical and emotional, were far too obvious almost from the moment I reached the camp; and I shall always be grateful that in those first crucial hours the man I married did not set my inadequacies down to my lack of an earnest, even an eager, desire to be a good wife in every sense of the word. He was not offended because I was bewildered and bemused now that everything was so different. He had known, better than I did, that I would suddenly find this difference strange and frightening. Also he recognized, before I was ready to admit it to myself, much less to him, that I was almost frantic with fatigue. I had long been under a severe strain and the antagonism between him and my mother, the wedding preparations, made under adverse circumstances, the houseful of guests, too little rest and too much excitement had increased this. I was deeply ashamed of my shattering exhaustion and did my best to fight against it. With great tact and tenderness my bridegroom convinced me that I had not failed him as a bride and that there was nothing disgraceful about exhaustion; under the circumstances it was the most normal thing in the world, and the best way to overcome it was to give in to it; he was going to insist that I must. However, he thought I would rally from it very quickly, and as soon as I had, he would effectually put an end to my sense of bafflement and insufficiency. He would have to do this as seemed best to him. Didn't I love him enough to let him have his way? It would make him very happy if he found I did.

Of course I wanted him to be happy and of course I loved him enough to let him do whatever he thought best, in his own way. After my glad affirmative, there was no further reference to his question. The time for "a little talk," which my mother had avoided, had passed, never to return, and this was no time for talk, either, beyond a few kindly but compelling directions, or for casual caresses which could lead nowhere. Only decisive action would put puzzlement and dread behind me, and my bridegroom was wise enough to take it. My much needed rest was neither interrupted nor cut short, but afterward there was no question as to what should happen. Harry put his arms around me and drew me close to him, encompassing me with his embrace. I knew I belonged there and suddenly was no longer afraid. I understood that this way, which was his way, was the best. He rent the last barrier between us so swiftly that the pain of its severance was only a prelude to the magnificent gift of union.

Possessed of this bounty, I no longer feared that I would not be capable of doing and being everything my husband wanted and required of me, and I was as overwhelmed with the conviction and joy of this as I had previously been overwhelmed with dismay and doubts. Besides, it was not only a question of what he desired and needed and the privilege I would have in meeting those desires and needs. Soon I was gladly conscious that I myself had desires and needs, of which I had not known before. Marriage was no longer a mystery, but a revelation.

Even the simplest workaday aspects of marriage became part of its enchantment. Every morning, while I was still half asleep, Harry left me to build and light the living room and kitchen fires. He easily convinced me that this was essentially his job: he knew just what kind of wood he wanted to use, since he had always selected and provided it for this and other camps, often felling the trees as well. By the time the fires were burning briskly, the savory smell of frying bacon had reached the bedroom; Harry had further convinced me that the preparation of this and his eggs was another thing he preferred to do himself, because he had been doing it for so many years on his hunting trips. There was no hurry, but I might as well get up to set the table and make coffee for myself and toast for both of us. After the first few mornings, I made biscuits too, as I had actually learned to do that in the month before my wedding. My biscuits were a great success, and Harry seemed as proud as if I had produced puff paste. Later, he even boasted to several of his friends about them.

After a leisurely breakfast we washed the dishes together, and then it was conceded that I should make our bed, sweep and dust before we rowed across the lake for the supplies left by prearrangement at a nearby farmhouse. Theoretically, dinner represented a joint effort, though my husband was really the chef and I was only his humble apprentice; but again I set the table and helped with the dishes. As I became more accustomed to them, these household tasks took much less time than they had at first; and I was never given a sense of inferiority because I did not do them more rapidly and skillfully, or made to feel that I was not doing my share.

The afternoons passed in a variety of pleasant ways. Sometimes we took a canoe ride and explored parts of the shoreline that were unfamiliar to me. Sometimes we went swimming; sometimes Harry, whose passion for "improving" things never left him even at such a time as this, worked on the grounds or in the boathouse. Daily outdoor exercise was as essential to him as reading was to me, and his physique was still as splendid as when he was captain of the Harvard crew. He was six feet tall and beautifully built, with wide sloping shoulders and narrow hips. His coloring was striking: ash-blond hair, very blue eyes, ruddy cheeks and, except where directly exposed to the weather, the whitest skin I had ever seen on any man. His teeth were very white too, and when he smiled you saw that they were strong and even; but though his expression was almost always uniformly pleasant, it was cheerful rather than jovial, and he would have considered the wide fixed grin of the present-day politician unnatural and undignified. When he came in after congenial physical labor, he did not look disheveled or dirty, nor did he seem tired. Instead, there was a sort of glow about him. He looked as if he wanted to share this sense of vigorous well-being with whoever had not been with him in the sun and air.

While Harry was working on the grounds, I continued the embroidery of monograms on my trousseau linen which had not been finished before my marriage. (What dozens and dozens of towels and sheets and pillow slips, tablecloths and napkins were then considered necessary for the well-equipped bride!) It was pleasant work but it was not exciting and every time Harry re-entered the living room after those outings he enjoyed so much, I quickened to his attractiveness and vitality. With an irresistible smile, he would say it was time we both stopped work for a while; besides, we had been separated long enough, it was time for us to be together again.

Our dinner had been hearty and late and we were seldom hungry at suppertime. So I was introduced to the custom, alien as far as I was concerned, of having whiskey and soda with crackers and cheese instead of a cooked meal; and though occasionally I substituted crackers and milk for myself, only two plates and two glasses were used, and these were rinsed and left to do with the breakfast dishes. Then came my only hard stint of the day: my husband insisted that all wedding presents for which I had not thanked the donors must be gratefully acknowledged before we left the camp; and since the wedding presents belonged to the bride, she must write these letters. This meant at least fourteen a day, but I agreed and settled down by the large lamp with a ruby-red shade, which we could see from a distance gleaming its welcome when we were out late and which made the living room radiant with its light. I wrote with good grace, except in one instance: my mother had given me fine old family silver—flat silver—as well as a great deal of jewelry and other valuables, but she had not given me a silver service; when this lack was made known, Harry's brothers had come forth with matching tea and coffee services which were very handsome, but which were marked with his initials! As a matter of fact, all members of the Keyes family had been extremely liberal in their wedding gifts: a baby grand piano, a supplementary set of flat silver, large, covered, silver vegetable dishes, huge silver vases and some very fine clocks had been among them. But to me the initials were their final gesture of defiance toward the match they had opposed from the beginning, and this gesture had hurt me out of all proportion to its importance, and far outweighed my appreciation for the value of the gift. Since it certainly had *not* been made to me, I contended that this was one present which definitely did not belong to the bride. We were closer to a quarrel than at any time for a long, long while and I still feel, after all these years, that I was right and that it was beneath my dignity to send a note of thanks to my brothers-in-law, considering the message they had so plainly sent me. But as I looked into my husband's face and saw its expression, I knew I had to choose between compliance on my part and anger on his. I could not bear to think of any rift in my newfound state of bliss. I wrote the letters to George and Charles Keyes.

The night I did so was one of those when I went for a second swim after finishing my stint—this time by myself, while Harry was banking the fires for the night and doing other small odd jobs which he considered peculiarly his province. I loved the freedom which our complete isolation gave me from the horrible bathing suit of the era. (I have never understood why many of us who wore it did not drown!) There was untold refreshment in the still cold waters at that hour and after my swim I went up to bed with a feeling of exquisite cleanliness.

The scrapbooks Harry had given me when I was fifteen had been kept up-to-date until the time of my wedding; but by then they were full, and though I haphazardly assembled a good deal of material for new ones, I did not resume routine clipping and pasting until some years later. The only contemporary record I kept during the early years of my marriage is in a *Line-A-Day* book, each of its pages evenly divided in fifths. It is described as "A Condensed Comparative Record For Five Years" on its title page, which also carries the injunction, in Latin, "No Day Without a Line." The entry for June 8, 1904, reads: "Wedding day. Married to Harry in Congregational Church. Reception at home. Left at two for camp."

After that, for a space of nearly three weeks, most notations read simply, "At camp." Since I well remember how that period was spent, I really do not need a detailed record, but there are a few illuminating exceptions to that brief entry:

June 12. At camp. Hamper from the Keyeses.

This was left for us at the farmhouse across the lake and was, no doubt, very welcome, after we had been doing all our own cooking since the eighth!

June 17. The Keyeses came out with a hamper of food.

This was not so welcome, at least as far as I was concerned, for they had found someone to row them across the lake and arrived unannounced at the camp. It might well have been an awkward moment for all concerned since, presumably safe from intrusion, lovemaking was not limited to our bedroom at night. However, the family was suitably received in the living room, though Gertrude Baker, Harry's nine-year-old niece whom he adored, after much whispering and giggling soon disappeared, obviously with the consent of her elders. When she returned, she was giggling harder than ever. I was suspicious of what she might have done, for I knew I had not been pardoned for trying to prevent the members of my new family from indulging in horseplay at the wedding. My suspicions were confirmed when I found that the child had torn my neatly spread sheets apart to make an apple-pie bed and had filled it with rice. I disposed of the rice and remade the bed, seething with rage and disgust. To this day, I have not been able to fathom why Harry's family, the most strait laced and prudish I have ever known, considered any vulgar prank played on the newly married quite permissible.

There was another visit, equally unwelcome as far as I was concerned. Three of Harry's friends from Woodsville, a precinct in the Town of Haverhill, who jointly owned a cottage on the other side of the lake, rowed over to the camp one afternoon. They stayed quite a long while and consumed a good deal of whiskey and soda. Though I did not dislike them, I felt their call was an intrusion under the circumstances and another which might well have been awkward! But I was thankful I had not voiced my feelings about this when Harry exclaimed, after their departure, "It did seem good to see some men again!"

June 20. Mother came out with Anne and a hamper of good things.
Anne cooked the supper and washed the dishes.

So that night there *was* a real supper, not just "something left over from dinner," as I later heard Harry define our customary snacks to his family. Though I would have been just as happy without my mother's visit, I did not resent it because it was prearranged and her maid Anne was not only capable, but unobtrusive.

June 23. Scrubbed half the living room floor.

Those were the days when bare floors, if unpolished, were regularly scrubbed, and though it had not been suggested that I should do this at the camp, I visualized it as the proper gesture and went to work on it with a will, instead of embroidering, one of the days when Harry was working at the boathouse. As I had never done anything of the sort before, I did not do it very efficiently, but I was commended for the effort.

June 24. Beautiful drive to Warren during afternoon and evening.
Scrubbed floors. Hampers from Mother and the Keyeses.

Evidently, the horse and runabout with which we had come to the lake were kept at the farm across from the camp while we were there; and evidently, having started to scrub the floor, I was determined to finish.

June 25. Swim, two paddles, one to 11 P.M. Perfect moonlight.

The thank-you notes were all written at last, so there was no stint to keep me indoors or force an early return to the camp; and the moonlight invited strolls ashore, because the transfigured trees sometimes parted to disclose shaded retreats and one such secret bower seemed made for lovers. It had never occurred to me before that a forest could give such privacy or that it could be used to such advantage. Indeed, I was lying comfortably relaxed, without conscious thought of any kind, when I saw that Harry was bending over me with a smile which I had come to recognize as a demand. There was something as primitive as imperative about his requirement; we were both in Biblical times again, when a man "went in unto his wife" simply and instinctively and she accepted his presence in her body without preamble as a matter of course. Instantly he had me in his arms and, without speaking a word, "entered in unto me." The memory of the long and passionate embrace that followed is one of the most hauntingly beautiful of my life, not only because of its own intensity but because it marked the discovery that it is not only in romantic fiction that "forest lovers" have a special endowment and a special reward.

June 26. Perfect day and night. Full moon and gentle breeze.

We returned to that same secret bower of beauty we had discovered the night before, and now it seemed even more permeated with magic. Hours passed before we could bring ourselves to leave it, because we had lost all consciousness of time as again we lay in each other's arms. Our only consciousness was in each other.

June 27. Came in from the camp. Heartbroken to leave.

I know that when I wrote those words I was suffering from real heartbreak. The stay at the camp had been more than an idyllic interlude; it had been a period of discovery and awakening and fulfillment. It had marked the end of troubled girlhood and the beginning of vitalized womanhood. I had gone there a bewildered bride and had learned it required only self-surrender to transform me into a wife who was radiant with happiness herself and whose husband felt and showed that his possession of her represented to him a victory in more ways than one. He had persevered against the opposition of his entire family and finally married the girl he had wanted ever since she had been fifteen years old. I was beginning to realize that my mother had been right when she said my immaturity was part of my charm for him, though his family considered it one of my main drawbacks (another was their dislike of my mother which Harry shared); and that, far from being disappointed in me as a bride, he had been relieved and gratified to find I was still the personification of innocence he had visualized and that it would be his undisputed privilege to teach me the facts of life by the most potent and direct method. There is no doubt that he exulted in having done this. He spoke of it often afterward and always as if it were the kind of primitive conquest which he had most desired. He emphasized more than once that the word "obey" in the marriage service had a very special meaning and that he would not hesitate to make me keep that part of my vow. He did not say this unkindly, but he left me in no doubt that his method of doing so would be just as direct and drastic as his method of putting an end to my bridal bewilderment. Fortunately for us both, far from resenting the dominance which meant so much to him, I had accepted it from the beginning as his right and, very soon, as a source of mutual joy. He could, and did, draw endlessly on the ardor he had awakened and find it boundless. I knew that I assuaged and delighted him and that he took personal pride, as well he might, in my transformation.

But now that he had achieved his conquest, now that I was wholly his, he had nothing more to strive for and might well be satisfied with fewer proofs of devotion than I would be only too glad to give him. I did not need to be told by a poet that love is in man's life a thing apart, while it is woman's whole existence. I would have found that out the day my husband welcomed to the camp the male visitors whom I regarded as intruders even if I had not realized it before. And now he must return to his political duties at the state capitol. He needed the additional twenty-five hundred a year this work provided, since his annual salary as president of the Woodsville Bank was only five hundred, and Pine Grove Farm, the family property in Haverhill, was barely breaking even, while the paper mill in Pepperell which Harry owned in partnership with his two brothers was not doing much more. The Keyes family managed to give an impression of wealth and one of the ways they achieved this was by jointly contributing to the maintenance of the same house, both in Boston and at the Farm, and this pooling of resources made them go further. Their credit was good and it did not trouble them to use it freely. It was not generally known that the assets of my husband's father, the first Henry Keyes and a prominent railroad pioneer, who had left his widow very comfortably situated, had been greatly reduced, partly by poor investments after his death and partly by the reorganization of the Atchison, Topeka & Santa Fe, of which he had briefly been president. Harry had told my mother, when we became engaged, that he thought he could count on five thousand a year, but actually he was hard put to meet that figure.

Besides their financial considerations, the duties in Concord were important and interesting in themselves and seemed to promise even more important and interesting prospects. He had twice represented the Town of Haverhill in the State Legislature (in New Hampshire called the General Court), and two years before our marriage had been elected to the State Senate, an office he still held. When the Legislature established a State Excise Commission to administer a new "local option" liquor law, the governor had shown his confidence in Harry's ability and integrity by appointing him to this commission. He had found his service, first as its treasurer and now as its chairman, a source of satisfaction and did not seem averse to the amount of time he was obliged to spend in performing it, even though it meant he was absent from home at least three days every week. Meanwhile, I must be an unwilling and unwanted resident at Pine Grove Farm, where a huge red brick house had been built after the original homestead, a fine old colonial dwelling, burned.

Why they did not build a facsimile of this, with a few additional conveniences, I never understood; it would have been characteristic of the North Country, adequate for all reasonable needs and comparatively inexpensive to run. Instead, they engaged Herbert D. Hale, son of the famous Edward Everett Hale and himself a well-known architect, to design a replacement for it. He was a great friend of Harry's who undertook to save the cost of a contractor by doing all the supervising personally, and the result of their joint efforts was a mammoth pillared house, shaped like a gigantic H, with the entrance at the center of the long hall constituting the cross section. In the arm at the left were situated the living room and the "morning room." The arm at the right contained the dining room and Harry's office, called the den according to the custom of the times; this had a separate side entrance, so that farm employes and business visitors could reach him without coming through the front door. Beyond the H stretched a wing embracing a butler's pantry, a kitchen pantry, a kitchen and a servants' dining room; the laundry was in the basement; on the second story were ten bedrooms, three baths, a very large linen closet, innumerable other closets and a storeroom; on the third, four more bedrooms, a playroom and two spacious attics. There were eight fireplaces, two large piazzas, one smaller piazza, two porches and a porte-cochere. The house had been built for the now almost unbelievably small sum of $12,000. I have been told that at present costs it could not be duplicated for $150,000. Though it belonged to all the family, and Harry and I were to live there the year round, the house had been designed primarily as a summer residence for my mother-in-law and her entourage: her unmarried daughter, Belle; her only grandchild, Gertrude Baker, the daughter of Harry's dead sister; her Swedish cook, laundress and chambermaid; Gertrude's German governess; and an English coachman. It was not an easy picture for me to fit into and _I_ had no work. Love had literally become my whole existence.

There was only one thought which, on the day of heartbreak when I left the camp, gave me courage. Perhaps I would not be alone very long. Surely in the course of that "perfect day and night" if not before, I must have been given a child. I had previously considered only what love itself meant to me, then and there, and not its possible consequences; there had been no room, in either my heart or my mind, for anything else. I have always been glad of this; I cannot help feeling that something has been lost, never to be recaptured, if the first weeks of marriage are complicated by reservations or intrusions of thoughts or acts that are not primarily concerned with the bride and bridegroom themselves. But now that my honeymoon was over and I instinctively knew there would never be another experience comparable to it anywhere, anytime, I wanted the memory of it with me in tangible and visible form.

Chapter 2

BUT it was not until several weeks later that I was assured of this, and then in a most unromantic way.

It was an extremely hot summer, and though I had always enjoyed warm weather, it did not now seem to agree with me as well as usual. I thought this was largely because I had to get up in the morning before I had had my sleep out; that might well be why I felt so tired, especially as these early hours made the day so long. Ezra Henry Baker, the widower of Harry's sister Gertrude, came to the Farm every week to spend Sunday with their little daughter, who had been named for her mother and who lived with her Grandmother Keyes. He returned to Boston every Monday on a train that left North Haverhill at six-thirty in the morning, and Harry took the same train when he went to Concord, which was generally on a Tuesday. So on those mornings breakfast was served a little before six. It was a three-course breakfast—fruit, cereal, bacon and eggs, toast, hot rolls and coffee—as against a four-course meal on the other days. Then breakfast was not until seven and doughnuts or pancakes with maple syrup supplemented the steak and potatoes, which replaced bacon and eggs—except on Sundays, when fish balls, brown bread and baked beans were always the substitute. All this hearty food was served by a waitress wearing a starched white cap and a starched white apron over a starched percale uniform, at a table spread with a spotless white linen cloth and set with heavy silver and fragile china. The entire family, fully and formally clothed, sat around the table. The ladies wore high-necked dresses with boned net collars that reached almost to their ears, and their long hair was carefully arranged on top of their heads. My mother-in-law, who had been a widow for thirty-five years, had never discarded her mourning; and though her summer dresses were made of cotton, they looked as heavy as wool. The men were always freshly shaven and always appeared at table wearing stiff collars and were never tieless or coatless even on the hottest days.

Everything about this meal was depressing to me: the hour, which seemed to me ungodly; the amount of food, which seemed no less so; the crackle of the maid's uniform; the sight of the little serpentine supports that kept the net collars in place; the somber tone set by my mother-in-law's deep black. I wanted to sleep until I woke up naturally, which meant not earlier than eight and often not until nine, and then I wanted a cup of coffee and a roll before I dressed or did my hair; and I wanted them in silence and seclusion, unless I could have a *solitude à deux* with Harry.

So I blamed my malaise on the Keyes family breakfasts rather than on the heat—and, I think, with some reason. But it certainly was very hot, and I had very little to take my mind off the weather. While Harry was away, I spent most of the time at my mother's house, where I could sleep as late as I wanted and where I took pride in surveying the garden and reflecting how superior it was to the one at the Farm. At The Oxbow, the garden sloped beyond the summerhouse on the south lawn and had a wide central flower-bordered stretch of grass between its rows of succulent vegetables. We always had fresh peas to go with salmon on the Fourth of July whether anyone else in Newbury had them or not— and usually they did not. We also had the first corn, the first butter beans and the first Brussels sprouts. We had a melon patch, a strawberry bed and an asparagus bed that was nearly one hundred years old and still richly productive. From the time the parsnips assured the arrival of spring, until the pumpkins heralded autumn, this garden provided luxuriantly for our table; and though it could not boast quite such an abundance of flowers, there were always plenty to decorate the house: peonies in the spring, asters in the fall and nasturtiums, sweet peas, petunias, Johnny-jump-ups, candytuft, moss roses and sweet Williams in between. Besides all these, there were the lilacs which bloomed in both front and back yards, lilies of the valley nestling on either side of the front door, beds of iris and hedges of tiger lilies and bittersweet bordering the lawns and tall-growing phlox and golden glow by the stable.

I had long taken all this productiveness and florescence for granted; now I really appreciated it. Except for their inexhaustible supply of sweet peas, the Keyeses had nothing to compare with any of it. Both their vegetable garden and their flower garden were less advantageously and attractively located than ours; they had no southern slope and they did not adjoin the lawn, but were in a flat expanse out near the fields. If I had been by nature a rabid gardener, I would have been excited to action by the challenge they presented, instead of being content to compare them, to their disadvantage, with my mother's. But as Evalyn Walsh McLean was to say years later, "I was not really a gardening sort of lady." As a girl, I had loved ranging through the woods searching for trailing arbutus and gathering violets and black-eyed Susans in the meadow, but when it came to garden flowers, I liked best merely to look at them while they were growing and to arrange them in vases when they were brought into the house.

My tastes in this direction had not changed now that I was married, so floral activities did not use up many hours out of the twenty-four and after I had packed my trousseau and wedding presents and taken them to my new home, I did not find much more to do at The Oxbow than I had at the Farm. My mother had had practically all the company she wanted for that summer at the time of the wedding, and she kept telling me how greatly it had tired her and how expensive it had been; from now on, she proposed to have only an occasional guest; it was necessary that she should rest and economize. It was not polite to remind her that she had planned the wedding to suit herself, and I decided she was probably feeling the heat too and that I must not be a burden to her.

When Harry was home, he was very much preoccupied with all the mail that had piled up while he was gone and with the endless matters that needed his attention on the Farm, at the bank and in the township. Townships, or towns, as they are generally called in New England, are locally governed by a board of three, called Selectmen, who are elected at Town Meetings. Harry had been a Selectman in the Town of Haverhill ever since he was graduated from Harvard and took the responsibilities of this position very seriously. The Farm was one of a thousand acres, more than two hundred under cultivation and the rest in woodland. Forestry did not need much attention at that time of year, but we were then at the height of the haying season. Work began at four in the morning and lasted as long as daylight; and there were extra hired men on hand for it, some less sober and industrious than the regular employes and therefore requiring more supervision. There were also over a hundred head of cattle. John Roorda, the wonderful Dutch herdsman who had come home with Harry nearly twenty years earlier, took competent charge of these, but they were Harry's special pride and joy. He had been one of the first importers of purebred Holstein-Friesians into this country. Not a day passed, when he was at home, that he did not go out to see the calves fed and make sure all was well with them; and there was a small office in one of the barns where the herd books were kept and where he and John Roorda conferred on questions of breeding and kept watch over maternity cases. In addition to all this, Harry was concerned lest the heat should kill all the shrubs and plants and flowers he had set out with such tender care around the house, and every evening after supper he watered these until it was too dark to see.

I really enjoyed visiting the calves with Harry, which was the only thing we did together on the Farm. I also enjoyed watching the reaping, which was still done with scythes: the long line of men moved in perfect unison the width of a great field of hay and, almost as if by magic, the tall upstanding grass lay flat and sweet smelling on the ground. The whole process was exciting to me. I could watch it from the rear piazza, where the Keyes ladies were accustomed to sit for hours every day, but they did not go for hayrides or romp in the hay after it had been put in the barns, and I found I was too young for the abandonment of these pleasures without regret. The hours on the piazza dragged for me.

I asked if I could not take charge of weeding the pansy beds and arranging the flowers afterward so that I might have some share in the gardening and household decoration. But it seemed that I did not do either the weeding or the arranging in the right way, so I gave up both. Once in a while Harry took me with him in the runabout; but most of his drives had a practical objective and it was tedious to sit in the heat outside the bank or someone else's barn while he was busy inside. There was no horse at the Farm which he considered safe for me to drive myself—though I rode horseback well, I had never been a good driver; and he did not regard a mere pleasure drive as a normal part of the day's activities the way my mother did, though there was a fine pair of horses in the stable and a comfortable carriage for my mother-in-law's use and she was driven by her coachman whenever she felt like it, which was only once a week or so. (As a young woman, she had been very beautiful; but she had never been mentally active, and now that she was no longer physically active, she had grown very heavy and avoided even the slight effort of changing her clothes or leaving the house. What she really liked to do was to help Belle separate the pink sweet peas from the purple ones and transfer them to vases from the milk pans in which they had been brought to the house early in the morning. The rest of the day she wished to devote to embroidery, which she did exquisitely and so extensively that it was almost impossible to find a smooth surface on which to rest your head if it ached and you wanted to lie down.) I spoke of resuming horseback rides and found that Harry had sold Tanglefoot, the mount he had bought when I was fifteen so we could ride together; and neither he nor my mother approved the transfer from The Oxbow to Pine Grove Farm of Kaweah, the old Kentucky

Thoroughbred that had belonged to my half brother James. Later on, Harry said, he hoped he could get us both new saddle horses, but not now. Again, it was a question of expense.

He had replied to his sister's urgent offer to install twin beds in his room with a decisive negative, so I could still go to sleep in his arms. But there was never the same sense of detachment from the rest of the world that there had been at camp. Indeed, more than once Belle came knocking at the door of our room, after we were in bed, on errands so trivial that it almost seemed as if she had purposely intruded on our precious privacy, but perhaps I do her an injustice.

On the twenty-first of July I was nineteen, but my birthday came and went without the usual festivity. I would have been proud to invite all the Newbury friends who had celebrated such occasions with me so many years and they would have been delighted to come to the Farm. But it was not suggested, and I had learned by then that the Keyes family took company very seriously. Since they had moved from Newbury to Pine Grove Farm—which was long before my day—they apparently preferred not to keep in close touch with most of their former neighbors. I felt there might be a certain awkwardness in trying to bring about a rapprochement.

I further realized it had been a mistake to enclose in the wedding invitations a card stating I would be "At Home" Thursday afternoons during August. I knew that Alma, my mother-in-law's peerless cook, would not fail to provide elegant and plentiful refreshments, and these would be impeccably served by Hilda, the waitress with the crackling uniform. But these "At Homes" would be much more formal in character than anything that was generally undertaken in the locality, and before I recognized the Keyeses' general attitude about company, I had invited some of my friends—none of them as yet out of their teens—to assist on these occasions and remain afterward for supper or overnight, depending on how great a distance they had come. Since my immaturity was so irksome to my family-in-law, I had every reason to believe that theirs would be also.

What was even worse, I knew my mother would take it for granted that she should come to all the "At Homes" and that she would be entitled to bring with her those "occasional guests" who happened to be staying at The Oxbow, and these proved to be more numerous than I had foreseen, with a new admirer among them. Until Harry's announcement that he wanted to marry me had hit his family like a bombshell, relations between The Oxbow and Pine Grove Farm in the summer and Commonwealth Avenue and Beacon Street in the winter had been marked by scrupulous courtesy and rare hospitality. Even as a little girl,

I had ridden my pony across the river to the Farm whenever I felt like it; when the fine old homestead caught fire, I had galloped through the valley seeking help; and many other episodes had confirmed my impression that I would always be made welcome by the Keyeses. But this was before I had been visualized as a possible bride for the eldest son, and my mother's divorce had precluded any close connection with her or her daughter as far as they were concerned. It was also before my mother had committed the crowning indiscretion, in their eyes, of countenancing further suitors, often men much younger than herself. She was still a very elegant and handsome woman, and most persons found her charming. It never occurred to the Keyeses that though she had approved Harry's suit in the beginning, she had so deeply resented their discourtesy in declining to welcome me as his fiancée that she too considered she had a grievance. She had done her best to make me break the engagement and honestly felt she was in a better position to condescend than they were.

I knew that very often the infatuation of her juvenile admirers took her entirely by surprise—there had even been one case when a youth fell in love with her voice before he saw her, and had made a nuisance of himself for several years. But there were also cases when she did nothing to discourage these unsuitable attentions and when her conversation was even more indiscreet than her actions. It was these aspects of her personality that obscured all others in the minds of the Keyeses, and for which I suffered the brunt of their unconcealed disapproval.

Their estrangement from Newbury acquaintances did not include their cousins, Mr. and Mrs. Thomas Keyes and Miss Hattie Keyes, who had large houses across the street from each other in the village. Miss Hattie was an austere, deeply religious woman, with a special penchant for foreign missions, who was much respected in Newbury, and she was also the only member of Harry's family who had shown me any sign of affection. Though I had known her all my life, I had stood somewhat in awe of her until we met one day shortly before the wedding and she greeted me with a cordial kiss and exclaimed, "So you are going to be my little cousin now!" She did not wait for one of those dreadful days "At Home," but came to the Farm to call one afternoon when all the family except Harry was gathered in the living room. "Cousin Hattie" drew me down beside her and asked if I were minding the heat.

"Yes," I said, "I'm ashamed to say I am, especially mornings. It's actually making me sick."

I could not imagine why a sudden hush fell on the group or why everybody then began to talk at once about matters which had nothing to do with the weather. I knew something was wrong and it troubled and puzzled me. As soon as Cousin Hattie had gone, I went out on the piazza for a few minutes before I went upstairs to change for supper, hoping that a breath of air would make me feel better. When, eventually, I reached the upper landing, I saw that Mrs. Keyes and Belle were standing near the door to Belle's room whispering. Then I was surer than ever something was wrong; whispering in that family always boded ill for me.

"Come here a minute, Fran*cese*," Belle said. No one else pronounced my name that way, but she often did. I walked over to her and her mother, inwardly quaking and feeling very sick indeed.

"Don't you *know* what is the matter with you?" Belle asked severely. I shook my head, and she and her mother exchanged glances.

"Hasn't anyone ever told you what it probably means when a young married woman feels sick in the morning?"

"No," I said, wondering if this were something else which should have been included in the "little talk" that had not taken place. "What *does* it mean?"

"I'm very much afraid it means you are going to have a baby."

I stared at her for a moment and then, quite involuntarily, I laughed. There was certainly nothing funny about the nausea and I did not mean to be rude. Besides, I was really sorry that I had embarrassed them. But I was so overjoyed to learn that I had not been mistaken in believing a child had been conceived while I was at the camp that the laugh became a natural part of my answer. "You're *afraid?*" I asked. "Shouldn't you be glad that someone in the Keyes family can have a baby?"

It was a home thrust. George and Emily Keyes had been married for two years and there was still no prospect of a child. Gertrude's mother was dead, my mother-in-law was seventy years old, Belle and Charlie were both past middle age and still unmarried. There were no children at either of the Keyes houses in Newbury. I knew it was whispered around that a fine old family was dying out. As far back as anyone could remember, though there were often sisters, there had always been three brothers in every generation, in each branch of the family, and now it seemed there was danger that the name might become extinct.

Seemed! But there wasn't really, since I had married into the family. I think I was the proudest girl in the North Country that day.

The most immediate result of the scene in the upper hallway was my independent decision that there was no good reason why I should endure those grim breakfasts any longer. The next morning I paid no attention to the great gong in the lower hall when it resounded through the house; when Belle, who could not resist the opportunity to come

knocking at my door, asked if I did not feel able to get up, I told her
that I did not, just then; if I felt better later in the day, I would go over
to my mother's and stay until Harry could come and fetch me.

That proved to be several days later, and meanwhile, I slept and slept
and spent my waking hours lightly and informally dressed, looking at
beautiful baby clothes that had long been stored away. There was the
first dress my mother had ever worn, which had been worn by her
mother and her grandmother before her and in which James, who was
fifteen years my senior, and I had both been clad for the first time. It
was exquisitely embroidered and in perfect condition still; of course it
must be the first dress *my* baby wore. Then there were all the clothes
that had been fashioned in Paris for James; the christening robe that
had been entirely of lace and had cost two hundred dollars when it was
bought—now it was worth much more—and five other dresses that
were only slightly less elaborate and valuable, plus a dozen more of the
finest lawn which my mother called nightdresses, though they were by
no means simply cut or unadorned either; and there were fragile, beribboned bonnets and soft Cashmere shawls. My mother gave them all to
me and I spread them out where I could look at them whenever I liked
and contentedly went to sleep again.

Until that visit I had always returned to the Farm so that I would be
there to welcome Harry when he came home from Concord, but this
time I did what I had told Belle I would do: I waited at The Oxbow for
Harry to come and get me. He arrived unannounced and sooner than I
had expected. I suspected that Belle might have telephoned him, suggesting that if he could, it would be a good idea for him to cut short his
stay in Concord; but at least she had not told him the news I was eagerly waiting to give him myself. His pride and pleasure more than
made up for her unfortunate remark that she was "afraid" I was going
to have a baby. It had been as much his hope as mine that we should
not have to worry about the possibility of never having one, and it had
never occurred to either of us that there could be any reason to welcome a delay. He was sorry I did not feel well, but after all, the unpleasant symptoms would probably not last long and I would soon forget all about them.

This cheerful statement was slightly more optimistic than the
situation warranted, and I think Harry realized this, for he wrote me
faithfully every day we were separated, urging me not to overdo. "Remember you must not only take care of yourself, we have our own little
family to think of now." He also managed to find more opportunities to
be with me when he was home than he had in the first weeks at the
Farm, as the *Line-A-Day* book testifies:

Went over to the Spooner place with Harry.... Drove to Haverhill
with Harry—tagged trees.... Took a paddle down the river with
Harry.... Went out to camp with Harry—perfect day.

Food continued to repel me, but I did no more early morning rising,
which helped a good deal. Otherwise, I was up and around most of the
time. I went regularly to church and to visit my mother, occasionally to
supper with my Newbury friends and even to one lawn party. I did my
best to be an adequate hostess on my days "At Home"; my worst fears
in regard to my mother and her latest admirer were realized, but fortunately, one of my school friends who came to assist not only proved acceptable to the Keyes family but actually made a great hit. This was
Theresa Helburn, who later was to become a mainstay of the Theatre
Guild.

When the time came for Mrs. Keyes and her entourage to leave (with
fourteen trunks and twice that many bags and bundles), I agreed to visit
employment agencies in Boston and try to engage servants myself. It
does not seem to have occurred to any of my elders that adequate domestic help might have been secured nearer home with less time, expense and trouble; both my mother and my sister-in-law (who relieved
her mother of all household cares) depended on Boston. It was necessary for Harry to be in Concord longer than usual just then, and since
this was the case, I actually welcomed the chance of making my headquarters for a few days with my dear aunt Fannie in North Woburn, a
Boston suburb, before spending a few more with friends who had pleasant summer places on Buzzards Bay. I was delighted to see them all
again, and during daytime trips to Boston I managed, with much trepidation, to engage a harried-looking couple whom I then shepherded to
the Farm. They seemed very doubtful whether or not they could give
satisfaction, which, interpreted, meant whether we could! However,
their attitude did not depress me; it was very exciting to be warmly welcomed back by Harry, who had sped the family on its way back to Boston and was obviously as glad to have me to himself as I was to have
him to myself. It was almost like being at the camp again, and there
was no concern lest anyone should come knocking on our door at night.
We had missed each other intensely, and this reunion was unrestrained
in its joyousness. Never had I been so eager for the full experience of
love, never had I so rejoiced in the prodigality with which it was offered me. If there ever was a time for love, it was now, or so it seemed
to me.

But afterward I was ill, really ill, not just sick in the mornings, and
my mother hurried to me, saying she had been afraid this would hap-

pen. A doctor was summoned, a trained nurse was hastily installed, and the newly acquired household help promptly left. It was not until I realized that Harry no longer looked happy that I knew he feared we were not going to have a baby after all. But I was sure we would. And I was right: at the end of a fortnight, all danger for the baby was past and I was allowed to sit up for a little while. In the meantime Belle, with her usual efficiency in household matters, had found us another couple. There was no question, this time, that they were experienced; but almost at the moment of their arrival, they burst into recriminations: they had supposed they were coming to a *cottage* and this was a *mansion*. It was *inexplicable* how anyone had *imagined* that two persons could do the work in such an *enormous* place. Harry tactfully calmed them: perhaps they had a friend who would like to join them? Surprisingly, they did; they would send for her right away. Until she got there, they would manage the best they could.

The best that Ida (the cook) and Charles (the coachmen) could do was very good indeed; and what Agnes (the friend who became the parlormaid) could do was even better. In fact, I cannot think of anything she was supposed to do that she did not do to perfection. Never since her day have I seen each fork and spoon, as it was dried, laid separately on a clean linen cloth before it was carefully replaced in its chest; never since then have I seen glassware and china so scrupulously washed in sequence—on no account at the same time—similarly rinsed and finally dried on an immaculate towel that was never used twice without laundering. Her cleaning, her bedmaking, her table service all had the same superlative quality; she herself was not only pretty but impeccably neat (without crackling). That Charles and Ida, who had each other and who were past middle age, should be content at a country place where they had no distractions did not seem too unnatural; that Agnes, who could not have been much older than I was, should be equally content without a beau seemed almost too good to be true.

Although I still was not strong enough to have the typical large family party on Thanksgiving, we made a festive occasion of it, with all the best china, silver and linen, and I wrote the little verses to go on place cards which have always represented almost my only parlor trick. Harry's was illustrated with a small picture of some of our own Holsteins and pleased him so much that he carefully kept it. I found it not long ago among trifles which to him apparently represented numerous treasure.

THE COW

Behold! The gentle, patient cow,
Who never speaks, but muses much.

We couldn't do without her now,
But then, our cows do beat the Dutch.

She sleeps, and chews her cud, and goes
Into her pasture green, and back,
And what she thinks about, she shows
Distinct and plain in white and black.
Thanksgiving, 1904.

In early December, I went to Boston again, but this time I stayed at my mother-in-law's big house at 88 Commonwealth Avenue (generally referred to simply as 88) under the watchful eyes of her and my sister-in-law, and there was no chance of overdoing. My great friend Helen Cutler was to be married late in January, and though it was obvious I would not be in presentable condition by then to attend the wedding, I did spend a day with her and saw her elaborate trousseau. I also spent a day with Elizabeth Sweetser, the friend I loved best of all, whose father was gravely ill. Naturally, I found her very sad and was saddened myself; so I was allowed to make no more personal visits, as sadness was supposed to be bad for me. I was, however, permitted to go to the theater, though *Romeo and Juliet,* in which Sothern and Marlowe were playing and which I especially wanted to see, was vetoed because of its probable depressing effect; a play entitled *The Harvester,* in which Otis Skinner starred, was chosen instead. I returned from this spectacle to report that the last act had been devoted to the hero's slow death following a stroke, and before this occurred he had fathered an illegitimate child in a household where he had been given shelter. Since I had suffered no ill effects from this type of entertainment, I doubted that *Romeo and Juliet* would harm me, as I was prepared for the outcome, having studied the play in school and having seen it several times already. I won my point.

Though there were no more social calls, Harry and I made a professional call on his old friend John W. Bartol, then one of the leading obstetricians in Boston. When my engagement was announced, he had written me a touching letter and he had been an usher at our wedding; I felt that I knew him pleasantly already, and his reception of us in the luxurious study of his fine old house on Chestnut Street was, after all, almost wholly social in character. Harry told him, conversationally, that I was expecting a baby and that it would mean a great deal to us both if he would accept the case. Just as conversationally, Dr. Bartol said he would be delighted to do so, made a casual note of the probable date when the confinement would take place and suggested engaging a nurse who would come to Pine Grove Farm at least a week before that. Well, the matter of a nurse had already received attention, Harry said: a friend of his sister's had just had a baby and Belle thought her nurse, a Canadian by the name of Miss McLeod, the best one she had ever seen, so she had engaged her at once for me. This was the first I had heard of it, and I was slightly aggrieved because I had not been consulted; and I had a suspicion that Dr. Bartol felt the same way. However, after a brief pause, he remarked that no doubt it would work out all right; would I send him a report about once a month? Having learned just what this report should cover, we left, with the understanding that the doctor would be expecting a telephone call about the twentieth of March and would catch the first train for North Haverhill he could thereafter.

Nothing was said about an examination of any kind, and no one seemed to feel there was any risk in waiting for a doctor who must take a five-hour train ride after he was summoned. I can visualize both present-day doctors and patients shuddering at this, but nothing went wrong, and personally I have always felt I had my children at the most ideal time in history: after anesthetics had come into general use but before mothers were wrested from their homes and hurried off to hospitals for their accouchements. In that era, the only girls who went to hospitals were patients who had no homes of their own where they could be suitably cared for, and sometimes no husbands, either.

After our visit to Dr. Bartol we returned to Pine Grove Farm, and I spent the rest of the winter there very happily. My mother stayed with me a great deal, usually when Harry was gone. Their long-standing mutual antagonism had not lessened, but as I had learned to keep them apart, it did not trouble me very much. My dear aunt Fannie, to whom he had taken an immediate liking during our engagement, was made as welcome by him as by me. Most of my guests were younger though: my former Boston schoolmates, cousins who were attending Dartmouth College and the Newbury friends I had missed so greatly the previous summer. With all this congenial company, it was easier to cope with loneliness while my husband was away, and I was in excellent health. It seemed more exciting to embroider towels and napkins now that we were using them ourselves, and these represented only a minor part of my needlework. I made baby clothes, simpler than those in that wonderful Paris layette, which would be too elaborate for every day, and worked with a seamstress on clothes for myself, since my Paris trousseau was of little use to me. While the house practically ran itself, I was gradually learning more about its mechanics; these interested me now that I had some voice in them, and for the first time domestic equipment and decoration intrigued me. I wanted to make a library out of the morning room where my mother-in-law had spent endless hours arranging sweet peas, and at my instigation additional bookcases were built there to hold the books I had brought over from The Oxbow and those Harry kept giving me.

> Harry gave me a rug for our room today.... Harry gave me a mahogany chair for my sitting room.... Harry gave me some more books. [The entries in the *Line-A-Day* book tell their own story. So do these:] Delightful day alone with Harry. Went to see the calves fed. ... Quiet Sunday alone with Harry.

These were still the happiest times of all.

Baby presents, now beginning to arrive, supplemented the gifts made to equip and embellish the house. I suppose any number of babies get as many or more, but they seemed to me almost countless and just as exciting as the engagement presents which had been coming in less than a year before: caps, bibs, jackets, bootees, blankets, little pillows, a bassinet draped in muslin and lace, and numerous ornamental bar pins known in those days as baby pins. Though I cannot remember anything we used them for, except to fasten down bibs, they were very much in vogue as baby presents.

Twice during the winter, I had occasion for grief: my wonderful grandmother Frances Parkinson Wheeler, for whom I had been named, died on New Year's Day, and very shortly thereafter Elizabeth's father, one of the finest men I ever knew. But I have no recollection of any other bad news.

Just as the summer had been one of the hottest I have ever known, the winter was one of the most severe, with storms so heavy and constant that every now and then we were snowbound for days on end, and the rest of the time we were able to have glorious rides in the red sleigh. I enjoyed these rides as much and took them as often as I had in my earlier teens. But it was a new experience to be completely snowbound, because I had never lived so far from a highway before, and I found this equally thrilling. Before I was married, my mother and I had spent only two winters in the country, and her house was near the main road which was kept open by snowplows, and life had been as neighborly at one time of the year as another. While the storms raged there were sometimes high winds, and if you tried to battle your way against them, they could be buffeting and blinding; then there were intervals when the snowflakes fell so softly and slowly that it did not seem they could ever make much of an impression; yet ground that was bare when you went to bed at night was covered with a smooth frosting the next morning. In either case, after the snowfall was over, a great silence descended on a land where everything was so white that it was dazzling

—the lawns, the trees, the fields, the mountains; even the roads and the river were engulfed in this white stillness; and at night, when the moon rose slowly above the highest peak on the horizon, our whole world was permeated with splendor. The snow and the stillness gave me a sense of complete detachment from everything that was soiled and turbulent, a feeling that no evil could penetrate an enclosure of such pristine purity. I was happy, not only in the recognition that my life had been enriched by love and that it would soon be further enriched by maternity, but in a sense of security and imperturbable well-being such as I had never known before.

In early March a telegram arrived from Miss McLeod, the nurse my sister-in-law had engaged without consulting me. The former was snow-bound in Nova Scotia; there was no telling when she would be able to leave there; she could not assist at my confinement. . . .

In a few minutes, another telegram was on its way, this time from Harry to Dr. Bartol. I had never voiced my feeling about this Canadian nurse, because I knew it would be interpreted as silly and morbid; but I had not forgotten that Harry's lovely sister Gertrude had died when her daughter and namesake was only a few days old and yet, over and over again, I had heard Belle extol her nurse. I could not help feeling that perhaps my sister-in-law, for all her executive ability, was not as well fitted as she should be to determine the qualifications of a nurse. My appreciation of snowstorms increased immeasurably when I heard the news from Nova Scotia, though I tried to conceal my satisfaction at the turn things had taken when the result of Harry's wire appeared two days later in the person of Miss Annie Jane Hilton, a graduate of the Boston Lying-in Hospital.

Unquestionably, she was one of the most efficient nurses I have ever known, and nothing could have exceeded the competence with which she assumed charge of the situation. The three rooms in the south arm of the H with their own bath, designed and furnished for my mother-in-law, sister-in-law and niece were of course vacant, and Miss Hilton chose these for our infirmary. The long hall that separated them from the other rooms on the second floor would ensure privacy and quiet, and no one else used that bath. I did not like the idea of moving out of the bedroom I shared with Harry, with my own sitting room opposite, which I had fixed exactly as I wanted it, in the north arm of the H, but when Miss Hilton pointed out that the other rooms not only were isolated, but had the advantage of connecting doors between them, I admitted the wisdom of her choice, though rather grudgingly.

Eventually, I grew very fond of Miss Hilton, for she not only took perfect care of me and my baby but also made herself generally useful in countless ways and shielded me from all kinds of petty annoyances. She became my friend, as well as my nurse, and so remained for years. Though she mellowed with time, at first she was a martinet of the most rigid type, and neither explained the reasons for her orders nor brooked any delay in their execution. When I was wakened around midnight on the twenty-first of March by slight intermittent pains which seemed to fit the description given me of labor's beginning, I was not at all frightened. I had gone peacefully to sleep in my own bed, and now I slipped out of it and went calmly down the hall to call her, as I had been told to do, the moment anything of the sort happened. But after I was installed in my new quarters, I was required to submit to a series of unexpected proceedings which seemed to me indignities, and I became increasingly rebellious, which made everything more difficult not only for her but for myself. If she had taken time to tell me why these measures were necessary, she would have saved us both a lot of trouble.

As promised, Dr. Bartol took the first train he could catch and reached Pine Grove Farm about seven in the evening. Though I had been in labor more than eighteen hours, I was still partially dressed, as parturient mothers were not supposed to give in to their pains by lying down, but to remain as active as possible until the closeness of these made it impossible for the patient to be active at all. I have a vivid memory of sitting in Harry's den, suffering greatly, and carefully observing the frequency with which Dr. Bartol consulted his watch; also of my thankfulness when he said, "Well, they're only five minutes apart now, we'd better get you to bed." I thought that must mean the end was very near; I could not have been more mistaken.

Two or three other pronouncements still stand out with startling clarity: Harry telling me that Dr. Bartol *could* shorten the labor by giving me ether and delivering the baby by high forceps, but that this would be bad for us both, and that I managed to say, "Oh no, of course not." And next, eons later, when all I wanted was to die, hearing the doctor say, "All right, you may have it now. Just hold this sponge to your nose and breathe hard, Miss Hilton will keep giving you more." Then, as I grabbed the sponge and pressed it against my face, hearing Harry say, "I'm sorry, I'll have to leave, the ether is making me sick." For a terrible moment I felt as if the world—my world—had indeed come to an end if he would desert me because he could not stand the smell of ether. After that, there was no pain, only a sense of time passing, though I had no idea how much or in what way. Later still, there seemed to be occasional waves of consciousness and during one of them I heard the doctor's voice saying, "Don't try to move just yet," and—as if of only secondary importance—"You have a fine big boy."

Chapter 3

I SUPPOSE no woman, however vital herself, can fully gauge the urgency that impels a virile man to precipitate the union between himself and his beloved. The experience is inevitably one of victory for him and one of surrender for her. Of course, after husband and wife have become one flesh, her joyous participation in the act of love is as essential as his for a happy and harmonious marriage. But his was the impetus, and he glories in it.

On the other hand, *he* can never know the glory that almost blinds her when she first looks at her newborn child. This, indeed, is bone of her bone and flesh of her flesh; if the father had died the day after conception, it would have made no difference. For nine long months she has carried this child in her body, and if she had not done so, he would not be there beside her now: a perfect and complete human being she can see and touch—his head, covered with soft fine down; his pink sleepy face; his tiny clutched fists; his plump warmly wrapped body. She has had months of discomfort, weeks of illness and, finally, hours of agony; she would gladly go through every minute of all that again for the sake of this moment. In becoming a wife, she fulfilled the first part of her destiny as a woman; but that destiny would not have been complete had she failed to become a mother as well. Now that she has, whatever happens in the future, nothing can rob her of the joy of that supreme hour; and when her baby is put in her arms and she holds him against her breast, she has another swift surge of joy if she knows he is still to draw on her for sustenance.

I think that a woman who does not nurse her baby misses a great deal. Next to the marriage relationship, it provides the closest and most significant tie two human beings can have. No one can take the place of the baby's mother, and he is very quickly aware of this; in a surprisingly short time, she becomes not merely a welcome answer to his demand for food, but a beloved person. As he feeds, he begins to study her face and to find something there he recognizes as precious to him; he does this almost as soon as he begins to knead her breast if he is not nourished rapidly enough to suit him. And not long after that, he begins to smile up at her, and to find his greatest comfort in her if he is fractious or ill, quite apart from his mealtimes. Of course, many women who cannot nurse their children realize what they have missed and strive to achieve the intimacy I have tried to describe, and very nearly succeed, though not so quickly. But I am afraid they are exceptions, and I shall always be thankful that I have three times known what it was to be a "nursing mother." I count it among the greatest privileges of my life.

My "fine big boy," promptly named for his father, throve from the beginning and was regarded with enthusiasm not only by his exultant parents but by our friends and relatives. I had been the first bride, both among my Boston schoolmates and my Newbury contemporaries; and the excitement caused by my engagement and marriage was revived now that there was a "class baby" on whom The Oxbow also had a claim. And when he was viewed in the latter role, the excitement was not confined to my companions, but included their parents and grandparents who nearly all claimed kinship with each other. Cousins hastened to call on my mother and tell her how delighted they were that a sixth generation was to be represented at The Oxbow; while she was almost beside herself at being a grandmother, and puffed with pride because it was her daughter who was not only perpetuating her own family strain but doing the same for the Keyeses.

Now that the baby was actually in the world and no longer an embarrassing subject to be avoided in conversation, the Keyeses all proclaimed their satisfaction that the name was continuing, and were lavish with gifts and attentive with visits. I was duly warned I must not let ten-year-old Gertrude see me nurse the baby and that, as she had never seen a little boy undressed, I must keep him carefully covered with a washcloth in case she was present at his bath. I felt these admonitions not only silly and prudish but shortsighted: what better chance could there be for a young girl whose mother was dead and who had no brothers, but who did now have a cousin whom she dearly loved, to find out how babies were fed and how little boys were made? But I complied and did not argue the subject, and in fact soon dismissed it from my mind. I was too happy and had too many other things to think about to let such trifling matters disturb me.

Those were the days when a newly made mother was kept in her room for a long time. (Dr. Bartol would not take a case unless the prospective patient agreed beforehand to stay in bed at least three weeks after childbirth and to nurse her baby, unless she proved unable to do so.) But my room was a big, sunny, pleasant one with a cheerful open fire in front of which the baby was given his bath; presents came in with practically every mail, and visitors at some time every day, though often these visits were cut short by the nurse; and the baby was fed every two hours in the daytime with night feedings at ten and two. Each feeding lasted fifteen or twenty minutes, so there was not much time between them, and the days passed rapidly and agreeably. I was not allowed to have the baby sleep in the room with me—in fact, his beribboned bassinet was in the room beyond Miss Hilton's, who occupied the one next to mine. But I *was* allowed to keep him beside me for an hour or so every afternoon and delighted in it. I sewed, I read, and my reading now regularly included a daily paper. During our engagement, I had followed Harry's political career when he provided news items relative to this, but my mother did not consider newspapers proper reading material for young girls, though she had no qualms about Cervantes and Fielding; and the items which had been interesting to me for personal reasons did not provide much general information. Harry was horrified at my ignorance of current events and begged me to give the Boston *Evening Transcript* at least a trial. My interest was stimulated because the editorial page always carried a poem and because the author of the department called "The Listener" was Betty Chamberlain's father, which gave it a personal connection; from these limited beginnings came my avid interest in the public prints.

I made the sort of recovery I was supposed to make, getting my strength back gradually and feeding my baby so successfully that he gained much faster than he was supposed to. For almost a month, there were no setbacks of any kind; then I developed a slight fever and could not eat my supper. Miss Hilton had insisted right along on heartier meals than I wanted, and though she did not force the supper on me, when she brought the baby for his ten o'clock feeding she said if I felt like it later to let her know and she would bring me some cocoa. About one in the morning I woke, feeling much better, and called to her. She left for the kitchen, saying she would be back in a few minutes.

When these lengthened into half an hour, I grew mildly curious; it did not take that long to prepare cocoa. When nearly an hour had passed and I could hear the baby beginning to fuss, I knew he must be getting hungry. I had been charged, on no account, to pick him up myself and really did not know how to do this or to change him, as I had not been allowed to do either; but when his fussing became a wail, I slid out of bed and groped for my slippers. At that moment, Miss Hilton re-entered the room with the cocoa and spoke sternly.

"Get back into that bed this minute," she ordered, "and drink your cocoa while I change the baby. I'll bring him to you, and if he finishes feeding before I get back, you will have to keep him with you. Agnes is sick. I've got to attend to her."

"Agnes is sick!" I echoed in surprise. "What's the matter with her? She was all right yesterday."

"Well, she's not all right now. I can't take time to explain. Drink your cocoa."

She brought the baby, removed the tray and disappeared. I was sorry Agnes was ill, but not worried. I knew Miss Hilton was capable of caring for her, whatever the matter was, and it was wonderful not to have the baby snatched from me the minute he had finished feeding. He cuddled down beside me and we both went contentedly to sleep.

When we woke, it was daylight and the baby was hungry again. Miss Hilton, who was back in her room, heard us stirring and hastened to do what was needed for both of us. But she was still silent and left abruptly. A few minutes later Harry came to my bedside, smiling the way he had at the camp when he wanted to win his point.

"Don't worry about Agnes," he said reassuringly. "We've taken her to the Cottage Hospital for a slight operation, but she isn't in any danger. When there's anything more to report, we'll let you know."

But I was not so easily put off. I insisted that he tell me *why* Agnes had been taken to the Cottage Hospital, *why* she needed an operation, and it was one of the few times when I won *my* point.

"You won't believe me when I tell you," he blurted out at last. "She had a baby."

He was right. I not only did not believe him, I *could* not believe him, and yet it was unthinkable that he would jest about so grave a matter. I stared at him speechlessly. If Agnes had had a baby, it had been born a scant month after mine and I had been visibly pregnant since Christmas; how was it possible that in a household of five, one of them a professional nurse, none had been aware of Agnes's condition? For twenty-four hours before my baby was born, I had gone through a series of preparations allegedly essential for safe delivery; I had had a physician and a nurse in attendance; I had endured hours of suffering and only the numbing ether had spared me supreme pain. How could Agnes's baby have been born with no such ministrations? And why, *why, why* should anything so dreadful have occurred in our house?

"She didn't expect it to happen quite so soon," Harry said miserably. "And Miss Hilton had just begun to have suspicions, when she saw Agnes leaning over to clean the tub. But even then Miss Hilton thought the baby couldn't be due for several months and that before then— before you were up and around or had to know about it—Agnes would find some excuse for leaving. I think Charles knew and planned that they'd all leave together. But Ida didn't know. She's had a terrible shock and wants to get away as soon as possible. I don't know what we'll do then."

"I don't either, but let's talk about that later. Now I want to know how Agnes could—"

"When she realized she was in labor, she locked the door. Obviously, she meant to go through the birth alone, but how she supposed she could conceal it afterward—if that's what she did suppose—I have no idea. When Miss Hilton went down to get your cocoa, she heard Agnes scream, and managed to force the door and get into the room. The baby had already been born—on the floor. You can imagine its condition— and its mother's. Or probably you can't, and it's just as well. Your fever may have prevented a real tragedy—much worse than what has happened. It was a close call. But I've told you the truth. Agnes is going to be all right and so is her baby. Please stop thinking about them and think about *our* baby. If you don't eat something, he'll go hungry."

I tried hard to stop thinking about them, but my own travail, safeguarded in every way, was too recent for me to dismiss from my consciousness the terrible suffering Agnes must have undergone all alone, and the deepness of the shame that must have impelled her to take such a frightful risk. It was my mother who put an end to my brooding. As soon as she heard what had happened—and of course news of this nature spreads through the countryside like wildfire—she went to the hospital and somehow persuaded Agnes to divulge what she had hitherto withheld: the baby's father was a gardener on the estate where she and Charles and Ida had been employed. She loved him, but was not sure he cared for her so she did not tell him she was pregnant; she did not want him to feel he had to marry her; she would manage somehow to take care of herself and her baby; she was very sorry for all the trouble she had caused. . . .

After that it was an easy matter, with Ida's help, to identify and locate the baby's father, though Agnes still steadfastly declined to reveal his name. A letter from my mother brought him promptly to the hospital: of course he cared for Agnes as much as she did for him, of course he wanted to marry her. He would have been glad to, even if there had been no question of the baby, but she had run away and never written him and he thought she was tired of him. As soon as she was able to leave the hospital, they were quietly married in my mother's house, and the baby was baptized at the same time. Then they returned to the estate where they had worked before and were given a small cottage of their own. My mother kept in touch with them for years. Apparently, they lived happily ever after.

My mother had done wonders for my shattered morale which no one else had been able to mend; but she could do nothing that would help me to run a servantless house while I was still physically incapacitated. She was having domestic troubles of her own, as her ménage, which did not share her charitable views, had been badly upset by the wedding, the simultaneous christening and the presence of two "immoral persons" in a respectable household. Belle hastened to assure me the Keyes exodus from Boston, complete with staff, could be made at any time and that she would be only too glad to take charge again. I was truly appreciative of this cooperative attitude, but I had not forgotten the full-dress breakfasts at six in the morning or the crises when I had my "At Homes," and I did not want to risk similar experiences. I also felt sure there would be differences of opinion about the care and feeding of infants and that when Miss Hilton was no longer there to defend me, my inexperience, like my immaturity, would be held against me. I was determined to take care of my own baby and to do it as my nurse was teaching me to, not as my septuagenarian mother-in-law and spinster sister-in-law thought I should. Besides, there was bound to be a laundry problem: in addition to diapers, the baby had a clean long white dress, long white petticoat, silk shirt and belly-band every day; and my white muslin dresses, frilled white petticoats, frilled muslin drawers, chemises and corset covers also had to be kept spotless. Though I had learned a little about cooking, I had not yet learned anything at all about washing and ironing; and I could imagine the baleful glances my mother-in-law's crusty laundress Edla would cast in my direction if I invaded her basement quarters, and her still more baleful tirade if these extra items were added to her already heavy load. The previous summer, when I spent so much time in Newbury, my laundry had been done there, but this was no longer practical. After careful thought, I finally had an inspiration: I told Harry I thought we should have a different kind of domestic help from his mother's and what we ourselves had had before, if we could get it. To begin with, I thought we could do without a coachman; surely one of the hired men on the Farm could look after the horses we used and drive for me when needed. Next, I thought we should ask Ina Danforth to come to work for us.

He agreed with me about the coachman, the plan I outlined should represent a substantial saving, and he did not need to have Ina identified for him. She had been my mother's cook when he first began to come to The Oxbow, and her husband Frank had been the hired man. They were both of sound Vermont stock and characteristically hard working, intelligent and self-respecting; they were never referred to as servants. When my mother decided I should cease having lessons from a governess and go back to school in Boston—which meant we would be at The Oxbow less than half of every year—an arrangement was made whereby the Danforths would work for friends of ours in Littleton. Unfortunately, Frank succumbed to asthma, and Ina brought him back to Newbury a chronic invalid; they were living with her sister and brother-in-law, Ida and Charles Greenleaf, in a fine old house the couples jointly owned. Charles was the village butcher and supplemented his shop with a horse-drawn cart in which he went from house to house so that his customers could make their selections without even leaving their back piazzas. Ida could keep an eye on Frank and, capable as Ina was, she could work for us and still go back and forth to Newbury in order to be with Frank when needed.

Harry agreed that we would be fortunate if we could persuade Ina to come to us, but he did not think she would consider it for a minute. However, if I insisted, he would telephone her. He went down to the den, where our only telephone was located, to place the call, and when he returned, he said Ina would come to see me that very afternoon. If she and I could reach an agreement about the work, he would pay her anything she asked—even as much as ten dollars a week, which was three dollars more than his mother paid Alma, who was virtually a chef. He knew Ina would be worth it, and we would economize somewhere else. . . .

I was back in my own room but still in bed much of the time, for, though the baby continued to gain by leaps and bounds, I kept developing slight fevers whenever I tried to hasten my convalescence. Ina came and sat beside me and we talked. It was agreed that she should have time off Sunday, leaving after midday dinner; she was to go home other days when supper was over if Frank especially needed her, but she would return to the Farm for the night unless some unforeseen emergency arose; and she was to be on duty all the rest of the time. She asked for the ten dollars a week, evidently expecting there might be some discussion about this; but when she found there was not, she accepted the sum as final and never asked for more. Only two things seemed to trouble her: she would have to wear a uniform and she would have to call me Mrs. Keyes. The first condition she accepted after only a slight hesitation, but when I mentioned the second, hating to do so, tears came into her eyes. She had not thought of me, until then, as Harry Keyes's wife. She had kept on thinking of me as the little girl who came to her kitchen asking for the pan in which frosting had been made or for the dasher of the ice cream freezer, and who had somehow grown up enough to go away from The Oxbow but was still a little girl that needed looking after. It was a hard moment for both of us. But then Ina leaned over and kissed me and asked if she should stay and bring up my supper. And I said no, Miss Hilton would do that as long as she was with us, and I was sure Ina would like to go home and have the evening with Frank and the Greenleafs and tell them about our plans.

She was back at the Farm early the next morning, ready to begin work. Between them, she and Ida had achieved a plain percale dress, and Ina had it on. She was slender and erect and neat as a pin, and I have never seen more beautiful hair than she had. It was pure golden in color, down to her knees when it was unbound, and worn in a coronet around her head. It took her fifteen minutes to comb it and pin up those braids, and they were always in perfect order if she was out of her own room. She had blue eyes and clear rosy skin and very white teeth. Her features were not beautiful or even regular, but you did not think much about those because it was her coloring you noticed, especially the coloring of her hair. I mean, that is what you thought about her looks; but when you knew you could depend on her as your friend and helper, you just gave thanks that she was part of your life.

I did so for ten years.

Chapter 4

WE decided to have the baby christened on the first anniversary of
our wedding day. Mr. Flanders, the rector who had married us,
was willing to perform the ceremony in the living room at Pine Grove
Farm, as we were eight miles from the nearest Episcopal Church. Miss
Hilton was still with us, but it was really time to dispense with her services, since these cost twenty-five dollars a week; and now that we had
Ina, I was sure of someone who was willing and able to help me with
the baby when and if I needed help, though at last I was beginning to
shake off my persistent weakness. Unquestionably, however, it would be
simpler to have a big christening party when *both* Miss Hilton and Ina
could help; and the first wedding anniversary seemed such an appropriate date!

Of course, we wanted everything to look its best for such an important event, and I had a special sense of obligation, since it was the first
party for which I had assumed full responsibility at Pine Grove Farm.
It was not enough for me that all the windows should be freshly washed
and all the brass and silver brightly polished. Somebody else did that,
under my supervision; I wanted to do something *myself*. It seemed as if
the logical procedure might be to clean some of the best things which
did not look to me quite fresh and which, in Boston, would have been
sent to Lewandos, the establishment that took care of delicate fabrics. I
knew that gasoline was the basis of their cleansing process and some
was always kept in the ell storeroom; so was an old tin foot tub. I did
not tell anyone what I had in mind for fear of the tiresome warning
about overdoing. When I was sure everyone was busy elsewhere, I went
to the storeroom, put gasoline in the tub and carried it to my bathroom,
where I had assembled the articles I meant to clean.

I knew that gasoline was inflammable and should be used very cautiously, but I had no reason to suppose that it would represent any more of a hazard in the bathroom than in the storeroom. Unfortunately, Miss Hilton, who naturally knew nothing about my project, had placed under the basin a small stove on which she prepared barley water for the baby. There was no electricity at Pine Grove Farm in those days; and the stove, like all our lamps, operated by kerosene. Immediately, the gasoline ignited.

As usual, in the summertime, I was wearing a white muslin dress and four ruffled white petticoats. I was enveloped in flames before I was even aware of danger. What I did next was one of the swiftest actions of my life and one about which I am most proud, for an instant's panic or delay would certainly have cost me my life, and there was no panic or delay. I picked up the bathroom rug, wrapped it firmly around me and went out of the door, closing it behind me, so that the fire would not spread beyond the bathroom. Then I walked down the hall calling for help.

Before it could reach me and I could be undressed and put to bed, I was terribly burned. My hands and face were the most painful and I could not open my eyes; but though eyelashes, eyebrows and my front hair were singed and the skin of cheeks and forehead badly scorched, through some miracle no lasting damage had been done to them. That was confined to my neck. I had defied convention enough to rebel against high collars, except when I went to the table, and my dress was turned down at the throat to form a V; as the folds of this had burned, so had the flesh beneath them, leaving bare bone. The rest of my body had been saved by the rug, but it had been impossible to hold that high enough to cover everything. I think we all knew, before night, that though the pain in my face and hands would lessen in a comparatively short time, the pain in my neck would increase and last for a long, long while and that I would bear the scar of it as long as I lived. But none of us mentioned that; instead, we dwelt on the degree of escape, which would make it possible for me to go on nursing my baby.

I know now that it probably would have been much better for us both if I had not, that he would not have sometimes gone hungry, as I am afraid he did, and that I would have suffered much less and my wound would have healed much more quickly if my meager stock of strength had not been constantly taxed. But in those days babies were fed nothing but milk until they were almost a year old, and it was considered unwise to wean a baby in hot weather. So I persevered until October, and though the baby did not gain by leaps and bounds any more, he never failed to hold his weight and slowly added to it. Miss Hilton, returned in the autumn to see him safely on his formula of pasteurized milk, lime water, freshly boiled water and milk sugar; and at her insistence, I went to the hospital in Hanover, so that a doctor in whom she had great confidence could prescribe a remedy other than carron oil —a half-and-half mixture of linseed oil and lime water—which was then the standard medication for burns. But this doctor had no substitute to offer, and even the simplest sedative was out of the question. I must continue along these lines if it took all summer, which indeed it did, before the open wound closed, and I was proud to prove I could do it. But I was never quite the same person again. I had learned in a hard way that love could not be my whole existence. Fortitude was what would have to count, much of the time.

Happily, with the coming of cool weather less fortitude was required, and the idea of spending some weeks in and around Boston seemed inviting. Delighted as my mother had been when her first grandchild was born, he did not prove a strong enough magnet to keep her in the country a second winter. In fact, she had sailed for Europe in August, while my burn was at its most painful stage, deciding, with characteristic impetuosity, that she had had enough of household cares to last for a long while; she wanted to return to Geneva, always one of her favorite cities, to buy new clothes from her favorite dressmaker before going to the Riviera for the winter, as her mother before her had so frequently done, to bask in its charms. This meant her house at The Oxbow would be closed indefinitely, so I could not go there when Harry was in Concord and I wanted a change for a few days; and much as I had enjoyed the previous winter at the Farm, I did not look forward to the long lonely evenings when he was away and my mother was not there to keep me company. Briefly, but nonetheless poignantly, I wished I could go to Europe with her—not for a long stay of course, but just for the ocean voyage, which I always enjoyed so much, and perhaps for a few days in Rome and Paris, revisiting the places and doing the things I had loved best. I yearned for a morning in at least one picture gallery and one cathedral, one drive through the Bois de Boulogne, one walk in the forest of Fontainebleau. I was ashamed of this yearning and succeeded in stifling it, but there was no doubt that too much solitude had begun to prey on me.

My Boston friends were not as free to visit me at Pine Grove Farm as they had been when I was first married, because they were now getting married themselves; and they wanted me to visit them instead, which I was more than willing to do. Besides, some dentistry which had been done while I was at school had proven unsatisfactory and had been too long neglected, first because I had been in Europe, where dentists were allegedly unreliable, and then because I had been pregnant, but there was no reason to delay treatment any longer. It was also a long time since I had gone to the theater or to a dance, and after all I was only twenty years old; it would seem good to do both. I had begun to miss the urban atmosphere in which most of my life before my marriage had been spent.

Harry, who had been captain of his varsity crew, went every year to the Harvard-Yale races at New London and frequently to football games, baseball games and class reunions in Cambridge. He also went at least every other year to Canada on a hunting trip with one or both of his brothers. Aside from these wholly masculine diversions, he never wanted to be anywhere else if he could be at the Farm, and though he was willing to go to the theater occasionally, he had never danced and steadfastly declined to do so; neither did he ever want to play cards. But from the beginning he had made it clear that as long as I did not question or ask him to change his design for living, he would not object if mine were different from his. Neither of us had realized, before our marriage, that a difference between our ages, as well as our tastes, might eventually lead to difficulties; we loved, trusted and respected each other, and that should take care of everything. Neither of us gave thought to the fact that urban activities came most naturally and pleasantly to me and rural activities most naturally and pleasantly to him. Nor had we recognized that as merrymaking is a normal occupation of youth and my time for this had been cut short by an early engagement, an early marriage and early maternity, I would sooner or later not only want but need to make up for the deficiency. Instinctively, I was now demanding a right to do so; and an unexpected and unsolicited letter from Dr. Bartol helped my cause immensely.

Dr. John W. Bartol
1 CHESTNUT STREET
Boston, September 23, 1905

Dear Harry:

After the weaning is accomplished and that husky boy of yours is fairly started on his bottle diet I think you will find it wise to give Mrs. Keyes a little change of scenery and air. There is often a reaction after giving up such intimate relations as she has held with him, and all the more so on account of what she has gone through in other ways.

Of course I make this suggestion only in a general way and leave it to your judgment to do what seems best, but before the winter sets in it occurs to me that you might like to get Miss Hilton or someone else to take charge of the baby so that his mother might feel easy in doing what she wants to.

Sincerely yours,
John W. Bartol.

With his approval, we made a slight change in the program the doctor first suggested: Miss Hilton did return to see the "husky boy" fairly started on his bottle, and it was just as well that she did, for the reaction from all I had gone through was even more prostrating than had been foreseen; but when I was well again, I planned three visits in and around Boston: the first to the Sweetsers' hospitable house in Brookline; the second to the beautiful old "Count Rumford house" in North Woburn where my aunt Fannie lived; and the third—at Harry's instigation —to my mother-in-law's big house on Commonwealth Avenue. I took the baby and Ina with me, and Harry joined us frequently, if briefly. I went faithfully to the dentist, but I also went to a round of luncheons and dinners and dances among my old friends and, more sedately, to symphony concerts and the theater while I was with the Keyeses. The dentistry was not completed when these visits had been extended as long as seemed advisable if I were not to impose on hospitality or be away from the Farm too long, so for the rest of the winter and the spring, entrusting the baby to Ina's capable care, I went to Boston every other week, taking the six-thirty train Monday morning and returning at six-thirty Wednesday evening. This permitted three dental appointments —Monday afternoon, any time Tuesday and Wednesday morning. But it also meant time for the theater, lunching with friends and other delightful pastimes. As I always visited, there were no hotel or restaurant expenses, and the round-trip fare was less than ten dollars. I was troubled because the dentistry was costing so much, and knew it was my mother and not my husband who should have been responsible for it. But it did not trouble me enough, nor were the sessions at the dentist's bad enough—though I am probably the world's worse dental patient! —to lessen my enjoyment of these trips.

Very often the friend with whom I stayed was Mary Tudor, who had been a classmate and good companion at Miss Winsor's School. As Mary had not come there until my final year, I had not previously felt as close to her as to the girls I had known longer. But she had stayed at The Oxbow while I was engaged and at my wedding had been one of the girls, all dressed in white, who preceded the bridal party and sat in the choir—a very attractive arrangement, and one which I saw repeated only once, when it was not nearly as effective, as the ladies in that cortege were not in their teens, but all middle-aged! Mary had also been among the first to visit me at Pine Grove Farm, and the more I saw her the fonder of her I became; intellectually she was brilliant, she was congenial in every sense of the word, she had a charming voice, and she was very handsome. An uncharitable schoolmate once remarked, "All the Tudor girls look as though they had been cut out with a pair of scissors," and it is true that there was a certain lack of softness about their clearcut profiles; but this was offset by their fine dark eyes, their beautiful complexions and their truly magnificent brown hair, which more than filled the then standard requirement of being long enough to sit on.

When Mary and her parents first urged me to stay with them as often as I would care to, I hesitated a little, but when I had gone to them once, I never hesitated again. They lived on the waterside of Beacon Street in a tall, narrow house which looked rather forbidding but was actually the scene of much free-handed hospitality. Instead of being exclusive, pompous or condescending, as was generally supposed by those not fortunate enough to know them well, the Tudors were so socially secure that they never needed to give a thought to whom they should select for associates; they could just take their choice and it did not matter if this led them far afield. I learned for the first time that my father and Mary's had been classmates and friends at Harvard, and obviously the poor Congregational minister's son had been made just as welcome by the Tudors in his generation as I was now. Mary's elder sister Elsa had recently married a French count, Alain de Pierrefeu, and they were visiting her parents; it was fun to speak French again and compare notes about places we loved in France. Mary's brother Henry had married Eleanor Gray, the daughter of John Chipman Gray, Royall Professor at the Harvard Law School, whose wife was a great beauty and whose house, also on the waterside of Beacon, was more elegant and spacious than the Tudors', though no more distinguished; and we were often invited there. Mary's next elder sister Delia, named for a great-aunt who was Charles Stewart Parnell's grandmother, was engaged to Louis Thatcher, still another Boston Brahmin; and Roland Gray, Eleanor's brother, was embarking on the dignified courtship of Mary which was eventually to make the relationship between the Tudors and Grays a double one. The circles in which they moved, though they were never the ones to point this out and the Keyeses would never have admitted it, were considered much more exalted and rarefied in Boston than those in which my family-in-law moved. I could not help being amused and somewhat satisfied because they were impressed with my easy entry into this milieu.

By June the dentistry was finished and the restlessness which had made the trips to Boston so welcome assuaged. I was perfectly satisfied to stay at home again and so intrigued by the rapid development of my baby, who was now walking and talking, that I did not want to be separated from him even for a day, for fear of missing some fascinating new aspect of his progress. But when Harry came home with the unexpected announcement that he had arranged "to let Concord go" for a little while and asked if I would not like to go to the camp with him, I knew there could be only one answer.

His public life had grown increasingly important to him, and I realized that if his private life were not keyed to meet this need, there would be disharmony between us. I had tried not to show any resentment of his absorption with politics which often precluded not only the leisure for a *solitude à deux,* but seemingly the longing for it. Now, suddenly, he wanted such solitude. Though I have always felt it is a mistake to try to recapture an illusion, I immediately consented; after all, our first stay at the camp had not been an illusion; it had been a reality which had changed my life. And this interlude would be different, in any case. I was older now and more experienced in many ways. I had borne a child and narrowly escaped death by fire; I had found how much suffering I could endure without faltering. I had also learned that I could and must make room for my friends as well as my husband in my life, because love could not be my whole existence any more than it was his. There would never again be the total self-surrender of supreme innocence which had meant so much before. But the tie between us was still very strong and he wanted to make it stronger. I realized this as soon as he spoke of going to the camp, and I also realized we would have only a few days to ourselves, instead of the weeks we had before.

Only too conscious of the little time we had, we tried to make every moment of it count. Far from leaving the camp brokenhearted, as I had two years earlier, I left it feeling that as a woman, I had truly come into my own. The ardor of a bridegroom may be taken for granted, but the yearning which prompts a man who is preoccupied with important affairs to break away from these, so that he may devote himself exclusively to his wife, is a tribute no woman can count on. The afterglow of my gladness lasted all summer. And there was no repetition of the scene in the upper hallway of Pine Grove Farm when my sister-in-law told me she was "afraid" I was going to have a baby. This time, I told her, with great pride, that I was going to have another.

This pride persisted despite the so-called morning sickness, which actually continued all day and which went on over a longer period than it had the first time. But at least no one expected me to get up for six o'clock breakfast; and I was fortunate in having for a visitor, whenever I felt able, one who was more than welcome. This was Mrs. Keyes's sister Mrs. Cobb, whom I was encouraged to call Aunt Mary, though my mother-in-law had made it very clear that I was never to address *her* except as Mrs. Keyes. Aunt Mary was lovely-looking, for besides having a wonderfully sweet expression, she had kept the almost perfect figure which had made her outstanding in her youth. She was spending a large part of the summer at the Farm, and from the beginning had shown herself affectionately disposed toward me. Aunt Mary was used to dealing with sick people and had a very soothing as well as very cheering effect on me.

And as I lay in bed, most of the time too exhausted to do anything but look out the window, my involuntary idleness resulted in an idea. Harry had long been troubled about one of the big barns for two reasons: its equipment was becoming obsolete, and it was too near the new house, which was so much larger than the old one; sounds and smells which had never bothered him before were a constant source of irritation to him. Our room was one of the nearest to this barn and after days of gazing at it, I finally asked Harry a question.

"Are you really going to tear down that barn as soon as you can afford to build a new one?"

"I certainly am. And put the new one a good deal farther from the house."

"What will you do with the empty space?"

"I hadn't thought about that yet."

"Why wouldn't it be a good place for a garden? A flower garden? It always seemed to me a pity that you can't see the flower garden from the house. It's an effort to get to it, and when you do, it isn't much to look at. It isn't part of the landscaping at all. I've always loved the garden at The Oxbow, even though I am such a poor gardener."

Harry looked thoughtfully at the barn and then at me.

"Why, you're right!" he said in a pleased voice. "It would be a fine place for a garden—a garden with trees at the rear, to shut out the sight of the other big barn, and a wide border of flowers all around a big grassy plot in the middle. I can see just how it would look. We'll economize in some other way so we can have a new barn and a new garden both."

We were always saying that we would economize in some other way so that we could do something which seemed more desirable at the moment, but this had not begun to trouble me then; I lay contentedly reflecting on my indirect contribution to horticulture at the Farm. Soon after I was up and around again, the framework of the new barn was rising; and in due course the garden became a reality, exactly as Harry and I had visualized it.

My mother was planning a very special "cousin" party that autumn to celebrate the centennial of her house at The Oxbow, and I held fast to the hope that I would be well enough to attend. Happily I was and did, and it proved to be a great occasion in the North Country. The local press devoted almost an entire column to the significance and history of the house built by Colonel Thomas Johnson of Revolutionary fame for his son David. Finally the chronicler approached the present:

> When a full century had rounded over the Johnson mansion, Mrs. Wheeler, the only child of Edward, the second son of David, bade a "goodlie Companie" assemble to help celebrate its hundredth birthday. The hovering spirit of the past must have smiled to meet its own once more.
>
> Sounds of old time music from fiddle and piano greeted the incomers . . . as hostess in smart array and colonial gentlemen received most graciously. . . . Candles lighted the dining room where the hostess's daughter—great, great, granddaughter of Colonel Johnson—presided at a table spread with ham, chicken pie, white and brown bread, doughnuts, pickles, coffee, butternuts, popcorn, apples and cider. . . .
>
> Who in the future years shall come and go? Who bid welcome and say adieu? And will the guest of 2006 take away memoirs more lasting and pleasant than those we have experienced today?

Fifty years later, at the sesquicentennial celebration of my mother's house, which by 1956 belonged to me, none of us attempted colonial dress, nor did our refreshments represent an effort to recreate colonial feasts. But two of my ten grandchildren—great-great-great grandchildren of the first owner—received our guests with me in the paneled parlor; and one of them, David Johnson Keyes, was his namesake. So we were proudly conscious, not only of the past's "hovering spirit," but of the future's bright promise. There have not been many houses in the United States where family possession has been so enduring, and even the elements seemed to be on my side in making the occasion memorable. In Vermont, it is not always warm enough to eat outdoors at night, even in July, and rain also must be taken into consideration; so as the invitation list grew, we began to worry about the well-being of our guests. But the weatherman could not have been kinder; the sky was clear and starry, the air was still and balmy. We scattered tables over the back piazza and on the lawn, and everyone ate in seated comfort by the light of Japanese lanterns. Certainly a "goodlie Companie" had again assembled and certainly there was again every reason to smile at the way the old house was holding its own and looking after its friends. Even without positive knowledge that it will still be doing so in 2006, I have faith that the future will be patterned on the past and that it will do so triumphantly.

Part Two

A Faster Pace, a Harder Time

Chapter 5

TIME began to go very fast. There were no more long leisurely winters when I lived entranced in a snowbound world, no more long painful summers when I waited and waited for a wound to heal. All my hours were crowded and many of them were glorious. I was neither a bemused bride nor a teen-age mother any more. I had grown up. I was the lady of the house and a figure in the community.

My second son was born two years, almost to a day, after my first and named John, for my father. Birth, as well as pregnancy, had gone harder this time, which I believe is unusual; but my powers of recuperation were better than formerly and there was neither a household tragedy nor a serious accident to complicate convalescence. Besides Ina, who did what was then called "second work" and helped me with the children, I now had a Nova Scotian cook, Mary Phillips, who was as good in her way as Ina was in hers. The children preempted much of my time. I taught Henry (who was not called Harry as his father was) his first prayers and began to read aloud to him when he was two years old, and after that an evening program developed rapidly, in which John soon had a share. This consisted of a story hour—tales from the Bible and children's classics—an early upstairs supper and bedside visits with prayers and hymns afterward. I never had any singing voice, but have always had a good memory, so my repertoire of hymns was a large one; and the songfests were an important part of their lives to the little boys and have been long remembered as such. Just a few years ago Henry told me his happiest memories of me during his early years at Pine Grove Farm centered around the "children's hour" when I first read aloud to him in the living room, and then sat beside his bed, hearing his prayers and singing hymns with him.

I also sang with Henry and John at the piano directly after breakfast, and since they were much more musical than I, the results were most enjoyable; even if I could not carry a tune, both my sons did so at a very early age; and they memorized the words of the hymns, as well as many biblical passages, with ease. As far as reading was concerned, Henry learned his letters from his blocks, and Ina helped guide him through his first primer, but he still liked to have the stories he read himself supplemented by others I read to him. John's progress was slower, because less eager; his interests lay elsewhere and required more varied guidance. In fact, it was quite a task to keep up with him.

Both boys loved to see the calves fed and began to go to the barn when they were so young they were carried over their father's shoulder. John Roorda, who was the mainstay of our dairy farm, became their devoted slave; and as he was also on very congenial terms with Ina, he was often with them in the house as well as in the barns and pastures. He was a man of exceptional caliber, and I knew I was lucky to have him taking a hand in the boys' development, especially as their father was away so much and they needed masculine as well as feminine guidance. It was a proud day for us all when Henry went for the cows by himself the first time and, thanks to John Roorda's training, brought each and every one of them to their stalls in orderly sequence.

One of the greatest treats for both boys, as they had been for me when I was a child, were the "sugaring-off" parties which took place in the early spring after the buckets of sap collected from tapped maples were brought for boiling and processing to a "sugarhouse" deep in the woods. Each guest was provided with a pan full of hard-packed snow over which the boiling syrup was poured, giving it the consistency of hot chocolate sauce ladled on ice cream. With this pièce de résistance, pickles and doughnuts were always served. Such parties usually took place in the late afternoon and the refreshments constituted our supper; but once Ina, the two boys and I went to a morning sugaring-off at the Dudley Carletons' fine farm in West Newbury and found we were expected to stay for noon dinner afterward! (The Carletons are relations of mine, through our common ancestor who was Governor General of Canada, and the names Guy and Dudley appear in almost every generation back to the time of William the Conqueror. I once took one of my Boston cousins, who was interested in genealogy, to the Carleton house, and as we went up the steps to the porch, he said with pride, "May I introduce myself? I am Dudley Carleton." Immediately two good-looking men, father and son, rose from their chairs and echoed his words with equal pride!)

Besides the hours I spent with the children, I managed to steal time for my secret vice, which was writing. This had to be done surreptitiously in odd moments, for neither my mother nor my husband approved, and there were not many odd moments. Those that I could steal were spent in the attic, where I had found an old abandoned typewriter. I persuaded the hired man to repair it, and when I had taught myself to type, after a fashion, I transcribed the stories which I first scribbled in the same kind of copybooks I had used in school. Then I hid the results beneath my underclothes in bureau drawers, where they lay undiscovered, while I continued my life of deception along with my life of good works and innocent amusements.

I looked after the upstairs rooms in our part of the house, did the mending and some personal sewing, and could have drifted along leaving other household cares in Ina's and Mary's capable hands; but I had the wisdom to realize I might not always have such a wonderful team and had better learn all I could, particularly about cooking, while they were there to teach me. As soon as I was really on my feet after John's arrival, I announced that unless I were flat on my back again, I would make all the bread, cake and pastry eaten in my house and would learn as much as possible about other edibles and their preparation.

This does not seem like much of a proclamation today, when so many young married women with children do most or all of their own work. But I have yet to meet one who does it in a twenty-five-room house without any appliances like vacuum cleaners, washing machines and driers. Until electricity was installed at the Farm, several years after our marriage, there were innumerable kerosene lamps to be cleaned and filled every day, and there were no electric irons either. The enormous amount of laundry necessitated by the kind of clothes we wore was done by washing with scrubbing boards and pressing with sadirons. Despite the amount of time and strength this took, the house was kept in a state of shining cleanliness. Rugs were taken outdoors to be beaten, and in winter, if the snow where they had lain showed any sign of dinginess, they were beaten again. The kitchen and laundry floors were scrubbed twice a week, and even the cellar stairs were washed regularly. Brass and silver were polished twice a week, and every door handle on the ground floor was made of brass. All jams, jellies and pickles were homemade, and no loaf of "boughten" bread or any store ice cream ever darkened the door.

Like practically everyone else in the locality, we had our own icehouse, which was filled every winter with ice cut on a nearby lake and carefully preserved in sawdust until the next supply was available. Anyone who was "running out of ice" was regarded as having been remiss in calculating family needs or improvident in filling them. The cracking of ice for the freezer was one of the first sounds associated with Sunday, for dinner without ice cream was unthinkable. We also took ice cream for granted when anyone was sick or had a party, not only in our own family but among our acquaintances. Baked beans, one of the staples of Saturday night suppers, did not come in cans; the beans had their own earthen pot; the accompanying brown bread its own mold. In fact, everything was prepared *sur place,* whether this was just for the family, for company, or for dress-up company; and dress-up company could mean anywhere from three to three hundred. When I made my ambitious announcement, I was undertaking to provide an average of from six to sixteen loaves of bread a week, from six dozen to sixteen dozen rolls, from one to four cakes a day and the same number of pies. And we had a variety of hot homemade bread at every meal; there was always toast for breakfast, but this was supplemented by biscuits, cornbread, rolls and different types of muffins in careful rotation. To this day, when I am at home, I expect to find a delightful surprise in the covered dish which accompanies my *café au lait,* and I am seldom disappointed.

In spite of—or rather, because of—the spaciousness and comparative luxury of my ready-made home at Pine Grove Farm, there was crying need for rigid economy in the present to make up for casual extravagance in the past. But my husband's family and political guests expected him to set a good table, which meant a lavish one, so I must be ingenious, as well as industrious and cautious.

New standards had been set for me, and I was very eager first to meet these and then to surpass them. For instance, all the married women with whom I was acquainted in Newbury except my mother—and then, she was only intermittently married!—made excellent pies, but none of them made puff paste. My mother-in-law's Swedish cook Alma made it to perfection; her lobster *vol-au-vent* was a masterpiece, and indeed there was nothing in the realm of pastry which she could not achieve. After her departure from Pine Grove Farm, I dismantled one of the washstands that had been relegated to the attic, had the marble top moved to the kitchen pantry and used this as the slab recommended by Fannie Farmer for the preparation of puff paste. But though the marble slab itself cost nothing, the *cannelons*—delicate pastry cornucopias filled with sweetened whipped cream—and the sweetbread and mushroom patties and dainty tartlets of all sorts which came into being thereon ran into tall money. I soon realized that vaulting ambition had o'erleapt itself. . . .

Mary Phillips had the perspicacity to realize that on a dairy farm the most economical way to make bread was with whole milk and no shortening. She also pointed out that the baked beans left from Saturday night's supper and Sunday breakfast could serve as the basis for both salad on Sunday night and soup on Monday. But it was Ina who helped most with economy. She did not subscribe to the theory that a free hand and no conscience are requisites for a good cook; on the contrary, she claimed the test of a really good cook is to contrive appetizing meals at minimum cost and never, never to waste a single scrap. I confess that I greatly enjoy the free-handed method, and the New Englander who can suppress his traditional—and inherent—conscience generally seems to me a much more genial companion than the one who cultivates it. But Ina's Spartan methods were certainly never obvious to anyone unacquainted with them; and without the curb she put on my flights of fancy, I doubt whether the family budget would have even approached balance.

Ina was a strict prohibitionist; and consequently the years spent under her tutelage were almost entirely unproductive as far as recipes for food or drink flavored with alcohol were concerned. There were two notable exceptions, however: frozen pudding and fruit punch. I evolved the recipes for both of these myself and was permitted to serve them, the pudding because Ina felt part of the curse had been removed since it was not a beverage, the punch on condition that I would always mix and pour it myself. The punch recipe was often doubled and redoubled in the course of a party; and after the remains of a large molded pudding which had provided the crowning glory at dinner had been repacked in the freezer and put down cellar, a group of revelers would descend and dig it out for a midnight snack!

I did not wait to become an accomplished cook before beginning, very hesitantly, but gradually more courageously, to mingle in community affairs. My first outside interest was in its religious life. The nearest Episcopal Church was in Woodsville, eight miles away; and though the Village Hall in North Haverhill was used for occasional services, these were infrequent, irregular and ill-equipped. There were, however, several middle-aged and elderly women who were willing to help improve this situation and two or three men who were willing and able to help financially. I persuaded the women to organize a guild and hold regular meetings, at which we sewed and made plans to raise money through the usual channels of fairs and chicken-pie suppers. Before long services were being held regularly; envelopes had been distributed among the parishioners to encourage weekly contributions and thus assure a slight salary increase for the rector; and the makeshift altar was covered with an embroidered cloth and illumined with candles.

Encouraged by the success of my first modest experiments in organization and fund raising in the community, I decided my next venture should be in behalf of a public library. One of the same ladies who had helped me to sponsor the church guild had already set aside the parlor of her house in North Haverhill as headquarters for a lending library, with trifling dues; but public-spirited and generous as the gesture had been, it did not begin to meet the needs of all the people who wanted to borrow books and borrow them without charge. Thanks to the generosity of a civic-minded native, Newbury had had a public library ever since 1897, a substantial brick building with two fireplaces and two reading rooms. It seemed to me a reflection on North Haverhill's cultural standards that nearly ten years later this village still had no kind of a public library; I was sure there must be some way of getting one.

There was: it could be done partly with money voted in Town Meeting and partly by private subscription. It helped to be married to one of the Selectmen, who would bring up the matter in Town Meeting; it also helped that there was now a horse at the Farm which was considered safe for me to drive, since Ina had needed such a horse to go back and forth on her evening visits to her sick husband. I started out in a covered buggy on a house-to-house canvass of the village, asking for money to help build the library. Some of the families I approached gave me only a dollar, but not a single one refused to contribute. The only couple in the community who as far as I know were themselves illiterate— and certainly they were the poorest—gave me five; they had children and could visualize what a library might mean to them. Many villagers, who were poor themselves but had relatives in more comfortable circumstances, enlisted their aid and some of them responded with a liberality beyond our fondest hopes. In three years the Village of North Haverhill had its library too, not as large, to be sure, as the one in Newbury, but designed by a competent Boston architect and built of brick in a style suited to its surroundings. It had a paid librarian with regular hours, and both the librarian's salary and the number of hours the library was open were gradually increased. It also had a fund for the purchase of new books, with a committee, of which I was executive chairman, responsible for their choice.

This perquisite was a great help to me. Unlike many people today, I did not need or yearn to be taught to read faster; my trouble always has been that I read so rapidly that books never last as long as I would like them to, unless they are so monumentally dull that I have difficulty reading them in the first place. Consequently, I have a constant craving for more books. Harry, not a great reader himself, had always recognized my need for them, and had been giving them to me frequently since the early days of our courtship. I had brought with me to the Farm, when we were married, de luxe editions of all my favorite poets, a complete set of Meredith and a complete set of Trollope, all of which Harry had given me; and for my nineteenth birthday he gave me a very handsome set of Kipling. Harry did not care for Kipling, and went to sleep when I tried to read *Without Benefit of Clergy* aloud to him. But he was determined I should read everything this author had published, in proper sequence. The next gift was a set of Dumas, when he found I had read only *The Three Musketeers, Twenty Years After* and *The Viscount de Bragelonne,* and those in French; fifty-odd carefully translated volumes were the answer to that, and I read them all, and much besides, that quiet winter before Henry was born.

But it was obvious that I was hard to keep up with and the library fund would help, if only a little. Naturally, my choices were not always approved and one of them was actually burned by an indignant reader. However, when I offered to resign from the committee and the self-appointed censor had to pay for the book, there was no more trouble; no one else wanted to assume the burden of selecting, from dozens of books sent on approval, the few we could afford to buy at a time, not to mention the task of wrapping and returning them. I welcomed it all with open arms.

With church and library work both going so well, and still time and energy to spare, it was natural that I should be on the lookout for some other outlet for both, and this proved to be dramatics. One of the men who had been most helpful in my previous ventures was Louis Kimball, a Dartmouth graduate who had enjoyed participation in college plays at Hanover. He had been recalled from a promising career as a teacher by the death of his father, a well-to-do local merchant, and had felt it his duty to remain in North Haverhill as the head of a family consisting of a clinging-vine type of mother, a painfully shy and almost tongue-tied younger brother and a sister married to a railroad conductor, who was gone much of the time. Louis could afford brief occasional absences, which he spent mostly in New York going to the theater, but he lacked any diversion at home. At some church or library meeting he happened to ask me if I were interested in the theater and, on hearing my eager affirmative, to ask a second question: had I ever acted myself? Why, only in school plays. Had I ever thought I might like to do more than that? Why, yes, I had. Then would I consider taking part in a play at the Village Hall in North Haverhill? A benefit, of course. . . . I didn't see why not. What kind of a play? When?

Louis chose the play—*Nance Oldfield*. What made him think of that one or believe I could act the part of the heroine or realize it would appeal to a very unsophisticated audience, I do not know to this day. But all of that happened. He himself acted the father's role, and a very attractive brother and sister, Will and Martha Clough, who were friends of his though strangers to me, were induced to play the young suitor and the famous actress's maid. We went quickly into rehearsal, and with no guide except Louis's limited experience and mine, which was still more limited, we learned to find our way across our makeshift stage and become letter perfect in our lines. The public performance took place without a hitch before a packed house and, for New England, tumultuous applause.

Harry congratulated the entire cast very warmly at the hall and continued to praise my performance after we reached home. The next day, he suggested that I should invite my fellow actors to dinner. The most charming of hosts, he was usually a reluctant one; whenever it was feasible, he encouraged me to do my entertaining during his absence. This was the first time I had ever known him to propose a party and then outdo himself in making it a success. It was evident from that evening that there would be more plays, and very soon it was clear that there would be a flourishing dramatic club.

If Louis Kimball and I were responsible for its foundation, several others were to a large degree responsible for its development and success. Dan Carr, another local Dartmouth alumnus, was soon courting the new grammar school teacher Sadie Reeves, and Sadie had had quite a little experience in high school and normal school plays. Helen Cummings, the daughter of the railroad superintendent in Woodsville, was a brilliant dramatic star at Wellesley. Will Clough was deeply in love with her, and though Helen made no secret of the fact that her heart was elsewhere, he welcomed any and every opportunity to be with her and the dramatic club seemed to offer the most of these. All contributed to our dramatic venture, but the greatest impetus probably came from Terry Helburn, whose prowess at Bryn Mawr actually surpassed Helen's at Wellesley and who was already earmarked for future success in New York. She continued to visit me frequently, for, like Mary Tudor, she was an erstwhile school friend who meant more and more to me as the years went on; if we were rehearsing a play when she came to stay with me, Terry coached it as a matter of course.

Though most of my readers will be skeptical, we eventually achieved a number of productions which would have done credit to a much larger place than North Haverhill, New Hampshire, and a much more experienced cast than such a locality could be expected to provide; and our presentations gave great pleasure. Many persons who otherwise never would have seen a Shakespearean play remembered with grateful appreciation *Twelfth Night,* given in a grove belonging to Miss Katherine Morse, a public-spirited neighbor; and *The Merchant of Venice,* presented in the hall at Pine Grove Farm. In the former, Helen was, of course, Viola, and I was Olivia; in the latter, Helen actually took the part of Shylock and brought down the house, while I portrayed Portia.

The dramatic club flourished for a number of years, despite the fact that Helen Cummings, our real star, left us for marriage in California. After Dan Carr and Sadie Reeves married, their joint enthusiasm spurred an upswing in dramatic activities. Sadie introduced old-fashioned melodrama, with great success, to our audiences in the Village Hall, which by this time the club had earned enough money to improve very noticeably, with good curtains and some stage settings. Moreover, the Carrs' home, on nearby Briar Hill, became one of our favorite places for club meetings. In a countryside which could count many fine old houses among its riches, theirs was unique in its murals, made by Rufus Porter, an itinerant painter in the days when American primitive art was at its most prodigal and intriguing stage. One of these murals had been recklessly whitewashed in a previous era of misguided improvement, but fortunately the others were intact. The meetings usually began in the original kitchen, which had become the living room but in which the old water box had been left undisturbed and still trickled and murmured gently and reassuringly; later we adjourned to the parlor, where the murals made a charming and picturesque background for beautiful old furniture and ornaments.

The club subscribed to a theatrical magazine which was circulated among its members, and Louis and I were nearly always able to report on one or more plays that this periodical featured. As I look back, it is amazing to realize how few outstanding operas, dramas and concerts I missed after the two boys had both emerged from babyhood. There was one dreadful summer when they had whooping cough with every imaginable complication and when I never left the Farm but once: to attend a pageant, which presented in dramatic form the history of the Town of Thetford, Vermont, from its foundation to the present. Other than this, my visits to Boston and New York were frequent enough, even though they were usually brief, to give me a great deal of sophisticated pleasure and to provide it vicariously for friends who did not have the same opportunities. I watched the *Evening Transcript* eagerly for announcements of coming attractions in both cities and was often able to plan my short holidays to coincide with the arrival of these. In New York, I stayed with Terry Helburn or with the Demings, a family whose association with mine dated back to the time when my father and Horace Deming were classmates at Harvard. There were five young Demings, just as there were five young Tudors, and in both families there was always someone only too glad to use my visit as an excuse for an outing. In Terry's case there was, naturally, no call for an excuse—it was taken as a matter of course we should go to the theater.

Many other friends whom I visited also helped me keep abreast of the entertainment world, as did my mother, between her sojourns in Europe. Harry could be lured into an occasional theatrical spree, and when we had been married nearly four years, he was persuaded to take me to New York for three days, which we spent mostly at the theater; and he himself sometimes suggested going to a play in Boston. His brother-in-law Henry Baker had season tickets to both the Boston Symphony and the Boston Opera and was most generous about sharing them. The crowning excitement came, however, in having the Theodore Vail's opera box put at our disposal.

Friendship with both Theodore Vail and his second wife, Mabel Sanderson, had thrived for a long time and for various reasons: Mr. Vail's only son had been a member of a Harvard crew that Harry coached, and though young Vail had since died, his father, the immensely wealthy president of American Tel and Tel, had always kept a warm place in his affections for my husband. Mrs. Vail had spent a good deal of time in Newbury with her mother when she was younger, and was on terms of great cordiality with both the Keyes family and my mother's. Mr. Vail had built a huge, palatial residence at Lyndonville, Vermont, some thirty-five miles north of Newbury, and made it his summer headquarters, and lived there in a style that savored more of upper Fifth Avenue than the North Country. There we had more than once been bidden to lunch, which the Vails called breakfast, and from which I went away hungry the first time because I neglected the opening homely courses with the expectation that some exotic dish would soon appear and I wanted to leave room to feast on that; then, before I knew it, we were rinsing our fingers in warm scented water, with flowers floating in the bowls, and the meal was over.

Though I left the table hungry, during the course of post-prandial conversation Mr. Vail gave me a piece of advice which I did not fully appreciate then but which has since stood me in good stead.

"I think Harry is headed for bigger things," he said, "and you'll be going along with him. You're very young, so perhaps you won't take it amiss if I give you a word of caution: never leave your subordinates to take the blame for what is really your fault. If you feel you have to reprove them for something that's been left undone or done wrong, do it privately, and if they don't improve, dismiss them and get someone who'll do better. But as far as the outside world is concerned, the head of any concern, whether it's just a household, or an office or a large organization, is responsible for what happens under him. And a good executive knows how to choose the people who help him. He can't do everything himself. But he can make sure that everything is done the way it ought to be by someone."

This was many years before President Truman put the sign on his desk which read, "The buck stops here," and many persons may say that it isn't as easy to get efficient helpers as when Mr. Vail was directing American Tel and Tel with such competence. But I have had good luck running both my household and my office along the lines he suggested; and am often irritated by executives who have no time for details and make no apparent effort to see that anyone else does.

Besides providing us with "breakfast" and good advice, the Vails invited us to take trips with them in their private railroad car, then the acme of elegance in travel, and we lived in it luxuriously while attending a series of functions in Burlington. All of this was thrilling, but none of it compared to basking in one of the best boxes at the Boston Opera House. Usually the performance was all-important to me, but on these occasions, it really did not matter much what I saw; it was almost enough just to have put on all my best clothes and to be there.

Meanwhile, our own local dramatic group, though it continued to prosper, began to undergo some significant changes. Several of our Newbury friends had joined, and socially they were a great addition. But North Haverhill seemed the more logical place to give most of our plays, and in winter the long cold drive between the two villages after a late rehearsal was undeniably a drawback. The Newbury members were hospitable and more than willing to do their share when it came to giving parties, but it was hard to persuade them to do more than that. Besides, these parties tended to feature two other diversions which distracted the charter members of the club. The first was bridge, which I had begun to play in Oxford during the autumn of 1903 but which had taken a long time to reach the North Country. The second was dancing, which, always a customary but not emphasized local amusement, was now assuming more status there, as in the rest of the world.

Naturally it was auction that we played, for Harold Vanderbilt was not to develop contract bridge until 1925; and I found the frequency and regularity of our games in the country of great benefit during my visits to Boston and New York, where it was taken for granted I not only knew how but would want to play bridge. I believe that bridge players are born, not made, and that whereas a knowledge of rules is useful, card sense, as well as moral and social sense, is essential. Considering the combined population of Newbury and Haverhill, the number of persons who had card sense and easily mastered the rules was surprisingly large. The elder members of many local families had been avid whist players, and that obviously helped to make them equally avid bridge players. Anyway, something did. My mother was among these, and she undertook to teach some of the younger women the game.

Many of my contemporaries had the necessary instinct and became willing addicts, but my special cronies (and distant cousins) Norman and Richard Cobb stubbornly held out against learning the game. Since it was almost unheard of to have parties without them, we gave thought, not to abandoning the bridge games, but to supplementing them with something the Cobbs would enjoy. The answer was a natural: I had given Richard, who was younger than I, his first dancing lessons when he was a little boy, and he had quickly surpassed his teacher in the art. Now the two brothers gave the effect of dancing as spontaneously as they walked. There breathed no female soul so dead that she did not want to dance with them. Ergo, we must have more parties with dancing. And we did.

Chapter 6

As I had not "come out," like my Boston friends, I had never known the thrill of a debut, and though I enjoyed a dance when it happened to come my way, I did not plot and plan to get to one, after I went to live at Pine Grove Farm, as I did in the case of the plays I wanted to see. Without any plotting and planning, I was apt to wedge in at least one dance every time I went to Boston or New York and an occasional one in the country, and that was enough to satisfy me.

Strangely enough, the person it did not satisfy was my mother. When I was born, she and my father had been living at the University of Virginia, where he was head of the Greek Department, and my mother had always intended to have me make my debut there during Easter Week, as was then a very prevalent custom among privileged Southern girls, and she had been disappointed because I had married too early to do so.

And so she came to a rather strange decision: she was going to spend most of the late winter and early spring of 1910 at the University with a friend of hers; she wanted me to join her there for Easter Week and do all the things that the debutantes were doing. She would pay all my travel expenses to and from Virginia, and she would give me five hundred dollars besides to spend on clothes; she had set her heart on having me do as she suggested.

It did not seem to strike her or anyone else that the program she outlined was absurd, but I was twenty-four years old, I had been happily married nearly six years, and I had one son five and another three. There was certainly no reason why I should try to compete with girls in their later teens for masculine attention or why I should want to. However, it was a long time since I had been to Virginia, which I loved, and

(63)

springtime there is one of those miracles which Vermont and New Hampshire can never hope to produce. (Virginia cannot achieve a miracle like autumn in Vermont and New Hampshire, but right now we are talking about spring.) What was more, it was a long time since I had had any new clothes to amount to anything, and my mother had not given me any since she furnished my trousseau. There was a really good dressmaker in Woodsville, whom I had been yearning to patronize but whose prices I could not meet. Five hundred dollars would go a long way with her. I especially wanted a pale blue satin evening dress and had wistfully secured a sample, just the right color, the last time I was in Boston. Now I could send for the material and have the dress—that is, if I accepted my mother's invitation. It had been made plain that the five hundred dollars was contingent on my consent to go to the University for Easter Week. Gradually, attraction outweighed absurdity.

On my way south, I stopped in Boston and went to see Dr. Bartol about an ailment which seemed minor, but was making me vaguely uneasy. It was never his way to be an extremist, much less an alarmist, and after questioning me about my plans, he said that since everything was scheduled for Easter Week, it would be too bad to upset the applecart; he thought it would do no great harm to go ahead as arranged. But he would like to have me see him again on my return north and call in a friend of his for consultation. I did not like the sound of this very much, but I succeeded in dismissing it from my mind without difficulty because I had so many pleasanter things to think about. I took a night train from Boston to Washington, spent the next morning wandering around the Capitol and the Congressional Gallery and boarded an afternoon train for Charlottesville.

Pine Grove Farm was still in the grip of winter when I left in late March. But in Virginia grass was green, fruit trees were all white and fluffy, other trees were in delicate leaf, flowers were blooming, creeks were in freshet, lambs were gamboling in the fields. Pink lambs! The mixture of red soil and creek water painted them pink. I had forgotten how charming they were. Both Town and Gown were in gala array, and the University seemed to me, as it still does, the most beautiful one in the United States if not in the world. My mother's hostess had several house guests besides ourselves, some of them young girls who were sleeping three in a bed because they really liked it that way—it was easier to whisper and share giggles and gossip if they were not too far apart. They were strikingly pretty themselves, and they wore strikingly pretty clothes, which they changed on an average of four or five times a day; but aside from that they spent practically no time in the house, and I made no new friends among them—I would have liked to, but there seemed to be no chance. However, my parents' old friends and their families all welcomed me warmly, and I went not only to delicious dinners and teas at their lovely old homes but for pleasant walks and stimulating horseback rides with them. The atmosphere was one of such abundant hospitality and carefree gaiety that it was impossible not to revel in it. I soon forgot that I had thought my mother's program absurd.

Every afternoon I went to a baseball game, except the day there was a special pilgrimage to Monticello; and every evening I went to a ball, except the night the musical comedy *Turvyland* was given. A supper party, at which chicken salad was the standard fare and the young gentlemen drank more than those at similar parties in the North did, but without obvious ill effects, always followed, and this meant that I seldom got to bed before daylight. I could not sleep late because I shared my mother's room, and she insisted on having her continental breakfast served promptly at eight-thirty. In the circumstances, it is not surprising that at the end of the week I went to bed with a sore throat and spent the next few days in the same place with the same complaint. But my indisposition was promptly succeeded by visits in Richmond, for a dinner, and in Washington to attend a military drill at Fort Myer and a play, and it was not until I reached Boston that I reluctantly faced the fact that something besides a sore throat had been the matter with me and obviously still was, and that I had promised to get in touch with Dr. Bartol on my return.

The consultation was with Dr. Davenport, a surgeon specializing in gynecology—Dr. Bartol did not perform operations—and surgery was indicated, indeed, was imperative if I were ever to have another child. As I wanted very much to have another child, this verdict was enough to speed me to a hospital. It was a private one, where Dr. Davenport liked to send his patients, and in the light of some subsequent hospital experiences I think I had remarkably good care, remarkably good food and an extremely pleasant room, the price of which—forty dollars a week—troubled me greatly. None of the rooms at twenty-five dollars a week, which is what I had expected to pay, was available. All kinds of tempting offerings came to me from Alma's kitchen, for "88" was just around the corner, and everyone there was truly kind. Moreover, I was in the midst of friends, so I had a great deal of agreeable company, as soon as I was well enough, except on Sundays, which were long lonesome days.

This was my first experience with a hospital, and I took it very hard. I was sicker from the anesthetic than I ever had been before, and at the end of the first week, any benefits derived from the operation were offset by my reaction to an overdose of morphine. Consequently, I was kept there almost four weeks and then at my mother-in-law's house for several days before Harry took me home. After that, many more days were spent in bed or very quietly, but this restricted life gave me an opportunity to indulge in my "secret vice" of writing.

I wanted very much to have a daughter, but this desire had never been shared by my husband; he wanted sons, and had been not only tremendously pleased but relieved that both additions to our family were boys. He would have been equally pleased and relieved to feel confident the family was now complete, and did so for several years. I accepted his viewpoint, without sharing it.

The winter of 1911–1912 proved to be a particularly severe one and Harry readily agreed that my wish to spend part of it in Boston was a reasonable one, considering the number I had now spent in the country. If I could find a small furnished apartment, it probably would cost no more to rent it for a few months than to heat the house at Pine Grove Farm in zero weather, and he could join me in Boston when he was not needed in Concord.

The best we could afford was the top floor—originally servants' quarters—of a four-story private house on Massachusetts Avenue, near the corner of Beacon, that had been sketchily remodeled and divided into flats; but we were also able to get one large room on the third floor for Ina and the two boys, and though we were very crowded, everything worked out smoothly. I reveled in the company of my old friends. Henry and John began school and dancing classes. Far from objecting to the latter, Harry was "almost pathetically pleased," as his sister put it, to have them go. Perhaps, subconsciously, he was beginning to realize what he had missed in not dancing himself. With great good humor, he came to "visit" us. I had expected, when he agreed to the arrangement, that he would merely tolerate it; instead, undistracted by the demands of office, bank or farm, he was more relaxed and companionable than in a long while. He took the boys to the dog show; he went regularly with me to the Church of the Advent, which for some time had been my favorite place of worship, and took me to the theater and symphony concerts. He made no more remarks about hoping the family was complete. Quite the contrary. Not long after our arrival, he told me he hoped he was safe in assuming that another baby was now on its way, but that he wanted to be sure. He was determined there should be no delay in fulfilling his desire and I responded with joy. Suddenly the crowded quarters of our nondescript little flat became permeated with the magic of the perfect days and nights in the freedom of Lake Tarleton, and the act of love had new meaning because it was not dependent on ideal conditions to give it splendor. And there was a new element in it. At the camp there had been no thought of anything except the joy that came with the union of lovers; the rest of the world did not exist —it did not matter to us there whether or not our mutual fervor should prove productive. But now my husband wanted proof positive that he could beget a child and sought this reassurance with greater and greater intensity. Not until my condition left no room for doubt could his yearning be assuaged.

It was soon evident, however, that there was not merely morning sickness to deal with this time; there was pernicious vomiting with a vengeance and it went on and on, while I lay racked and helpless. In those days, intravenous feeding had apparently not been considered in such cases, and the alternative to taking nourishment in the normal way seemed to be slow starvation, if the condition persisted. Much as I had wanted another baby, it was very hard to be patient and philosophical about this. Quite aside from the wretched discomfort, there were so many things I wanted to do and had counted on doing.

Newbury was celebrating its sesquicentennial that year, and Henry and John had been chosen to unveil the memorial marker honoring their great-great-great-grandfather, Colonel Thomas Johnson. I not only felt tremendous pride in this, but some trepidation lest they should not be equal, at their tender ages, to so important a function. Moreover, all summer long my mother's house was crowded with guests, among them the Governor of Vermont, the Honorable Allen M. Fletcher, and various other dignitaries whom she had expected me to help entertain. Suppressing his disinclination for such festivities, Harry did his best to play the part of host for her, and as usual left everyone wondering why a man with such great social gifts should be so averse to using them.

He went a step further and—in order to tell me about it—attended the wedding, in the church where he and I had been married, of my dear friend Katherine Cobb, younger sister of Norman and Richard, to Noble Foss of Boston, whose father was then Governor of Massachusetts. Newbury's excitement over the sesquicentennial mounted to fever pitch when the Fosses' private car was switched to a siding at the Newbury station and kept there during the wedding festivities. Nothing comparable to the presence of an entire gubernatorial family ensconced in a private railroad car, because one of its members was marrying a Newbury girl, had ever happened before. Besides, it was not just any girl, it was Katherine, beloved by everyone who knew her. Her disposition was angelic, and so were her looks. Her eyes were blue and her skin delicately rosy; her hair fell in clustering golden curls around a face always wreathed in smiles. Nothing angered her and nothing disturbed her, and she was always glad to do whatever anyone else wanted to do. She was the youngest in our special set, but no one ever felt she was in the way. She was our treasure and our pet.

On the night of that wedding to which I could not go, I kept thinking how lovely she would look as a bride, standing to receive her guests under the marriage arch in the parlor of her family's beautiful old house The Homestead, where I had spent so many delightful evenings. This time I would not be one of the guests she was greeting. I could not accept my disappointment without a pang.

As summer ripened into autumn and I was still no better, my husband—who, not unnaturally, had changed his mind again about another baby—and the local doctor tried to tell me I could not possibly go on this way, and eventually other opinions, both family and medical, were emphatically brought forward: I could not possibly live to get another child into the world; I already had two children who would be left motherless if I persevered on my sacrificial senseless course. This struggle happened so long ago that I had almost dismissed it from my mind when the current propaganda in favor of interrupting pregnancies for all sorts of reasons brought it back. But if I had not persisted in my faith that I could survive myself and produce a healthy child, I would not only have been burdened with a guilty conscience all my life; I would have missed one of the greatest joys that has ever come to me. My third son—formally christened Francis, but always called Peter—was born normally and weighed nine pounds, ten ounces; though I was emaciated, he was no sooner in the world than I was able to eat ample meals again, and I nursed him for seven months, during which he steadily gained. A happier baby or one who made those around him happier, it would be hard to imagine. His father became his devoted slave, and to the day of Harry's death he continued to feel that the sun rose and set on Peter's head. As for me, my disappointment that he was not a girl did not outlast my first glimpse of him.

With three sons, to whom my triple responsibility was that of nurse, companion and teacher, my days were fuller than ever; and my long period of physical inactivity during pregnancy had resulted in trouble with my feet, which meant more expense as well as considerable discomfort; but my disability was short-lived and Ina was standing by. As she was now a widow with no obligations to an invalid husband, she could relieve me in more ways than ever. After the boys were in bed at night, I was free to seek diversion, and I found it, not only in the ways to which I was already pleasantly accustomed, such as bridge parties and amateur theatricals, but, like most of my contemporaries, in dancing—not dancing as I had known it before, in which I had never excelled or especially wanted to excel, but something entirely new, in both form and intensity, in which I did want to excel.

While I was finding my feet again, everyone else in the vicinity had been devoting his to more and more dancing; the earlier plan of supplementing bridge and dramatics with dancing had been expanded with a vengeance. Newbury had stolen a march on North Haverhill by engaging a professional teacher from St. Johnsbury to give bi-weekly lessons in the Village Hall, and pupils flocked from both sides of the river.

We enjoyed these classes very much, and nothing in the way of a novelty was too ambitious for us to attempt. The tango and the *maxixe* —which we pronounced for some time as if it were an English word— expanded our repertory of the hesitation waltz, the foxtrot, the two-step and the one-step; even the older dances like the polka and the mazurka still flourished, for we were insatiable when it came to dance steps. And standards of performance were high. I have watched the *maxixe* many times since then, but I do not think I ever saw it more charmingly interpreted than when Elsye Hale, a recent bride, wearing her wedding dress, danced it with Richard Cobb on some very special occasion. Elsye was a skilled musician, and before her marriage she and her brothers had formed an orchestra and had often played for our dances. Now she became one of our star performers and Richard Cobb was well qualified to be her partner. Though I agree with John Gunther that Manuel Quezon, the statesman who later became the first president of the Philippine Commonwealth, was one of the best ballroom dancers in the world, I would still put him second to Richard Cobb.

The dancing lessons were only episodes in a general scene. The Village Halls in both Newbury and North Haverhill were always available for private "benefits." We also began to consider the feasibility of dancing at private houses, where we could have informal parties with no question of a benefit. Cousin Agnes Bayley Cobb would not let us use The Homestead for such a purpose; she claimed that so much motion would shake the old house more than was good for it and that her handsome hardwood floors would all get scratched. Then Mrs. Charles Darling came home from a visit to Boston, during which she had left her daughter Jeannie to keep house, and was very much puzzled at the condition of the parlor carpet; it looked as if mice had got into it; after that, Jeannie made no further attempts to shield the Axminster with sheets. My mother, on the other hand, was more than willing to remove the heavy furniture, which had been in my father's study at the University of Virginia, to make space in her library; but, though we appreciated her good will, we were rather crowded there. However, the big hall at Pine Grove Farm, which had served to hold an audience for *The Merchant of Venice,* now proved equally adaptable for dancing. It was a simple matter to roll up the rugs and put the Victrola on the chest which stood under one of the windows. Unscheduled interruptions sometimes occurred when my eldest son, by then eight or nine years old, appeared on the stairway in his pajamas and yelled indignantly, "Change that needle!" The Victrola was his property, a highly valued Christmas present, and he rightly resented the absorption in other aspects of the party which had made us careless about a detail that was then of great importance.

Other places for private parties were soon available. For instance, Mr. Warren Bailey, in order to provide a suitable place for his sons, Warren and Horace, and his daughter Clara to entertain their friends, put a fine hardwood floor in his shed chamber, which had the same generous proportions as the rest of his big white farmhouse, and otherwise spruced it up. There was no question of limiting ourselves to Victrola music, for Mr. Bailey had bought an old square piano and installed it in the shed chamber. A pianist from St. Johnsbury was secured to play it, supplemented somewhat haphazardly by Horace, who played the violin, and Warren, who played the horn, when they were not dancing. Horace had just become engaged to a very attractive Boston girl, Ruth Muggett, and she made her first appearance among us at a dance in her fiancé's house, wearing a beautiful emerald green evening gown, and created quite a sensation. I can still see her, blonde and smiling, moving gracefully among us; and I can still remember my sleigh ride home at two in the morning, on one of those winter nights when we lived, breathed, moved and had our being in a world transfigured by snow and stars.

This was before the snow plow swept the roads bare immediately after a storm, leaving them suitable for wheeled vehicles but totally unusable for those with runners. Instead, a powerful snow roller, drawn by four horses and preceded by a lead horse, started out early in the morning; and by evening, when the drivers came in, cold and hungry and weary, there was a smooth solid surface of tightly packed snow perfectly adapted to sleighing. Since Mr. Bailey, in addition to his other activities, had charge of the snow rollers in Newbury, he made a special effort to see that his guests should not only find conditions for the dancing itself delightful but enjoy getting to it and going home from it.

During my first winter at the Farm, I had been fascinated by the silence of the snowbound nights. But this was a different experience, for, instead of being engulfed by the stillness, I was moving through it to the sound of sleigh bells, which rippled with the same effect of belonging to it as, earlier, the dance music had rippled through the place where it belonged. Then, with each successive partner, there had been a sense of shared rhythm, of flow and movement, and this still lingered, but now there was an even greater sense of harmony.

By 1914 we were quite at ease, as far as the new dances were concerned, though none of us had lost his taste for early favorites, which included square dances as well as waltzes and two-steps. I have very happy memories of an evening at the Village Hall in North Haverhill, featured as an Old Fashioned Dance, to which I went with Richard Cobb. We all danced the Virginia Reel at my mother's "cousin parties," for which music was supplied by the tinkling old square piano; and we took and changed our places without any formal prompting. But the Old Fashioned Dance in the Village Hall was the McCoy, not just a reel danced in my mother's parlor or an incidental Portland Fancy. There were nothing but square dances—Lancers, quadrilles, minuets and so on—and they were called by a prompter, who stood near the orchestra and who, next to the floor manager, was the most important person there.

We had had good sleighing that year, well into April as usual, but this Old Fashioned Dance took place in May, so I went to it, and numerous others, in a Model T Ford. Automobiles were slowly coming into more general use, but they were still put up for the winter and such a thing as a snow plow was far in the future. To this day, I think sleighing is the best possible form of transportation, though eventually I grew more appreciative of Model T Fords.

That year my birthday party was a light-hearted dinner with dancing afterward, and I recall very few parties that were completely unconnected with dancing. One was a candy pull at the Carrs'; two others took place at the camp when Harry and I entertained groups of friends. Increasingly, the camp was used for such purposes instead of for a retreat from everyone else. I felt we had lost something by the change, but I did not grieve as much as I would have if I had not been present when the original building, which meant so much to me, burned to the ground. Harry was in Concord when this happened, and I was summoned to the lake by a telephone call from the fashionable club into which the friendly farmhouse across from us had now been transformed. Our property was on fire; would I please come out immediately? By the time I could reach the scene, there was nothing left to save. No one knows how the flames started—probably because some unauthorized visitor dropped a cigarette; but whoever was to blame for the beginning of the blaze, no one was to blame for its end. With only a trail through the woods and rowboat by which the camp could be reached, no one could possibly have put out the fire once it had caught. I stood watching the smouldering ruins, feeling as if I were looking at the funeral pyre of my youth, and my grief was deep and poignant. When Harry decided to rebuild and created a log camp which, architecturally, was much more important than the first, I knew I would never feel the same way about it as I had about the other. This time, there was no question of trying to recapture an illusion; it was better to have everything different.

Chapter 7

WITH few interruptions, our good times continued through 1915. In 1916, the story was very different.

Prior to the summer when Henry and John both had whooping cough, none of the children had been seriously ill. There had been a good many hard colds, apparently impossible to avoid in our climate, but nothing worse, and Peter had been an exceptionally healthy baby. Then, one night around the middle of January, he was taken violently ill with acidosis. There was no question that he was at first seriously ill and then dangerously ill. I watched over him day and night and, before the end of the week, became obsessed with the fear that I was going to lose him. I kept telling myself how thankful I was that I had sold a diamond bracelet—one of the most valuable ornaments my mother had given me at the time of my marriage—so that I could afford to have his portrait painted. I would always have that, whatever happened. . . .

I did not dare undress, but sat close beside the crib watching for any sound or movement which might indicate a cause for fresh alarm. There seemed to be none; nevertheless, I did not mean to relax my vigil. I must have done so one night, however, for I came to my senses with a start, conscious of another presence in the room. A figure draped all in white and with a veiled face was bending over the crib with outstretched arms. I screamed, snatched up the child and held him close to me for the rest of the night. In the morning he was better, and from then on his improvement was steady. But I did not doubt then, and have never doubted since, that the figure I saw, or seemed to see, was a warning that my child would have been taken from me if I had gone to sleep.

Unlike The Oxbow, which, as far as I know, can lay no claim to being haunted, Pine Grove Farm, in common with most old dwelling places, has its traditional ghost, or rather ghosts, for there are two. One is an Indian trying to force his way into the blockhouse, which was the first building on the site; and that there really were such attacks was unmistakably revealed when the front lawn was plowed to permit the planting of wheat during the First World War and numerous old arrowheads were turned up. The other ghost is a benevolent spirit, sometimes said to be John Roorda, who goes quietly up and down the stairs and through the corridors in the dead of night, making certain that everything is secure. The Indian I have never seen, nor have I ever felt anything suggesting his presence; but Mary Tudor, by then Mrs. Roland Gray, was once so certain he was crouching outside her bedroom door, which mysteriously opened on a perfectly still night, that she insisted on leaving the Farm the next day; and one of my granddaughters refuses to occupy that room because she was similarly startled—before she had ever heard about the Indian. The benevolent spirit I have heard again and again. But certainly neither of these apparitions has any connection with the figure I saw in my child's room and was destined to see again more than two years later. The second time, it was a benign, not a malignant spirit, and I saw it, not in a shadowy room at midnight, but in a pine grove on a beautiful April afternoon, under very different circumstances.

Peter had hardly recovered from his illness when the entire family came down with the grippe, and by late spring it was evident that something far more serious was the matter with me. I suppose there is never a convenient time to be sick, but this seemed particularly inopportune from the moment Harry came, stood beside my bed and asked a question that would have sounded abrupt and mercenary if it had not been accompanied by such a pleasant smile.

"Do you think your mother will leave you any money?"

"I suppose so," I answered, trying to sound casual. "But you know she never gives me any—just a special treat once in awhile, like the trip to Virginia or another piece of jewelry. Do you need some extra money?"

"Very much."

"Can you tell me why?"

"I'm thinking very seriously of running for governor. I've got to decide within the next few days."

Then this is a pretty poor time for me to be running up more doctors' bills, I said sadly to myself. I knew that finances were at very low ebb. The mill, the bank, the Farm—those traditionally solid, dependable sources of revenue—were not as infallible as I had been taught to believe. At the mill there were costly disputes between union and non-union labor; at the bank, the previous cashier, who was a close personal friend, had embezzled a considerable sum, and though insurance covered most of the actual cash loss, it did not cover the withdrawals which resulted from the loss of local confidence. At the Farm, the tragic and sudden death of John Roorda from a rare disease had deprived the herd of its wisest, most experienced and most faithful overseer; Harry was away from home too much to give the cattle the same close supervision. Moreover, the precarious state of my health had made it impractical for me to remain at the Farm the last few months prior to the birth of my youngest son and the first few months after it; Dr. Bartol had said very frankly that he could not take the chance of failing to arrive on time to deliver me, even if there had not also been the need—at last recognized —of both prenatal and postnatal care. So we had taken a suite at the Hotel Vendome for the winter, which cost one hundred dollars a week. This included all meals for Ina, Henry and John; Harry and the trained nurse when they were with us; and myself when I was able to eat again. The suite had only one bathroom, which was inconvenient, but it was spacious and sunny and also served as my hospital when the new baby was born, so—by today's standards—it was ridiculously cheap. But there had been no way of stretching income from the "dependable" sources to cover it, and some of our best cattle had been sold to make up the deficit.

I grieved over this, but that did not help the situation and I tried to console myself with the realization that I had no personal extravagances with which to reproach myself. My doctors' bills and related expenses were the only ones incurred expressly for me, and those apparently had been inevitable. I attempted to make up for them by facing other economies cheerfully, and this cheerfulness was not assumed. The refreshments served at local parties were all homemade and unpretentious, and bridge was never played for money. I did not mind very much that my trousseau had never been substantially replaced or even supplemented, except for my trip to Virginia. I could make nearly all my clothes with the help of a seamstress who came to the house twice a year; in fact, when occasion demanded, I could cut out a dress after breakfast and have it ready to wear to a dance that evening, and it would be a very pretty dress at that. I did not mind much, either, that it was no longer possible to squeeze out money for the theater whenever a particularly good play came to Boston or New York. But I minded very much when bills came in over and over again marked, "Please Remit," and my husband told me he did not see how he was going to pay them. I did not see how I could do so myself, though I tried hard to think of ways and means. My mother had always given me handsome presents but had steadfastly refused to give me even a small allowance which I could call my own. Deeply embarrassed, I appealed secretly several times to Mary Gray for financial help, and never in vain. But the sad fact remained that the big house and the proud position and the rising political fortunes were not only without any solid financial foundation; they were actually in jeopardy.

However, Harry's brothers, who were proud of him, wanted to help him and fortunately were in a position to do so. George had married a very wealthy girl and it was not of vital concern to him, just then, whether or not the mill in Pepperell made money; Charlie was still unmarried and could afford to take chances. Encouraged by them, Harry announced his candidacy on June 23rd. I lay in bed, gloating over the complimentary notices that appeared in practically every New Hampshire paper, and was particularly pleased with an editorial in the Manchester *Union:*

> Mr. Keyes is one of the best known and best liked public men of the state. He has rendered conspicuously able and fearless service in a difficult and arduous post—that of chairman of the State Excise Commission. In addition to this, he has demonstrated in several other public capacities his ability, integrity and patriotism. One of the best tests of a man's real fitness and real quality is the test of home support and endorsement. No man in public life in New Hampshire could present a better record in this regard than Harry Keyes. And this, we predict, is but an earnest of the high regard and respect in which he will be held by all of the people of the state after he has served them all as their chief executive.

As far as the campaign was concerned, there was every reason to be hopeful, almost from the start, that Harry would get the Republican nomination. As far as I was concerned, it was increasingly evident that I could not avoid surgery much longer. Dr. Bartol had told me several months earlier that he did not think I should try to do so. Somewhat hesitantly, I had asked if it would be all right for me to consult a different surgeon this time. Not that I hadn't liked Dr. Davenport; but he was a good deal older than I was, and practically a complete stranger. With my anxiety about expenses, coupled with my knowledge that this was a crucial point in Harry's career, I felt it would mean a great deal to have a surgeon who was personally close to me and also more or less a contemporary; I would be able to speak more freely. I mentioned an old friend, Foster Kellogg, and was relieved when Dr. Bartol approved my choice. But it was not until the fifth of July that I consented to have

Harry interrupt his campaign and take me to Boston, where he installed me comfortably at the Vendome to await the outcome of an examination.

Foster Kellogg and I had become good companions during one of my vacation visits to Buzzards Bay. We had gone sailing and swimming and dancing together during the summertime, sometimes by ourselves and sometimes in groups, and had spent many quiet evenings together in the wintertime, while he was at Harvard and I was at Miss Winsor's School. In those days, boys and young men seemed perfectly satisfied to call on a girl and spend the evening in conversation, and the girls were equally contented with this arrangement. Foster and I talked a great deal about what we were reading, for we were both natural bookworms, but we also managed to cover other subjects, and we got to know each other very well. The bond of congeniality and understanding, which I had recognized from the moment I met him, increased rather than lessened with the years, and neither my marriage nor his, which took place several years later, affected it in the least. The girl from Chicago whom he eventually married, Rosalie Hanson, had also been a good friend of mine for a long time, and it seemed perfectly natural to continue the friendship with her as Foster's wife. I often dined with them when I was in Boston, and they with me, and I knew that Foster and I still spoke the same language.

By this time, he was, of course, through college and the medical school and I had heard references to him as a promising young surgeon. I had not thought of him in that connection until Dr. Bartol made his shattering announcement. Then I felt that no one could help me face surgery as wisely and understandingly as Foster could; and from the moment he agreed to take the case, I was convinced that I had been right. He chose the Faulkner Hospital in Jamaica Plain for the operation, performed it successfully and was scrupulous in his after care. As a faithful and cheering visitor, he did everything I had hoped for my morale. Also, in so far as it is ever possible for me to be comfortable and contented at a hospital—since I seem to be allergic to them—I was comfortable and contented there; and though this was a far more serious operation than any I had had before, I was sent home, apparently in good condition, two weeks after it had taken place.

Surgeons were just beginning to shorten the length of time they kept their patients quiet, and I had a modern surgeon. I did not question his judgment, especially as I knew he would be deeply distressed, as a friend no less than as a surgeon, if anything went wrong with my convalescence. But I did not seem to be regaining my strength very rapidly. There were some contributing factors that had nothing to do with surgery. On the fifth of September Harry received the Republican nomination for Governor of New Hampshire, and two days later his mother died in Pepperell, where she had spent that summer. Four days after she was buried in the family plot at Newbury. The house was full of people, the telephone rang incessantly, the details surrounding the funeral seemed endless, and Harry, who had adored his mother, was grief stricken. The general atmosphere was certainly not conducive to calm recovery.

Even so, there seemed to be no good reason for so much pain where the incision had been made. Eventually I discovered that the scar tissue, instead of healing evenly, had split. When I reported this by telephone to Foster, he said he thought he and Rosalie had better take a short trip to the mountains and put Pine Grove Farm on their itinerary. He did this as soon as it was feasible, without apparently regarding it as an emergency; and when he removed the dressing over the sensitive area, he seemed slightly surprised and vexed, rather than anxious.

"You're losing a stitch," he said.

"Is it serious?"

"No, just uncomfortable. Don't let anything irritate it and keep it clean. It'll heal presently."

But it didn't.

Chapter 8

FOR a week after the Kelloggs' visit I tried, not very successfully, to carry on as I had before the operation. I was tired all the time, my side hurt, and my mood was one of unrelieved despondency. My mother, who had already been married three times, had married again, this time a man even younger than I was. Harry said emphatically that he would never receive her new husband and that he hoped I would not do so. Under the circumstances, a certain degree of estrangement and a good deal of friction between my mother and myself were inevitable. At first, I stood up under them fairly well, but eventually they began to tell on me. I did not actually grieve, as if I had sustained a loss by death, but the strain added to my general sense of futility and failure.

I think now I might have put down on the credit side that despite my inexperience, I had managed to run a twenty-five room house with half or less than half the domestic staff my mother-in-law required, and that I was able to take both company and illness in my stride, which she had never been able to do. Neither did it occur to me that besides teaching my sons to read and sing, I had acquainted them so early with biblical and classical stories that they had a head start on their knowledge and enjoyment of both and never had to go through the painful process of "learning to like literature." Instead, I dwelt on the fact that I was ill much of the time and was not contributing a cent toward the cost of these illnesses. I was in almost constant pain. I felt I was a burden, financially and physically, to my husband. It has been said many times that the passion of a strong man is loving and taking and the passion of a good woman is loving and giving, and I was giving nothing, because he had become indifferent to taking anything. Harry's attitude toward me had so completely ceased to be one of ardor that I thought I must have involuntarily failed to meet the requirements that he had stressed in the first days of our married life and that I was still eager to fulfill. Though I had early realized that the time might come when he would be satisfied with fewer proofs of devotion than I would be glad to give him, I had not visualized a time when we would occupy separate rooms because this was his preference, or when references to the act of love would bring forth the comment that I was "attaching too much importance to that sort of thing." He had led, for the most part, a healthful, vigorous outdoor life and had retained, to a surprising degree, his fine physique as a young athlete; moreover, from the time he was seventeen years old he had run a successful stock farm where he raised horses and sheep, as well as cattle, and their breeding was of constant concern and paramount importance. Both his early dismissal of sex from his personal life (for there was never any other woman involved) and his reluctance to consider it part of a normal adult relationship are, in some ways, hard to explain. On the other hand, the number of celibates and marriages occurring at middle-age in his family, its extreme prudery and his own disinclination for mixed society might have warned an older and more experienced woman that though his feeling for me was abiding love and not, as my mother claimed, a brief infatuation, its urgency would be assuaged by possession and paternity. It did not occur to me, either, that the fact that I was just over thirty and he was over fifty had anything to do with the difference in our emotional conditions and needs. No one clarified this for me. Lacking this and other enlightenment, I was disheartened and unhappy. I did not see where the courage to go on was coming from.

As is so often the case, it came from a wholly unexpected source. My friend Mary Gray had gone to California the previous spring, since a summer there had been recommended by her husband's doctor for Roland's health. They now had four children and had taken them all with them and it had become advisable, especially for the sake of the youngest, who was delicate, for Mary to prolong her stay. She had been concerned about my slow convalescence and had recognized some of the factors, besides my operation, which partially accounted for this; she saw no reason, if a change were good for the Grays, why it should not be good for me. She wired, asking if I would not come and make her a visit. She would be responsible for my traveling expenses up to a certain sum, which she mentioned, and it was a generous one.

My first reaction to this invitation was a negative one. I had never left my family for any length of time or gone any distance from them; I took it for granted that my husband and my children needed me. As a child and a young girl I had traveled a great deal, because that was what my mother loved to do and was free to do. I had enjoyed the many trips I had made with her, including one we took to California when I was sixteen, but I had ceased to think of travel *per se* as a normal part of everyday life, and California now seemed to me like the other side of the world.

Little by little, as I lay on the sofa in front of the living room fire fingering the telegram, my viewpoint changed. Only one member of my family really needed me at present, and that was my eldest son Henry. For some time he had been having serious trouble with his eyes, and all the previous winter, had been forbidden to use them more than an hour a day; but he had kept well ahead of his scholastic schedule through brief lessons from Sadie Carr, supplemented with much reading aloud on my part. I knew of no reason why I could not undertake all his teaching, and do it as well in California as in New Hampshire. I also knew Mary would be glad to have me bring him and I would not need to ask her for extra money if I did so. Henry would not be twelve until the following March, so he could travel half-fare; and he had enough money in his savings account, made up from the five- and ten-dollar gold pieces which were then standard Christmas and birthday presents, to more than pay for that. I could not think of a better way for him to spend this golden hoard; he would get a great deal out of such a trip.

Ina had remarried after ten years of faithful service, but again the gods had been very good to me: two friends, Carrie Greene and Catherine Argo, who were losing a position in Cambridge because their employers were going to Europe, had advertised in the Boston *Evening Transcript* for a position where they could be together. They were willing to go to the country and to accept moderate wages if this did not involve separation. By great good luck, I had noticed the advertisement and had written them; the response to my letter had been so favorable that I had made a hurried trip to Boston to interview them. Carrie was a Nova Scotian in her early thirties. Cathie was a much younger and very attractive Scot who had been brought to the United States in her teens by relatives whom she had found so uncongenial that she had struck out for herself. She had found, through employment in the same house with Carrie, the affection she had missed. Both young women were well trained and willing to work hard; their references were impeccable. I did not hesitate to engage them, and the day Ina left they came to the Farm.

They had now been with us a year and a half and had given complete satisfaction. They had acquired acceptable suitors, so they were finding that life in the country surpassed their fondest expectations. They were

impressed by Harry, good to John and slavishly devoted to Peter. I
need not hesitate to leave on account of the two younger boys, and this
was equally true as far as Harry was concerned. He was home less than
ever since he was devoting most of his time to campaigning all over the
state. He subscribed to every paper published in New Hampshire, both
daily and weekly, and was assured of gratifying editorial support. Politically, there was nothing I could do to help him; such a thing had never
been suggested by him or anyone else. In fact, the press had mentioned
me just once—in connection with my illness. Reference had been made
to the candidate's three sons—"all eventually destined for Harvard"—
so, indirectly, marriage was established. But no one gave that a thought
as a factor of any importance. If anything, it would be a relief to Harry
to know that I was not moping around the house, as I had been doing
so long, but had found something to cheer me up.

   Once the decision had been made to accept Mary's invitation, Henry
and I were on our way very quickly, he in a state of great excitement, I
in a state of release from tension and depression. As a polio epidemic
was raging in Boston, we went via Montreal and, though delayed seven
hours by a freight train wreck near Toronto, reached Detroit in time to
take a drive through the city and have tea at the Statler before leaving,
at eight in the evening, for Chicago. We arrived there at the untimely
hour of four in the morning and presented ourselves, rather apologetically, at the elegant Blackstone. But we were received with the utmost
courtesy and given a beautiful big room where we slept until lunchtime;
then we went to spend the night at Highland Park with my old friend
Helen Cutler, now Mrs. Russell Mott, and her family. I had seen her
only once since she had been a bridesmaid at my wedding, but found
her as lovely to look at and as interesting to talk to as ever. There was a
fine game of bridge that evening and the next day Helen and her eldest
son, who was about a year younger than Henry, went into Chicago with
us for lunch at the University Club. Afterward, while the two boys were
at a football game, Helen and I went to a superb performance of *Justice*
with John Barrymore starring. And at eight that evening, Henry and I
were on the Overland Limited of the Santa Fe headed for Los Angeles.

   We were both fascinated by everything about the trip, and now that
twilight has descended on the great railroads, I am doubly glad that I
knew them in the days of their ultimate glory. Henry's first ambition
was to become actively associated with one, and by way of preparation
he had long since abandoned the electric train in the playroom for an
outdoor route between the barns, manned by his carts and his brothers'.
He had already traveled many times on the Connecticut and Passumpsic
Railroad connecting Boston and Montreal, which had been built by his

grandfather Keyes, and had read everything he could find about its creation and operation. To travel on the great road of which this grandfather had been president seemed to him like the next step toward the achievement of his dream. The service and cuisine of the diner were impeccable; our compartment provided us with every possible comfort and the observation car gave us every possible opportunity of enjoying the scenery. My first trip to California had been made by a different route, and I had not seen the Painted Desert before; no arid region that I have seen since, in any part of the world, compares with its splendor. As soon as we drew to a stop in Albuquerque, the train was surrounded with picturesque Indians hopefully waiting to sell their wares—woven blankets, beaten silver, turquoise jewelry. We could hardly believe these people and their products were real. It all seemed too marvelous to be true.

The morning of the third day we began to see orange groves; then the city of Los Angeles swallowed them up and we were caught in a tide of popular excitement a hundred times more powerful than our own. This was Election Day and it meant, to that state, at that time, not only the election of a president, with Hughes and Wilson running neck and neck, but also a frantic struggle between the wets and the drys. We thought we were well acquainted with local option. After all, hadn't New Hampshire set such a notable example of handling this that its methods had been copied in Massachusetts and various other places? Wasn't it my husband—Henry's father—who had been responsible for a large part of its success, as chairman of the State Excise Commission? Now we realized that we knew practically nothing about this vital question, by California's criteria. New Hampshire was not a wine producing state; it was the people's standards of sobriety, not the livelihood of thousands, that was at stake there, and this made all the difference. It was fortunate that we had two hours to spare between the time the Overland Limited arrived in Los Angeles and the time a local train left for Ventura, from a station on the other side of the city; otherwise, it is doubtful that we could have made the connection. The shouting, pushing crowds had overflowed from the sidewalks into the streets, and paid no attention to the vehicles that were trying to pass through them. It was all very exhilarating, but it was also very dangerous to ignore the belligerent mood of people at fever pitch. Stimulated though I was, I became increasingly conscious of my responsibility to my young son. In one way, I wanted to continue as part of such a scene; in another, I was relieved when our train pulled out of the station and started up the coast.

The atmosphere was still charged with excitement. Countless bonfires were burning along the way, and apparently no one had gone to bed in the towns through which we passed. They were all as noisy and crowded and electrified as Los Angeles. When we reached Ventura, Morrison, Mary's conservative and reliable chauffeur, who was standing on the platform when we descended from the train, shepherded us expertly through the crush and stowed us securely in the waiting car. Almost directly across the street election returns were being flashed on a huge screen. I had caught the fever myself by that time. I wanted to know what was going to happen next.

"Couldn't we stop and watch a few minutes, Morrison?" I pleaded.

"Well, I don't know, madam. Mrs. Gray's instructions were that I should bring you straight to Nordhoff. She's waiting up for you."

"Just a few minutes! I'm sure she won't mind."

"Well, madam, if you insist."

He was reluctant, but he was efficient. Inside of five minutes, he had maneuvered the car into a place where we could have an unobstructed view of the screen. Henry and I leaned forward eagerly, determined to miss nothing. And as if we had been meant to arrive neither a moment earlier nor a moment later, this is what we saw:

KEYES CARRIES NEW HAMPSHIRE BY 5,000.

In a large state five thousand votes do not represent much of a majority, but in New Hampshire they meant a very substantial victory. Henry and I were pleased and proud without believing that it affected us very closely; at no time had we been made to feel part of the campaign, and nothing had ever been said about moving the family to Concord in case Harry were elected. I did know that New Hampshire was one of the few states which did not provide a gubernatorial mansion and that the governor's salary was only three thousand a year; so I more or less took it for granted that Harry would take a room at the Eagle Hotel, as he had when he was a member of the State Legislature and Excise Commission, and that the children and I would remain at the Farm. We were still very far from being part of the political picture, and at the moment Henry and I were very far away geographically. To add to our sense of separation, we received no answer to the immediate wire of congratulation which we sent or to any of our letters, nor did telegrams or mail of any description reach us during our entire stay in California. Why this happened still remains a mystery, for we were later assured that both had been sent and there had been no mistake about the address. To be sure, we had given this beforehand as Nordhoff, for we did not know until after our arrival that the Grays and their house guests were to move to Hollywood in less than a week; but of this change in plan my husband and staff were immediately notified, and everyone was cautioned that the words "Care of Mrs. Roland Gray" must appear on all communications. Whatever the reason for the baffling silence, it did not contribute to my peace of mind or raise the low spirits which my devoted friend was trying so hard to improve.

She continued to be much concerned about my health and, since I was averse to consulting a strange doctor if it could be avoided, insisted that I let her dress the scar, which was no worse but still showed no signs of healing. I spent most of my time in bed or on a sofa until we moved, while Henry for the first (and, I am afraid, for the last) time in his life enjoyed some horseback riding.

Mary, who drove as efficiently as she did almost everything, decided I would find the trip to Hollywood by car less tiring than by train; but on the way we were caught in a vicious sandstorm which would have tried almost anyone's endurance, and I was in a state of collapse when we reached our destination. And contrary to expectations, the climate proved an added ordeal. I could not adjust myself to wearing a muslin dress in the middle of the day because it was so warm, and then going to bed in a flannel nightgown with a hot water bottle and a mound of blankets because it was so cold at night. Despite my failure to improve by leaps and bounds as soon as I had reached California, the split in the scar tissue did not spread, and in other ways I began to gain enough to enforce daily lessons in ancient history upon a pupil who was finding a good deal to divert him, and I got considerable enjoyment out of my visit.

We went to the races at Santa Monica and saw Dario Resta break the world's record in automobile racing. (I suppose now his pace would hold up traffic because of its slowness.) We went to Universal City and to St. Gabriel's Mission and up Mt. Rubidoux to see the cross planted there by Father Junipero Serra. Mary and I went to a concert given by Percy Grainger, in which he played nothing but Chopin and played it superbly; and Henry and I went, via San Juan Capistrano, to San Diego and saw the illumination of the Fair in the evening and its principal buildings the following morning. I took Henry and two of the Gray children to the ostrich farm in South Pasadena, and we all celebrated Thanksgiving together with a mock turkey, as Mary had become a confirmed vegetarian. Henry found it hard to forgive her this masquerade, and it helped reconcile him to our departure when we left on the first of December for Idaho Springs in Colorado, to visit my half-brother James Underhill and his wife Lucy.

As a little girl there was no one in the world whom I loved as much as James. He was fifteen years older than I was, and no child ever had a kinder or more thoughtful elder brother. When he was at Harvard, he came back to Beacon Street every week end to build me a new house with my stone blocks—demolishing the one he had built the week before—and to take me for a long walk. The first time our mother took me to Europe he was doing post-graduate work at the University of Geneva, and he always had time to give me a boat ride on Lake Léman or one on the funicular to the top of Mt. Salève. After that, he went west to pursue his profession as a mining engineer. The year I was sixteen, when my mother and I went to California, we spent several months in Idaho Springs, and I went to the bottom of numerous mines and the top of numerous mountains with him. He had declined to come to my wedding and give me away. The Keyeses would have been surprised to learn that he felt just as strongly as they did that the marriage was a mistake, because he did not approve of my future brother-in-law Charlie. (They had been in the same class at Harvard, and there had been a widespread jest to the effect that Charlie's middle name, not Harry's, should have been Wilder.) I had missed James very much all these years, and it meant even more to me to be with him and Lucy in Colorado than it had meant to be with Mary in California. Now I was not able to go to the bottom of mines and the top of mountains with him, but Henry did and learned a great deal in the process, besides having a wonderful time. We did not get very far with ancient history in Idaho Springs.

One day Lucy took Henry on an outing, leaving me alone with James, and I gathered this was to give me a chance to talk confidentially with my brother. In fact, despite his natural reserve, he went so far as to ask if anything were troubling me, and I have always been sorry that, after a moment's hesitation, I said, "Nothing much," and changed the subject; it would have been a great relief to discuss all my problems with him. But I did not want him to know I was worried about money, because he would then offer to help me and he had none to spare; and since he had not approved of my marriage, I was afraid if I told him about my feeling of futility, he would blame Harry for something for which I myself was possibly to blame; it would have been disloyal to take the risk. I brought the conversation to a close and turned all my attention to getting the dinner. Although by then I knew how to prepare a good many different dishes quite efficiently, I never had put a whole meal on the table, and I was ashamed to confess this and appalled with fear lest I could not. I was also very much surprised to find with how little effort I succeeded and how much James enjoyed chicken the way I fixed it!

Though I had not confided in my brother, it was evident that he and

Lucy were both concerned about me. They were devout Christian Scientists, but since I was not, they felt I ought to see a doctor, and I did not succeed in stalling as I had with Mary Gray. A kind physician by the name of Dr. Morehouse came to see me twice and looked rather thoughtful; it would be a good plan, he said, for me to stay quietly in bed until that split scar had healed.

Lucy and James kept house very simply, not to say sketchily, because they were more interested in other things, and I knew it would be very inconvenient, as well as awkward, considering their faith and that of most of their friends, for them to have an invalid in the house. Besides, by now I had heard from Harry: He had found a house in Concord which he could rent and which he liked; he thought I would like it, too. He would meet me in Boston and show me the plans. I must stay at the Vendome long enough to shop for whatever I felt would be necessary in the way of clothes; he would like me to let him know about how much that would cost and he would arrange to meet the bills. Henry and I left Idaho Springs as soon as I could send an answer and get packed, though Dr. Morehouse had paid me another troubled visit and I agreed to stay in bed on the train, which I did, even when it made a stop at Niagara Falls, where Henry did his first independent sightseeing. Presently, we were back in Boston and again installed at the Vendome.

My first caller was Foster Kellogg, and his visit was strictly professional. He took one look at me and told me I had better stay in bed.

I obeyed without argument, but afterward we discussed not only my health but the general situation at some length, and his adivce sounded precautionary rather than mandatory. In fact, the only definite order I can recall was not to move too many grand pianos around. I confessed that I had come to Boston on purpose to shop, and he had no trouble in understanding that the inauguration of a governor undoubtedly indicated a more ample wardrobe for his wife than I had on hand. In those days, I could slip easily into ready-made clothes, and could choose what I wanted and needed very quickly. For the first time since my marriage, a definite sum for an outfit had been approved by my husband and I would undertake to keep within it, going to stores where I knew I could find what I liked at reasonable prices and not spend hours looking around for something cheaper. (In fact, that has never been my way of shopping. I have always preferred going without to wasting time.) I also had to take Henry to see his oculist, though his eyes were definitely better, and if the oculist's report were as good as we hoped, then we were to go to Milton and see Mr. Field, the headmaster of the Academy, where Henry was entered for the following year. Provided I could do that much, I could and would stay in bed all the rest of the time I was in Boston. Of course when I went back to Pine Grove Farm, I would have to be more active, closing the house, and getting the maids and the children moved to Concord, since there was no one else to do it.

Foster agreed that it looked that way, and though it was then he made the remark about grand pianos, showing he did not feel quite easy about Pine Grove Farm, he seemed to think I ought to be able to manage the shopping, the oculist and the trip to Milton all right if I kept my word about staying in bed the rest of the time. So, two days later, I began my search for a new wardrobe. I had set my heart on getting my dress for the Inaugural Ball at Hollander's, then quite the most elegant specialty shop in the city. I could hardly believe my good luck when the first thing I tried on—a pink and silver brocade, which was the dress of my dreams for the occasion—fitted me as if it had been made for me. I gave the charge address and stopped, on my way out of the store, to buy a petticoat. As I stood at the counter, a good-looking man, formally dressed, who seemed deeply embarrassed, came up to me.

"Mrs. Keyes?" he said. It sounded like a question, and I thought he was merely trying to identify me, so I nodded and smiled and went on with my purchase. "I'm very sorry," he said, and I could tell from the sound of his voice that he really was, "but our accounting department tells me it can't authorize the charge on the dress you just selected."

"Why it's the same charge address I've had for years! Lots of my clothes came from here when I was just a little girl."

"Yes, Mrs. Keyes. We appreciate that. And your mother's account is still in order. But since your marriage you've made very few purchases here. And the last one—a velvet suit—has never been paid for. We try to extend every courtesy to our old customers. But when bills are unpaid for years. . . ."

The velvet suit was already so old that I had forgotten when I bought it; I realized it must have been in the era before I began to be troubled by those communications marked "Please Remit," which occasionally strayed by mistake from Harry's desk—where they belonged, since the accounts were in his name and not in mine—and which he showed me occasionally of his own accord and said he did not know what he was going to do about them. Neither had happened in the case of Hollander's, so when I was authorized to spend what I needed on clothes for Concord, I had taken it for granted that everything was in order. By now there were several interested shoppers, besides the clerk who had been waiting on me, listening to our conversation and the manager's embarrassment was more than equalled by mine, but I tried to speak calmly.

"I'm very sorry," I said. "Will it be all right for me to have this petticoat I've just chosen? I have enough cash with me to pay for that, but not enough to pay for the brocade."

"Certainly. We'd be very glad to sell you the petticoat for cash," the manager said. I paid for the petticoat, took the package containing it and walked out. I did no more shopping that afternoon. As far as I knew, the accounts at Stearns, Hovey's and Chandler's might be in no better order than the one at Hollander's. When I got back to the hotel, I did what was, for me, a very unusual thing: I put in a long distance call for Harry, who was in Concord. I hope and believe I did not speak disagreeably, but I did speak firmly. I told him what had happened, and though he admitted he had never paid for the velvet suit, he said he was sure a great many people owed Hollander's as much as he did, if not a good deal more.

"Perhaps that's just the trouble," I replied. "Anyway, unless you can get a check in the mail this evening, I'm not going to do any more shopping. I won't go to Concord. I'll stay at the Farm with the children and I won't reproach you because you can't afford to have us join you after all. But if I'm going to be where people can see me, I'm going to try to look the way they think their governor's wife ought to look. I'm not going to the Inaugural Ball in a dress I've run up myself between breakfast and supper. You wrote me you thought I'd mentioned a very modest sum in telling you what I'd need to spend, but you didn't write me that you still owed money on the one suit I've bought in the last six years. If you had, I'd have told you that had to be paid for first and the money for it couldn't come out of the sum we allotted for this winter. Just let me know."

The next afternoon I received a telephone call from Hollander's. They were very sorry there had been a misunderstanding—they had not realized the occasion for which I had chosen the dress was such an important one. They were sending the dress to me at once. And, yes, the account had been settled.

"Settled and closed," I said.

I did not have the strength to give up that dress. But it was useless to pretend that bills would be paid as promptly as they should be, and the episode had been too painful to risk repeating. For the time being, I must shop at less expensive stores. And somehow, as soon as possible, I must find a way of paying for my own clothes.

There was nothing the matter with the accounts at the other stores to which I went. I bought a burgundy-red wool suit, a blue serge dress, a red velvet evening dress and what we then called an afternoon dress of garnet-colored velvet. Gertrude Baker, who had made her debut the year before and had had more clothes than she needed for it, contributed a beautiful pink satin dress, a sage-green evening dress and a rose-colored velvet evening cape with a fur collar. The latter was especially welcome, as I had meant to make a sealskin coat do for both day-time and evening wear.

The report from Henry's oculist was encouraging, the reception at Milton Academy very cordial. Harry, who had been in Concord all week, came to spend Sunday with us and brought with him the plans of the house he had rented. I agreed with him that it could not have been pleasanter or better suited to our needs. No reference was made either to the Hollander episode or to the doubtful state of my health. On Monday, he went back to Concord, and I went to Pine Grove Farm.

I tried to remember Foster's jesting remark about grand pianos, but there seemed to be so much for me to do, and there was no doubt that the inflamed area around the scar was spreading and turning darker and that I was feeling much worse generally. On the first of January, I started the elder boys off to Concord. They were very proud at being allowed to make the trip alone, and there was no question that they would be well looked after on their arrival, as Harry, Belle and Gertrude were already at the rented house and the owner's cook was staying on. After the boys had gone, I sent for the local doctor, who told me I had blood poisoning, that I must have a trained nurse at once and that it would be foolhardy for me to attempt the journey to Concord. In return, I told him that foolhardy or not, that was what I meant to do, and he accepted my decision as inevitable under the circumstances.

By great good fortune, I was able to reach Miss Griffin, one of the nurses who had cared for me at the Faulkner Hospital and had come back to the Farm with me afterward. She left Boston at once, and though she agreed with the local doctor's opinion, she did not refuse to help me prepare for the trip. Harry had been home for just twenty-four hours during the week of moving and, as he was leaving, had leaned over my bed with tears in his eyes and said, in a strained voice, "I hope very much you'll be able to come. I need you." It was the first time he had ever told me so, and after that nothing would have kept me from going. I was important to him after all. Not in the same way as at first, but in a way that Carrie and Cathie mattered a great deal to us both. I was satisfied with that.

Miss Griffin, Peter, Carrie, Cathie and I took the train for Concord on the third, though I traveled, only partially dressed, in a drawing room. At the end of the trip, I was cordially greeted with cheers of, "We knew you'd make it!" But I was too sick even to listen, and I knew I had fever and that something was given me to ease the pain a little.

After that, my impressions began to blur, but I was aware of a strange doctor and then of a second nurse in the room and next of Foster Kellogg, so I realized they had sent to Boston for him. Somewhere, a long way off, my husband was being inaugurated Governor of New Hampshire, and my friends, who had come to Concord from Newbury, were dancing at the Inaugural Ball. But all that day and all the next night the two doctors and the two nurses watched beside my bed. I heard them talking to each other in whispers, and once in a while one of them came and spoke gently to me and did something they thought might ease the pain. I cannot remember how any of them looked or what any of them said, except Foster. But I do remember seeing his stricken face and hearing him say something that sounded like, "I couldn't believe it could be bad as this until I saw her. I'd have given anything in this world—" And then I must have slept. But I do remember that the room was banked with flowers, that it was completely surrounded with long-stemmed red roses and that I declined to release a bunch of violets with a red rose in the center which had been sent me to carry at the ball and which I held fast in my hand.

Part Three

Parallel Destinies

I<small>T WAS</small> several days before I was considered out of danger and a week before it seemed wiser to move me to Boston. Miss Griffin remained in charge, but the Concord nurse did not accompany us; instead, a replacement was waiting for us at "88," where I was installed in a huge, chilly guest room at the rear of the second story, which had been deemed the best place for me. Belle remained in Concord to run the house and supervise the children, and before I left, had managed to convey to me her feeling that Harry was a better husband than I deserved, which, of course I knew had always been her opinion but which I thought might have been left unexpressed just then. Also, as a rabid homeopathist, she had made it clear that she hoped my doctors would soon stop giving me that "horrid stuff," i.e., anything to relieve pain. Fortunately, as I was not nursing a baby, I was not again forced to undergo the agony of the summer I had been burned. Aside from the fact that such remarks, which Gertrude Baker frequently repeated, were no more beneficial to me than they would have been to anyone as near a nervous breakdown as I was, everything possible was done in the household for my comfort and well being.

Foster had insisted upon calling in another doctor for consultation. I took an immediate dislike to him and doubt to this day that he did me much good, although he stood very high in his profession. The first time he was summoned, he was at table, and evidently he had not only dined very well but wined along with his dinner. He was not really intoxicated, but he was certainly high. His breath and his manner were alike obnoxious to me, and though he never came in this condition again, I could not forget that he had done so once or dismiss the fear that he might do so again.

I wanted very much to die, and though naturally I was told that such a yearning was not only abnormal but sinful, no one said anything sufficiently cogent to overcome it. Strangely enough, a dream effected what no individual had been able to do, and it was not even a dream which dealt with realities or with personalities that I could recognize. I seemed to be dead and lying in an open coffin, past which my grief-stricken friends were filing. Then one of them stopped and spoke, not sorrowfully but reproachfully: "You've always told me that nothing was too hard to face. You've persuaded me to believe that and act on my belief. Well, I don't believe it any more. I'm not going to keep on struggling. You didn't have to die. You just gave up because the going was hard. That's what I'll do, from now on."

Miss Griffin heard me calling "No, no!" and came quickly to my bedside. I was sitting up, more than half awake. "I'm not going to die!" I said firmly. "Why, of course not!" she answered, and then added the cliché I was so tired of hearing, "Just think of all you've got to live for!"

"I've got more than I realized," I told her. After that, nothing was said about dying. We talked, instead, about how long it would take to get well.

The person who was of the most help and comfort to me during this troublous time was Elizabeth Sweetser, now Mrs. Kenneth Moller. She was then living just around the corner on Marlborough Street, and every day she came to see me at "88"—sometimes for only a few minutes, sometimes for a long visit and always at odd hours. I never knew when she would come, but I did know she would come before the day was over. She gave me no sanctimonious advice, and indeed no advice of any kind; she listened quietly and understandingly to whatever I said to her and commented on it if I asked her to. Aside from this, she merely chatted. about what she and our mutual friends were doing or about Kenneth's business and their little daughter's progress in school—anything she thought would interest and amuse me. When she had gone, I lay still, thinking over her latest visit and anticipating her next one.

After nearly three weeks it was decided I did not need a second nurse and was well enough to discuss my case a little. Foster was convinced that between the time he saw me in Boston on my return from California and the time he saw me in Concord on the day of Harry's inauguration I must have scratched the inflamed area around the scar and the scar tissue itself; it had been irritated but certainly not septic when he first saw it; but when he next examined me there was widespread infection. I admitted it was possible I had done this, when half asleep and wretchedly uncomfortable, in a drowsy effort for relief. But I could not remember doing so. In any case, was that really the root of the trouble? If the scar tissue had been normal in the beginning, would it have split? Yes, it could have, under the circumstances he outlined. Well, shouldn't I have been put back to bed then and there? No, that was not the way such cases were treated nowadays. . . . We looked at each other unhappily, conscious that after years of unalloyed friendship we were losing confidence in each other and, what was just as bad, that each of us was losing self-confidence. I was unsure that the sad state of things was not partly my fault; Foster was unsure that it was not partly his. I had turned to him in trouble and the result had been close to tragedy. I was more than willing to assume my share of the blame or all of it, if what had happened really was my fault; but I knew that never, as long as I lived, would I rely unquestioningly on anyone again. (Though the scar tissue seems to be normal now, it was not normal as recently as eighteen years ago. I wrote nearly all of my novel *Steamboat Gothic* in bed because it had split again, and it did so periodically for more than thirty years, though blood poisoning never resulted a second time.)

At the end of four weeks I was dressed for the first time, and three days later Miss Griffin and I returned to Concord. I still had to be very careful not to irritate the scar, for though it had healed after a fashion, it was still sensitive and the slightest strain threatened to break it. Besides, I had of course lost a great deal of strength. It was a long time before I really recovered, but during my slow convalescence, my Concord doctor made a suggestion that proved invaluable. "I am afraid you are not going to be very strong for quite a while," he said, "but if you will make up your mind as to what is the most important thing for you to do in a given period, and do just that, I think you will be able to do it. You may have to stay in bed beforehand and go back to bed afterward. But the public's general impression will be that you are doing a good job as a governor's wife."

He was absolutely right. Comparatively soon, I was able to preside informally at a tea table every afternoon, and it was made known that I would be glad to have callers at that time. Next, I began to go regularly to church, where Henry and John were both singing in the choir and where, on Palm Sunday, Henry was confirmed; to accept invitations to small dinners; to join other young mothers as they looked on at their children's dancing classes once a week; and to join a similar group studying first aid under the auspices of the Red Cross. Everyone was very kind and cordial and understanding, both of the effort I was making and the handicap I had to overcome; and I quickly came to feel I was among friends and not critics. It was my first experience in a small city,

where life was as different from life in the country as it was from life in
a metropolis, and it was a very happy one. To this day, my memories of
Concord are among the happiest of my life.

The inauguration had taken place in January. By late spring I was
well enough to return calls, to give a large reception and several dinners, at one of which Admiral Peary was the guest of honor, and to
take—and pass with a grade of 95—an examination qualifying me to
teach Red Cross First Aid. I was no longer teaching either Henry or
John, as Henry—now permitted to use his eyes for three hours a day
—was being tutored by a member of the St. Paul's faculty, and John
was going to a public school. The experiment of private lessons was a
great success; Henry passed his examinations for Milton, "showing
marked excellence in Latin," early in June. The experiment with the
public school was less successful. Evidently, all sorts of epidemics were
rampant, for in swift succession John came home with measles,
chicken-pox and German measles, generously distributing them to his
brothers and keeping the governor's house in and out of quarantine all
winter. Nevertheless, as this drew to a close, I not only was giving the
effect of being active, I had really achieved activity.

On the sixth of April the United States declared war on Germany.
Before the end of May we were all back at Pine Grove Farm for the
summer, and combining my knowledge of Red Cross Surgical Dressings
and First Aid, I had begun to teach both; I took an active part in the
Liberty Loan Drives, the work for food conservation and many other
wartime endeavors. Service and not amusement had become the chief
objective of American women everywhere.

It was when the spell of this spirit of service was very strong that I
received a letter one day from the editor of a New York magazine, asking if I would state my views on the wearing of mourning in wartime.
The magazine was not an important one. It owed its brief existence to a
group of wealthy women who desired a channel for the expression of
their views; subscriptions were by invitation only and cost twelve dollars a year. I had not been invited to subscribe to it, nor should I have
felt I could afford to do so. (Twelve dollars, in those days, meant almost half the cost of a "baby bond" and quite a few skeins of heavy
khaki-colored yarn!) Nor was the editor writing me because in some miraculous way he had become aware of my hidden manuscripts and was
eager to give their creator a chance to express herself publicly. He was
simply sending a form letter to every governor's wife in the Union.

I did not regard this communication as one of much consequence and
cast it into the scrapbasket and went to bed. I was very tired. I had
spent the day collecting the knitted outfits the women of Haverhill were

giving to the battleship *New Hampshire,* and I had no energy or enthusiasm left for the pile of mail on my desk. But somehow I could not dismiss that letter from my mind; and at last I got up again, salvaged it, wrote a few swift sentences on the back of it, slipped it into an envelope and put it in the mail bag. Then I forgot all about it.

Several weeks later, in the course of a visit to Boston, my memory was suddenly jogged by Mary Gray.

"That was a very good little article of yours in *The Chronicle,* Frances," she said, "and the idea you presented seems to be meeting with fairly general approval."

"Chronicle? What article? What idea?" I gasped.

She calmly handed me a magazine. On the page she had turned down I unbelievingly read the lines I had written, hurriedly but with great conviction, suggesting that a gold star rather than black crepe might serve as a suitable symbol for those bereaved by the war.

"Very good," Mary repeated. "You know I always told you not to give up trying to write."

"I know," I said dazedly, "but you're the only person that believes I can do it."

"This editor evidently believes it," Mary retorted. "I shouldn't be surprised if he asked you for something else."

I dismissed the idea as fantastic. But I returned to the Farm to find a letter from him saying there had been such a wide response to my article on mourning that he would be grateful if I would send him another, this time outlining my views on playing bridge during the war, and asking for its delivery before a certain date.

I glanced at the calendar. My mail had not been forwarded to me during my absence, and the editor's letter had lain on my desk for several days. In order to have my reply reach him on time, it would have to be posted in Woodsville, seven miles away, before two in the morning when the New York express left. It was already past midnight. I woke up our long-suffering hired man, who, like Ina and Cathie, never failed me in any emergency.

"I want you to take a—a letter to Woodsville for me," I said through the crack of his door. "Please! It isn't written yet, but it will be, by the time you've dressed."

A fortnight later, my second effort appeared in *The Chronicle.* Shortly afterward, the *New Republic* published a scathing satire on it, and the *Literary Digest* reprinted it with favorable comment.

I sat down with the three periodicals in my lap and did some very hard thinking. Quite by accident, I had penetrated rather extensively into print. What, I asked myself seriously, would happen if I *tried* to penetrate? I decided to find out.

The attic was not only the one quiet place in a house full of children but also the only spot where my occupation was unlikely to meet with discovery and consequent ridicule. With several "town histories" and some yellowing family papers for reference, I wrote—rewrote—and rewrote again—a sketch of the first Frances Parkinson's life. Then, as secretly as possible, I dispatched it to the editor of our state magazine, *The Granite Monthly*.

His reply came by return mail. I read it with incredulous eyes. "I have much pleasure in accepting your story of your grandmother," the letter ran, "not only because of its historical value, but because it is exceedingly well written."

After that, I spent every minute I could steal in the seclusion of the attic. The story of Frances Parkinson was followed by other historical sketches; some articles and verses inspired by the war were also written, revised and sent out to seek a welcome. None of them was published in a magazine of wide circulation or national importance, but all were accepted by minor periodicals, and one or two were reprinted. *The Chronicle* continued to ask for articles and used all I submitted; and the mere fact that any magazine should like what I wrote gave me the courage and self-confidence I had lacked before. Emboldened by the extremely modest success I had achieved, I walked into the ground floor office of a well-known publisher the next time I was in Boston and asked a startled clerk how to submit a manuscript for book publication. He disappeared, but returned after a few minutes still looking rather dazed, and said the editor would like to speak to me.

I climbed a flight of seemingly endless steps and was ushered into a large room, gloomy except for its open fire, that looked out on an ancient graveyard. A gentleman of scholarly appearance, who was barricaded behind a large desk, invited me to be seated and regarded me with evident amusement.

"I understand that you want to send us a story," he said. "We would prefer that you should not roll it up tightly and tie it with pink ribbon, but otherwise we try not to be unreasonable in our requirements. However, one of these is for typed scripts, double-spaced on standard-sized paper."

With pride, I told him that I already knew that much and had taught myself to type. Then he began to question me. So I had been writing for years and hiding the evidences of my crime in bureau drawers? And now I had had a few articles and verses published, and that had given me the idea there might be a real story in at least one of those hidden manuscripts? Well, one never knew. At least it would do no harm to try. . . .

I went home with gritted teeth. It did not seem possible to squeeze out an extra moment from my overcrowded days to spend at the typewriter. The children were four, ten and twelve years old respectively. I was deeply pledged to war work of various kinds, and my health, though infinitely improved, was still far from dependable.

How, with all these complications, could I attempt any more? I did not see, but unseeingly I resolved that fifteen minutes a day, taken when and where I could find them, would probably not be very much missed by anyone. I began a systematic effort to show the amused-looking editor what I could do.

It would be gratifying to relate that he was greatly impressed by the first typescript I sent him. Far from it. He sent it back with a note which was a masterpiece of delicate irony. Nevertheless, he added a postscript to the effect that I might try again.

It was almost a dare. I accepted it as such. But the second manuscript also came back. So, incidentally, had every short story and article I had submitted to a major magazine. To this day I cannot look at a long slender envelope—the so-called "commercial" size—without a distinct sensation of nausea. They are irrevocably associated in my mind with rejected manuscripts.

Early autumn of 1917 found me in a fighting mood. It also brought to light a novel which I had written in odd moments when Peter was a baby—a simple story about the kind of life and kind of people I knew best, entitled *The Old Gray Homestead*. It had been revised and transcribed from my grubby copybooks to smudgy typed sheets and transcribed again to neatly typed and numbered pages. When it was properly tied up and dispatched, I felt much better. Miraculously, I happened to have a spare evening on my hands, and in great exuberance of spirit I sat down and wrote a very light-minded essay which I called "The Satisfied Reflections of a Semi-Bostonian." Then, spurred on to mischief by the laughter of a friend to whom I read it, I sent it off to a very highbrow magazine, the last place on earth where I thought it would be welcome.

The essay and the book were both accepted, and this time I was paid for the essay—all of seventy dollars. Harry was away when the check came, but I put it on his desk so that he would find it as soon as he reached home, together with a note I had proudly typed on the rejuvenated Remington:

Dearest,

Here is my first check—not a very large one to be sure, but much bigger than I expected, since the little article for which I received it did not take me over three hours to write and, of course, I am entirely unknown as an author.

I am very anxious that this should be used, not for some little luxury that I could not otherwise feel justified in buying, but in the family budget. If you feel you can put enough with it to pay Dr. Ladd's bill for Peter, I should rather that it should go for that than anything else. If not, it would pay our pledge to the last Red Cross Fund—$25—and leave quite a little over for something else. Perhaps it would pay a grocery bill as well. These are just suggestions. It is *yours*, every cent of it, to do exactly what you think best with, and I am reasonably sure now that I shall have more like it, or larger, to give you from now on.

I cannot help taking a certain pride in the fact that, after grieving for many years because I, unlike my two sisters-in-law, brought no fortune to my husband, the first money I am giving him is not inherited, or a present to me from my parents, but something I have earned myself, without the help of anyone.

All good fortune go with you. I believe the hardest days are over for us both.

Yours as ever,
Frances.

The letter announcing that the "Semi-Bostonian" was regarded as "extremely attractive" at *The Atlantic Monthly* where I had expected its levity to be condemned was encouraging and gratifying, especially as most of the reasons I had given for being satisfied were that I had escaped from Boston. But the letter announcing that *The Old Gray Homestead* had pleased and touched the amused-looking editor was a landmark in my life.

I picked it up at the post office one September morning when I was on my way to an outdoor grange meeting which lasted all day, with a picnic luncheon in the woods between the sessions. It was nearly evening when I reached home again and quickly assured myself all was well with the children and the household and that no message had come from Harry, who was campaigning in the south of the state. Then, taking the limp envelope which contained the all-important tidings, I went into the south grove and sat there for a long time.

The sun went down behind the Vermont hills, the river and the meadow grew dusky, the tall trees turned black against the starry sky, the stillness of the autumn evening deepened. The silence, the peace, the beauty around me strengthened my conviction that I had received an accolade and that I must keep a vigil of consecration. It seemed to me there could no longer be any doubt what tools God meant me to use in my lifework; I was going to be a writer. And I made a pledge—partly to myself but mostly to Him—that I would look upon this work not only as a trade but as a trust; that I would never write anything simply for what I could earn by doing so, no matter how much I needed money; that I would never write anything shabby or scandalous, and that I would never consciously write anything inaccurate or unfair or unkind; that I would never let even a scrap of paper leave my hands if what I had written on it was not just as good as I could make it— not as good as I should like to make it, of course; not as good as I hoped to make it some day; not as good as what most other writers were doing; but the very best that was in me.

When at last I rose and went home through the night, it was with a heart singing with happiness, and a strengthened, uplifted spirit. And I recognized that the second great change had taken place in my life. The first had occurred when I became a bride and merged my being with my husband's. Now this union still existed, and I had, besides, a destiny of my very own.

Chapter 10

From that day I knew I was going to be a writer. But it did not occur to me that my writing would ever develop into an independent career. I visualized it only as a measure for helping my husband financially while I went on doing my best to fulfill the obligations of Harry Keyes's wife, whatever they might prove to be. The first of these was to speak at a flag-raising in North Haverhill, which formally inaugurated organized Red Cross work. Two days later I began the distribution of Red Cross and Navy League supplies. The following morning I drove to Hanover with Harry and proudly watched him receive an honorary degree at the Dartmouth Commencement exercises before we went on to Newport, New Hampshire, for luncheon with his staff members.

But the personal records I kept during the summer of 1917 confirm my recollections that war work of one kind or another was regular and frequent:

> Sent David [the current hired man] to deliver 10 Navy League outfits. . . . Spent most of the day telephoning about war funds. . . . Red Cross surgical dressing work in Woodsville all day. . . . Did up wool in the a.m. and delivered it in the p.m. . . . Home nursing 7:30. Canning demonstration in North Haverhill.

Undeniably, we were becoming more and more war conscious; but sometimes patriotic efforts dovetailed with festivities:

> Decorated Town Hall in a.m. . . . Captain Keene's lecture, "Life in the Trenches," and dancing afterward. Splendid time.

Other events were connected with the governorship, and had no direct relation to the war effort:

Staff ladies came here to spend Sunday while their husbands went to the camp with Harry. Dinner and bridge party for them Saturday evening. Church at Woodsville. Lunch at Tarleton Clubhouse. Long drive afterward. Guests departed 11 a.m. Monday. Awfully tired.

On the following day:

Farmers' Association 9:30 a.m. 75 people here.
Farmers' Association—160 people here 3:00 p.m.

We fed these groups, not elaborately, but plentifully; and the coffee, biscuits and doughnuts for the morning party and all punch, sandwiches, salads and cakes for the afternoon party were made in the house. Greeting, feeding and speeding on their way again such groups was obviously regarded as part of my job; and this did not exhaust me, for I went out to lunch informally with my next-door neighbor after the morning party, made calls in the evening and organized a Red Cross Auxiliary in North Haverhill the day after.

In August I went to Littleton, New Hampshire, for the Hospital Fair, as this was an event in which the Glessner family was deeply interested, and my friendship with them went back a long way. George Glessner had been my brother James's best friend at Harvard and had often visited us at The Oxbow. As a small child, I had become exceedingly fond of him. Flinging myself into his arms as he arrived for one such visit, I had exclaimed, "Oh, George, I am so glad you are an old man, because Mamma says I should kiss only old men from now on!" As he must have been all of twenty-one at that time, there was general amusement over my outburst and I was not allowed to forget it for a long while. Then, after he and James were graduated, I completely lost track of him. But though the Glessners were Midwesterners, closely allied with the McCormicks of harvesting-machine fame and fortune, and resided regularly in Chicago, they became greatly attached to their fine estate near Littleton and soon ceased to be known disparagingly as "summer people." George's parents became outstanding for philanthropy and civic improvements, especially for their benefits to aid the local hospital and for the fine stone walls they built, not only on their own property, but along adjacent roadsides; and eventually George, who had married a charming girl named Alice Hamlin, established a year-round residence nearby—a structure of great elegance where a Mexican butler, Román Ovando, gave an exotic as well as experienced touch to the meals he served. George became deeply absorbed in politics, entered the State Legislature and was one of Harry's strongest supporters; it was in this capacity that I renewed my friendship with him, and found him as congenial as ever. As for Alice, she quickly became one of my most valued friends and was the inspiration for the heroine of my "Satisfied Reflections. . . ."

For the Fair that year Alice had chosen as assistants at her table, besides myself, Mrs. Charles Evans Hughes and the famous violinist Maude Powell Turner, who were both spending the summer in the White Mountains.

The autumn proved to be one of maternal duties and anxieties rather than of war work and gubernatorial obligations. I left for Boston with Henry, expecting to see him safely installed at Milton the next day. On the train, he suddenly became ill and by the time we reached the Hotel Puritan, where we had planned to spend only one night, he was delirious with fever. He had been stricken with bronchial pneumonia and it was nearly two weeks before he was well enough to start school. In the meantime I could not leave him as I was his only nurse much of the time. Soon after Henry's recovery, it became apparent that Peter would have to have an operation on his throat: a small lump, which gradually increased in size, was diagnosed as a cyst that might be malignant. The opinion was that the sooner it was out of the child's throat, the better. The operation was performed at the Hotel Puritan, for hospitals were still regarded as a last resort, and all went well, but a great deal of time and money were expended before we were satisfied on that score. All three boys were sick in bed the day before Thanksgiving, which we spent at the Farm, and where we decided to remain for the rest of the winter since the Legislature was not in regular session.

The weather had now become an omnipresent problem. We had almost no fuel and could not get any more—a situation which served to weaken, for me anyway, the argument that if you have enough pull, you can get anything. It took about a ton and a half of coal each week to heat our house, and the best we could do for quite a while was to have it sent in hundred-pound bags by express from Boston. We had our own wood, but only a little of it had been properly seasoned; we had not expected to spend that winter in the country and to need so much. One of my gloomiest memories is that of sitting in front of the living room fire, where the green logs hissed and smouldered, holding Peter in my lap and wondering how I was to get the little boy comfortably through the winter. He had proved to be one of those with whom the various substitutes we were using for white flour did not agree, so that food as well as warmth was a problem as far as he was concerned. Meanwhile, the cold became more intense. Just before New Year's, when I went to Woodsville to do errands, the thermometer stood at thirty-five below zero with a strong wind blowing, and for over a week the mercury never rose to zero. In many places near us all records for cold weather were broken.

Yet on New Year's Eve there was a military ball at Littleton and, for some reason that I have never understood, Harry was perfectly willing to attend it, despite his usual aversion to such functions and the problems which the coal situation and the arctic weather were creating for us at home. We spent the night with the Glessners, and this was also an exception to a well-established rule—indeed, it was the only such visit, outside his family, that I ever knew him to make. The Littleton *Courier* featured the occasion as a "brilliant military ball with . . . crowded hall, fine music, attractive decorations. The social event of the winter. . . . Gov. Henry W. Keyes and Mrs. Keyes were the honored guests of the evening, enjoying the dancing until a late hour."

I am afraid that Harry did not enjoy the dancing on this occasion any more than on others; certainly he did not take part in it, though he actually did lead the Grand March with me and remain at the ball until the end. As for me, I did enjoy it, and was one of the large number who were still on the floor for the good-night waltz. I wore my red velvet dress and had a glorious time.

Chapter 11

DURING the early part of 1918 my activities were subject to frequent interruptions because of illness, both my own and the children's. However, these periods of confinement to the house gave me an opportunity to consider a very important problem.

It was not then customary—though it has since become so—for a governor to seek a second term in New Hampshire; but Harry had been assured of ample support if he would like to succeed himself. He had also been assured of a certain amount of support if he decided to try for the United States Senate; but as there were sure to be other contenders from both parties for the seat of the Democratic senator who was retiring, this attempt might be more of a gamble than the other. Harry paid me the compliment of consulting me as to which I thought would be the wiser course.

Personally, I had been so kindly received as the wife of the governor that I knew I would miss the friendships with which I was now surrounded if I left the milieu in which I had begun to feel at home. On the other hand, I knew I would be greatly thrilled by Washington, so I would be happy whatever way the die was cast. I was not so sure about my husband. It was more natural for me to take chances than it was for him, and it would not have worried me to do so in a case like this. I would have cheerfully assumed that I was going to win until there was definite proof to the contrary, and if I lost, I would go on to the next opportunity that was offered, confident that this time everything would be all right. Very early in life I had learned the truth of the Spanish proverb, "Every time a door closes, another one opens." Harry did not feel that way. He had never been defeated for any office and could not endure the thought of it; defeat and disaster were synonymous to him.

There were other considerations. In a small state like New Hampshire the governor is, or can be, very close to his constituents, and there was no doubt that Harry had achieved and could continue to enjoy this pleasant relationship. "It is one proof of the popularity of Governor Keyes that up in New Hampshire almost everyone calls him Harry," the Boston *Transcript* said in a feature article. But its further statement that this proved he was "a natural mixer" was less true. His mother was painfully shy all her life and never saw anyone outside her own family if she could help it, and Harry had inherited a streak of this shyness. Mrs. Theorore Vail averred that when he was a boy, "he blushed and sat on his hands if he were obliged to meet strangers." Of course, that had long since become a figure of speech; but though he had every social grace, he disliked society, especially mixed society, and it was only with close associates in the athletic and political worlds of which he had been a part practically all his life that he was really a willing mixer. Even in Concord he had gone to only one of the dinner parties given in our honor by members of his staff and their wives; from my own slight experience in Washington as a child and a young girl, I knew it would be much harder for him to withdraw into his shell there whenever he felt like it.

Still another very important consideration lay in the fact that for more than a year now he had been the chief executive in every sense of the word. While in his own state, a governor outranks everyone except the president, even the vice president. In the Senate, everyone outranks a new member, except others who enter at the same time. He would be given one of the most undesirable seats. His name would appear last in the panel of those committees he was called to serve on, and he would have little or no choice as to which these should be. His position as one of ninety-six men, all of them strangers and some of them uncongenial, would be very different from his position as governor.

On the other hand, Washington undoubtedly had more opportunity to offer than New Hampshire. For one thing, to be practical, it offered more money. A senator at that time drew the princely salary of $7,500 a year as against the $3,000 paid the Governor of New Hampshire. As it was now time for John, like Henry, to go away to school, we could not help making that a major consideration. And Washington, which had been regarded by foreigners as one of the minor world capitals before the war, was now taking its proud place as a major one; it would be a very exciting and very important place to live. (And possibly that was another drawback instead of another advantage; I love excitement and thrived on it; Harry hated it!)

When it came to the ethical aspects of the case, which I knew weighed heavily with him, only he could decide whether he could be of more use to his state and his country in Washington or in Concord. His decision, made on that basis, was in favor of Washington. In March he announced his candidacy for the Senate on the Republican ticket, and George H. Moses, a former Minister to Greece, ex-Governor Roland H. Spaulding and Rosecrantz W. Pillsbury, member of a prominent family and a former owner of the Manchester *Union,* all announced theirs at about the same time.

It was evident from the beginning that this was not going to be another case when I could unconcernedly read the words "Keyes carries New Hampshire by 5,000" as they were flashed on a screen.

At the moment, however, there was nothing I could do to be useful, and during the next month I spent considerable time in Boston off and on, as the scar tissue was causing trouble again and Mary Gray had persuaded me to consult, at her expense, a female physician in whom she had great confidence. I followed this doctor's instructions, and though they may have averted more serious trouble, they did not effect a cure, so it was agreed that the benefits received did not warrant leaving home for prolonged treatments, which I was very unwilling to do. However, I did spend some time in Concord, finding, as I had before, much warmhearted hospitality in that pleasant little city. These visits were evidently not without a certain amount of therapeutic value, perhaps because they were made under very luxurious conditions and I had a great deal of needed rest and no responsibilities in the course of them. At all events, I returned to Pine Grove Farm for good early in April and plunged at once into work for the Third Liberty Loan with even more vigor than I had been able to put into the first two.

I had only been home a few days and was already deeply involved in this drive when I was greatly moved by a strange supernatural experience which seemed like a sequel to the one that had occurred in Peter's sickroom more than two years earlier. Richard Cobb had departed for Camp Devens in September, but I had seen him several times since then. One night when I was having supper with Norman Cobb and his wife Maria at The Homestead, Richard had unexpectedly come home on furlough and we had all sat and talked until very late before we parted with the comfortable feeling that this was such a long-established custom it would take more than a war to break it; and we had had other incidental meetings. In January, Richard had been listed among the members of the 302nd Field Artillery eligible for officers' training camp; and in April his name appeared on the roster of those who had qualified for an appointment as a second lieutenant. But nothing had indicated that his departure for France was actually imminent when he arrived at Pine Grove Farm in the middle of a bright and beautiful April afternoon and made the abrupt announcement that he had received his overseas orders; he was leaving the next day and had come to say good-bye to me.

Our friend Earl Greer was driving him on a round of farewell visits, and I invited them both to come in, but Earl said they must hurry and that he would wait outside. I called Harry, who was in his den; just then the telephone rang; he answered it and was held up. Richard and I stood in the front hall, looking at each other but not saying anything; there was so much we wanted to say and we could not say any of it. He put his arms around me and kissed me and said, "Be good." That was all. The next minute he was gone.

I was still standing in the hall, just as he had left me, when Harry finished speaking on the telephone and came out of the den. He knew that I would take this parting very hard, and he tried to say something that would comfort me. He had always understood how much Richard meant to me, that there had been an accord between us into which distant kinship and close friendship both entered, but which had added something special, though undefinable, to those ties, ever since we were children. And much as Harry wanted to help, he was powerless to do so. I told him that and then, ungratefully, I ran out of the house and hurried down the driveway to the south grove, crying bitterly. I sat down on the carpet of fallen pine needles and tried to stop sobbing. At first I couldn't, but when I dried my eyes and looked up, I saw a white figure standing in front of me—the same one I had seen more than two years before bending over my baby's bed. And while I gazed at it unbelievingly, it spoke and, substantially, this is what it said:

"You have nothing to grieve over. Nothing will happen to the man who's just said good-bye to you. He'll be at the Front for six weeks or more, but he won't even be scratched. Tell his mother what I've told you, so she won't be afraid either."

The next day, I went to see Richard's mother and told her what had happened. She had taken to her bed upon Richard's departure and was hysterical. Instead of calming her, I only increased her hysteria. She thought I had imagined or even invented the scene in the pine grove and said it was cruel of me to hold out such false hopes. Nothing could convince her that her son was not going to be killed.

In May a letter I had written to its editor was published by *L'Impartial,* one of the leading French language newspapers in New Hampshire, where there are several excellent ones, for a large part of the population in both Manchester and Nashua is of French-Canadian background, and proudly clings to its linguistic heritage. Previously, *L'Impartial* had commented very gratefully on one of the several political appointments Harry had made among the French Americans. At the same time, it gave considerable space to an article based on his slogan, which had already become very popular in English and which translated smoothly into French, "I'm sowing wheat—are you?" (*"Je sème de l'avoine—et vous?"*)

This seemed to be something on which I could comment with a reasonable degree of intelligence, because of the rich harvests I had seen in France and my sincere belief that our soil and climate in the North Country were as well adapted to the cultivation of wheat as these were abroad; also, since wheat fields in France were by no means always vast, I saw no reason why we should allow ourselves, as Americans, to be persuaded that only the huge farmlands of our West were suitable for such cultivation. I wrote conservatively, suppressing the impulse to mention the arrowheads we had discovered when our lawn was plowed so we might plant it with wheat, lest the connecting link with our ghost story should be regarded unfavorably by those opposed to psychic phenomena. I was rewarded for my caution. *L'Impartial* not only published my remarks in full but commented on them in a very flattering manner.

Now I had tried another literary subject and had managed to carry it off, though composing in a foreign language. My self-confidence received a tremendous lift, and early the following month I began regular work on a book.

But it was still wartime and a war governor, even in a small state like New Hampshire, had heavy responsibilities and a crowded schedule; and as soon as it was not expecting too much of me, physically speaking, Harry asked me not only to go out myself but to represent him at meetings which were mainly social in character. Among these was a large one of affiliated women's clubs held at a Congregational church in Nashua. I was taken to the platform and ensconced in a substantial clerical chair; there I leaned back, hoping and believing I looked the part of a governor's wife to the assembled ladies. I had on a dress of soft white brocaded silk, its decolletage outlined with a fine lace bertha, and wore a bunch of violets with a red rose in the center at the trim waistline—the most approved floral adornment before the day of corsages. I smiled complacently and fingered my fan, and just at that moment, I heard the chairman of the meeting announce, "Mrs. Keyes will now address us."

I rose, feeling that the earth was rocking around me, and gripped the rostrum; never before or since has the solid pulpit of a Congregational church looked so good to me. Through my confused thoughts one idea forced itself: "If I could just make these women laugh, while they are laughing I can think of something to say to them."

The speech was not only an overwhelming success; it marked the beginning of a new era. When I returned to Concord, Harry met me wreathed in smiles. "If you can do that once, you can do it again," he told me confidently. "Henceforth, you're the speechmaker in the family." The state accepted me as such and nicknamed me the "Lieutenant Governor." (There is no such official in New Hampshire.) Somewhere, at the back of my dazzled mind, came an astonishing and confusing realization: *speakers, really good speakers, got paid.* Of course, I could not ask for money, or even accept it, for the speeches I made when I was pinch-hitting for Harry. But after he was no longer governor. . . .

That year the midsummer outing of the New Hampshire Weekly Publishers took place at the Lake Tarleton Club, by then a well-established resort. After gathering at the club on Saturday morning, the members with their wives and friends, numbering around forty, started on a drive which took them to both sides of the Connecticut River and included Pine Grove Farm on its itinerary, where Harry and I welcomed them. Then we hastened out to the camp, where we had agreed to receive the group late that afternoon. These visits were fully described in the friendly New Hampshire press, such as the Rochester *Courier:*

"By invitation of Gov. Henry W. Keyes, the newspaper party was entertained at his log cabin on Saturday afternoon. . . . The governor, who was a champion oarsman when in Harvard, has not forgotten how to row, and his boat, himself at the oars, led the long line of boats and canoes through the white capped waves which separated the boat house from his camp, on that windy afternoon. A few of the timid ones walked around the shore, for the governor made a fine trail from the club house to his camp so that his mother, who feared the water, might walk in safety and comfort along the shore. Mrs. Keyes met the party at the log cabin where she proved a most delightful hostess, serving a delicious lunch, including some 'war cake' which she had herself made, using neither white flour, butter or sugar. The boats were rowed back just ahead of a big thunder shower, which appeared to hold off until the last canoe had come alongside the wharf. And then it poured. Later, the governor and his wife rowed across and spent the evening at the club house."

The publishers' meeting was a natural for a great deal of informal political discussion, and the senatorial campaign was a favorite topic. It was generally conceded by most newspapers that the race would be such a close one that they could not risk predictions. Shortly thereafter, however, any conjectures made at the meeting would have been swept aside in any case because of the sudden death of New Hampshire's senior senator, whose term still had two years to run. This unexpected vacancy in the Senate posed a question as hard to answer as the one in which the governorship and the senatorship were balanced against each other. Since Harry had the power to appoint whomever he chose to the vacant seat, there was nothing to prevent him from choosing one of his rivals, thereby greatly reducing the odds of the race. Rumors as to whether or not he would do so flew about the capitol.

Again Harry paid me the compliment of consulting me, and again I worried lest my feeling in the matter might not be to his best advantage; I could not rid myself of the conviction that though such an appointment might be good politics, it would not be good sportsmanship. While Pillsbury was admittedly not much of a menace, Spaulding and Moses were both major contenders, and both were respected and experienced men; it seemed to me that the only way to win fairly would be to continue the race with both of them in it; to eliminate either one by appointing him to a position he coveted seemed to me comparable to scratching a horse on the ground that it was disabled when actually there was nothing the matter with it. Harry was at first inclined to think the comparison extreme, and I admitted that it probably was. But several days passed in which he took no action. Then came a totally unexpected announcement, which did a great deal to clear the atmosphere and improve Harry's chances: Mr. Moses withdrew from the four-cornered race and announced his candidacy for election to the unexpired term of the recently deceased senator. This meant hurried and complicated work in the New Hampshire Department of State, to provide for his election and an abrupt change in the ballots for the primary, which had already been printed. If Moses were successful, he would be assured of only two years in the Senate, instead of six. On the other hand, he would be the senior senator, with good committee appointments and an excellent chance of re-election; and as the latest indications were that two of his opponents were running ahead of him, his present prospects were also better. As far as Harry was concerned, the only loss he had to face in the Senate was that of seniority, and in the present struggle there was one less rival to overcome and a conclusive answer to the tempting idea of an appointment which would not have measured up to his high standards.

I left the Farm early in the week of Moses's declaration, in order to go on with the obligations of Lieutenant Governor as Harry visualized

these, including a stay in Peterborough to attend a large official luncheon and a pageant given under the auspices of the National Civic Federation, and a Patriotic Field Day at the University of New Hampshire
in Durham. There the program began early in the morning and lasted
until late in the evening, but I reached Wentworth-by-the-Sea with a
day to spare for various official duties before the launching of a ship
which I was to christen the following noon at New Castle. I failed to
enjoy these activities much, because I was obsessed with the fear that I
would get a message from Harry saying he had been detained by important matters in Concord, and in view of the turmoil caused by Mr. Moses's announcement, I should have been obliged to forgive him if he had.
We had already attended together a much heralded triple launching
which had taken place at the shipyard on the Fourth of July, and I was
afraid he would say that he had proven his good will by going to one
such function.

I need not have worried. He had been tremendously pleased because
Mrs. Woodrow Wilson, who named all the ships of the emergency fleet,
had decided that this one should be called the *Haverhill* in honor of our
home town and also because I had been chosen as its sponsor; he arrived in a beaming mood, accompanied by most of his council and staff.
I had not confessed to him that I had written some verses which I
hoped and believed were appropriate for the occasion, though I had timidly told Mr. Robert Jackson, the Master of Ceremonies about them.
The latter had accepted, in a rather gingerly way, the sheet of paper on
which I had typed them, and after a moment had looked up at me with
an expression of great surprise, exclaiming, "My God! They scan!" He
had then hastened to have copies made and given to all the papers and
had prevailed on me to recite them as soon as the launching prayer had
been delivered by the clergyman who was employed at the shipyard. I
have always felt great scorn for versifiers who have needed to read their
own compositions, so I folded the paper Mr. Jackson had given back to
me and triumphantly recited:

> "Go forth, sturdy ship, from the shores of New Hampshire,
>   As stalwart and strong as the state of your birth,
> And bear on the ocean, wherever you venture,
>   The message she sends to the rest of the earth. . . ."

As verse, it did not amount to much. But its effect that day left nothing to be desired by me, not only because of the applause that came
from over six thousand people, but because of the expression on my
husband's face when he looked at me.

We went back to Concord together in the official car, which he was driving himself, and there was no one else with us. As we approached Concord, he informed me that he must go straight to the capitol, that he did not want any supper. He seemed to take it for granted that I would not want any either, but I was hungry. Though the launching had not taken place until nearly half-past two, it had been set for one-thirty, so we had had a light and early lunch. Now it was late evening and we knew the dining room at the Eagle Hotel, which kept conservative hours, would be closed. But as we went by Angelo's Restaurant on Main Street, I saw it was still open and asked Harry to let me out; I would get a bite to eat and then walk to the hotel. It was only a short distance.

I was still wearing the big hat, the pink satin coat and the embroidered white dress I had worn for the launching. I went in and sat down on the first vacant stool in front of the counter and asked for a chicken sandwich and a coffee ice cream soda, as those were then my favorite form of sustenance when I wanted something nourishing in a hurry. However, they were unavailable here, so I ordered something else, I have forgotten what, and devoured it eagerly. Meanwhile, a young man who was sitting on the next stool entered into conversation with me.

"Been to the launching?" he inquired, taking in my gala attire.

I acknowledged that I had.

"See all the swells?"

I said I thought probably I had.

"I hear the Governor's wife is quite a girl," my newfound friend remarked casually.

Something in his voice made me suspicious. I had been very angry the first time I saw a photograph of myself publicly displayed, having been brought up to believe that a lady's name appears in print just three times—at her birth, at her marriage and at her funeral—and her likeness never. But a courteous photographer had explained to me that unless I specifically objected to a certain print, he had a right to display photographs of me because of my husband's position, and by now there had been a good many on view. I slid off the stool and smiled pleasantly.

"She would be pleased to know that's the way people feel about her," I said. "I'll tell her. Thank you for telling *me*. Good night."

Chapter 12

THE primaries took place only ten days after the launching and necessitated an entirely new form of activity on my part. Returns from the polls in those days were telephoned to the candidates, and if the instrument in Harry's den had been a rattlesnake preparing to strike, he could not have recoiled from it with greater horror. Nothing could persuade him to touch it, so I was the one who answered it.

As evening came, and with it the news from the larger districts, it became increasingly evident that the race was too close for comfort and that Harry might well lose it to ex-Governor Spaulding. We had regretfully decided that if Harry were not nominated, we could not afford to send John away to school, and all through supper Harry kept casting mournful glances at the boy and finally looked toward me with a question prompted by a title of Mark Twain's.

"The prince or the pauper?" he asked lugubriously.

"I'm sure it won't be either one," I retorted. But as the night wore on, I found it harder and harder to look on the bright side of things. I have always been allergic to telephones. As far as I am concerned, they are very seldom time-savers and very often the destroyers of schedules. The months I have kept house in Spain without one have been among the happiest of my life, and I have never doubted that one of the reasons was the absence of interruptions to a heavy working program; but I have rarely felt such loathing for a telephone as I did that night. At one in the morning it looked as though Spaulding were ahead. At two he seemed to be holding his own. It was not until three that this glorious news came through from the Manchester *Union:* Keyes leads by

302 votes on returns from 264 towns and wards with 30 still to hear from. An hour later we knew the battle was won.[1]

On the way to my own room I looked in on John, who was sleeping soundly and peacefully, unaware of how fateful the night had been for him. I then crept into bed, exhausted but triumphant.

It had been decided if John did go away to school, he should not go to Milton, much as we liked it, because he kept complaining of having Henry's good marks "flung in his face" and his father and I thought there was so much truth in this that he probably would be happier somewhere else. Since this was the case, the Morristown School, of which Harry's old friend Alfred Butler was headmaster, seemed a logical choice; and my mother, in one of her sudden bursts of generosity, invited John and me to spend a week end in New York as her guests before I delivered him safely at his eventual destination. In those days there was a very good through train from Montreal to New York which stopped at Woodsville, then quite an important railroad center; we could take it late in the afternoon and be in New York early the next morning. Plans had been made so late that we were not able to secure a drawing room, but my mother had engaged a section for John and me and a lower berth opposite for herself and had been assured there was a good chance that the upper berth would not be taken and in that event she could have the whole section. We installed ourselves comfortably and went into the dining car, and had an excellent supper. When we returned to the sleeping car, we found that another passenger—or rather two—had boarded the train in our absence: a very attractive young woman, wrapped in a long cloak, and her two-year-old child. As no other space was available, she had been given the berth above my mother.

I did not see how she could possibly be comfortable there and offered to change places with her. But she insisted she would be all right, and very soon she and the two-year-old went to bed. I never sleep well on a train, and I was even more wakeful than usual because I was excited about John's school and the prospect of theater-going in New York, and I was just recovering from a bronchial cold and still coughing a good deal. Besides, I could not help thinking about the young woman with the child and feeling that somehow all was not well with her. When I heard the porter's bell, I immediately guessed it was she who had rung and sat up, listening. After a slight delay the porter came shuffling

---

[1] There was a very general belief that *Queen Anne's Lace,* my first really successful novel, was largely autobiographical. However, this was true of only two chapters. The one in which Anne takes election returns is the first.

down the aisle and stopped where I had expected. Then I heard an anxious question and an indifferent reply.

"Do you suppose there's a doctor on the train?"

"I don't know, ma'am, and there's no way I could find out. I couldn't wake up everyone asking, not at this time of night."

The porter went away, obviously unconcerned. Next I heard something that sounded suspiciously like a groan, followed by a sob. At that period, ladies were not supposed to undress on a train, unless they had a drawing room, but merely to "loosen their clothing," that is, take off their corsets; and though I did not always observe this priggish rule, I fortunately had done so that night. I put on my shoes, parted my curtains and stood up.

"Can I do anything to help?" I asked.

"I don't suppose you can," came the agonized reply.

"What's the matter?"

"I'm having a miscarriage," gasped the poor girl.

I thought rapidly. Because of my cough, I had two kinds of medicine with me, either one of which should act as a pain killer; one of these was chloroform water and the other was a sweet liquid mixture with codeine in it. I also had an ample supply of absorbent cotton and gauze, for certain sanitary accessories were homemade in those days. And I had toilet water, which could be used as a disinfectant because of its alcoholic content. With this much equipment I certainly could be of some help, even if it were not the most expert. I took the bottle of chloroform water from my Victorian bottle bag (the ancestress of the modern train case!) and thrust it into the hand of my prospective patient.

"Take a drink of this," I ordered. "It'll relieve the pain, even if it doesn't stop it. I've got some other things that may come in handy too. I don't dare try to move you, but I'm going to lift your little boy down and put him in my berth. I'm sure I can do it without waking him. But if he cries I'll wake my mother and she'll look after him. . . . Where are you planning to get off? Because I think we ought to send a wire from the next stop and have an ambulance meet you. But don't worry. I'm sure everything will be all right."

It was. My supplies proved more than adequate. I had no trouble using them, and my patient, who stopped sobbing after her second drink of chloroform water, was cooperative as well as appreciative. When we reached her destination, her husband, a doctor and an ambulance were waiting for her. The next week I had two gratifying letters, one from the husband saying he didn't know how to thank me and one from the doctor saying he didn't know how I could have done a better job.

Not long afterward Katherine Cobb Foss, who was expecting a baby, invited several of us to go on a trip through the mountains in her car, which she drove herself. Her mother-in-law tried to dissuade her, insisting that in her condition she should not attempt anything of the sort. News of my recent experience on the train had spread, and Katherine used it as an effective argument in favor of her outing.

"I've taken the precaution of asking Frances Keyes," she said. "If she can cope with a woman who's having a miscarriage in an upper berth, she can cope with me, wherever we are in the White Mountains. Don't give it another thought."

We had our excursion, and though fortunately nothing went amiss, my reputation as a gynecologist seemed to be established.

The trip to New York was a pleasant one. We stayed in great luxury at the Knickerbocker Hotel, shopped all day Saturday and went one evening to a testimonial concert for the boys of the 165th Infantry, at which the principal singers were Amelita Galli-Curci and John McCormack, and the second evening to a "mammoth musical spectacle" appropriately entitled *Everything* at the Hippodrome. On Monday I went with John to Morristown, where I had already made a preliminary visit of inspection, stayed to supper at the school and left feeling that everything was well with the new student.

I returned from New York expecting to begin active work immediately on the Fourth Liberty Loan drive, only to find that it had been postponed because grippe was raging everywhere and schools and churches had been closed. But this onset of the deadly disease which soon became known as Spanish Influenza—quickly shortened to flu—was not recognized as anything more than a passing epidemic, and after a few weeks the precautions were relaxed or disregarded, the "Fighting Fourth" was in full swing, and I was working harder than ever to sell bonds. New Hampshire had been the first state to go over the top in the Third Liberty Loan drive, and this record was a challenge; on the other hand, people had given so frequently and so generously by now that many of them felt they could not do any more just then, and I began to despair of meeting my quota. When I received an eleventh-hour message from headquarters, asking if I would undertake to sell ten thousand-dollar bonds, autographed by the President, which had suddenly become available, I groaned and started to say I was afraid it was impossible. But I then remembered the maxim attributed to Napoleon, "If it is possible, it can be done; if it is impossible, it must be done." "All right," I replied. "Ten, you said? I'll do my best."

This time the telephone was not a curse, but a salvation. The hours that I now sat beside one were almost as long as those I had spent taking returns the night of the primaries; however, I spent them much less anxiously. Almost from the first I found a ready response, and presently I began to feel not only as if I were playing a game but as if I were winning it. I tore off a sheet from the pad on which I had written my victims' names and telephone numbers and began to scribble on it:

Ten thousand-dollar bonds
Standing in a line,
I hailed the Chief Executive,
Then there were nine.
Nine thousand-dollar bonds
Didn't have to wait.
I'phoned a Vermont Democrat,
And then there were eight.
Eight thousand-dollar bonds
As the clock struck eleven,
I got the Woman Chairman
And then there were seven.
Seven thousand-dollar bonds
Don't seem hard to fix.
A famous writer heard of them,
And then there were six.
Six thousand-dollar bonds
As sure as you're alive.
A Portsmouth lady heard of them
And then there were five.
Five thousand-dollar bonds!
Not so many more!
Manchester's a dead game sport,
And then there were four.
Four thousand-dollar bonds
Left to trouble me!
Littleton came up to scratch,
And then there were three.
Three thousand-dollar bonds!
I'm not feeling blue.
Littleton held another friend,
And then there were two.
Two thousand-dollar bonds,
Going on the run.
Someone said, "A neat idea,"
And then there was one.
One thousand-dollar bond!
This is really fun.
Orford cried, "Of course I will,"
And then there were none.

Before I had finished my parody on "Ten Little Indians," which came to me in a rush, I was interrupted by an incoming call.

"For heaven's sake, I told you *ten!* That's all that were autographed! And now people are calling in asking for more! Please stop right away!"

It seemed too good to be true, but it was true. I had sold all the available autographed bonds and, as it turned out, I could have sold double that number. With my official report I turned in the jingle I had written and promptly received another call: would I sell that for a fifty-dollar bond? I would and very gladly did.

Chapter 13

I WAS still exhilarated by my coup in the Fourth Liberty Loan drive when Election Day came, and certainly everything about this was calculated to increase a sense of triumph, though this time it was my husband's and not my own. He regarded the telephone with less revulsion than he had on the night of the primaries, and there was every reason why he should have, for the news was good from the beginning. Occasionally he consented to take the telephone himself, and each time he left it looking better satisfied than he had the call before. However, I stood by and it was my good fortune to take the message that spelled victory.

"You've won by a handsome margin," I told him exultantly.

"What do you *call* a handsome margin?" he demanded, snatching the receiver from my hand.

It was well over six thousand, a higher figure than that by which he had won for governor. The telephone continued to ring all the next day with messages of congratulation, and telegrams and letters poured in. It was all very exciting. Then, besides the great news of my husband's success, there were again signs that I was making modest but encouraging progress in my writing. I had had another article published in a second French newspaper, *Avenir National;* two more historical sketches in *The Granite Monthly* and a "human interest" article, "The Educated Woman and the War," in *The Cricket on the Hearth,* Concord's newest venture in the publishing field. Furthermore, some verses entitled "The Soldier's Wife," which I had sent to *Association Men,* the official magazine of the Y.M.C.A., had been accepted immediately, and I had been really touched by the response to them. Since relatives, especially young male relatives, are apt to be rather caustic on the subject of literary efforts, at least in my experience, I was particularly pleased by the comments in a letter to my husband from my cousin Royal Carter, who was then in the Philippines: "The poem is good, *good, good;* no mawkish sentimentality, but strong emotion, a poem for us all to be proud of."

Messages of congratulations on the election were still coming in when we were wakened very early in the morning with the news of the Armistice. The first official report had hardly been received when the telephone rang with a summons from my friend Clara Worthen in Newbury.

"We're getting up a parade," she announced. "Put on your Red Cross outfit and hurry over. We want you to march in it."

I reached Newbury in record time. A good-sized crowd was already assembled before the Worthens' house in the center of the village—actually, it was a source of amazement to me afterward that there was anyone left to view the parade, because just about everybody seemed to have been summoned to march and to have obeyed the summons. Just what inspired Clara to organize the parade, I had no idea, nor have I even now. But she did a fine job. It was a beautiful day, Indian summer at its best—the sun bright, the air crisp and still. Presently, in orderly fashion, preceded by a makeshift band, we circled the Common, stopping to salute the monument to Newbury's Revolutionary War hero General Jacob Bayley, and then went up the so-called Montebello Road to the cemetery. There we paused before the decorated graves of Colonel Thomas Johnson, Indian Joe and various others of Revolutionary fame, continued on to The Oxbow to halt before the marker in front of the house that "Colonel Tom" had built and then retraced our steps to the village. We sang all the current war songs and finally, without prearrangement, "Onward, Christian Soldiers." I have heard it sung and have sung it myself countless times, but I have never heard it sung with such soaring spirit and such deep emotion as it was that day.

I was glad to have the parade to look back on in the weeks that followed, for they were very grim in many ways. The flu had now shown itself in its true colors and was rampant everywhere. Henry had gone from Milton Academy for Thanksgiving with my mother, who now spent her winters in Andover, Massachusetts, at the Inn, and had been smitten while he was there. I was troubled to be separated from him when he was ill, though I knew she would see that he had good care, and actually it was better than I could have given him, for a sufficient number of nurses and doctors were still readily available in the larger places. Our own kindly and efficient doctor was so overworked that he could not give any of his patients much individual attention, and there were no trained nurses to be had in our locality or brought in from outside—where they were in even greater demand. Cathie had married her faithful suitor, Henry Deming, the previous spring, and though she could come in for an occasional day's work, we had only Carrie in the house for domestic help. One after another, Peter, Harry and I were felled with the flu, and John shared our fate when he came home from school for Christmas. The messages which arrived now were not those of pleasant congratulation, but of upsetting news about the progress of the epidemic throughout the nation and among our friends. I had managed to crawl into my clothes for the first time and get as far as the nearby room where Harry lay sick when the telephone by his bed rang and I answered it. The speaker was my old friend Frank Sweetser, his voice almost unintelligible with grief.

"My sister Elizabeth—" he began, and stopped. But I knew before he went any further the gist of what he would say. She had three little girls and she had tried to take care of them, because Kenneth was sick too. Their one faithful maid could not cope with everything alone, though she had tried. They had not been able to get a nurse. Pneumonia had set in. The funeral would be. . . .

Everything went completely black around me as I replaced the receiver and toppled over on the bed beside Harry. I had never had a sister, had never particularly wanted one; but for years Elizabeth Sweetser Moller had been an integral part of my life. Something had gone out of it with her death, I knew only too well, that I would never be able to replace. The old adage that for every door which closes, another will open would not help this time. No matter how many other doors opened, none would make up for the one that had closed. Mary Gray did more for me, materially and psychologically—in fact, more than any woman has a right to expect of another—and my gratitude to her, my affection and admiration for her were boundless, as my gratitude to Genevieve Walsh Gudger and my affection for her were later to become and still remain. My intimacy with Jeannie Darling began earlier—actually, in the days when we were so young that we took our naps together in a trundle bed; and I was only a little older than that when Marion Burdett and I, living a block away from each other on Beacon Street, and the Edmands sisters and I, separated only by a few more blocks and a cross-over into Commonwealth Avenue, became "best friends." From later schooldays on, Terry Helburn was my liaison officer with the dramatic world, where, but for her, I would have been merely an onlooker. These are only a few examples of what I am trying to express: no matter how many friends I had, and I was blessed with many, there would always be an element in my friendship with Elizabeth which did not exist in others, just as there was in my friendship with Richard Cobb an element which did not exist in association with the other men I was glad and proud to know. Among the earliest of the statements which brought fame to Byron was his declaration that "Friendship is Love without his wings," which would generally be taken to mean that friendship does not end, as if in sudden flight, whereas love has been known to do so. But Byron was not given to dwelling much on loyalty, either in fact or in fancy, and I have always felt he actually meant that while friendship lacks the iridescent quality we associate with wings—and with love!—it has or at least can have many of its other attributes. Perhaps among those is the element I have been seeking in vain to define.

I could not give way to my grief over Elizabeth's death; I had to pull myself together and try to do what I could to help Carrie, which was not much, for I was terribly weak; and Harry, who was himself getting worse by the minute, kept begging me not to do the same thing Elizabeth had done. Didn't I realize that if I killed myself, the rest of them would be in even more dreadful straits? But he had pneumonia now, and if Carrie could manage to feed us and take care of Peter and John and bring up all the trays, she could not do any more than that, with all the good will in the world. I found I could keep on my feet for fifteen minutes at a time, then for half an hour, then for an hour; and, mercifully, I did not have a relapse. I hated to get the mail and to hear the telephone ring and even to read the newspapers, because almost every time I did, it was to have more bad news. Within a few weeks, six of our friends died, among them the husband of one of my classmates. I tried to tell myself that I should not dwell on this, but on my thankfulness that my own husband had passed what was then called "the crisis" for pneumonia and that, if *he* did not have a relapse, the worst was over. Fortunately, I did not know that there were more fatalities from influenza that winter than the United States had suffered in the war.

Little by little, the situation began to improve. Harry sat up in bed and he and I worked on his farewell address as governor, which we knew, by then, he would not be able to deliver in person. The galley of *The Old Gray Homestead*—the first galley proof I had ever seen—was coming in gradually, and I was thrilled beyond measure as I sat and read it, marking it with the symbols I was just beginning to learn. In those days, galley was very carefully checked by a competent copy reader, and the author's labors on it were light; more than anything else, it provided me with a chance to see my story as a whole and without further anguish as to what I could do to make it better before it was finished, because now it *was* finished! I really enjoyed my proof reading of *The Old Gray Homestead*. It was a bright spot in a picture which, over all, was rather gloomy.

Another cheerful aspect of this situation was furnished by the fan mail. There had been gratifying public recognition of *The Chronicle* articles and the articles in *The Granite Monthly* and the French newspapers; there had also been complimentary letters and flattering comments in conversation from friends. But until "The Satisfied Reflections of a Semi-Bostonian" was published in *The Atlantic Monthly* that dark December, I had never received an avalanche of mail from total strangers. Indeed, I had never so much as heard of this by-product of creative work, and I was even more thrilled with it than with the galley. I stopped dreading the arrival of the postman on our Rural Free Delivery route and watched eagerly for his coming. The letters were all agreeable, and some were music to my ears. One of the latter type ended with the words, "I realize by the text of your article that you are married, and I am old fashioned enough to believe that, when addressing a married lady, her husband's initials should always be used. However, as I have no idea who your husband is or where you live, I am sending this to Frances Parkinson Keyes in care of *The Atlantic Monthly*."

Obviously my correspondent had overlooked the "Contributors' Column" at the front of the magazine, in which the identity of those whose work appeared in its pages was disclosed; and as I thought Harry was now sufficiently convalescent to enjoy a little levity, I showed him the letter and told him I was going to have it framed for his office in Washington. "For a long while everyone called me 'the girl Harry Keyes married,'" I reminded him, "then eventually they changed that to 'Harry Keyes's wife.' Naturally, my old friends refer to me as Frances Keyes, but they never use the Parkinson. I'm sure this is the first time anyone has thought of me as Frances Parkinson Keyes—a writer—and not as the wife of a local celebrity who became his state's governor and is about to become one of its senators. Perhaps it's also the last time. But at least it's happened to me once."

Harry laughed and said he didn't think it would be the last time. He had been pleased with the fan mail too. I had heard him bragging to his family about it over the telephone. "Why, she's had letters about that article from as far away as Missouri!" he kept saying in a bewildered voice. He was also duly impressed with the galley and asked if there was anything he could do to help me with it. I didn't think there was, that belonged to my new province, but I appreciated his offer, just as I did the one to share his "fan mail," particularly one communication that had come addressed simply:

Mr. Kise Esq.
The Man That Keeps Mewles
N. H.

Of course, he had never kept mules, and the contents, like the superscription, remained a mystery. Another correctly addressed communication sent us into gales of laughter. It came from a Midwestern state and read:

"Our plan is to sell at a large public auction kitchen aprons made from the shirt tails of famous men. Entire proceeds will be turned over to the Red Cross. It is our desire to secure a cast off shirt from the governor of every state in the Union. We are wondering if you have a shirt which has outlived its usefulness as a shirt, which you will mail to us. We urge the patriotic purposes back of our campaign and the publicity for our sale should every governor respond."

It was good to have something to laugh over after all the dark days we had shared. And it was good to know that we were both getting well again and that, pretty soon, we would both be going forward together.

Part Four

The Great World of Washington

Chapter 14

I T WAS February before we were actually on our way to Washington. Convalescence was a slow process that year, and attempts to hasten it were usually disastrous. Another handicap lay in the housing situation; Washington was terribly overcrowded, and rents were sky high. We had almost given up hope of finding a place to live when we heard of a rented house in Chevy Chase which the tenants wanted to leave before their lease expired in June and had permission to sublet. It did not sound ideal, but it did sound feasible, and Harry, who had made a more rapid recovery than I had, started off to inspect it. His report, though not enthusiastic, was sufficiently favorable for me to believe we could manage, and Peter, Carrie—who still represented our entire domestic staff—and I joined him there.

The house was well located, diagonally across from the Chevy Chase Club, and had pleasant grounds; but it was very sparsely furnished and so small that it provided no place except the unfinished attic in which to put the two older boys when they came home for vacations. The departing tenants had left us the names of their laundress and the man who allegedly took care of the hot-air furnace. Neither was conspicuously reliable, and Carrie was overworked, for I was still not well enough to help much with household tasks, and there were a good many days when I could not get up at all. Peter was soon ill again, this time with extreme earache, and a general practitioner turned him over to a specialist who proved to be actually brutal in his treatment. Inevitably, the next step was a hospital and a mastoid operation. Fortunately, the hospital was one where the mothers of young patients were permitted to stay too, and Peter's care there was kindly and efficient. At last there was real improvement, and he began to resemble the same child he had been before the flu struck us. There was an excellent school near our house and, very happily, he started going there. On Sundays, he went regularly to Sunday school in the morning and to the Zoo in the afternoon, and I accompanied him to both. When Henry and John came home for their spring vacations, they began a zealous round of sightseeing in which they felt Peter should be included; actually, his cultural interests were bounded by his school and the Zoo.

My own were not quite so limited, though they were by no means as extensive as I had planned and expected, and the one really glamorous social experience was a dinner at the Larz Andersons' palatial house, then the most distinguished private residence in Washington. Anderson had married a tremendously wealthy Boston girl, Isabel Weld Perkins, who had been graduated from Miss Winsor's School several years before I was. She was talented and charming, had written several books and had been active in war work abroad. Before his retirement, Anderson had been Chargé d'Affaires in Rome, Minister to Belgium and Ambassador to Japan. He had been decorated by all these governments, and Mrs. Anderson had received the Belgian Order of Queen Elizabeth and the French Croix de Guerre. The effects of all this were evident in their mode of life and their entertainments. The door was opened for us by an English footman in livery; a bowing, kimonoed Japanese conducted us to the cloakroom, and an even more imposing functionary, of still a third nationality, announced our names when we reached the drawing room, which was separated from the entrance by countless other apartments and a stairway almost as overwhelming as the one in the Paris Opera House. The immense flower-decked table in the dining room gleamed with priceless porcelain and glittered with a display of crystal and silver that was actually dazzling. The elegance with which the Glessners entertained, the assurance and dignity of the Grays and the Tudors, the inflexible pattern of propriety mingled with etiquette which ruled the Keyes family, the mellowness and symmetry that permeated the old Virginia houses—all these paled before this pageant of splendor. I have not the slightest recollection of our fellow guests, because my surroundings, in themselves, were so engrossing; but I somehow gathered that our bluff, blond host was making a special effort to be cordial to me and put me at my ease, either because he and Harry had been friends at Harvard or because he guessed that this was unfamiliar territory to me. His solicitude had exactly the opposite effect; I felt as if I were eighteen years old again, back when I was "the girl Harry Keyes married," and not the poised and self-confident woman who had apparently been a success as a governor's wife. I was wearing the pink and silver dress I had bought for Harry's inaugural and had not been able to wear then; I knew that the diamond necklace my mother had given me when I married went well with it, that as far as appearances went I could hold my own with the other women in the room; and conversation, either in English or in French, had never presented any difficulty. Yet obviously some touch of sophistication which should have been there was lacking, one that probably would have been present if I had "come out," like my Boston friends, and mingled in adult society before my marriage instead of going practically from my own nursery to my children's, as one observer had put it with exaggeration but still with a grain of truth. I determined to find out what this aspect of sophistication was and remedy the lack. Evidently I was successful, in Larz Anderson's opinion. I do not remember what I wore the next time I went to the Andersons', but the dinner was in honor of the then Vice President and Mrs. Coolidge, and I sat next to Henry Cabot Lodge, who had been a classmate of my father's and had always shown himself most kindly disposed to me. Before the evening was over, Mr. Anderson whispered to me that it was unbelievable how much I had improved. Meanwhile, I had been to a good many dinners where the hosts and guests were quite as distinguished and the table equally splendid, even if service and setting were less exotic than at the Andersons'; and I felt that he was the one who was lacking in savoir-faire or he would never have made such a remark. Nevertheless, I was glad to realize that I probably *had* improved—from his viewpoint.

I had been duly informed beforehand that in Washington it is the newcomer who makes the first calls and that if the newcomer is a senator's wife, she must call on all the senior senators' wives, the ambassadors' wives and the Cabinet officers' wives without delay and promptly return the calls made on her by congressmen's wives and the unofficial ladies prominent in resident society, generally known as the "cave dwellers." However, it was a literal impossibility for me to begin this arduous program before autumn, much as I wanted to conform to all the regulations of my new position; I had no car and I was either ill myself or taking care of a sick child, or both, a large part of the time; and as the new senators did not take the oath of office until late May, I hoped and believed my delay would not count against me in the future. When the so-called Continental Congress convened, I gave a luncheon for the New Hampshire delegates at the Shoreham, then by far the most fashionable hotel in Washington; and attended some of the sessions at Continental Hall, shepherded by Harry's cousin Elizabeth Pierce, who was the Chaplain General of the organization. I had not met her before, since she lived in Washington and seldom left it. Like my sister-in-law Belle, she had sacrificed her own romance because her mother did not approve of it, but, unlike Belle, she had not become bitter or critical. She was deeply religious and still lovely looking, though she was already an elderly woman. I became greatly attached to her and saw a good deal of her in the next few years.

That first spring I also went to one meeting of the Colonial Dames, a very exclusive gathering in a musty old house on Lafayette Square, and, though I have always been very proud to be a member of that organization, experienced the same sense of inferiority that I had at the Larz Anderson house. I was persuaded by Mrs. Daniel Lothrop, the mother of my childhood friend Margaret and the author of the famous children's book *Five Little Peppers and How They Grew,* to become the national historian of the Children of the American Revolution, which she had founded. With more enthusiasm than I felt for membership in these patriotic societies, I accepted an invitation to join the League of American Pen Women, pleased and astonished that I was considered eligible on the strength of a few articles and a brand new novel which had not yet proven its worth. I was equally astonished to receive a communication from A. N. Marquis & Company, Publishers, requesting that I "kindly furnish data for a brief personal sketch" for *Who's Who in America.*

I also agreed to serve on the World Services Council of the Y.W.C.A. and to act as chairman for New Hampshire on the recently organized Theodore Roosevelt Memorial Committee to restore and preserve Roosevelt's birthplace in New York City. All these connections brought me into contact with a great many pleasant and intelligent women and provided me with a number of agreeable experiences, but eventually I made the sad discovery that—for me at any rate—it was almost impossible to do justice to both executive and creative work at the same time. I also discovered that I found working entirely with women was less satisfactory, as well as less stimulating, than work in which men and women cooperated. Larger and larger feminine groups became increasingly overpowering and increasingly unproductive to me personally, as far as my writing was concerned, and that, next to my family, was what mattered most.

The Old Gray Homestead was published on Henry's birthday, which I considered a good omen, and in one sense it was. I had received no advance royalties on this book, but shortly after it came out I was amazed by the receipt of a check for something over four hundred dollars, and this time I did not offer it all to my husband. I went out and bought new spring clothes, the lack of which had constituted an additional reason for my delay in making calls and receiving company. I paid cash for everything, so there would be no bills to worry me, and experienced the typically feminine uplift of spirit natural to a woman who feels she has the right thing to wear.

Unfortunately, in other ways, the publication of my first book didn't do as much to cheer and encourage me as I had expected. On the whole, the reviews were favorable, even though they were not enthusiastic, and the setting especially had been much praised. "It is not upon the intricacy of the plot that the genuine success of Mrs. Keyes's first novel depends, but rather upon the absolute truth of the picture which she paints of New England life and character," *The Granite Monthly* had said. Moreover, the novel had been sold to an English firm, which liked it very much. But my rural scene, wholesome and peaceful for the most part, had been marred by the introduction of an indiscretion committed by a minor character. This was, unfortunately, quite as typical of the scene in question as its more moral aspects, and the reference was very discreetly worded; but it had an adverse effect on my publishers, on two reviewers and, worst of all, on my husband. The publishers had raised no objections to it until some of the purchasers returned the book with protests. My editor had written me, when he accepted the book, "I hope we have made you understand that we think very highly of this book, of its authenticity and of its emotional appeal." I could not understand why he did not feel the same way a few months later, and I was baffled and astonished, for I felt—and still feel—that I had written nothing indelicate. When Harry told me it would be more helpful if I were strong enough to do the washing and save money that way, instead of trying to earn it by writing, I was deeply hurt.

The remark was made in a moment of anger brought on by a combination of circumstances, most of them unconnected with me. I had been right in believing that Harry would find the atmosphere of the Capitol in Washington, where he was still a stranger, less congenial than the Capitol in Concord, where he had been the central, most powerful, and most admired figure. His committee appointments were, on the whole, agreeable to him, and two of them—Naval Affairs and Public Buildings and Grounds—were to prove especially important as far as his later work was concerned. He really liked Kendrick of Wyoming, Hale of Maine, Frelinghuysen of New Jersey, Gay of Louisiana, McNary of Oregon and Harding of Ohio; he regarded several with respect—Lodge of Massachusetts, Calder and Wadsworth of New York, McLean of Connecticut, Lenroot of Wisconsin, Underwood of Alabama, Kellogg of Minnesota, Swanson of Virginia and a few others. He found, as many have remarked, that conservatives of the North and the South have much in common, and was liked and respected by his colleagues on committees. On the other hand, he disagreed so violently, as to policy,

with the "progressive" element typified by many Midwesterners—
Kenyon of Iowa and Norris of Nebraska, for instance—that he had no
common meeting ground with them. France of Maryland and LaFollette
of Wisconsin he dismissed as Communists; Reed of Missouri he disliked actively on personal grounds, while admitting his great gifts; and
he never referred to Walsh of Massachusetts in private except as "that
flannel-mouthed Mick." And though I feel sure he did not say this publicly, the feeling must have been evident!

In a small state like New Hampshire, the political picture is very
close and very important to all the people, and Harry had been surrounded by friends, many of them lifelong friends. He missed them, and
he missed Pine Grove Farm.

Senator Harding and others invited him to play golf at the Chevy
Chase Club, but he had never cared for golf and he understood that golf
—like bridge, which they also invited him to play and which he also
declined to do—was played for high stakes, which he could not afford.
In short, he did not completely fit into this political picture; and it did
not help when he came home at night to find he must be the one to cope
with an old-fashioned furnace and perform other such tasks when he
was tired and out of sorts. I knew he did not really mean what he said,
but the fact remained that he never praised the book and I knew he
never would. This made me fearful lest he should be no better pleased
with the next one, which somehow I had found time to transcribe from
the scribbled pages of copybooks to neatly typed sheets and sent to the
Boston publisher.

But, as far as my writing was concerned, Harry did pay me what I
considered a very high compliment:

> *United States Senate*
> COMMITTEE ON
> EXPENDITURES IN THE POST OFFICE DEPARTMENT
>
> July 14, 1919
>
> Dearest—
>   Should I decide to speak in Senate on League of Nations I would
> appreciate your suggestions and recommendations. No hurry. Appar-
> ently a long controversy.
>
>   As ever,
>   Harry.

The issue of the League was the most burning one of the current session, and Hamilton Holt of the New York *Independent,* in sizing up the
way senators might be expected to vote, correctly placed Harry in the
group of eight Republicans "who do not want to see the treaty rejected,
but who favor reservations or amendments to safeguard the interests of

the United States." If this group could have prevailed, there is no question in my mind that membership in the League would have been assured before adjournment; it was not "a little group of wilful men" who defeated it, but the President's insistence that he would not countenance a change in "the crossing of a t or the dotting of an i." Therefore, no compromise could be reached between the Republicans who were outright or near isolationists and the forty-five Democrats who were willing to accept the treaty as it stood. A minor but still important factor in the case lay in the Senate's resentment because Wilson had failed to consult it before doing the drafting. Actually, according to the Constitution, treaty-making powers lie with the Senate and not with the President, and Wilson had deliberately and publicly disregarded this fact. The Senate took umbrage because its prerogatives had not been respected, and this feeling influenced more votes than it should have. Over and over again, in years to come, I was to see such a reaction to what was considered a dare, or an indignity. Rejection of the League was one of many disastrous but very human results of this attitude. The final vote was thirty-five for and forty-nine against ratification.

It had been agreed I should stop off in Boston on my way north for the summer and have a further consultation with the editor whose office looked out on the old graveyard. He received me pleasantly and said that, after all, the sales of *The Old Gray Homestead* had been well above the average for a first novel and that he thought the new script, entitled *The Career of David Noble,* showed promise of better sales— eventually. But he did not think the time for it had yet come. He would put it in his safe for the present and we would talk about it again later on. Meantime, he hoped that while I was at home I would write him a different kind of a story: one with the same setting as the first (the second had strayed to Europe in its scene!) but without even a hint of scandal. He made two or three casual suggestions about characterization and wished me well. I left the office believing I understood how to please him and determined to do so if I could. I was not altogether happy about the script that had been left behind, but decided to dismiss that from my mind.

At the Farm I found conditions for writing more propitious than they had ever been before, and I was happy to improve them. Both the older boys went away to camp for the first time, and Peter was now old enough to play outdoors for hours at a time with his carts under only casual supervision from Carrie. One of our pine groves was not far from the river, and the only road that went near it was used just when crops were stored or removed from our meadow barn, which was not being done that summer. The weather was perfect, and almost every day I took a copybook, a dictionary and some pencils and went immediately after dinner to that isolated grove. Then I sat down on the pine needles and wrote until almost suppertime. I had greatly missed my Newbury and Haverhill friends and had looked forward to being with them when I got home; but I voluntarily withdrew in order to write—in fact, I found I did not want to do much of anything else. It was the first of only three times in my life that I have been able to do so under ideal conditions and without interruptions of any kind, the others being in Lisieux, when I was writing *Thérèse* at the Abbaye des Benedictines, and in Avila, when I was writing books with a Spanish setting. For these, however, I needed to consult a great deal of reference material, most of it in a foreign language, and to seek advice from the best living authorities I could find. None of this was necessary in the case of the writing I was doing in the grove, and I have never written so fast and made so few changes. The work was a source of unalloyed pleasure. In two weeks the entire first draft of *Lady Blanche Farm* was on paper; two months later I had finished typing it and it was on its way to Boston.

Meanwhile, though I did not seek out my old friends, I did not try to avoid them, and one day I received a telephone call from Mrs. Alexander Greer, the mother of my friends Charles and Earl, saying she would like very much to come and see me on an important matter whenever it would be convenient for me. She was not one of the older women whom I had known well all my life and whom I saw frequently, like Cousin Mary Johnson and Cousin Ellen Bayley, and by no stretch of the imagination could she have been called a cousin. Furthermore, as far as I knew, we had no special interests in common, though she was active in community affairs. But of course I said I would be glad to see her and set a time for tea. She was always exceptionally well dressed, which took time as well as money before ready-made clothes were easily available, and had a sense of style rare in a woman who had spent all her life in the country. I had heard rumors that she possessed an independent income and that this had been of great assistance to her husband when they were first married, for he was entirely self made. There had also been vague murmurs to the effect that the source of this income was a mysterious one, but I had never been much intrigued by these reports. She arrived for her appointment looking, as usual, as if she might have posed for a recent fashion plate, and carrying a neat package which suggested by its size and shape that it might contain diaries or letters or both. I quickly found that my guess was correct.

"I have read *The Old Gray Homestead*," she told me. "I enjoyed it very much." Of course, those words were music in my ears after its reception in some other quarters. "It is the first book I ever read with the setting in rural New England," my caller continued, "that seemed to me true to life. You didn't make fun of the 'natives' and, on the other hand, you didn't get sentimental about them. I've been wishing, for a long while, that I could find someone to write the story of my grandmother. It's a wonderful story, but until now I haven't felt I could trust anyone with it. I do feel I could trust you. I've got the necessary documents to prove it's true, even though parts of it may sound improbable. I've brought papers with me for you to see. I hope very much you'll write the story."

I was extremely touched. Fortunately, I did not then foresee that hardly a week would pass when someone did not offer me a wonderful story about members of his family which he did not know how to write but which he would be glad to have me write, sharing the profits, the proposed division being greatly to his advantage. I explained to Mrs. Greer that at the moment, I was writing a story already on order and that I could not attempt anything further just then. But if she would leave the material with me. . . .

That night I read the letters and diaries she had entrusted to me. She was right. The story was as improbable as it was true, and I would be very proud to write it. The only question was when I could. I fully expected that publication of *Lady Blanche Farm,* the story I had written on order, and *The Career of David Noble,* which was reposing in the safe, would keep me busy for some time.[1]

It had not occurred to me to ask for a contract or advance royalties from the Boston publisher before committing myself to a summer's work. I felt confident I had followed instructions carefully and that, this time, editor, reviewer and husband were all going to be pleased. The letter which reached me a few days after my talk with Mrs. Greer struck me with the force of a body blow.

The editor was very sorry, but the new script did not come up to his

---

[1] The story based on the material given me by Mrs. Greer, and entitled *The Safe Bridge,* was serialized in *Home* Magazine in 1934 and published in book form the same year. It has never gone out of print, and according to the Newbury librarian it is still in greater demand there than anything else I have written. Like my other novels, it was published in England, but the Foreword, stating that the book contains no imaginary characters, settings or major episodes, was omitted there. The English reviews were almost uniformly uncomplimentary, and one was especially severe: "This American writer is one who hitherto showed some promise of developing into an able novelist. It is therefore doubly unfortunate that she should have descended to writing such an utterly fantastic tale, which bears not the slightest resemblance to anything which possibly could have happened."

expectations. Technically, it was amateurish: the reader was introduced to one girl, whom he assumed to be the heroine, only to find, after a couple of chapters, that her cousin commanded an equal amount of attention; this would be confusing to the reader; it was contrary to all the rules to have two characters of the same sex of equal importance in the same story. (I had just read *Anna Karenina* for the first time and had become actually dizzy with mental calisthenics that took me in rapid succession from Anna and Vronsky to Kitty and Levin; and I had been told over and over again that it was one of the greatest novels ever written; so I could not help wondering why that special aspect of my story was labeled "amateurish.") There were other drawbacks to acceptance, of course, but this in itself had sufficed to bring about an adverse decision. By way of conclusion, the letter informed me that the other script, the one which had been reposing in the safe all summer, was being sent back at the same time, since there was now no question of having it follow the one I had just finished.

I did not even open the package containing the spurned scripts. I was ashamed to confess to Harry what had happened, and the confession was made doubly hard because, though he did not actually say so, I gathered that he had expected the rejection. He indicated that he thought the acceptance of *The Old Gray Homestead* had been more or less of an accident and not a very fortunate one at that; personally, he would be just as glad if there were no more books, if there were some other source of additional income. He did not mention the washing again, but I felt he might just as well have done so.

It was not until I began to pack for our return to Washington that I forced myself to unwrap the package which had caused me so much misery. It might just as well be put in one of the bureau drawers where I had so long hidden my attempts at fiction. As I undid it, a small piece of paper fell from the script of *David Noble* and fluttered to the floor. It did not occur to me that it was not meant for me, and I read it with a growing sense of desperation. It was an interoffice memo written months previously by one company employe to another, and it stated quite clearly that as far as that publishing house was concerned, the novel was unacceptable. "However," the scribbled message continued, "there is no doubt that the author shows some promise and we do not want to lose her yet. If we send this back, she may submit it somewhere else and then she'll be gone for good. Better hold it until we see what she sends next."

I made a copy of the note and sent the original back to the editor with no comment other than that it had apparently been left in the script by mistake. His reply was not an apology, except for an oversight; obviously the man who had written the note and the man who had followed his instructions felt nothing unethical was involved, and as this was (and still is) one of the most reputable publishing houses in the world, I could only conclude that these are not governed by the same rules that apply even in politics. I also concluded that, from then on, I must never undertake any writing for a publisher which involved time and effort unless the verbal request that I should do so was reinforced with a written one and at least a token payment of hard cash. In this respect, the experience was indeed of sterling worth. In almost every other, it was disillusioning and disheartening.

But it was also another challenge. For more than a year I had been satisfied to find a welcome in periodicals of good but not prominent standing, and limited circulation. Now I wanted to aim higher. I interrupted my packing long enough to write an article on the suffrage question—I still felt at the time that the benefits which would be derived from giving women the vote were debatable and I called the article "On the Fence," which correctly expressed my viewpoint. I sent it to *The Atlantic Monthly* and it was promptly accepted.[2] The check for it arrived most opportunely shortly after my return to Washington. It was of great help to me in paying for the taxis in which I rode while making the six hundred and fifty calls that represented the first of my official obligations. It also prevented me from feeling that these, rather than further efforts to become a real writer, must be my greatest concern.

---

[2] This was later included in a book entitled *Youth and the New World,* which was used as a textbook in my son Henry's English A class at Harvard—he claimed, much to his embarrassment!

Chapter 15

MY TARDINESS in meeting the obligations of a new senator's wife weighed rather heavily on my conscience, unavoidable as it had been. I tried to make up for it by plunging with all the vim and vigor of which I was capable into the multiple stereotyped activities of the following autumn.

We had at last found a small, well-located, furnished apartment at Meridian Mansions—later known only by number and street as 2400 Sixteenth Street—in Washington itself. For our needs this was a great improvement on a crowded, inconvenient house in the suburbs, though it was even more of a strain on our budget—five hundred dollars a month—and it required a formidable amount of cleaning to render it fit to live in, from my viewpoint. This took a good deal of my time and strength. The previous tenants had evidently departed in some haste and with little thought to their successors' comfort. We found soiled linen on the beds, rubbish in the bureau drawers and even spoiled food in the refrigerator. Quantities of boiling water, antiseptic soap and disinfectant were indicated, and all were unsparingly used. Harry, Peter, Carrie and I took possession early one Saturday afternoon, and my first caller arrived about ten minutes after we did and climbed unconcernedly over the clutter in the front hall. It had not occurred to me to leave word at the desk that I was not receiving, since this was not the day of the week when I was supposed to do so, but thereafter I was more careful. The following Thursday I had my first "At Home." It was not as well organized as I would have liked, but I was right in believing I would not have to provide for as many visitors then as later in the season; and I did not commit the almost unforgivable sin of declining to receive all callers who did come (unless I was sick in bed or out making calls myself) if they presented themselves between four and six Thursday. From then until April, except when completely incapacitated or prevented by some emergency, I faithfully received every other Thursday, making calls on the alternate Thursday and on every other day of the week.

These were then officially allotted, with a degree of rigidity which would have done credit to the laws of the Medes and Persians: Supreme Court ladies received on Mondays, congressional ladies on Tuesdays, Cabinet ladies on Wednesdays, Senate ladies on Thursdays, diplomatic ladies on Fridays, resident society—"cave dwellers"—on Saturdays and Sundays. The new senator's wife called first on all her superiors in rank: the wives of all senators who had been members of the Chamber longer than her husband, the Supreme Court ladies and the ambassadorial ladies, of whom there were, fortunately, not nearly as many as there are now, for fewer countries were represented. Whether she should take the initiative in calling on the Cabinet ladies or they should call on her was a debatable and often a burning question. They outranked her at parties —that is, if a senator's wife and a Cabinet officer's wife were both present at the same luncheon or dinner, it was the Cabinet officer's wife who sat at the right of the hostess or host, unless she in turn had been outranked by an ambassador's wife; in return for this prerogative, the Cabinet ladies were theoretically supposed to call first. However, most Cabinet officers' wives did not then support this theory, and unless a senator's wife called first, she was apt to remain a comparative stranger to the Cabinet ladies, to her disadvantage. I have always been glad that I swiftly numbered friends among them.

The senator's wife also returned, as soon as was humanly possible, calls made on her by congressional ladies and cave-dwelling ladies. I did my best to conform to this system, using up all the money I had earned for writing "On the Fence" and also a little nest egg Mary Gray had given me for "an emergency." I was afraid expenses incurred for taxi fares might not seem to her an emergency, but they certainly did to me as I went doggedly on my way without a car of my own.

I have never been shy, in the sense that it is hard for me to meet strangers under what for me are normal conditions; indeed, I have always taken pleasure in making new friends that way. But it was very hard for me to overcome my reluctance to go into completely strange houses to which I had not been invited, in the way I understood an invitation—an official obligation was something else again—and explain my identity to completely strange hostesses. I had lived most of my life among people who had known me a long time, many of them from childhood, and in not a few cases the friendships were inherited ones; I found the very words, "I am Mrs. Keyes, the wife of the new senator from New Hampshire," difficult to form. Eventually I learned that very often a senior senator's wife accompanied the newcomer on her first rounds, and I took pains to do this when I achieved seniority myself; but owing to the rather strange political circumstances occasioned by the death of her husband's predecessor, Mrs. Moses had been in Washington only a little longer than I had, and she was in very poor health. Even if she had wished to assume additional responsibilities, it would have been hard for her to do so. Usually a hostess did her best to relieve the strain—in many instances she had been through the same ordeal herself, sympathized with me and showed this by her tact and cordiality. But there were times when the indifference to making my acquaintance was only too obvious and one in which there was downright rudeness. This was in the case of the Baroness de Cartier, whose husband was then the Belgian Ambassador.

"Really?" she said in response to my hesitant self-introduction, her tone of voice showing that she could not possibly have cared less. "Well, I hope you don't expect me to return your call. I can't go as far as senators' wives."

One of the ladies near me happened to be Mrs. Chandler Anderson, a sister of Mme Riano, the wife of the Spanish Ambassador, who, like the wives of several European ambassadors in Washington just then— including, I am sorry to say, Baroness de Cartier—was an American by birth. Mrs. Anderson duly reported the episode, and the following Thursday almost every ambassadress on whom I had called by then appeared in my apartment, as well as Mrs. Lansing, whose husband was then Secretary of State. The attempted rebuff had been a benefit, as far as I was concerned; as far as the Baroness was concerned, it proved a boomerang. Very definitely, she was not one of those women who are an asset to their husbands' careers. She had been a widow when she married De Cartier and, as such, had been acceptable to the Belgian government; but she had neglected to mention a previous alliance which had ended otherwise, and when this came tardily to light, it was very *mal vu* in a predominantly Catholic country. Since her tenure of the position of ambassadress was precarious at best, she would have been wiser to guard it carefully; instead, besides various relatively minor acts of rudeness, she declined to accept the seat assigned her, in order of precedence, at a White House dinner, because it would have placed her next to the German Ambassador. Granted that feeling after the war still ran very high, the seating was done according to protocol, and it was a serious offense to upset a table plan for seventy guests. Such unbecoming conduct not unnaturally had serious repercussions, and everyone welcomed the arrival of De Cartier's successor.

There were a few loopholes in following the code for the calling system and a few compensations for it. It was not unusual for a large number of congressional ladies who all lived in the same apartment house to pool their resources and receive together. When this was done, the visitor who had called on one could consider that she had called on all, unless each had provided a basket labeled with her name in the entrance hall for the cards left on her. Some doormen had their favorites, and it was not uncommon to see them take a fistful of cards from one basket and drop them in another, permitting their pet tenants to brag the next day that they had had more visitors than their fellow hostesses. Two senators' wives sometimes received together, and when they did, there was no question: the call was made on both. And calls could be very brief, especially if the drawing room led into the dining room; then the visitor could go in one door and, quite unobserved by her hostess, out another. She did not need to stop for tea at more than one place, and no matter how voracious her appetite, she could not possibly drink it everywhere she went. Mrs. Charles Hamlin, whose husband was a member of the Federal Reserve Board, told me she had once made seventy calls in one afternoon; I think that must have been a record, but it was no great achievement to polish off twenty or thirty.

If a caller actually did pause, it *was* tea that she drank, supplemented sometimes by coffee or chocolate or both, but never by alcoholic beverages; and the tea was reinforced with sandwiches and cakes, which varied in quantity and quality, according to the ingenuity or wealth of the hostess, but which were almost always attractively set forth. Such fare was, in a very true sense, a refreshment; and while making her rounds and stopping in the course of them for tea, the caller gradually met many of the men and women with whom she would most frequently be thrown, and among them she met a few who would really become her friends.

Indeed, without stepping out of Meridian Mansions, I soon found that I was surrounded with friends—it had actually been nicknamed "The Senatorial Beehive," for eleven senatorial families lived there during the postwar period. The ladies in this group were constantly in and out of each other's apartments; they played a great deal of bridge together; they cooperated in calling and in entertaining.

I became very fond of my fellow tenants in the "Beehive"; but by far the closest and most enduring bond I established there was with Montana's Senator Thomas J. Walsh and his daughter Genevieve, who acted as his hostess. Her mother had died shortly before I came to Washington and how Genevieve, the wife of a young naval officer, Emmet Gudger, and the mother of a pretty little girl named Elin, managed simultaneously to run her father's establishment and her husband's I have never understood, but she did. This was comparatively simple when Captain Gudger was stationed in Washington, for then they all lived in the same apartment; but she made it seem equally simple when he was stationed in Newport or in Norfolk! Taking a night train or a night boat, she would suddenly appear on the capital social scene, tiny, tidy and tight-lipped, and without the least apparent effort proceed to fulfill all official obligations. Then, having galvanized her father's immense and indolent Negro servant Irene back into vigorous action, Genevieve would vanish as swiftly as she had come. Even when Captain Gudger was ordered to the Philippines and Genevieve accompanied him there, she turned up in Washington the following spring, concentrated her talents on a brief but effective social program, and then retired temporarily to a hospital where, without the slightest ado, she produced a second daughter, who was named Gloria and added, as if automatically, to her mother's smooth-running dual household!

Undoubtedly, it was Genevieve Walsh Gudger's extraordinary efficiency which first attracted me to her so strongly. The caliber of her mind was comparable to that of her father, and through the crowd of vapid chatterers in which the capital abounded, her intelligence, her self-control and her driving purpose clove like an arrow. She had been Senator Walsh's companion throughout his campaigns from the time she was a child; she was familiar with every angle of the political picture, and her astuteness intrigued me from the moment I met her. Moreover, she was about my own age, while most of the women with whom I was thrown were at least old enough to be my mother, and her youthfulness and zest for life were another great attraction to me. Age also accounted for my footing with her father, which was that of a friend and contemporary of his daughter's, rather than that of the wife of one of his own colleagues. He was always extremely kind to me, revealing none of that sternness and ferocity which many persons regarded as an integral part of his nature.

He loved to play bridge and could hardly take time to devour his dinner before sweeping up two decks of cards from his desk and setting up a collapsible table with a snap; the way he pounced on his tricks was very like the way he descended on the trembling witnesses who appeared at the investigations he conducted. Being a devout though tolerant Catholic, he also loved to go to church; and I had a standing date to attend the Thanksgiving Pan-American Mass with him. This was a brilliant and beautiful service, held in Washington every year at St. Patrick's, in honor of the representatives of Central and South American countries, who turned out for it in full force, dressed with the utmost formality and elegance.

Besides the advantage of making friends, the conscientious caller benefited in those days by the standardized visiting hours—usually from four to six and never later than five to seven. This meant she was home early enough to see her children before their bedtime, if that was what she wanted and needed to do, or to rest and change her clothes without haste before going out to dinner, if that were next on the program. I always managed to have a story hour with Peter, just as I had done, first with his brothers and then with him, in the years at Pine Grove Farm. Personally, I liked this schedule of tea, even if taken in a crowd, and a period of relaxation before a seated dinner, where the guest list automatically ensured interesting conversation and widened horizons, much better than the frantic cocktail buffets which, to a large degree, have supplanted and succeeded both tea and dinner without achieving the best characteristics of either.

After the story hour, with increasing frequency, came the eight o'clock dinners which I enjoyed so much. An outstanding one of that season was given at the Army and Navy Club by Colonel and Mrs. Charles Patterson in honor of the Italian Ambassador and Baroness Romano Avezzana, who became my very good friends. "There were forty of us at table, which was in the shape of a hollow square," I wrote in my diary. "The center was filled with pussy willows, daffodils and narcissi; all held together with pale green gauze. Broiled live lobster was the pièce de résistance. I sat between the Italian Ambassador and the Marqués de Bernezzo and did not pass a dull moment. We went on after dinner to a *concert diplomatique*—one of a series of four—at the Belasco, where we had several boxes." A Peruvian contralto and a violinist were the performers of the evening, and the enthusiastic audience —"one of the smartest of the season," as it was somewhere described —included the majority of well-known names in Washington.

An important side issue of the calling system was the question of pourers. Obviously it was not practical for a woman who was called upon to greet large numbers of guests, arriving in close sequence, to attempt presiding at her own tea table. She therefore asked friends to do it for her, and though this was not actually a matter of protocol, it assumed many of the same aspects. It was considered more or less an obligation to make sure the pourers were themselves a sufficient attraction to give added importance to an "At Home." Consequently the wives of ambassadors, Cabinet officers and the more prominent senators were in

great demand as pourers; and since these ladies all had crowded schedules of their own, they could not be expected to devote an entire afternoon to one "At Home"; the best they could do was to give it half an
hour. They served in shifts, and someone had to make sure they were
relieved when their period of service was over. This meant an additional helper for the hostess—one who, besides relieving the pourers,
must always be sure they had something to pour, for tea and coffee had
a way of giving out suddenly. Then there was the further necessity of
seeing that the guests circulated, so they would not block traffic or be
stranded in a corner with no one to talk to, which could easily happen
when a great many strangers were thrown together. To further assist the
hostesses, "floaters" were invited to supplement the pourers. These were
usually younger woman, or even young girls, and it did not matter so
much whether or not their names were sufficiently well known to adorn
the social columns. The overall picture, however, was considered extremely important.

Some official hostesses liked to have their assistants come to their
"At Homes" hatless and wearing especially elegant afternoon dresses or
even dinner dresses, in order to set them apart from the general run of
guests and identify them as persons who would be of help and also—
though less admittedly—persons of importance with whom strangers
would be impressed. Mrs. Josephus Daniels, whose husband was then
Secretary of the Navy, was among those who followed this practice and
who expected her assistants to comply with it, less as a favor than as a
requirement—at least that was the way it sounded to me when I received a telephone call from her secretary informing me that I was
scheduled to pour for her employer the following Wednesday between
five and five-thirty and that I should wear a dinner dress. The beautiful
pink satin which Gertrude had given me and I had worn for my one and
only formal reception in Concord was still in good condition, and I
donned it with satisfaction, but with the hope that there would not be
many demands similar to Mrs. Daniels' made upon me, for it was the
only dress of that type I owned and I felt it would not bear repeated appearances in the role of hostess's assistant as easily as one less noticeable. On the other hand, I did not in the least mind wearing over again
the same outfit when I was only a caller and not an assistant—my black
velvet suit, with ermine collar and cuffs and matching hat and muff. I
received several compliments on it with no strings attached, and several
others which indicated that its chief merit was one of easy recognition
and that, until everyone had identified me, this could be a help.

Mrs. Daniels was what is often known—sometimes in a complimentary and sometimes in a disparaging way—as the "motherly" type:

full-figured, good-natured, easy-going. I found a common bond with her when she told me she never liked to let anybody leave her house without offering them something to eat, for I have always felt exactly the same way.

Calls on the wives of Assistant Secretaries were not on the first list of "musts" for senators' wives, since the latter outranked the former, but sooner or later, the formers' calls had to be returned, and occasionally, a fortunate chance brought about a welcome acquaintance. Young Mrs. Franklin D. Roosevelt—he was then Assistant Secretary of the Navy —represents a particularly favorable example of this: though her five children, to whom she was devoted, were still small, she managed to find time even then for the civic and philanthropic activities in which she later became so outstanding, and the living room of her sunny, spacious home on R Street was often thrown open for parlor meetings in connection with these. My first remembrance of her is at one of these as she sat knitting beside a cheerful open fire equally attentive to the presiding officer and to her various guests.

Her attitude toward me was one of great friendliness from the beginning. Of the Assistant Secretary himself I saw very little in those days, as he did not attend the parlor meetings; but the little I did see of him confirmed as correct the three comments I heard most frequently about him: that he was exceptionally good looking, that he was genial and humorous, and that he was devoted to his wife. He was immensely popular, with both men and women, but no breath of scandal touched his name. Recently, a great deal has been said and written about his association with a certain other woman, then and thereafter; but I never heard it in those days. Indeed, though stories of *political* scandal were freely bandied about, stories of sexual scandal were very rarely voiced among the people I met. Later Roosevelt came in for his share of it, but not, I firmly believe, with justification. Among the senators, there was only one whom I heard criticized for lack of marital propriety, and as Mrs. Roosevelt once said to me herself, "Would it be possible to find *any* group of ninety-six men among whom one such charge could and would not be made?" Accusations of hard drinking were much more frequent, and though these were generally exaggerated, unfortunately there was a good deal of truth in them.

After I had started Peter in day, Sunday and dancing schools and begun my inflexible schedule of making and receiving calls, enrollment in the Ladies of the Senate became my next logical step. This group, organized as a Red Cross Chapter during World War I, owed its formation primarily to Mrs. Key Pittman, the lovely wife of the Senator from

Nevada—himself one of the most charming as well as one of the most brilliant members of the Chamber. Since a slight but somehow very attractive vagueness about matters that seemed to her easily dismissed was one of Mrs. Pittman's amiable traits, the creation of this organization seemed rather out of character. Nevertheless, she deserves every credit for it.

In those days, the Senate Ladies met to sew every Tuesday morning in a room assigned them in the old Senate Office Building and remained for luncheon afterward. The table was set for them and ice water, rolls and butter were furnished by the Senate restaurant; aside from this, the Ladies had no service or help. Six of them acted as hostesses each time, their names chosen in alphabetical order, and they vied with each other in bringing specialties of their own localities or that had proven outstandingly successful in their own kitchens. For instance, Mrs. Harding, who was then a senator's wife, contributed two very different dishes— waffles and chicken pie—which I remember as especially delicious. My contribution was a cream of cucumber salad which was so popular that I had the recipe engraved on Christmas cards for my fellow members of the Ladies Senate.

At first, each member could bring a guest to these luncheons, but pressure for invitations soon became so intense that only the hostesses of the day were allowed this privilege, and then it was abolished altogether. Eventually, so were the weekly luncheons, though the Red Cross program of weekly sewing still continues; now there are only two luncheons a year, one given at the Capitol by the Ladies of the Senate in honor of the President's wife and the other given by the President's wife at the White House in honor of the Ladies of the Senate.

I enjoyed the Senate luncheons immensely and went to them more or less regularly for years, though I decided at the very beginning that they could not be taken too seriously. The day I was welcomed at one for the first time, the wife of Senator John Sharp Williams of Mississippi greeted me warmly and added, "You don't know how much these luncheons come to mean! I simply live from Tuesday to Tuesday." Then and there I resolved that whatever I did with the rest of my life, it would not be ordered in such a way that I would live from one Tuesday luncheon to another. However, I do not wish to disparage the importance that luncheons played in my schedule; I went to them or had luncheon guests myself until the time came when I simply could not do this and keep abreast of my work—and that was then far in the future.

I found it virtually impossible to go out in the morning, except for taking Peter to school; otherwise, the hours from eight to one were barely long enough for routine housekeeping and desk work, and I reluctantly turned a deaf ear to invitations for morning lectures and musicales and, with even greater regret, to a suggestion that I should join the Bible Class conducted by Mrs. Selden C. Spencer, the wife of the Senator from Missouri, which had met with such a wide response that it was finally quartered in the ballroom of the Willard Hotel, after having outgrown the double drawing rooms of the Washington Club. Only once, that first whole season, as far as I can remember, did I abandon my domestic duties; and this was to go to the Senate Chamber to attend proceedings which were of great interest to me personally. It was Lincoln's birthday, and Harry read to the Senate the Gettysburg Address, from one of the two existing copies written throughout in Lincoln's own hand. President Lincoln had given this manuscript to Edward Everett, who had presented it, together with the manuscript of his own address delivered at Gettysburg on November 19, 1863, to Mrs. Hamilton Fish to be sold at a benefit for Union soldiers held in New York during March of 1864. The two documents had been purchased there by an uncle of Harry's and had been in the family ever since.

Thanks to the graciousness of Senator Lodge, who introduced Harry at the opening of the proceedings, they took a form very complimentary to him, and for the first time since our arrival in Washington he seemed genuinely pleased at something that had happened in the Capitol. After adjournment, I remained for lunch with him in the Senate restaurant, and many of his colleagues and their wives came to our table to greet and congratulate us, and of course we were asked again and again to display the famous document. It was a proud day for Harry.

Chapter 16

AT THIS period Russia was still represented in Washington by the Kerensky government, and as the Ambassador, Boris Bakhmeteff, was unmarried, his sister was his hostess. I had called on her in the course of my diplomatic rounds—naturally on a Friday—and was astonished to receive, the following Monday, an invitation to lunch the coming Wednesday. Like invitations to the White House, invitations to embassies take precedence over any other plans, and usually these are quite willingly altered to suit the occasion. Mine certainly were in this case. The Bakhmeteffs' house was much less pretentious than the one which later became the Soviet Embassy; but it was suitable for its purposes, and because of its extensive library and its general atmosphere of quiet culture, it seemed to me more like a house on the waterside of Beacon Street than any I had so far seen in Washington. The luncheon, featuring several Russian dishes, was delectable and the group of guests small but very distinguished. My pleasurable astonishment grew when I found I was placed beside the Ambassador, and it increased still further when I found out why I had been invited.

"I have been wanting very much to meet you," he told me as soon as we were seated. "That is, of course, I met you last Friday, but I did not have a chance to talk with you then and, to tell the truth, I did not place you until later when I went over the cards that had been left. That was when I realized we had been honored by a visit from the author of 'The Satisfied Reflections of a Semi-Bostonian' and 'On the Fence.' I was so pleased when the latter appeared recently. I had been watching for something more from the pen of the semi-Bostonian. I hope that before long there will be something from the viewpoint of an adopted Washingtonian."

Naturally, his remarks delighted me, and they also gave impetus to an idea which had begun to germinate in my own mind. Very soon thereafter came another similarly significant luncheon, given on a Sunday by Representative and Mrs. Frederick C. Hicks of New York. This time I was not seated by an ambassador, but by an official of the State Department who, though younger than I was, had already become Chief of the Division of Latin-American Affairs. I had not met him before, as he had only recently returned from Argentina, where he had been Second Secretary of Embassy and where he had managed to achieve an understanding of Latin-American psychology which went far beyond a thorough knowledge of its history, customs and language. But I did not feel he was a stranger, partly because, as a product of Groton and Harvard, he personified a type of well-born and well-educated young man I had been familiar with since childhood; partly because I had heard so much about his extraordinary diplomatic talents; and partly because he had married a Boston girl, Esther Slater, whom I knew slightly and who was a great friend of my friend Marion Burdett. I thought him extremely attractive and felt sure I was going to like him before he further predisposed me in his favor by beginning his conversation in much the same way the Russian Ambassador had when I lunched with him. The name of this promising young man was Sumner Welles.

"I have been hoping for a chance to talk to you," he said amiably. "The trouble is, at a luncheon or dinner I don't usually sit anywhere near a senator's wife—I'm way down below the salt. But I can't help telling you how much I enjoyed the 'Semi-Bostonian' and how much I hope you are going to write about Washington."

"Do you really?" I asked, wondering if I were justified in taking this as a genuine compliment and not as casual lunch party conversation. "You're the second man who's said that to me lately."

"I'm sure a great many would have told you so if they'd had the opportunity. . . . Who was the other one?"

"The Russian Ambassador."

"I might have known. Bakhmeteff reads everything, and incidentally, he has very good judgment."

The conversation switched to other topics and after luncheon Mrs. Welles and I chatted about mutual Boston friends until the party began to break up and her husband joined us.

"Don't forget what I said," he told me as we shook hands. "We'll be very much interested in what you do next."

"Just what do you mean by 'we'?"

"Why, everyone who hopes you'll go on writing! And I should say, at a guess, that means everyone who's read what you've written so far." He hesitated a moment and then added, "Specifically, I think I'm safe in saying anyone who's connected with official life at home and abroad or interested in learning more about it."

I have long since ceased to feel that many things happen merely by chance. I believe that far more often they are a part of a pattern. Moreover, I think the pattern is controlled and perfected by some Power higher than our own. I cannot define it with any greater exactitude, any more than I could define with exactitude the element that makes a certain kind of friendship different from all others. But I have felt its force and its truth over and over again. I was not only getting compliments at luncheons that season after the publication of "On the Fence"; I was having my second thrilling experience with fan mail. Some of it came from readers of "Our Doctor," a tribute to our local country practitioner, which appeared in the first number of *The Penwoman,* the magazine which the League of American Pen Women had started; some from readers of "The Story of 'Master' Henry Parkinson," a historical sketch about my great-great-grandfather, which had appeared in the official magazine of the D.A.R.; some from the *Atlantic;* and a little more from editors of other magazines and of books, who wrote cautiously that they might be interested in my work. And when I saw a gray envelope from *Good Housekeeping* lying on my desk, I honestly thought it was a communication of the latter sort, though it was addressed to *Mr.* Henry W. Keyes and not to *Mrs.* Henry W. Keyes. I believed the first word to be a typographical error, and my belief was all the more logical because my husband's mail, except from members of his family, customarily went to the Senate Office Building, not to the apartment, and was usually prefaced by the title Honorable. Though never before or since have I opened a letter which I was not *sure* was meant for me, I opened this one without hesitation.

I was appalled to find that I had been mistaken. The letter *had* been intended for my husband. *Good Housekeeping* was proposing to start a campaign through its pages in favor of the Sheppard-Towner Maternity Bill, which was shortly to come before the Senate for action. The editor of the magazine, Mr. William Frederick Bigelow, hoped very much that Senator Keyes would support the bill.

As soon as Harry came home that evening, I explained and apologized for opening the letter. Far from being angry, he thought I was taking the matter much too seriously: Probably the communication was nothing but a form sent every senator to back a publicity stunt. He did not believe in federal help for such measures; he felt the states should handle public welfare individually. He did not know Representative Horace Mann Towner of Iowa, though he had heard him well spoken of, but Senator Morris Sheppard was an inoffensive man, except when roused over the subject of Prohibition, of which he was rabidly in favor; no doubt this was another of his impractical schemes. Harry was surprised that Sheppard had taken time from his pet complaint to consider maternity aid. He, Harry, would certainly not vote for this bill. As for the letter I was worrying about, the place for that was the scrapbasket.

I did not see it that way. I had learned enough through my Red Cross work, both in New Hampshire and in Washington, to feel very doubtful that the separate states were really doing enough for maternity and child welfare; and if they had not managed to do it by this time, how could we feel sure that they would in the immediate future? Anyway, if Harry were not going to answer the letter, would he mind if I did?

Harry shrugged his shoulders and said he thought I was wasting my time. But, for once, he was mistaken.

Mr. Bigelow's reply to my letter came by return mail. It was not only courteous, it was grateful—in fact, he went so far as to say that he thought perhaps I was an answer to prayer. Briefly dismissing the subject of the Sheppard-Towner Bill for the moment, he told me he had been trying in vain to get permission for a reporter to see Mr. Edwin Meredith, the Secretary of Agriculture; he wanted to print a statement clarifying Mr. Meredith's contention that the Department of Agriculture was more closely related to more of the people than any other Cabinet department; but so far, Mr. Meredith had declined to give such an interview. Did I by any chance know him personally? If so, did I think Mr. Meredith would be willing to talk to me on this subject?

My answer also went off by return mail. I did indeed know Mr. Meredith personally, and most pleasantly. I often saw him and Mrs. Meredith socially and was on very friendly terms with them. I had telephoned the Secretary's office and found that he would be glad to talk to me about an article for *Good Housekeeping*. Unless I had immediate instructions to the contrary, I would go ahead and write it.

No instructions to the contrary arrived, but in due course a letter which seemed pleased, though a little bewildered was delivered. It had not occurred to Mr. Bigelow that everything would—or could—move so rapidly in official circles. The article was very good. He was scheduling it for August and calling it "The Fortress of the Farm." He had instructed his treasurer to mail me a check for three hundred dollars. He thought perhaps he had better send his associate editor, Miss Toombes, to see me. He had an idea that I might write something else for *Good Housekeeping*.

The check came in almost as soon as the letter, and I decided it should be divided in a way which proved so satisfactory that I followed it for many years in handling every check I received: ten per cent went into the savings bank, ten was given to church and charity, ten was devoted to a special little luxury that I had felt I could not afford, and the rest went straight into basic current expenses. I had hardly put this plan into operation when Miss Toombes appeared and remained in Washington for a week. She was personally not quite so depressing as her name, but I knew she was there to find out, if possible, how much value I might have to *Good Housekeeping,* as a regular contributor, and the only way I could enlighten her was to include her in as many of my activities as possible. I happened to be pouring at the Congressional Club that week, so I took her to a reception there, which seemed to impress her very favorably, as did a couple of luncheons. But of course I could not arrange to have her included at formal dinners, for which the guest lists had been made up far in advance, and, taken by and large, I did not feel it was a particularly exciting week. However, I had already forgotten that the social pace in Washington is so much swifter than in most other places that even a glimpse of it often amazes outsiders. At all events, when Miss Toombes's week was up, Mr. Bigelow joined her in Washington and we spent the evening at my apartment engaged in a three-cornered conference.

I had formed a mental picture of Mr. Bigelow as a very large man, ruddy of countenance and emanating forcefulness. I could not possibly have been been more mistaken. He was slightly built, with very little color in his face and with hair and eyes and expression all so unremarkable that I could not have said the next day what I had noticed about them. But even though the forcefulness was so well concealed, it was only a matter of minutes before I knew it was there. The caliber of his voice was unmistakable. He spoke as one having authority and being accustomed to exercising it. Though I was thrilled at the mere possibility of becoming a regular contributor to *Good Housekeeping* and even had a definite plan to submit for approval, my self-confidence was shaken.

I wanted to write articles slanted to the tastes, talents and needs of "the woman I used to be," I began hesitantly; a woman whose earlier years had included travel and urban life, as mine had, and could not help missing the opportunities they offered when she no longer had them; or she might be a woman whose life had been singularly deprived of such opportunities and who longed to take part in them vicariously. I was finding Washington an inexhaustible source of pleasure, privilege and enlightenment; I thought I could help other women see it through my eyes. Automatically my husband's position gave me an entree to official circles, and I was trying to make the most of them by faithfully living up to the obligations established by protocol for a senator's wife, in as far as my limited financial means and the amount of time I had to give my little boy would allow me to go out in society. I had already made quite a few friends. I liked to have company and had had a good deal of experience in entertaining large groups, with insufficient funds and household help. If I could do it in New Hampshire, I believed I could do it in Washington, where social life and political life were so closely interwoven that it was hard to tell where one began and the other left off. I felt I would see enough of both to write about them in any proportion the editor preferred. Two quite prominent and distinguished gentlemen, who had read my articles in the *Atlantic,* had told me they hoped I would follow up my impressions of Boston with impressions of Washington. . . . Naturally, Mr. Bigelow asked me who the gentlemen were and seemed to give the matter careful thought.

Although nothing was settled then and there, I have always felt that the pattern for the "Letters from a Senator's Wife," which were to be a regular monthly feature in *Good Housekeeping* for the next fourteen years, began either that night or the following Wednesday when, unexpectedly, I was asked to speak before a hearing on the Sheppard-Towner Bill. I was seemingly as little prepared to do this as I had been at the meeting of the New Hampshire Women's Clubs when I earned the title of Lieutenant Governor; but the results were equally pleasing and even more portentous. Mr. Bigelow attended the hearing on the bill and so did Mrs. Maude Wood Park, the national President of the League of Women Voters, which was strongly in favor of the bill. The next day she came to see me and told me she and Mr. Bigelow had "had a talk." Whatever its details may have been, I was unquestionably its main subject, and Mrs. Park, like the Russian Ambassador and Sumner Welles, had inadvertently done me a very good turn. To all intents and purposes, I was already slated as a regular contributor to *Good Housekeeping.*

Chapter 17

A LETTER from Mr. William Morrow, then editor-in-chief of the publishing firm of Frederick Stokes, was among those received during the spring which had led me to believe, merely from seeing the envelope, that the one from *Good Housekeeping* might be for me. If I had another novel in the course of construction, Mr. Morrow had said, and was not under contract for it, he would be very much interested in seeing it. As a matter of fact, of course I had two, not under construction, but in virtually completed form, which I had sadly put away as unlikely to find a welcome anywhere; I had yet to learn that one editorial rebuff is by no means conclusive evidence that a story will never be marketable. Besides, for the time being, I found that my activities, present and prospective, with *Good Housekeeping* seemed to be about all I could handle, in addition to my domestic, maternal and social duties; but, as I prepared to leave Washington for Pine Grove Farm in early June, I unearthed the parcel, which had been stowed away since early autumn, and sent *The Career of David Noble* to Mr. Morrow without any attempt to refurbish it. In due course, I received a very pleasant letter from him, saying he thought the story had distinct possibilities; would I feel like talking it over with him the next time I happened to be passing through New York?

Despite the inclusion of my essay, "On the Fence," in an anthology, I was still gunshy, as far as book publishing was concerned, and I did not leap on the next train for New York as I certainly would have done before my experience in Boston the previous year. I went back to Pine Grove Farm and spent a busy but unremarkable summer there. My sister-in-law Belle had died in Boston the previous spring and, as in the case of her mother, the final burial had been postponed until it could take place in the family lot at Newbury; this meant a gathering of the Keyes clan at Pine Grove Farm with heavy responsibilities for me. The boys were now old enough to want considerable company of their own, and this required some attention if not actual supervision from me. I drove several times to Ryegate, the nearby Vermont village that was featured in the story Mrs. Greer had suggested to me the previous summer. I also made several speeches in the vicinity and since there was no longer any reason, as there had been when Harry was governor, why I should not accept an honorarium, I gladly did so.

I was still a frequent and apparently welcome guest of both the Demings and the Helburns, but I now had an additional foothold with Harry's cousin Kitty Colby and her husband Charles, who spent at least part of their winters in New York. Certain "little experiments" which the Keyes family had regarded disparagingly as taking Charlie's time away from his teaching at McGill University had at last been justified; he had invented the noiseless typewriter and was on his way to becoming a rich man. Having myself been told more than once that I could not earn a dollar to save my life, I had secretly sympathized with Charlie's ambitions; now that I was beginning to realize my own, I had a special fellow feeling for him. He and Kitty were comfortably installed in a suite, large enough to accommodate a guest or two, at an excellent hotel. They insisted that my first visit to New York that fall should be with them, and I was delighted to comply.

I took advantage of my stay with them to telephone Mr. Morrow, who promptly invited me to lunch. Nothing could be more indicative of the sad change that has come over the publishing business than the decline of this then characteristic technique of beginning an association with an author. If a manuscript reached an editor-in-chief at all (having first been carefully screened by his readers), he himself generally wrote a letter stating (1) that he was sorry to say the material did not quite fit into his list but he would be glad to see something else (and he really meant this!) or (2) that he thought the material had possibilities and he would like to discuss them. Since the letter Mr. Morrow had written me fell into the second category, a quiet luncheon was the next logical step.

He made a few rather hesitant suggestions: he would like to see a certain character developed a little further; he thought one conversation dragged a little but others could profitably be prolonged, as well as certain descriptive passages; in his opinion, the script needed to be about ten thousand words longer to achieve the status of a full-length novel. He had no other changes to suggest; if I would be willing to make those he had mentioned. . . . I said that of course I would, and almost as

though it were an afterthought, which required apology, the crass subject of money was wedged into the cultured conversation. This time
there were to be advance royalties—at the risk of seeming unladylike
and grasping, I made that point timidly but firmly, and was infinitely relieved when Mr. Morrow said, why most certainly. Then came a brief
discussion concerning the scale of royalties after the advances had been
earned. We shook hands, I thanked Mr. Morrow for a delightful luncheon, he thanked me for giving him a chance to bring out my book, and
we parted the best of friends. Three days later the contract was signed.
That was all there was to it.

Almost immediately after I arrived in Washington in a jubilant
mood, Harry, with several other members of the Naval Affairs Committee, left for the Pacific Coast on official business, but I resumed my
place in the social whirl at a pace which steadily became more brisk. I
entertained at luncheon myself in honor of Baroness Romano Avezzana, the first of a series of luncheons I was planning for the winter,
since Harry, running true to form, still preferred me to entertain without him whenever this was possible, and in the case of dinners that was
not suitable in Washington. (Luncheons had the further advantage of
being more economical than dinners, since a menu inadequate for the
latter tended to seem lavish in the case of the former. Also, luncheons
were considered acceptable legal tender for honoring a couple, only one
of whom would actually attend; and with limitations of space and service, this was still another advantage.) I made all my Supreme Court
calls, I dined at the Press Club and the Chevy Chase Club—and as I
returned from the latter around midnight, the telephone was ringing and
Mr. Field, the headmaster of Milton Academy, was on the line.

"I am very sorry to disturb you at this hour," he said, "but you were
out when I called earlier and I felt I must speak with you personally.
The school doctor is a little concerned about Henry. He isn't in pain
and he hasn't asked for you or his father; in fact, we thought it better
not to let him know we'd telephoned you. He's—well, there's a lump
under one of his knees. As you know, he's been playing football, and
we thought some sort of blow might have caused the swelling. But we
called in Dr. Maynard Ladd, who, I believe, operated on your younger
son, and Dr. Ladd thinks this lump should be removed. There's a
chance it may be sarcoma."

"I'm afraid I don't know what sarcoma is."

"It's—it's cancer. But, of course, we won't know until the lump is removed whether it is malignant or not."

"And if it is cancer—what then?"

"Why, I'm afraid it means amputation. But as I said. . . . And Dr.

Ladd couldn't operate until the latter part of next week at the earliest. If you could get to Boston by Tuesday and talk things over. . . ."

I said that I most assuredly would, and the connection was broken. For a few moments I sat still, because I was too stunned to move or even think clearly. The possibility that my fifteen-year-old son might have to go through life with an artificial leg or, if the malignancy should spread, that there would be very little life left for him to go through seemed too dreadful to contemplate. But, obviously, it must not only be contemplated but faced—calmly and competently. And it would be costly in hard cash, as well as in every other way. I had no idea where to reach Harry, as he was traveling from place to place in California and had not been able to let me know where he would be or when; but I knew that even if I could get in touch with him, it would be very hard for him to send me as much money as I needed without considerable maneuvering. To offset this difficulty, another letter expressing editorial interest had reached me, this time from the *Ladies' Home Journal*. If I could only stop and see the editor on my way to Boston, perhaps. . . . But I had an appointment with Mr. Bigelow scheduled for Monday morning, and I still had those ten thousand words to write for Mr. Morrow with their deadline the next week.

This was Saturday morning, but fortunately for me, week ends which began on Friday at the latest and often lasted until Tuesday were not then standard practice for editors. I reached Mr. Bigelow by telephone and asked if I could see him as early as nine on Monday in Washington and found that I could. Still telephoning, I learned that Mr. Currie of the *Ladies' Home Journal* would be very happy to have me lunch with him in Philadelphia on Monday. We could discuss a possible Washington article while we ate. I found that Alice Glessner's cousins Judge and Mrs. von Moschitzker would meet me in Philadelphia, take me to their house for an afternoon break and dinner and engage space on the Federal Express for Boston that night. I would be in Boston Tuesday morning, the earliest time Dr. Ladd could confer with me, and if the Fates were propitious, by then I would be assured of enough money to take care of the operation. I called Mr. Field, told him when to expect me and went back to my desk.

It was now nearly noon. At four o'clock Sunday afternoon I finished inserting the ten thousand extra words in different parts of *The Career of David Noble*—a few hundred here, a couple thousand there—which, for me at least, is one of the hardest things on earth to do in expanding a novel; as soon as the script was in the mail I began to pack so that I would be able to leave for Philadelphia the minute my appointment with Mr. Bigelow was over.

Everything went smoothly in Washington and Philadelphia. I reached Boston on time and went directly to Milton Tuesday morning. Henry was attending classes as usual. I had decided not to make up any tall tales about having been called to Boston unexpectedly for some emergency, but to say in a matter-of-fact way that I had come to accompany him to Dr. Ladd's that afternoon and what we did next would depend on what he told us. Henry's reception of me was equally matter-of-fact, and he expressed no concern when Dr. Ladd said we had better plan to check in the following night at Massachusetts General, where he would make arrangements for Henry's room in Phillips House, and plan to operate Thursday morning. I spent Tuesday night with the Fields, and then Henry and I went into Boston and saw a matinee before proceeding to Phillips House. I had still not said a word to Henry about my anxiety or the cause for it, and I knew he had not been told how serious a situation he was facing. As I gave the matter more thought, I decided that he should be—that if he came out of anesthesia minus a leg, the shock would be worse than any he might suffer from dread beforehand. So, as quietly and tactfully as I could, I reminded him how troubled we had all been when the cyst had developed in Peter's throat, for fear that it might be malignant, and said that though the lump under his knee was not exactly a cyst, it could cause trouble, so. . . .

"I knew that the moment I saw you yesterday," he said quite calmly.

It was not until he was actually on the operating table that he lost his nerve. I had been allowed to remain with him, and I could see that he was shivering.

"Suddenly I'm frightened," he said in a low voice.

I was frightened, too. But somehow I managed to say what proved to be the right thing to reassure him, though what it was I do not know— it is the only detail about the entire episode that I have forgotten. Fortunately, he did not fight the anesthetic, and as soon as he was unconscious, I went back to his room and waited. It was a long hard wait, one of the days that inevitably left its mark, even though it ended in relief: the lump removed from under Henry's knee was as large as an orange, but it was nonmalignant.

His convalescence was characterized by the ease with which the young generally recover. When his nurse appeared shortly after the operation with the menu for the next day and said he could check his favorite dishes, I shook my head; I did not see how it would be possible for him to tolerate anything more solid than orange juice. But when I waked myself the next morning, I could see through the open door between our rooms that a laden tray was being taken to Henry, and presently, he had demolished everything edible on it. By Sunday he was well enough to be moved from Phillips House to the Milton Infirmary, and I was not needed any more. I went back to Washington and sank into bed myself. I was completely exhausted. But my exhaustion was permeated with increased self-confidence. I had proved that I could indeed meet an emergency calmly and competently if I had to and, what was more, that I could go on writing at top speed, no matter how upset I might be emotionally. The discovery was to stand me in good stead in the future.

For several days I did not even try to leave my bed. Then I was up and doing again—to give the second luncheon in my series, to dine out myself; to attend the opening session of Congress, at which Harding spoke, as a senator who was President-elect. And after that, over and over again, to go to the Senate Chamber to hear the discussions on the Sheppard-Towner Bill, since it had been agreed that this was to form the subject matter of the first "Letter from a Senator's Wife" for *Good Housekeeping*.

I had felt very optimistic all fall that the "Sheppard-Towner Bill for the protection of maternity and infancy" would get to the floor of the Senate almost as soon as Congress convened, but my optimism did not meet with much definite encouragement. So I was delighted when I received a telephone message from Mrs. Park late Monday evening, the thirteenth of December, telling me the bill was likely to come up the next day and that she hoped I would be at the Capitol. I assured her that nothing would keep me away, and at eleven o'clock the next morning I started off, for I thought the galleries might be crowded. There was one especially reserved for the wives of senators, but this reservation wasn't always as strictly observed as it might have been—when Harry took his oath of office, there were six nuns sitting placidly together on the back row! On another occasion, it was rumored, a lady came to the entrance and said she was Senator So-and-So's wife, only to be told by the doorman that he couldn't possibly let her in—Senator So-and-So had three wives there already! As the gallery was very small, this violation of the rules meant that many senators' wives found their places occupied if they arrived late for some event of unusual importance, and this is what I feared might have happened.

I need not have worried. The gallery was absolutely empty. I sat alone, listening to the order of morning business—the reading of petitions and memorials, the introduction of pension bills, et cetera. At one o'clock, knowing that this would last another hour, I decided it would be safe for me to go over to the Senate Office Building for the weekly luncheon of the Ladies of the Senate. As I pressed the bell for the private elevator to take me down to the subway between the House and the

Senate Office Building and the Capitol, Mrs. Park came out of one of the other galleries looking tired and discouraged and spoke to me.

"Our bill isn't coming up today after all," she said. "I tried to send you a message, but you'd already left. Of course, we're hoping now for tomorrow, but there's nothing to do but wait."

With a good deal of difficulty, I rearranged my plans for Wednesday and started bright and early for the Capitol. It was not until after four in the afternoon that Senator France, Chairman of the Committee on Public Health and National Quarantine, rose to move the consideration of Senate Bill No. 3259.

The motion was finally agreed to. Senator France asked that the bill might be passed quickly, without debate, since it was "a measure that should commend itself to the Senators," and Senator Sheppard asked that the formal reading of the bill might be dispensed with. To this Senator King objected, and Senator Smoot brought forward the question of some amendments that he wished to offer and to have read with the bill. Senator France expressed his hope that the bill might be passed that evening, and was promptly and flatly told by Senator Smoot that it could not be, and Senator King moved to adjourn. The "consideration" which the Senate had given the bill had not lasted ten minutes.

In spite of Wednesday's disappointment, I again took my seat in the otherwise empty gallery on Thursday, for the women whom I had met in the corridors of the Capitol—representatives from organizations all over the country who had been working hard for the bill the entire fall —had told me they had every reason to expect an early vote. I was delighted when, early in the afternoon, Mrs. Sheppard, who was one of the youngest and prettiest of all the Senate wives, joined me in the gallery. The Senate Chamber was dreadfully dingy and ill-ventilated and needed all the brightening it could get!

Promptly at two o'clock, Senator France again asked the Senate to consider the Maternity Bill. There was, as usual, a little skirmishing. One or two gentlemen had not yet had time to study the bill thoroughly; one feared that an absent colleague might feel disappointed if it were read while he was away, and so on. Two years earlier I would have been much touched by such thirst for information and consideration of absent members, but I had come to realize that a senator is apt to plead ignorance of a bill when he wishes to delay its passage; so I was re-lieved when the bill and the amendments to it were finally read by the Clerk of the Senate and Senator Sheppard obtained the floor to speak for his bill. His speech, beautifully delivered, was clear and concise and dignified. When he finished, Senator Harrison asked him if this bill in any way repealed the law preventing the dissemination of information concerning birth control, and was told that it did not. Then Senator Thomas rose to his feet with the following remark:

"Mr. President, with fifteen senators present, the Secretary, the reading clerk, the doorkeepers, the pages, and spaces filled with unoccupied and deserted seats, I shall occupy a few minutes of your time and the senators' time in expressing some of the reasons which compel me to oppose the adoption of this measure—"

My heart sank. There was no law to prevent a senator from speaking for or against a bill as long as he chose—until he dropped from exhaustion, in fact; and having heard the gentleman from Colorado—who was very able and could be very delightful—speak previously when he wished to oppose a measure, I knew that he was not easily exhausted. As the afternoon wore on, he talked, pacing up and down, about Herbert Spencer and the government of Great Britain, about the happy condition of the United States a quarter of a century earlier, about the great Republican victory the previous November and various other things. When I was beginning to wonder how he could possibly remain on his feet another minute, he said quite calmly, "And now let us come to this bill!" Then he dwelt on the great dangers lurking in bureaucracy and extravagance and the violation of states' rights. He said that if twenty-three thousand women were dying annually in childbirth, it was "probably a normal mortality and would persist." He felt it safe to assume that not one per cent of the women in the country had read this bill which so many were said to be advocating. And when he had finished with the bill, the day was finished, too, and the Senate adjourned—which of course had been his intention from the beginning.

On Friday the first speaker against the bill was Senator Warren. He was deeply concerned about the awful state of the United States Treasury and the danger of having "emotional" legislation introduced into the Senate. He spoke of the "recommendations that come from women —dear souls!" He asked—in the name of God—whether, if we were spending eighty thousand dollars a year to investigate Child Welfare, we were not mindful enough of the matter of maternity and the care of infants. It seemed to him that this sum was quite sufficient.

Senator Pittman spoke next, in favor of the bill, echoing a suggestion of Senator Sheppard's that if we could not afford the two million dollars for which it called, we might possibly rob one of the unopposed appropriation bills for the Army and Navy to that extent. Then he added that he distinctly remembered when the Senator from Colorado had done him the kindness to vote for a bill of his. "He spoke on this floor for two hours against the bill, and probably lost me five or six very good votes, and then he voted for the bill." Senator Thomas asked if the bill was carried.

Mr. Pittman: "The bill carried in spite of the speech of the Senator."

Mr. Thomas: "That is the usual result of my addresses in this body." But finally Senator Pittman completed his remarks and Senator France asked for a vote.

By the time it had been ascertained whether or not there was a quorum present, Senator King and Senator McCumber had both risen to oppose the bill. Other amendments were offered, in many cases involving only the change of a few words here and there and discussion of the bill became general. There was considerable difference of opinion as to the exact meaning of the terms "experts" and "infants"; as to whether the Children's Bureau or the Bureau of Public Health Service should take up maternity work. And so another day was used up. And then, after one more long hard day was spent in technical discussion, in making small amendments, in striking out a phrase here and putting in another one there, the Sheppard-Towner Bill for the Protection of Maternity and Infancy *passed the United States Senate*. It was shorn, to be sure, of much of its power; its appropriations were reduced; its original purposes were, in some places, thwarted and changed—but *it was not defeated!*

In one way, I wished it had gone through with not a hand or a voice raised against it; in another way, I was glad it passed the way it did, fighting for its very life, exactly as so many of the women and children it was going to help had to fight for theirs. To me there was something deeply symbolic about the manner of its victory—something, too, that strengthened my deep-rooted conviction that while we must have faith that the right always conquers in the end, it is only the hard-fought conquest which afterward seems worth while, and great and holy.

For me personally, there was another great point of significance in the bill's passage: it was the first important legislation of more interest to women than to men that had been passed since the Nineteenth Amendment. But I do not believe it would have passed if women had not had the ballot; the thousands of letters they sent their senators, urging them to support the bill, would have carried far less weight if their writers had not been voters. I had neither sought nor desired the right to vote; I had felt that the ballot for women would bring only doubtful blessings in its train. But if it could bring about the passage of bills like this, I was willing—and glad—to confess I had been mistaken.

Chapter 18

I WAS still greatly preoccupied with the Sheppard-Towner Bill for a week after it had passed the Senate; the task of writing my first *Good Housekeeping* "Letter" on this subject took precedence over everything else. This was my first attempt at recording anything of the sort, and I realized how much depended on my success—or lack of it. My efforts were rewarded; Mr. Bigelow liked the article, Mrs. Park liked the article, and a senator whose opinion I valued very highly told me: "It is a wonderfully vivid picture of the Senate and what takes place there. You have done a real service in showing the people back home, who never have a chance to come to Washington and see for themselves, why it often takes so long to pass bills."

The bill had yet to pass the House of Representatives before it could become a law, and hearings on it began the following week. I attended these and was again asked to make a speech, which I did with more self-confidence this time. Mr. Bigelow was not present, but Mrs. Park reported to him that I had "made a perfect speech." It was nothing of the sort, but her judgment was gratifying and valuable. When I welcomed my sons home for their Christmas vacations, my spirits were as high as theirs, and Harry returned from his western trip in good spirits too. His friend Gordon Woodbury, who had succeeded Franklin Roosevelt as Assistant Secretary of the Navy, invited us to be among his guests for a day's cruise on the *Sylph,* the yacht which was one of his official perquisites. Everyone was in a genial mood and a holiday atmosphere prevailed; the knowledge that a change in administration would inevitably soon mean Mr. Woodbury's retirement was not allowed to depress us that day.

The first change in the official picture that was of real regret to me and a foretaste of many such future pangs was the departure of the Romano Avezzanas, which was precipitated by an abrupt shift in the Italian government. I had become really attached to Baroness Romano, who was, before her marriage, Jacqueline Taylor of St. Louis. She had an impregnable social position in her own right and possessed so much grace and charm that she overshadowed many women who were more beautiful; she excelled in the art of dress, an art facilitated by the wise policy which granted a special allowance to Italian ambassadresses for their wardrobes. She also excelled in the writing of cordial personal notes, for which she always seemed to find time no matter how crowded her days.

The article I had written for *Ladies' Home Journal* as the result of my luncheon conference with Mr. Currie the previous October was published late in January. It was entitled "A New Senator's Wife" and was couched, for the most part, in a rather minor key, for it was composed when all my first grievances against Washington were still fresh in my mind. I felt better when I had publicly aired my opinion about the housing situation, the shopping situation and the official calling system, and a chorus of praise arose from fellow sufferers. On the other hand, the Local Board of Trade was furious, and I was somewhat peremptorily summoned to appear before a meeting of its representatives. I could have insisted on being represented by counsel instead of going personally, or I could have taken someone with me. I decided to do neither; I had made no statements which I could not prove and none of which I was ashamed. I went alone, and climbed up on a platform to confront a sea of angry faces. It proved to be much the best course I could have pursued. I was able to answer calmly and promptly every question hurled at me, and gradually the atmosphere cleared. Mr. Julius Garfinckel, the head of the most fashionable department store in the city, rose and said he thought a motion was in order to thank Mrs. Keyes for having come to the meeting, and Mr. Frank Jelleff, the head of a similar establishment, seconded the motion. Adjournment took place with much cordiality and hand-shaking. Mr. Garfinckel and Mr. Jelleff both gained a faithful customer in me, and in many wealthier women who had shared my grievances, and for months Washington rang with echoes of the article, both pro and con. In fact, not until I wrote about high prices in Ireland has my pen produced such an immediate reaction.

The new year began with an accelerated social schedule, though I would have said the year before that this was impossible: I was one of the hostesses at the first luncheon held by the Ladies of the Senate, I gave the third in my series of luncheons at home, I went to innumerable luncheons elsewhere, and dinners figured more and more frequently on my program. Toward the end of February I wrote to a friend, "I ate just two meals, besides breakfast, at home last week, and at one of those I had company myself; and yesterday, which was my receiving day, I had more than three hundred callers and stood on my feet four hours which, on top of everything else I had done, was an endurance test. So I think I have a right to be tired."

But tired or not, I was still setting aside an hour every morning for Peter and doing more and more writing of various kinds, including a review of Honoré Willsie's latest book, *The Enchanted Canyon,* for the New York *Herald Tribune,* which resulted in an offer to do reviewing regularly for that paper. I was delighted and hastened to tell Mr. Bigelow this news, but to my great disappointment he did not regard it as such; the *Herald Tribune* and the Hearst empire, to which *Good Housekeeping* belonged, were bitter enemies and if I became a contributor to the former, I would jeopardize my position with the latter. As the "Letters" meant more to me than anything else, I was obliged to give up the reviewing.

I was faithfully following the fortunes of the Sheppard-Towner Bill. Subsequent to its passage in the Senate, it had been favorably reported out by the Interstate Commerce Committee of the House, but after a considerable delay it had still not got to the Floor. One day I received a hasty message telling me that the bill was coming up for a hearing before the Rules Committee, to see if it could not be given precedence and passed before the current session ended. Would I please come to the Capitol at once?

It was raining in torrents, but I went, and reached the Committee Room bedraggled and damp. And certainly nothing happened there to make me feel any less gloomy. Judge Towner and others pleaded for his bill, and finally I spoke—begging that the committee would not call it a "woman's bill" but a national bill. The chairman, Mr. Campbell of Kansas, came and shook hands with me after the hearing was over, and told me that what I said was sensible and that he wished to thank me for it. But fifteen minutes later we learned that the committee had adjourned without taking a vote, and that consequently there could be no hope that the bill would pass this session.

I paddled home from the hearing terribly depressed and convinced that I wasn't much of a speaker after all; but fortunately, I did not have either the leisure or the solitude in which to foster a spirit of gloom. Over and over again, I have discovered that if something goes wrong when I am in the country and there is nothing to take my mind off it, I brood over it all day and all night; but in almost every city things happen so fast that I have no time to sit and brood by day, and by night a dozen new problems or pleasures have taken my mind off the original one. In this instance, it was the Midwinter Convocation of George Washington University which temporarily took my mind off the Sheppard-Towner Bill.

This Convocation is always a great event in a Washington season; but since 1921 marked the centennial of the university's founding, it naturally achieved special significance. Furthermore, my interest in it this year was quite personal, for three acquaintances of mine—Mabel Boardman of Red Cross fame, Senator Moses and Senator Pittman— were to receive honorary degrees, and, even more to the point, I was going to get one myself!

The degree ceremonies were preceded on Monday by a dinner at Rauscher's, then Washington's leading restaurant, at which the speeches were, I think, the best I've ever heard on a similar occasion, and I sat between the Chilean Ambassador and Senator Pittman, both charming and brilliant men, so I could not have been more agreeably placed. Moreover, in the course of dinner, Senator Pittman kindly suggested that since he and I needed to arrive early for the exercises the next day, perhaps it would be a convenience for me to go with him and Mrs. Pittman, in case Senator Keyes had trouble in securing a pair (the arrangement by which two members of opposite parties mutually agree not to vote on a given question during a specified time), and was detained.

As it turned out, Harry *did* have trouble in getting a pair and did not arrive until after the exercises had begun. Thanks to the Pittmans, I reached my destination in plenty of time to struggle into my unfamiliar robes and take my appointed place in the academic procession. And I began to realize in the course of the drive that I was forming two new and significant friendships. Until I had listened to Senator Pittman's tilt with Senator Thomas during the discussion of the Sheppard-Towner Bill, the former had been hardly more than a name to me. Then I recognized him as a presence, conspicuous for his tall, slender and graceful figure, thick dark hair and elegance of dress in a gathering where so many were overweight, balding and poorly tailored. I had also begun to recognize him as a man who could be formidable in any argument, because he knew how to make himself convincing with a few deft sentences and gestures. On the other hand, I knew very little about him personally. Though I saw Mrs. Pittman regularly at the Senate Ladies' luncheons and had found her lovely looking and congenial, no mention had been made about backgrounds. The dinner at Rauscher's had given me the opportunity to ask a few questions, and it had seemed quite in order to begin by asking his university, since universities were a major topic.

"Southwestern Presbyterian at Clarksville, Tennessee," he answered casually.

"Clarksville, *Tennessee!* All the way from Nevada!"

"Well, you see, I hadn't hit Nevada then. I was born and raised on a plantation in Mississippi."

"That explains a good deal. You seem more like a southerner than a westerner," I said, and added hastily, "That was meant as a compliment, so I hope you took it as such."

"I assumed it was, and I did. I didn't go directly from Tennessee to Nevada. After an attack of typhoid, I went to Seattle for my health and began to practice law there. But I got sidetracked and went to Alaska."

"Alaska!"

"Yes. I was interested in gold then, silver came later. I see the Ambassador is trying to divert your attention and it's quite a long story. Perhaps you'll let me tell you some other time how I happened to wind up in Nevada."

The drive the next day had hardly begun when Senator Pittman began to question me. "Where does the Parkinson come from?" he inquired. "It wasn't your maiden name, was it?"

"No. It was my paternal grandmother's maiden name. I was Frances Parkinson Wheeler the second. . . . You promised to tell me the rest of the Klondike story," I reminded him.

"Some other time. We'll be seeing more of each other."

Meanwhile, we had reached the school, and the exercises seemed endless. As usual on such occasions, there were too many speeches, and they could not compare in brilliance with those that had been given the night before. Then the students who were completing their courses at mid-year instead of in June were given their degrees. Last of all, the honorary degrees were conferred—all twenty-seven of them, each with its own little speech. I felt guilty because I was so tired and wished the ceremony would end so that I could go home. But at last my turn came and my hood of fine black alpaca, edged with white velvet and lined with yellow and blue-striped silk, was draped carefully over my robe by a member of the faculty, and I listened unbelievingly to the citation that was read as the President of the university handed me my diploma. It did not seem as if it could be about me:

> "Doctor of Letters, Frances Parkinson Keyes:
> Vice President of the League of American Pen Women; frequent contributor to many reviews and periodicals of the highest literary standards; author of novels that are filled with the breath of that pure

wholesome rural life which is the strength of America and its institutions."

I felt then, and have never ceased to feel, that I had not accomplished
enough at that time to deserve such a citation and that if the President
of George Washington University had not known and liked me personally, it would not have been awarded, or at any rate not so soon; and he
admitted afterward that the award was based less on what I had done
than on what it seemed obvious to him I was going to do and that he
wanted his university to be the first institution of learning to recognize
this publicly. But he also said that the question had been thoroughly
discussed with various faculty members, and they had all agreed my articles in *The Granite Monthly* and the *D.A.R. Magazine* had shown a
capacity for very careful research and had been a real contribution to
Americana. The experience confirmed my feeling that authors often
make a great mistake in declining to contribute to minor magazines of
limited financial resources and circulation because these do not pay
enough or reach enough people. Taking the way that opens, even if it
seems hardly more than a footpath, not infrequently leads to the highways of heart's desire, if not to fame and fortune. At least it has been
so in my case.

Chapter 19

O N MARCH 4, 1921, the breathless crowd cramming the dingy Senate
Chamber saw the great clock over the rostrum turned back three
times in order to maintain the fiction that the new Congress begins at
twelve noon. It listened with a sense of bewilderment as Mr. Marshall,
the retiring Vice-President, involuntarily 'stole the show' from Mr.
Coolidge, the incoming Vice-President, by making one of the most
moving speeches ever delivered in Washington. It shivered, with a sense
that supernatural forces were at work, when a shaft of splendid sunshine fell full on Harding's handsome upturned face as he took the oath
of office in the classic portico. It rejoiced as, surging up Pennsylvania
Avenue, it beheld the long-locked gates of the White House flung wide
open again. Never did an administration begin more buoyantly."

These words, written long ago, epitomize more vividly than I could
do it now the events and sensations of the first inauguration I attended.
And it was with a feeling of real excitement that I myself drove through
the gates leading to the enclosure of the White House a few days after
the ceremony.

To be sure, I was going there merely for the purpose of leaving
cards. But after seeing those gates closed the two years I had been in
Washington, because of Mr. Wilson's illness, I suddenly felt that the
whole atmosphere of the city had been changed by this one difference in
the scene. As the car stopped under the portico, a servant in livery immediately came out of the door, bearing a small tray. I put the cards on
it and drove out through the gates again. That was all there was to it.
But it was enough to give me a sense of having the right to approach, in
the same way that I did an embassy or any other official establishment,

the great mansion from which I had been excluded so long, as practically everyone else had been.

Promptly thereafter a note, engraved on heavy white paper and surmounted by a gilt crest, was delivered to me by hand. It read:

> *Mrs. Harding*
> *Will be glad to receive*
> *Mrs. Keyes*
> *On Tuesday afternoon*
> *March 22nd*
> *At five o'clock*

This was the way in which Mrs. Harding—and Mrs. Coolidge after her—expressed her readiness to receive individual callers. The visits, efficiently controlled by the Head Usher, who announced your arrival and signalled your departure, were spaced fifteen minutes apart and so did not allow much leeway for varied discussion. But they did permit time for any one topic of special interest to the caller, and Mrs. Harding never failed to know what this was likely to be and enter into conversation that was sprightly, well informed and timely. Shortly before the inauguration she had, at my request, joined the National League of American Pen Women, in which she was eligible for active membership because of the work she had done on her husband's paper, the Marion *Star.* Now she told me she would be glad to receive the organization as a whole in the course of its coming national convention and talked with me about tentative arrangements, all of which were pleasantly confirmed the next day. She asked about the progress of my own writing, showing genuine interest, and told me she hoped to see me almost as often in the future as she had in the past.

Of course it was for her and not for me to determine whether or not she would do this, and I am happy to say that she did. In my case, and in the case of every other senator's wife with whom I am familiar, that first formal call—a single concession to protocol—was simply a prelude to a resumption of much the same camaraderie we had enjoyed before. She continued to attend the Senate Ladies' luncheons; at a Congressional Club reception given in her honor she managed to wedge in a few words of personal greeting to every guest presented; and when she learned the club's last festivity of the season was to be a picnic in Rock Creek Park, she immediately sent word that *of course* she would be there; and just as we were unpacking our baskets at the picnic grounds, she drove up. The next instant, she was in our midst, laughing and joking and cutting ham and making herself generally useful. She was fond of arranging afternoon cruises on the *Mayflower,* in the course of which she helped pass the sandwiches at tea time and intermittently joined in our bridge games, though generally she asked to be excused, so she could spend more time on deck.

All such contacts with Mrs. Harding meant a great deal to her senatorial friends; but nothing she did earned more heartfelt gratitude than her efforts to lessen the burden of official calling and still give the women on whom it fell the opportunity to know and enjoy each other. Because the International Conference for the Limitation of Armaments was being held that winter, she realized the stress of social duties would be greater than ever, and since the wives of all the Cabinet members had not planned to be in Washington for the season, the demands on the few who were there would be particularly strenuous. It had occurred to her that if the ladies of the Senate would receive with her at the White House some autumn afternoon, the ladies of the Cabinet could make their call on her and be presented to them at the same time.

"I have lived in Washington twenty years, and this is the most gracious thing I have ever known a President's wife to do," the wife of a prominent Democratic senator who invited me to go with her that afternoon said to me as we drove down Sixteenth Street. But since thoughtfulness and graciousness seemed as natural to Mrs. Harding as fragrance to a flower, I was not at all surprised.

The party began even before we were inside the front door, for everybody arrives at the White House on the very tick of the hour at which they are invited, and the file of cars stretched the length of the driveway. We all began to visit together as we walked across the porch and into the big hall where we left our wraps. Mrs. Coolidge, dressed in pale gray, was standing at the door of the East Room—beautifully decorated with autumn leaves and palms and ferns—to receive us, after which we formed an immense circle—about sixty of us in all. Presently, Mrs. Harding, in soft dark blue with a pink rose at her belt, came in and we each went up and spoke to her, resuming our places in the circle afterward. Next the wives of the Cabinet members who were in Washington, each escorted by an aide, came into the room, greeted Mrs. Harding and then went around the circle shaking hands and chatting a minute or two with each senator's wife. When this ceremony was completed, we went out informally to the dining room for tea. It was the first time many of us had met that season or had an opportunity to discuss plans and events of the wonderful winter before us. I think we were all sorry when Mrs. Harding came and shook hands with us again, with a personal message for each one, and went upstairs, which was our signal for departure.

Admiration of Mrs. Harding was general, irrespective of political party. It has now become the custom—I might almost say the fashion —to find absolutely nothing good to say about the Harding Administration; I am glad to tell the other side of the story, for there *was* another side: many of the big things were well done and so were many of the little things. For instance, I never had a day "At Home," as long as the Hardings were in the White House, that I did not receive flowers from there, with a pleasant little note. Granted that Miss Laura Harlan, the daughter of a Supreme Court Justice, was a fine White House secretary; but Mrs. Harding was responsible for her choice, exemplifying Theodore Vail's maxim that competent executives should be able to enlist competent assistants.

The promised reception for the National League of American Pen Women took place on a beautiful spring morning, with the Harding blue we had heard so much about beforehand in the skies, so Mrs. Harding received outdoors, and writers from all over the country, many of them making their first visit to Washington, saw not only the Executive Mansion but its grounds under ideal conditions. This was only one of many similar functions that first spring the Hardings were in the White House which meant much more to the guests than they did to the hosts. But one that meant a great deal to both, and was outstanding among all others, was the reception given Mme Curie, the discoverer of radium, in the East Room of the White House. Packing it to the doors were ambassadors and ministers of foreign countries; members of the Supreme Court and the Cabinet and their wives; heads of the Congressional Committees—Foreign Relations, for instance—especially entitled to be present; and a few individuals who had been invited because of personal generosity or achievement. All sat waiting to pay homage to the frail little woman, as she walked up the narrow aisle and turned to face the assembly: utterly unassuming and retiring, with a sweet, shy, gentle face, very pale and a little haggard, but lighted with a wonderful smile. M. Jusserand, the French Ambassador, made a little speech of welcome; next Mrs. William Brown Meloney, the editor of *Delineator,* who was accompanying Mme Curie on her trip through the United States, gave a most graceful speech; and then the President spoke.

". . . As a nation whose womanhood has been exalted to fullest participation in citizenship, we are proud to honor in you a woman whose work has earned universal acclaim and attested woman's equality in every intellectual and spiritual activity. . . .

"We bring to you the meed of honor which is due to preeminence in science, scholarship, research and humanitarianism. But with it all we bring something more—we lay at your feet the testimony of that love which all the generations of men have been wont to bestow upon noble woman, the unselfish wife, the devoted mother. If, indeed, the simple and common relations in life could not keep you from great achievements, it is equally true that the zeal, ambition and unswerving purpose of a lofty career could not bar you from splendidly doing all the plain but worthy tasks which fall to woman's lot."

Listening to the President then, and sitting at the meeting given in Mme Curie's honor at the National Museum that evening, when slides showing the poorly equipped and bare laboratory where, working beside her husband, she made her great discovery were viewed, and the story of her frugal, retired life was retold, I thought how true it was that those who complained, "If I could only have had a chance, I might have amounted to something," were only offering poor apologies for their lack of determination and persistence and courage.

After the President finished speaking, Mme Curie rose and, in excellent English, thanked him for the gram of radium he had presented her in behalf of the women of America—an idea conceived by Mrs. Meloney.

"I accept this rare gift, Mr. President," Mme Curie ended, "with the hope that I may make it serve mankind. I thank your country's women in the name of France. I thank them in the name of my native Poland. I thank them in the name of science. I thank them in the name of humanity, which we all wish to make happier. *I love you all, my American friends, very much!"*

Before the afternoon was over, Mrs. Meloney created an opportunity to chat with me. The previous month she had bought my first short story about Washington, which was published early in the fall under the title "Sheridan Circle"; now she told me that she hoped I would come to see her the next time I was in New York and discuss the possibility of more fiction; meanwhile, did I have any ideas that she could be considering for *Delineator?* I asked her what she would think of a series of such stories, each with its setting in a different part of the city—Lafayette Square and Meridian Hill, for instance—but featuring some of its main attributes. She thought it sounded like a very good suggestion, and we could talk about it later.

There was no chance for lengthy conversation then, but I needed no urging to go to New York. I not only enjoyed the brief trips that took me there but found I was getting a great deal out of them. Thanks to Terry Helburn, I went to opening nights at the best theaters; and thanks to her and other old friends and to editors who were becoming favorably disposed toward me, headwaiters at several very good restaurants were beginning to recognize me. The visit that was marked by the sale of

"Sheridan Circle" had been made during the latter part of Henry's spring vacation, and I had had the happy experience of sharing with him my pleasures and the sights that meant the most to me—a foretaste of many such experiences in the future. On the day Henry had accompanied me to Mrs. Meloney's office, an assistant editor who was escorting us to the elevator had said to him, "You have a very wonderful mother." I was very much embarrassed when Henry retorted, "I knew that long before you editors did," and did my best to rebuke him severely as the elevator slid toward the ground. But I was not in a rebuking mood. I had been able to finance this trip for my son, as well as for myself, and believed—as it proved, quite rightly—that I would be able to finance many more. And in my handbag I had checks totaling a thousand dollars, all of them representing money I had earned through writing. Another thing had happened that was quite unbelievable, but true.

I would have found it still harder to believe something I did not discover until long afterward: that Mrs. Meloney had sent a form letter to hundreds of women asking them to name their favorite magazine and to tell why it was their favorite. An overwhelming majority answered that their favorite was *Good Housekeeping* and that the reason for their choice was "Letters from a Senator's Wife." After receiving this report, she became determined to lure me away from Mr. Bigelow.

From the beginning of the Harding-Coolidge Administration my relations with Mrs. Coolidge were just as cordial as my relations with Mrs. Harding had been for years. Shortly after the inauguration, Miss Mabel Boardman invited me to be a fellow guest with Mrs. Coolidge at the showing of an educational moving picture Miss Boardman was promoting. She called for us in her huge Pierce-Arrow, and ensconced us in straight box seats, but nothing was ever stiff about the atmosphere Mrs. Coolidge created. That afternoon I happened to mention that the first thing my husband said to me when we arrived at an evening reception was always the same, "You needn't feel you have to stay long on my account." "You're lucky," Mrs. Coolidge retorted with a laugh. "All Calvin says is 'Grace, we're leaving.'" She had a great gift of mimicry and imitated the Vice President's nasal twang in a way that made everyone join in her laughter whenever she did it.

My final official luncheon that spring of '21 was in her honor, and every few days I went to one which someone else was giving in her honor. She always gave the impression that she was having a wonderful time; as a matter of fact, I believe she really was. She had inexhaustible joie de vivre, and apparently she was also inexhaustible physically. For instance, several afternoons in the week she went to Mrs. Thomas F.

Walsh's immense house, which was patterned on the lines of a North German Lloyd luxury liner.

This tremendously wealthy woman was the widow of a Colorado gold mining tycoon, whose initials were so much like those of the Senator from Montana as to cause considerable confusion. She first became well known to the country at large through the book entitled *Father Struck It Rich* written by her daughter Evalyn Walsh McLean; but she was already well known in Washington for her kindly hospitality, and everyone on her visiting list could count on a welcome between four and six at her daily tea dances. Like the rest of us, the new Vice President's wife was glad to avail herself of such largesse.

Mrs. Coolidge accepted very few evening engagements without the Vice President, but I saw so much of her in one way or another that I screwed up my courage and asked her if she would be my guest of honor at a buffet supper for the Women's National Press Club, which I had recently joined, when *The Career of David Noble* came out. I need not have hesitated; she not only accepted the invitation to supper, but wrote this by hand when she received an advance copy of the book:

Dear Mrs. Keyes—

The enclosed doesn't express half my enthusiastic admiration of your book. Adequate brevity isn't my long suit. This is brief, but not adequate. I should like to go on and on and touch upon every character in the book, each seems to me to be drawn so true to type. I personally know every one of them.

I am thrilled to the core to be asked to participate in the birthday celebration of David and I'll be there promptly at 6:30.

With love,
Grace Coolidge

"The enclosed" I was authorized to quote:

You have made David Noble so real to me that in thinking of him I almost lose sight of the fact that the delineation of his character and the shaping of his career are due to your genius. He is a true Vermonter with a singleness of purpose and a determination to win that is characteristic of those sturdy, persevering, hard-working people. Only a severe jolt could have brought him to a realizing sense of his narrowness of vision and you supplied the jolt. . . .

To the buffet supper she brought a package wrapped in tissue paper and tied with bright ribbon—the kind one takes to a child's birthday party. When I opened this, it proved to contain a small gray wooden elephant on wheels. Around the middle of this symbol Mrs. Coolidge's card was fastened with red, white and blue ribbon, and on the card was written:

This funny old gray elephant
With tusk and tail and ears
Will lead you right, where'er you go
Throughout the coming years.

Mrs. Coolidge gaily explained that she had been hearing so much about my accidental—but influential—Virginia birth and had been seeing me in close and congenial company with so many prominent Democrats that she felt the time had come to remind me where my affiliation really lay. I promised her I would not forget and placed the elephant in a prominent position on my desk.

It so happened that the following day Mrs. Sheppard, with whom I had become very good friends, came to lunch with me. She surveyed my elephant unenthusiastically, and when I told her why it had been given to me, she made no comment. But before the end of the afternoon another package was delivered to me, also wrapped in tissue paper and tied with bright ribbon. Out of it dropped a small gray donkey, girdled with red, white and blue like the elephant. To its belt was attached Mrs. Sheppard's card, and on it was written:

To be with you yet
Lest you forget—that you are really a southerner!

I put the donkey on my desk opposite the elephant, and there they faced each other amicably, a constant though whimsical reminder that I must write without party bias, until 1928. Then came the holocaust. The elephant was constructed solidly, all in one piece; but the donkey was jointed, like a doll. When I returned to Washington after the fall elections, the elephant was still standing proudly upright, but the elastic which held the donkey's joints together had disintegrated, and he was lying prostrate, a pitiful wreck of his former jaunty self. I called in Mrs. Sheppard to see the wreckage, and she agreed there was nothing to do but bury the remains. It was a sad moment.

But in 1932 she gave me a new donkey. It was made of glittering metal that looked as if it would last for some time. In fact, it was not only far more dashing but far more substantial than the elephant, which, though still solid, had become somewhat weatherbeaten. However, I still keep them side by side.

Chapter 20

I WAS disappointed not to get home for my birthday that year, but on the twenty-second of July the Sheppard-Towner Bill finally passed the Senate by a vote of sixty-three to seven, and I thought that was the best birthday present I could have had, after all the weary months of setbacks and disappointments since its introduction. And before the month was over, I was involved in another undertaking that meant still more to me personally.

I had been spending a good deal of time in Virginia for various reasons, and in the course of my visits there had been several occasions to discuss a speech made by the Honorable Bill G. Lowrey of Mississippi during Confederate Day Exercises at Arlington Cemetery. This speech had made considerable impression on me, and one section had been especially moving and provocative:

"Let the home of Lee, as the home of Washington, be held sacred in the hearts of the people. Let it be kept in its original form and beauty, the peculiar care and treasure of the Daughters of the Confederacy, as Mount Vernon is kept by a band of noble women."

I had first visited Arlington when I was only thirteen years old, and had been deeply shocked to find the home of Robert E. Lee, my favorite figure in American history, in such deplorable condition. A caretaker was living there in very sketchy fashion; the spacious entrance hall and dining room were dirty and dismantled; and the beautiful double parlors, where the wedding ceremony of Robert E. Lee and Mary Parke Custis, granddaughter of Martha Washington, was performed, were the repository of hideous metal wreaths which had been sent to decorate the graves of soldiers who died in the Spanish-American War. To my mother's consternation, I was very close to crying; she had not dreamed that at my age I could be so deeply affected by a sight which to her was regrettable but not personally tragic. She tried to quiet me, but I broke away from her and rushed to the front gallery, where I gazed out at the splendid scene of nearby hills and Washington across the river with eyes that were overflowing. When I brokenly made a solemn declaration it is not surprising that she could not take it seriously:

"When the time comes that I have some influence, I'm going to make people see what a disgrace it is that General Lee's home should be left in such a condition. I'm going to do something about it."

"But, Frances, what could *you* possibly do?"

"I don't know. But *somehow—some time—*"

As I have said before, I do not believe things happen by chance; I believe there is a pattern. Mr. Lowrey's speech seemed made to order for *me*.

The reaction to my first articles in *Good Housekeeping* had been so favorable that Mr. Bigelow, instead of telling me what *he* wanted me to write about next, asked me if there were anything special *I* would like to write about, any cause I would like to advance. My answer was prompt: the restoration of the Lee Mansion at Arlington. Though Mr. Bigelow was the son of a Union officer, his reply was equally prompt: "Go ahead. I don't know that we can do anything, but we can try." Consequently, the next "Letter" in *Good Housekeeping* contained the following paragraph:

> The shocking neglect of the Lee Mansion at Arlington, which is government property, as compared to the fostering care which has been bestowed on Mount Vernon by the Mount Vernon Ladies' Association who, seventy years ago, rescued the estate from ruin and have preserved it with intelligent devotion ever since, is an object lesson deserving reflection. The Lee Mansion is an even more stately one than Mount Vernon and might well harbor as many valuable and beautiful historical objects. Whatever our opinions and traditions may be, moreover, we all realize now that Robert E. Lee was one of the greatest generals and one of the noblest men who ever lived. To every American woman the abuse of his home must seem a disgrace; to every Southern woman it must seem a sacrilege.

Mayme Ober Peak, a fellow member of the Women's National Press Club, who lived in Upperville, Virginia, mentioned my concern about Arlington at a meeting of the United Daughters of the Confederacy and wrote me that "everyone was much interested," and shortly thereafter I had a letter from Mrs. M. G. Richardson, the president of the Upperville Chapter, inviting me to be her guest at Corotoman, her ancestral estate, and to address the local members. I accepted her invitation with pleasure and enjoyed myself thoroughly at her lovely old place with its white pillars and green shutters. But Upperville is in the heart of the hunt country and is not a large urban center; in addition, many of the ladies I had expected to address were away for the summer. I was astonished the following day, when I was leaving Washington for Pine Grove Farm, to find that the Associated Press used this item:

> Upperville, Va., July 30.—A movement has been started here to restore the Gen. Robert E. Lee mansion at Arlington to its former beauty. . . .
>
> Mrs. Henry W. Keyes, wife of Senator Keyes, of New Hampshire, and a native of Virginia, is one of the prominent leaders of the group of women who will attempt to obtain permission of the government to reclaim the historic old residence and make of it a shrine somewhat on a parallel with Mount Vernon.

At Pine Grove Farm, reminders that my speech in Upperville had attracted a good deal of attention kept arriving in the mail, including a long letter from Representative Lowrey which said in part, "I am sure that you, through the Daughters of the Confederacy, can lead this move more effectively than I could do. Of course, however, there will be important points upon which you will need the co-operation of men who are in political position. Especially when you need this in the House I crave the honor of serving you and the cause."

Meanwhile more articles appeared in the press, among them an editorial in the Washington *Herald,* supporting the renovation and beautification of the Lee Mansion, and early in the fall I received an invitation to attend the twenty-sixth annual convention of the Virginia Division of the Daughters of the Confederacy in Richmond on the thirteenth and fourteenth of October. I accepted and was asked to address the convention, and everyone I met made me feel that I was among friends and collaboraters. But again, it was the written word that meant most to me in the end. This time, it was an editorial by the great historian Douglas Southall Freeman in the Richmond *News Leader,* in which he very kindly said, "It is singularly appropriate that this undertaking should be the task of a magnetic woman who represents, in a sense, North and South. She can accomplish what many Virginians have desired, but have not felt they could urge. To many, Arlington is in some sense what Reims is to millions of French: It is a desecrated shrine that many have thought should be allowed to fall into ruins, if the North so elected, because it had been seized and wrecked by Northern troops. If Mrs. Keyes' exceptional position enables her to prevent this, surely she will have deserved the thanks of patriots. The thanks of Virginia already are hers for a visit and an address that were an inspiration."

I naturally returned to Washington glowing with joy, and satisfied that I had indeed received a big response to my suggestion; and also that while awaiting the next developments regarding Arlington, I could throw myself wholeheartedly into the other activities which were crowding in on me. But as so often happens when the outlook seems exceptionally bright, it was suddenly darkened, by an article distributed by the NEA Service:

> *Mrs. Keyes' Earnings Exceed Husband's Pay As Senator*
> To be the wife of a United States senator would satisfy most women's ambition.
> To mother three lively boys would keep most women occupied.
> But this is only part of it with Frances Parkinson Keyes, whose revenues from her writings exceed the salary of her husband as senator from New Hampshire.
> Mrs. Keyes is putting a new novel, *The Career of David Noble,* on the market in October.
> Also, she is vice president of the League of American Pen Women and business manager of their magazine, "The Penwoman"; vice president of the Children of the American Revolution; adviser on the National Council of the Y.W.C.A.; state chairman for New Hampshire of the Woman's Roosevelt Memorial Association; head of the publicity work of the Congressional Club, which issues a weekly bulletin; and—
> But to exhaust the list would merely exhaust the reader.
> It was the triple duties of writing, and rearing her boys and carrying out her social obligations as the wife of the governor of New Hampshire—for it was from the governorship that the senator stepped to his seat in the Senate—that prepared Mrs. Keyes for her many present duties.
> "I made more than a thousand calls in the capital last year," she says—and this is the more remarkable when it is noted that the Keyes do not keep a car.
> Friends speak of her as "the woman who always has time"—for no matter how many or pressing the demands on her, she always seems to find the precious minutes for any duty.

Every statement in this article could be supported by fact, and I have no doubt that its author meant to be complimentary; but if it had been submitted to me before publication, I would have done my best to see that it was ruthlessly edited. Harry had never harbored the strong feeling, characteristic of many forceful men, that he should be able to support his wife without help from her. On the contrary, he had not hesitated to say from the beginning that he resented the fact my mother would not give me an allowance, and his remarks to this effect had intensified the antagonism between them; furthermore, he made no secret

of the fact that he hoped and believed her death would make a difference in our resources. The marriages of his brothers to heiresses, whose
fortunes were of substantial help to their husbands in both cases, was a
frequent topic of conversation. So was the fact that he was paying out
more than five hundred dollars in interest charges on his debts every
year and that as the date to meet these charges approached, he could
talk and think of nothing else. Knowing that financially I was a burden
to him had been a source not only of embarrassment but of grief to me,
and this had reached a climax when I was taunted with the humiliating
reproach that I could not earn a dollar to save my life.

Because I knew that Harry would have given a good deal to erase
those words from my memory, I tried to lean over backward in my efforts not to remind him of them, either directly or indirectly, and I
would have bitten out my tongue rather than volunteer the information
that I was earning more than he was. But somehow it had been found
out, and someone had lost no time in broadcasting the fact. It was Harry's turn to be deeply hurt, and it was hard to convince him that I was
not responsible for the leak. I tried my best to soften the blow to his
pride by reminding him, as gently and tactfully as I could, that my
earnings were a godsend. I could take over the rent of our apartment,
which had now been reduced by furnishing it with our own belongings,
which were much more substantial than our ready cash; soon we could
have a car in Washington; and I could pay the wages of Cathie and
Henry Deming, who now constituted our staff, as Carrie had married
and left our employ, and Cathie had persuaded her husband to work for
us too. I had paid for all my own clothes ever since *The Old Gray
Homestead* was published; I could now pay for the boys' clothes too, as
well as provide them with pocket money and contribute to their school
bills. I was getting a generous allowance from *Good Housekeeping* to
cover the expense of going to events which I must attend as its representative and the entertaining I must do in connection with my work for
the magazine, and this would be a great help from now on in official entertaining as well as in traveling. Surely if I could do all this, Harry
could begin to get rid of those overpowering debts and we would both
be much happier!

We did not bring up the subject a second time, and as my earnings
increased I simply took over more and more of our living expenses. I
was very happy that I could do this for many reasons. One of them was
that I felt, at last, I was doing more for my husband financially than my
sisters-in-law were for theirs, because they had simply *inherited* their
money, whereas I had proved my ability to *earn* mine. It was also, of
course, a great release from nervous strain to believe that I would be re-

ceiving no more duns for overdue bills; my accounts were settled every month, and Harry should have plenty now to take care of the statements that came to him. And this release from strain meant more abundant energy for doing all sorts of things that I enjoyed, quite apart from official obligations.

More immediately, Robert Lansing paid me the great compliment of reviewing *The Career of David Noble* for the New York *Times,* and Honoré Willsie reviewed it for the New York *Herald Tribune.* Nearly all the critics were very complimentary and I was very happy about everything connected with the book. Even the reviews that condemned it did not unduly depress me, because they nearly always arrived at the same time with some that praised it; and not the smallest element in my happiness lay in the fact that Harry liked this book very, very much. I had been wrong in believing, after he criticized *The Old Gray Homestead,* that I would never be able to write a novel that would please him.

And by now he himself was much happier in Washington than he had been at first. He had found his niche on the Committee of Public Buildings and Grounds for he could no more help trying to improve any site with which he was associated than he could help breathing. When he inherited Pine Grove Farm, though the first groves to give it a name had seeded themselves, Harry continued to supplement this growth with more pines and redeemed great stretches of sand and stubble; waste places became garden land, as he toiled over them. By the time of our marriage he had not only transformed his heritage into a place of beauty, he had been chairman of the first Legislative Committee on Forestry in New Hampshire, and good roads and forest reservations had become a passion with him. Before he became governor, he had been instrumental in the transformation of a state, where comparatively little had been done to preserve and enhance its natural charm; and even his preoccupation with the war did not divert him from this purpose. What he accomplished for the beautification of Washington and its surroundings was, as I see it, the direct outgrowth and natural expansion of the work he had done for the beautification of his own home and his own state.

The first significant step he took in this direction after reaching Washington was to introduce a resolution for the enlargement of the Capitol grounds. At that period, the area between the Capitol and the Union Station—both beautiful in themselves—was still cluttered with the barnlike structures which had been built to house government workers during the First World War and which detracted greatly from the spaciousness and dignity of the location. From the beginning, Harry viewed these jerry-built monstrosities with an indignant eye and, in the family circle, frequently voiced his regret that strangers coming to Washington were given such an unfavorable first impression because of this sordid sight. Consequently, when Colonel Clarence Sherrill, Director of Public Buildings and Parks in the nation's capital, assailed the entrances to this as "atrocious," Harry saw a heaven-sent opportunity. With a zeal which astonished the Colonel, Harry proposed a plan for making them attractive instead.

C. K. Berryman, the cartoonist whose drawings did so much to enliven the pages of the *Star,* promptly depicted Harry in shirt sleeves and standing knee deep among buildings designated "Government Apartments" and "U. S. Lodging Quarters," amidst which only one scraggly tree was visible and behind which the Capitol was obscured. The legend ran, "Colonel Sherrill is right, the entrances to the National Capitol *are* atrocious."

They are no longer atrocious. The stranger coming out of the Union Station gazes across a serious of gracious terraces toward a dome rising above a vast structure of dazzling whiteness. By day, it glitters in the abundant sunshine with which Washington is so singularly blessed. By night, it takes on even greater splendor, for floodlights stream upon it from every side. In the foreground, the spray of a triple fountain adds a touch of iridescence to the scene.

Harry's enthusiasm for the beautification of Washington never abated and in time led to his work on the Supreme Court Building Commission and the Arlington Memorial Bridge Commission, and the importance of this is also visible to every visitor to Washington.

But he did not become preoccupied with it to the exclusion of interest in his other committee assignments; and he was always especially absorbed in everything connected with the Navy. From the start of his first term in office, he was a member of the Naval Affairs Committee and introduced the bill providing for a Bureau of Aeronautics in the Navy Department. Aviation is now so casually taken for granted that it is hard to realize that as late as 1921, its right to serious recognition was still regarded as highly debatable; but belief in its value was considered so progressive that it could not be lightly assumed.

While the bill providing for the establishment of a Bureau of Aeronautics was under consideration, a young lieutenant commander who had recently come to Washington with his Boston bride and established himself in a small apartment not far from ours was one of our frequent visitors. He often came to see Harry early in the evening, remaining for hours on end; and he was a great favorite of our son Peter, who was then still a small boy. Hardly had the visitor been announced when the door of Peter's bedroom began to creak and open inch by inch. Then through the crack a pajama-clad form would appear, bound across the room and land with a leap in Richard Byrd's lap.

I had my own serious pursuits, Arlington and others, and I was deeply interested in them. But much of my time was spent in more glamorous ways, and it was then that I began to think of Washington as a kaleidoscope, with brilliant colors that shook into strange shapes that were always striking and sometimes startling. "When you were a little girl did you ever turn a kaleidoscope and marvel at the beautiful designs which succeeded each other as rapidly as you moved your hand, and call the rest of the family to share the gorgeous pictures with you?" I wrote to a friend. "I have constantly been reminded of that lately, for Washington has been truly kaleidoscopic in variety and beauty." And then I tried to describe some of these wonders to my friend.

The first picture was deep purple—the purple which is the color of mourning, and yet of royalty as well, and so much more poignantly suggestive of noble grief than black: the rotunda of the Capitol on the night of November 10, 1921. The afternoon before the body of the Unknown Soldier had been brought there and placed upon the catafalque where the bodies of Lincoln, Garfield and McKinley rested. In the evening, President and Mrs. Harding, Vice President Coolidge, Speaker Gillett and the Secretary of War had laid the first wreaths upon the flag-covered casket, while the guard of five soldiers around it had begun their silent vigil. Early the next morning, the public—already waiting in a line more than two blocks long—was admitted and allowed to pass through the rotunda. Dawn was breaking on Armistice Day before the last of the one hundred thousand men, women and children who made up that vast throng of mourners had gone; for no one was denied admittance. . . .

The next picture was white—the dazzling white of pearls and snow and lilies—the white of the marble amphitheater at Arlington. The ceremonies attending the burial of the Unknown Soldier were on the morning of November eleventh—Armistice Day. There was a faint haze over the blue skies early that day, but it fluttered away; and when I took my seat in the immense structure the sun was shining brightly. It fell on the wreaths given by every state in the Union, each exactly alike except for the coats-of-arms which formed their centers; on the still more magnificent wreaths which decorated the boxes occupied by the members of the Supreme Court, the Diplomatic Corps and the Cabinet; and on the great mass of wreaths brought from the Capitol rotunda and grouped together at the foot of the stage. . . .

My third picture was green, the green of springtime, of new ideas and fresh hopes, of dull earth suddenly shooting forth vigorous young plants which will feed hungry bodies and restore broken spirits: the picture of the opening session of the Conference on the Limitation of Armaments in Continental Hall. The flags of the nine nations represented at the conference stood on the stage in two groups: those of the United States, Great Britain, France, Italy and Japan together—the five powers invited to participate in the conference; and those of Belgium, China, the Netherlands and Portugal together—the nations invited to participate in the discussion of Pacific and Far Eastern questions because of their interests in that part of the world. On the floor, separated only by a narrow cord from the open square of green baize tables at which the delegates sat, were the "accredited writers" for the conference—authors and journalists from all over the world—and that was where *I* was sitting. . . .

Now the picture has turned to blue, the blue that the old Italian masters used when they painted the Madonna's robes—the House of Representatives on the eighteenth and nineteenth of November. For two long hard days, the House talked and argued and fought over the Sheppard-Towner Bill, that measure for the protection of maternity and infancy for which I had worked so long. Seldom, I believe, had a more spirited combat taken place in that turbulent body. But at the end of the second day there was a call for the "ayes and nays," and the vote was two hundred and seventy-nine to thirty-nine in favor of the bill, a proportion fairly close to that in the Senate vote the previous July. A few minor changes necessitated the return of the measure to the Senate, but there it was promptly accepted without even being sent to a conference. That battle was over—and it had been won. . . .

In my final kaleidoscopic picture, all those wonderful colors were blended—the great "arch of jewels" hung like a necklace, with the coats-of-arms of the nine nations at the conference as a sunburst in the center, between two tall white obelisks, also studded with gems, erected near the Pan-American Building and illuminated on the nights of November tenth, eleventh and twelfth. The Marine Band played, the President turned the switch which released the searchlights—long shafts of ruby, emerald and amethyst radiance shining from every direction upon the thirty-seven thousand Novagems that were used in the construction of that dazzling portal of brilliance. Could it be, I wondered as I looked at it, a symbolic gateway of light through which we were walking to higher things? I hoped so. . . .

Chapter 21

BRILLIANT parties were almost incessant that winter, but the plenary sessions of the Arms Conference were quite as exciting, at least to me. I was very thrilled over my credentials, which only eight ladies of the press succeeded in achieving for the opening session, to which no other women were admitted except those who were members of the Executive Committee or whose husbands were among the conference leaders. Entrances were so zealously guarded that sometimes rather amusing mistakes were made. For instance, Mrs. Coolidge left the Willard Hotel in such haste one morning for a plenary session that she forgot her ticket. Undismayed, she accosted the doorman at Continental Hall with her customary bewitching smile. All Washington had been beguiled by this and had become familiar with it—with the exception, apparently, of this doorman. He viewed her suspiciously.

"I am Mrs. Coolidge," she said pleasantly.

The doorman regarded her impassively. "What's your husband's first name?" he inquired.

"Calvin."

"What's his business?"

"He's Vice President."

"Vice president of what?"

Later, the rules were relaxed and the wives of senators and representatives were given gallery seats to some of the sessions, as were an increasing number of officials. But I preferred to remain in the one I had secured on my own, because it was much more desirable as a vantage point and Sumner Welles, with whom I was on very good terms by this time, called out to me enviously as he passed by on his way to a much less privileged place. Also, the seat next to mine was allotted to H. G.

Wells, whose persiflage was very engaging and whose asides were most amusing. He had long been one of my favorite authors, and I enjoyed his company immensely, both in and out of working hours, and was very much thrilled when he presented me with a copy of *Ann Veronica,* beautifully bound in limp leather. On one occasion, however, I was somewhat embarrassed when he insistently offered to relieve me of my fur coat, and I wrapped it still more closely about me, declining his help with a haste and nervousness I could not explain. Tickets were issued separately for each session and doled out at an office in the Navy Department Building near the Potomac; sometimes very little advance notice was given as to when these sessions would take place, and we had to be in our seats when they began. That morning I had been wakened from a sound sleep by a telephone call informing me that a session would begin in thirty minutes. It was something of a feat to get from Meridian Hill to the Navy Department Building and from there to Continental Hall in that length of time, and though I managed to do it, all I had on under my coat was a nightgown!

With the years the feeling has inevitably grown that the Washington Conference actually accomplished very little toward the reduction of armaments and that the United States was adroitly "taken" by the guests it had invited to its round table. At the time, however, the attention of the country was certainly centered on Continental Hall, and the world waited breathlessly for tidings of what was being said and done there. The press was feted almost as much as the delegates themselves, which was not surprising, for each nation had sent the cream of its journalistic and literary crop, and altogether the press made a notable showing. The fact that it was so overwhelmingly masculine was no disadvantage in the eyes of the few women who had been included. The party of which I have the most vivid recollections is the one which the Dutch Minister, Dr. Everwijn, gave at Rauscher's for the Dutch delegates and the entire press.

The ratio of men to women that evening was about twenty to one, and the former vied with each other in giving the latter a good time and certainly succeeded. Besides, the beverage that was being circulated was well calculated to restore drooping spirits. Fruit juice had been blended to produce a delicious punch; and though this had been spiked, it had been so smoothly and skillfully done that only a connoisseur would have detected it. I had been so tired before I started out that I had hesitated about going; and as my limited wardrobe was beginning to show the strain of so many festivities, I did not feel that the dress I was wearing was worthy of the occasion. But after I had had a glass of this mixture, I revived considerably and went to find my car and change my instructions to the driver: instead of leaving at eleven, after what amounted to little more than a courtesy call, I was now prepared to stay until two.

On my way, I met William Jennings Bryan, who was just coming in —late, according to his custom, which permitted a more impressive entrance than an earlier arrival. As usual, he was wearing a flowing cape and carrying white gloves and a tall silk hat. Both he and Richard Oulahan, at that time head of the New York *Times* Washington Bureau, always appeared in this regalia at evening parties, and the latter invariably managed to look more ambassadorial than any ambassador present. Mr. Bryan, being considerably heavier and also less sophisticated, was less imposing. He bowed to me briefly—from the beginning, he had been more aloof than most of the gentlemen of the press, perhaps because the role of correspondent was new to him—and continued on his way to the party.

I still had no car of my own, but thanks to a suggestion from Miss Harlan I was nearly always able to secure a shabby Ford which was owned and operated by a man named Walker, whose prices were modest, though he stipulated that he should always be addressed as Mister. It took me some time to find Mr. Walker, whose insignificant vehicle had been displaced by an officious policeman in order to accommodate a gleaming Rolls-Royce, and when I finally rejoined the other guests, a startling sight met my eyes.

Mr. Bryan was the center of a spellbound circle; his golden voice was ringing melodiously through the ballroom; in his hand was a glass of punch. As I approached, he drained this. Just as I wedged my way into the circle, a waiter appeared bearing a beaker-laden tray, and Mr. Bryan graciously consented to accept a second glass.

"Delicious!" he exclaimed enthusiastically as he drained this one also. "There is nothing more refreshing than a good fruit punch, nothing in the world! And I am gratified indeed that our host of the evening"—and here he bowed in the direction of Dr. Everwijn—"is limiting himself to this."

Mr. Bryan's geniality increased apace. By the time he had had a third glass of punch, even I was benefiting vicariously by it. No one saw fit to enlighten him as to the true content of the beverage he was imbibing. The Dutch Minister was unconscious of his involuntary perfidy, since he was quite unaware of the views held by America's most celebrated teetotaler and believed he was showing a distinguished guest the honor which was his due.

I afterward heard that Mr. Bryan was livid when he read the accounts of the party the next morning. He categorically denied the episode, but the denial did not carry much conviction; after all, there had been about three hundred witnesses! As for me, I was so elated that I went out and bought a new dress!

Though the reception held at the White House on New Year's Day, which was attended by all the most prominent delegates to the conference, set the tone for all similar functions that season, I felt the one held at the British Embassy was almost as splendid. The comfortable old mansion with its mansard roof and porte-cochere in which the Embassy was then housed has now been demolished, and a sprawling monstrosity has been erected on upper Massachusetts Avenue to replace it; but none of the entertainments given there can surpass in elegance of appointment or refinement of atmosphere those given in far simpler surroundings.

The old Embassy had one really imposing feature—a massive mahogany staircase, surmounted, at the point where it divided in two graceful branches, by a life-size portrait of Queen Victoria, painted when she was at the very crest of youth and power. On all great occasions this portrait was brilliantly lighted and profusely banked with flowers; and it seemed to the guests, who faced the picture as they entered, as if a regal hostess was actually waiting to welcome them. This impression was never more vivid than on the night of the Arms Conference reception, when white chrysanthemums were massed in front of the portrait and soft music was heard in the background.

The afternoon reception given in honor of the delegates by Senator and Mrs. Pittman was somewhat less spectacular in character but almost as brilliant. At that time the Pittmans were living in a large house on upper Sixteenth Street, next door to one occupied by several young diplomatic bachelors; but because of a communicating door halfway up the stairs, it was possible to make the houses into one. The guests entered through the Pittman house, were received by Mrs. Pittman in the large second-floor drawing room, and found refreshments in the dining room beyond. In the library above, Senator Pittman ministered to those whose views were not in strict conformity with the Volstead Act. When the guests had been duly refreshed, they were guided next door where the dancing was in progress.

Mrs. Pittman had asked me to receive with her and to make myself generally useful in steering distinguished guests in the right direction; I had such a good time in the process that it was very late when I finally tore myself away to go on to an eggnog party which the Prince de Béarn was giving that same evening, feeling that my own pleasure, like virtue, had been its own reward.

However, when I reached home the following day after my usual rounds, I found my refrigerator bulging with game, my bathtub filled with flowers and my three sons gorging themselves on all sort of forbidden delicacies. A note lying on my desk explained the felicitous windfall:

Dear Frances—

We cannot find words to express our gratitude for your kindness and sweetness to us on Sunday.

We just could not have gotten along without you. You had such a perfect understanding of the situation and took things in hand so gracefully. But we realized that your efforts must have prevented you from getting much personal pleasure out of the occasion and that you must be terribly fatigued.

We are sending you some ducks from Key's hunt and some candy and cake for your young sons. Also some roses which I am afraid have not wholly retained their freshness, though I kept them in a box on purpose all night.

I am sorry we didn't see you at Prince de Béarn's. We couldn't go, it was so late when all our own guests had gone.

> Yours with much love,
> Mimosa Pittman.

From that time on my friendship with the Pittmans was increasingly cordial. The gift of ducks became an annual one, and often when I took the Congressional Limited to New York, the head waiter in the dining car sought me out and asked, "Will you let me know about what time you will be wanting dinner, Mrs. Keyes? Some very nice game has been sent with instructions to have it cooked specially for you."

Then, in the fall of 1922, Mimosa, or Peg, as she was usually called, sent me a characteristic telegram:

KEY WAS ELECTED WITH GREAT MAJORITY AND WE ARE DOUBLY HAPPY BECAUSE WE CAN BE MORE WITH YOU IN THE FUTURE STOP BUSHELS OF LOVE FROM BOTH OF US

The Arms Conference and its correlative activities were my main preoccupation during the winter of 1921–1922, though they by no means crowded the question of Arlington's restoration from my consciousness; accounts of the Upperville meeting and the Richmond convention had been included in my *Good Housekeeping* "Letters," resulting in an increase of fan mail, with only one communication, among the dozens that reached me, critical of the movement which was now well under way.

I went to all seven plenary sessions of the Arms Conference and wrote about them at length. "On the left of the table, you would especially notice the noble face and figure of Srinivasa Sastri, India's representative, dressed in a gray costume that is rather clerical in its appearance, his head covered with a snowy turban. . . . At the foot of the table and most compelling of all is the young and brilliant Dr. Wellington Koo of the Chinese delegation." Mrs. Coolidge brought her knitting to the sessions and sat placidly plying her needles. Mrs. Alice Roosevelt Longworth, who hated hats as much as I hated gloves, sat at ease, with her bright hair uncovered. Mrs. Harding and Mme Jusserand, on the contrary, held themselves erect and rigid; their manner was formal, their attire conventional. I recorded these and many other details of the scene, but I also covered in full the work done at the plenary sessions right up to the last one on the sixth of February.

Continental Hall never looked more lovely, decorated with palms and the flags of the nine nations, the boxes filled with distinguished women, beautifully dressed, the balconies and floor packed to the last inch of standing room, the delegates, as they gathered for the last time around the green baize table, shaking hands and chatting with that perfect friendliness and lack of restraint which had been apparent from the beginning.

"The treaties which have been approved by the conference," Secretary of State, Charles Evans Hughes, the conference chairman announced, "will now be signed in alphabetical order—the United States of America, Belgium, the British Empire, China, France, Italy, Japan, the Netherlands and Portugal." I still have not decided which was the most impressive—the unrestrained, joyful clapping, or the tense, electrified silence with which it alternated, as one after another, the groups of delegates left their seats and walked to the place where the treaties lay, the big white sheets, with their red seals, crackling slightly, as the pens moved slowly across them.

Then, after the President had spoken and the benediction was pronounced, the chairman's gavel fell, and the Washington Conference came to an end.

As long as the conference lasted, I was obliged to limit the number of invitations I could accept, unless they were directly connected with it. But when it was over, there were no strings attached to the notes I sent expressing pleasure in acceptance. One of the dinners that spring, to which the mere invitation thrilled me, was given by Mr. and Mrs. Frederic Delano—Franklin Roosevelt's uncle and aunt—in honor of Associate Justice and Mrs. Oliver Wendell Holmes. The Holmeses were both elderly and feeble and went out very little; Mrs. Holmes took her airings in a small closed brougham, in which she circled slowly through Potomac Park; it was almost the last vehicle of its kind to be seen in

Washington. But the scintillating wit and polished presence of the Great Dissenter and his wife remained undimmed until the last, and any group which they honored with their company automatically took on an exciting aspect.

Miss Mabel Boardman was another outstanding figure in Washington life who entertained us that spring. Her figure was unalterably "straight-fronted," and her pompadour remained unflattened by the changing demands of fashion which brought in bobbed hair. On every possible occasion, this pompadour was surmounted by a tiara, and her general resemblance to Queen Mary was so striking that it startled the Prince of Wales—later the Duke of Windsor—when he first beheld her. But her appearance was far more forbidding than her character. She was full of good works for the Red Cross, of which she was national secretary, and for many other philanthropic enterprises; and, with the single exception of Mrs. Medill McCormick, she came closer to establishing a salon than any other woman in Washington. That year I received from her, with an engraved card of invitation, a neatly typewritten note which read:

Dear Mrs. Keyes:

Some one said to me the other day that in Washington one met in a social way only at dinners and balls and it was unfortunate there were no informal evenings "at home" after the rush of the season was over.

Therefore I am asking some friends to come in Monday evenings in March for a very simple "at home." A postprandial cigar and a prohibition sandwich may not be very tempting, but I trust pleasant company will be, and that you and the Senator will be among the number.

I hope the men will wear a dinner jacket and black tie if they wish, as it is so informal and that you will come early and often.

We did not go "early and often," for March was a crowded month for us that year. But we did go on the last of these Mondays, and the company we found was certainly pleasant. Senator Lodge was there. Alice and Nicholas Longworth were there, the former, as usual, the center of an admiring group; the latter wandering amiably about, creating an atmosphere of genial warmth wherever he paused. And Chief Justice Taft was there, his smile as expansive as his person, his enormous bulk comfortably disposed in the corner of a capacious sofa from which he was not once dispossessed. He and Harry were already discussing the feasibility of a separate building for the Supreme Court, which then still held its sessions in the famous Chamber of the Capitol; and for once Harry did not murmur, "You needn't stay long on my account."

In late April and early May the third annual Convention of the

League of Women Voters and the Pan-American Conference of Women took place in Baltimore, and at the request of Mrs. Park, Mr. Bigelow asked me to cover it for *Good Housekeeping*. It was a giant meeting for the League had invited women from all the Americas to confer on subjects of special concern to them—education, child welfare, women in industry, prevention of traffic in women, civil and political status of women and international friendliness. The response had been tremendous. Thirty-three official delegates from twenty-two countries were present, and at the opening meeting they marched upon the stage, which was surmounted by a huge disc bearing a map of the western hemisphere, each carrying a tall staff topped with a white placard on which was written the name of the country from which she came. One after another, they told about the work done for children in the country where each lived, speaking, with only two or three exceptions, in faultless English; and they presented a most distinguished appearance in their smart black dresses and large black hats.

Unquestionably, the foremost drawing card of the conference was Lady Astor. She made a great hit by coming to a meeting straight from the train on which she had arrived in Baltimore and making an impromptu speech. I met her several times, but most of all I enjoyed a quiet visit I had with her at the lovely country house where she was staying. I could hardly believe my good luck when the message came that she would be glad to see me; much less did I imagine I would have a whole hour with her and her husband, who was quite as charming and interesting as she was. She told me of the bills she had introduced in the House of Commons, for instance, those on equal guardianship of children and the legal position of women. But most of the time she insisted on discussing the questions in which I was interested, and after covering the Sheppard-Towner Maternity Bill we drifted—not unnaturally, for she was a very loyal Virginian—to the subject of the Lee Mansion at Arlington. I found that she was deeply interested in this restoration project, and she kept reiterating in her earnest, outspoken way, "Oh, you must make people see that it should be done." I promised her that I would at least keep on trying.

A few days before this conference opened, I began to have trouble with the scar tissue which had never been normal and which had bothered me intermittently ever since my operation six years previously. Now the scar split open again. I knew that if I sent for my doctor, he would order me to bed and make me stay there, so I patched myself up as best I could and went to Baltimore anyway. Why I did not die of blood poisoning is still a mystery; but I had a strange feeling that this meeting was destined to be extremely important to me in ways I had not yet visualized, and I had long since concluded that nothing would kill me except old age. I did, however, suffer intensely, and when the conference had been in session only two or three days, I fainted at the press table.

When I first began my work for *Good Housekeeping,* many of my fellow reporters had given me the feeling—not from what they said, but from the way they acted—that they thought I was a good deal of a dilettante, that the financial aspects of my job were unimportant to me and that I would not last long. The episode in Baltimore, painful though it was, put an end to that impression: no woman in my condition would persevere unless it meant a great deal to her. Nothing could have exceeded the kindness and helpfulness shown me from then on. Winifred Mallon, who was then with the Chicago *Tribune* but later joined the New York *Times* Washington Bureau, on which she was the only woman, was the first to come to my rescue, and we remained friends until her death. Another woman who was covering the conference and was inexpressibly good to me was Millie Morris, whom Ishbel Ross described in *Ladies of the Press* as the "redhaired, erratic star of I.N.S. —generous, brilliant, indifferent to money and her own interests but gifted and alert in her profession." She taught me more about journalism in a week than I have ever learned from anyone else in a year, though she did it in a very casual and offhand manner. I had never met anyone like Millie Morris before—in fact, there have not been many persons in the world like her, and that applies to her kindheartedness and her brilliance as well as her stained finger-tips, her queer clothes and her gorgeous hair. I liked her from the minute I laid eyes on her, and this liking quickly ripened into grateful affection as she corralled handouts and wrote rough copy for me while I gradually grew better. "Nothing has happened to excite the world today," she would assure me, perching on the edge of my bed and lighting one cigarette from another, after having piled reference material all around her. "Some of the others will be along after a while. Anything else I can do for you in the meantime?"

The last great event of the spring was the dedication of the Lincoln Memorial. The exercises on Memorial Day were as severely simple as the temple itself, and as the man which it commemorated. There was no military parade, no floral display. But nearly a hundred thousand people were assembled and there were more than five thousand in the reserved section on the platform, including members of the Grand Army of the Republic and also—I am glad to say—the United Confederate Veterans, the American flag fluttering between them. Chief Justice Taft, who was the chairman of the Lincoln Memorial Commission, stood in the center of the stage with the President and Mrs. Harding, the Vice President and Mrs. Coolidge, and Mrs. Taft on one side of him, and on the other Robert Lincoln, the only living son of the great President, and Representative Cannon—"Uncle Joe"—of Illinois, who was a member of the convention nominating Lincoln in 1860.

Dr. Robert Moton, the President of Tuskegee Institute paid the tribute of his race to its emancipator; he was followed by Edwin Markham, who read his poem, "Lincoln, the Man of the People." Finally came the address of presentation for the Lincoln Commission by the Chief Justice and the speech of acceptance for the nation by President Harding.

The latter was hailed as one of the best the President had ever made. But I have to confess that the only part of it I have remembered is a quotation from Lincoln himself, and later, the fact that Harding had chosen to lay so much stress on it seemed sadly prophetic. " 'If I were trying to read,' Lincoln said, 'much less answer all the attacks made upon me, this shop might as well be closed to other business. I do the best I know how, the very best I can, and I mean to keep on doing it to the end. If the end brings me out all right, what is said of me will not amount to anything. *If the end brings me out all wrong, ten angels swearing that I was right would make no difference.'* "

Chapter 22

O
N LEAVING Washington for the summer, I headed for Boston, where the entire family was congregating for Henry's graduation from Milton; and his father and I swelled with pride when he won the Reading Prize—he had already captured the Latin Prize—and received a diploma "with distinction for high scholarship." Though he had now spent five years at preparatory school and parts of several summers at camp, I had remained extremely close to him through constant correspondence and by keeping a good deal of time free for him and his friends during Christmas and Easter vacations in Washington, as well as for the longer periods at Pine Grove Farm, and he was already accepted as a near-contemporary by many of my friends. If his father was absent, he acted as my host, and we played bridge together, frequently danced together and took short trips together. There was very little consciousness of a generation gap between us—which is not strange, if we accept thirty years as the average for the difference in generations, since he was born when I was nineteen. I am convinced that one of the chief advantages of having children when you are young lies in the lack of difference in viewpoint which inevitably arises when there is more difference in age. Mothers understand their children's problems better when they do not have to look back too far on those they had as children themselves; and perhaps equally to the point, children understand their mothers' problems better if they do not have to look too far forward to visualize these. At any rate, that is the way it worked out for me. The far greater difference in age between my husband and his sister and brothers and myself was much more of a problem.

After Henry's graduation, Harry was obliged to return to Washington, as the Senate was still in session, and I went with the boys to the

Farm, where I stayed for three weeks. In that length of time, I managed to see more of my old friends than I had in a long while. I found that the craze for dancing seemed to be a thing of the past in Newbury and Haverhill and that interest in dramatics had entirely died out. This was something of a shock to me, as I still participated in both with enjoyment. I often went in the afternoon to dance at Mrs. Walsh's hospitable home in Washington. Also, I had recently had a very good time at a period ball there, to which I had gone in hoop-skirted green satin, adorned with my grandmother's jewelry and lace, impersonating Balzac's "Woman of Thirty"; and I had just taken the part of Guinevere in a pageant entitled "The Cross Triumphant," wearing a medieval costume that my dressmaker had created from the rather battered remains of the dress which I had not been able to wear to Harry's inauguration, but which had now seen me through three Washington seasons. It simply had not occurred to me that there would be no dancing or any kind of theatricals at Pine Grove Farm.

However, I was relieved to find that enthusiasm for bridge—except in the Cobb family—was stronger than ever, and the Darlings, Carrs and Hales were my guests at a pleasant dinner followed by a good game. Then the Cobbs came en masse to a supper party, and afterward all ten of us went to see *The Four Horsemen of the Apocalypse*. In those days, the advent of television had not yet resulted in the closing of all moving picture theaters in a radius of thirty miles, as it now has, and we could see a good film as often as we chose. I was glad that Richard not only went to this one willingly, but wanted to come and talk it over later on, dwelling at length on Rudolph Valentino's part in it. When Richard first returned from France, nothing would induce him to talk about the war or anything connected with it, but on every other subject we were as congenial as ever. He seemed interested in everything I was doing and we spent several enjoyable evenings together. The special fellowship was as close as always.

Mary Gray, who was dividing her summer between Santa Barbara and the Ojai Valley that year, had urgently invited me to visit her in California again, bringing one of the boys with me; it seemed the logical thing for Peter and me to accept. Congress was still in session and there was no chance for Harry to come home until fall; the two older boys were both going to camp, and Peter at ten was old enough to get a good deal out of such a trip. Our first stop was for a three-day visit with friends in Kansas City, where the chief event for Peter was a prolonged —and repeated—visit to the Electrical Park, and where I quickly became involved in a series of interviews and speeches. From there, we went to stay with James and Lucy in Idaho Springs and had the same wonderful kind of a visit in this mining center that Henry and I had had six years earlier. Then we headed for California and a much more active interlude there than I had anticipated.

Mary had numerous plans for me, all of them completely unrelated. She had become increasingly interested in extrasensory perception and such kindred subjects as astrology and palmistry; she felt that I should be more closely in touch with these. She was also extremely eager to have me make acquaintances in Hollywood, as she was convinced these would be of great help with my career as a writer. She had been the first to say that I would have one; and though she was pleased with the modest success of the two books and the numerous short stories I had written so far and the greater popularity of the *Good Housekeeping* "Letters," she wanted to see me succeed in a more important way financially and otherwise, especially as she realized how hard I was working to help with the family expenses. Mr. Bigelow, on the other hand, had not been particularly impressed with the California visit from a *Good Housekeeping* standpoint. He conceded that perhaps it would be a good plan for me to have a vacation, or something resembling one, but I did not even mention astrology and palmistry to him, as I was quite sure he would be non-receptive to them; and when I did mention Hollywood, he was not only cool in his attitude toward it, he was actually frigid. Later in life he unbent somewhat in his position toward remarriage after divorce, but at that stage he was denunciatory. "She may be a perfectly charming hostess," he said in referring to one of the stars Mary hoped I might meet. "But, as far as I am concerned, she has broken the laws of both God and man and her name will never be mentioned in a magazine I edit."

Under these circumstances, it was obvious that I must concentrate on something else if I were to continue to be a wage earner during the summer. Fortunately, I had been asked if I would serve, in my capacity as a member of the World Services Council, as one of the hostesses at Asilomar on Monterey Bay, the only conference ground owned by the Young Women's Christian Association. I was especially glad to do this, as it was impossible for the other senators' wives who were council members to attend and as Asilomar owed its very existence to one of the most remarkable women who ever came to Washington as a senator's wife—Mrs. Phoebe Hearst. And of course as far as *Good Housekeeping* was concerned, this was an ideal solution.

I enjoyed being at Asilomar, and my visit there logically led to one at the Girls' Studio Club in Hollywood, and since that was also under the management of the Y.W.C.A., I was equally delighted at an invitation to see its headquarters. Any girl working for the movies in any capacity was eligible for membership, and it was a very light-hearted attractive group that I found waiting to greet me when I arrived for the dinner and reception given in my honor.

After this introduction to movie land, I spent days going through the big studios, for though Hollywood, despite Mary's hopes, showed no interest in my books and never has done so, it welcomed me warmly, both as a private individual and as a reporter of its activities. I spent a morning with Harold Lloyd and a whole day with Mary Pickford; best of all, at a luncheon I met the screen writer Frances Marion, whose friendship was to mean a great deal to me in years to come. So Mary Gray had her way about making Hollywood contacts, and even though I did not write about the stars for *Good Housekeeping,* I did write about many of them for other periodicals, including articles about Mary Pickford which were featured in *McCall's* and *Better Homes and Gardens* and which led to several additional and very pleasant visits with her both in Hollywood and New York.

Nor was Mary disappointed about the preternatural aspects of my sojourn. Without in any way revealing my identity, she made an appointment for me with Grace Boughton Voce, an astrologer who lived secluded in the Ojai, and I spent a whole day with her. In the course of easy and seemingly almost casual conversation, she "read" my life—past, present and future—with an accuracy which to this day leaves me speechless with astonishment. She seemed to know everything I had done or wanted to do in the course of my life so far, and the predictions of others seem vague and general compared to the startling exactness, as to time and place, of those Mrs. Voce made. She foretold events of which I could not possibly have given her the slightest hint, because I had no inkling of them myself. One of her prophecies was that a change in religion was coming; another, that my greatest success in my chosen work would come after I had lost the prerogatives which seemed to facilitate this. Both of these portents and several others came true; nothing she foretold remained unfulfilled. When this happened, I was not surprised and in some cases the fact that I was forewarned was a help, which of course had been Mary's idea. How much was due to astrology, how much to clairvoyance and how much to sheer chance I do not know. I only know it happened.

Late in August, Peter and I left the hospitable Grays and, before starting back home, spent a few days in San Francisco, unquestionably one of the most intriguing cities in the United States. I had been there once before, as a sixteen-year-old girl, but that experience was very tame beside this one, which resulted in various new acquaintances of whom I was destined to see more in the future, and various side events, among them my introduction to Gump's Store, an adventure in itself, and a hesitant session with the photographer Boyé, who took the best pictures of me that had ever been made up to that time and have remained the best ever since!

Chapter 23

THE autumn of 1922 was studded with speeches. Shortly after my return from California, while my headquarters were still at Pine
Grove Farm, I spoke in Plymouth and Littleton, New Hampshire, and
Hartford, Connecticut. After my arrival in Washington, I made
speeches in Fredericksburg, Alexandria and Lynchburg, Virginia, and
in Columbus, Ohio. Most of these talks (except those made in the interests of Arlington) were professional in character and the expansion of
my budget which they made possible was very welcome. I also met a
great many interesting women (and a few interesting men!), and being
naturally gregarious, I always enjoy meeting interesting people.

But the physical and mental strain was much more exhausting than
taking care of children or keeping abreast of a Washington calling
schedule. During my days as "Lieutenant Governor," I had discovered
that I had no trouble in making myself heard, even before large groups,
because my voice carried well; but I had never been taught to use it—
or, rather, to save it—and when a speech was over, it was badly
strained, especially if the address had been preceded by a meal. Since
breakfast to me had meant coffee and rolls in bed from the time that
Peter did not need me early in the morning, I found convivial matinal
gatherings accompanied by course after course of very hearty food extremely hard to take. There were two of these at Columbus, and the
second time that four courses beginning with fruit cup and ending with
tenderloin steak were solicitously offered me, still without coffee, it was
just too much. The lady next to me, seeing that I was doing scant justice
to the food, observed rather caustically that I did not seem to like the
breakfast the Athletic Club had provided; I replied apologetically that it
was all very nice, but quite different from the breakfasts to which I was

(205)

accustomed. "Why, you're from New England!" she exclaimed. "Of course, we should have remembered that you want pie!"

Besides, days that began with early breakfasts were apt to extend to evenings with very late dinners. After that memorable breakfast at the Athletic Club, it was one o'clock the next morning when I got to my feet, as I was the third speaker at the dinner and both my predecessors had talked at great length. Sometimes I wondered if the main purpose of these gatherings was not the social side issues, rather than the speech itself, as far as the lioness of the occasion was concerned. This feeling was especially strong at Hartford that year. My talk was scheduled for a Monday afternoon, but my hospitable hosts had begged me to come on Saturday in order to give plenty of time for parties beforehand, and I did not feel I could decline; so a succession of these took place all day Sunday, Monday morning and Monday noon. Hartford is a focal point for a large number of smaller towns, in many of which preparatory schools are located—Connecticut is actually a stronghold of these! Large numbers of teachers, their wives and pupils had paid me the compliment of coming to hear me speak; but they were iron bound by supper hour regulations; and the club meeting I was to address was the annual one. Before I was called upon, the committee chairmen had all been asked to give their reports, and there were a great many committees. By the time they were finished, the afternoon was practically gone and so was more than half of the audience! But the evening was still young for the Hartford contingent, and I went to several more parties before I sank wearily into bed.

I would not feel it fair to mention these episodes, if similar experiences all over the country had not, in time, brought me to the conclusion that I must choose between making speeches and writing books, because the speeches consumed too much time and strength, not primarily in themselves, but in their side events, and because the books meant more, not only to me, but to other people. Five hundred persons represent a goodly number at a speech; a book with only a modest reception is read by at least five thousand, and a reasonably successful book by at least fifty thousand. If you really have something to say, you want to say it to as many people as possible; and even my first book, *The Old Gray Homestead,* sold more than five thousand copies the year it came out—and over fifty years later is still in print and selling a few copies every year.

That fall, just before I went to Lynchburg, Katherine Cobb Foss paid me a visit—the first one I had had from an old friend since coming to Washington—and I was especially eager that she should have a good time. I need not have worried. Though the season was hardly under way, she was breathless with the round of luncheons, teas and dinners which were already following each other in swift succession. The beauty and amiability which had made her such a favorite when she was a child and a teen-ager were more than fulfilled now that she was approaching thirty; and I was delighted to find that though her brothers had lost their enthusiasm for dancing, she had not done so. I took her to dance at Mrs. Walsh's, where she made an immediate hit and was favored with many attentions, among them a very attractive invitation to visit the Naval Academy. Besides going to Annapolis, we enjoyed a horse show, a theater party and numerous other festivities, and Katherine departed for New England saying Boston just never would look the same to her again.

In December of 1922, the Pan-American Union was again in the limelight with a conference which lasted two months. It began with a plenary session at which were signed a treaty, eleven conventions and three protocols affecting the relations of the United States with Central America and the Central American republics among themselves. In other words, it accomplished a good deal more than most conferences, and the earnestness and good will which marked it were apparent from the very first meeting.

The most beautiful dinner I went to that winter also took place at the Pan-American Union. The time had passed when the sight of gold plates thrilled me. Mrs. Walsh had a complete gold service for sixty, and I had come to take such lavish accoutrements, if not as a matter of course, at least as a logical part of the design for elaborate entertaining by the very wealthy; originality of decoration and charm of setting, together with distinction of guests, meant a good deal more. This dinner was given by the Minister of Uruguay and Señora de Varela in honor of the Ambassador of Great Britain and Lady Geddes. The representatives of seven countries—geographically as widely separated as Persia and Norway, Italy and Argentina—were gathered in the Council Chamber where we dined, and we drank our coffee in the wide gallery overlooking the patio and its lighted fountain. Our hostess was one of the most beautiful women in the Diplomatic Corps, and that evening she wore a dress of filmy lace with quaint jewelry clasped about her throat and hanging from her ears, and a red rose stuck in her dark hair. I never saw this dinner surpassed in elegance among the many I afterward attended at the Pan-American, though some were larger and more sumptuous.

Following hard upon the delegates from Central America came the famous "Tiger," Georges Clemenceau, the former War Premier of

France, to plead his country's cause before us. His visit was an informal one, but I think he made an even more favorable impression than if he had been sent by his government, for his unofficial status placed his sincerity and devotion to his cause absolutely above suspicion. He was a small man, over eighty years old and yet as charged with vitality as if he had a battery inside him; though rather hunched and shriveled, he was extremely genial; and he never appeared without his hands firmly incased in a pair of gray mocha gloves. (Of course, there were all sorts of speculation as to why he did this, and I loved the answer he gave: "I wear them because my hands get cold, but my feet never do!") He spoke perfect English, and I was fortunate in being invited to meet him at the French Embassy and to hear his principal address in Continental Hall. One newspaper for which I have great respect described this speech as "a delicately worded invitation to the United States to call the great powers to a new world conference where a new League of Nations, acceptable to the government and yet capable of insuring permanent peace, might be framed." It seemed to me, however, to be neither that nor a plea for imperialism nor an excuse for militarism nor even a veiled appeal for help, financial or otherwise, but merely an honest and convincing explanation of France's postwar attitude.

Early in the new year, two very important conventions were called by my friend Mr. James Davis, the Secretary of Labor—a meeting of the National Executive Board of the General Federation and a conference of Women in Industry. The Executive Board endorsed a national uniform marriage and divorce bill, which was later introduced into the Senate by Mr. Arthur Capper of Kansas. *Pictorial Review,* then one of the four leading women's magazines in the United States, was advocating it as intensely as *Good Housekeeping* had advocated the Sheppard-Towner Bill—though, sad to say, not with the same fortunate results.

The bill provided that the laws covering both marriage and divorce should be the same in every state of the Union. It set the legal marriageable age, with parental consent, at sixteen for girls and eighteen for boys; and at eighteen for girls and twenty-one for boys without parental consent. It prohibited the marriage of imbeciles, the insane, feebleminded, epileptics, paupers and those afflicted with venereal disease or tuberculosis, of blacks and whites and of first cousins. It provided for divorce for five causes, applicable alike to men and women: adultery, cruel and inhuman treatment, abandonment or failure to provide for a period of one year, incurable insanity and the commission by either party of an infamous crime. It required that in all cases a year must elapse after divorce before remarriage could take place.

The *Pictorial Review* campaign failed to hold public interest very long, and Mr. Capper's bill did not pass; but both had the merit of calling attention to glaring defects in certain state laws, many of which have since been rectified; I went on record as believing that "next to the Sheppard-Towner Bill and the Labor Bill, it is the most important measure of special interest to women that has yet been introduced into Congress"; and my outspoken approval of it incidentally and unexpectedly widened my own bailiwick, for Mr. Arthur Turner Vance, the editor of *Pictorial Review,* asked me to write an article about it. This was published under the title "The Average Woman and the Uniform Divorce Bill," and became one of a short series—"The Average Woman and Social Success," "The Average Woman and the Servant Problem," and others—as *Good Housekeeping* and *Delineator* did not share the *Ladies' Home Journal's* aversion to having me contribute Washington material to another magazine, and I was very glad of the increase in both audience and revenue which *Pictorial Review* provided.

The Conference of Women in Industry was called by the Secretary of Labor to formulate standards which should promote the welfare of wage-earning women, improve their working conditions, increase their efficiency and advance their opportunities for profitable employment. "The duty devolves upon the whole people to see that their employment is safeguarded, so that the general welfare of the nation may not suffer," Mr. Davis said in his opening speech. "I trust, with all my heart, that the day may never return when we shall see, as the people of my native town of Wales have seen, a woman at work in the steel-rolling mill . . . wrestling with one hundred or two hundred pounds of iron. . . ."

The Secretary's speech aroused not only great enthusiasm, but considerable discussion, and one part of it which touched me especially was not in his prepared address and was told very simply. "Not long ago I was with a group of men who began an evening of reminiscence by telling, each in turn, what the pleasantest experience of his childhood had been. I dreaded to have my turn come, because there were not many pleasant experiences in my childhood of which I could tell. But at last I thought of one: when I was eleven years old, my younger brother and I changed places on the twelve-hour shift which began at two in the morning and ended at two in the afternoon. It was very dark between our little home and the mine. So, every morning at two o'clock, my mother used to get out of bed and put some tea on the stove and light a kerosene lamp—we were considered quite well-to-do because we had this one kerosene lamp—and open the door and sing in her native Welsh. She stood there singing, near the little twinkling light, until one boy had safely reached home from the mine and was sheltered beside her drinking his hot tea and the other boy, wakened to begin his work and cheered with the tea before he started out, had trudged off into the night and safely reached the mine. Neither of us ever had to take that trip without the comfort of the tea and the song and the light. The picture of my mother, singing in the darkness, is the brightest memory I have."

The story was one of the "land of promise" indeed—the small boy groping his way home at two in the morning, now a member of the President's Cabinet—but it was more than that: it was the most vital plea against child labor I had ever heard. I was not surprised that after it every speaker I heard at the conference expressed himself in favor of a constitutional amendment to abolish child labor.

To those who knew nothing about the Secretary's past, this story was surprising as well as moving, for his status in Washington gave no hint of straitened circumstances, much less of actual poverty. Mr. and Mrs. Davis lived with their rapidly increasing family in a large hospitable house on Massachusetts Avenue and were both hearty, good-looking and outgoing. When the Secretary rejoined his wife after a day at the office, he always kissed her fondly, whether they were at home or at some official gathering. At one reception, a comparative stranger who was standing nearby happened to hear a reference to "the baby" and asked Mrs. Davis how old the baby was. "Almost a year," she said, and when the questioner exclaimed with surprise, "Why I didn't know you had a child that age!" Mrs. Davis replied, "I always have a child of that age," which was very nearly true: a new little Davis came along annually.

The family was so happy, wholesome and united that Mrs. Davis's death when she was still a young woman seemed doubly tragic because apparently it could have been avoided. She decided that she needed to lose weight, though she was the type to whom plumpness is becoming. But she went on some sort of crash diet and overstrained her heart, because she did not eat enough to keep up her strength, though she did keep up all her usual strenuous activities. This tragedy was far in the future when the Secretary made his memorable speech about his mother, however.

On January nineteenth—the anniversary of Lee's birth—I attended a luncheon and meeting of the Daughters of the Confederacy in Philadelphia and had the great pleasure of being the house guest of Mrs. Francis du Pont during my twenty-four hour stay. Though I did give a talk, everything was so beautifully planned and executed that instead of returning home exhausted as I usually did after a speech, I actually went back refreshed, feeling the break in the normal routine had been beneficial, as well as delightful. Scranton, where my cousin Elizabeth Hill Conrad, then president of a women's club, lured me a little later in the season, and Baltimore and Manchester, which were also on the schedule, were more of an effort, but all seemed to repay this, both from the financial standpoint and from the standpoint of making more worthwhile acquaintances.

But I did not have sufficient stamina for such a strenuous program without frequent minor breakdowns in the form of trouble with my back, with the stubborn old scar and with insomnia, which had always plagued me and which was an increasingly persistent problem. Finally, a doctor told me he thought that if I were not hounded by the consciousness that it would soon be time to get up though hour after hour had passed sleeplessly, this relief might not only reduce the insomnia but incidentally help to take care of other handicaps. Would it not be possible, he inquired, for me to organize my household in such a way that I would not be called in the morning and, after I woke naturally, to have coffee and rolls in bed and go through my mail in a leisurely fashion? Harry, who liked to get up "in good season" anyway, immediately volunteered to take Peter to school in the mornings, which was a tremendous help, and so I adopted this plan. But no matter how many conferences I covered, no matter how many dinners I attended and no matter how many speeches I made, I still always managed—except during my brief absences—to spend at least an hour reading aloud to Peter every evening and to take him to dancing school once a week.

I also managed, though I confess I do not see how, to write at least a little every day, in addition to the requirements of *Good Housekeeping* and *Delineator*. Even though my faith in my future as a novelist was very faint, it still survived; and I had by no means forgotten the promise I had made Mrs. Greer four years earlier that I would try to write the story of her grandmother. On February 25, 1923, I finished *The Safe Bridge*. That, we had decided, should be the title of the story, based on the old Scotch proverb, "You must always speak well of the bridge that carries you safely over"; and now it was ready to show Mrs. Greer when I went back to Pine Grove Farm and, if it met with her approval, to show to a publisher. Its completion was a turning point.

In those days, Congress remained in session until March fourth, and members of both Houses who had not been re-elected still held their seats until noon, when the new Congress began. These Lame Duck Sessions resulted in many impasses, for the outgoing legislators could not only introduce and often secure the passage of bills completely contrary to the policies of their successors, but block the passage of bills advocated by members who had retained their seats; and no one who could get into the Capitol as a spectator missed the last-day sessions, for they were fantastic. In the Senate, some men sang their own swan songs, and others listened with appreciation to eulogies spoken by men who in a matter of minutes would cease to be their colleagues; still others were receiving congratulations because their defeats had already led to appointments, by the President, to posts which compensated for their loss, as a mark of gratitude for past services to the party. It was therefore possible on March 4, 1923, to gaze down from the gallery on Senator Miles Poindexter of Washington and behold in one and the same person the new Ambassador to Peru, upon Senator Harry New of Indiana and observe the new Postmaster-General. There was considerable surprise that no new appointment was announced for Senator Joseph Frelinghuysen, for he was known to be one of the President's most intimate friends, and indeed the treaty of peace with Germany had been signed at his house. The conclusion that Mr. Frelinghuysen had declined an appointment was probably correct. At all events, he was one of those who sang his own swan song, in a way that was so dignified and so lacking in any hint of bitterness or recrimination that it made a deep impression: "My ambition to represent New Jersey has been fulfilled, and I have been privileged to sit in the Senate during the most eventful period in my country's history. It was also my ambition to represent my state as acceptably and capably as the three senators of my name and family who have preceded me in this body, and I hope I have measured up in some slight degree to the high standards they set. As I go forth again as a private citizen, I know that I have the respect of my constituency. . . . I regret leaving the splendid fellowship of my friends here."

As soon as the Vice President's gavel had thudded down, accompanied by the announcement, "Sixty-seventh Congress is adjourned without day," all onlookers in the Senate Chamber streamed to the doors in their haste to reach the far more hilarious celebration characterizing the closing of the House of Representatives. At eleven o'clock it had taken a recess; a tremendous farewell ovation had been given "Uncle Joe" Cannon; and the Marine Band had grouped itself about the Speaker's desk. Mrs. Winifred Mason Huck, Congresswoman from Illinois, had borrowed a violin from one of the musicians, and galleries and members had begun to sing and cheer together. "The Old Oaken Bucket," "Farewell, My Own True Love" and "Dixie" followed each other in quick succession. Then the families of members began to surge out on the floor; this is forbidden in the Senate, but it is part of the show at the House. Children were lifted high in their fathers' arms above the semicircle of desks. Mrs. Mondell, Mrs. Longworth, dozens of other women were standing beside their husbands. The first hilarity passed; some people were still laughing, but more were growing a little choky. "Home, Sweet Home" came after "Auld Lang Syne." And the final song which the band played caught up and echoed a spirit which was mighty, not only in its patriotic but in its devotional strength:

Praise God from Whom all blessings flow,

the melody swept over us all like a triumph of thanksgiving.

> *Praise Him all creatures here below;*
> *Praise Him above, ye Heavenly Host,*
> *Praise Father, Son and Holy Ghost.*

A year earlier Constance Drexel, a staff writer for the Philadelphia *Public Ledger,* had written an article which began, "Mrs. Harding has been mistress of the White House exactly one year. Has she been a success? Yes, an unqualified yes." The article went on to outline her efficiency as an executive and an organizer and did not neglect to mention her dignity and distinction as a hostess and her taste and judgment in dress. As far as I know, there was not a single woman in official Washington at that time who would not have agreed with Miss Drexel or who was not stricken the following fall when Mrs. Harding's serious illness became known. Again, it was a member of the press—Maude McDougall, also a correspondent for the *Ledger*—who voiced the general sensation of impending tragedy. After being called upon to write a feature story about Mrs. Harding which could be rushed into print in case she died, Maudie told me, "As I sat pounding out the words, 'Mrs. Harding *did,* Mrs. Harding *said,*' the tears rolled down my cheeks so fast that I could not see my keyboard. I had to stop writing."

Somehow Mrs. Harding was kept alive, through her own inherent courage and determination, as well as the skill and vigilance of her personal physician, Dr. Carl Sawyer; and near the end of her second year in the White House just before leaving Washington for a long period of convalescence in Florida, she received a small group for the first time since she had been felled by the illness that nearly cost her life. "She wants to see you before she goes away and to have you see how much better she is," Miss Harlan told each guest as about twenty women gathered in the sitting room on the second floor. "She will not be able to entertain for some time, but she wanted you all to come in and have a cup of tea with her before she leaves."

The guests included the newspaper women on the White House list, nearly all of them, like myself, members of the Women's National Press Club, and also Mrs. Miles Poindexter, the wife of the defeated Senator from Washington who had just been appointed Ambassador to Peru. Mrs. Poindexter's presence came as a surprise to me and, I think, to most of her fellow guests. She had been contributing to her home-town paper for some time, but as she had not affiliated herself in any way with press activities in Washington, this was not generally known until she wrote a very bitter article outlining the privileges accorded a cabinet officer, but not a senator—no car provided, no regular provision of flowers for his wife's entertainments and so on. All this was true, but she had certainly chosen a strange time to say so, when the charge of being a poor loser would surely follow, and the contrast between her attitude and Senator Frelinghuysen's made it all the more remarkable.

But Mrs. Harding had obviously decided that she must be recognized as a serious craftsman, and no one was disposed to resent anything the First Lady did or said that day, when we were all so overjoyed at her recovery and so glad to see her again. As soon as we had assembled, Mrs. Harding joined us in the sitting room, which was gay with spring flowers, cozy with deep comfortable chairs and huge sofas upholstered in chintz, warm with a bright wood fire, homelike with books and magazines and photographs scattered about. I never saw her look so pretty as she did that day, without her glasses and the black velvet band she always used to wear around her throat, and dressed in a tea gown of coral velvet and silver lace. She perched on the edge of the piano bench and joked and chatted in her old lively way, treating her recent illness, for the most part, lightly and cheerfully. But she said she had been so deeply affected by the letters and messages that were brought to her when her convalescence began that she had broken down and wept— with the result that she was not allowed to see a letter or newspaper for several weeks. She was reading again now, for about fifteen minutes a day, but for the rest, the President read to her. One of the great compensations of her illness was that she and her husband were seeing more of each other than at any time since they had come to the White House. She also said, quietly and with the deepest sincerity, that she believed her life had been saved by the prayers of the American people. And I, for one, was inclined to think that she was right. We did pray for her recovery—every man and woman that I knew—and our prayers were answered. "More things are wrought by prayer than this world dreams of." This is not merely a quotation, but a statement of fact.

Part Five

European Correspondent

SHORTLY after the Industrial Conference ended, I had an unexpected visit from Mr. Bigelow. We had frequent conferences about the "Letters," in New York and sometimes in Washington, and he enjoyed coming to the capital for special events, such as the dedication of the Lincoln Memorial. Harry could nearly always squeeze an extra seat from his senatorial allotment, and Mr. Bigelow was most appreciative and never failed to reciprocate with invitations when I was in New York. At the moment, however, I knew of nothing about which we needed to confer, and no event of outstanding importance was taking place. I was completely in the dark as to what had brought my editor to see me and was thunderstruck when he told me.

"Mrs. Park was so pleased with your account of the Pan-American Conference in Baltimore," he told me in a pleasant but calm manner, "that she has asked me if I would not consider sending you to Rome for the Ninth Congress of the International Suffrage Alliance, which is to take place in May. Would you care to go as *Good Housekeeping's* representative?"

For a moment, I was absolutely speechless. Then I managed to make it clear that I would be overjoyed to do so.

"If we are going to the expense of sending you to Europe," Mr. Bigelow went on, "it seems to me you might as well stay there long enough to take in a few other events, in a few other countries. No doubt, you have enough good connections or could establish enough valuable contacts to keep you busy all summer. Is there any place where you would especially *like* to go?"

"I've always wanted very much to go to Spain," I answered, finding my voice quite easily this time.

Mr. Bigelow looked at me pensively. "I hadn't thought of Spain," he said slowly. "But yes, I believe you might find material for a very acceptable article there. Not many people include a visit to Spain when planning an European itinerary, so you'd have the advantage of writing about a country that isn't as well known as others you'd visit. . . . Well, think it over and talk it over with your husband. If he's in favor of the plan, he might have some helpful suggestions too. I shall need to have your decision within a week, because if you can't cover that conference in Rome, I'll have to let Mrs. Park know."

The first person with whom I talked over this plan was not Harry, but Cathie. To begin with, I couldn't wait for my husband to get home from the Capitol without telling somebody; in the second place, I couldn't think seriously of leaving Peter for so long unless I had her solemn assurance that *she* would never leave him, for a single day or night, while I was gone. She promised instantly and gladly, and I knew she would keep her word, and that he would be happy with her. Needless to say, this was before the era of the eight-hour day and the five-day week for domestics; if it had not been, I could not possibly have embarked on a foreign program while I still had a young child. I have always felt that Cathie Deming deserved no small share of the credit that came to me for my work abroad.

Harry, far from raising objections, recognized Mr. Bigelow's project for just what it was—a wonderful opportunity. He had friends at our embassies in both England and France, and he would be glad to write to them. But it would probably be a good plan for me to have a talk with our friends William R. Castle, Jr., Chief of the Western Division in the State Department, and Juan Riano, the Spanish Ambassador. . . .

Nothing could have exceeded the cordiality and cooperation these gentlemen showed me and they immediately wrote very flattering letters of introduction for me: Señor Riano's was addressed to King Alfonso's Private Secretary, and Mr. Castle's, somewhat less formal in tone, was written to our Ambassador to Italy:

Department of State
WASHINGTON

March third,
1923

Dear Dick:

This will introduce to you Mrs. Keyes, wife of Senator Henry Wilder Keyes, of New Hampshire.

I am not sure whether you know Senator Keyes but you undoubtedly know him by reputation as one of the excellent men in the Senate and a great friend of the President.

Mrs. Keyes has published some books and now writes about things in Washington for *Good Housekeeping*. Her articles are very widely read and tremendously liked and—different from other writers along similar lines—Mrs. Keyes never seems to "put her foot in it."

Mrs. Keyes is to be in Rome for an international suffrage meeting and will probably write several articles. I hope that you can open the doors for her in order that her time in Italy may be both pleasant and profitable.

Yours as always,
W. R. Castle, Jr.

The Honorable
Richard Washburn Child
American Ambassador,
Rome.

I wrote on my own initiative to Baroness Romano Avezzana, whose husband was now Italian Ambassador to France, and had an immediate and affectionate response: I must take one of the new Italian ships of which they were so proud and land in Naples; her husband had several relatives there, they would meet me at the dock and welcome me in their homes; and letters would also be dispatched at once to Rome, to make sure I saw everyone I wanted to meet there; then, when I got to Paris, she and her husband would be expecting to see a great deal of me.

As the time for departure approached, I naturally grew more and more excited. Passage was duly engaged on the *Conte Rosso*, and I learned with pleasure that Mrs. Gaillard Stoney, whom I had liked very much when we met in San Francisco the year before, was taking the same ship, since she was going to Rome as a delegate to the conference, and that she would be spending a little time in Naples first and would be at the hotel where I planned to stay. But I did not attach any great importance to this prospective companionship. I had no hesitation about striking out by myself, for I felt that with all the letters I had, I was well fortified against loneliness, besides being well provided with help in my work. It was Charlie Colby, now so frequently my host in New York, who put an entirely new idea into my head.

"Who's going to be with you after you and this Mrs. Stoney part company?" he inquired casually when I next went to visit him and Kitty.

"Why, nobody."

"You hadn't thought of having Henry join you—as your secretary?"

I was almost as much amazed as I had been when the trip was suggested to me in the first place. "Mr. Bigelow would never consent to all the extra expense that would mean," I objected, "even if Henry were qualified to be a secretary—which, as you know, he isn't."

"He knows how to type and certainly should be able to manage for one summer, even if he can't take shorthand—he could take your dictation direct to the typewriter if there wasn't time to write it out in longhand. He's done enough traveling in the United States to know how to handle tickets, take care of baggage and so on, and there couldn't be a better time for him to learn more—after all, he's eighteen years old. And how do you know Mr. Bigelow wouldn't consent to the extra expense? You haven't asked him. If he objects, you might point out to him that in most of the places you'll be going, it's considered much better form for a young or even a youngish woman to have a male relative with her than to travel alone. It shouldn't be necessary to mention that, but in case it is. . . . You look a lot younger than you are. And he wants you to make a good impression everywhere. He'll find—and you will too—that the conference in Rome is only a prelude. You have bigger and better things ahead of you than that."

Charlie's calm assurance was convincing. I telephoned Henry then and there and found he would be only too glad to go, and then, timorously, I broached the subject to Mr. Bigelow. He did not turn a hair. He said he thought it was an excellent idea. Henry must join me as soon as his freshman year ended in June.

It would be an understatement to say that everything went according to plan. Everything went much better than planned, and I knew before I left the United States that Charlie Colby had been right: bigger and better things *were* ahead of me. Not that I underestimated the importance of an international gathering of earnest and intelligent women striving to improve the lot of those less fortunate. But attendance at such a conference was mainly feminine, and accounts of it would be more interesting to women than to men. Before long, I would be, or at any rate should be, dwelling more on questions of general significance and meeting more of the leaders responsible for them. I even had an inkling of where I might begin: the Romano Avezzanas had laid the groundwork for my stay in Italy with great thoroughness, and right then the spotlight of the world was centered on its Premier, Benito Mussolini. Postwar Italy had been the prey of unemployment, strikes and general disorder. The Fascists dealt efficiently and rapidly with these unsettled conditions, and in May of 1921, Mussolini, their recognized leader, was elected to Parliament. A year and a half later, the Fascists marched on Rome, and the King, exhausted by the struggle to maintain any kind of government, not only made no effort to halt them but invited Mussolini to form a cabinet. As one diplomat put it, "The King had just fifteen minutes in which to turn around and managed to do it." By the time I was leaving for Rome in the spring of 1923, Mussolini's authority was supreme, and Italy was no longer the fourth-rate power it had been, but a first-rate one. Dirt and disorder had been succeeded by cleanliness and efficiency; trains ran on time; beggars had disappeared. There were fine new roads and a new merchant marine. The Pontine Marshes, long a source of disease, were being drained and transformed into beautiful productivity; the Lateran Treaty would result in harmony between the Vatican and the Quirinal for the first time in many years. Now no one speaks of these and similar accomplishments, but only of the vaulting ambition which eventually brought so much national and international disaster in its wake. Hitler, originally Mussolini's pupil, became his master and brought about his ruin. I am thankful that these coming events had not yet cast their shadows when I started so happily for Italy and that, in what proved a triumphant visit for me personally, there was no sign of future tragedy.

The voyage on the *Conte Rosso* seemed magical to me from beginning to end. My cabin was so crowded with flowers that I could hardly get into it myself, much less find room for one of the two good-sized trunks without which I would not have dreamed of traveling in those days. But none of the flowers, not even Mrs. Harding's, meant as much to me as the letter Mr. Bigelow had written me:

Dear Mrs. Keyes:

Now that you are actually on your way, I hope that everything still looks rosy to you. I realize that it is no light thing for a wife and mother to tear herself away from her family for several months, and I appreciate your great interest in the work you are doing, which I naturally assume is the prime reason for your being willing to do this. My last word to you as you leave is that if I have seemed to leave a number of things rather indefinite, it is because of the confidence that I have that you will meet every occasion as it should be met and will perhaps do better if left uninstructed than if you had to decide whether or not to carry out instructions. My best wishes go with you, and I hope that you will never have anything but the most pleasant of recollections of the things that you are to do and see during the next few months.

If at any time you feel that you need to get in touch with the office, just remember that while it is a long way off from where you will be at the time, messages go either through air or under water in such a rapid way that, so far as communication is concerned, the two continents are practically one. Our cable address is COSMOTOR, NEW YORK, and we shall be here to do anything we can to assist you in any way that you may have need.

Mrs. Stoney and I were given seats at the Captain's table and every meal seemed to me the realization of a gourmet's dream. The traditional Captain's Dinner, at which the host made a gallant speech, was a feast worthy of Brillat-Savarin. The weather was perfect throughout, and I would have regretted the voyage's approaching end if the first sight of land had not been so beautiful: the quiet Azores, mantled in gray-green, cultivated to the very tops of their sloping hills; the low white houses lying close against them, the high surf foaming off the jagged shore. Then came the Straits of Gibraltar—at three in the morning, in the congenial company of the ship's doctor and a group of kindred spirits. The sky was a network of stars, the lights of Tangiers so brilliant that it seemed we needed only stretch out our hands to touch the African shore. The Rock loomed like a huge sentinel on the coast of Spain; ships passed each other silently in the narrow channel. Next came Sardinia, rugged and grim, when the sun was setting in riotous glory behind a lighthouse high on a black hill, and at last an opalescent dawn illuminating the curving Bay of Naples, the thin smoke from Vesuvius curling upward on one side of it, peaceful Ischia sleeping on the other. Then the Romano Avezzanas' relatives, the Scariglias, met me, as promised, and invited me to a sumptuous luncheon, including Mrs. Stoney in their hospitable gesture. They also found a dentist for Mrs. Stoney, whose attentions she badly needed, and Signora Scariglia took us shopping, to tea at a pleasant seaside park with a fashionable restaurant and on a round of excursions.

In Rome, though Mrs. Stoney and I stayed at the same hotel and saw each other frequently, our paths separated somewhat, as her program was largely directed by the Countess of Aberdeen, an old friend of hers who was also a delegate, and mine by the American Embassy, where Mr. Castle's letter to "Dear Dick" had been very fruitful. The Ambassador and Mrs. Richard Washburn Child were an attractive and urbane couple living in the *Palazzo* Orsini—one of the most famous old Roman palaces—and on the best of terms both with the new Fascist government and the old aristocracy; and I had the pleasant surprise of finding as Second Secretary of Embassy, Copley Amory, Jr., the individual who did more than any other one person to make my stay in Rome enjoyable. His father was an old friend of Harry's; and once, in the early days of our marriage, when father and son were taking a canoe trip down the Connecticut River, they had stopped off at Pine Grove Farm and I had made friends with them. At that period the teen-age gap between me and the son was very great, but by the time we met in Rome, we were practically contemporaries, and I was delighted to find him there.

Many of the glories of springtime Rome would have escaped me if it had not been for Copley. It was thanks to him that I had my first glimpse of the Knights Templars' garden and several other spots off the beaten path; he asked me to lunch at a *ristorante* on the Aventine, he invited me to tea at his apartment.

And shortly I received an exciting invitation to attend the gala performance of *The Barber of Seville* at the Constanzi Theater, given in honor of the King and Queen of England, who were making a state visit to Italy. Invitations to this had been very carefully restricted to the Italian aristocracy and the heads of the Diplomatic Corps; I knew that even the American Embassy would not have an extra invitation available and had not regarded attendance as a possibility. Then an invitation dropped into my hands—thanks, of course, to the Romano Avezzanas. Even if there had been nothing on the stage worth seeing and hearing, the audience itself, in full evening dress, with jewels, orders and decorations galore, presented a splendid sight; and the Queens were more dazzling in their apparel than any I had ever seen before.

The formal inauguration of the Congress took place about a week after this gala performance, in the great assembly hall of the *Palazzo dell' Espozitione*. The place was packed to the walls, and hundreds of persons were turned away. Mussolini addressed this meeting, and the press and the delegates had an excellent chance to observe the Premier before he began his speech, as he sat in a tall carved chair at the center of the stage—though I thought that wherever he sat would automatically become the center of the stage. He was a man rather above medium height; very dark, with a face that was stern and almost gloomy in repose but that lighted to charm and radiance when his eyes kindled and his teeth flashed in a rapid smile. He was extremely quick in all his movements, without losing dignity and force, and was faultlessly dressed in formal clothes.

There had been many pessimistic remarks beforehand, to the effect that this Congress would not be recognized in any way by the Italian government, and that there was not the slightest hope of political enfranchisement for Italian women. But the Premier began his remarks by saying, "The Government *Fascista,* over which I have the honor of presiding, wishes to express to you first its great pleasure that you have chosen Rome as the seat of your Congress, and to welcome you in the most cordial and warmest way," and before he finished speaking stated, "I feel authorized to declare that the Government *Fascista,* if nothing unforeseen happens, can vouch to grant to several categories of women the right to vote, starting from the administrative vote."

The reports of the four standing committees—Equal Pay and the Right to Work; Moral Questions; Nationality of Married Women; and Economic Status of Wives, Mothers and Children, Legitimate and Illegitimate—began the first day of the Congress, and the discussion that arose in connection with them was extremely interesting. And as I watched and listened to this and later sessions I realized how absolutely right one of the speakers had been in ascribing the greatness of Carrie Chapman Catt, who was retiring from the presidency of the Alliance that year, to her "world-consciousness." There was not one of us women there who would not have been a greater woman than she was then if she had had more world-consciousness. It is rather an Anglo-Saxon trait to be extremely well-satisfied with ourselves and all that we have and do and are, and I would have been the last to say that we did not have good reasons for our self-satisfaction. But it was good for us to see that other peoples had cause for self-satisfaction also. It was extremely wholesome for us to hear women whom we had thought of as "poorly educated" speaking easily and fluently in four or five languages about world conditions, when we could only flounder through one or two and often knew far too little of national, not to mention international, affairs. It was wholesome, too, to have spread before us the culture and refinement and wisdom of those women of the ancient races whom we complacently described as "heathen" and "barbaric." And it was important, since it made for better international relationship—which, when you came right down to it, was only another phrase for universal peace. We shall never abolish war by merely stating, pompously and blindly, that war shall be no more. But we *shall* abolish it when we recognize—and follow—the everlasting truth of the universal "Fatherhood of God and the fellowship of all mankind."

I attended the first few sessions of the conference faithfully; but early in the week it opened, I received a letter from our Ambassador, informing me the Premier would be glad to grant me a private audience on Thursday morning at half-past eleven. I knew this was much more important to me than anything else I could do, so, at the stated time, I went to the Chigi Palace, accompanied by Copley Amory, and was ushered into an enormous antechamber, where a large number of men and women were sitting. Two or three extremely smart Fascist guards were pacing alertly to and fro, and a fumbling, stooping, little old man was going in and out a door with the cards that were handed him. It was, I afterward learned, only about fifteen minutes—though it seemed about fifteen hours—before a young man came through another door and told me Baron Russo, the Minister of Foreign Affairs, was ready for me. I parted from Mr. Amory and was taken into another antechamber—a smaller one where there was no one else.

Baron Russo greeted me courteously, saying he was glad to see me and that he had heard pleasant things about me from mutual friends. Then he asked if I spoke French. He seemed much relieved when I assured him that I did.

"Good. Then it will not be necessary for me to act as interpreter for you with His Excellency; you will be able to speak with him directly and alone. He is expecting you," Baron Russo announced, and opened a second door.

The room into which he led me was wainscoted in dark oak and hung with priceless tapestries, draperies and paintings. Two great sixteenth-century globes stood near the entrance, and at first I was not aware of the room's other furnishings; I was too overcome by its vastness. Its splendid length was unbroken by any cluttering furniture, and I was appalled to realize that I would have to traverse this immense space before I was within speaking distance of the Premier. He was standing beside a mammoth flat-topped desk piled with documents arranged in precise order, with a high-backed chair behind it and two similar chairs facing it. In the brief interval before he shook hands with me, dismissed Baron Russo and invited me to sit down, I had the feeling he had been attentively sizing me up while I was taking that seemingly endless walk. I was sure of it when he sat down himself and waited for me to speak.

It is never easy to start an important conversation with a severe man who gives you no lead at all, and it is especially difficult if you must do so in a foreign language and with the consciousness that the person with whom you are to deal is charged with electric force. I knew I would never again need an explanation of this man's rise to power or his present supremacy; and I was so desperately anxious not to fail in handling the situation acceptably that I feared my anxiety would be a stumbling block. However, fortune favored me.

"You speak excellent French," the Premier flung out, not as if stating a fact, but as if expressing relief; then, swiftly: "You do not need to tell me who you are or what you do. I already know all that."

"If you had not," I retorted mentally, "I should not be here." But aloud, I naturally said nothing of the sort. It was the time, I saw, to match his rapidity with my own, if I could, so I asked him a number of direct and leading questions about current politics and conditions, especially in Italy.

"I am going to give you your answers in writing," he said. "Then there will not be any doubt in your mind as to exactly what I have said, or in anyone else's as to whether I have said anything at all."

I thanked him, of course, though I was disappointed at not being able to quote some of the striking things he said to me. Then, without stopping to catch my breath or give myself time to think, I asked him the favor that had been in my mind from the beginning—whether he would allow me to go and see his wife. I had asked Mr. Child if it would cause the Embassy any embarrassment if I were to do this, and had been told that it would not cause *him* any embarrassment, but that it might cause me a good deal, as I was bound to meet with a curt refusal —since that was what always happened.

However, nothing of the sort happened to me. The Premier hesitated for a minute before he answered. Then he told me, very simply and with great dignity, what I already knew, though it was the first time I had heard it so well expressed: that his wife was not in Rome with him, but in their own city of Milan with their three children, where he joined them whenever he could for a week end; that her time was entirely given up to her family and her household; that she did not concern herself with politics and that she did not receive visitors, either socially or officially; that she, like himself, came of very plain people. He paused again, and then continued, "I do not know what a lady like you would find to say to my wife. Are you quite sure you want to visit her?"

I knew that the interview's outcome depended on the way I answered, and fortunately I was able to do so in the only way that could have worked. "There were a good many years, *M. le Président*," I said, "when I lived very quietly at home, on a farm, taking care of children, not concerning myself with politics and seeing my husband only when he came home for week ends, as he could. It was not until we had been married thirteen years that he took me with him to the capital of our state and then to the capital of our country."

There was a third and longer pause, and the Premier's gaze was even more searching. But at last he said, "I should be very glad to have you go and see my wife. I shall telephone her that you are coming and ask her to give you some pictures of the children, if you would like to have them. She will expect you and I am sure will be delighted to see you. As I have been."

For the first time, he smiled, and his whole face was transfigured. Then he touched a bell and a secretary appeared. "Take this lady to the elevator and have the porter see her to her car when she gets downstairs," he said in Italian, which I was beginning to understand a little. Then, in French with that wonderful smile, *"Au revoir, madame."*

When I rejoined Copley Amory and told him what had taken place, I could see he was extremely doubtful that I would really be permitted to visit Signora Mussolini; he was convinced that the Premier had merely chosen the most graceful way to conclude our conversation. But I felt confident that if the Premier had not been willing for me to do so, he would have told me so, as he had told others; I did not think he would break his word after having given it to me. So I hardly needed the message which reached me two days later, through the astonished Embassy, that Signora Mussolini was expecting me. I was told that I should start for Milan at once, without telling anyone where I was going or why, and I caught the first possible train. A member of the Consular staff was at the station to meet me, having been instructed to accompany me on my visit, which he was obviously doing with some bewilderment and, if I am not mistaken, even more reluctance. He was convinced that there would be some last-minute difficulty.

At first it looked as if he were right. I had expected, I do not know why, a suburban cottage. But I was conducted instead to an unpretentious apartment house in the center of the city, and there met my first obstacle in the person of the *concierge*. It was apparent that, though the Premier had doubtless telephoned his wife, nobody had telephoned the *concierge*. With perfect composure and great volubility we were assured that *Madame la Présidente* was out of the city, that there was no prospect of her return, that she was, alas, extremely ill, and so forth. Official credentials of the most complete and satisfactory order were immediately produced. It was some time before the *concierge* could even be persuaded to look at them. But at last he remembered that he *had* been notified such a visit was to take place. He admitted that *Madame la Présidente* was at home and in good health, and motioned us up the stairs. There were four flights of them and no elevator, but we finally reached the top and confronted a door bearing a white porcelain plate on which was lettered in blue the name BENITO MUSSOLINI. And once inside that door, the welcome we received from Benito Mussolini's wife was cordial and instantaneous.

There was no woman in the world just then about whom there had been more unsatisfied speculation than this one, none of whom more inaccurate statements had been made, none who had been more assiduously secluded, partly because of her own wishes and partly to ensure her safety. The small simple drawing room into which we were ushered might have passed for the front parlor in a New England farmhouse of the humbler type. There were the crayon bridal portraits and the framed marriage certificate hanging on the wall, the center table with its bunch of flowers, the "best" ornaments of china and bronze, the plush-covered furniture placed primly around. And—as unmistakably as the hostess of such a farmhouse would be—I found my hostess a lady in every sense of the word, with the additional graciousness and ease which only the woman of Latin race is apt to possess when she has not had what we speak of as "advantages"; she was a blonde—and if there is anything prettier than a dark Italian woman, it is a fair one—her soft yellow hair caught in a carved ivory comb, her cheeks pink and dimpled, her smile quick and gay and gentle. She was wearing a brown satin dress, simply but very well made, with a plain gold locket on a chain around her neck.

We sat side by side on the stiff little sofa and began to visit as unceremoniously as it is possible for two women to do. I called her *"Madame la Présidente"* once; after that, I called her "Signora Mussolini." And we talked almost exclusively about her husband—and mine; about her children—and mine; about her intimate interests—and mine. At the end of half an hour, I thought perhaps I ought to go, and said so— though I did not want to, because I was having a good time and thought she was too. Then she surprised me.

"If you really would like to see the children—if you really are disappointed that they are out—will you not come back again at six?" she asked. "They will be home then, and I shall be very glad."

This I shall always think of as the real invitation—the one that came because she hadn't disliked me, hadn't found it hard to talk to me, hadn't minded, after all, being disturbed by this stranger from another world. I went back at six—receiving a smile of welcome from the *concierge* this time—with yellow roses for Signora Mussolini, because they reminded me so much of her, and three boxes of candy—I knew better than to take one, no matter how large, to be divided into three portions by small and eager hands. One was for Edda, who was twelve, one for Vittorio, who was seven, and one for Bruno, who was five.

The eldest was strangely like her father in looks, and the gentle motherliness which seems to characterize all little girls who help bring up their younger brothers contrasted oddly with her appearance of severe brilliance. The boys were light and vivacious, like their mother, and all of them thoroughly delightful. Edda told me that she was beginning to study French at school; we tried it out. Vittorio imparted the glad tidings that in Bologna there were a thousand "little *Fascisti.*" Bruno, at first resentful because Edda had made him wash his hands before greeting me, melted somewhat as a bonbon melted in his mouth. . . . Children are about the same the world over. Again, I found it difficult to tear myself away.

That evening I went to Vespers at the Milan Cathedral, the largest and in many ways the most beautiful Gothic cathedral in the world, and then to a fine performance at La Scala with Toscanini conducting. The next day I was back in Rome, where a report on my experiences in Milan was eagerly awaited and enthusiastically received. "He liked you," the Ambassador remarked. Then Mr. Child suggested that, for safety and speed, I might like to send my article in the diplomatic pouch.

I had gotten my first scoop.

Chapter 25

I LEFT Rome reluctantly, which is chronic, no matter how long I stay there, even when Paris is my destination, as it was that time—but only to catch my breath before hurrying on to London. President Harding had given me a letter of introduction to present to Ambassador Harvey as soon as I reached London, but the Childs thought it would be wiser to mail this from Rome, so that Mr. Harvey would have more time to arrange for my participation in the current London Season.

The White House
WASHINGTON

March 4, 1923.

My dear Mr. Ambassador:

This note will be presented to you by Mrs. Henry W. Keyes, wife of the Senator from New Hampshire. Mrs. Keyes is a very good friend of Mrs. Harding and I am glad to tell you that I hold both the Senator and Mrs. Keyes in very high esteem. I shall be especially pleased, therefore, if you will show such courtesies as are becoming to Mrs. Keyes on the occasion of her London visit. I assume, of course, that she will wish to be presented at Court, and I will be very glad if you can arrange to meet her wishes in this matter.

Very truly yours,
Warren G. Harding

Hon. George Harvey,
Embassy of the United States of America,
London, England.

I found Paris looking its sunniest and loveliest, as it is apt to do in late May, and it seemed wonderfully unchanged in many pleasant ways. But there was one difference that filled me with joy: the mourning wreaths were gone from the statues of the Alsatian cities in the Place de la Concorde—they were French again! However, it had taken a war to make them so, and a reminder of this was in the hundreds of flags, American as well as French, hung out together to mark Memorial Day, and at the tomb of the Unknown Soldier heaped with flowers.

The Romano Avezzanas had engaged a room for me at the Hotel Meurice, where I was provided with every possible luxury but where I spent less time than I did at the Italian Embassy, then located in a marvelous old house on the rue de Varenne, allegedly the first meeting place of Napoleon and Josephine. A large luncheon party had been arranged for me there the day after my arrival and a quiet visit with the family the next, and that was all the days there were, for the following one I was taking the tedious trip to London, with its change from a train to a steamer and then a second change back to a train. It took only seven hours, but it was more exhausting, to me anyway, than a transcontinental crossing in the United States, and in those days there was no alternative. To make a bad matter worse, a bitter wind rendered the Channel very rough, and London itself—huge, gray and overpowering at first sight—was colder than Washington generally is in midwinter.

However, I had neither time nor disposition to be depressed about the weather, since all this haste had been indicated by an impressive-looking envelope with my name written in a bold and dashing hand across it and the words, "Lord Chamberlain," imprinted in the lower lefthand corner. Inside it two cards were clipped together, the smaller one reading:

To be presented, Mrs. Henry W. Keyes

while the larger one was engraved:

The Lord Chamberlain is
commanded by Their Majesties to invite
Mrs. Henry W. Keyes
to a Court at Buckingham Palace
On Wednesday the 13th of June at
9:30 o'clock P. M.
LADIES: *Court Dress with feathers and trains.*
GENTLEMEN: *Full Court Dress.*

Since "commands" like this were issued to only twelve American women at each court, they were not lightly prized or often disregarded, and the fulfilling of them required a good deal more preparation than was necessary for attendance at the White House or, for that matter, at any other court. Any handsome evening gown was permissible, but it must have a court train hanging from the shoulders and lying on the floor exactly eighteen inches. Any hair style would do, but on top of it three small snowy plumes had to wave and, over it, had to float a white tulle veil reaching to the knees. There had to be long—very long—white gloves; there had to be either a bouquet or a fan; there had to be a limousine with a footman as well as a chauffeur. The gathering of all these necessities was no quick or easy task. So, with some trepidation and all possible speed, I began to secure them immediately after the receipt of that "command."

On the Monday before the court, Mrs. Post Wheeler, the wife of our Chargé d'Affaires, acting in the absence of the Ambassadress, Mrs. Harvey, invited the American women who were to be presented to her lovely house on the Chelsea Embankment to receive their final instructions, practice the all-important curtsy and have tea. It was a hilarious occasion, with two of us enthroned as the "King" and "Queen" and five others representing Gentlemen-in-Waiting and the Lord Chamberlain. The remaining "presentees" passed before them in mock solemn procession, keeping far enough apart to avoid each others' imaginary trains and making our bows with as much state as we could muster. After this rehearsal, my sinking heart revived a good deal, for I found the ceremonial was not half so elaborate as I had feared. On the all-important night, I arrayed myself quite happily in a white and silver brocade dress trimmed with silver lace and ropes of pearls, its white chiffon train edged with silver; put on white silk stockings and silver slippers; had my hair done by the court hairdresser; wrapped around me a white brocaded velvet cloak with a pink satin lining and mink collar and cuffs; picked up my long gloves, feathery white fan and set out for Buckingham Palace in the broad daylight which prevails at seven-thirty in the evening during an English June.

Early as I was, there were dozens of cars in line ahead of me, and the wait before the palace doors opened was much the hardest part of the entire experience. For the British public walked slowly up and down on either side of the halted cars, pausing leisurely beside each, even thrusting heads in open windows and making such comments as it felt the occupants deserved. There was no disorder, and for the most part, this was merely a display of friendly interest and kindly curiosity, sanctioned by long custom. But there was an occasional caustic remark or coarse jest, and even apart from these, I did not find it a pleasant sensation to sit, helplessly and alone, between two rows of meandering strangers who regarded my predicament as their lawful—and free!—means of amusement. So I was thankful when the mounted police appeared and signalled for the cars to move. After that, it was not so bad.

At last came the stop at the outer gate; the inspection of the invitation; the entrance to the gray inner courtyard; the doorway, blazing with light and wide open; the dressing rooms with the friendly attendants—"The train over the *left* arm, if you please, madam; there now, you have it exactly right—quite lovely, I'm sure. Can I do anything else to help you? Thank you, madam." And then I approached the wide carpeted staircase with the guards in scarlet and gold on either side, and beheld misty veils and snowy feathers and fragrant flowers, the sparkling jewels and lovely gowns of the women, the black velvet knee breeches and quaintly buttoned coats and lace ruffles, or the magnificent uniforms of the men. Nothing I saw seemed to me more beautiful than that thronged staircase, nothing was more "courtly" in every sense of the word.

In Victorian days, the "commanded" ladies had to stand, sometimes for hours, crowded together until their turn for presentation came. But in my era seats were provided, so that the process of waiting was not only perfectly comfortable but decidedly interesting. Promptly at half-past nine, the King, in the uniform of an Admiral of the Fleet, wearing the Orders of the Garter and the Bath, and the Queen, in a beautiful black pailletted dress, with a tiara and other ornaments of pearls and diamonds, and also wearing the Order of the Garter, arrived, and the band played the national anthem. A procession was formed, headed by Their Majesties and preceded by the Lord Chamberlain and other officials carrying their staffs of office and walking backward, and progressed through the state rooms to the throne room; the King and Queen took their places, with Princess Mary, the Marquis and Marchioness of Carisbroke and the Infanta Eulalia of Spain behind them. First came the presentation of diplomats and officials, who then took their places not far from Their Majesties—a throng glittering with beautiful jewels, with gold and silver lace and spangled tulle, with decorations and orders, with medals and brilliant braid. And then the presentation of the general circle began.

The throne room was a large oblong apartment, its walls simply decorated in white and gold, with a few handsome tapestries; tiers of seats covered in crimson brocade were on four sides of an open space in the center; a pipe organ was at the end opposite the crimson-draped thrones. In single file, the ladies to be presented (gentlemen were not presented at courts, but at levees) entered by a door at the right of the organ, and walked slowly past it and out a door at its left, into a corridor which ran the length of the throne room. Then they approached the throne room again by a door at the left of the thrones. Here each candidate paused while two Gentlemen-in-Waiting took her train, which up to now she had carried over her arm, and spread it carefully and at exactly the right angle on the floor behind her. Next she stepped inside and handed the card with the words "Being presented Lady [or Mrs. or Miss] So and So," to the first Gentleman-in-Waiting beyond the door; and he passed it down the line of the four others who stood between her and the thrones until—wonderfully timed—she heard her name called in a loud clear voice exactly at the moment she curtsied before the King. After that, she took three or four steps to the right and curtsied before the Queen; then, still walking to the right but with her head turned to the left, she reached the door at the other side of the thrones, felt, as she walked out of it, her train being gently laid back on her arm —and suddenly realized that the presentation was over!

"And what did it all feel like?" Well, it felt much less complicated and much more enjoyable than I expected! Every detail was so carefully carried out, everyone in attendance was so kind and experienced that it would be a very nervous or socially untrained woman who would run the slightest danger of making a mistake or even feeling anxious that she was not doing the right thing. The British Court was the most beautiful and brilliant in the world and also the most perfect and complete. But it was much more than that. There was an atmosphere of dignity about it which increased its beauty a hundredfold and formed the basis, I believe, for the enjoyment of its guests. In spite of the large number of people—there were eight hundred at that particular court—there was no noise, confusion or haste. There was room for everybody and time for everybody, and everyone seemed to be made genuinely and personally welcome. I shall never forget the sweet and gracious and *cordial* dignity of the bow and smile with which the Queen acknowledged my curtsy. I could not take my eyes from her face—her photographs gave only the slightest idea of its loveliness—in my slow passage out of the room.

Nor shall I cease to remember gratefully the friendliness of the Yeoman of the Guard from whom I inquired the way to the supper room: "The supper rooms downstairs are open now, madam. But it's sometimes a bit hard to get back upstairs once you go down. If you'd wait here, until the King comes out—it won't be long—there'll be one open on this floor too. And you could sit quite easy in that chair and watch the crowd, if you'll excuse me for suggesting it, madam. Thank you, madam."

I took the friendly advice and watched the sumptuous pageantry of the scene until the upstairs supper room opened; then I joined some friends and talked it over while I ate an excellent and very hearty meal, for I had had neither tea nor dinner. And finally, I found that Mrs.

Keyes's footman had been summoned to the palace door, as I went to get my cloak, so there was not an instant's delay in leaving. Almost before I knew it, I was back at my hotel again, taking off my white and silver finery and wishing a little that Harry and boys could see it and tell me they thought it was pretty and becoming; realizing, too, that this was the third time I had prepared, and laid away, a white veil: for my First Communion, for my wedding, and now for Court—all such great though such utterly different events, all landmarks in my life, all approached with a good deal of forethought and some foreboding and all, in the fulfillment, so much more joyous than I had dared to hope.

Presentation at Court was, of course, the "Open Sesame" to everything which, in a social sense, a woman could possibly wish to do; so the next impressive-looking envelope which reached me did not give me quite so much of a surprise. It contained a voucher for a lady's badge to the Royal Enclosure at Ascot.

Though slightly chilled to learn from my English friends that I must wear a "pretty lacy frock—what you'd use for a summer garden party at home, you know," as I'd been comfortable only in wool and fur since reaching London, I gritted my chattering teeth and presented my cherished voucher on the opening day of the races, and in spite of the fact that it was typical of an English June—that is, cold and foggy and drizzling—I wore the requisite gala attire.

Miraculously, I was rewarded, for the sun came out before I reached Ascot. It did not come out the way it does in Italy with a hot triumphant brilliance, but hesitatingly, wanly and faintly warm. However, as this was the first time I had glimpsed it since leaving Paris, I welcomed it enthusiastically and agreed politely that it was a glorious day. And glorious in one sense it certainly was: His Majesty's horse won the third race, and the Aga Khan's won the sixth—by more than ten lengths. As a spectacle, the Ascot races certainly *were* the most glorious sporting event I had ever seen: the fragrant turf, as soft and green as moss; the long rows of coaches and tally-hos; the striped tents of the private clubs where lunch was served (at the Marlborough Club, where I had mine, the stripes were pale green and white, with baskets of geraniums hung along the openings); the festive tea at Torwood, the lovely house near the course which the Post Wheelers took for Ascot Week; the wonderful clothes in the Royal Enclosure—every man in a tall hat and cutaway; every woman in an exquisite creation; the East Indians in vivid turbans or gauzy scarves; the guards in green velvet and gold lace.

But most of all, the "Royal Procession" was glorious. First came three mounted policemen, next two outriders in scarlet livery on white horses; then Their Majesties, with the Prince of Wales and Prince George, riding in the first of the long line of open landaus drawn by four gray horses, the postillions in the Ascot livery of blue coats with scarlet sleeves, white breeches and black jockey caps. Then came another carriage—and another—and still others, curving out of sight near the entrance to the Royal Box, decorated with pink hydrangeas and tall lilies. Something of the gaiety and leisure and splendor of another age seemed to envelop it all and I have always been glad that I was part of it.

Next to going to Court and to Ascot, I wanted most of all to go to the House of Commons, so I was delighted when cards reached me, first for the Members' Gallery, and then for the Speaker's own private gallery. To begin with, I heard a good deal about soldiers' pensions and inadequate housing, all of which sounded so familiar that I might have closed my eyes and almost believed myself in the Senate again.

But next came a distinct contrast: the installation of the new Lady Member, Mrs. Hilton Philipson, more generally known as Mabel Russell, for she had had a very successful stage career before she married, and her own name had stuck. She was a most attractive figure in her simple blue dress with white collar and cuffs, as she entered the chamber at the moment the Speaker began to intone, "Members desiring to take their seats. . . ."—and made the three low deliberate bows which are required at this ceremonial before she signed her name and took her place. There was a great deal more etiquette in the House of Commons than in Congress!

Aside from my visits to Parliament, the presentation at Court and attendance at Ascot, it soon began to seem as if I were doing very much the same sort of things in London that I would have been doing in Washington: going to a succession of luncheons and dinners at charming houses. There I met large numbers of distinguished persons and was entertained cordially and pleasantly, but I began to have a vague feeling that England just then was less important to me, as a writer, than Italy had been and France might well be, and that I should not linger too long in London.

This feeling took definite form one Sunday afternoon when, being committed to nothing special, I decided to visit the tomb of the Unknown Soldier in Westminster Abbey. It was a cold gloomy day, and the great church was dark and chilly and almost empty. This surprised me, for I had supposed there would be Evensong fairly soon and wondered if I would have time to make my pilgrimage before it began. The pilgrimage was never completed, but not for the reason I had foreseen: a verger suddenly appeared before me and sternly told me I must leave the building, as he was on the point of closing the last door.

"But surely you keep the Abbey open for prayer and meditation, even if not for services!" I protested, really aghast.

"Not on Sunday, madam," he said severely. "Never on Sunday!"

I went back to the Hyde Park Hotel in the pouring rain and after some minutes of deep thought took a cable form from the desk and addressed it to Henry, who was already on his way across the Atlantic aboard the *George Washington,* which stopped at Cherbourg before docking at Southampton. I wrote:

PLEASE MEET ME IN PARIS INSTEAD OF LONDON STOP
ACKNOWLEDGE RECEIPT.

Chapter 26

BEFORE my precipitate departure from London, I had received a pleasant letter from Harry's friend, Mr. R. W. Boyden, a member of the Reparations Commission in Paris. He said he would be glad to do anything he could to help me and I had replied that I wanted especially to meet some of the great ladies of France, and that I wanted to see some of the cemeteries. Mr. Boyden answered promptly and approvingly, but he began his letter with the suggestion for an enterprise of which I had not even thought: "You asked me to send you a memorandum of the subjects which occurred to me as possibly worth your while. First, the Ruhr. . . . The actual day to day incidents and the whole thing as a great historical event ought to be most interesting."

From that moment on, I gave the Ruhr a great deal of thought. The friendliness between the United States and France was so self-evident then that it required very little comment, at least from me; but the relations between France and other nations were not so well understood by Americans generally, and I had stressed them twice in the *Good Housekeeping* "Letters"—first during the Arms Conference and later during Clemenceau's visit to Washington. Now it seemed to me they needed stressing again, and I wrote:

> Suppose you had a neighbor, a rich neighbor who had wronged you so greatly that you were going without much you needed and who had been commanded by law to repay you. Suppose you were convinced that he was able to do so, and still he would not. You would "attach his property," wouldn't you? You would not retaliate by trying to injure him as he had injured you, but you would certainly collect that debt if you could—or you would be a spineless and unbusinesslike individual. That was exactly France's intention when she entered Ger-

many's rich coal regions and took them under military control—since there was no other way she could take them. And that is what she is still doing when she sends into France the coal in which Germany agreed to pay her war debt—and failed to do, until forced in this way. . . .

I had no sooner announced my decision than I began to encounter obstacles and opposition. I was told the occupied regions were no place for a woman, that no woman could get there and that even if I did manage to, I would be so wretchedly uncomfortable and so moved by the misery I would see around me, I would be extremely unhappy. That the strained relations between Great Britain and France, in regard to their relations in Germany, were going from bad to worse, and that no one knew what the result would be. That it might be difficult for me to communicate with the outside world if something unpleasant occurred, since telegraph, telephone and postal service were all under military control. That sabotage was becoming more and more frequent—sentinels were being killed at their posts, bombs were exploding in all sorts of places. That the slaughter of ten Belgian soldiers by one of these bombs, in a train, ended any possibility of traveling through the Ruhr by train, even if the train service were not so irregular that it could not be counted on. That it would not be feasible to go from Paris to Cologne by train and try to hire a car there, since practically no automobiles were available and those that were available were naturally German cars driven by German chauffeurs, and an abomination to the French authorities.

Most of these discouraging facts I knew and had already considered, but I listened politely. Everyone had told me I would not be able to see Signora Mussolini and I had had two nice visits with her! While I waited for the necessary laissez-passer and official letter of introduction, Henry arrived, full of enthusiasm for his trip in the *George Washington* and excited over the prospect of his first sightseeing and opera going in Paris, which I enjoyed with him. I went to a magnificent state dinner at the Italian Embassy; I attended several sessions at the French Chamber of Deputies and Senate and heard the Naval Treaty for Disarmament, proposed at the Washington Conference, ratified by a vote of four to one. I went to the dedication of Alan Seeger's statue on the fourth of July—a statue erected entirely by French subscription to honor the American volunteers who entered the French Army before we joined the Allies; and I called on the three great ladies whom I especially wanted to see:

Mme Raymond Poincaré, wife of the former President of France; Mme Alexandre Millerand, wife of the then President; and the Maréchale Foch.

By the time I had done all this, the laissez-passer had arrived, and so

had a favorable reply to a letter our military attaché, Colonel T. Bent-
ley Mott, had written General Degoutte, Commander in Chief of the
French Army of Occupation, at Dusseldorf. Besides these, I had Ambassador Herrick's letter of introduction, which was to prove of inestimable value—especially its postscript, which he added at my instigation.
Translated from the French, the letter read:

Paris, July 7, 1923.

I am happy to certify by this letter that Mrs. Henry Wilder Keyes,
my very distinguished compatriot and a writer of note, wife of the eminent statesman, Mr. Henry Wilder Keyes, Senator from the State of
New Hampshire and intimate friend of President Harding, is at present
traveling in Europe, in order to authenticate a series of articles which
she is proposing to write for important publications in the United
States.

I shall be personally most appreciative of the favorable reception
which military and customs authorities may be good enough to give
Mrs. Keyes and for all the facility which they may kindly accord her
while complying with formalities in the course of her trip.

Myron T. Herrick
Ambassador of the United States of America
in Paris.

P.S. Mrs. Keyes will be accompanied by her son, Mr. Keyes.

Armed with these credentials, Henry and I started out early one July
morning in a French car, with a French chauffeur named Codifero, on
our journey to the Ruhr. My aversion to the necessity of passing
through the devastated regions vanished like the mist which the hot sun
cleared. Codifero, who had been a *poilu* all through the war, earnestly
desired us to behold his country—not only its physical aspects, but its
spirit as well—through his eyes.

We stopped in the Paris suburbs while he told us how the city's taxi-
cabs were commandeered to bring out the troops to defend it, because
there was not time for them to march, and how the invaders, practically
within sight of their coveted prize, were driven back. He insisted, as we
passed field after field of rich crops, stained scarlet with poppies, on
stopping at every American monument that had been erected, on our
drinking at the fountain built in Quentin Roosevelt's memory at Cham-
ery, on our walking down the long lines of white crosses, fifteen thousand of them, which marked the resting places of American boys at
Romagne. The desolation of the shattered villages faded in the friendliness with which we were everywhere received—children waved as we
passed, women ran to bring us water—and at the sound and sight of
building everywhere, building which, I discovered at the cost of brief

nights of sleep, began at four in the morning and did not stop before ten at night. We lunched at Château-Thierry and reached Rheims just as the sun was going down behind the broken spires and empty window frames of the cathedral; dined like princes in the tiny garden of the hotel where we spent the night. After another early start, we lunched at the Hostelry of the Argonne, circled Verdun and crossed the frontier into the independent Duchy of Luxembourg just as the customs were closing, at eight in the evening.

The next morning on reaching the frontier of the German territory under French control, at Trèves, we encountered our first opposition. There was some flaw in our *triptyque*—the customs pass for the temporary importation of our car—though I had been assured, before leaving Paris, that it was completely in order. The unhappy Codifero remained in the customshouse for an hour, vainly beseeching the officials to let us through, before he came out and told us what the matter was. My temper was not at its best after sitting all that time in the broiling sun in close proximity to the belligerent Zouaves on guard; but I have discovered there is nothing more effective and disarming, when everything is going all wrong, than to pretend it is going all right. I descended with my special passport, my laissez-passer, Ambassador's Herrick's letter and a pleasant smile, and entered on the scene with a good deal more apparent composure than I actually felt. A few minutes later, we were on our way again. After that, at every village we entered, at every bridge we crossed, we were stopped by a sentinel, sometimes a Zouave, sometimes a native French soldier. Every so often they read my letter straight through, occasionally they merely glanced at the envelope which held it; but in the end it was always handed back to me with a smile and a gesture to go forward. Near the university city of Bonn, where I saw more French soldiers than anywhere else, a doubtful, *"C'est pour une personne seulement"*—"This is for only one person"—was followed by an expression of relief when the postscript, which I had suggested at the last minute, was reached—*"Madame Keyes sera accompagnée par son fils"*—"Mrs. Keyes will be accompanied by her son." We entered Cologne without mishap as the Angelus was ringing.

Meanwhile, quite aside from my numerous interviews with sentinels, I had passed a very interesting and instructive day. The difference in attitude of the inhabitants was the first thing that struck me. We had left the land of friendly smiles behind us. Such route directions as we requested were grudgingly and chillingly given. In one of the mountain villages, three men suddenly appeared in front of the car, and one of them—about six feet four and proportionately broad—demanded a ride to Coblenz. I quickly decided it would be wise to grant his request. For three hours he sat on the front seat beside the shrinking Codifero and I shall never forget the delighted expression with which the little chauffeur, after we had deposited our unwelcome passenger (who, to do him justice, offered to pay for his ride and seemed genuinely grateful when I declined) rose and saluted the French flag flying over the ancient citadel.

At Wittlich, where we stopped for lunch, we were very well fed at the small inn. That was business. But we ate in an atmosphere of silence that fairly bristled with antagonism. I made no effort either to speak French or to pay for our meal in French money. Codifero unfortunately did both, and was obliged to come to me for rescue. I was thankful for my slight command of the German language, rusty after nearly twenty years of disuse, but still comprehensible, and my suitcase full of German marks, which I had procured with some difficulty before leaving Paris. (This is not a misprint. The mark's devaluation increased so rapidly that thousands were necessary to meet routine expenses, and because of the paper currency's bulk, it had to be secured daily from the banks.) Without them we certainly would have gone hungry, yet French money was at a premium, and French and English so familiar in Germany that I did not, for one minute, believe we were not understood. The German patrons passed us, as they left the dining room, without the salutation of *"Gemahlzeit,"* which is their custom at the end of a meal. Only one young man in a far corner, who had been completely aware of the situation—a young man of unmistakable breeding and military bearing, though he was not in uniform, which was forbidden all German officers in occupied territory—returned my bow, when Henry and I went out, with perfect courtesy and a charm of expression and manner which I have not forgotten, because this was the only such gesture I received from a German during our entire stay.

Another thing which interested me was the general appearance of the countryside. On a question of military tactics, I could easily make a mistake; but no woman who has lived for years on a farm can fail to recognize good crops or adequate farm equipment. The crops were magnificent, and the splendid machinery much more abundant, expensive and in better condition than it usually is in New England. In like measure, no woman who has brought up children and interested herself in child welfare can fail to recognize malnutrition. The robust youngsters swarming everywhere showed very plainly that neither they nor their mothers had gone hungry during or since the war.

We reached Dusseldorf about eleven in the morning and went at once to General Degoutte's headquarters at the Stahlhof, its unmistakably German architecture swathed in French flags, its sentry boxes striped like candy in red, white and blue. A letter and telegram had already announced my imminent arrival, and almost immediately, I was shown into the presence of the kindly and capable man who had commanded our troops at Belleau Wood and who was so respected, admired and trusted by America. Almost immediately also, as I had somehow felt sure they would, the difficulties which I had been told would beset my path vanished.

Yes, it was true they did not encourage ladies to come into the Ruhr just then, but they were glad to make an exception in my case, especially as I was accompanied by my son. (How right Charlie Colby had been! I never would have been allowed to make this trip without Henry.) Of course, the car could have a permit to "circulate" wherever I chose to go, with a French officer to escort me as often as I wished— but I was entirely at liberty to make such investigations and ask such questions of the native population as I desired, absolutely unhampered; there was nothing to conceal. And in what conditions did I have the greatest interest—child welfare, food supplies, economic affairs? Naturally! But the military questions would also be explained. Yes, the French authorities had taken over the hotels, but they were really very good, the servants and managers in them entirely *"convenable."* The General ventured to hope that, with the orders he would issue to have us put up, we would be comfortable. He was, unfortunately, about to leave for Mayence, but before he went he would like to present to me the officers of his staff, especially the one who would act as my escort; and then, when I had lunched and unpacked, I would like to go— where? I had only to say! Certainly. . . .

No one could have asked for a pleasanter escort than Major Maurice Tencé; and to say that I was made comfortable at the hotel is putting the case mildly. I found myself in possession of by far the largest and most luxurious room and bathroom I had had all summer, and Henry was equally well quartered. I descended to the dining room, expecting to lunch sparingly and simply. After five courses, including such items as fresh butter and milk, white bread, fresh vegetables, salad, fruit and ice cream (supposedly nonexistent in the region), I was almost too well fortified to go out and begin my investigations.

That I began them with a suspicion that the reports of hardships endured by the native population had been exaggerated is not surprising, and this suspicion did not diminish, but increased. I did not make my trip either hastily or superficially. I went to Essen, Kettwig, Werden, Bredeney, Gelsenkirchen, Wanne, Herne, Dortmund, Syburg, Witten, Hattingen, Mettmann, Duisberg and Krefeld. I stayed as long as I liked and saw whatever I liked in each of these cities and in the intervening country. I saw the mines and the soup kitchens, the Krupp mansion and the workmen's quarters. I went by boat around the fine harbor of Duisberg, into the Herne canal and into the Rhine and saw throngs of long low boats bearing rich freight. Everywhere I found the same lush, beautiful countryside with its splendid harvests, its handsome estates and comfortable stone farmhouses—with many others in the process of construction. Everywhere I found the same great dusky, powerful cities; the Ruhr region was only about forty-five miles wide and twenty-five miles long, but it contained four cities with a population of over 250,000— Essen had 500,000—and ten with over 100,000, with foundries and factories, manufactures and mines. Coke and coal were not the only products of the Ruhr; the great Krupp works, the finest of their kind in the world, were there; steel plants, woolen, cotton and silk mills were plentiful; the velvets of Krefeld were famous; there were immense chemical dye houses; toys, musical instruments, aluminum utensils and tanned leather were all manufactured.

I can say with truthfulness that I never saw so much wealth and prosperity crowded into one small area in my life. The streets were lined with shops—jewelry shops, clothing shops, candy shops, fancy bakeries —all doing a flourishing business. The native restaurants were so crowded that it was necessary to engage tables long in advance; and in those restaurants the Germans sat for hours on end and ate their enormous meals and drank their enormous mugs of beer—men, women and children alike. The drastic devaluation of the mark had apparently made little difference in the amount of money people were willing and able to spend. Workmen emerged at closing hours in white shirts and wellcut suits; working girls in silks; all wore excellent shoes. Never, in factory or mining towns at home—and I had been in many—had I seen such good clothes. I looked in vain—and carefully—to find a child who was either ragged or thin, and I had never seen so many children in so brief a time in my life. I think it is safe to assume that whatever other propaganda flourished in Germany, that of birth control had not!

It was possible that there were some conditions I couldn't see, some situations I couldn't, with my rusty German, understand. But since it *was* possible, I was especially glad of a long talk I had with four American women and one Englishwoman, whom I found established at Essen, where they had a canteen—the only time I saw any compatriots during the entire trip, the only time I heard English spoken. They had gone there with completely neutral sentiments, they had been there for some time, they had seen nothing with the help or under the direction of French officers, and they were perhaps better fitted by previous training than I was to make careful observations. In turn, and without a dissenting voice, they told me the same story: that day after day they had difficulty in getting seats at the crowded restaurants, that all around them people were eating four times as much as they could manage comfortably. That they had never seen opera so magnificently or so extravagantly given, with changes of bill every evening and changes of scene every few minutes, before audiences attired in full evening dress and blazing with jewels, who packed the opera houses to the doors. They referred to the frequently made comment that the lavish expenditures being made in Berlin were all those of foreigners—but since there were no foreigners resident in the Ruhr or even passing through it, except in the rarest cases, it was undoubtedly native Germans who were spending all the money there. They said that they had offered a prize to the one among them who would be able to find, and point out to the others, a single undernourished child, or even a little girl without a bright hair ribbon—and no one had won it. One of these women I had already known personally in Washington; all of them I knew by reputation. Their word and their evidence were to me indisputable.

It chanced that the French national holiday—the fourteenth of July —fell in the course of my visit, and on that day, accompanied by the charming Major Tencé, who had seen the destruction of Rheims Cathedral and had lost one of his children through malnutrition, Henry and I drove to Herne to have lunch with General Caron, who commanded several of the divisions in the Ruhr. At his headquarters, we found not only the General, but ten other high-ranking officers drawn up to receive us. They had planned a little celebration in honor of the day before they knew that *"une dame américaine"* was coming there, so they had gone on with their preparations "venturing to hope" that she would act as hostess for them! A little dazed at this unexpected compliment, I took my place at the head of the flower-decked table. And almost instantly my slight discomfiture at discovering myself in the presence of this handsomely uniformed and bemedaled group—not one of whom spoke a word of English!—disappeared before the sincerity and cordiality of its welcome. Only one woman had visited them before—and no American! Never in my life have I tried harder to live up to what was expected of me. And when, at the end of the delicious meal, accompanied by champagne served in pitchers, the General rose to propose a toast to "a day dear to all French hearts and made doubly happy for those gathered together in a foreign country by the presence of a representative from the United States," I managed to rise and say how much it had meant to such a representative to be privileged to be with them. And I thanked heaven—for the thousandth time that summer— that I could speak French!

By then, everything was on a very friendly footing indeed, and the General suggested that we go to the celebration which General d'Anselme, the Commander of one of the occupying divisions, was holding that afternoon beside the colossal statue of Kaiser Wilhelm on the summit of Hohensyburg. We could go in his car and Henry could follow in ours; a message to expect us could be telephoned ahead. The rapidity and completeness with which the arrangements were made was overwhelming. At the exact moment when we reached the top of the mountain commanding a glorious view of the entire valley, General d'Anselme and his staff drew up to receive us. Simultaneously, a blue-clad military band burst out with the *Marseillaise,* which echoed and re-echoed across those German hills. As usual, when very much moved, I wanted to cry and probably did a little.

I would have cried much harder had I known the musicians' camp would be the target of hand grenades that night, because they ventured to play their national anthem beside the statue of a German Emperor, and that some of them would never play it again. . . .

After the ceremonies, we had tea, with me at the head of a military table again, one general at my right and the other at my left, the chaplain at the foot and the two staffs and a beaming Henry somewhere in between. At last, and very reluctantly, we found it was time to go down the mountain and start back to town. At the foot of Hohensyburg was a stand where souvenirs were sold and my newfound friends laughingly insisted on presenting me with some of them—postcards, a paperweight, a scene painted on wood. But, when we said good-bye, General Caron gave me the *real* souvenir of the day—the most wonderful souvenir ever given me yet, perhaps the most wonderful I would ever have.

"You have shown your love for the flag of France, madame—would you care to have the standard which I carry on my car? I have used it for a long time and it has been decorated with the *Croix de Guerre.* If you will permit me, I would like to give you our *Croix de Guerre. . . .*"

Of course I was barraged with questions about the Ruhr during the rest of the summer in Europe and after I reached home. I answered these frankly and freely, and since I have not changed my mind about any of them during the intervening years and they still shed light on Franco-German relations, past and present, I think it is perhaps in order to repeat both questions and answers here.

"Did you think that the attitude of the native population was hostile

to the French?" It seemed so at first. But I thought most of the outrages
—that they were being committed was indisputable—had been perpe-
trated by outsiders, hired by directors of organized crime. The children
played with the French soldiers; the men and women in the shops and
streets behaved civilly enough. There was though an atmosphere of con-
straint, of a sharp line of demarcation between two nationalities in some
cases, of smothered or open resentment.

"Did you think the French were insolent?" Not in the least. In the
Ruhr itself, I did not see a single French officer or enlisted man who
was not polite. The complete sympathy and understanding, the lack of
harsh and perfunctory military discipline existing between officers and
their subordinates were extremely significant and pleasant. This relationship differed so greatly from that between German officers and
those under their command that it was often wrongly interpreted by the
latter as a lack of systemization.

"Did you think France did right to enter the Ruhr?" Decidedly, yes.
I have no more respect for a nation which does not insist upon its rights
than I have for an individual who behaves in a flabby fashion.

"Did you think that Germany could pay her indemnity?" Still more
decidedly, yes. If that one small district practically shut off from communication with the outside world—without train, postal or telegraph
service and with practically no automobiles, for they had been used for
sabotage and permits to "circulate" were consequently difficult to obtain
—was rich enough in its own resources to maintain itself in such luxury, what must the resources of the entire nation have been? Besides—
and we are apt to forget this—not one foot of German territory had
been occupied during the war, not a single building destroyed, no
women and children killed.

Chapter 27

B<small>Y THE</small> time I announced my intention of going to Spain in August, I was immune to discouraging advice, considering what had happened in Milan and in the Ruhr. So I listened unmoved when everyone tried to dissuade me from going there in that month on the varied grounds that the climate would be unbearable, that there would be nothing to do and no one to see, that the rules of Spanish etiquette were so strict and severe I would never be able to understand or observe them and, besides, that it took weeks to secure any kind of audience. I had begun to learn that nearly all the important things a foreign correspondent wants and needs to do are apt to be pronounced impossible, dangerous or forbidden. I therefore mailed the letter to King Alfonso's Private Secretary that Juan Riano had given me before I left Washington, stopped declaring my intentions and, accompanied by Henry, took a night train from Paris to Madrid, thus putting an end to objections.

We had hardly crossed the frontier from garden-like France when I began to realize the tremendous difference between the two countries. Dawn was just breaking as I raised the shade and looked out of the window; but the sunlight, though it only tinged the sky, already had warmth and brilliance in it; and I began to visualize something of the strength and solitude, something of the imperishable dignity and rugged beauty of Spain. Bright sand and tawny rocks stretched out in an apparently limitless expanse. Then, in the midst of this immensity, rose a monstrous building, seemingly from nowhere. This was the Escorial, that strange aloof structure, created by a strange aloof man, Philip II, who made good his claim that he could rule the world on two inches of paper and who, in creating his palace and his tomb, captured and consecrated the spirit of Spain.

Within another hour, we had reached Madrid, a capital as fascinating as Paris and as unlike it as Castile is unlike Provence. The lovely women in the streets were nearly all black clad; they carried fans and wore mantillas, instead of hats. The tiny tramcars had fringed curtains at their windows; oxen with crudely constructed but brightly painted yokes drew their heavy loads through the main streets, their drivers walking in a leisurely way beside them. But there were no such contrasts at our hotel; it was the last word in modern elegance, and its spacious shaded garden was just across the street from the Prado.

We had found French Codifero so satisfactory as a chauffeur that we decided to seek a Spanish counterpart and discovered him in Leopoldo —a swarthy, courteous and completely efficient *madrileño*, with a passion for speed and a genius for exploration. He spoke no English and only a little broken French, and at the time I knew very little Spanish, and Henry none at all; but from the beginning we understood each other perfectly. Whether it was a matter of a prime minister or a shopkeeper, a cathedral or a calling list, Leopoldo knew exactly what to do and saw to it that we did it.

The first place he took me, within twenty-four hours after my arrival in Madrid, was to call on the Secretary of State, Señor Don Santiago Alba, who with wonderful promptness had sent me a message that he would be glad to receive me at once. I walked up the broad staircase of the Foreign Office, pausing to admire the splendid and touching picture of Queen Mother María Cristina presenting to his subjects the young King Alfonso XIII, for whom she had acted as a wise and devoted regent since his birth six months after his father's death. The waiting rooms of eminent personages had begun to have quite a fascination for me after the summer's varied experience and I was almost sorry that my stay in this one at the top of the stairs was so brief, for not only was it very beautiful, but I was intensely interested in two others sitting there: a friar with an austere spiritual face, and a comfortable bourgeois who must have weighed at least three hundred and fifty pounds and who was refreshing himself with a tiny tasseled fan about six inches long. But a polite assistant came almost immediately to tell me the Secretary was waiting and in the kindness of his welcome, I could see that any fears about the success of my visit to Spain were groundless.

"Of course, you have come at a bad time," he said, "no one is in Madrid just now—except the Ministry and a few others who have to work. But you will find us all more than glad to do everything we can to make your visit pleasant. However, before we begin to arrange a schedule, I must offer you my heartfelt condolences on the great loss you have sustained in the death of your President."

I stared at him in stupefaction. I had not seen a newspaper since the day before I left Paris, for I had not then formed the habit, now an invariable one, of reading at least one daily paper in the language of whatever country I happened to be visiting; and of course this was before the days of trans-Atlantic airmail. When I had last heard of President Harding, he had been making whistle-stops across the United States and pleasantly acceding to every request made of him, even to the point of riding on mowing machines, if that was what his local hosts wanted him to do, in order to show his interest in their way of life. It had occurred to me that he must be overtaxing his strength, but as he laughingly said of himself—and later, alas! as it was to be said in criticism and not in praise of him—he had never learned to say no. I was thunderstruck, as well as grief-stricken, by the Minister's announcement, and it took me a few minutes to recover. He recognized this and refrained from hurrying me; then he outlined a program for me.

The following week I received a telephone message from him saying the King had returned from Santander for a council meeting and would grant me an audience if I would present myself to his Private Secretary, the Duke of Miranda, at noon.

With much less red tape than surrounded a visit to the White House, I was admitted to the palace and ushered into a small room which contained a desk, a few chairs, a collection of silver cups—apparently polo trophies—and two extremely clever caricatures of His Majesty. As I sat there, all my dread of Spanish Court etiquette melted away. It was not the apartment of a man who took himself, or who was taken, too seriously, whatever his rank. I had hardly reached this comforting conclusion when a tall slim gentleman with a delightful smile entered and introduced himself as the Duke of Miranda.

"I am very glad indeed to meet you," he told me. "Our Ambassador to the United States has cabled us about you, our Ambassador to France has telegraphed about you, our Secretary of State has spoken to us about you and we have received various other communications. It appears that you are interested in Spain and we are very glad. . . . His Majesty works hard—all the time, practically; this morning he has already seen the Secretaries of the Navy and the Interior, as well as several others, in regard to important measures—"

"Then by now you feel he might be almost glad to see a lady?" The Duke had been so friendly I could not resist replying in kind.

"Exactly, Madame. I think that, when you have seen the King, matters will arrange themselves. . . . It is too bad you have had this dull week in Madrid."

I tried to tell him that though it had been saddened by the news of

President Harding's death, it had not been dull by any means. My son and I had spent several mornings at the Prado and then gone back to the Ritz for lunch in the garden—a delightful combination of the best in art and an introduction to delicious drinks and dishes, hitherto unfamiliar to us: *sangría, gazpacho* and *paella.* We had eaten so much lunch every day that we had been practically comatose for a while afterward; then we had gone for a drive in the Retiro. Besides, we had not stayed all the time in Madrid—we had spent a day at the Escorial and a day and a night in Toledo, and had thoroughly seen and greatly enjoyed both. Though I had been unfamiliar with his art before, I felt I would now recognize an El Greco at sight. And I had really met a good many delightful people, among them the Marqués de la Vega Inclan, who had arranged to have me see the Duke of Alba's Liria Palace and had given me a beautiful set of illustrated books, each featuring a different Spanish city; he had also told me of his plan for converting old palaces in out-of-the-way places into guest houses, so that tourists would be assured of clean, comfortable and attractive accommodations wherever they went. (This was the movement that started the conversion of old palaces into so-called *paradores* and also the building of simpler, modern *albergues,* both of which have completely transformed travel in Spain.)

"I am glad you enjoyed meeting the Marqués and thought well of his plan. But it is too bad you should have seen the Liria Palace when it is closed for the summer and all the beautiful furniture shrouded in white covers—really quite tomblike. I still feel you must have found Madrid rather depressing; but you will soon go, of course, to Santander and will find it very pleasant there. Meanwhile—"

He was still outlining all the enjoyable things he would arrange for me to do when a liveried page appeared and bowed. "That means the King is at liberty," the Duke said, rising. "Just here, across the hall."

He waited for me to precede him through the door and disappeared after a murmured word of presentation to another tall, slim young man, also with a delightful smile, who shook my hand, said he was glad to see me and asked me to sit down.

If I had not sat with his portrait smiling down on me at the Spanish Embassy in Washington many times, I never would have been able to convince myself that he really *was* the King, that it was possible to transform a royal audience into such an informal and stimulating conversation. The gentleman with whom I was talking was fascinating, not because he was a king, but because he was very much a man. Of his charm I had heard a great deal and for a long time, but I was entirely unprepared for the quality of it. It was not only the charm which comes from the highest possible quality of savoir-faire; it was also the charm which comes from an exceptionally fine-fibered personality and the glowing health associated with open air and clean sport, the charm of clear eyes and skin and physical and spiritual no less than mental grace. And back of the grace there was force—force that was quiet, even casual, but nonetheless force—and a rare degree of magnetism. Meanwhile, as the pleasant cultured voice went on, I was so completely at ease that I felt as if I were talking with an old friend and was not surprised when he echoed my thought.

"We talk like old friends. Your home is New Hampshire? That is one of the New England states, isn't it? But now you live in Washington practically all the time? Tell me a little about it, what a senator's wife is expected to do. . . ."

"Your son is a student at Harvard? And your husband and your father and brother went there, too? I have many friends—members of the Marblehead Yacht Club—who went there. Perhaps you know Mr. Charles Francis Adams?"

"I do, indeed. He is one of my husband's best friends."

"Where else have you been this summer? Italy—England—France— tell me about it. Do you smoke? Do you mind if I do? . . . What are you planning to do next in Spain? Why don't you come to Santander?"

"To pay my respects to Her Majesty?"

"Certainly, whenever you like. Can you get there early next week? I shall be back by then."

I told him the Marqués de la Vega Inclan had given me a letter of introduction to Doña Margot Bertran de Lis, one of the ladies in waiting to the Infanta Isabel, who was at her country palace of La Granja, and that I was waiting for a reply to a request for an audience before making any plans.

"But there is no earthly reason for you to wait around for that. The Duke of Miranda will telephone my aunt and let you know at once. She would probably be delighted to have you for lunch or tea tomorrow. Then you can get started for Santander without delay. . . . It has been so nice to have this talk with you. . . ."

I had been there, I realized, for a solid hour, and having already had some sad experiences with Spanish telephones—which are not one of that country's best features—I hesitated to wait for the call to come through; but as the door opened to admit the Duke of Miranda, another gentleman was revealed in the hall, and the King motioned for me to sit down again and spoke to the new arrival.

"Come in, Jimmie, and meet an American lady I am sure you will like. Mrs. Keyes, may I present the Duke of Alba? He and I are going to have a drink before luncheon. We hope you will join us."

Next to the King himself, the Duke of Alba was unquestionably the most outstanding, attractive and dynamic figure in Spain, and in some ways he was unquestionably more remarkable. I could hardly believe the good fortune which had enabled me to meet him in an atmosphere so completely cordial and unconstrained. Very rarely has a man of exalted lineage *himself* proved gifted and great in so many ways as Jacobo María del Pilar Carlos Manuel, Fitz James Stuart y Falco, seventeenth Duke of Alba and also tenth Duke of Berwick. He began his public career as a Member of the *Cortes,* the Spanish Parliament, and this was his official position when I met him that day at the palace in Madrid. By the time I met him at the Marlborough Club in London some years later, he had filled almost every important position his country could give him, including that of Foreign Minister and of Ambassador to Great Britain. But his talents were by no means confined to statesmanship; he was one of the foremost historians of his day, and his command of history took both executive and literary forms; he was the Director of the Royal Academy of History and the author of at least a dozen books of historical importance. He was equally well informed about art and architecture and equally active in organizations connected with them; and all these talents and graces were so internationally recognized that he had the most outstanding decorations of ten foreign countries. Quite incidentally, he was, like the King, a thorough-going sportsman and a crack polo player, which meant that both were eagerly heading for Santander where the next matches were to take place.

All of this, of course, I did not gather over one cocktail. Much of it I already knew, for the fame of such a glamorous figure, a hereditary duke in England as well as Spain, was naturally the frequent subject of conversation in the Court circles of London, where I had so recently been; and some of it I have learned since, as one achievement after another has come to my notice. But this much I did realize during that brief encounter in the palace: I recognized the man who would some day be the prototype of the hero in a novel I should write about Spain.

My sense of genuine welcome continued and the Duke expressed regret that he had not known I was in Madrid and would like to see his palace; he would have been delighted to take me there himself, and the Duchess would have been delighted to receive me; but I would see them both in Santander. I assured him, quite sincerely, that I had enjoyed and admired the palace, despite the covered furniture and that anyway the palace did not matter so much now that I had had the greater pleasure of meeting its owner and was looking forward to meeting the Duchess. Meanwhile—wonder of wonders!—the telephone call had come through, and I realized it was high time I said good-bye. I went out to the sunny courtyard, where I found Leopoldo slumbering, as usual.

"We are going to La Granja," I said, shaking him into consciousness. "To see the Infanta Isabel. Tomorrow, at half-past three."

"*Sí, Señora*. It is a pretty drive over the mountains. We can do it in two hours."

"Three," I said firmly.

"*Sí, Señora*. I will be ready."

Accordingly, the next day, Leopoldo and I, accompanied by Henry and a friend of his who had turned up in Madrid, set out over those tawny, rugged mountains I had so quickly learned to love. We lunched at Segovia, with its encircling Roman aqueduct, its mellow-hued cathedral and its turrets towering to the sky—what a treasure house of beauty even the smallest Spanish city can be!—and then drove to the famous old palace where the King's aunt, the Infanta Isabel, spent her summers. I had meant to ask if the boys could not see that portion of La Granja which is sometimes open to the public while I had my audience, which I supposed would last about half an hour. But the golden-haired Doña Margot Bertran de Lis was at the threshold to welcome me and refused to hear of such a plan, as she cordially shook hands with us all.

"Of course the Infanta will wish to receive them too. And then you are all to see the palace, every bit of it, and afterward go for a drive through the gardens, and then we will have tea."

The stately white-haired Infanta, then over seventy years old, was equally insistent and cordial, and two embarrassed young men were catapulted, so to speak, into the presence of royalty without further ado.

The Infanta took us first into her own bedroom and sitting room, unpretentious, homelike apartments, gay with pretty chintzes and with family photographs and books much in evidence; next we were conducted through the palace and chapel. Then a high carriage, drawn by four bay horses, with two seats facing each other in back and a short raised one in front, drew up at the front door, and a plump coachman, clad in a tall polished hat with a red cockade on the side and a blue uniform that had red trimming and gold buttons stamped with a crown, descended with breathless dignity from his perch. The Infanta motioned the lady-in-waiting, the two boys and myself to the back seats and then pulled on a pair of stout brown gloves and took the driver's seat herself —the coachman taking the place to her left! With infinite skill and dash, she drove those four horses through the magnificent park and gardens, covering hundreds of acres and containing the most exquisite fountains I had ever seen, turning from her high seat to chat with us as casually and pleasantly as if she were sitting in an easy chair at home. Afterward tea was served, with white and gold china and gold spoons. With it, some crystal vases with finely etched scenes of La Granja were brought in for me to choose among, "as a souvenir of the afternoon," and to the vase was added an autographed picture. Finally, when we were ready to start back to Madrid, we had our last glimpse of the Infanta, waving to us from an upper window and urging us to "come again."

Unfortunately, few days in the course of a lifetime can be absolutely perfect—some wise man claimed that no one was entitled to more than fourteen—and I had waked that morning with a bad sore throat. Naturally, I was determined not to let this interfere with my outing that day, but by the time we got back to Madrid I was really ill, and the next morning it was evident the throat was septic. My first experience with a Spanish doctor was not a happy one, as almost the only advice he had to offer was that I should not sleep with the window open! And this was August, with the temperature in the nineties!

The next few days were pretty wretched, but the first of the following week I managed to drag myself out of bed, into my clothes and then into the car with Leopoldo at the wheel. Before night, Henry and I were installed in another luxurious hotel, this time at Santander, where I found awaiting us a card for a box at the polo matches, good for a week, and a message saying the Queen would receive me on Thursday.

Santander on the Bay of Biscay was not a town where one went sightseeing in the usual sense of the word, as it had no historic monuments; nor was it a fashionable watering place like San Sebastián, where the Diplomatic Corps and many of Spain's most prominent officials automatically go every year for the month of August. In fact, it was hardly recognized as a seaside resort until Alfonso XIII decided that its climate, its beach and its very lack of ostentation made it just the spot for him and the Queen and their young family to spend their vacations and built a modern, unpretentious palace there, instead of going to the ancient and magnificent one at Aranjuez, as his forefathers —less sportsminded—had done. Actually, though the fine public beach was thronged, very few Spaniards went swimming in those days and Henry was often hard put to find someone to go with him. I was still feeling under the weather after my illness, so I was glad to have a quiet week and, for once, enough time to write without a sense of pressure;

and I feel I cannot interpret the experience better than by quoting from a letter, just as I wrote it then and there:

> Imagine, for a background, a bay of ultramarine, with a gray cruiser, flying a red and yellow flag, anchored in the middle of it and dozens of sailboats plying back and forth, separated from an ultramarine sky by a range of ultramarine mountains, shading to emerald and dotted with scarlet-roofed white houses. In the foreground is a polo field of vivid green, its stables partly covered with glossy ivy and with mounds of yellow iris in front of them; at its left, a white marble hotel de luxe. . . .
>
> The King in white shirt and breeches and riding a piebald pony is playing a swift and skillful game; struck on the cheek by a misdirected ball with such force that I expect to see him reel off his horse, he simply jams his helmet securely into position and gallops away swinging his mallet. Twice he rides up to the Royal Box, which is nothing more elaborate than a row of wicker chairs under a big umbrella, to talk for a moment with his beautiful Queen. His two small daughters, as lovely as their mother, are dressed alike in white silk dresses and big straw hats trimmed with yellow daisies, and are comfortably stretched out in front of the box playing with a dachshund puppy. A few ladies and gentlemen-in-waiting are with the Royal party; some of the other spectators, admitted by the magic lavender-colored cards, ourselves among them, are seated in adjacent boxes, the others on collapsible camp chairs or on the ground.
>
> There is a tie, then a conference as to whether the game shall be continued in the deepening shadows and rising breeze. The final decision is to do so. A luminous moon, grown to only a fourth of its future splendor, appears in the sky, no longer ultramarine, but pearl gray. Lights come out on the cruiser, on the drifting sailboats, on the white marble hotel, friendly and twinkling. Suddenly there is a quick goal, a stir of pleased applause and the crowd turns to salute its adored King, his vivid animated face still kindled with the excitement of the game, as he comes from the field with his fellow players, who are presented to Her Majesty. Then Alfonso XIII puts on a serviceable-looking hat and coat and strolls off toward the palace, arm in arm with a friend, laughing and chatting. The little princesses return the puppy to the stables and climb into an automobile with a lady-in-waiting. The Royal sport is over for the day. . . .

We went to another polo match that was even more interesting, because all the royal children were there—the two larger boys and the two younger ones, besides the two girls who were between them in age, a vigorous and delightful family of youngsters—and the beautiful Duchess of Alba was presenting the gold cups which her husband had offered as trophies. And, best of all, as I had been promised in Madrid, I went to see that lovely, golden-haired, pink-cheeked, blue-eyed princess, still essentially English, without the slightest sign of Latin transformation, who was her very gracious Majesty, the Queen of Spain.

The hour for the audience was fixed for half-past eleven in the morning; and the Queen received me in a charming room overlooking the sea and cool with its breezes. Two ropes of magnificent pearls hung around her neck, and there were pearls in her ears and gorgeously-hued jewels —sapphires and emeralds and rubies—on her hands. But her dress— pale gray crepe de Chine—had the supreme and deceptive simplicity which only the greatest dressmaker can achieve and only the most sophisticated women wear with distinction. Her manner was completely courteous, but it was much more formal than her husband's, her conversation much less easy and cosmopolitan. She did not have the same degree of magnetism. But she had infinite dignity and poise and almost flawless beauty. I shall always remember her as one of the most beautiful women I have ever seen. She was truly a vision of loveliness.

Six years later, during a visit to Barcelona, I met Alfonso XIII again, in his pleasant study at the Royal Palace there. That time, knowing how crowded his days were, I had expected the audience to be very brief, but the King had nearly an hour at my disposal, and we conversed unhurriedly. If I had been seeking enlightenment on a puzzling policy from a friendly senator in his office, the atmosphere could not have been kindlier.

In spite of his hospitable and delightful manner, his energy and vitality, I gathered that Alfonso XIII was tired and that his courtesy in receiving me was all the greater on that account. He had just opened two expositions in different parts of Spain; he had driven two hundred miles that afternoon to dedicate a monument (my audience had been officially set for "half-past seven in the afternoon"); and he had not for a moment neglected affairs of state. He was a monarch who took his responsibilities seriously and conscientiously; he drove himself hard; his working hours were long, and his alert and intelligent mind was constantly striving for more knowledge on more subjects, though his grasp of any one was so swift, his understanding so complete, that it was a privilege to watch his mental processes. Those who regarded him only as "the best sport in Europe," a dashing and fearless motorist, a crack polo player and yachtsman, had formed a very incomplete picture of him. He was always a "good sport," always dashing and fearless; but it was work and not amusement that dominated his life.

He was graver than when I had met him in 1923 and, recognizing the reason for this as I glanced at his mourning, I wished there were some way I could express my sympathy. The King had recently lost his mother, whom the whole world had regarded as one of its most outstanding women because of her devotion and dedication to her son. I have already mentioned my admiration for the painting in the Foreign Office which depicts María Cristina's presentation of her son to his people; and as we sat talking, I was very conscious of the part she had played in his life, very conscious of the effect her loss had had upon him. But before long, his gravity gave way to increasing animation, and he began to ask questions eagerly and enthusiastically—questions about everything I ordinarily did at home, about everything I had done in Spain and everything I proposed to do in South America, where I was going after leaving Spain. I could not change the character of the conversation with questions of my own, nor did I wish to; I was not seeking an interview, but an impression which would help me interpret the King to others; and he was giving it, beyond my every expectation, though it was only when I spoke of "understanding Spain" that he furnished me with a quotation.

"You have spoken of the industry of my people you observed during your trip through Andalucía," he said. "Do you think, in the United States, it is generally known that this is a working country, a country which recognizes that to survive, to advance, you must labor? I am afraid not. And I am afraid—excuse me—that Spain is regarded as being illiterate as well as indolent. Do you know that in the last two years ten thousand new schools have been opened in Spain, the salaries of teachers increased, the number of pupils in a classroom limited so that every child may have proper attention? That is the sort of thing I wish you would think of us as trying to do—and doing. I wish you would think of a monarchy as a government of responsibility rather than display; of a king, not as a remote personage with a scepter and a crown, but as a human being in clothes like these"—he touched his black sleeve. "Pomp and ceremony, of course, where they belong. They have their proper place in the scheme of things. But—"

He came to the door of the study with me, opened it and walked out into the anteroom before he said good-bye. "Have a good time in South America," he added, "and afterward—come back to Spain again."

I am glad to say that I have been able to do so, over and over again, and to say this after having lived with Spain through sad and tragic days, as well as happy and triumphant days. Her heritage is glorious, her destiny more glorious still. The Spanish playwright Benavente, Nobel prize winner, said, "There is something more sacred than a

grave: a cradle. There is something greater than the past: the future."
Turning from the graves of Spain to her cradles, turning from her past
to her future, we will find that her supreme fulfillment still lies beyond
the present day.

Viva España!

Chapter 28

ALL things being equal, I think it is a mistake to visit Switzerland directly after visiting Spain, unless scenery is the main objective of the trip. Geneva was my maternal grandmother's favorite continental city, because she enjoyed buying jewelry and there was certainly no better place for that than the Quai de Mont Blanc. It was also my mother's favorite continental city, because she claimed that the best dressmakers in the world were there, not in Paris; and the year I spent there as a child was the most serviceable and important one of my entire education, partly because it enabled me to grow up trilingual—which has proved invaluable in my line of work—and partly because it taught me early in life that New England and Virginia were not the only places in the world where congenial and cultured company could be found. If picture galleries, cathedrals and general glamour are of greater interest to a tourist than high mountains and quaint villages, I believe he does better to put Switzerland first on the list of his European sightseeing and not last.

My own reasons for going there in 1923 were twofold and had no connection whatever with any of Switzerland's above-mentioned attributes. I had been told in Paris that our legation in Berne could well serve as a model for American legations throughout the world because, as occupied and run by the Honorable and Mrs. Joseph C. Grew, it was practically perfect from a diplomatic standpoint, so I naturally welcomed an opportunity to go there. I was also eager to see something of the Swiss *écoles ménagères* (domestic science schools) for I had heard that every Swiss girl was obliged to attend one of these before her marriage. I myself had married without the slightest knowledge of housekeeping, and I had in consequence arrived at the heartfelt conclusion that it is almost criminal to allow a girl to marry in so helpless and ignorant a condition. As far as I knew, nothing had ever been done (officially) in the United States to remedy this. I wanted to see what Switzerland had done.

In addition to other letters, Mr. Castle had given me one to Mr. Grew, which I had sent on to him soon after Henry and I reached Santander.

Address Official Communications to
 The Secretary of State
  Washington, D. C.

> *Department of State*
> WASHINGTON
>
> March 5, 1923.

Dear Joe:

This will introduce to you Mrs. Henry Wilder Keyes, wife of Senator Keyes of New Hampshire, who will probably be in Switzerland sometime this spring or summer.

Mrs. Keyes is well known as a writer of articles and I hope that you can discover something for her to write up in Switzerland which will be interesting to her readers and at the same time of advantage to Switzerland and to this Government. . . .

Henry and I chose a rather roundabout route for reaching Switzerland when we left Spain. We went from Santander to San Sebastián, where we regretfully said good-bye to Leopoldo, by train from San Sebastián to Paris and then from Paris to Geneva. An invitation to visit the Grews had come from "Dear Joe" with the same promptness that the one had come from "Dear Dick," so almost immediately after descending from the Paris-Geneva train, Henry and I found ourselves installed in the one for Berne. Nothing that had been said to me of the legation's atmosphere and efficiency was in the least exaggerated; socially, it was delightful, and practically, it functioned with dispatch. Mr. Grew had already arranged an appointment for me with the President the day after my arrival, and accompanied me when I kept it.

I suppose there is no country in the world where the President is surrounded with as little pomp and ceremony as in Switzerland. He is not strictly a President in our sense but the senior member of the Federal Council of Seven, a body not unlike our Cabinet, except that its members are elected instead of appointed. He holds the title of "President of the Federal Council" for one year only, when the next member in order of seniority takes his place. The then current President, M. Karl Scheurer, was also the Minister of War. Unattended and unquestioned, Mr. Grew and I entered the beautiful Federal Building, walked up the marble staircase without encountering a soul, found—not without some searching—a small room where two or three guards were chatting and asked the way to the President's room.

"Over there," said one of them with a wave of the hand.

We thanked him and knocked on the designated door. A smiling secretary admitted us, but no one else was visible.

"The President is expecting you. Go right in," he said, opening another door.

The room into which we were ushered was no larger than the average family living room and, though furnished and decorated in perfect taste, not a whit more elaborate. A fair rather heavy man stepped forward and greeted us cordially, motioned to seats at a small table and sat down with us. A nation which can preserve its neutrality and its honor for four hundred years has something great in its form of government and the men who direct it; and I was glad to learn something of both. The President's conversation was largely governmental in character: he talked of similarities between our countries, the laws and problems of both, the reasons for the abiding friendship between them. No one came to bother or interrupt us, to suggest that the audience was over, and when I finally rose to go, it was at my own instigation.

"I'm so sorry that I cannot join you at dinner, as Mr. and Mrs. Grew so kindly asked me to; unfortunately, I am leaving town within an hour. Some other time, I hope," the President said, as we parted.

Though I had learned that the rumor about obligatory attendance at domestic science schools was considerably exaggerated, I had also discovered that it had sufficient foundation to make investigation worth while. Switzerland is made up of twenty-two cantons, much as our country is made up of fifty states. In two of these cantons—Fribourg and Solothurn—every girl between sixteen and twenty, whether contemplating marriage or not, was required to study domestic science; and the necessity for providing girls with a practical knowledge of domestic arts had been generally accepted and *écoles ménagères* had been established in many cities. I entered the prim little parlor of the one in Berne, and was received by the director Mlle Trüssel, a small white-haired woman with a sprightly and businesslike manner. She asked me to be seated and gave me a résumé of the school's work before we began our tour of inspection. According to law, if any five girls formed a group and advised the city authorities they wished to study domestic science, a course had to be instituted for them. There were three types of courses. First, for working girls who could attend only in the evenings and could pay no tuition. They were taught plain cooking, the most advantageous ways to prepare cheaper meats and vegetables, which materials washed and wore best, and what kind of small home could be made most attractive and most easily maintained. Second, there were courses for girls who worked in stores and factories and also had to attend evening classes, but could pay some tuition and were likely to have a bit more to spend, though they must learn to do so wisely. Third, there were courses for wealthy girls, who could pay well and were required to do so, and who, if they were to direct large and elegant households wisely, needed more intricate instruction.

"Of course, all girls are taught sewing in the regular schools," Mlle Trüssel told me. "Beginning in the first grade, there is a required course for each year, which must be covered and passed as in the case of other subjects. I supervise this sewing, and knitting as well. Each girl must make a complete layette—that goes without saying. And her husband's shirts and trousers she should also be able to fashion. The school boards tell me I teach more than is required. But look—" She led me to a table where lay beautifully tailored garments of various sizes and cuts. "More than is required in the grades," she said with a slight sniff, "but when I get letters from my former pupils, living far up in the Alps, telling me they have clothed their households, what do I care for that?"

After another week in Paris, Henry and I sailed for home in the *Leviathan,* the erstwhile *Vaterland* of the Hamburg-American Line, which the United States had seized from Germany in 1917 and used as a transport before restoring the ship to her former splendor and adding to this. In those days, there were no facilities for American ships to embark and disembark passengers at Le Havre, and at Cherbourg they had to go far out in the harbor by tender, a complicated and wearisome process when there was an immense passenger list and when practically everybody traveled with one or more trunks. It was two-thirty in the morning before we finally got aboard ship, after so many crowded and uncomfortable hours that I vowed I would never leave the United States again—a statement naturally received with great derision by my eldest son, but which I honestly believed when I reached my stateroom, almost frantic with fatigue. Though I was quite conscious of the wonderful opportunity the summer had offered and had derived untold satisfaction from it, I had worked hard, too, and kept not only long hours but late ones. This farewell to France was both too long and too late.

However, I had great powers of recuperation, and sea air was in itself a restorative before air conditioning was introduced and portholes were tightly sealed. Presently, I was following what became a fairly regular shipboard practice for me in the next years: work until late afternoon; an hour's walk on deck and a swim before dinner; bridge and dancing afterward (on this voyage, with Paul Whiteman's orchestra furnishing the music). And there never was a gayer crossing, both in the number of diversions available and in the number of delightful passengers with whom it was possible to share these.

We reached New York at the comfortable hour of noon, and Henry left at once for college. John, whose school began the next day, arrived early the following morning and went out to Morristown that afternoon. After his departure, I taxied to the *Good Housekeeping* office to hand in my final European article and my expense account and report on anything Mr. Bigelow wished to hear about.

He drew toward him the envelope containing the expense account and relevant receipted bills, and in a bold flowing hand wrote across it: "Okay. Attention of Business Manager." Then, without opening it, he handed it to his secretary. Next he laid the other envelope containing my article carefully to one side and said he would look forward to reading it that evening; then he coughed slightly.

"The circulation of *Good Housekeeping* has gone up a hundred and fifty thousand in the last few months," he said. "Of course, that is largely due to our serial. Still, I think your articles have had something to do with it too. I believe we must take it for granted that you are suited to present foreign situations capably. Where would you like to go next?"

Part Six

American Chronicle

Chapter 29

AT THE moment, Washington was obviously my indicated destination. Congress was in session, with Harry in faithful attendance. I
was very much afraid he might have been upset by an article of Mrs.
Poindexter's, who had already caused much feeling by her claims that
Cabinet officers had too many prerogatives. During my absence, she
had published the statement that Harry was planning to withdraw as
a candidate for re-election in my favor. Fortunately, he had taken this
as a good joke, since he was well aware that I never wanted to hold office, even in a women's club, and that my ambitions lay in quite a different direction. There were no minor notes in his warm greeting.

Peter, whose school was about to open, was hale and hearty, and
Cathie and Henry Deming were also in faithful attendance. As far as
housekeeping was concerned, I had no more onerous task than to walk
into an apartment already swept and garnished. It was a wonderful
homecoming in every way, and there was, so to speak, frosting on the
cake. Within twenty-four hours, Mrs. Coolidge sent flowers from the
White House with the message "Love and welcome" on the card that
came with them; there was also an immediate invitation to luncheon at
the Spanish Embassy, where reports of my stay in Spain had been enthusiastically received; and a few days later came a message from Mrs.
Coolidge's secretary, Miss Harlan, saying the former had suggested that
I might like to pour tea for her when she received the wives of the
Heads of Missions. Alice de Riano, the wife of the Spanish Ambassador, had become acting *doyenne* of the Corps in the absence of Mme
Jusserand, and Mrs. Coolidge felt that under the circumstances—my
great friendship with Alice and my recent sojourn in Spain—my presence on this occasion would be especially fitting. The thought was a

kind and gracious one, which pleased both Alice and myself very much. The tea table was set out informally in the Red Room and there were no other pourers. The whole occasion was intimate and delightful.

And almost immediately after this reception, Miss Harlan telephoned to say that Mrs. Coolidge would like to have me come informally to luncheon with her. There was a small and very pleasant group in the family dining room, and afterward we went upstairs for a long quiet visit. Later on, other guests joined us and we all went to a concert by Mme Schumann-Heink.

The President was not on hand for either of these occasions, but thereafter he was present more frequently than absent at the functions I was invited to at the White House during that administration. I have read recently that Mr. Coolidge "did not display any affection whatever to Mrs. Coolidge in public. As a matter of fact, Coolidge, both in public and in private, seems to have treated his wife more coldly than any President's wife was treated before or since." [1] I venture to disagree for several reasons. One is that most New England gentlemen traditionally feel it extremely ill bred to show affection to their wives in public, but this does not necessarily mean that they treat them coldly in private or that they underrate them. A second reason lies in the fact that Mr. Coolidge's daily walks almost always took him in the direction of Connecticut Avenue, where many of Washington's luxury shops were located, and he frequently paused before windows specializing in women's wear. If he saw a dress he liked, he would enter the shop and order the garment sent on approval to the White House. This was not a rare, but a very usual occurrence; and a man who takes that much interest in his wife's appearance is not apt to be indifferent to her. A third reason lies in the fact that Mr. and Mrs. Coolidge almost never made separate engagements for the evening and said quite frankly that they counted on having this time together, whether alone or in company. Certainly they personified a complete antithesis to each other, but far from denoting lack of affection or congeniality, this often represents the opposite. I believe it was so in their case and my belief is founded on a continued friendship which permitted me to see them not only in Washington during two administrations, but also in Plymouth, where I was their guest, and at Pine Grove Farm, where they were mine and my husband's.

I may add that I never found conversation with Coolidge as difficult as it was alleged to be. True, he did not go in for "small talk"; but he spoke both willingly and well on subjects that interested him—

---

[1] Jules Abels, *In the Time of Silent Cal.*

education, for instance. When he first came to Washington, both his sons were at preparatory school, as were two of mine; and with this as a topic of mutual concern, it was easy to go on to others. He was, moreover, an omniverous reader and a very discerning one; he was well qualified to discuss both classic and current literature and all the main events, national and international, of the day. I cannot help feeling that persons who complained about his silence as a dinner partner never really tried to get beyond the trivialities to which he did not think it worth while to respond.

The week after that pleasant luncheon at the White House, I went to New York for the dedication of the Theodore Roosevelt birthplace and a conference with Mr. Bigelow and the editor-in-chief of Appleton's—since that publishing house wanted to bring out the *Good Housekeeping* "Letters" in book form—and then on to New England to keep speaking engagements and see my old friends. My conference with Mr. Bigelow was extremely important. I had thought over his wonderful offer of more travel for *Good Housekeeping* and had talked it over with my husband. I did not feel I should be absent from home for any length of time in the near future; but Representative Towner, one of the authors of the bill which had inaugurated my association with *Good Housekeeping,* had been defeated in the last election and had been offered the governorship of Puerto Rico, and he and Mrs. Towner had urged me to visit them at *La Fortaleza,* the wonderful old palace which for centuries had been the home of the Spanish governors. I felt that such a visit, besides giving me pleasure, would provide material for a very interesting article and would be glad to write it in the spring, if this would be satisfactory. The following year, I would be glad to go around the world if all the circumstances were propitious, as I had every reason to hope they would be; but it would take a lot of planning, a lot of preparation, and I would need a lot of time for it. I thought I might need to have a little regular secretarial help—perhaps once a week—and would appreciate an allowance to take care of that.

Mr. Bigelow agreed with everything I said, including the need for secretarial assistance at *Good Housekeeping's* expense, and I went on to Appleton's very happy in every way. I undertook to abridge the "Letters" slightly, in order to reduce them to customary book length, but not to change them in any other way; there was no problem about illustrations, and I did not feel that the amount of extra work involved would be very heavy. This was usually my optimistic viewpoint in those days; and it was more justified than usual, for I had been fortunate in finding an excellent secretary, Miss Margaret Shufelt, who had a job with one of the government bureaus but was willing to work for me all day every Sunday and additional evenings, as needed, for fifty dollars a month. I had already made up my mind that since it was now really decided I was going to Puerto Rico, I must study Spanish during the winter, and the Rianos had promised to find me a teacher. But that, also, I expected to take in my stride.

I spent three days in Boston among old friends and left on an early morning train for Manchester, New Hampshire, where my program included a luncheon, a speech, a dinner and an evening party, besides interviews with several reporters that day and breakfast the next morning —a breakfast of such proportions that I missed my train for Littleton, where I was to speak next. I was obliged to hire a car to get me there (of course, at my own expense) in time to address an audience of eight hundred, for the North Country had turned out in full force to hear what the local girl who had made good thought of foreign parts. Naturally, Pine Grove Farm was closed for the winter, but I stayed two nights with the Glessners in Littleton and one with the Greers in Newbury, and managed to see old friends, besides making a new one and conferring with Mrs. Greer on the story of her grandmother, the script of which I handed over for her inspection.

The new friend was Richard Cobb's bride. When I wrote him six months earlier that I was going to Europe, he replied that he had news for me too: he had at last decided to marry and was very sure that the restlessness and discontent he had felt ever since his return from the war would soon be over. Lisle Southworth, the girl he had chosen, was certainly qualified to accomplish that end; she was very pretty, musically talented, the graduate of an excellent secretarial school, but domestically inclined; and she adored him. Her family lived in Newbury, but she had not been a member of our Old Guard because she was so much younger than the rest of us—fifteen years younger than I was, to be exact; and though I knew her by sight, it was hardly more than that until now. Lisle had already fitted in easily with the rest of the Cobbs and all the Greers, and on the festive evening we spent together, the whole group enjoyed itself.

Mrs. Greer did not join us in these festivities, but my talk with her was highly satisfactory. She was apparently not only very much pleased but very much moved by what I had written. "It's all *true,*" she said, looking at me with tears in her eyes, and added, "You've told it just the way it *was.*" Conversations, of course, had to be imaginary; but there was not an imaginary character in the book or a major incident that was fictitious. In regard to just one of the latter—the most dramatic in the book, where lovers parted for many years suddenly find each other again—Mrs. Greer wanted two slight details changed.

"You say he offered her a glass of sherry," she remarked, pointing to the place in my script. "Well, I have no doubt she needed that, after the shock and all. But a few minutes later he offers her another. I think the second glass of sherry should be deleted. My grandmother was a very temperate person. And then the way the man greeted her—taking her in his arms. I think a cordial shake of the hand would be more appropriate."

I agreed to eliminate the second glass of sherry, but I called in Mrs. Greer's sons and daughters-in-law to help me with the cordial shake of the hand. With their earnest cooperation, I was able to convince her that lovers, long lost to each other, did not exchange greetings that way when finally reunited.

After I was back in Washington there was another speech to make, this time in Frederick, Maryland, and then came the National Convention of the Daughters of the Confederacy, meeting at the capital and, for the first time, north of the Mason and Dixon Line. I attended several sessions, spoke hopefully about Arlington and helped arrange to have the delegates admitted to the mansion, still dilapidated, but now cleaned up, which most of them had never seen. I also undertook to give a small but elegant reception for the Virginia delegates.

By now, my "Days at Home" had become a good deal of a trial, despite Cathie's wonderful efficiency. She was always ready for an emergency; and she was not dismayed when visitors climbed the fire escape and entered through the rear door. She quickly assimilated the fact that anyone who wished might barge in upon a senator's wife at a Thursday reception, by fair means or foul, and she made the best of it. Only once did I see her daunted. She came up behind me while I was shaking hands and whispered anxiously, "Mrs. Keyes, one of your guests is taking all the fruit out of the silver epergne on the sideboard and putting it in a paper bag. I am afraid that, in a minute, she may try to take the epergne, too. What had I better do?"

I confessed that I was startled myself. Fortunately, one of our assistants, who was standing near by to lure callers into the dining room, took the situation in hand. The offender was an elderly drug addict, who had known better days and who scanned the social columns for announcements of "Days at Home." Then she went to the houses that were open, watched her chance to slip by the doormen and wormed her way in, thus securing much of the food on which she existed. Most

Washington hostesses and their helpers knew her and left her unmolested, since she had never been known to take anything except food;
once fed and supplied, she left willingly; but I had not been in the capital long enough to know this. I was not alarmed after that first experience, and for a time I too suffered her intrusions; then, finding she was
becoming actively offensive, I gave instructions to offer her money and
send her away. When that did not prove effective, I finally ceased to announce my "At Homes" altogether.

It was an extreme measure and deprived me of the pleasure of seeing
many persons I should have been delighted to receive; probably I
should not have resorted to it if she had been the only abuser of my
hospitality. But there were numerous others: an elderly man of sinister
aspect, whose habits were similar, came early and stayed late; so did a
number of hard pressed young foreign attachés who, though they did
not carry food away, devoured enough to see them through until morning if they had no invitations to dinner. The schoolgirl groups, at first
limited to thirty or forty, increased when the rumor spread that they
could meet a senator's wife and a "real live author" at one and the same
time. They arrived bubbling over with flattery and armed with autograph albums; the receiving line came to a standstill while I repeatedly
signed my name. Also, would-be writers began to appear, asking if I
would tell them why their manuscripts had been rejected when mine,
obviously no better, had been accepted. As patiently as I could, I tried
to explain that Thursday afternoons did not afford the best opportunities for such conferences. But it made no difference; the siege continued.

I had almost decided I should have to take the still more extreme
measure of not receiving at all, at least for the time being; but I had
many friends among the Daughters of the Confederacy, and they had
showered me with hospitality in Virginia, besides making me an honorary member of the organization and bestowing a silver cup upon me because of my efforts toward restoring Arlington. I was eager to show
some return for so much kindness and courtesy, and planned a party of
which I was really proud when preparations for it were complete. My
scheme of decoration featured the Confederate colors: red and white
roses, white frosted cakes studded with cherries, vanilla ice cream and
strawberry sherbet, red and white mints. And Mrs. Harris of Georgia,
who received with me, and I both wore white dresses and red scarves.

I was determined that on this occasion at least there should be no
gate crashing, and cards had been sent to all members of the Virginia
delegation. But some of them forgot to bring their cards, and after one
or two, to my great regret, had been turned away, there was nothing to

do but give instructions that all who presented themselves were to be admitted.

Eighty-five had been invited; three hundred and fifty came. Inside half an hour no one would have known there had been a color scheme in the table decorations or anywhere else. The beautiful red and white cakes were devoured almost at a gulp. Cathie put a bread board in the center of the kitchen floor—the only uncluttered place in the apartment —and frantically cut fresh sandwiches. One of my distinguished assistants called a taxi, hastened to the nearest caterer and returned with reinforcements, including a vast number of stale macaroons. A friend who occupied the apartment under ours set her staff to work. Somehow we managed. But when it was over, Mrs. Harris and Cathie and I looked at one another and exclaimed, "Never again!"

Despite our frustration, I was glad I had persevered with my party, for it attracted enough attention to stimulate flagging official interest in Arlington, and the following spring the first bill, recommending Congressional action, was introduced by Representative Louis P. Cramton of Michigan. But the bill contained no provisions for funds, and there is often a long wait between a bill's introduction and its passage, and then another long wait for an appropriation. It was not until March 4, 1925, that a joint resolution passed, without a dissenting voice.

Then two more years went by before a bill asking for an appropriation of ten thousand dollars was introduced, and this met with a sad fate. "I am sorry that the appropriation for Arlington . . . perished in a filibuster during the last days of the session of Congress," I wrote a friend. "Most disgraceful scenes were enacted there, for which both parties were to blame, and I am thoroughly ashamed of them. Of course, I am disappointed that the appropriation didn't go through without further delay, but I am not going to allow myself to be permanently discouraged, for I know it will go through sooner or later."

I was right. I had found an unexpected ally in my husband. He too had become interested in the preservation of Arlington. And he was a member of both the Appropriations Committee and the Committee on Public Buildings and Grounds. With his cooperation assured, I instinctively felt that success was only a matter of time.

Meanwhile, the winter of 1923–1924 itself was not without political drama, including the Teapot Dome scandal.

Though I do not agree with Mr. Abels regarding President Coolidge's attitude toward his wife, I am in thorough accord with the following observation:

Soon after Coolidge became President, the Teapot Dome scandal erupted, the facts having been brought to light by a Senate committee headed by the bulldog Senator Thomas J. Walsh. This concerned the transfer of valuable government oil reserves to private oil companies, the principal one being at a queer-shaped hill in Wyoming called Teapot Dome. Albert B. Fall, Harding's Interior Secretary, had been bribed to make the transfer.

Coolidge professed his holy indignation. "If there has been any crime, it must be prosecuted—no one will be shielded for any party, political or other reasons . . . if there has been any guilt, it will be punished, if there has been any fraud it will be revealed." At the same time, with consummate skill, he tried to minimize the involvement of Republicans. "A few public officers were guilty participants, but the wonder is not that there was so much and so many, but rather that there have been so little and so few." Members of the Senate demanded that Attorney General Daugherty be fired since he seemed to be implicated. Coolidge rode out the storm of protest, and after weeks had gone by and public interest had become stale, he dismissed Daugherty on an unrelated issue, that the Attorney General refused a Senate committee access to Justice Department files. . . .[2]

Harding had been dead only three months when Walsh unleashed his blistering attack on the Secretary of the Navy, Edwin Denby, who had allowed the transfer of the reserves—an attack that was unfortunately only too well merited—and in the Senate there was an outcry for the resignation not only of Daugherty, the Attorney General, but also of Denby himself. (Fall, the Secretary of the Interior, who was equally involved, had already resigned.) But this outcry was soon hushed. Coolidge not only declined to ask for either of these resignations but took pains to point out that the Executive office was in the White House and not in the Capitol. Neither the people nor the press were ready to believe the worst, especially as Charles Evans Hughes, Herbert Hoover and Andrew Mellon, fellow Cabinet members of the accused and of unquestioned personal integrity, were all silent on the subject and apparently never raised the issue either publicly or privately. This was a phase of the situation which Walsh confessed in private conversation that he had never been able to understand.

But if Walsh himself was discouraged at the lack of response to his efforts, he showed remarkable self-control in his refusal to betray any such sentiment. As usual, I saw a great deal of him that winter, for I went to church with him on the occasion of the Pan-American Mass Thanksgiving Day, the Midnight Mass of Christmas Eve and several

[2] Jules Abels, *In the Time of Silent Cal*, pp. 23–4.

other special services, which permitted quiet conversation en route between St. Patrick's Church and Meridian Mansions, where we both lived. Moreover, the bridge games, when neither the Walsh family nor I had a formal dinner engagement, had become a habit; and these evenings were unmarred by any outbursts of ill temper or other visible signs of strain. Sometimes the Senator seemed to pounce on his cards with greater ferocity than usual or to bid with more implacable firmness, but never did his intensity take on a political tinge.

Aside from covering public events for *Good Housekeeping,* my own life in Washington followed the pattern of official luncheons, receptions and dinners which was now fairly well established; and my social schedule was crowded and exciting, and on the whole, I took great pleasure in it. But it was darkened by bad news from abroad: Jacqueline Romano Avezzana, who had become one of my most cherished friends, died suddenly and tragically during an operation for suspected peritonitis. A mutual friend wrote me, "I am the poorer by a sweet and amiable friend and a charming and distinguished house to go to." I knew I was poorer in both these ways, too, but took some comfort in the realization that Jacqueline Romano had made a place for herself which reflected credit on all her countrywomen, for no continental who had known her would ever be guilty again of generalizing that all American women lacked poise, graciousness and savoir-faire. I managed to keep up by correspondence my friendship with her daughter Yolanda and her husband's relatives in Naples, who had been so kind to me, though I did not have much time for personal letters, as I was studying Spanish intensively and writing regularly for both *Good Housekeeping* and *Delineator.*

I continued to type my own articles and short stories from my first pencil draft, as I had always done, but I dictated all professional and some personal letters to Miss Shufelt, who proved to be an excellent stenographer and who also assumed responsibility for keeping my scrapbook up to date. All of this lightened my desk work perceptibly.

But the boys' engagements, as well as my own and my husband's, now required a good deal of attention. The flapper had just come into her own, not only in John Held's cartoons, but in real life; and to this day I have not been able to rationalize the transformation of the giddy, teen-age girls who were my guests at that period into the gracious ladies —wives of generals and ambassadors—who, a generation or less later, became my hostesses in various parts of the world. Though Henry was only seventeen when he entered Harvard, he was eligible as a freshman to attend many debutante parties and, by his sophomore year his social calendar was almost as full as mine. Normally, John, who was still in preparatory school, would have had to wait another year for inclusion in such festivities, but he got under the wire for our parties and frequently for other peoples'. This was the era of the tea dance; there was always one at the White House, we always gave one, and there was rarely an afternoon when there was not one somewhere else; then there was a rush for the two older boys to get into their first tuxes and be off to a dinner dance. Moreover, gone were the days when a visit to the Zoo every Sunday afternoon fulfilled Peter's requisites for amusement and enlightenment. At the age of twelve, he had his own set with its own special involvements, and he also went with us, as a matter of course, to the theater, which we managed to do at least two or three times during each vacation period. In addition, he made numerous all day trips to points of historical interest in nearby Virginia with us, besides seeing the main sights of Washington itself.

Nor were religious and scholastic obligations neglected. We all went regularly to church every Sunday, and often I had an appeal for help with an academic difficulty and somehow or other was able to cope with the demands of the moment. For some unexplained reason, John's mind went completely blank as far as his Latin was concerned. Though he had done reasonably well in it up to then, he simply could not recall one word of anything he had been taught and stared miserably at the baffling pages of his textbook. Though, as a girl, I had read both Ovid and Nepos for pleasure, I had not looked inside a Latin grammar for twenty years and felt very doubtful as to how proficient a teacher I should prove. But I suggested that we should try to see what we could do by working together, starting at the beginning of the book and covering as many pages as we could every day. Just how we did it I do not know; but when John's vacation ended, we had reached the place with which his class was struggling and everything was clear to him as far as we had gone. He muttered that he had learned more with me in two weeks than he had at school in two years and went back to Morristown to make the same report, where it was naturally received with mixed emotions.

All in all, I honestly do not believe that any mother ever had a better time with her children when they were young than I did, or got more out of the varied forms of shared association. All senators were furnished note pads of bright pink paper for casual jottings and I have treasured a page from one Harry used to answer a query concerning my outstanding characteristic in his eyes. It reads:

> Your question last evening has been on my mind even if I appeared indifferent at the time.

I am inclined to think my answer would be your interest in and devotion to the welfare of our three fine sons.

He may have been right, but I certainly did not deserve any special credit for this. They had become the source of my greatest joy. I was genuinely sorry for women who had not experienced maternity; and more than one confidence affirmed my impression that many who were not generally regarded as bereft deserved much sympathy.

A striking example of this occurred in the course of a visit with Mary Pickford at the Ritz in New York the autumn after I had first met her in Hollywood, when we had discussed at some length the motion picture industry as a whole and her special place in it. She complained that we had not talked about me at all and asked what I had been doing.

I answered that I had just come from Sweet Briar College, where I had spoken to the students, and that when I told them I was going to New York to see Mary Pickford and asked if I should take her their love, they had all cheered and shouted for joy.

"It's very wonderful to have the young girls of the country feel that way about me," she said, "very wonderful to be privileged to succeed while I'm alive—and young—and able to enjoy it all. I've worked hard and gone through some bitter struggles, but I think my career has brought me everything I could possibly want—except one. There's one thing I haven't had that every woman—every real woman—wants most of all."

The room seemed to have become very still. The lump in my throat was large. But I asked, feeling sure as I did so what her answer would be, what this missing thing was.

"Didn't you guess? I haven't had a child. . . . And you have *three!* I'd give up my career tomorrow for what you have and I haven't!"

Some way, across the shining silver of the tea table, our hands met. And I knew that after this, despite every difference of tradition and environment and viewpoint, Mary Pickford and I were going to be friends —that we spoke the same language, the language which all "real women" all over the world speak to each other.

Chapter 30

As always, I was delighted to be aboard ship again, whatever my destination, though I had no idea how thrilling I was to find my first sight of the tropics and, indeed, the entire experience of my initial stay in Puerto Rico.

We left New York harbor at noon on a still and sunny April day, the Goddess of Liberty engulfed in a golden mist as we slipped by her. The sea was calm and friendly to begin with, but lashed itself into a turbulent rage as we neared Cape Hatteras; and the ship rolled and pitched so for nearly twenty-four hours that it seemed incredible it would be able to hold together. Every time I tried to get up, I was hurled back toward my berth with such violence that I could not keep my footing, and repeated efforts were required to get into my clothes and out on deck.

The United States Mail Steamship *Ponce* had space for only twenty first-class and thirty second-class passengers, with one bathroom for each class; and my tiny cabin, with its folding wash basin and an overhead tank into which water was poured twice a day by a solicitous steward, was reminiscent of those in which I had traveled during my childhood, but never since then. Two hooks over the bunk represented the total provision for hanging clothes, and though there was a narrow sofa on which baggage could be placed, there were no chairs. However, everything was spotlessly clean; the bill of fare was surprisingly varied and appetizing; the officers and most fellow passengers, including several nuns, were congenial; and the steward was a mine of information about everything that was happening during the rough weather when I could not get about.

"We got two old maids aboard, sisters, that's takin' the one great trip of their lives," he told me. "They ain't been sick, but the lungs and liver has been scared clean out of 'em by this storm we been havin'. Their names is Hattie and Mattie. 'Ain't you frightened?' says Miss Hattie to me yestiddy, clutchin' at me as I went past her deck chair. 'No, ma'am, I ain't,' says I. 'It always blows up a little fresh around Hatteras.' It don't always blow so fresh the *Ponce's* backside is out of the water half the time, but natchelly I don't tell the old maid that. 'Well,' says she, 'I have been plenty scared'—or words to that effect. 'I was so frightened in the night, I called to my sister in the upper berth and told her I thought we both better get up and put our boots on. She agreed with me and we done it and, after that, we felt better.' I dunno why it should make 'em feel better to put on their boots in the middle of the night, ma'am, unless they figgered it would be easier walkin' on the bottom of the ocean if we should happen to hit it, which I admit looked more'n likely around eight bells."

Our progress was retarded for nearly two days by the storm, for it did not entirely spend its fury until we were almost in sight of land again. By then, when I stepped out of my cabin, it was to transfigured surroundings: curtains of snowy dimity had supplanted the crimson rep with which the windows had been draped; slip covers of fresh linen had been neatly tied over the dining salon chairs; uniforms of navy blue had disappeared and officers and crew were clad in spotless white. The color of the sea and sky had changed too. These were no longer a virulent gray. The lapping waves were a translucent sapphire, the sky a disc of turquoise; the balmy air was permeated with the first languor of the tropics. Flying fish and porpoises had begun to play around the prow of the *Ponce*.

Pearl-hued clouds, shot through with flaming arrows of sunshine, were massed along the horizon under a crescent moon as the *Ponce* slid into the harbor of San Juan late in the afternoon, past a Spanish schooner with all sails set, putting out to sea and riding like a great snowy swan over the rippling waves. Beyond the lights of the city, twinkling through the iridescence, the revolving beacon of *El Morro* gleamed and glowed. Standing high in the bow of the upper deck, I gazed over the panorama spread out before me with a growing sense of unreality and excitement. Little dagger-like thrills seemed to stab at my throat and strike at my spine.

I passed swiftly down the gangplank and across the wharf toward Mrs. Towner who was waiting for me beside a big car with the crest of the island on one door. Two minutes later we were acknowledging the salute of the guard at the doorway of *La Fortaleza*. This was the residence of the Spanish governors from 1639 until Puerto Rico was ceded to the United States after the War of 1898, when it became the residence of our governors. We mounted the broad stairway under the Moorish dome of its entrance, where Governor Towner was waiting to welcome me. Hovering slightly in the background was another figure who was briefly indicated to me as Magdalena, "who will show you to your room and help you in any way you wish as long as you are here."

Magdalena's slippers padded softly up the state staircase of polished mahogany; then she went down a long corridor with multicolored windows, over a floor of black and white marble that looked like a mammoth checkerboard—marble brought as ballast in the Spanish galleons four centuries ago. Next she turned to the right and preceded me down another corridor tiled in smaller squares of red and yellow and, finally, threw open the double, swinging shutters, extending over only the middle of the doorway, of one of the most entrancing rooms it has ever been my good fortune to occupy; twenty-five feet square at a conservative guess, with four deep windows, blinded and shuttered but without glass, set in arched embrasures, blue tiles on their wide sills; a lofty beamed ceiling painted white, with a chandelier of gilt and crystal suspended from the central beam; small braided rugs on the marble floor; cupboards and wardrobes of colossal proportions; a dressing table and desk that conceded little to modernity, gay with crimson roses; and, in the middle, a big bed of inlaid wood shrouded in mosquito netting.

La Fortaleza contained many other attractive rooms. Among them was an immense and magnificent apartment across the entire front of the first floor, which had been called the Throne Room in Spanish times, as it was used for audiences with the Governor General, the direct representative of the Crown. The house was equally fascinating outside too. It was built around an open patio, and in the rear there was a walled garden with a dripping fountain; a mass of fragrant flowers bloomed in the shade of coconut and mango trees, and a vine-covered gate led to the sea wall beyond. In one of two towers was a room formerly used as a chapel, with an underground passage leading to a spring near San Juan gate—to be used in case of siege—and a subterranean vault where treasure could be concealed. But it was the long corridor on the second floor that really held me spellbound. Every afternoon that we were in town, at the hour when the sun streamed in through its stained glass windows and made changing patterns on the floor of black and white marble, I managed to get back to it and linger until the light faded; and ever since then I have kept a picture of it on the wall of a room I use constantly.

Mrs. Towner had been a valued friend ever since I went to Washington. Intelligent, gracious, tactful and finely balanced, she was one of the most notable presidents the Congressional Club had ever had, and an outstanding Regent of Iowa for Mount Vernon. But the Towners had lived very simply in a small apartment, and their entertaining had been circumscribed, like that of so many legislative families, including my own, by a limited budget. There was a fresh thrill in seeing them established in such a delightful and important setting as *La Fortaleza*. Moreover, until then, I had associated the Governor largely with the Maternity Bill in which his name, as the Representative from Iowa, was coupled with that of Senator Sheppard of Texas. I had seldom seen him except in the Capitol, and I had not previously known how extensive and varied was his interest in welfare measures and his ability to promote them, or that he was an accomplished musician, who managed to spend a little time at the piano every day, and an omniverous reader whom little escaped in either classical or current literature.

The Towners gave a large reception for me the day after my arrival, thus providing me with a chance to see the Throne Room put to elegant modern use and also to meet most of the pleasant persons with whom I would be thrown in the course of my stay; and I was included in the Towners' invitation to a wedding which was held at ten o'clock the following evening and united two families of great prominence. The little Gothic chapel where the religious ceremony took place was beautifully decorated with white flowers and the wedding procession was one of the most elaborate I have ever seen. The whole setting affected me deeply. The chapel was attached to the Convent of the Immaculate Conception, where the bride had been educated, and, reigning in its luxuriant garden was one of the loveliest statues of the Virgin I have ever seen. Possibly daylight might have revealed some flaws or inadequacies in the scene; but by moonlight none was apparent or even imaginable. After the magnificent reception at the bride's home which followed the ceremony, I asked if we could not pass through that garden again; and when we had done so and I had retired to my great airy room, I was quite unable to sleep or even to lie still and quietly enjoy the scent of the gardenias which were always placed at my bedside. Finally I rose, went to the desk and, without forethought, hesitation or erasure, wrote a sonnet about the statue. Then I went back to bed and fell peacefully asleep.

The next morning, I ventured to show the Towners what I had written, and the Governor asked for the original draft, so I do not have this.

The Virgin of the Immaculate Conception

Mother of Heaven! bathed in silver light,
Serene and pure and radiant you stand,
A crystal glory streams from either hand,
And crystal stars, celestially bright

Encircle your veiled head, a glittering band.
Your robes are spotless as the driven snow,
And fragrant flowers grow about your feet;
The perfume which they cast is not more sweet
Than the sublime divinity you show
To every passing stranger in the street.
Beneath the splendor of the tropic moon
I see you waiting; may both soiled and shriven
Who seek for comfort, find your presence soon
And finding you, find too the road to Heaven!

It seemed almost unbelievable to Governor Towner, as indeed it did
to me, that anything in sonnet form—one of the most complicated in
the realm of poetry—could have been composed so spontaneously; yet
he knew I had never seen the statue until the previous night, and the
draft, the only one in existence, was in his hand. I am usually skeptical
on the subject of sudden inspiration, in creative writing, which normally
represents untold hours of drudgery before satisfactory results are
achieved, but in this instance I was forced to believe in it. I have, of
course, written other sonnets, both before and since, none of them very
remarkable (nor is this one, except for the circumstances under which it
was devised) and none of them composed without blood, sweat and
tears.

Both Governor and Mrs. Towner were not only conscientious in their
efforts to become and keep fully informed about everything that was
happening on the island; they were genuinely interested in sharing these
activities. Shortly after my arrival, an industrial and agricultural fair
was held in the city of Arecibo and they took it for granted that they
should attend and that I should go with them. But also, besides *La For-*
taleza, the fortunate Governor was provided with *Jajone Alto,* a quaint
old Spanish roadhouse adapted for modern official needs, perched on a
high mountainside some sixty miles from San Juan, where he could go
for rest and recreation; and one weekend of my visit was spent in this
way, quite free from official duties. Those picturesque roadhouses of
yellow plaster with trimmings of red brick, situated at frequent intervals
along the old military roads of the island, dated back to the time when
messages had to be sent by hand from city to city in relays, and the
bearers were given an opportunity for rest and refreshment at points
not too far distant from each other. We passed a number of them as
we sped along the twisting macadam roads to our destination: through
Santurce, one of San Juan's fashionable suburbs; through Río Piedras,

where the beautiful University of Puerto Rico and the equally beautiful government gardens were situated; through Caguas with its festive plaza and Cayey with its military and naval radio stations; down valleys and up hillsides dotted with cabins built on stilts and thatched with dried palm; past quaint, primitive warehouses where tobacco was dried and *tiendas* gay with fluttering muslins and laces or solidly stocked with prosaic groceries.

San Juan had given me my first glimpse of a beautiful tropical port; this was my introduction to tropical countryside: bamboo trees waving like tall green ostrich plumes; coconut palms and royal palms, slim straight sentinels on quiet mountains; coffee plants shaded by guava trees and the omnipresent bananas; sugar cane rustling in the wind, shining in the sun; flamboyant, the only tree on the island which loses its leaves, sere and dusty, bereft at that season of the scarlet blossoms which are its flaming glory from May to August; finally, the first glimpse of the shimmering Caribbean through a cleft in the luxuriant hills, and then the friendly little house with its wide veranda in the rear, its green shuttered door swung wide to receive us.

Affairs of state called the Governor back to San Juan early Monday, but Mrs. Towner and I went on to Coamo Springs, which had been a favorite resort for over a hundred years. Long before the day of automobiles or American possession, the Spanish governors with their retinues and the beauty, fashion and wealth of the island betook themselves there in coach and four to drink the waters and take the baths, staying at an excellent hotel. This had lost none of its charms; the brave green and crimson were still on post and pillar, shutter and fence; the dining room, gay with bright porcelain flamingos, is the only one I ever entered where the menus assured the diner that "extra portions will be served without charge." The cell-like bedrooms were still austerely bare and clinically clean. A peculiar feature in some of the bathrooms—two tubs in a room, known as *baños matrimonios*—was still retained and was extremely popular.

After another day at Coamo Springs, we drove on to Ponce, where we visited the bustling market and bought countless strings of scarlet beads, bowls carved from gourds and other treasures. I had been lamenting that San Juan was so thoroughly modernized that there were no ox teams left in the streets, as there still were in Madrid; but we found them in less progressive Ponce, and quantities of goats as well. The automobile was not omnipresent, either; top buggies with embossed brass straps looking like huge starfish across their backs and drawn by two horses were stationed around the plaza, and were the most accepted means of transportation. The *bomberos*—firemen—clad in black helmets, tall black boots, red shirts and blue trousers, with axes over their shoulders, seemed equipped to start a conflagration rather than extinguish it—they certainly fired the imagination, if nothing else!

We stayed two days in Ponce and then struck eastward to San Germán. It was Good Friday and therefore a holiday. Everywhere the country roads were crowded with people going to the nearest town, dressed in their Sunday best—girls in white and gaily colored crisp organdies, men in white duck. The plazas were, of course, more crowded still, not only with the inhabitants but with merry-go-rounds and Ferris wheels and pushcarts from which cakes, cold drinks, dry goods and knickknacks were being sold. I confess that all this was something of a shock to me, for I had never seen so solemn a day observed in so festive a fashion. But the famous Good Friday procession—"The Funeral of Jesus Christ"—which, following ancient custom, took place at five o'clock in all the island's provincial towns, had nothing grotesque or irreverent about it; it was, on the contrary, extremely beautiful.

According to then universal practice, the church bell was not rung from Holy Thursday until Holy Saturday, but three times within the hour before the procession began, a curious muffled sound was made by spinning large pieces of wood arranged in pinwheel fashion. Then altar boys, bearing lighted candles, and several men with musical instruments emerged from the side door of the church, preceding a group of veiled girls. Next came a portable altar, surmounted by a plain wooden cross, tied with purple ribbon and encircled with a lace scarf; candles burned before it and it was followed by a long line of men and boys, women and girls walking before a glass receptacle, resting on the shoulders of four men, in which lay the image of the dead Christ, lightly shrouded in white gauze and surrounded by lilies. The coffin was lidded with an ornate decoration of gold and surrounded by more lighted candles shielded with glass globes. Last of all, also borne by four strong men, came the figure of the *Mater Dolorosa,* her robe of black velvet edged with silver, her long train embroidered in silver stars; she held the crown of thorns in one hand, a lace-edged handkerchief in the other. This statue was also encompassed by shaded and lighted candles, and I saw women on balconies drop flowers gently down as it passed. The procession, which extended four blocks, moved along the principal streets, encircled the town and finally re-entered the church by the main door. In absolute silence it made its way, not a sound coming from the hundreds who took part in it or those who stood watching as it passed. Later, when it had grown dark, there was a moonlit procession in which no men took part. In it, only the image of the *Mater Dolorosa* was carried, preceded and followed by women and girls holding lighted candles and singing the "Ave Maria." It was supposed to be symbolic of the lonely Mother searching for Her Son.

In rather strange contrast to these celebrations, we took supper between the processions with the Presbyterian minister and his wife who were in charge of the small evangelical mission at San Germán and who, finding us stranded with no meal in sight and a keen desire to prolong our stay, received us with a kindly and sincere hospitality I have rarely seen equaled.

Late evening found us at Mayaguez, overnight guests of a charming Puerto Rican family with a beautiful home; but much as I enjoyed this, it called attention—as did every similar visit—to the sharp line of demarcation between the very rich and the very poor. Wealth, deep culture and a high degree of civilization were everywhere found almost side by side with poverty, ignorance and primitive existence. I saw more beggars in the short time I was in Puerto Rico than I did in six months spent in five different European countries. There were said to be nearly ten thousand homeless children on the island. Wages were very low. The schools were doing splendid work and were rapidly adopting a system of free lunches; nevertheless, they were often teaching children who were hungry—a man who was earning fifty cents a day could not feed his family in a very lavish fashion. I noticed that the fourth grade children were not much larger than those in the first grade. The doctors were doing excellent work, too, but were often prescribing to patients who could not afford to follow their instructions. Hookworm and tuberculosis—the two greatest health problems—are both diseases of poverty. An abundance of fresh milk and fresh eggs could not be secured for nothing. A latrine costing thirty dollars could not be built when there was not the wherewithal to pay for it. The grinding season in the sugar *centrals* lasted only about half the year; during the other half employes had to search for new positions—difficult to find—or subsist on half wages.

I do not wish to imply that the situation was worse than it really was or that it was not improving. While wages were less than in the states, it also cost less to live. There was no problem of fuel and none of the necessity for supplying warm clothing. A law had been recently passed establishing minimum wages for working women and regulating the employment of women and children. And I found the Puerto Ricans to be, in instinct, a very clean people. I was constantly amazed at the appearance of the men and girls who emerged from humble little huts along the country roads—the girls in white cottons, quite evidently fresh from the tub, the men in white duck that was spotless. But the poverty I also observed distressed me.

In the course of my travels with Mrs. Towner, I had seen a good deal of both the police force and the schools, and both had aroused my admiration. The police force was an insular, not a local, institution and was by far the most efficient, vigilant and courteous I had ever seen. Its members were chosen by competitive examination, with captains men of standing in their communities. The Colonel in Charge at San Juan was in his leisure moments a writer of thrilling detective stories and at all times a very delightful gentleman. Policemen were in evidence everywhere, even in the smallest villages, directing traffic, maintaining order and supplying information. As for the schools, they were certainly the largest and most beautiful, in proportion to the size of the places in which they were located, I had ever seen, except in California. This was true not only of the cities, large and small, but of the villages; you could not ride more than a mile or two on any country road without passing a "rural school," the older ones made of wood, the newer ones of cement and stone. *Four-fifths of the insular budget was devoted to education.* And the children had the great advantage of growing up bilingual. Through the fifth grade, instruction was given in Spanish, with English as a special subject; after that, all the textbooks were in English, and Spanish became the special subject. It was literally impossible for a boy or girl to be graduated from high school without equal facility in two languages, and this, I am sorry to say, was and is not the case of any school I know of in the United States. With the commercial, industrial and social relations which connect us with the Spanish-speaking countries, a thorough knowledge of their language is, in my opinion, extremely important for us to acquire.

There were more than five thousand Spaniards on the island, and their position since Puerto Rico was ceded to the United States had been peculiar. By the terms of the Treaty of Paris, signed after the Spanish-American War, residents of Puerto Rico who had been born in Spain were allowed to retain their Spanish citizenship if they so desired, but those born on the island were not. This brought about a condition extremely unsatisfactory to many of those concerned. Spanish subjects had often taken up their temporary residence in Puerto Rico, for business or other reasons, and reared their families there; and while it was true that, from the moment the first American troops arrived, the majority of the Puerto Rican people welcomed the conquerors with open arms, there were many examples of allegiance to the old flag. Finally a test case arose: a gentleman whose parents had belonged to ancient and distinguished Spanish families but who had been born on the island went to Spain, established residence there, married one of Madrid's reigning beauties and became a member of the Spanish Senate, where he served with distinction for some time. Then he returned to Puerto Rico, triumphantly proclaiming his Spanish citizenship. It was denied. He took the matter to court and, after delays and complications, won his point.

My friend Juan Riano, Spanish Ambassador in Washington, who had done much to make my first visit to Spain the previous summer pleasant and profitable, had advised the Spanish Consul in Puerto Rico, Señor Freyre de Andrade, of my imminent arrival. The latter, aware of my deep interest in the situation generally and in this particular case, arranged to have me become acquainted with both. We started out bright and early one shining morning for Barranquitas, a mountain resort in the heart of the island, where the Senator's family had a country residence. We stopped first at the Spanish Hospital, supported entirely by the Spanish residents of Puerto Rico and staffed by Spanish doctors and nurses—a magnificently equipped building, immaculately clean and very attractive. Then we went into a high rugged part of the island new to me. The Senator and his family gave us a warm welcome at Barranquitas. The lady of the house was even more beautiful than reported, and I found the Senator the same fine type of Spanish statesman I had first met last summer. We had a delicious supper in an airy dining room overlooking the shadowed mountains, then went for a walk in the rustic garden surrounding the house before, very reluctantly, I felt constrained to say good-bye. There had been a shower during our visit, and the heavy brilliant flowers through which we passed were drooping with fresh, wet perfume—purple passion flowers, golden roses, snowy gardenias. Over them all, on a sturdy staff, two flags were lifted—the crimson and gold of Spain beneath the Stars and Stripes.

That, in my opinion, was as it should be. For no civilization is complete in itself. Each much learn from another, must help another. In Puerto Rico, the Latin and the Anglo-Saxon had an opportunity for merging which gave promise for a dual civilization which few people could equal. There was no enlightened and fair-minded Spaniard or Puerto Rican who would not admit—who would not willingly declare —that the island had made tremendous strides in education, in sanitation, in general progress for all sorts and conditions of persons since American possession. But, by the same token, no fair-minded American should have failed to admit and declare what we had derived from the power and beauty and culture of Spain.

Chapter 31

I N THE usual course of events, the publication of a third book is less thrilling than that of a first or a second, but the publication of *Letters from a Senator's Wife* shortly after I returned from Puerto Rico did not follow in the usual course of events. Now Mrs. Coolidge had become the First Lady, and she had again agreed, evidently with real pleasure, to preside at another book party—this time a large luncheon which I gave for my fellow members of the Women's National Press Club, and which the Washington press reported in detail. The New York *Times* gave the book a front-page review in its Book Section, the book made the bestseller list in Portland, Oregon, and briefly in several other places, and again there was only one brickbat among the forty-five reviews which reached me.

This brickbat appeared in—of all papers!—the Washington *Post* and read, "Under the title *Letters from a Senator's Wife* comes from the press of D. Appleton & Company, New York, a volume of correspondence that may be interesting to the writers of the included epistles, but can claim little interest from the general reader. The authoress or compiler, or both, Mrs. Frances Parkinson Keyes, has included in her offering a number of communications or exchanges that are rather dull and dreary."

This did not depress me unduly for several reasons. One was that it was hard to believe a reviewer for a metropolitan paper—particularly a paper in the Capital—could be so naive as to suppose that these "epistles" consisted of private correspondence among several writers, haphazardly assembled in book form by a publisher, when as a matter of fact they had been written by me alone and had already been appearing for three years in a national magazine as a series of articles dealing in letter form with public and semipublic events. If the reviewer of some provincial paper had written with so little basis for his remarks, they would have been dismissed with the contemptuous comment that critics seldom bothered to read what they were writing about; it was harder to take this position with a prominent paper like the *Post,* but other Washington comments more than made up for it, especially those from Mrs. Robert Lansing, whose husband, then Wilson's Secretary of State, had so kindly reviewed my second book, wrote me, "For a long time I have felt there should be a record written of Washington—socially—and you have supplied the need. I only wish you covered the period of the War —from '14–'19. But you have done it well and I believe your book will be a book that will live, as a portrayal of the times and customs." I was also delighted when Mrs. W. R. Castle, Jr., the wife of our Assistant Secretary of State, whose husband's letters to "Dear Dick" and "Dear Joe" had helped pave my way in Europe, wrote, "I started the book last evening . . . and could not put it down. I sat up far too late for my health and today, instead of being out of doors, have finished the book."

As I look over the reviews, carefully pasted so many years ago in the then current scrapbook, I find a great many contrasting opinions, which it is interesting rather than discouraging to compare. None have malice, and though some lack enthusiasm, others still give me a real glow of pleasure. "This book will appeal to only two kinds of people—women who expect to live in Washington and to enter its social life, and women who are interested in the trivial doings of the near-great." . . . "Many people will get a better idea than they ever have had of some of the more important facets of the many sided life of Washington." . . . "They are graceful and illuminating letters, sometimes even fascinating." . . . "No Asquithian titillations need be looked for in this limpid dish of gossip." . . . "There is a freshness and simplicity in Mrs. Keyes's style that raises her book far above others of its kind." . . . *"Letters from a Senator's Wife* are dreary reading for the average mortal." . . . "Mrs. Keyes has a keen and clever mind. She understands political movements and how to tell about them." . . . "Mrs. Keyes writes with more circumspection about social affairs in Washington, with which she is entirely familiar, than about politics, with which she being less familiar speaks with more confidence." . . . *"Letters from a Senator's Wife* should be on the required reading list of every woman who contemplates living in Washington." . . . "This is not a book especially for women. I enjoyed it, too." . . .

A fortnight after the book came out, I was on my way to Cleveland to cover the Republican National Convention, having just moved my household from Washington to Pine Grove Farm for the summer and assured myself of the welfare of each of its members, including Peter's five goldfish.

The Cleveland Convention was my first assignment of the kind, and I had looked forward to it with a good deal of pleasurable excitement, despite numerous warnings that it would be a very dull affair because everything had been cut and dried beforehand. I did not find the experience dull, since, fortunately, I am very seldom bored, but I did find it irritating in several respects. To begin with, I was allotted a hotel room on a court, as gloomy as it was stifling, and provided with plumbing which was out of order. (Several years later when I returned to Cleveland to autograph books, the same room was assigned to me and the bathroom was still out of order, but that time I was able to change hotels.) Of course, there was no hope for changing this in an overcrowded city, and I was already in a bad humor when I went to the Public Hall to present my press credentials and get my ticket. There I was confronted by Jim Preston, who ruled over the Press Gallery in the Senate but with whom I had never tangled before, as I naturally had always sat in the Senators' Gallery. Now I found he had decreed that only reporters who had to file telegraphic accounts would be accommodated in the press section. I tried to argue with him on the grounds that most of the men and women who were representing magazines would reach millions of readers to the newspapers' thousands and that such unjust discrimination would not only make them his bitter enemies but greatly reduce the coverage of the convention. He was completely unmoved.

I was not worried about myself, for I felt reasonably sure that someone would offer me a seat on the speakers' platform, and sure enough, Mr. John Bartlett, who had been Governor of New Hampshire and was now Assistant Postmaster General, promptly came forward with one. But I feared that the representatives of other magazines deserving recognition would not be so fortunate and that hard feelings, with unpleasant results, would follow, and I was right.

My next experience revealed a viewpoint very different from Mr. Preston's. My old friend Alice Glessner, now National Republican Committeewoman for New Hampshire, had suggested that I go with her to a reception given by some local socialite. When I told Alice I had not been invited, she said there must be some mistake; she would telephone and let me know the outcome. In a few minutes she called back, obviously embarrassed. Mrs. X had discovered that I was a reporter, and she made it a strict rule not to admit reporters to her house. I laughed and begged Alice to relay this verdict to Jim Preston; for twenty-four hours I had been trying without success to convince him I was a reporter; perhaps Mrs. X would be willing to do that for me.

This episode had a rather amusing sequel. The following winter, when I reached home one day after making my usual round of calls, Cathie told me that a lady from Cleveland, briefly in Washington, hoped I could "spare time" to see her, "as there was no one in Washington she wanted so much to meet." I returned the telephone call and found that my would-be visitor was none other than Mrs. X.

"I'm sure there must be some mistake," I said quietly. "When I was in Cleveland last June, you sent me word you did not want me to come to your house because I was a reporter. I am still a reporter." There was a gasp, followed by a short pause, and then Mrs. X said apologetically, "Of course, I didn't know you were *that* Mrs. Keyes."

This, naturally, was the worst possible thing she could have said, and I was sorely tempted to say that I didn't have a free minute—which was very nearly true. But I realized that this would seem as if I were bent on taking revenge for a social slight and giving it more importance than it deserved, so I suggested a late hour the following afternoon. Again I went out to make calls, and when I returned the door was opened by an impeccable butler, the living room was adorned with flowers, and my best afternoon dress was spread out on my bed ready for me to slip into. Cathie, from whom there were few secrets, had heard my side of the conversation the day before and had connected it with a story I brought home from the convention; she was determined to impress Mrs. X; it was she who had engaged the butler and bought the flowers, besides spending most of the day preparing delicacies for tea. This she presented with a full silver service, wearing her best black uniform, lace apron and lace cap with long black satin streamers.

I was tremendously amused, and so, on his return from the Capitol, was Harry. But Cathie did not consider it a laughing matter. She was bent on upholding the prestige of the family, which she felt had been slighted.

As usual, there was no dearth of semisocial, semipolitical parties to which I was invited in Cleveland but none of them were very exciting, and neither were the sessions of the convention. The keynote speech, delivered by Representative Theodore P. Burton of Ohio, took an hour and fifty minutes to read, but I find nothing in it that has stood the test of time well enough to quote. He duly noted that this was the first national convention to which women had come as delegates, with the right to vote. His reference to the fact that his party was on the defensive when it came to the Teapot Dome scandal was so delicately worded as to be scarcely recognizable.

Immediately after Mr. Burton's speech, the four convention committees—on Resolutions, Rules, Credentials and Permanent Organization—were appointed and began to function. It was one of those times when you wished you could be in at least four places at once. I decided to go to the hearing the Resolutions Committee was giving to those who wished to submit planks to be inserted in the party platform. This was largely because I wanted to hear the resolutions, which I knew would differ very widely, presented by the League of Women Voters and the National Women's Party; but I found many of the other subjects equally absorbing. The plea made by a Negro— Christine Maura of New Jersey—for enforcement of the Fourteenth and Fifteenth Amendments was dignified, brief and poignant. The greatest excitement was caused by the reading of the progressive bloc's proposals, presented by Governor Blaine of Wisconsin, which were radical in the extreme. They were greeted with hoots and hisses, and criticism on the part of one committee member at even giving them a hearing; but Senator Reed Smoot reminded the committee that it had announced *all* proposals would be given consideration, and the chairman upheld him.

On the third morning of the convention President Coolidge was nominated to succeed himself by Marion Leroy Burton, head of the University of Michigan—a slim, spare man, redhaired and slightly stooping, not unlike the President in general appearance, except that he was larger and more animated. His address was a masterpiece, not only in subject matter and literary form but in its delivery. Dr. Burton spoke without notes, cutting the prepared speech already given the press almost in half but adding spontaneous epigrams, quotations and allusions. There had been a demonstration lasting twenty minutes at the first mention of President Coolidge's name when the platform had been read the night before, but it was nothing to the demonstration which greeted Dr. Burton's remarks about him. Steadily the applause grew as he made point after point of his speech. At his final words, "I have the distinction to present as candidate to succeed himself—Calvin Coolidge," the delegates and alternates began to stream into the aisles; the galleries shouted, waved fans, programs, handkerchiefs; colored lights began to flood the hall. The organ boomed "Onward, Christian Soldiers" and everyone took up the refrain. We sang, not only because we wanted to but because we simply could not help it.

The convention had taken on significance and vivacity at last. But these attributes were fleeting. The final sessions were sadly anticlimactic. In Washington it had been common knowledge that Mr. Coolidge had sounded out Senator Borah on his availability for the Vice Presidency and that Borah had declined to consider the proposition; he knew very well that he wielded far more power as senator than he could otherwise. Now Governor Frank Lowden of Illinois, who was nominated for Vice President on the second ballot, vehemently declined the nomination. It was no secret that he had long coveted the Presidency, and there was a general feeling that his refusal to accept second place lacked good sportsmanship. It was not until a third session was called for the evening that Charles G. Dawes was nominated on the third ballot. He was in so many respects well fitted for the post that it was both unfortunate and incomprehensible that he had been pressed into service only as a last resort. But there was never anything the matter with his sportsmanship.

I went straight from Cleveland to New York to attend the Democratic Convention, and it would be hard to imagine a greater contrast than existed between the two experiences in every way. I was at once comfortably installed in one of the small suites at the Commodore, which I had previously discovered were ideally suited to my needs. they were situated at the end of long corridors, the bedroom led only into the sitting room, not into the hall, so that noise never penetrated to it, and there was never anything the matter with the plumbing.

In the suite I found a message asking me to call Mrs. Edwin T. Meredith immediately and was fortunate in making prompt connections with her. We had been good friends ever since she first came to Washington when her husband was appointed Secretary of Agriculture, and as they had frequently returned there to visit after his retirement from official life—which meant more time for his highly successful publishing activities—it had been easy to keep in touch with them. They were giving a luncheon for the members of the Iowa delegation the next day, Edna informed me, and they wanted very much to have me for their guest of honor; if it would not be an imposition, they would like to have me make a brief speech. Meredith was now among the "favorite son" candidates for President and, before the convention was over, proved to have a good deal of strength. Both husband and wife would have graced the White House. I was very touched at the invitation; even on such an occasion as an otherwise wholly Democratic luncheon, the Merediths had singled me out with friendship and pleased approval of my writing and speaking. And, as usual, their party was delightful.

Slightly apprehensive after my experience in Cleveland about tickets, I left my comfortable quarters and went promptly to Madison Square Garden. A greater antithesis to Cleveland Public Hall with its austere simplicity and lack of decoration could hardly be conceived. The Garden was literally covered with flags, large and small, from top to bottom. Japanese lanterns, blue and yellow, mingled with portraits of Jefferson, Jackson, Cleveland and Wilson suspended from the rafters; and the press, in all its branches, was receiving a hearty welcome. The sections devoted to it stretched out in two great whitewashed divisions— like a huge bird with its wings spread—on either side of the speakers' platform and immediately below it; and radio, for the first time, had come into its own—announcements were already being broadcast with the earnestness and directness which revealed the closeness of the speaker with his unseen audience.

Eventually I ended up, though I do not remember just how, with five tickets, all apparently legitimate, and was consequently enabled to invite my editors, my son John and several friends to various sessions and to a party at the Garden. But I had hardly taken my seat in the press section for the opening session when Senator Walsh, the Permanent Chairman of the Convention, leaned over the rostrum and snapped out, "What are you doing down there?"

"I'm covering the convention," I answered meekly.

"Well, you could cover it from up here, couldn't you?"

"I suppose I could. But I thought I'd better not intrude. After all, this is a Democratic Convention and I'm a Republican Senator's wife."

"After all, you're a friend of mine and of my daughter. Come up here this instant."

He seized his gavel with such force that he appeared about to pound out his summons. Without further delay, I ran up the steps from the press section to the platform. He snatched my ticket and scrawled across it swiftly, "Admit bearer to the platform at all times. Thomas J. Walsh, Permanent Chairman."

"There!" he said with finality. "From now on you had better come and sit beside me."

There was no more discussion about it. I spent most of the next four weeks seated not far from the presiding officer's side.

The convention's first real thrill came with the opening song and prayer; the second, to me at least, with the speech made by Franklin Roosevelt placing the name of New York's Governor Smith in nomination for the Presidency. Hard as this is to realize now, it was then taken for granted that Roosevelt's public life was at an end, and I wrote,

> Mr. Roosevelt, formerly Assistant Secretary of the Navy and candidate for Vice President in the elections of 1920, whose own notable career has been cut tragically short by an attack of infantile paralysis,

cannot walk without crutches or stand without support; but the earnest beauty of his fine, clear-cut face, the splendor of his delivery and the literary perfection of his sentences rose triumphant above his broken and crippled body.

The tremendous demonstration which crashed though every pause and thundered and roared for nearly two hours when he had finished was thrilling, too; and the thrill was not materially lessened for me by the fact that such demonstrations are carefully planned beforehand and engineered with equal care. It had spontaneity and sincerity and strength just the same—a touch of bravado, a touch of rowdiness, a fine show of recklessness and pride—New York "showing the world." The lilting gaiety of "The Sidewalks of New York" rang in my ears not only all day and all night, but for many days afterward. I shall never forget it.

And I shall always count it as one of the great experiences of my life that I saw Franklin Roosevelt manage to take the seven steps that were necessary to reach the rostrum, which was too narrow to accommodate his wheelchair, and that I sat within a few feet of him while he made the so-called "Happy Warrior" speech which failed to win the presidential nomination for Al Smith, but which—I shall always feel—went a long way toward making Roosevelt himself a presidential possibility.

I had discovered before I was invited to the speakers' platform that Will Rogers's seat in the press section was not far from mine. (He had been at Cleveland, too, but I had been separated from him there by Preston's edict about the telegraphic and nontelegraphic press.) No one could possibly have been more friendly and helpful than he was at the time and I frequently returned to the press section in order to take advantage of his good sense and good cheer. I still find the comments he wrote on the convention for the New York *Times* not only the most amusing, but the most discerning of any I have kept:

> It was a beautiful Sunday here. The New York churches were crowded with New Yorkers. Coney Island was crowded with delegates. It may have been a coincidence, but every preacher in town preached on "Honesty in Government."
>
> My sidekick, Mr. Bryan, arrived and sent his three trunks full of resolutions direct to the stage door. One trunk was leaking.
>
> Well, the Democratic scandals got started yesterday.
>
> Cordell Hull, the Chairman, announced that Cardinal Gibbons would offer the opening prayer. He was informed by some Republican that Cardinal Gibbons had been dead for three years, but that he might prevail on Cardinal Hayes to act instead. Hull evidently knows more about politics than the ministry. . . .

One guy from Montana, Maloney, forgot his speech and didn't say anything. He was the hit of the day. They applauded for five minutes. . . .

One day and up to two thirty in the Night they fought and argued the Klan. . . . Alaska voted one Ku Klux away up there. Can you imagine a man in all that Snow and Cold with nothing on but a thin white Sheet and Pillow slip?

Every time the speaker nominated somebody, why the Band would strike up what they thought was an appropriate tune. The bird that nominated Brown of New Hampshire kept talking and referring to "The Old Granite State. That Glorious old Granite State." When he finished up the Band played "Rock of Ages." There was granite for you.

I enjoyed Will Rogers, but I was fast reaching the point where I enjoyed no one else. Personally, I felt the speakers had publicized the Klan as it had never been publicized before—the last thing they would have wanted to do. The week end before the balloting was to begin, it was three o'clock Sunday morning when I finally sank wearily into bed after a continuous session which lasted eleven hours. The next day I did not even have enough energy to walk around the corner to the Church of the Heavenly Rest, which I had selected, from its name, as being the one best suited to my needs. I pulled the sheets more closely around me and stayed where I was until it was time to go to another session on Monday to listen to the balloting.

It lasted for ten days, with only one interruption, which occurred on the evening of July 7th. There were rumors that Calvin Coolidge, Jr., had injured his foot while playing tennis with his brother John on the White House court. Just a blister on his heel, the first rumors said; then there were vague reports about an infection; then others, not so vague, that the boy's condition was serious. At ten-thirty a radio announcer hurried to the speakers' platform and whispered to Walsh. Even before his gavel fell, the tumult in the Garden was hushed. He spoke without raising his voice and everyone heard him.

"It is with profound grief that I must tell you Calvin Coolidge, Jr., has just died. The convention stands adjourned."

There was a low murmur which gathered intensity, as hundreds in the Garden recognized the tragic force of his words and shared the sorrow of the bereft parents at the White House. Except for this murmuring, the great crowd dispersed silently.

The next morning, the prayer with which the exercises opened was in a different key from any that had preceded it: "This convention of the Democratic party gathers this morning under the shadow of the grief that has come to the home of the Chief Magistrate of our nation together with all our fellow Americans. We bow our heads in sympathy and reverence by the side of our President as he and his family pass through the valley of the shadow of death. We pray that the divine comfort and healing may be vouchsafed to the sorrowing parents. May the father and mother of the lovable youth who has been called from life to life find solace and strength in the thought of the loving sympathy of the American people. In token thereof this convention silently bows its head with loyal and affectionate regard for the President and mother of Calvin Coolidge, Jr."

After this, the balloting was resumed. It went on and on. I began to have the feeling I have sometimes experienced during a long uncomfortable journey that it was never going to end. One hundred ballots were cast before I had another thrill. But finally, at two-thirty one morning a letter from William G. McAdoo was read, releasing the delegates pledged to him. Earlier, Franklin Roosevelt had read a letter from Smith, saying he would withdraw his name when Mr. McAdoo did. After the elimination of these two, one more ballot was taken; it showed that their strength was drifting somewhat aimlessly in several directions. At four o'clock an adjournment was called until noon.

Exhausted, I climbed into bed at five and out again at ten; when I reached the Garden, it was to find there was no more polling of delegations; no more booming of favorite sons. The torpid atmosphere was electrified again. Presently, Underwood of Alabama and Davis of West Virginia were leading, then Davis shot ahead; next the Governor of Alabama, whose resounding chant had started every roll call was shouting, "Al-a-abamm-er casts twenty-four votes for John W. Davis." Chairmen of state delegations were yelling, "Mr. Chairman— *Mr. Chairman*— MR. CHAIRMAN! I desire to announce that Illinois—Virginia— Georgia—New York—wishes to change its vote. Mr. Chairman—I move that the nomination be made by acclamation!" The march of the state standards started again, the band played. On the platform were raised the standard and flag of West Virginia and a huge picture of the nominee.

It was a great demonstration, but the afternoon session closed with another, hardly less clamorous and even more touching. Ex-Secretary Daniels had moved to adjourn until evening before considering the selection of a vice president. From the floor arose a murmur of protest which swelled to a roar:

"No—no—no—we know now we want Walsh for Vice President— Walsh—Walsh—Walsh!"

If ever a nomination was made by acclamation, that one was, and the convention thought everything was over but the cheering. Then the slim Walsh, gray haired, gray clad, looking almost pathetically spent, raised his hand and controlled once more the uncontrolled mass, as he had already done so many times. He had brought such distinction to the difficult office of Permanent Chairman that he had enhanced his already high reputation for ability with every day that passed.

"I thank you for the great honor you have done me," he said, steadily but in a voice curiously hushed. "I am deeply appreciative, deeply touched. But the selection of a vice president is not a matter for sudden decision. The convention stands adjourned until eight o'clock this evening."

"We'll get you yet," someone called out, and there was another cheer.

But I knew they would not—guessed the reason before Walsh's dignified and formal letter of declination was read at the final session: that he felt he could serve his party and his country better on the floor of the Senate, where he was reasonably sure of retaining his place, than as its possible presiding officer.

"The two outstanding personalities revealed by the convention," said the New York *Times,* "are Walsh and Roosevelt—the two who did, and did perfectly, what they tried to do and what they should have done."

For two days after the convention ended, I stayed in my comfortable quarters writing my own article and reading and rereading those that Will Rogers had written. On the evening of the second day, the Pittmans, who had also stayed over, declared I had been incarcerated long enough and insisted I should dine with them. It happened that I had not seen as much of them as I had of many other friends during the convention, and I was glad of the chance. As not infrequently occurred now that I was on terms of easy companionship with them, we argued a good deal. I could not persuade them to admit that the Democrats had thrown away the election, even though I knew they agreed with me; the most they would concede was that if Walsh had only been on the ticket, their chances of victory would have been much greater. As it was, four weeks had been wasted; without his constant reminders all through the summer, of the last administration's misdeeds, there would be nothing to stop a Coolidge landslide. Davis, unquestionably a man of great ability and unimpeachable integrity, was very generally characterized as a "Wall Street candidate." Charles Bryan, the vice presidential nominee, was known outside his own state largely as the brother of William Jennings. The ticket could hardly have been weaker. The gravity of Harding's faults and failings had still not made a sufficiently deep impression on the public mind to swing the vote away from his party.

I reached home thankful for the peace and quiet of the countryside, and though I was exhausted when I arrived there, I revived enough to have eighteen of the Old Guard for dinner on my birthday, and since I had brought presents from Puerto Rico for everyone, a picturesque new note was added to the festivities. As usual, Labor Day was the occasion of a celebration in Newbury, the main feature this time being a performance of the comic opera *Cox and Box* with Henry, John and Sidney Johnson as the spirited actors and singers. Sid was the son of Laura Chamberlain and Ervin Johnson, both distant cousins of mine, at whose wedding I had first been unquestioningly accepted as "Harry Keyes's girl" by the North Country; now another ancestral friendship was being continued and another abiding kinship honored in the next generation, according to our custom.

Between these two major celebrations, I actually had the courage—or rather the bravado—to start a new book. *The Safe Bridge* had not found a welcome anywhere, and *Lady Blanche Farm* was still in the wrappings which had enclosed it on its return from the publisher; moreover, after considering the possibility of using short stories during the summer months, when Washington would provide little or no news, Mr. Bigelow had returned those I sent him with the comment that he was afraid I would never be able to write fiction that was up to the *Good Housekeeping* standard. Mrs. Meloney continued to publish my short stories in *Delineator,* but this was frankly because she could not lure me away from *Good Housekeeping* as far as articles were concerned. She had made another effort during the Democratic convention, and I had been sorely tempted to accept it, for she offered me a better price than I was getting from *Good Housekeeping* and a long-term contract, which I did not have with them. But Mr. Bigelow had given me my first big chance and I was grateful to him. I felt that as long as he wanted me for a regular contributor and his readers continued to respond—without quite visualizing the two as synonymous—I should stay with him. On the other hand, I had been greatly incensed by a book entitled *Revelry* —an "exposé" of the Harding Administration—which Horace Liveright had sent me with a request for a review. It presented an aspect of Washington I had never seen and which I still could not believe existed. For the first—and I may add for the only time in my life—I responded to Mr. Liveright's request in a letter that was consciously discourteous. I said that nothing would induce me to review this horrible book; it was obviously written by an outsider who knew little or nothing about Washington; some day I would write a novel that gave a true picture of official life, and when I did, I would send him a copy. . . . I did not for one moment suppose that Mr. Liveright would answer this unpardonably rude letter, but he did so promptly. Without referring to my comment on *Revelry,* he said he would be delighted to see my novel when I wrote it. I started it the next day and named it *Queen Anne's Lace.*

It did not get very far beyond the title. Mr. Bigelow decided to fill in the summer months with so-called human interest articles, which I detested. One of them was a "Letter on Everyday Good Citizenship," one a "Letter to Every Mother," one a "Letter on Friendship." Inevitably, no matter how hard I tried to avoid it, there was an involuntary note of condescension in such articles; they sounded as if I imagined I knew more about and could deal better with citizenship, motherhood and friendship than the readers to whom they were addressed. As a matter of fact, Mr. Bigelow himself was not satisfied with the one about friendship, as I originally wrote it, and for the first time made me rewrite an entire article. The telephone call making this demand came to me at six o'clock one evening, when I had been at my desk all day dictating letters, hitherto set aside in favor of work on the article. Lisle Cobb had stepped into the breach and was helping me intermittently with my secretarial chores, as Miss Shufelt had not been able to leave her position in Washington to come north with me. After hearing my side of the conversation, Lisle exclaimed, "Why, you can't possibly do that tonight. You're too tired!" "But I have to," I replied. "It's all in the day's work. The revised version has to be in New York Monday morning or it won't make the deadline. Come on, tell me what you think might improve this."

She stayed until nine and was very helpful. By midnight I thought I had the situation under control, and our cooperative hired man took the script to Woodsville, as there was no mail out of either Haverhill or Newbury on Sunday. Mr. Bigelow was pleased with the final results; but, though I usually read what I have written after it is published— some times with modest pride, often with wonder as to how it was ever accepted—I have never looked at that miserable article on Friendship from that day to this, though many people have been kind enough to tell me they liked it.

Of all the human interest articles published that summer, however, none brought in such wide and varied response as the one presented under the title of "How I Learned to Write," which was not of my choosing. It was meant to encourage would-be authors who, like myself, had not been to college or taken any special journalism courses and who seemed to hold the idea that they were doomed to failure on these accounts. I tried to convince such aspirants that there are many different ways of learning to write and mentioned some that had been helpful to me. It never entered my head or Mr. Bigelow's that the article would be interpreted as an arrogant and unfounded claim to literary craftsmanship. But the Des Moines *Register* did interpret it that way and printed a blast of derision, headed "The Need of Discrimination":

> We notice in the October *Good Housekeeping* an article by Frances Parkinson Keyes, the "Senator's Wife," on "How I Learned to Write," in which with great solemnity and earnestness she explains just how she conquered the art. All of which would be sensible enough if Frances Parkinson Keyes were in any way important as a writer. Her gossipy letters from Washington are entertaining reading and certainly worth doing, but given the same opportunity, a hundred other women that we know could produce letters quite as entertaining. Mrs. Keyes's short stories and novel (we have read only one—perhaps she has written more) certainly do not entitle her to regard herself as a creative writer. If her recent article had been on "How I Got Myself in Print," or "How I Learned to Punctuate," or "How It Feels to See Your Picture in a Magazine," there would have been point to it. Mrs. Keyes evidently lacks humor.

I took this review very much to heart. I do not know why I should have been so stricken by a midwestern reviewer's statement that I wrote nothing but gossip when various people of great distinction had thanked me for making current history so real and the New York *Times* had considered a book of mine worthy of its front page review. Perhaps it was because this Iowan gave me a feeling of such complete helplessness. He said he knew a hundred women who could do as well as I could, given my "opportunity," and I longed to ask him to identify them and their "opportunities." Would they all labor under a severe physical handicap, heavy family responsibilities, straitened financial circumstances and only seven years of formal education? It was not just that he could not understand a writer like me; it was that he could not understand a woman like me and nothing I could say or do would make him.

As I have said, I was brought up to believe that a lady's name appeared in print only when she was born, when she married and when she died; but this reviewer would simply laugh at the suggestion that it was hard for me to disregard this maxim, and that I personally would not have done so if it had not been necessary for me to become a wage earner. No woman turned loose, as I was at the age of six, to browse in her father's library with volumes written in five languages, deludes herself into believing she has "conquered the art" of authorship; she grows up surrounded by too many examples of what this means. Nevertheless, her early work can be original creative writing. I might have been willing to grant that my punctuation needed improvement and that an article entitled "How I Learned to Punctuate" would be as incorrectly headed as one entitled "How I Learned to Write." The first thing I wrote—at the age of seven—was a pageant to be enacted in my mother's drawing room. It had very little punctuation and its spelling bore no resemblance to Webster's. However, it *did* have a perfectly recognizable plot and twelve separate scenes which worked out very well. In other words, it *was* creative writing.

I suppressed the urge to answer back, realizing its futility (as I have since learned the futility of arguing with the Internal Revenue Service). But I really did not need to in this instance. The *Register's* reviewer was immediately inundated with protests, one of which he was sporting enough to publish:

> *In Defense of Frances Parkinson Keyes*
>
> "A little while back," writes Clare Drees, "I read a short disparaging article on the book-page in regard to the popularity of Frances Parkinson Keyes's literary efforts.
>
> "I wish to take issue, in a friendly vein, in favor of this writer, who, according to a number of paramount critics, ranks with our best modern writers. . . .
>
> " 'How I Came to Write' is a document teeming with human sympathy, super-efforts to overcome all obstacles to reach her literary goal, and above all displays a brilliant mind, a loyal wife and a fine loving mother.
>
> "She is a writer one would love to have a chat with, deriving great mental benefit from the privilege."

My mail and Mr. Bigelow's were also flooded with letters from enthusiastic readers. I needed the reassurance these gave, for I was very tired and correspondingly depressed, but this was the summer of all others when Harry, who was up for re-election, required the sort of support I could give him, and I was determined not to let him down.

I had more and more requests for speeches, and I tried hard to make as many as I could, not only because I knew we needed the money, but because these talks seemed to be helpful in the general political picture. I spoke in Randolph and St. Johnsbury, Vermont—near enough to the New Hampshire line to bring a good many people over it. I spoke to big audiences in several New Hampshire cities and went over state lines again to Connecticut, to appear at Hartford, and to Massachusetts to appear at Lawrence, Belmont and Littleton, where the crowd was so large that I had to move from a hall to a church. All this was very gratifying, and it was easier for me to get about now because, for the first time, I had a car of my own that I had bought and paid for in full with money I had earned. It was a maroon-colored seven-passenger Stude-baker, which I affectionately named "Studey." I took immense pride and pleasure in using it myself and inviting my friends to use it with me. It was decided that when we went to Washington after the election, Studey would go, too, and Henry Deming would be our chauffeur; just as Miss Shufelt would ease deskwork, Henry Deming would ease getting away from the desk.

Meanwhile, much as I enjoyed using Studey and proud as I was of my well organized household, things seemed to have a way of going wrong if I left home. During one of my brief absences, Peter fell from his pony and broke his arm; during another, Harry was in a bad auto-mobile accident; his car was demolished, a horse was killed, and Harry himself was severely shaken up. With two invalids in the house, it was necessary to recall invitations to one party of political significance, but usually I managed to see them through somehow.

> Members of four chapters of the Daughters of the American Revolu-tion in this vicinity . . . were guests at the home of the U.S. Senator Henry W. Keyes, Pine Grove Farm, North Haverhill, Thursday after-noon, Aug. 14.
> There were about one hundred ladies present and they spent a plea-surable afternoon with their hostess, Mrs. Frances Parkinson Keyes.

> Senator and Mrs. Henry W. Keyes sponsored a most successful polit-ical meeting Monday afternoon at their estate in North Haverhill, there being 500 in attendance, about evenly divided between women and men. . . . Mrs. Keyes acted as the presiding officer and spoke briefly on the purpose of the gathering, which was to urge the people to vote at election time, and more especially the women.

I had, to be sure, two capable and willing domestics, to help with the housework and entertaining, but as I look back, I wonder how we man-aged. There was no caterer anywhere within hailing distance, and re-freshments were served at these gatherings. They were relatively simple, but five hundred people can eat a lot of salad, a lot of sandwiches and a lot of cake, and everything they ate was made in the house. By the first of November, I had begun to wonder how many more times I could rally, but on the fourth I crawled out of bed and, somehow, despite the terrible pain of sciatica, went to North Haverhill to vote. Then I told Harry that this time he would have to take the returns himself and crawled back to bed, to rise no more for a week.

There was no reason why I should. He was re-elected to the Senate by the largest majority ever given a candidate of either party in the state of New Hampshire.

Chapter 32

I WAS pledged to a new series of speeches after the November election, and did manage to keep all my engagements, though I was still in considerable pain when I started out on the eleventh. I went in swift succession to New Bedford, Waltham, Somersworth, Malden and New Britain, stopped briefly in New York and reached Washington in time to go to the Pan-American Mass on Thanksgiving Day with Senator Walsh and to the Army-Navy Game in Philadelphia with Harry on the twenty-ninth. A letter I wrote Mary Gray shortly thereafter not only refers to a very fine game but gives an account of a strange psychic experience which occurred immediately afterward:

I have quite definitely avoided, since I returned from California, going into that state of semi-trance which I experienced when you and I were at the Ambassador. I have felt on the verge of it many times, but have had to work under such heavy pressure all the time that I have not dared risk the exhaustion that came to me with that. I have not been able to control dreams, of course, of which there have been many, and then came this waking experience.

A week ago—November 29th—I went with Harry to the Army-Navy football game. It was the best game I ever saw and the trip, made on a special train provided for official people, was a very pleasant one, but in no way extraordinary. As we were driving home from the station—a little after nine in the evening—I was conscious of the sound of distant cheering and asked Harry if he heard it. He said he could hear nothing. It grew in volume and apparent nearness, so I asked him again. When he replied in the negative three times, I became aware that I was hearing something he was not meant to hear. It seemed almost like a chorus of heavenly hallelujahs—or what I should imagine such a chorus would be like. When we got out of the car at

(304)

our front door, I could see a bright light in the sky, something like northern lights. I heard the music even more clearly then and every time I wakened during the night I could hear it, and the room was very bright—not light exactly, but still illumined.

It was years before I had a repetition of this experience, and I have no explanation for it. There had been several instances of extrasensory manifestations after the two which had so deeply affected me at Pine Grove Farm; but I had decided that though I could not deny the existence of these, it was unwise for me to make any attempt to develop them. I had even gone so far as to decline socially to make any experiments with an ouija board. I had the feeling, perhaps exaggerated, that I had no right to use, with the help of a device and as a means of amusement for groups, whose views on the subject ranged from the skeptical and the derisive to the credulous and the awed, what was apparently sensitivity to forces I respected without understanding them. The very fact that my private experiences had been rare, unsought and significant strengthened the feeling that they should be valued but guarded and that they should be accepted as factual, but extraordinary and never sought.

During November, two deaths occurred which affected me very deeply: Senator Lodge died on the eleventh and Mrs. Harding on the twenty-second. By then, of course, President Harding's weaknesses had all been very fully discussed, but no one had come forward with a criticism of his wife; and it is hard for those of both political parties, who knew her well, to accept as justified the present generally adverse appraisal of her. That her husband did not deserve her unquestioning devotion is unfortunate, if we are forced to the conclusion that he did not. But many marriages have been happy and successful, even though they were marred by faults and failings that are hard to forgive. "A woman knows there is always something [good] left in the man she loves. And, even if she did not know it, it would be the same. She would rather give all for nothing than never give at all." This statement, quoted from *Home,* a novel anonymously published by the Century Company in 1914, is certainly true of many women; and I am sure it would have been true of Mrs. Harding even if the man she loved had given her nothing. But he had given her a great deal. He had, indeed, carried her to the White House, justifying the faith she had in him, and it is unthinkable that there was ever a lack of kindness in his attitude toward her or a lack of appreciation. To say that Harding is the worst President we ever had because he was (lamentably) unfaithful to his marriage vows is as ridiculous as it is to call him our worst President because of the Teapot Dome scandal. It must be admitted, however reluctantly, that the normal adult male who is completely continent before marriage or wholly satisfied with monogamy after marriage is the exception and not the rule. As far as political scandals are concerned, I strongly recommend that Harding's most virulent critics make a thorough study of the Grant Administration and then come down to the present day. As I recall it, there was no accusation—or any chance for one, considering the size of his landslide—that Harding's election had been stolen; nor was it necessary to force the resignation of any member of the White House staff, because of proven perversion.

The boys' vacations were always crowded because their engagements overlapped mine and their father's, and this year there was an added complexity. John announced he would like to be confirmed before he went back to school. To this day, I have no idea what caused the sudden resolution, but his father and I were agreed that his strong desire should be met, if possible. I telephoned at once to our Bishop's office, asking for an appointment, and found him most cooperative. He said he would be very glad to have me bring my son for a talk, and if this proved satisfactory to all concerned, he would confirm John in his private chapel on Saturday, the twenty-seventh. This seemed most appropriate, as it was the feast day of St. John the Evangelist. The simple ceremony, at which our entire family and the Bishop's wife were present, was most impressive, and the fact that the rest of the day was spent in a way typical of the holidays—two tea dances and a third dance from nine to eleven—seemed not at all incongruous. Henry had been confirmed before we left Concord, and just before I started on my trip around the world, Peter, who had been going regularly to catechism classes for weeks, was confirmed in a large class at St. Andrews, our parish church in Washington. After this, all three of my sons not infrequently managed to go to Communion with me.

Early in the new year came the farewell banquet tendered the Ambassador of France and Mme Jusserand upon the former's retirement after twenty-two years of diplomatic service in Washington, at that time a record tenure for an ambassador. This was certainly a "superdinner," and it had unusual significance for us, since the Jusserands had been our next-door neighbors and very good friends from the time we went to live at Meridian Mansions. The banquet was attended by over a thousand persons, among them many of the most distinguished in the nation, and was held just one hundred years after the famous farewell feast for Lafayette, and in his tribute to Ambassador Jusserand, the Speaker of the House, who was the toastmaster of the evening, said:

A hundred years ago a poem to Lafayette ended with this couplet:

A nineteenth-century primitive painting of Pine Grove Farm.

(Top) HWK, Sr., and Jr., 1906. (Bottom) The author at the age of twenty-three.

The author reading to John and Henry, 1910.

The author at the time of HWK's Inauguration as Governor of
New Hampshire, 1917.

(Top) The author in her Red Cross uniform, 1917. (Bottom) Richard Bayley Cobb in World War I uniform.

Poster used during HWK's first campaign for the United States Senate.

BOYÉ OF SAN FRANCISCO

Photograph taken by Boyé of San Francisco in 1922 and regarded by the author as "the best picture ever taken" of her.

(Top) The author with Peter, 1922. (Bottom) Senator Keyes, the author, Peter, Henry and John in Washington, 1927.

The author at the time of her presentation to King George and Queen Mary, 1923.

C. VANDYK LTD.

A later portrait by Boyé, circa 1925.

*The author as she appeared at a Japanese tea party given in her
honor at Kyoto, 1925.*

(Top left) The author at the Great Wall of China, 1925. (Top right) Govern-ment House, Singapore. (Bottom) Princess Kil Chang Whe, Princess Eu and an American nurse, Seoul, 1925.

The author and HWK, Jr., in Venice, 1926.

Car in which Russ Thayer, John and the author drove to the
Christ of the Andes.

COURTESY: WASHINGTON POST

HARRIS & EWING, WASHINGTON

(Top) President Coolidge signing the Child Labor Bill, June 4, 1924.
(Bottom) Senator Keyes during his second term of office.

Pine Grove Farm as it appears from the Vermont side of the Connecticut River.

FOWLE

"We bend not the neck and we bow not the knee,
But our hearts, Lafayette, we surrender to thee."

You, Sir, carry back with you to the same country the same conquest.

There were other eloquent tributes, and then, last of all, except for the *Marseillaise,* came the Ambassador's own speech, in the course of which he said:

Looking back across the years that have been, it seems to me that I see in the distant past a very young man, looking even younger than he was, asking a police officer on the Place de l'Odéon in Paris the way to the Foreign Office. Duly informed he began walking toward it, unaware that he was starting on a journey which would make him see many countries, and end half a century later in a city whose very name symbolizes uprightness, nobility of purpose, love of independence—the city of Washington.

Soon after this dinner, I was a delegate to the Conference on the Cause and Cure of War. This was not convened by any of the so-called peace societies, but by nine great women's organizations representing a membership of over five million and many different lines of thought and endeavor. The purpose of the gathering was to make a dispassionate study of the causes of war and their possible cures, not to hold a meeting of propagandists; in a word, the convention was presumably largely educational, and the speakers chosen to address it were selected because they were experts—military, legal, political, administrative, scientific —and not well meaning but uninformed or emotional persons who might do more ultimate harm than immediate good to the cause of peace.

The conference considered many ways to end war. I liked Rabbi Stephen Wise's suggestion that we "religionize the churches, educate the schools, liberate ourselves in the matter of textbooks. Work through the women's clubs and the men's clubs and through the homes, which are in danger of shifting too many of their burdens." I liked much less the recommendation of nonresistance under any and all circumstances and the hisses which greeted former Attorney General George Wickersham's remark that there have been righteous wars. We owe our national life to a righteous war. Birth control as a preventive for war—the discussion of which occupied most of one afternoon—seemed to me to fall rather wide of the mark; so did a prolonged dissertation on the relations between Turkey and Armenia. I was also sorry when some rather sweeping statements made by Rabbi Wise, David Hunter Miller and Mr. Wickersham that were derogatory to Congress, and especially to the Senate's stand on the World Court, were greeted with applause—an attitude toward a great legislative body difficult for me to understand, coming as it did from a group whose avowed purpose in meeting was the substitution of law for force. As the applause continued, I realized my resentment was developing into anger, and suddenly I found myself on my feet asking the Chair for recognition.

"Have any members of the Senate been invited to address this convention and explain their stand?" I inquired. I cannot remember whether the answer was a definite no or a rather vague mumble to the effect that one senator had been approached, through a secretary, and did not seem receptive to the idea. At any rate, it was obvious that no thorough attempt had been made to have legislative action or the lack of it interpreted for the convention.

"If I can persuade one to come, will you make room on the program for a *senator* to clarify the Senate's position on the World Court?" I asked impetuously.

The Chair, while expressing doubts about my persuasive powers, said that in such an event time would of course be created on the program. I hurriedly left the meeting and headed for the Capitol. I felt reasonably sure that either Senator Pittman or Senator Walsh would make the speech if I asked him to do so. Either one would be more than adequate; it was just a question of which I could locate first. This happened to be Key Pittman.

"You are not in a position to ask favors," he said banteringly as soon as I had been ushered into his office. "You talked to Senator Ransdell twice as much as you did to me at the Jusserand dinner and wrote a jingle for him."

"I wrote one for you too."

"Yes, but I'd have been better pleased if mine had been the only one you wrote."

"Oh, for heaven's sake, Key, I don't play favorites at a formal dinner, even if I feel like it! If you don't want to come and speak to these women, say so! I'll go and ask Senator Walsh."

"Of course, I'll talk to them," Key Pittman said pleasantly. "When? Where? How long? Come and have lunch with me; we'll discuss it then."

At the next session of the convention, he made a splendid speech which, because of his position as a member of the Foreign Relations Committee, carried great weight; but his personal magnetism probably had even more to do with its overwhelming success. He explained, without apology or praise, the handicaps under which such a committee functions, the inevitable delays and difficulties. His own approval of the League of Nations had long been known; but he paid a well deserved compliment to his colleagues who disagreed with him, asking the conference to recognize that though we sometimes differed as to means, the end desired by all patriotic Americans was the same. He ended with a high tribute to President Coolidge. As I listened to him, bursting with pride that the Senate should have so compelling a spokesman on this occasion, a statement made earlier in the conference kept coming back to me, one made by Dr. Manley Hudson of the Harvard Law School in his account of the League's achievements—that it had taken two years to settle a dispute over a boundary line in Albania, which neither he nor anyone else seemed to think an unreasonable length of time. Since this was the case, were two years—or even twice two years—an unreasonable length of time for the Senate to consider the World Court?

Senator Pittman accepted and promised to deliver to the Foreign Relations Committee a resolution which the conference had passed, declaring its "earnest wish that the Senate of the United States shall take immediate action to provide for our national membership in the Court by its prompt adoption of the resolution providing for such adherence with the Harding-Hughes-Coolidge reservations"; and the speech which President Coolidge made to the delegates when he received them later that same day must have reassured them greatly, with his reiteration in favor of the World Court.

Just four days after the Conference on the Cause and Cure of War ended, another great meeting began: the Foreign Missionary Conference. It was the largest gathering of the kind ever held, numbering more than five thousand persons, of whom about a third were women—and it was the first time that women had been recognized to such a degree in a large missionary assembly. At it were represented practically all the Protestant denominations, with delegates not only from the foreign field, but from churches all over the United States and Canada; with a membership of seventy million.

As soon as the convention had been called to order, the congregation rose to sing a wonderful old hymn, one that I learned before I even learned to read, for my grandmother, who taught me almost everything that I acquired in those days, believed children should not only thank God but praise Him. So as the first lines of "All Hail the Power of Jesus' Name" rang out, I felt a thrill that carried me far away from Mrs. Coolidge, who had come on the platform with the President and the officers of the day and who was singing with great spirit and enthusiasm, away from the soberly clad song leader and the great mass of humanity surging around me. It carried me back thirty years to an old New England parsonage; and then it swept me clear around the world —"from Greenland's icy mountains to India's coral strand," in the words of another fine old hymn which we sang later. From start to finish of the conference, there was no one feature of it that I enjoyed more than the singing, nor one from which I derived more spiritual exaltation. There was no accompaniment save a piano and a clarinet; but five thousand people, singing with their whole hearts and souls, do not need much accompaniment; they are sufficient unto themselves; and they reveal a power which shows them to be sufficient for much else besides.

The week was one of great inspiration to me—a week in which, at the very height of the Washington season, I slipped away entirely from luncheons and dinners, receptions and calls, and sat at the feet of great teachers and listened—and learned. It had for me only two flaws. First, not *all* the denominations which publicly professed to believe in "God, the Father Almighty, and in Jesus Christ, His only Son, Our Lord" and carried the gospel to distant lands with that profession on their lips and in their hearts were represented at the conference. I learned from sources so authoritative that I could not doubt them, that those missing were not invited to attend this conference because they had declined to come to others in the past. I hoped they would be present at the next one, both by invitation and by their own desire. Long before I ever heard the word "ecumenicity," I was a strong believer in it!

The other flaw, in my opinion, was the nature of some references made to men in public office. For instance, Toyohiko Kagawa, "the saint of the slums," whose twenty years' work in the worst districts of Kobe and Tokyo and his writings describing it had become famous, said he had decided there were two kinds of persons in the United States— Christians and members of Congress. Perhaps these allusions would not have made so deep an impression upon me if I had not heard them so many times, in regard not only to members of Congress but also to other persons of high degree. I did not imagine for a moment that these were all miracles of righteousness; but I felt that on the whole they were a great deal better than the country at large gave them credit for being, that religion occupied an important part in their lives and that the still small voice of conscience was heard above the clamor in legislative halls and the murmurings of the executive chamber. My previous discovery that every single woman on the Executive Board of the Congressional Club at that time was a church member inspired some careful thinking along these lines; and having begun to think, I began to study and to investigate.

Many of our Presidents have been church members; and according to the Methodist Board Survey ninety per cent of the members of the then incoming Congress were church members and several were outstandingly devout. But there was still prevailing prejudice against men whose form of faith was not the same as that of their critics. A storm of criticism had swept over the country when Edward Douglass White was appointed to the Supreme Court. Because he was not an able lawyer, a scholar and a gentleman? Not at all. Because he was a Catholic. Both as Associate Justice and as Chief Justice he served with honor and glory to himself, his country and his church; the second time a Catholic was appointed to the Supreme Court it occasioned no more comment than if a Presbyterian had been. The same storm raged over the appointment of Mr. Brandeis—because he was a Jew. It will never rage again for that reason. Mr. Smoot's election to the Senate was bitterly denounced— because he was a Mormon. He proved himself one of the most faithful and efficient of public servants; his junior colleagues did not have to breast the same wave. "There are more ways than one to Heaven, perhaps more Heavens than one." We can, and should, choose our own paths; we cannot, and should not, attempt to choose our brother's, or penalize him for keeping to the one of his choice. As soon as we do, we undermine that spirit of toleration and brotherhood which, as President Coolidge said, must, both at home and abroad, serve as the cornerstone of true Christianity.

The weather man had frightened us with prophecies of rain for the Inauguration; but the fourth of March dawned mild and bright—a gentle sort of day. I was in the Senate Chamber early, for I always loved to watch it fill up on such an occasion.

The Senators were crowded on the Republican side of the aisle with the visiting governors, and Governor Nellie Tayloe Ross of Wyoming, the first woman governor in the United States, received a tremendous ovation when she came in. The Members of the House, twenty minutes late, took their places, followed by the Diplomatic Corps in dress uniforms; the Cabinet in formal morning attire; the Army Chief of Staff, the Chief of Naval Operations and the Commandant of the Marines scarcely less resplendent than the foreign dignitaries; the Supreme Court, their black robes voluminous and lustrous. Mrs. Dawes, in vivid blue, was sitting in the front row of the Senators' Gallery, her children on either side of her, the Cabinet ladies behind her. There was one empty place in the row, between a spare elderly man and a small elderly woman in a black dress who was talking to a slim, tall boy with dark hair on her other side: the President's father, the President's mother-in-law and the President's son. Then a lady all in gray came down the aisle and took her place in the vacant seat, and every man and woman in the Chamber rose, suddenly silent in tribute to the President's wife.

This tribute was no empty one, and it was significant that it took the form of silence, not of applause. Mrs. Coolidge had lines in her face and silver in her hair that had not been there a year before. But her fine courage had never failed her; her poise, her cordiality, her humanity had not fled before grief.

Finally, the Vice President-elect entered to the roar of tempestuous clapping, shook hands with Senator Cummins, the President pro tem, advanced briskly to the platform and seated himself in the presiding officer's chair. It was several moments before the uncontrolled amusement on all sides brought him to his feet with the realization that he was the only person not standing to receive the President. An instant later, President Coolidge, escorted by the joint Congressional committee, came in quietly and took his seat. There was a reserve, a dignity, about President Coolidge which stood him in good stead at such times, and he faced the audience with something strangely compelling in his composure.

But as the proceedings continued, I could not help remembering the ceremony four years earlier when the retiring Vice President, Mr. Marshall, made a speech which I thought one of the finest I ever heard, and Mr. Coolidge, the incoming Vice President, gave me "faith in Massachusetts" to hear him; and it was therefore a disappointment, and also something of a shock, when General Dawes seized a flimsy manuscript and, with great excitement and no reserve whatever, began a Philippic against the Senate's rules, conduct and procedure. His arms circled about and his fists beat the air; a lock of hair waved across his heated brow; and when the diatribe was concluded and four new senators were called to take the oath of office, the General exclaimed, "Bring 'em up faster, bring 'em all up!" Then, without awaiting a motion from the floor to adjourn, the Vice President announced that we would proceed forthwith to the front of the Capitol for the inauguration of the President.

The boys' spring vacation began shortly after the Inauguration and John's classmate and distant cousin Sidney Johnson, who had cooperated so successfully with my two older sons in their riotous presentation of *Cox and Box* at the Labor Day observance in Newbury, came to stay with us during the holidays and suggested that I spend part of these "joy riding" with John and himself in Virginia. The idea was in every respect a happy one, which resulted in the first of many trips on which he was our good companion. We went part way down the Shenandoah Valley, stopping overnight with friends in Winchester and Lexington.

I had a lovely time and what the trip meant to John and Sid can be reckoned in neither days nor dollars. Never again would "Sheridan's Ride" mean to either of them a verse to be memorized between Friday and Monday; they had seen the dignified old house from which he started and traveled the road over which he had galloped. Never again would the streams and mountains of Virginia be blue lines and double caterpillars on a map, or the Shenandoah a "new dirigible named for some place." Never again would the courtesy and hospitality of the South be a graceful legend after such a happy experience.

The League of Women Voters was holding its annual meeting in Richmond that spring, and as this has always been one of my favorite cities, I welcomed an excuse to prolong my stay in Virginia and attend it, though I was beginning to feel less and less enthusiasm for meetings held by large groups of women. It seemed no matter how worth while the cause they sought to promote, the proportion of really earnest and dedicated women to those who were merely seeking a new outlet for their energies or an expansion of their social life was lamentably small. I was glad that this one would be my last for some time to come. But Mr. Bigelow, who had made a special effort to attend it, seemed disturbed because he had found no one to represent *Good Housekeeping* at such meetings during my long absence, which was now impending. He asked me for suggestions, and after giving the matter careful thought, I made one.

"She hasn't enough contacts," he answered briefly.

I tried again, mentioning a woman who I believed knew practically everybody.

"Yes," Mr. Bigelow agreed, "she has a wide acquaintance, but I don't like the shape of her jaw. She has a grim expression. It puts people off."

I tried a third time, mentioning a woman who knew everybody and who had a pleasant smile. He shook his head.

"She doesn't know how to dress," he objected. "That's important too."

I laughed and reminded him that a reviewer on the Des Moines *Register* had said there were a hundred women who could do my job just as well as I could, given my opportunities. Surely Mr. Bigelow ought to be able to find one. He shook his head again and made blistering remarks about the *Register,* which were music to my ears.

My preparations for departure were taking more and more of my time and were by no means all pleasant. I had not been vaccinated since I was seven years old, and then I had been vaccinated in three places at once on the theory that only one would "take"; all three took and I nearly lost my life. It was the conclusion of all the medical advisers to whom I had reported this that I had practically had smallpox and that no vaccination would ever take again. At the time, it was not necessary to show a certificate of recent vaccination if only going to and from Europe, but it was necessary if going to and from China; so I submitted to the inevitable, and again I was quite seriously, though not dangerously, ill for more than a week. Three inoculations for typhoid were no kinder, or dentistry done under an anesthetic that did not quite work. I must confess that there were moments when my courage faltered, as far as taking the trip was concerned. But I could not confess this in the face of the dinners given in my honor at the embassies of the countries I was to visit, and the wonderful farewell party the Women's National Press Club had planned for me.

This dinner was a very happy, not to say hilarious, occasion. It was held in a suite at the Hotel Hamilton, where we gathered around a long oval table, decorated with roses sent from the White House. The delivery of a series of fake telegrams from newspapers, read and answered at intervals, enlivened this feast; in these, my size, my old-fashioned hair style and my tendency to gather about me groups which grew in size like snowballs, as well as various other characteristics of mine, were all the targets for good-natured raillery. "Wire at once if true Mrs. Keyes has bobbed her hair. If so get photograph and mail special delivery," said a dispatch purportedly from the Cincinnati *Enquirer*. The reply was, "Not yet. Hopefully watching developments." . . . "Is it true that Mrs. Coolidge and John have joined Keyes party to go as far as San Francisco while White House is being renovated? Rush reply." This came "from the Washington *News*" to Martha Strayer, who answered, "No truth Coolidge report Stop Party to San Francisco still limited to Mrs. Keyes her son Henry and Henry's friend her son John and John's friend her son Peter and Peter's friend." The climax was a "wire from the Christian Science *Monitor*" asking, "Will Mrs. Keyes comment on joint statement Senators Borah and Jim Reed to be published all Hearst papers in morning that her trip is result of plot international secret agents working through League Women Voters and Thomas Jefferson Memorial Association to get United States into League of Nations?" To this Catherine Hackett made the emphatic response, "Mrs. Keyes refuses comment Borah Reed Stop Says you couldn't print it in the *Monitor* if she made one."

The menus were printed on telegraph blanks and concluded with the words:

So long, Frances. Frances, we will miss you so.
So long, Frances. How we hate to see you go.
And we'll be longing for you, Frances, while you roam.
So long, Frances, don't forget to come back home.

This dinner was one of the few occasions in my life in which I have really had the last word, and I brought my remarks to a close in this fashion:

Of course you all know that I am
About to leave you for Siam;
In short, that I am on my way
To take the road to Mandalay;
And thereby to secure a firmer
Impression on the state of Burma. . . .
But whether I am near or far
In Washington or Panama,
Whether I'm here or boldly gone
To find the treasure of Ceylon,
Remember that I love you all,
And that from every port of call
I'll send you greetings in those "Letters"
Which tell you all about my betters—
All that I can, of course I mean,
Put in that prudent magazine,
Upon whose stuff I strive to shine,
Because I believe it fair and fine.

Remember too I shall return
From Athens, Naples, and Lucerne;
From castles I have found in Spain—
And then I'll see you all again,
Whenever I can get the chance,
For Persia, Palestine and France
Can give me nothing much, I guess
That I'll love better than the Press
Club, so for Monday lunch
I'll soon be back here with the bunch;
And don't let anybody cry
Because I now must say good-bye.

Some time prior to my departure on my round the world trip, I had been promoted to the rank of Associate Editor, with numerous perquisites, and it had been decided that Peter would make the first part of the journey with me, which would include stops at Cuba and Haiti; it would do him no harm to miss the last few weeks of school, and he was old enough—twelve—to get a good deal out of such a jaunt, and my allowance from *Good Housekeeping* for expenses was large enough to include him. Henry and John would join us in Panama, and Peter and John would go home overland from California while Henry and I continued to the Orient, the Near East and Europe. His marks at Harvard were good enough to permit a year's absence from college without loss of scholastic standing, which meant that he had two summers at his disposal as well as an autumn, a winter and spring. He had taken shorthand lessons each morning before his regular classes, and had been doing quite a little reporting on college activities for the Boston *Globe,* to supplement his allowance. His editor, Lawrence Winship, had told him the paper would be glad to publish brief pieces giving his impressions of the places we visited and these proved to be a success from the beginning, while his earnings from them were more than welcome in providing him with spending money, for though all his expenses were paid as my secretary, no salary was included. John was scheduled to enter Harvard in the fall, and it did not seem wise to postpone this; but though we did not yet think of him as the student of the family, he had written me, shortly before his graduation from Morristown, "I got my Historical Thesis prize—a set of Parkman comprising 13 vol. I also got the prize for reading aloud—consisting of a volume of Kipling's verses. I was chosen valedictorian and got Daddy to help me on my speech. I got my gold baseball and letter also my basketball letter." All this seemed to indicate that John was entitled to a trip too, and I was glad that I could afford, through my earnings, to give him this.

Everyone kept telling Henry what "a wonderful opportunity" he was having, which of course was true, but it was an opportunity in which all the family, including myself, were to share, culturally and financially. It was these benefits that Harry and I were able to keep in mind, rather than a long separation. Besides, my husband was good enough to say and, I knew, to feel that I had helped him with his career, and now he wanted to help with mine, in which he had gradually become more and more interested as he recognized more and more clearly that it complemented his and harmonized with it. He and John came to see Peter and me off in New York and there was nothing gloomy about the leave-taking. And as I later wrote to Genevieve Walsh Gudger:

I wish you could have seen my stateroom on the *President Garfield* as I saw it—filled with the tangible expressions of good will and affection from the kind friends who were wishing me bon voyage for my world trip. It bloomed like a garden with fragrant flowers. . . . Then there were hampers of fruit and tins of sweets, dozens of telegrams and letters; a writing case; all the books I wanted to read last winter and had no time for; even a lace-edged, handmade negligee; and four lovely bags, among them the elegant gold-clasped one of white moire, richly embroidered, lying in a white satin box with a card reading, "With fondest love from Genevieve." . . .

We left New York on a still, sunny afternoon, soft with smoky haze, and Peter and I stood on deck, listening to new sounds and looking at new scenes. A Chinese orchestra was playing on strange thin-sounding instruments and the passengers stood casting streamers of colored paper out over the ocean long after the pier and the friends, toward whom they had originally been directing them, were lost to sight. And so we left our first port and faced the open sea. . . .

Part Seven

Letters From Afar:
Panama and the Orient in the
Mid-1920's

Chapter 33

I WAS awakened by Peter, who was protruding from a porthole in a perilous position and calling to me that this was the greatest day of his life. I was thus drowsily aware that we must be entering the Panama Canal, which he had been clamoring to visit ever since he first saw a picture of it in a geography; a few minutes later we were both on deck, clinging to each other in excitement.

The banks of the canal were green, greener than anything I had ever seen—as brilliant as if they had been lacquered. It was raining, softly, mistily, and the gentle gray of the skies was reflected in the gentle gray of the water as we were lifted smoothly into the first lock. I had not dreamed it could be so quiet—and so wonderful. I thought of those beautiful lines in Browning's "Andrea del Sarto":

> *All is silver gray,*
> *Placid and perfect in my art.*

I thought of them repeatedly after that. And I wished I were a poet myself, that I might describe Panama as she should be described—a woman lovely in her grays and greens, gray draperies, emeralds on her fingers, tourmalines in her ears, jade about her throat, a gracious, wise and silent lady.

It was then only a little more than twenty years since Panama, previously a province of Colombia, had achieved her independence and become a republic, been promptly recognized by the United States and, shortly afterward, signed a treaty granting to us five miles of land, to be known as the Canal Zone, on either side of a proposed canal. In addition, the treaty "granted to the United States in perpetuity the use, occupation and control of any other lands and waters outside the Zone

above described, which may be necessary for the construction, maintenance, operation, sanitation or protection of the said canal."

The sanitation of the city of Panama, which merged into the Canal
Zone without apparent boundary line, was under the direction of an
American official, whose power in his department was absolute; and the
Panamanian government had secured the services of American experts
in road building to assist in the development of its highway system.
Aside from those two departments, we did not have, and should not
have had, control of the affairs of the republic; and we sent a Minister
to it, as we did to other independent countries. In the Canal Zone, however, we had our own governor; it was an independent establishment in
the government service, directly under the President, though as a matter
of executive arrangement the Secretary of War represented him in the
administration of canal affairs. The organization on the isthmus employed about ten thousand persons, while as many more officers and enlisted men of the Army and Navy were stationed there. And our policy
in regard to the Canal and the Zone was very different from our policy
in regard to the Republic of Panama. The former policy had been
clearly defined by Charles Evans Hughes, the former Secretary of State.
"By building the Panama Canal," he said, "we have not only established a new and convenient highway of commerce, but we have established new exigencies and new conditions of strategy and defense. It is
for us to protect that highway. I believe that the sentiment of the American people is practically unanimous that in the interest of our national
safety we could not yield to any foreign power the control of the Panama Canal, or the approaches to it, or the obtaining of any position
which would interfere with our right of protection or would menace the
freedom of our communication."

There was substantial reason for this view of the case. For centuries
the great nations of the world had contemplated and attempted the
building of a canal. For centuries their contemplations and attempts had
borne no fruit. At length the great French engineer of the Suez Canal,
Ferdinand de Lesseps, undertook the project and failed. Yellow fever
and malaria raged, and in a single year there were twenty-two thousand
deaths. Finally the United States succeeded. The English writer Stephen
Graham, in his entertaining and illuminating book *The Quest of El
Dorado,* called the Panama Canal "the greatest advertisement of America in the world. Its construction was a superhuman task. . . . What was
one of the most pestilential swamps in the world is now something like
a health resort. . . . The Panama Canal . . . is a monument of America's
executive power, of her technical knowledge, and of her readiness to
use that knowledge and stake millions upon it. Every foreign ship pass-

ing through the Canal bows to the Stars and Stripes and, though paying
a money due, yet acknowledges a debt of civilization to the American
people. . . . The ships . . . come as guests through American waters.
America is the hostess of the world."

My own information in regard to the relations between the Republic
of Panama and the Canal Zone had been so scanty before I went there
that I was very grateful for this lucid explanation; and in passing
through the Canal, I was conscious of what Mr. Graham had said of
America as a great engineer and, even more, a great hostess and conqueror of death and disease.

We had entered the Canal at daybreak and at two in the afternoon
Peter and I were still hanging over the rail of our ship, afraid to glance
away for a single second lest we should miss a single sight; we had not
left the deck at all, except to change into our best bib and tucker. For,
while we had still been twenty-four hours out at sea, a radio message
had come from Admiral Latimer, who had been a fellow guest in Haiti
and who was then in command of the special squadron stationed at Panama, inviting us to lunch with him aboard his flagship, the *Rochester,*
immediately upon our arrival in Balboa. So we went from one kind of a
thrill to another, as literally as we went from one kind of a vessel to another, and found blended with the gray of Panama the gray of our own
battleships. It was a charming party, with that added flavor of festivity
which always seems to mark an entertainment on shipboard, and it was
not until late afternoon that we tore ourselves away. Then we went
ashore in the Admiral's launch and took our first drive through Balboa
and around Ancon Hill on our way to the Hotel Tivoli.

Everywhere the soft slopes were covered with the same brilliant verdure, everywhere the hard gray highways were bordered with it; and
both hillsides and roadsides were dotted with small gray houses
mounted on stilts and swathed in screened porches. I looked in vain for
the pretentious dwellings described to me beforehand; even the governor's mansion would scarcely have been called a fair-sized house in
New England, and in the South it would not by any means have ranked
as such. Most of these bungalows, as I soon discovered because of constant hospitality, contained a living room and dining room—often one
and the same apartment, though sometimes divided by a small hall—
and a kitchen downstairs, and two or three bedrooms upstairs. With a
few concrete exceptions—literally!—they were frame buildings, guiltless of plaster, almost guiltless of partitions; they contained a few rugs
and pictures, as little furniture as possible and almost no books, books
being the prey of bookworms—another literal fact! These houses were
provided by the government and could not be individually owned; no

amount of private fortune or public pull could improve one's quarters, which were allotted according to rank and length of service. I must confess that I missed the high ceilings, white plaster walls and colorful tiled floors of Cuba, which seemed to me infinitely more beautiful, as well as much cooler, but which seemed nonexistent in the Zone (though I found them again in Panamanian houses). I also pined for electric fans and thermos bottles, which the government did not provide, either in the private houses or the hotel which it owned and operated. And I never was so hot in all my life. The dryness which redeemed Haiti and the breeze which redeemed Havana were both wanting. The atmosphere, with the exception of a few brief hours of respite, seemed to me heavy laden and relentless.

But it is only fair to say that Americans living in the Zone did not seem to feel this way about it. I sat panting on many a porch while my hostess assured me it was always cool there, that she frequently had to close the windows and pull a blanket over her at night because of the wind. She would quote statistics about a heat wave in New York and ask if I did not feel fortunate to have escaped to the Zone, or, more conservatively, she would assure me that "the dry season is different," that the past week "has been unusual" or that "the sense of oppression ceases after one has been here for a time." I never argued and I never contradicted. I remembered all too well the years I spent in explaining that New Hampshire really wasn't cold in winter. The thermometer goes down to thirty below and stays there; but it is so *clear* and so *still* and so *dry* that of course . . .

Besides, there were many conditions, entirely aside from the climate, which the American woman living in the Zone could and did enjoy. Housekeeping in those small bare houses was extremely simple, and it was rendered doubly simple by the fact that servants were inexpensive, plentiful and excellent. A modest salary permitted the employment of two experienced maids, a laundress and a seamstress; consequently, many a woman who at home was obliged to do all her own housework, washing and sewing had an abundance of leisure. The social life was delightful, partly no doubt because there was plenty of time for it and partly because human beings naturally feel more disposed to gaiety when it does not have to come at the end of a hard day's work or represent an expenditure they can ill afford. Rents were reasonable too, and there was no coal to buy, no necessary change from summer to winter clothing with its attendant bother and expense. And children, as well as adults, throve. Never had I seen more husky children; they were swarming everywhere, tearing around apparently as oblivious of the heat as they were unaffected by it, while their parents followed a program which sent me to bed in a state of complete exhaustion. The adults began their day's activities at dawn and often ended them about the same hour; and in spite of this, there was no time sacred to the siesta; they swam and walked and danced; they played golf and tennis and bridge; they lunched out and dined out and in between they went out to tea; and all this was done not only without fatigue but without the slightest ill effect.

And while it is true I did not enjoy the climate or the quarters, I did enjoy everything else. I loved the water, the most delicious I had ever drunk, the softest I had ever bathed in. I loved the jitneys, invariably cars of expensive make with very inexpensive rates, their seats covered —as required by law—with clean washable material neatly buttoned over them. If you soiled your dress in a hired car in Panama, you could take the matter to court and the taxi driver could be forced to pay your laundry bill and sometimes more than that. I loved the beautifully paved streets where there was never an offensive sight or an offensive smell. I loved the sight of little children being taught to swim almost as soon as they learned how to walk, so that they dropped in and out of the water with the unconcern of small mermaids and mermen, in the big pool of the Balboa clubhouse, open and free to all. I loved the outdoor market in Panama City, and the sailing boats which brought the produce to be sold there. I loved the great golden altar in the Church of San José, which made me think of the city paved with gold, and the superb statue of Balboa, standing "silent upon a peak in Darien," which faced the sea in front of the hospital of San Tomás. I loved the Union Club, built squarely over the ocean so that you saw nothing but water on three sides, with fortified islands in the distance, and on the fourth side glimpsed a quaint street and quainter houses, like the mise en scène for *The Barber of Seville.* I loved the *tertulius* (informal parties) that took place at this club, the Americans and Panamanians mingling more than at any other place for dinner and dancing on the open terrace—the men all in white, the women and girls in soft sheer dresses. I loved the graceful native costume, the *pollera,* which some of the ladies still wore to parties, and my frankly expressed admiration of it resulted in the commencement of a collection of dolls, for a beautiful one, authentically clad, was one of many presents I received in Panama. I loved the Plaza Francia with its wide low steps mounting to the promenade on the sea wall; the arcade where stone tablets tell the story of the Canal from 1529 to 1914 and where the monuments to De Lesseps and his colleagues stand, defeated but still great—a tribute to the "glory of the conquered." I loved the *Presidencia,* with the snow-white egrets nestling against the mother-of-pearl columns in the patio.

I was introduced to the *Presidencia,* not casually but in due course. Among the very first of my callers were Señor and Señora Alfaro, the

Minister of Foreign Affairs and his wife. He was the brother of our friend the Panamanian Minister in Washington, and there was much similarity between them. Both had the same delicacy and high breeding, the same quick and quiet courtesy, the same thoughtfulness, kindness and attention to detail—in short, the same rare degree of real statesmanship. And at the end of our conversation, the Minister of Foreign Affairs asked me when I would like to be presented to President Chiari, quite as if it were a matter of course that I should be. If ten-thirty on Monday would be agreeable, he would be glad to come for me then.

Punctually at the hour appointed, we started for the *Presidencia,* which was located directly on the waterfront. A guard of soldiers was patrolling its columned portico, and gleaming bayonets were stacked at one side. But, once past its wide doors, I promptly forgot this formidable array in the sheer beauty of the patio. Its supporting pillars were gleaming, opalescent mother-of-pearl. In the center there was a white marble fountain in the midst of a shallow pool, with turtles and goldfish swimming in it. Threading their way daintily from column to column and from one side of the pool to the other were a family of egrets, two parent birds and three babies, all as white as the fountain and at the same time ephemeral, almost gauzy in their delicacy. The mother wears the gorgeous plumage—the *aigrettes* for which she used to be so indiscriminately slaughtered—only during the mating season; and since both she and her fledglings perished when she was killed to satisfy woman's vanity, these exquisite creatures—real birds of Paradise—had nearly become extinct before legislation for their protection was passed. I was thankful that these I saw were safe in such lovely surroundings as the courtyard of the President's house.

When we reached the top of the wide carved staircase at the rear of the patio, Señor Alfaro and I found ourselves facing the door of the President's reception room, which he opened for us himself. Would we come in and sit down? Never had I been in the presence of a great personage who made me feel more truly welcome, more instantly at ease —it was another case of that wonderful Panamanian kindness! There was no exchange of formalities whatever; instead, there was immediately a friendly, even jovial conversation under way. On the walls of a simple cottage in the village of Aquadulce which I saw later was a bronze tablet bearing this inscription:

> Here was born, on the 15th of November 1869 Rodolfo Chiari,
> indefatigable warrior, master of optimism and energy, model
> citizen of his country.

The writer of that inscription, I am sure, knew his subject well.

Eventually, the President asked if I would not like to see something of the palace and, acting as guide, he took us first to his private office and then to the magnificent state drawing room, where the walls were hung in pale blue, the furniture was covered in gold brocade, and crystal chandeliers were suspended from the high ceiling; from there we entered the banquet hall, wainscoted in superb dark native wood, the chairs surrounding the immense polished oval table intricately carved.

At this point, I began to watch for a signal of dismissal, but it did not come, and it was I who suggested I should not trespass upon the President's time any longer.

"I am sorry that Señora Chiari was ill this morning and could not receive you," he said, "but we will arrange for that some other time before you leave. Meanwhile—are you fond of motoring? If you will telephone my secretary, Señor Calvo, at any hour, he will send one of my cars to take you out. And would you care for a trip to the interior, to see what we are doing in the way of road building? I have a launch large enough to accommodate several persons over night. If you and your young son would be interested?"

Speaking for Peter as well as myself without feeling I was taking much of a risk, I assured the President that we would be delighted. And twice within the next week a breathless bellboy came to tell us the President's car was waiting. In it we went through the quaint and ancient city with its tempting shops and gay plazas; through the former exposition grounds which had become the finest residential section and the park where a marble Cervantes sits forever pensive; past the Juan Frango racetrack; past the rude wooden cross, erected on a boulder and surrounded by coarse cotton cloth, before which candles burn perpetually for that son of the great Espinosa family who became a leper and who, by his humility and patience throughout years of agony, became sanctified in the minds of many patient and humble sufferers, so that in all the time that had passed since his release, they had never failed to remember him with their flickering lights. There were market gardens along the way, with thrifty Chinese stooping over their carefully tended plants; villas of the wealthy; institutions for the poor; cottages and cafés. The *chivas* whizzed by—literally, *chiva* is the Spanish word for goat, but in the vernacular it meant a native motor bus. The laden donkeys plodded past. We might turn to the right and go down to Old Panama, where stood the ruins of the pomp and majesty of Spain, as they had stood since the days of Morgan's raid centuries ago, with thatched huts teeming with new life built in the very shadows of their crumbling walls. Or we might go straight ahead to the *barrio* (village) of Juan Diaz, where the good roads ended and where model cottages and farms, a school, a church and a telegraph system were being built by the government to supplant the primitive shelter of former times.

Then, on the appointed evening, we went down to the dock where the launch *Almirante* was waiting for us; and soon we were chugging out to sea—not very far out, but far enough to make it seem a real adventure. There was only one cabin at the foot of a small hatchway, and Peter and I settled ourselves there very comfortably while the President's son —a quiet, pleasant young man a little over twenty—and the captain stretched out in cots on deck. In the morning, as we had our *café con leche,* we entered the Aquadulce River, broad and placid; an hour later we were at the Port of Aquadulce—sweet water or gentle water, whichever way you choose to translate it, it is rightly named. On the dock another son of the President's, the one who acted as superintendent of his father's great sugar *central,* was waiting to greet us, a most engaging figure. He was wearing riding clothes, and though his wide gray sombrero shadowed his vibrant face, we soon learned his black eyes could be sparkling or melting and that his even white teeth added to the charm of his frequent smile. With that same never-failing Panamanian courtesy, he soon had us installed in a waiting Ford and drove us to the village of Aquadulce. The first thing I noticed was the schools, crowded to the very doors—five of them in that one small town. We were driven to the house which was the President's birthplace, where a young lady, a cousin, was waiting to receive us. Then, after a pleasant visit with her, we started for the ancient city of Santiago. We saw fertile country, capable of vast development, with massed mountains faintly blue in the distance—mountains which assumed the fantastic shapes of medieval castles. Much of the land was unfenced, and there the government allowed the poor to pasture their cattle free of charge—cattle uniformly sleek and strong. There was no shortage of either good milk or good meat in Panama, as there is in so many tropical countries, and beside each cow fluttered the little "cow bird" that devoured the insects which would otherwise annoy her. The roads were perfect, with strong culverts and iron bridges, for Panama was building, building, building, and her proposed highways and schools promised to do much to bridge the chasm that existed between the highly cultured classes and primitive people of which the population was comprised—for there was no great middle class.

It was all tremendously interesting to us—the open country, the somnolent city of Santiago, the quaint inn where we ate lunch, the *Casa Blanca* (White House) where the Chiari brothers, in their mother's absence, kept bachelor hall, the cool, stone-floored house in Aquadulce where we rested—and all too soon, it was time to return to the launch.

After that, much too soon again, Peter was shaking me into consciousness with the announcement that the launch was passing Fort Amador. The President's car was waiting for us at the dock in Balboa, the workmen were just starting out for the day as we circled green Ancon Hill, and the sun was staining the gray sky behind it with a shower of golden glory.

Venturing afield again, we went, through the kindness of Governor Meriweather Walker, to Colón in his "scooter"—a shrieking, bouncing, tearing little hybrid painted bright yellow and most appropriately nicknamed the "Yellow Peril," which rushed along on the railroad track but was operated like an automobile. Peter and I both lost our hearts to the "scooter." No roller coaster, no Ferris wheel, could possibly compete with it when it came to a joy ride. Its antics and its prowess sent us into howls of laughter. Moreover, without it we would have missed our one glimpse of Colón, on the Atlantic side of the canal, for engagements were packed so closely together that I had only one evening to spare, and though there was a late train over from Balboa, there was none back.

We went also, in the Governor's launch, to the island of Taboga, where the one highway—paved with concrete, lighted electrically, too wide for a sidewalk, too narrow for a street—wound its way through rows of multicolored plaster houses roofed with red tile, set in the midst of tangled gardens and shaded by trees from which hung great clusters of the loveliest of all orchids, the Lady of the Night—waxen white and heavy with scent. There was not an automobile on the island, or, apparently, a vehicle of any sort; the hotel, which had flourished in the past as a week-end resort, was closed; and there were less than a thousand inhabitants left. But there was a pretty plaza, artistically planted and lighted, and a serious little gray church, to the top of whose tower we climbed by a winding stone stair. And late in the afternoon we walked across the narrow strip of sand which at low tide connects Taboga with a tiny neighboring island of Urabá and went swimming.

Best of all, we went up the Chilibri River. Starting at daybreak with a congenial party we drove to the Chagres, whose wide waters flow into the Canal, and there we took a motor launch. At first there seemed nothing distinctive about the scenery—we might almost have been going down the Connecticut from Pine Grove Farm to White River Junction. Then suddenly, as we turned from the Chagres into the Chilibri, we were in the heart of the jungle. Water hyacinths, softly blue, choked the stream; wild fig trees met overhead, their bulb-like fruit floating on the water; scarlet orchids reared like giant coxcombs on bending branches. The dense green growth of tropical forests was all about us—feathery ferns, wide glossy leaves, tight twisting vines. Now and then in a small clearing we passed a cluster of huts surrounded by a banana plantation; once we went aground, directly opposite a low shelter roofed with boughs of coconut palm, where a young girl was doing her laundry. The wet white clothes were piled in twin bowls made from a gourd, and she was using a flat stone for a washboard. She was delectably pretty, her dark hair curling in little tendrils above her oval face, her lips parting over perfect teeth; she was barefoot and her damp cotton dress clung to her figure like a statue's drapery. I regret that one of our party did not photograph her, but I still see her in my memory.

At length the Chilibri became so narrow and so shallow that the launch could go no further; however, there were some native *cayucas* (canoes hollowed from tree trunks) drawn up on the bank, and we hailed their apparent owner, and asked him to take us upstream. The transfer was made, and then we went on, further and still further, into the mighty silence of the jungle river.

The contrast between taking such trips as these and then, within a few hours, going to dinners and dances and teas left me as breathless as a cold shower. And yet that is what I did constantly. There was an evening reception at the Governor's when Dr. William Beebe, who had just returned from an expedition to the Sargasso Sea, spoke in a lucid and interesting way on his discoveries, illustrating his talk on the "poor fish," as someone jokingly called it, with truly remarkable pictures. There was an afternoon reception at the Alfaros', where we drank tea from antique Chinese cups, as well as rich Spanish chocolate and fruit punch into which ice cream had been whipped, and ate great cakes with nuts imbedded in their luscious fillings, and marrons glacés and translucent candied fruit—all these besides the sandwiches and wafers one would naturally expect. And I also had the pleasure of meeting several charming Panamanian women who were good enough to ask me to their houses—invitations which I gladly accepted.

On my last evening of all came a *baile* (ball) at the *Presidencia;* and though I felt I might be caught like Cinderella, I resolved to take a chance and go. My ship sailed at eleven, and the *baile* did not begin until nine, which meant, as I was very well aware, nearer ten. Moreover, Henry and John, who had been joined by Sidney Johnson, had arrived at three that afternoon in the same ship in which Peter and I, as well as they, were to leave. In a few brief hours we crowded in a visit to the powerhouses to see the operation of the locks, with Admiral Latimer, and went to the Plaza Francia, the Church of the Golden Altar and Old Panama. Somehow we dressed for dinner in fifteen minutes, and to dinner with us came Cecilia Alfaro, the lovely daughter of the Minister of Foreign Affairs, and two attractive young friends of hers. It would never do, these young ladies insisted, for the boys to leave without a glimpse of the Union Club, and surely—all six clamored at once —I would not drag my sons and our cousin away from the *Presidencia without a single dance!*

I did not. We went to the Union Club and from there to the *baile.* At the head of the wide stairs leading up from the patio of the *Presidencia* stood our guide from Aquadulce transformed into a *grand seigneur;* he had come into town especially for the event, and gone were the riding breeches and wide sombrero; he was resplendent in a white uniform with brass buttons and gilt braid; but the smile was unchanged. The Minister of Foreign Affairs was waiting to escort us inside; and at the door of the reception room, beside the President, stood Señora Chiari, a handsome woman, strikingly dressed in that severe and faultless black which can be so much more elegant than any other costume in the world. I tried to express my appreciation for all they had done for me, to tell them, as I presented my own sons, how much I had enjoyed theirs; and they increased my sense of gratitude and indebtedness by leaving the receiving line to go and get photographs and autograph them for me; they had not realized, they said, that I was going so soon. Then they sent us, with their pretty daughter for a guide, to see the private apartments on the third floor: the Moorish room with its jewel-like lights; the state bedroom with its two great carved, crimson-covered beds, a sacred image beside each; the cheerful flower-decked dining and living rooms. When we went downstairs again, the orchestra was ensconced in the balcony at one end of the banquet hall and the flag of Panama, illumined by colored lights, was suspended across the other. Between them, the great oval table was laden with tempting delicacies. The boys had been promised one dance before we left, but somehow this became two, and three, and four. I would locate Sid and then Henry would be missing; then I would find John and Sid would have disappeared. "My, can those girls dance!" was the only explanation they gave for their slippery conduct. But now it was *ave atque vale* with a vengeance. The Alfaros' car, which had brought us to the *Presidencia,* fortunately had not stirred from the front door. As we leaped into it, the Minister, in rapid Spanish, impressed upon the chauffeur the absolute necessity for haste. Peter, greatly upset by our seeming desertion and with a collection of miscellaneous baggage heaped around him, was watching anxiously for us at the hotel entrance; quickly we reassured him, assembled the luggage, somehow stowed it in the car and sped away. The passenger gangplank had already been raised, so we made a human chain at the baggage gangway and passed suitcases, hatboxes and paper packages along to each other. Then we dashed up ourselves, while prompter passengers leaned over the deck rails and cheered or jeered, according to their humor. Cinderella's gold brocade dress, with its train floating from the shoulders, was not the most suitable traveling costume and inevitably provoked further mirth from the onlookers. And we did not have a minute to spare. But we had missed neither the ship nor the *baile!*

That was the manner of my farewell to the lovely gray and green lady of Panama. But I hoped it was only *hasta luego* and not *adiós,* and so, happily, it has proved. For she is a very lovely lady, indeed.

The voyage between Panama and California, which began so hectically, remained turbulent throughout.

There were several reasons for this. Among them was the prevalence of passengers in their later teens and early twenties, who proved so congenial that they were reluctant to be parted; they danced until all hours and then they sat or strolled about on deck, sometimes in hilarious groups and sometimes in suspiciously silent couples; the members of the crew, whose duty it was to holystone the decks, found that the wee small hours no longer afforded them an opportunity to do their work. The situation became so serious, in the Captain's opinion, that he called all the young fry together and told them they were welcome to dance until midnight, if they chose, or to amuse themselves on deck until that hour, if that was their preference; after that, however, lights would be dimmed and everyone must go below.

The dimming of lights seemed to no one in the "gang"\an obstacle to the pursuit of pleasure, but those who decided the Captain did not really mean what he said were in for a sad surprise; the culprits were again summoned before him and sternly told that any further unruliness would be punished by confinement. This time he got results. The lounges and decks were deserted and the holystoning was resumed according to schedule. Well pleased, the Captain decided to give an evening party, on the open afterdeck, for some of the passengers he considered outstanding. It was a beautiful moonlight night, the air was balmy, and everything pointed to a most agreeable interlude. Then the Chief Engineer came striding into view, obviously much upset. They were not getting enough air in the boiler room, he announced, something must be the matter with the funnels. The Captain, at the moment in a mood of pleasant relaxation, replied that he did not think anything serious could be wrong—possibly just a lack of breeze? After all, it was a very warm night. The Chief Engineer departed, muttering; in five minutes he was back, dragging with him the villains of the piece: my son John and a girl named Judy, in whose company he had spent practically every waking moment since leaving Panama. They had discovered the netting stretched across the funnels near the top and had seen no reason why they should not sit on it, well concealed by the funnel's overhanging hood. It had not occurred to either of them that they were shutting off ventilation or that, if the netting were not strong enough to hold them, they would have a disastrous fall. Judy's mother, as well as myself, was among the carefully chosen guests, so I will draw a veil over the rest of this deplorable scene, except to say that I later fictionalized it in my novel, *The Great Tradition.*

During the next few days, the "gang," somewhat subdued, devoted more time to bridge, and loud were their lamentations when the chairman of the tournament—who happened to be Judy's mother—declared that they were too young to take part in it. As sympathy was on the side of the protestors, despite their wrongdoings, the lady was overruled and, greatly to her discomfiture, Sid won the men's prize, with Henry and John coming in second and third, while her daughter took first place in the ladies' division! Meanwhile, the inevitable fancy dress party had taken place, in which Henry—clad in a barrel to caricature the ship's laundry, which was out of order—had won the prize for the most original and amusing costume and Peter had won the prize, from bewildered judges, for the most beautiful one. I had found a wig of blond curls, which was extremely becoming to him, and arrayed him in a white brocade dress of my own, and no one could discover the identity of this lovely young girl who had suddenly appeared in our midst. He was inclined to be somewhat sulky about it afterward; he never would have consented, he said when it was too late to change his mind, to masquerade as a girl. All the "other fellows" were making fun of him and he took no consolation in his prize. But John was jealous of both his brothers; and when he learned there was to be a second costume party just before we landed, he resolved that he would get a prize for some kind of a costume—and he did. He descended to the quarters of the Chinese crew, found there some discarded rags, which had once been a shirt and trousers, and with these (partially) covered his person, which had been stained a deep bronze. No one recognized him either, for he had also dyed his blond hair and very skillfully made up his face. He was unanimously voted deserving of the prize for the worst costume; he also achieved a high fever and a septic sore throat so severe that he could not conceal how very ill he felt; it remains a minor miracle that his condition was not detected and we were not held in Quarantine.

I myself was not in the best condition to deal with a sick son and the various complications and changes of plan in which his condition involved us. The first week at sea I had been working very hard on my next contribution for *Good Housekeeping,* not leaving my cabin, except for lunch, until evening, when I had a walk and a swim, played bridge and danced, in accordance with the program I had adopted on the *Leviathan* two years earlier. But toward the end of the week I injured my back in some way and was soon in terrible pain and completely unable to move. The ship's surgeon insisted on sending a radiogram to a specialist in Los Angeles, who came aboard at San Pedro and confirmed the diagnosis that the sacroiliac joint was out of place. It did not seem to occur to anyone to have X-rays made, but the specialist strapped me with adhesive tape and the following day, able to move about a little though still in considerable pain, I went by ambulance to make a prearranged speech at Long Beach. The trip was not as short as had been expected, but the ship was held for my return. The next morning, we were in San Francisco, where we hastily transferred to the St. Francis Hotel—surely one of the world's best—and sent for another doctor. Without a moment's hesitation he announced that John was very ill, that I ought to be in bed myself and that it was fantastic for me to think of sailing for Hawaii on Saturday of that week.

As rapidly as I could, I reorganized our schedule. There seemed no reason to postpone the departure of Sid and Peter overland—in fact, it seemed better to remove them from possible contagion without further delay—and, not without some heartache on both sides, I parted from my youngest son and devoted myself to the care of his brother John. Henry, also warned of possible contagion, went out to see the town and kept clear of the sickroom.

Late that same afternoon, I was conscious of a subtle, unfamiliar change in the atmosphere and unnaturally early darkness; then the glass chandelier began to tinkle. We were on the fifteenth floor, facing San Francisco's Union Square, and it did not take long to realize we were in the midst of an earthquake and that there was nothing I could do except sit still and continue reading aloud in the hope that John's feverish condition would blur his consciousness of what was happening. If he took fright, he could easily become much worse. My hope was vain. He sat up in bed, suddenly alert.

"Is this an earthquake?" he inquired eagerly.

By this time, the chandelier was not only tinkling, it was swaying to and fro. There was no use in pretending.

"Yes," I replied, hoping I spoke calmly. "But it may not amount to much. Don't pay any attention to it. It's nothing to worry about."

"Worry! I'm not worrying. But I don't want to miss seeing those buildings on the other side of the square when they begin to rock."

Before I could stop him, he was out of bed and at the window. I felt the chandelier was providing quite enough excitement. Gradually, the swaying subsided, and after another tinkle or two there was a welcome silence. Deeply disappointed, John climbed back into bed. The next morning, I needed a doctor more than he did. His fever was practically gone, and he was ready to eat solid food—in fact, the heartier the better. With the resilience of the young, he had made an almost complete recovery. I was the one in need of recuperation.

This, however, was not too long delayed. In my opinion, San Francisco is one of the most charming and individualistic cities in the United States, and I was soon able to enjoy many of its attractions, besides making three promised speeches and being photographed again by Boyé, as my family and friends thought the pictures taken by that firm three years earlier were the best I had ever had made. I celebrated my birthday, if not with the Old Guard, at least with a very satisfactory substitute for it, led by my good friend Florence Prag Kahn, who in February had been elected to succeed her husband, the Honorable Julius Kahn, in Congress. Larry Knowles, who had been a classmate of Henry's all through school and so far—through college, had been offered a world trip by his parents and had now joined us to make this. We saw John off to visit Mary Gray and her family at Ventura; and then, one Saturday in July, the three of us sailed for Hawaii and Yokohama.

Chapter 34

THE first sight of Japan came at dawn—a low gray range of hills, scarcely separating the clouds above it from the surf below it. There was no sign of life, not a village or a vessel. By noon, however, the single scoop-like sails of tiny craft had begun to bob about us, and then Larry came rushing in to say he had just seen Fujiyama and that I must come on deck at once! It rose before me, partly misted over with clouds —a bride-mountain, or thus I saw it, so pure and stately that evil could not touch her, so lofty that she could easily touch the heavens.

After that, nothing would have induced me to go below again—and indeed there was no time. We were lined up for inspection by the Quarantine doctor and rushed into the smoking room to file before the immigration officials. Here I found myself somewhat delayed and, I must say, somewhat troubled, for the individual who examined my special passport began to ask very thorough and searching questions. So I was a writer and a senator's wife; was my husband with me? No, my eldest son and a friend of his. Where was my husband? To the best of my knowledge, at our farm in New Hampshire. Why was he not in Washington? Well, Congress was not in session. What had I written? Three books and numerous magazine stories and articles. What were the names of the books and the magazines in which the stories and articles had appeared? Was I going to write about Japan and if so, when and where would my impressions appear? Where had I been before coming there, how long was I going to stay, and where was I going next? Perspiring freely and conscious of the line of passengers behind me, I answered these and what seemed to me innumerable other questions put to me with perfect courtesy but unescapable authority. At last the stamped slip permitting me to disembark was handed me; I seized it and fled.

And fleeing, I tumbled almost literally into the arms of reporters, who seemed much better informed about me than the immigration official. One of them singled me out in a group of about a dozen women, made a beeline for me and, bowing from the waist, exclaimed, "Mrs. Keyes!" in tones of triumph. Before I could admit my identity, nine more of his colleagues had descended upon us, all but one attired in European costume, all bowing and all efficiently armed with information, large notebooks and cameras. Before such an example of journalism's power, I abandoned my contemplation of Fujiyama and posed and prattled. No woman could have done less.

Meanwhile, customs officials had come aboard to examine our baggage, so there was not the long tedious delay after landing which makes disembarkation at many ports a nightmare of fatigue and annoyance; and this examination, like everything else, was conducted with efficiency, thoroughness and courtesy. When we walked down the gangplank, we knew we were free to go wherever we chose, as soon as we chose. We were greeted by Mrs. Coleman, a charming Quaker whom I had met at the Missionary Conference in Washington the previous winter, and by Dr. Vance Murray, the Chief of Quarantine for the United States Public Health Service in Yokohama, to whom Dr. Hugh Cumming, the Surgeon General in Washington, had given me a letter of introduction.

After some discussion regarding plans, we decided to proceed at once to Tokyo, only forty minutes distant by electric railway, and establish headquarters there; then to start forth the following day with Dr. Murray for our first trip by car. The fact that cholera was prevalent in Yokohama and Tokyo when we landed and the details of Dr. Murray's work that we saw, which insured the detention of any ship without an absolutely clean "bill of health," both brought home to me the important part the Public Health Service plays in safeguarding the health and welfare of our country. It seems a simple matter when we are sitting safely at home to say casually, "I see by the paper that there is another outbreak of cholera in Japan." It would be another story if we had to say instead, "I see by the paper that there is cholera in New York and San Francisco and it's spreading. Brought in, from all reports, by a ship from the Orient." Thanks to the Public Health Service, we rarely read anything of the sort any more.

Some of this we discussed during our first drive with Dr. Murray the next day, but mostly we were too enthralled with the sights and sounds all around us to think of anything else. After lunch at the Imperial Hotel—certainly the most artistic hostelry at which it was ever my good fortune to stay, and except for its beds one of the most comfortable—

we started "over the road" to Yokohama. Part of this road, built since the great earthquake, was a broad boulevard which would have been a credit to any country; part of it was in a sad state of disrepair, though it was a marvel that this should be so small a part—only two years had elapsed since that holocaust of death and destruction had taken place, and now, everywhere, there was building, building, building. It took me back to those devastated regions in France through which we had driven and where the same indomitable courage and determination had been so evident.

All along the way, we saw the vivid color, the teeming life character-istic of Japan. Apparently, everyone had a bicycle, whether he had enough rice or not—for some of the riders looked as if they could do with more; they darted through the streets with a dashing disregard of such traffic laws as there were, and these, I judged, were neither numer-ous nor rigidly enforced. At twilight paper lanterns tied to the bicycles' handlebars began to glow, illuminating the lily and lotus and leaf with which they were decorated. Automobiles were less numerous, most of them were very dilapidated, and all had wide flat brushes attached to their axles. Horses were less numerous still, and almost invariably far too heavily laden; in the mass of bicycles, automobiles and horses, the rickshaw men trotted calmly along, placid and seemingly tireless. Most of the rickshaws were shabby affairs which looked ready to tumble apart, though they never seemed to; but some of the privately owned ones were quite smart and shining, with black side-curtains and aprons which could be snugly buttoned in case of rain—and I feel sure the say-ing that it never rains but it pours must have originated in Japan, for such downpours I had never seen anywhere else!

Bicycle and automobile, horse and rickshaw hurried and harried each other; but they paused as the *mekura* (blindman)—an omnipresent figure, for there was much blindness in Japan—proceeded quietly along tapping with his stick. They also paused for the street cleaner, who, in his straw hat, straw cape and straw apron, looked like an animated three-story pagoda! They turned aside, too, when a celebration of the *matsuri*—the propitiation of evil spirits—was taking place and en-shrined images, supported on the shoulders of struggling, swaying, shouting bearers accompanied by musicians, were carried through the streets. We encountered our first *matsuri* on the way to Yokohama, but a kindly soldier, seeing our difficulties, ran beside the car and facilitated our progress past the procession. In front of houses tiny strips of white cloth were suspended, to ward off evil spirits; and the festival decora-tions were lavish and gorgeous: bright cloth and metal, artificial flowers and crinkly lanterns, twisted and twined and floating from shop and shanty. The children had a special ceremony of their own, and they too shouted and sang as they stumbled along over the cobblestones.

We drove by so many small open shops that Larry decided the Japanese must spend their lives in exchanging commodities! There were more bookstores, proportionately, than I had seen in any other country, but this was true of everything: more china shops, more shops where dried fish was spread in neat rows, more tailor shops, more tea shops, more barber shops. The Japanese, to an even greater extent than the Neapolitan, seemed to feel there was nothing he needed to conceal, and all the processes of life were revealed before us. But there was much that was not only interesting but lovely, and nothing that was in any way unclean or revolting; and to my great surprise, for sewers were non-existent, there were no unpleasant odors.

At Yokohama we swung through the *yoshuwara,* or "licensed district," which existed in every Japanese city except in the Province of Gumma. There was a temple at the entrance where the girls went to pray, then rows of houses presenting unwindowed facades to the street, each with its guardian. During the earthquake these houses were locked to prevent the escape of the inmates, who all burned to death. Later, the government was petitioned not to rebuild this *yoshuwara,* and though the petition failed, many of the younger members of Parliament voted in favor of it. (It is greatly to the credit of Japanese womanhood that the women who attended the memorial service for those poor girls were from the noblest families in the country.)

We continued on our way, slipping through the crowded streets and passing along the waterfront to Kamakura and open country, or as open as it ever is, for with the density of population, there are few great spaces in Japan. Fields of rice and lotus-covered marshes lay about us; we saw the deep beauty of rich greens through the shadows of late afternoon. Beyond the gate of a temple where we stopped, a branch of vivid pink quince-flower scattered its blossoms and the singing of locusts was the only sound in the silent air. When the highway narrowed, we left the car and walked through a village and across thick white sand, into which we sank ankle deep, to the long fragile foot bridge which connected Enoshima, the "picture island" where no man ever died, with the mainland. The sun, a ball of liquid flame, lay lightly against the azure slope of Fujiyama—a bride no longer, for she had cast her veils away and stood fully revealed—rising resplendent against a resplendent sky. And as the molten ball vanished, shooting long rays of fire below it as it went, a crescent moon, the merest thread of silver in that golden arras, dipped across the heavens.

The little moon was very near the horizon when we returned from the island, having dimly glimpsed its beauties, and I had no idea where we were when Dr. Murray stopped the car before a lighted gate of glowing red lacquer. As we passed beneath it, he suddenly exclaimed "Look!" Looming through the dusk, massed fir trees about it, stars above it, the bronze figure of the Daibutsu—the great Buddha—rose fifty feet above us, as it has risen for nearly seven hundred years. It had been too dark to read the inscription on the entrance gate:

> Whoever thou art that enterest here, and whatever thy own faith may be, enter reverently, remembering that this has been a place of worship to multitudes for generations.

But none of us needed the admonition; the supreme beauty, the supreme solemnity of the spot were overwhelming. I could not imagine that a light word could ever be spoken there or an irreverent thought conceived.

We dined late and well at the Kaihin Hotel in Kamakura—an excellent one, as were all but one of the hotels we visited in Japan—and as we drove homeward, passed through the *Eta* town of Izawa. There were over a million of the *Eta*—special caste people—in Japan, who, though they had been given the same legal status as ordinary people fifty years earlier, were still regarded as outcasts and continued to live apart in their own communities. The *Eta* never were a caste in the sense of caste in India, but had hereditarily been undertakers, butchers and tanners— trades considered unclean by the Japanese; and though this "dirty village" looked no dirtier than any other we saw, a strange atmosphere of mystery and gloom pervaded it, so we were glad when the twinkling lights of Yokohama came into view. Shorn of its former beauty as the city still was in the daytime, it glowed with loveliness at night, and its vitality, like its charm, was too great to be burned or shattered away.

Later there were also trips to Miyanoshita, nestling among the hills, and to Nikko, on the clear mountain top. Never shall I forget lying on my bed beside the window which extended the width of my room at Miyanoshita, after a late swim in a pool of limpid water, and watching the stars come out, one by one, above a distant wooded slope. If the soul of the East abides at Kamakura—as I believe it does—surely the peace of the ages descends upon Miyanoshita; and no less surely is the beauty of holiness enshrined at Nikko.

We went there in a funny little car, so small that the boys—both six feet tall—were obliged to double up like jackknives to make room for their legs. We had made up our minds to do most of our traveling packed in this toy car, in preference to the railroad, so we bumped along over roads none too good as roads go, but very charming in regard to scenery. Indeed, the high walls and thatched cottages, the verdant country and clipped hedges were often reminiscent of rural England, especially as most of them were seen through a mist of rain!

About twenty-five miles outside Nikko we came to an avenue of cryptomeria trees, not unlike our own California redwoods in majesty, which had been planted three centuries earlier as a worthy approach to the temples erected at the same time. Finally we crossed a gorgeous red lacquer bridge, closed to ordinary traffic, and saw dense groves of the same trees covering the mountainside on which the temples stood.

Leaving our shoes at the thresholds, where we were greeted by priests in flowing garments sometimes pure white, sometimes jade green, we passed very slowly, but still far, far too fast, from sanctuary to sanctuary, pausing before the petals of the sacred lotus flower, great and gilded; before the five-storied pagoda, with the signs of the zodiac wrought about it in glowing color; before the famous carving of the three monkeys, one covering its ears, one its mouth and one its eyes in the command, "Thou shalt hear no evil, speak no evil, see no evil"; before the *Yomai-mon*—the "day-spending gate," where many days, indeed, would prove insufficient to study its exquisite workmanship. In one temple prayers for the dead were being offered; in another we saw a holy-water cistern cut from solid granite, where the faithful were cleansed before going on their way. In many faiths we find the same symbols, the same ceremonies—and find, too, the deeper and holier principles that lie behind them. Surely, Nikko is a place of prayer for all people, and one in which I have always been thankful I was privileged to pray.

When the rain was over—and that was not until we had decided it never would be—it was over with honors, so to speak, and the sun came out in a smiling cordial sort of way, which expanded into hospitable radiance as we started for Lake Chuzenji. At Umagaeshi we were obliged to leave our mini-car, neatly parked under a bamboo tree; and, not feeling sufficiently frisky to attempt a four-mile uphill walk—though of course my companions did—I was persuaded for the first time to get into a rickshaw. To me, there was something most unpleasant in being the burden of another human being, and I was much surprised at hearing the rickshaw was invented by the early missionaries. But in this case the labor was divided between two husky specimens, and I probably minded it a good deal more than they did, for their spirits seemed to improve as the day wore on. Neither was the ascent made without refreshment; three times we stopped at teahouses, where we sat on spotless matting and drank delicious clear hot green tea without cream, sugar or lemon—served in tiny cups with no handles and accompanied by small crackers in size and substance very like the animal crackers of my childhood, and fat cushionlike cubes of peppermint candy.

And finally, after nearly two hours of climbing, we came upon the rainbow radiance of Kegon Falls, with its mist of spray and its tumbling music, and eventually to a stretch of plateau with a little village at its far side and, at the end of the village, Lake Chuzenji: lovely as a fairy mirror, with here and there a tiny sail, light as a powder puff, floating over it.

Our travels over for the time being, we settled ourselves in Tokyo, a huge drab city unbeautiful except in spots, with most of its streets unpaved and consequently very muddy and very dusty by turns. There were innumerable students everywhere, all in uniform, a uniform very like that of a bus conductor—but there the bus conductors were girls, extremely neat, pretty and demure. The kimonos of the women, instead of the sumptuous garments of my imagination, were almost invariably black or very dark gray; only the children and the geishas wore bright colors, at least, in public. But the women were much more attractive in their somber kimonos than when they adopted foreign dress, in which their taste seemed to be uncertain and which, at best, was unbecoming to their type.

In the center of the city a wide deep moat, fringed with pine trees and banked with high stone walls, separated the grounds of the Imperial Palace from the rest of the world and created an impression of medieval strength and grandeur. On the outskirts, the Crown Prince's handsome palace, resembling a French chateau, stood in the midst of large formal grounds; and there were glimpses of many handsome residences behind high walls and beyond covered entrances. The Ginza, the Fifth Avenue of Tokyo, was hectic rather than harmonious, and the shops, except for a few large new department stores, were tiny; but beautiful things could be bought in them, and at night, with lighted windows and open booths along the pavement, the Ginza sparkled with color and life.

But there was very little apparent revelry anywhere. By order of the government, foreign dancing had to stop at ten in the evening, geisha dancing at twelve. After the shops closed, also at ten, the streets were almost deserted, and as early as eleven we found it impossible to get a sandwich and a drink at our hotel. The gentleman who said New York was a dull place because there was nothing to do there between midnight and bedtime would have had a hard time in Tokyo!

It was still very early in the "season," exactly as it would have been in Washington at that time of year, but I began to have callers almost immediately. The first to come was Baroness Ishimoto, one of Japan's leading feminists, who appeared the very day of my arrival. She was only twenty-seven and exquisite in both person and dress. Her face was very serious in repose, but when she smiled, as she was apt to do at the conclusion of a sentence, the smile lighted not only her lips but her eyes. Her kimono was of black brocade, shot with silver, and her *obi,* also silver shot, of pale lavender. When she raised her arms, the sheer embroidered sleeves of her under-kimono were visible, while her spotless white socks ended just above her ankle. She was hatless, of course, and her perfectly dressed hair was unadorned; completing her street costume were *getas,* the wooden sandals which the Japanese removed when entering their own houses and whose clatter in crowded streets made a continuous clap-clap on the pavement.

Baroness Ishimoto's English was as perfect as her costume, and as we had many common interests, we were instantly absorbed in conversation. She was an ardent suffragist and hoped to see the vote extended to Japanese women without delay. Herself the mother of two lovely children, she was also a believer in birth control, wisely used, as a partial solution for Japanese overpopulation. "Now that the United States, as well as Australia, has closed its door to our emigration, we must give that subject careful consideration," she said. "But I believe that contraceptive information should be government controlled, as it is, I believe, in Holland, that there may be no risk of exploitation by midwives, by whom most of the obstetrical work in Japan is done."

When I asked if she would be glad to see some of our social usages introduced, she answered, "If we could have the advantages without the disadvantages, but not everything introduced from America *is* excellent. We have, for instance, brought in some very wonderful machinery. We have also"—and her delicious illuminating smile flashed—"the chewing gum!"

I also began to make calls and to be entertained at Japanese houses, and soon we received our first invitation to attend the Japanese classical theater, the *Kabuki-za.* The theater was finished inside with natural wood, and I thought it one of the most attractive playhouses I had ever seen. And a theater party in Japan proved much more comprehensive than one at home! In the first place, the performance began at three-thirty in the afternoon and lasted until eleven; and instead of seeing only one play, we saw four or five, all superbly staged and acted, and with a different but equally ornate curtain lowered between each one. There were ample periods between each play, which were used for strolling about the beautiful foyer, greeting acquaintances or relaxing on the comfortable sofas, upholstered in Pompeiian red, which were scattered about. One intermission was devoted to dinner—a delicious four-course meal served in the building. At the end of the evening, a visit was paid to the shops in the building, and sweetmeats in lacquered boxes were purchased to take home. On the night we went, the performance began with *Othello,* in translation—all the tragedy left in, but all the lovemaking taken out, for Orientals did not kiss! It was acted entirely by men—as were all the dramas in this classical school—with settings surpassing any I had ever beheld in the many times I had seen this play.

Our first wholly Japanese meal in a wholly Japanese house was in the home of Mr. and Mrs. Tsunekichi Asabuki, the former a so-called "merchant prince of Nippon." Mrs. Coleman and her husband took us to the Asabukis' in their car, and at the entrance of the house, we all sat down on the polished step and removed our shoes before putting on the soft felt slippers which bowing, waiting servants handed us. Then we passed through a narrow corridor, sniffing the sweet scent of matting and fragrant wood that greets you upon entering a Japanese house, and into the drawing room. Here beautiful Chinese rugs were spread over the matting, and there were deep sofas and armchairs. Our host and hostess, with Countess Watanabe, one of Japan's great poets as well as one of her great ladies, were waiting to greet us. Mr. Asabuki was dressed in a flowing black kimono of rich silk; and Mrs. Asabuki in striking green crepe, the skirt of the kimono decorated with pale flowers —dyed to order in the fabric, as is the unique and costly custom of Japanese ladies, her *obi* confined with a superb jewelled pin.

Very shortly dinner was announced and, leaving even our felt slippers behind, we entered the dining room in silk-stockinged silence. On the floor, thick square cushions covered with dark green brocade were arranged in a hollow square, open at one side; and the seat of honor, which was given me, was not beside the host, who sat at one end, but in the center, before the *kakemono*—symbolic picture—hanging in an alcove, with a low desk of gold lacquer and a vase of flowers in front of it. The *kakemono* is changed according to the seasons, as are the flowers, so this one was decorated with an autumn scene and the autumn theme was carried out in almost everything put before us: first, in the tiny black lacquer tables decorated with golden leaves, which were placed in front of each of us, next in the dishes—even to the golden cups painted with fall fruits in which our coffee was served. We were immediately given little bowls, holding no more than a thimbleful of *sake,* and these were refilled, as often as we would permit, with the same warm sweet liquid. Then came soup, made of beans, in covered containers; brook trout, fried whole, with a tart sauce in separate dishes to go with them, and a paste of fish besides; a decorated gelatin compounded of chestnuts; partridge finely ground and molded into small cakes; macaroni and green vegetables, and steak cut into infinitesimal pieces; luscious melon and Japanese pears, which tasted like our own but had the texture and shape of apples; then soup again with the rice. And all this, except the soups which we drank and the fruit which we took in our fingers, we ate with chopsticks! And we managed very well indeed!

When we returned to the drawing room, we saw that one of the priceless rugs had been covered with a cloth and on this were spread porcelain paint boxes, porcelain bowls filled with water and a number of sheets of gold paper, fans and other small articles. Before this array was kneeling a young man, who proved to be Mrs. Asabuki's painting teacher. She knelt beside him and the two proceeded to paint. With swift sure strokes, the fans and panels were rapidly illuminated with flowers, birds and other decorations—cherry blossoms, bamboo branches, chrysanthemum clusters, a glimpse of Fuji beyond a pine grove; and when we made our adieus, these lovely things were given us! Meanwhile, some "poem cards" had also been brought in—slim panels of cardboard with gold designs on colored backgrounds; and very shortly Countess Watanabe was composing and reciting verses, and we were asked to do this too! My "one parlor trick" helped me out, as it has many times before and since. The boys insisted that my contribution counted for them, and found the later part of the evening less of a challenge than I did.

"Next time you give a dinner," Henry remarked, as we drove away, "why don't you *really* entertain your guests? Paint a few pictures, write a few poems and so on. My, what a good time we had!"

Not long after this dinner, the boys and I received similar cards from the Vice Minister of Foreign Affairs and his wife, Mr. and Mrs. K. Debuchi, inviting us to luncheon at the Maple Club in Shiba Park, where our entertainment varied from that at the Asabukis'. Here we did not immediately go in to dine. First we sat on flat cushions facing a low, white-covered table which stood before a magnificent golden screen. At its right was a small stand on which two jars covered in black wicker, two shallow bowls and cut flowers, berries, leaves and ferns had been placed. A large elderly man appeared and bowed; he was a "flower man," the most famous one in Japan, and was prepared to show us arrangements, according to different schools. The first, in the larger jar, was in classical and ancient fashion; weirdly beautiful—yellow chrysanthemums, red berries and quantities of thick black stalks tipped to one side and set triumphantly on the table. There were bows and applause. Then the bowls were arranged in a softer and more modern style, with peonies predominating; the smaller jar was filled last of all, in a way suggestive of both the previous styles—ampler than the first, taller than the second. Finally, the table holding them all was moved into the dining room.

My chopsticks were bundled neatly in a white cloth, and the Vice Minister, watching me unroll them with an amused twinkle in his eyes, asked if I would not prefer a knife and fork. I declined, indignantly. "Very well then, not until you ask for them." I had not the slightest intention of asking for them, and, thankful for the practice I had now had, picked them up and got along even better than the first time! "You deserve a diploma," murmured my host, "or a medal. A medal, I think, with chopsticks rampant on an azure field. When you return from China, we shall have a presentation ceremony."

But he did not jest all the time. Quite suddenly, shifting from excellent English, he asked me a question in German. A little startled, I managed to reply in the affirmative—and in the same language. Next he stated, rather than inquired, "You spent the winter before your marriage in Berlin?" After some small talk several more questions, the answers to which he knew perfectly, were quickly posed in French: *"Et vous êtes allée à l'école à Génève?"* Here I was on surer ground and quite fluently even managed a hint of revenge. *"Hablo también un poco español, señor."* And was rewarded by having the conversation revert to English! But it was disconcerting to have a complete dossier unexpectedly tossed at me in several different tongues.

Then while I was still considering how very thorough the Foreign Office must be in acquiring information, there was a tinkling sound, followed by a light drumming, and six geisha dancers came tripping into the room. Their kimonos, vermilion lined and fastened with vermilion *obis,* had a pattern of brilliant red and yellow leaves on an azure ground. This was the famous "maple leaf" dance. The first movement was performed with fans for accessories, the second with "flower hats" —artificial blossoms attached to wire frames; the third with what appeared to be slim bamboo poles, their upper parts wrapped in red and white silk. However, in a moment I guessed they were flags and I was right, for the performance ended with the waving of the Stars and Stripes, alternating with the red sun in a white heaven which illumined the banner of Nippon.

"Well," said Henry on the way back to our hotel, "if I ever hope to have a better time than *that!* Do you think I can keep these flowers straight until we get upstairs?"

Another letter with the *Gaimusho* (Foreign Office) stamp came from the admirable Mr. Kishi, the Vice Minister's Secretary: the wife of the Minister of Foreign Affairs, Baroness K. Shidehara, was inviting me to tea on Saturday at half-past three at her residence in Tokyo, and hoped my son and Mr. Knowles would come with me. There was no danger in this respect. As long as invitations of this nature continued to pour in, I was perfectly sure of two very eager escorts. And the prospect of the tea ceremony in one of the most famous and beautiful gardens in Japan would certainly have filled anyone with delight. We had a long drive and began to fear we had mistaken the direction and would commit the unforgivable sin of being late when a high brick wall rose beside the road and glancing about, we were reassured by seeing Mr. and Mrs. Edwin Neville, our Chargé d'Affaires and his wife, in a car directly behind us. So we all entered the gate together and found Baroness Shidehara—joined shortly afterward by the Minister—waiting to receive us, with the Debuchis, the Kishis and a Mr. Saburi.

The garden of the Shideharas was over three hundred years old, and its age, like its size—it covered acres—made itself felt at once. So did its stillness; the great city just outside the brick wall might have been a thousand miles away. There was a large pool with lily pads floating on its surface and little mandarin ducks swimming in it; and we saw a minute waterfall—christened "Niagara" by the irrepressible Mr. Debuchi! —beyond a stone bridge above a tiny stream which divided one grove of trees from another. There was emerald green moss so brilliant it looked painted, so soft and spongy the footfall made no sound upon it, and we glimpsed ancient gray stone lanterns through feathery boughs. From the top of a small hill, Fuji could be seen on a clear day, and a simple pedestal marked the place where the first shogun had once stood. Everywhere there was beauty—beauty and peace.

There were several pavilions in the garden, and in the first one we passed we found a woman painting, as Mrs. Asabuki and her teacher had painted; later on, we were again given matchless fans and panels, decorated before our eyes, to take home with us. The second pavilion, near the tiny waterfall, was empty, and we paused for a moment to admire the view; the third was the teahouse. Normally the teahouse is apart from the main one in Japan, and on this large estate it stood in the very depths of the garden. Near it was a small shelter where in ancient times warriors removed all insignia of rank and laid down their weapons before approaching closer—for to the tea ceremonial all must come without pretense or power. There was also a gray stone basin where the hands were cleansed before entering; and the doorway itself was very low, so that all must stoop, as a sign of humility, when they went in. At it stood the "teaman" who acted as master of ceremonies; he motioned us to enter and take our places in a circle, with Mrs. Neville and myself on either side of the *kakemono*. In one dim corner were a brazen kettle, a lacquer box filled with fine green tea powder and a lacquer bowl with a small wire brush resting on it; here two women prepared the ceremonial tea, helping each other in a definite and ordered way. Some of the green powder was emptied into the lacquer bowl, then steaming water was poured on it, and the two were whipped to a froth with the brush. This, accompanied by a small cake of chestnut paste, was offered first to the guests of honor and next to each of the others. The tea was thick and foaming, much like frothed chocolate in consistency, and strong enough to be bitter, although most agreeably so—quite unlike the clear green tea of everyday usage; and it was sipped, as it had been prepared, according to a prescribed rite.

The simple little house, almost concealed in the quiet woods and unadorned save for the *kakemono* and a single vase of flowers, the dim light, the soft drizzle outside—for it had rained soon after we entered —the shining brass and smooth lacquer, the silence, the solemnity enveloped us like a garment. And I felt, even before I knew—the "teaman," the only person who spoke, told us—how this tea-ceremonial originated, centuries ago. It was to show the beauty and holiness that could surround and abide in the simple and necessary things of everyday life.

We were invited by the Ambassador of Belgium and Mme de Bassompierre to the wedding of their daughter, and a wedding in the Diplomatic Corps of any capital is always a thrilling event, but doubly so in Tokyo, where there was such a blending of Oriental and Occidental society. And at the reception in the Belgian Embassy there was such a friendly atmosphere, so many guests present whom we already knew, that it seemed impossible we had been in Tokyo only a few short weeks. But, despite our eagerness to linger, Mrs. Neville and I were watching the clock—with eagerness, too. For, several days before, notes had come to both of us—with, for me at least, a needed translation from the invaluable Mr. Kishi—asking us to tea with her Imperial Highness Princess Higashi Fushimi at her palace at half-past four on the day of the wedding.

Mr. Kishi left the reception early so he could precede us to the palace and "make preparations"; Mrs. Neville and I followed in the company of Mrs. Kishi. At the palace entrance, we were met by Mr. Kishi, two Gentlemen of the Household, a steward and a number of servants and escorted to the drawing room, where a slender lady, very simply dressed in gray but very elegant and distinguished looking, was seated on a sofa, surrounded by a semicircle of similarly dressed ladies, who were standing.

"Your Highness," Mr. Kishi said, "may I present to you Mrs. Keyes and Mrs. Neville?"

We had not been instructed regarding procedure beforehand, but it was all made so easy for us that we did not have the slightest difficulty or even embarrassment. We bowed to the slender elegant lady on the sofa—the Princess Higashi Fushimi—and she rose and shook hands with us both, smiling very sweetly and cordially. Then, as one of the ladies-in-waiting motioned Mrs. Neville to a seat beside her, the Princess said, in perfect English, "Will you not sit down beside me here, Mrs. Keyes, that we may talk together?" The first thing she did was to compliment me, very kindly, on some of my verses she had read that morning, saying she had enjoyed them so much she hoped I would write a poem and dedicate it to her some time. Then, leaving me speechless with pleasure at being honored with such a request, she began to ask me about my visit to Japan, where I had been, whom I had met, what I had enjoyed most. After a short while, the conversation became general, the other ladies in the group joining in, and a little later the lady-in-waiting asked, "Would you not like to look at this screen, Mrs. Keyes, which was painted by Her Highness?"—the skillful signal that Mrs. Neville and I were to change places. The screen was delicately decorated with scenes characteristic of the twelve months of the year; and there was also another very beautiful screen in the room, which I thought was painted too, but which proved to be *embroidered*—a mass of dark glowing waves with a soft dark sky above them. This had been a present from the Emperor, as was a choice gold lacquer box handed me for examination.

"Look inside as well as out," I was told, "and see that the design, though concealed, is continued there. That is characteristic of such workmanship—it is perfect, whether it is to be seen or not."

I had learned by now that a cooperative guest was nearly always expected to write something extemporaneously and the remark instantly gave me the clue for my next verses. "Isn't that rather like a Japanese lady?" I asked. "She is so modest and so secluded that only a few are privileged to see how lovely she is. Her greatest beauties—and they are very great—are not carelessly revealed. If I am to write a poem for Her Highness, could it not be about this lacquer box, comparing it to a Japanese lady?"

The suggestion seemed a pleasing one.

As we sat down again, tea was brought in—"foreign tea" with sugar and lemon in compliment to the foreign visitors. It was served on separate tables for each lady, with dainty sandwiches and a variety of sweets, as we would have had them at home. One of the ladies asked me about Mrs. Coolidge and the customs prevailing at the White House —how an "audience" there would be arranged, for instance. So I told her of the pleasant custom our First Lady had instituted, of receiving groups of about thirty for tea twice a week, and that any official lady could occasionally ask to take a house guest with her to one of these teas. We next drifted to the subject of larger receptions, garden parties and so on, and the entertaining done by the wives of Cabinet officers and senators. The sympathies of the ladies-in-waiting seemed to be very much stirred—as well they might have been—at the recital of what we underwent in the course of calling and receiving!

The following day, I sent these verses to the palace:

> *The Princess has a box of lacquer ware—*
> *A golden casket very old and rare*
> *Her waiting lady handed it to me,*
> *And smiling said, "I wonder if you see,*
> *Under the cover, that the skilled design,*
> *Although concealed, is very fair and fine."*
>
> *I hardly dared to touch it, as it lay,*
> *So cool and smooth before me there that day,*
> *An Emperor's gift, a palace ornament—*
> *But as I held it, and before I went*
> *Out of the gracious presence, I had told*
> *My thought about this box of lacquered gold.*
>
> *"Your Highness, it is given me to know*
> *That in Japan, a lady does not show*
> *Her sweetness like a spendthrift, nor her grace*
> *For careless comment, to each passing face.*
> *Her wisdom, like her loveliness, is such*
> *That she does not reveal nor give too much*
> *To many. For the honored few, she locks*
> *Away her beauty, like the lacquer box.*

Chapter 35

I WANTED to see something of industrial conditions before I left Japan, and Chigasaki, where silk filatures were made, seemed a logical place to go first. Setting out from Tokyo by train early one morning after a heavy rainstorm, the boys and I were met at the Yokohama station by Dr. Murray, who had offered to take us in his car for the rest of the trip. He informed us that the typhoon the night before had resulted in several landslides across the highway, so there was nothing to do but wait until they were dug out. This news was imparted with nonchalance, and I accepted it in the same spirit. Ever since a very charming lady had told me calmly that she had not accomplished as much as she had expected on a certain morning, because "there had been three or four earthquakes and the garden was in rather a mess," I had ceased to gasp at anything. The Oriental mind is composed. It needs to be. But we finally started on our way again.

Even apart from the landslides, still not completely cleared, the road contained many elements of excitement. In places where the mud was too deep we had to get out and push; and, once, the planks of a bridge across a swollen stream cracked as we sped over it. As we penetrated further inland, conditions became somewhat less hair raising and, by the time we reached the placid stretches of the mulberry farm, they were nearly normal.

At the factory, we were taken first to drink, not tea, strangely enough, but *café au lait,* with rich little cakes. Then our tour of inspection began. The cocoons were brought in by the farmers in large baskets, just as any farm produce might be offered for sale, and paid for according to weight. Then they were plunged into a steam oven, from which they were removed at the further end, the worms having been killed instantly by the immersion, and placed in huge sacks in a warehouse until needed for the process of manufacture. This began with a bath in a large vat of boiling water that lasted seven minutes, by which time the fine silk threads were in condition to be separated, unwound and rewound on shuttles into skeins; this was being done by girls in the next rooms we visited. Finally the skeins were twisted for packing and each one scrupulously weighed. There were two crops, spring and fall, with the spring silk considered superior, and they were carefully labeled according to grade.

I was deeply interested in this factory not only because of the process, but also because the conditions in it were so much better than I had expected. I had heard terrible tales about industrial plants in the Orient, so had rather dreaded to visit any; but like most of my other fears this one was groundless. The silk filature at Chigasaki was spotlessly clean, well lighted and well ventilated; the machinery, almost entirely made of wood, was safe and simple to operate. The four hundred girls who worked in the factory slept and ate there too, and their living quarters were immaculate. The large dining room also served as a hall where Christian services were held twice a week, and prominent lecturers spoke once a month. There were six teachers at the filature, pianos and other musical instruments were provided; and there were several athletic fields. The working day seemed very long—six in the morning until six in the evening!—but time off for meals and rest periods made it actually a ten-hour day—no longer than it was in many of our states then. The pay—forty cents a day—seemed very small, but its purchasing power was much larger than it would have been with us; and it was almost clear gain, as neither food nor lodging had to be paid for with it. And I did not see a single girl who looked under eighteen or one who seemed to be in poor health.

Our jaunt to Chigasaki made the weaving factories in Kyoto, where we next went, twice as interesting to us, for there we welcomed the skeins as old friends when we saw them emerge, multicolored, from the dye rooms and find their way to the looms. The tapestries, velvets and silks made in Kyoto were absolutely peerless in their beauty, and the brocade woven especially for *obis* was superb. A length of about ten yards is required for one, and the cost varied from fifty *yen* to five thousand—twenty to two thousand dollars! So, considering that the kimono, with its dyed-to-order design, cost at least two hundred *yen* and the under-kimono and accessories were no less expensive in proportion, it was easy to see that the costume of an elegant Japanese lady ran to tall figures.

The lustrous brocades, rich with their intricate patterns, heavy with gold thread, increased the curiosity I had felt ever since reaching Japan as to just *how* a Japanese lady dressed—I mean the mechanics of it. I therefore literally jumped at the chance when an invitation to tea at the Kyoto headquarters of the Y.W.C.A. requested that I wear Japanese dress. I grew even more enthusiastic when my costume was shown me —an under-kimono of flamingo silk; a kimono of pale dull blue, with a dyed-in-the-fabric design of black and white birds; an *obi* on which a thick pattern of green and red and gold lay against a cream-colored ground. When I was divested of everything but bloomers and chemise (I am probably the only woman left in the world who still wears a sheer linen chemise!) the under-kimono was tied securely around me with a knotted cord; while the kimono itself was folded at exactly the right angle, a crosswise pleat over the hips, one side lapping far over the other, and fastened with no less than four more cords, all tied very tightly in various places above the waistline. In addition to the cords, a scarf of bright red crepe was wound around the waist and a broad, strong black and green checked ribbon over the breast. These were so tightly drawn that it was almost impossible to breathe. Last of all came the *obi,* reaching from breast to waistline, also drawn very tight, fastened in an intricate bow in back and secured —or, rather, ornamented —in front with a jewelled pin. There was absolutely no support over the abdomen and too much restriction, I thought, above it. The Japanese women certainly had very lovely figures, very slim and straight, though whether it was because of the way they dressed or in spite of it, I could not say.

It was in Kyoto, rather than in Tokyo, that I found time for study and contemplation and discussion, but the city also was favorably situated for a center while making excursions in the vicinity, and one of these took us to Nara, the first permanent capital of Japan. The road skirted along the Uji River, broad and placid; the scene was so peaceful that it was something of a shock to learn that the tall chimneys on the other side were those of gunpowder factories! At Uji stood the Ho-o-do (Phoenix Hall, so called from its shape of a bird with outspread wings and a long tail) of the Byodo-in Temple, which had been pronounced one of the twelve perfect buildings in the world by the great architect Ralph Adams Cram. Uji was also the district where the choicest tea was raised and where we saw it growing for the first time— not unlike laurel bushes in appearance. Small quaint warehouses rose in the midst of the fragrant and beautiful teafields, and beyond them were feathery bamboo forests.

In the villages we drove through, the houses, more primitive than those further north, were nearly all of baked mud called, strangely enough, *dobe*. Pilgrims trudged along, tall staffs in hand, wide straw hats on their heads, blowing on conch shells or ringing tiny bells as they walked. Friendly children lifted their arms and lustily greeted us as we sped past; patient black oxen drawing crude heavily-laden carts turned slowly aside to let us by. The roadsides were red with *shirei*—lilies of the dead—which bloomed at the time of the equinox and were considered symbolic of the soul passing from one side to another like the season. Here and there a lone fisherman bent over his pole in a lotus pool; rice grew thick and rich in the swamps or hung, already harvested, from wooden bars above the moist fields.

It was noon when we entered the park at Nara and had an enchanting surprise: we had heard of the "sacred deer of Nara" and had pictured them penned in some sort of glorified zoo. When we found there were *eight hundred of them* roaming absolutely unconfined through the temple groves of cryptomeria, peeping in and out among the stone lanterns and feeding from our hands, our delight knew no bounds. I made up my mind that when I went back to Kyoto to buy brocades on that glorious occasion when my ship came in, I was also going back to Nara to pet the deer! Alas! the ship has never yet been sighted.

Our last jaunt was to the port city of Kobe, where we spent the night, and the next morning we were on the *Chosa Maru,* the smallest vessel in the way of a steamboat I have ever seen, watching the busy port disappear behind us. Then came a voyage of magical beauty through the Inland Sea, with mountains and sky and water, tiny islands and tinier sailboats all dipped in liquid silver for it was a gray day, but the sort of gray day that glows and shines; and it ended in a blaze of fiery pink, with a night of wide-scattered stars after all.

The next morning, when we stopped at Moji to take on and unload cargo, the sun was bright again, the sails vivid white, the ocean vivid blue; then, after only a partial day of open sea, we entered the Inland Sea of Korea, and there were mountains and islands about us again. Here was bleaker beauty than that soft loveliness of Japan's Inland Sea, more rocky, more precipitous; but it was beauty nonetheless, and I was very happy lying on the small uncovered deck and watching it.

Henry, Larry and I were the only foreigners on board, and I was the only woman. The frugal steward came down every morning to make sure we were not seasick, before preparing the "foreign food." The cabin accommodated only sixteen passengers, and had practically been preempted by the Japanese delegation to the Customs Conference in Peking, headed by a Mr. Hioki. They played mah-jongg all day, so there was little to interrupt either my letter writing or my dreaming. And, dreaming, I had time to assimilate and assemble some of my impressions of Japan.

Chapter 36

T HE toy boat in which we had embarked at Kobe pushed its way up the river to Tientsin five days later, and we had our first sight of the wide drab-colored stream and the wide drab-colored land on either side of it, with huts of baked mud fringing the banks of the river and squatty little ships plying about in it. As we went further, we passed Italian, British and French gunboats; and, when we neared the city, we saw that the signs on the substantial buildings were in French and English quite as often as they were in Chinese. About ten in the morning, the boat slid up to the shore and we disembarked with as much ease as we would have stepped ashore from a canoe on the Connecticut River. There were no customs, no Quarantine, no passport examination. A brass band, gorgeously attired in sky-blue and crimson, was playing stirring airs, and a company of khaki-clad soldiers with fixed bayonets stood at attention. This display of the military, however, had no further significance than a respectful welcome to Mr. Hioki and his fellow delegates by the local officials, according to Mr. William Hunt of the American Consulate, who took us into his kindly and efficient charge and casually informed us we would find our multitudinous baggage on the train that afternoon. Then he took us for a rickshaw ride through the French and British "concessions," provided us with an excellent lunch at the Consulate Mess and, a few hours later, saw us installed in a first-class though rather dingy compartment on the late afternoon train to Peking.

The sky-blue and crimson band—or its twin—was playing again, as a send-off to the Japanese delegation, and at each station where we stopped duplicates gave vent to their musical, hospitable and patriotic sentiments. A member of the military police posted himself in the corridor outside the compartment, wearing the most enormous revolver I had ever seen and a knapsack ample enough to contain equipment and clothing for months of combat. His smile, however, was as disarming as his apparel was formidable and he and the bands furnished our only diversion as we rode through miles and miles of flat dismal country, with the same kind of muddy streams and mud huts we had seen in the morning and hundreds of little mounds which we knew were graves— for the Chinese bury their dead above ground. Yet this sad, silent country had dignity and grandeur; it was not monotonous, it was restful; it was not lonely, it was spacious. A woman born and bred in our own great plains would, I thought, have found herself suddenly homesick, looking at it. And even I, used to mountains and valleys all my life and loving them beyond expression, sensed its sober splendor and significance as I looked across to the distant place where earth and sky met in a gray horizon, or looked above, where a pale sickle moon cut a gray sky. I was almost sorry when the smiling guard signified that Peking was the next station. On the platform stood Mr. John MacMurray, our Minister to China, waiting to welcome us. He looked very tired, I thought, and much older than the previous spring when he was still Chief of the Division of Far Eastern Affairs in the State Department and I went to confer with him—the cares of office do not sit lightly on anyone who takes them conscientiously and gravely. But his quiet courtesy, his respose of manner —two characteristics which, no less than his knowledge and love of all things Chinese, must have endeared him greatly to the Chinese government—were unchanged. He saw us safely to our hotel and assured himself that our reservations were in order before he hurried off to an official dinner in honor of the conference delegates.

That is the true story of the "hardships" I had been told I must endure in penetrating to Peking, and more such "hardships" followed! Every morning I woke and stretched myself across my huge soft bed (the only really good bed I had had since I left San Francisco, except in Nikko) as the bugler at the fort across the way blew reveille. He blew this bugle frequently and loudly, early and late. At first I resented this, though I realized he had some good reason for doing it, but I soon ceased to feel resentful, largely no doubt because, for the first time since I could remember, I slept soundly and dreamlessly all night. So I would touch the bell swinging over my head, and in would come that justly famed ministering angel—the Chinese "boy." The term "boy" had nothing to do with age—that one must have been well over sixty. He was tall and dignified, clad in a long white robe and bearing a tray, and he murmured, "Good morning, Madame. It is a fine day." He poured coffee and hot milk and dropped lumps of sugar in a cup and buttered the toast and looked at me in pained surprise when I tried to do any of these things myself. Then he went to the window and pulled back the damask curtain and opened the Venetian blinds and the sunshine streamed in—not occasionally, but every single day, flooding the room, flooding the city beyond that great window. No matter at what time of day or night I rang, service was equally prompt and equally perfect. Once, by mistake, I touched my bell at three in the morning; instantly my "boy" appeared in the doorway, fully clad in his long white robe, and calmly awaited orders. Where he slept I cannot imagine. But of one thing I am very sure: he never heard of an eight-hour day!

When I had finished breakfast and was dressed and at my desk trying to write letters, I found it almost impossible to do anything but sit and bask in that sunlight, as I gazed out over the city. In the linden grove facing the hotel there was a flute player sitting under a tree, and a barber shaving a customer, and a vendor of small sweet cakes calling his wares, and several weary coolies who had curled up and gone to sleep on the dusty ground. Beyond lay the Italian glacis—the space between the Legation Quarter and the Tartar city, which was opened after the Boxer Rebellion and which thenceforth had been kept open as a measure of protection. Up and down it went funny closed cabs, mostly painted bright green and drawn by shaggy Mongolian ponies with bright bells and driven by mustachioed personages wearing round black caps and flowing robes. Up and down it also went the rickshaws, and the patient mouse-colored donkeys, and the caravans of camels. The first time I saw one of these caravans, I nearly fell out of the window with excitement; and several weeks later, after seeing hundreds of them, I was still impelled to follow them with my eyes until they were out of sight. They stepped slowly, with a swaying motion, a narrow cord passing from the nose of the leader to that of each camel behind it, their wares arranged over their humps and against their tawny sides. Their driver trudged beside them, a long stick in his hand—impassive and imperturbable even when he had to turn his train aside for a shining limousine.

Beyond the glacis was the Legation Quarter, surrounded by a high gray wall, a sentry at every entrance and exit and the coat-of-arms of each country blazoned above the gate that admitted you to its compound, where another sentry was stationed. There, in the Anglican Chapel of the British Legation, many missionaries found their only home for six weeks in July and August, 1900. Past the Italian, Japanese and other legations was our own, where we were delightfully entertained again and again, and still further on rose the City Wall. We went there to walk and found it largely occupied with the coming generation of diplomats in the care of their *amahs,* who were among the best nursemaids in the world, devoted to their small charges. From the wall, we could see Peking spread out before us—the Forbidden City inside the Imperial City, both with their soft red brick walls and their massive gates; then the Tartar City and the Chinese City, each with its own wall. Out of the great city gate poured a ceaseless stream of humanity; on the thronged streets the Mongolian and Manchu ladies bargained and strolled, the vendors of persimmons squatted by the pavement and offered you their golden fruit. You had to go quickly if you were to resist the temptations of fur and porcelain, brass and jade spread out before you. In the distance, beyond the open markets and noisy theaters, the Temple of Heaven loomed against the sky—and all this was bathed in that streaming, stimulating sunshine. Rome is the only city I have ever visited where the autumn sunshine was as brilliant and as all pervading as it was in Peking that year.

Ko, my rickshaw man, was always patiently waiting to take me wherever I chose to go—snowy ruffles on the cushions of his chair, a small rug of Ming blue for my feet, worth a fortune at home. Though I disapproved of rickshaws and rarely used one in Japan, in Peking I had no choice, for that cheerful savage Ko attached himself to me and sat endlessly waiting for me at the hotel entrance. If I went in a car, he still sat there, looking at me reproachfully as I passed; when I succumbed and had his number called, he came trotting up grinning from ear to ear. "Good morning, missy, velly fine day. Where you go lunch? Yes, I know." And he was off, swift and strong, passing every other rickshaw. When we returned from lunch, it was, "You go out tea? File o'clock? Yes, I know." And later still, "You go out dinner? Half-past eight? Yes, I know." Last of all, when he had trotted home with me through the narrow unpaved streets, bordered with small gray houses, whose blank facades gave no hint of the lovely open courts beyond their shiny red doors, the moon no longer a crescent but a brass medallion lighting our way, he would bid me farewell with, "Good night, missy. You want in morning? Yes, I know."

The first dinner to which Ko carried me, padding softly through the Legation Quarter late in the evening—for Peking dinners were held later than any except Spanish ones—was at the home of Mr. Clarence Hewes of Louisiana, First Secretary of our Legation, a rising diplomat and the accomplished head of an elegant bachelor establishment. At his table we were introduced to that most delectable confection, "the wall of Peking with Peking dust inside"—a hollowed circle of glacé fruits and nuts, heaped high with powdered marrons covered with whipped cream. We found among our fellow guests Mr. Frank Lockhart, our Consul General at Hankow, then acting head of the American Secretariat for the Conference, with his pleasant sweet-voiced wife and pretty daughter Maurine—great friends of Senator and Mrs. Sheppard, at whose Washington house I had first met them. Before the evening was over, Mr. Hewes offered us his invaluable "number one boy," Yung, to take us to the Great Wall, and Yung, looking very sleek in his velvet jacket and silk skirt, came into the drawing room to receive his instructions. We asked Mrs. Lockhart and Maurine to join us, Mr. Lockhart being too busy, and arranged to start the following Tuesday at seven in the morning.

Promptly at the time and place appointed—the Hsichihmen station —Yung appeared, and from then on, as far as lay within his power, our path was strewn with roses. Afterward, Mr. Hewes confessed he had told Yung I was an Imperial Duchess, which may have accounted to some degree for the perfection of the service he rendered. I must admit we were thankful for a little rose strewing, for the train in which we went to Chinglungchiao—the nearest approach to the Wall—was absolutely unheated and crowded to the point of suffocation, and the one in which we returned was unlighted except for one small oil burner; and both were dirty beyond description. Nor was Yung's smiling efficiency limited to the trains; from the howling rabble at Chinglungchiao station he selected the most promising coolies and bargained with them, and soon we were on our way again—Mrs. Lockhart and I in rude sedan chairs, their long poles supported on the bearers' shoulders, and the young fry on donkeys. Even Yung could not disperse the beggars, itinerant vendors and a group of persistent small Mongolians who attached themselves to us; and thus we proceeded, a meandering cavalcade, through the rocky ravine leading to the Wall.

Suddenly it was coiled before us—a great tawny serpent sprawling across a great tawny country and basking in the warmth of a brazen sky. From the highest mountain to the lowest valley and then up and down and beyond again it stretched, as it had stretched for two thousand years, silent and sinister and splendid.

We climbed to the highest watchtower and sat on its loftiest parapet, gazing into the melting distance; far away, in a bowl made by the hills, lay a little walled city; flocks of sheep, droves of donkeys, caravans of camels threaded their slow quiet way through the massive gates and along the narrow passes. A sense of storied unreality, of drenching antiquity, an awesome realization of limitless expanse and immense power filled our souls, and it did not leave us even when we descended and stopped to eat lunch at a lower tower, where smooth stones had been covered with taut white cloths to serve as tables and piles of smaller stones served as seats. It did not leave us even when, as the mellow afternoon wore on and still no breath of breeze ruffled the calm air, we took out a traveling bridge set and played five rubbers while we waited for the tardy train. The ragamuffins and peddlers gathered about us in a surprised circle and watched us. So perhaps, hundreds of years ago, their ancestors watched kings a-pleasuring.

Ko took me, wrapped in the fur robe which the snap in the sunshine now made necessary, to pay my respects to the Minister of Foreign Affairs, Shen Jui-Lin, who received me richly attired in gray and black brocade and conversed with me in fluent French. A few days later his Private Secretary, Mr. Hwang, escorted me to an audience with the Chief Executive of the Provisional Government of China, Marshal Twan Chi-Jui, who was not properly referred to as President. The reception room for such audiences—a high, dim, narrow apartment with beautiful Chinese rugs on the floor and formal foreign furniture—was in the Ministry of War; when Mr. Hwang and I entered, escorted by Mr. Ru, the Master of Ceremonies, Marshal Twan rose from a small sofa, acknowledged the deep bows we all made and shook hands with me, which was a great surprise, since I had been instructed that one bowed out of his presence, as in the case of royalty, and I did not dream the two courtesies would be used together. Then he reseated himself, a crimson and gold cushion at his back, motioned us to sit down and, concealing his hands in the voluminous folds of his brilliant blue robe, listened gravely, his face masklike, as Mr. Hwang talked to him about my husband and myself. For a few moments he responded only in monosyllables, but with the appearance of tea he began to ask questions and, finally, to talk fluently and forcefully on all sorts of subjects. His extreme gravity vanished and his face, brightened by a smile, was strangely attractive.

The audience, which lasted an hour and a half, was the first, he told me, that he had ever given an American lady visiting China, but we freely discussed conditions in China and world conditions. "China has never been an aggressive nation. The teachings of Confucius, by which we have been guided, have counseled patience and submission rather than force. It is only as a last resort that we assert ourselves and demand our rights. . . ." To the subject of peace he reverted again and again. And it was with the expressed hope that I would do my share, in writing about the different nations, to make them better known and better understood and consequently better loved by each other, that he finally bade me "farewell—a happy journey—and a safe return."

Aside from that audience, there was no experience that gave me quite such a thrill as the opening session of the Customs Conference, to which I was the only woman admitted as a member of the press. It may seem to some that the question of tariff alone would not be a sufficiently important one to justify the calling of an international conference, but they forget the revenue our government derives from this source and the weary months of debate in the Senate which the discussion of each new tariff bill consumes. "China is the only country in the world now," Dr. C. T. Wang, formerly Prime Minister and later director of Sino-Russian negotiations, had written, "that has been deprived of the freedom of adopting an independent fiscal policy and fixing a tariff for herself, in spite of the most profuse professions by the powers to respect her sovereignty, independence and territorial and administrative integrity. The Chinese people have awakened to this wrong done them ... and they are now demanding in a chorus that this infringement should be blotted out." Since the Hanking treaty of 1842, China had been paying both an export and an import tax of five percent—that is, the government had been obliged to charge its own people, as well as foreigners, for the privilege of exporting—in order to meet expenses, while foreign goods had come in at the extremely low figure of five percent—compared to the ninety percent we levied on some imports! China certainly had something on her side in suggesting she would prefer to increase her revenues from an income tax and that she, rather than foreign powers, should determine the degree of taxation.

Dr. Wang laid before the conference, in behalf of the Chinese government, its "proposals for the removal of the restrictions imposed by the existing treaties affecting the Customs Tariff," first among which was that "the participating powers formally declare to the Government of the Republic of China their respect for its tariff autonomy, and agree to the removal of all tariff restrictions contained in existing treaties." The other representatives, except those of Great Britain and Japan, confined themselves to brief, gracious and noncommittal expressions of pleasure at being present and hopes for a happy solution of all problems. Sir Ronald Maccleay, the British Minister, went somewhat further and offered fewer felicitations, and I thought his statement that his delegation was "prepared to discuss the question of tariff autonomy either at this conference or, if that cannot be arranged, at some later date" savored of a preference for further postponement.

All this time, Mr. Hioki, the head of the Japanese delegation, had been drinking cup after cup of hot tea, which was brought in and placed on the green baize table before him. But finally he rose—and proceeded to unburden himself of the contents of a bulky document which consumed as much time as all the other speeches combined. I hardly suppressed a gasp of dismay when he began to trace Japan's progress from the toils of extra-territorial restrictions and unilateral engagements in the matter of customs tariff from 1858 onward! "The difficulties, the embarrassments and the perplexities that confront China today have been ours. . . . *However,* an immediate duty is encumbent upon us who are here assembled." He proceeded to point out flaws which, in his opinion, existed in the Chinese viewpoint and to offer an alternative: "The inauguration of tariff autonomy in China," he concluded, *"implies the existence of an adequately strong and unified government and presupposes a complete removal of all restrictions which might impede the freedom of intercourse and trade between China and other powers."*

There, in a nutshell, was the other side of the story.

It was true that there was no stable government in China then, that civil war was rending the land and that other unsettled conditions existed. China was deeply in debt, and the creditor nations could not be blamed for wishing to ensure collection of what was due them. There was terrible poverty, too—beggars on almost every street, squalor on every hand. Even the historic landmarks of unmatched beauty—the Temple of Heaven, the Summer Palace, many others—were falling apart from neglect, whereas most nations would have treasured, restored and guarded them; a small thing in itself, perhaps, but significant of many greater things. It had made me sad to go through these palaces and temples.

On the other hand, who could say that China unrestrained, unfettered, might not rouse herself and rise from the ashes of former greatness to a supreme future glory? Which was cause and which was effect? Was she undeserving of autonomy because of her condition, or was her condition the suffering expression of her need for autonomy? Here was a people with a population nearly four times as great as ours, industrious, sober, calm, patient and intelligent. I never met an American long resident in China who did not tell me that the more he saw of the Chinese, the more he respected them, admired them and recognized their grandeur. In the light of what has happened since, the Customs Conference of 1925 seems more and not less significant than it did then.

Chapter 37

DURING the autumn of 1925 my plans became very uncertain. Part of this uncertainty was caused by wars and rumors of wars which did not make traveling in China either easy or safe; but most of it was caused by my own conflicting emotions. Should I stay in Peking, which bewitched me—and go to the garden party in the old Imperial Palace of the Forbidden City—or should I return at once to Tokyo, which had charmed me—and go to the Imperial Chrysanthemum Party in the garden of the Akasaka Palace?

I finally compromised by doing both.

The invitation to the Forbidden City arrived late one evening after the Civil War had reached a stage where it seemed advisable to take the first train out of Peking or make up my mind to remain there indefinitely and, perhaps, uncomfortably. Despite all the noble statements to the effect that peace, and only peace, was the aim of the Chief Executive, the Minister of Foreign Affairs and various other officials, it looked less and less as if we could count on their attainment of this aim, or even strenuous efforts toward it. There was very little coal in the city, and that was being "conserved"; I had caught a frightful cold in the rooms which, according to our standards, were grievously underheated. Reports that food would soon be no more abundant than coal were persistently circulated and, watching the amount consumed by two healthy young males in the course of every twenty-four hours, I grew thoughtful. But as I read that the "Commission of the Ancient Imperial Palace" begged me "to be so kind as to visit the Palace and its Museum," this visit to be followed "by a reception at the Pavilion Chiang Hsueh Hsien," I hesitated, and then I succumbed to the temptation of availing myself of an opportunity—and giving the boys the same opportunity, for they were both kindly included—which few persons had ever had. In the days of the Empire, the Forbidden City was indeed literally forbidden to all save those of most exalted rank; and since the fall of the Empire, it had been closed and deserted except for one or two buildings which, out of its hundreds, were opened to the public twice a week. Now, at last, the high officials of the Provisional Government had decided to open it as a whole and admit to its sacred precincts the members of the Diplomatic Corps, the other delegates to the conference and a few fortunate guests besides—some two hundred in all. Laying the invitations for Henry and Larry on their pillows so they would find them when they returned from a dance they were attending, I canceled our travel reservations, unpacked my best hat and went to bed determined to remain, war or no war!

All my life, I shall be glad that I did. On the appointed afternoon our rickshaws took us along the tile-capped moat, with its pink walls opposite, to the great gate Shen Wu Men, where we had to leave them. Before the day was over, we were thankful they had taken us that far, for no less than five miles of walking over stone-flagged courts and through stone-flagged passages and up long flights of stone steps awaited us! But it was walking made easy by the gorgeous if ruined splendor that was on every side: the splendor of tiled roofs, green and gold and blue, glowing in the late sunshine, and the carved ceilings where the same brilliant colors were mingled—for these, as characteristic as the red and black lacquer of Japan, are the vivid hues of temple and tower, palace and pavilion in China; the splendor of thrones and screens, wonderfully wrought, of paintings and draperies and garments that glittered and gleamed. One robe of deep yellow, heavily embroidered and edged with sable more than a foot deep about the hem, was the most truly regal costume I have ever beheld. And jade and bronze and porcelain, imperial seals and documents and tablets filled one vast hall after another.

We went through the Hwang Chi Tien, the throne room of the palace, and the Shang Shu Fang, formerly the Imperial School, and the Chiao T'si T'ien, where the Imperial marriages were celebrated—and all of them were filled with splendor. But there were relics of tragedy as well in the Forbidden City, for the Ning Shov Kung—the hall in which sacrifices were offered—still contained the implements which were employed in their performance, and in the first courtyard we entered was a small stone well with the inscription:

> Princess Chen, one of the wives of the Emperor Kwang Hshi,
> was forced by the Dowager Empress Tsi Hsi to throw herself
> in this well in 1900.

At last we came to the spacious Imperial Garden, where the stately trees were scattering bronze and yellow leaves over the ancient ornaments and carved stone seats—a place full of dignity and repose. Just beyond stood the painted pavilion where the Emperor Chien Lung used to write poems, where the Empress Lung Tu spent her leisure and where the Emperor Hsuan Tung gave banquets to foreign guests. Appropriately, the reception was being held in this pavilion, called Chiang Hsueh Hsien. Tea and punch, sandwiches and cake, and other delicacies were spread invitingly on long tables decorated with chrysanthemums.

At this feast we met once more many of the men and women who had done so much to make our stay in Peking delightful, among them the Minister of Foreign Affairs, Mr. Shen Jui Lin, and the Vice Minister, Mr. Tseng Tsung Kien, in fashionably cut foreign dress, a huge powerful man with great diplomatic talents as well as a gift of sparkling repartee and uncanny skill at bridge. (Never have I seen bridge played as fast as in Peking. The shuffling and dealing seemed almost like sleight of hand, the bidding was so rapid that it required great alertness to follow it; and then very soon Mr. Tseng Tsung Kien, or one of his almost equally skillful compatriots, would say, "I believe I have all the rest," and spread out his cards, and never once did I know him to make a mistake!)

Other fellow guests, who had entertained us and whom we were glad to see again, were the American Minister and Mrs. MacMurray, and Dr. John Calvin Ferguson, American adviser to the Chief Executive, very cordial and jovial. In one of the vast courtyards of the Forbidden City, we also discovered some Tokyo acquaintances, among them a member of the Japanese Delegation, who promised some eventual reassurance about the next step on my journey.

"This is a wonderful party, isn't it?" I asked. "But you don't think, do you, I've jeopardized my chance of getting to *your* garden party by staying for it? I know I'm running close to the wind, but the date for the Chrysanthemum Festival hasn't been officially announced, as far as I can discover."

"I shall be glad to find out the date for you. You are leaving tonight? And going through Korea? When you get to Seoul, you'll find a wire. Close connections, but I hope they will work out for you."

"I hope so too."

There was not much time left in which to repack my best hat, but it was stowed away somehow and, with it, vivid memories of one of the most distinctive functions I had attended in a republic—comparable to the *baile* at the *Presidencia* in Panama and the most lovely of our own

White House parties. We sped to the station and past laden cars of a troop train to the private car at its end which the efficient railway commission had secured for us, where we found almost as many gift-bearing friends waiting to see us off as we would have at home. We were thankful beyond words, for the trip before us would have been difficult—to put it mildly—without the car, which had once been a fine one, with a sitting room, a room with two berths, a room with a real brass bed, and a bathroom with an actual tub, besides the service quarters. Unfortunately, the plumbing was out of order, so we had no running water during the trip; the brass bed shook violently and threatened to fall apart every time I turned over; and, apparently, no house cleaning had been done since the car's maiden trip. The "boy" in charge, unlike most of his kind, spoke no English, and his only idea of ministering to us was to bring us tea at half-hour intervals. However, we were grateful for that, as we had no vestibule connection with the rest of the train. Next to us was an ammunition car—a juxtaposition which provided food for *thought* every time a few sparks flew! And that was the only food I did get until we reached Mukden, except sandwiches we had brought from the hotel and candy which had been a farewell gift!

Even more frequently than the tea service came stops to let other troop trains pass—trains with open cars full of fur-hooded, gray-clad soldiers and cars full of mules and guns and cannon and airplanes. We counted over fifty of these trains; others went uncounted during the night. Twice the stops were rather long and courteous officers entered our car, saluted and asked for my "name paper," which, I discovered, meant my visiting card; after reading it, they smiled and saluted again and we were on our way once more.

We reached Mukden only three hours late, to the sound of *getas* clattering through the windswept station and the sight of a Japanese hotel looming before us, with its prices all in *yen*—for Mukden marked the starting point of the Japanese-run railway and the station hotel was under the same management. An hour later, after hot baths and cold drinks, we were all tucked in clean hard beds, sound asleep.

Mukden was a city of wide, well-paved streets, bare and bleak, but with a sort of starkness not devoid of magnificence. The Russian influence was evident in costumes and architecture and vehicles, and wonderful furs, crudely cut and cured, hung heavily in the small dark shops which lined the pavements. We drove past them into the walled city, stopping on the way for Mr. Sokobin, our Consul, and came eventually to a handsome doorway, heavily guarded, where he and I alighted—the residence of North China's military idol, Marshal Chang Tso Lin, commander in chief of one of the warring armies. Before I left Peking, a telegram had reached me telling me he would receive me at noon on this day.

We went into a small office where several soldiers were gathered around an air-tight stove and maps and charts were spread out on a table. With the soldiers was a gentleman looking very elegant in black brocade—a striking contrast to the others' bulky uniforms—who rose hurriedly, greeted Mr. Sokobin with enthusiastic cordiality and introduced himself, before Mr. Sokobin could present him to me, as Mr. Kao of the Foreign Office. He bowed us out of the room, hastened ahead of us across a courtyard and ushered us into a high imposing house with richly colored tile on the walls and huge pots of colorful flowers standing about. Then, somewhat breathless, I found myself in a drawing room furnished with ebony inlaid with mother-of-pearl, tall cabinets filled with treasures of jade and porcelain and two enormous stuffed tigers with wide-open mouths! A puffy brocade sofa and arm-chairs were clustered about a table covered with fringed red plush, on which stood tall dishes of bright blue pressed glass laden with pastry, baked barely past the dough stage and filled with strange jams!

For one bewildered moment I fancied I was back in my quivering brass bed dreaming the whole thing; that such contrasts could be displayed within the walls of one room and that I had been led to view them by a Chinese Mercutio like Mr. Kao did not seem possible. Then, without announcement, the Marshal entered and it was harder than ever to realize my imagination was not playing me tricks. For here, instead of a large and imposing military figure in a resplendent uniform, stood a gentle looking, smiling person whose hand, as he placed it in mine, was as smooth and small as a young girl's, whose speech was as soft and slow as that of an elderly gentlewoman and who was dressed in a brocaded robe of ultramarine—the favorite color of the Chinese, glowing in the poor's ragged cottons no less than in the rich silks of the wealthy and their rugs, roofs and porcelains. He seated himself on the sofa and began to drink tea and smoke a long thin pipe, packing the bowl tightly at frequent intervals with his delicate fingers. And he talked, in that soft slow voice, very fluently indeed.

He did not discuss military tactics at length; in fact, when he said his main object was not so much to gain control of South China himself as to prevent the control of all China by the Bolsheviks, he dismissed them entirely, until I asked whether he had a family. Then he told me he had seven sons, the eldest of whom, "the young General," was evidently his father's idol, as he was the idol of his men. The Marshal naturally reverted to the subject of warfare as personified for him in his first-born, but only for a moment. "The other boys are all too young to be in the army, and I have six daughters also. The youngest is only two. But I rather hope I shall never have a really large family. It is so expensive to rear and educate and establish them suitably."

And the Marshal and I, mutually sympathetic, discussed the high cost of living!

Not for one moment did he make me feel that the audience had been either a condescension or an inconvenience for him, though I knew it must have been both, especially during a crowded pulsing week when history was fast being made. Instead, he kept reiterating his regret that my stay in Mukden was so short that it gave him no opportunity to offer me any real hospitality, much less a suitable entertainment.

Short it certainly was. For within an hour after I left the Marshal and bade farewell to Mr. Kao, I was on the train again—the best train, I am impelled to state (except its twin, with which I later made acquaintance), in which I have ever ridden in my life. For the Japanese, whose trains in their own country left so much to be desired, used cars very much like our Pullmans from Mukden through Korea to Seoul and on to Fusan—the embarkation point for Shimonoseki—to whose comfort they added their own perfection of service and cleanliness. I leaned my weary head against the white linen "tidy" covering the neat green plush seat with a sigh of contented relief.

It had begun to snow, and we moved along, hour after hour, through a desolate countryside where even the smallest villages were few and far between. At last we stopped at a tiny station whose illumination, though scanty, permitted us to see the outlines of two or three insignificant houses near by. A moment later I was aware that a rather slight but very distinguished-looking Chinese, handsomely dressed in sapphire blue brocade, was coming through the car toward the drawing room. When he reached the open door, he bowed and presented a card which read, "L. M. Sun, Attaché, Bureau of Foreign Affairs, Amtung."

"We are approaching the frontier," he said. "Of course, we do not expect any disturbance, but these are troublous times. It was the suggestion of my friend—and yours—Mr. Tseng Tsung Kien that I should come and give myself the pleasure of conversing with you until we have actually entered Korea."

It was very late and I was very tired, and that there could be two episodes in the same day as fantastic as the audience with the Marshal and the unexpected arrival of this dignified gentleman on the edge of nowhere was difficult for me to grasp. It required all my self-control to thank him for his courtesy and invite him to be seated. He settled himself, as if everything were so natural as to need no further comment, and began to question me about my impressions of Peking, which he hoped had been favorable. To this, at least, I could respond enthusiastically; but from time to time I eyed Henry and Larry, who were sitting opposite us, with some anxiety; so far, they had been silent, except when addressed directly. I was afraid that sooner or later one of them would burst out with a question and reveal his astonishment at the latest turn of events—and I was right, but the query was far from the one I expected.

"What was your class at Harvard, sir?" Henry inquired without preamble.

"Ninety," our visitor replied. "I was a freshman when your father was a senior." After that, the conversation switched from the Customs Conference to the Harvard Yard and I managed to get my second wind.

The next morning when I raised my curtain and looked out the window, I decided again I must be dreaming—or at least seeing ghosts! We had come to rugged mountainous country, and stalking about the bleak landscape were tall stately figures clad in white draperies. Some of them wore draperies over their heads as well as their bodies; these, I afterward discovered, were women. The men had on the strangest hats I ever beheld: a cap which looked exactly like a fly-trap overtopped by an undersized stovepipe, both made of very fine split bamboo painted black or, in the case of the wealthy, of fine black horsehair. Even in the cities the men wore this weird headgear—unless they were in mourning for their parents, when they wore an enormous mushroom-shaped straw, that the sun might not shine on their countenance during four years.

I had been told I would find Seoul a disappointment after Peking, but this was not so. It was a beautifully located city, cupped by hills. It had fine wide streets, abundant light, pure water and excellent school buildings—and all these benefits, let us grant, Korea owed to Japan, for she did not possess them before she became part of Japanese territory. To Japan she doubtless also owed her appearance of scrubbed cleanliness, for it did not seem to be indigenous elsewhere on the Asian continent. But all her own was the still beauty of the Twelve Tombs of the Korean Emperors on a cluster of molded hills outside the city, where stone figures of priests and soldiers and animals kept silent watch about the graves of the illustrious dead. All her own was the still splendor of the lofty pillared audience chamber in the East Palace, with its golden hangings and turquoise screens and the plum blossom, instead of the chrysanthemum, embroidered on its throne. All her own was the quiet loveliness of the palace garden, where a yellow ginko tree towered—as it had since prehistoric times—above the scarlet splash of maples and rainbow-hued pavilions which overlooked the placid lakes. All her own was the homely comfort of the heated stone floors, overlaid with heavy waxed paper, which were warmed by flues running beneath them from an outside open oven. All her own was the strong solid brightness of her chests, bound and studded with brass or inlaid with mother-of-pearl, and the imprisoned sunshine of her flawless amber. When a pendant and earrings of this liquid light were given me and I knew I had three bits of Korean color to keep the rest of my life, I was so pleased I nearly cried.

The good angel who gave me the amber was Mrs. Herbert Welch, the wife of the Methodist Bishop of Japan and Korea, and to the Welches and the Millers—our Consul General and his fragile wife and talented daughter—were due much of the pleasure and success of my visit. It was Mr. Miller who secured for us the permit to see the East Palace, where Prince Yi, the eldest son of the last Korean Emperor, now lived in deposed state; and it was Mrs. Welch who took me to the Union Social Center, established by Methodists and Presbyterians together on an old Imperial property, where still stood the building in which the treaty ceding Korea to Japan was signed; as well as the building where the manifesto known as the Declaration of Independence against Japan was signed in their own blood by thirty-three Koreans. And at this Social Center I had a special thrill: I met a Korean princess and kissed her hand—a princess who was exactly six years old!

Near the Center stood a palace—less grand than the East Palace but still very beautiful—in which resided a younger brother of Prince Yi. Close to this palace, in an establishment of her own, lived one of the younger prince's wives, the Princess Kil Chang Whe, with her only child, the Princess Eu. She and her mother had become deeply attached to the nurse in charge of the Center's Health Clinic; so when the latter presented herself to the Princess Kil Chang Whe and told her an American lady was at the Center and would like to see the little girl, her mother replied, "All the servants are making *kimchee* today and cannot be spared to take Eu to the Center; but she may go with you and Lavinia, the Biblewoman,[1] to see the American lady. I am pleased that she should go."

So, when I reached the Center, there sat little Princess Eu, on a bench in front of the fireplace, holding tightly to the hand of Lavinia, the white-clad Biblewoman. Eu had left her small embroidered shoes by the door, and her full skirt of crimson brocade fell in rich folds to her tiny, white-stockinged feet. Her tight fitting bodice was of yellow satin trimmed with crimson, and on her head she wore a black velvet cap embroidered in colors, from under which her long thick braid of dark hair

---

[1] *Kimchee* is the Korean sauerkraut. A Biblewoman was a native who had become a convert to Christianity and went among other Koreans doing good works and spreading the Gospel.

hung to her waist. She was lovely, with wide-set dark eyes, smooth rosy skin and a small nose and mouth which already had the slightest trace of hauteur in their sweetness, for she was very much the princess even if she was only six—very poised, very calm and collected. As Mrs. Welch and I entered the room, she got down from the bench and extended her little hand to each of us to kiss, quite as a matter of course. Then to each of us in turn she swept a deep curtsy—her skirt spreading out like a fan, her head bending like a top-heavy blossom, her hands, like smaller blossoms, falling against the hem of her dress. These formalities having been fulfilled, she reseated herself with perfect composure and sat silently and politely receptive to our unbounded enthusiasm. However, when Mrs. Welch presented her with some entrancing paper dolls, she seemed to feel the occasion required a suitable expression of gratitude. She rose again and began to dance, singing as she did so, without the least self-consciousness or embarrassment—an exquisite little dance that would have done credit to a princess thrice her age. Then, when it was time to leave, she gave each of us her hand and swept us her deep curtsy again before she walked to the door and put on her small shoes.

I should have been glad to linger much longer in Seoul, but the promised telegram giving the date of the Chrysanthemum Party in Tokyo was waiting for me there, and to reach Japan in time we had to be on our way. So we boarded a train (the aforementioned twin) for Fusan where we caught the night boat to Shimonoseki. But we realized we were in Japan again twice before we got there: when the cabin boy indicated our staterooms and in the same breath asked, "What time you want your bath?" and second, when the passport officials detained us for an hour, asking futile and superfluous questions before they allowed us to land. Then came a hard ride, twenty-eight hours long, with accommodations which, though described to us beforehand as "very special," were exceedingly uncomfortable; and only the matchless sight of Fuji's perfect purity rising above the scarlet maples and harvested rice kept our weary spirits from drooping before we reached Tokyo.

There the long-promised invitation awaited me—thick and stiff and wide and surmounted by the Imperial crest, the conventionalized chrysanthemum, in heavy gold. It was engraved in Japanese, but with it was a smaller card, which read:

> Gentlemen are requested to wear Frock-coats and Silk hats, Military and Naval Officers their Uniforms corresponding to the above, and Ladies, Visiting dress.
> Guests in Mourning dress will not be admitted.

Guests are requested to arrive at the Akasaka Palace by 1:30 p. m.: those by carriages or automobiles to enter by the Main Gate of the Palace, and those by jinrikishas or on foot by the East Gate (Higashi-mon) at the top of Kinokunizaka.

The card is to be handed to the officials in charge at the entrance.

In case of rain, the party will not take place. The guests, however, are admitted to the Gardens on the same day from 1 to 3 p. m. (same dress).

This final paragraph confronted me balefully. There was, it appeared, no provision for postponement or for holding the festivities indoors, and since it rains so much of the time in Japan, I felt the chances for fulfillment were very slim. My worst fears were realized. On the morning of the party, it poured in torrents, and before noon the news was spread that "the Empress, the Prince Regent and the Princes of the Blood" would not grace the occasion with their presence—that there would be, in fact, no visible hosts or hostesses at all! Mr. Neville, our Chargé d'Affaires, telephoned however, to ask if I would not like to go with Mrs. Neville and himself to see the beautiful gardens just the same; and, armed with umbrellas, rubbers and topcoats, we started on our way.

At the entrance our cards were taken from us by officials dressed in blue velvet knee breeches, red velvet vests, black coats trimmed with gold braid and white stockings. They held huge umbrellas over their heads, while the guests concealed their frock-coats, uniforms and "visiting dress" beneath mackintoshes to protect them from the rain, which dripped and splashed to the ground, as we progressed.

The Akasaka Palace, which was the residence of the Prince Regent, was a handsome building, constructed like a French chateau, with a magnificent garden in the rear—brilliant at that time of year with the Japanese maple, with which even our own New England maples cannot compete, and late camellia blossoms flowering on high trees. Snow-white swans floated on the quiet surfaces of wide lakes, and shaded walks wound from one breath-taking vista to another. At the further end of the garden, refreshments were served in split bamboo pavilions, and similar pavilions sheltered the precious blossoms which rose symmetrically from earth as smooth as brown satin, in every color, size and shape. Some clustered thickly on the same plant, others displayed a single superb blossom tipping from a long slender stem. The tiny pink and white and yellow daisies which, through infinite skill and patience, have been developed into the chrysanthemums of today were not the most imposing, but there was something starlike and pure and radiant about them, and I returned to look at them again and again.

When we had walked through the gardens and looked at the chrysan-themums, we went home. It was a great pleasure—a great privilege—to see them, but I was disappointed because the party to which I had so looked forward did not, in one sense, take place at all; that there was no one in any of the pavilions to greet us and give us a feeling of wel-come. Even if no member of the Imperial family could do so, it seemed as if somebody might have been chosen to represent them. Had it not been for the fact that my return to Japan had given me the chance to meet Chang Tso Lin and Princess Eu, I should have been sorry that I had not gone straight from Peking to Shanghai. The second stay in Japan was somewhat anticlimactic in character.

There was also an occurrence—new in my experience at that time, though a few years later I was to have a similar one in Germany—which upset me a good deal: one day, on returning to our hotel suite after an absence of several hours, I found that it had been thoroughly ransacked and that no effort had been made to restore order after what had appar-ently been a very intensive search for something incriminating among my belongings. My clothes were strewn about in every direction, dresses taken from their hangers, bureau drawers emptied of their contents, desk drawers of correspondence and notes. Only my dispatch case had been locked, and its lock had been forced; all my letters of introduction for the rest of my trip had been disarranged; it took hours to get them back in proper sequence. Nothing was missing, and I have not the slightest idea what the intruders were looking for; but I recalled that both times I had arrived at a Japanese port I had been closely ques-tioned as to what I meant to write and why; for no apparent reason, I was suspected of something. This distrust made me distrustful in my turn and I reported the search to Mr. Neville. He very wisely advised me to make no complaint, since nothing was missing; but I had an un-comfortable feeling in Japan from that day on, and I did not try to put my next article in the ordinary mail, though there was not a word in it which could be considered critical. I had Henry take it to the next ship bound for the states and entrust it to the purser.

But in saying good-bye to Japan for the second time on that trip—and probably for the last time in my life—there were other memories which went with me, memories which I did not expect to gather, memo-ries which I have never ceased to treasure. I came to know the courtesy and refinement of the Japanese people. I saw the Daibutsu massive in the dusk, and Fujiyama with a ball of fire resting on her slope at sunset, and the red temples of Nikko rising at the top of rain-washed gray steps, and the silent hills of Miyanoshita by starlight. I fed the deer at

Nara, and I wore, for once in my life, that exquisite and modest garment, the kimono of a Japanese lady. I drank ceremonial tea in the heart of a dim and ancient garden and, in their own homes, saw men and women and little children. The beauty of all these things is, happily, unforgettable.

Chapter 38

THE days of my second stay in Japan, except for the Imperial Garden Party and a few farewell dinners and receptions, were crowded with such humdrum and necessary details as packing and shipping, doing accounts and mending clothes. Then we sailed for a second time from the drab city of Kobe and, after a rather drab passage of seventy-two hours, entered the turgid waters of the Yangtze early in the morning and made our slow way up the mighty stream, churning off into the Whangpoo River later in the day. Craft of every conceivable kind choked the passage—junks and sampans, teeming with life and crowded together like schools of fish, foreign gunboats, fussy tugs, coalers, freighters, sailing vessels, ocean liners. Up and down it tilted and seethed, that vast vanguard of vessels great and small; beyond it rose the city of Shanghai, flashing and flaming—with hard cold sunshine by day and with darting lights that blinked and blazed in the evening.

It was evening when we saw it first, for the landing process, like the progress up the river, was a difficult one: we had to go far upstream in our ocean liner to the docks, and then go far downstream in the liner's launch to the customs jetty. But there were no formalities of Quarantine or passport—surely in this respect, as in many others, China was a traveler's paradise! After a casual examination, we saw our trunks depart, slung in a cradle of stout ropes from a thick bamboo pole, carried by two coolies—coolies who, in spite of the stinging cold, had nothing but straw sandals on their feet. Then we were free to get in our car. We curved along the vibrant Bund and swung up Nanking Road, past shop windows full of sparkling silver images and shimmering silks and shawls and porcelains as delicate as the laces they crowded. Sikh policemen with their turbaned heads and gleaming eyes loomed before us, huge powerful dictators of the tumbling traffic; and presently we were rounding the race course and the lights we had left behind were towering, a tremendous tiara, against the soft dark city-head which they clasped. It was a swift ride, for the streets were wide and well paved; and soon we were on Bubbling Well Road and the specialty shops and florists were being supplanted by fine residences set on wide lawns behind high iron gates; and then we found ourselves in the soft-carpeted silent hotel, which did not seem like a hotel at all and which was Shanghai's latest pride, as it might well have been the pride of any city which possessed it. Another night we would dance and dine in its ballroom, the largest I had ever seen, but that night, since we were tired and cold, we went straight upstairs to the comfort of our tapestried, oak-lined sitting room and dined quietly under shaded lights in front of an open fire before drifting off to sleep in downy luxury.

I didn't know beforehand that I could buy French dresses and American shoes and books and go to Italian opera and have a permanent wave by the latest process in Shanghai! But that was because I'd been thinking of it as a Chinese city, rather than as a Treaty Port, which it had been since 1842, when the Treaty of Nanking was signed by Great Britain and China. The Chinese city was there too, of course, and anyone who wished could go and see it, as we did. But most of our time was spent in the International Settlement, which was governed by a Consular Body, where not only Chinese but citizens of many other countries resided, and which was one of the most brilliant and cosmopolitan cities in the world. Not unrelatedly, foreigners were subject to the jurisdiction of officials of their own nationality, under the "principle of extraterritoriality" (now often called extrality), which was then a subject of much controversy. There was a British Court and a French Court and, although most Americans in Shanghai lived in the French Concession, any offenses they might commit were tried before a United States Court for China.

I was anxious to learn more of the Courts and, also, to see something of them; and I was most fortunate in having for my guide Miss Viola Smith—a very able as well as a very attractive person, herself a lawyer by profession, though not by practice, and the first woman appointed to our Foreign Service's Department of Commerce. She took me to still another court, the International Mixed Court. As originally formed, this was a Chinese Court and became a Mixed Court only when a foreign interest was involved. When the Revolution of 1911 threatened to leave the city without any court, the Consular Body governing the International Settlement took the court over and continued its administration.

Thus cases involving no foreign interests were sometimes watched over by both a foreign assessor and a Chinese magistrate. This was quite the busiest and most important court in Shanghai. In addition to caring for all the criminal and civil litigation of more than half a million Chinese, it tried several hundred of the mixed cases of foreigners versus Chinese each year. The Chinese were handed over to their own authorities only when the verdict was execution. *There was no jury trial and there was no appeal from this Court.*

On the afternoon of our visit to the Court, held in a dingy dirty room both cold and close, five unfortunate coolies were being tried for stealing coal. Such dejected and forlorn specimens I had never seen; the profiles of the four waiting at the dock were all different in form, but all alike in misery, numbness and fear, and quite as expressive as the face of the one who was testifying. The Chinese magistrate and the British assessor seemed on excellent terms and wearily detached from everything taking place, except for a brief and biting tilt between the Britisher and the Eurasian lawyer for the defense, who ill advisedly lost his temper, thereby laying himself open to the scathing sarcasm of the prosecuting attorney. A Chinese stenographer sat slowly drawing characters with his soft brush; a Chinese interpreter with a taste for drama allowed himself the luxury of oratorical fireworks. In the rear of the room, on dark narrow benches, sat other prisoners awaiting their turn, mostly women accused of kidnaping, and thieves. Other than the Supreme Court in Washington, this was my first experience in a courtroom. I left it feeling sober and soiled and sad.

More happily, one of my first callers in Shanghai was Miss Mayhew, the official hostess for the Y.W.C.A. in that city; and the first dinner we attended was at Hostess House—a succulent meal with meltingly roasted partridge, to help us appreciate the delicacies which China offered, and caramel ice cream, to remind us of home. Miss Mayhew had invited an interesting group to meet us, among whom was Miss Mayling Soong, the Chinese member of the Child Labor Commission. When she first slipped through the door, I caught merely a glimpse of long pendant diamond earrings and a tall, slim graceful figure wrapped in a sable cloak which fell to her heels. Then the cloak dropped, like leaves around a flower, and in a flash of gray and scarlet she sank to a low stool in front of the open fire and began to speak, weaving her way through the repartee of one of the most brilliant conversations to which I ever listened. All the world knows her now as Mme Chiang Kai Shek, the wife of the President of the Republic of China, but I like best to think of her as I first saw her, an exceptionally lovely and charming young woman. For as we left Hostess House that night, Mayling Soong invited the three of us to take tea with her and meet several friends. A few days later, we presented ourselves at the big "foreign" residence on Seymour Road—the Chinese in Shanghai, for the most part, did not live in the fascinating houses of high thresholds, many courts and several buildings which so intrigued us in Peking, but in houses very like our own, except that they had no steam heat, which, I confess, I missed very much. But it was warm and cozy before the glowing coals of the drawing room's open fire, and while we drank rich *café au lait,* followed later by hot clear tea, and ate rich sweetmeats and listened to the delightful music made by another guest, I discovered that my hostess had been a classmate of my cousin Elizabeth at Wellesley and that her youngest brother would be at Harvard the next year. Then she took me to another room and showed me photographs of her two elder sisters, both graduates of Wesleyan in Georgia.

I already knew that one of these sisters was the widow of Sun Yat Sen, the late President of the Republic of China, and as I looked at the pictured face before me, so sweet and lovely and calm, I found I could not stifle any longer the expression of a growing desire.

"Where is Mrs. Sun now?" I asked as casually as I could.

"Here in Shanghai."

"Would it be presumptuous if I asked if she would receive me?"

"Of course not. I am going there to dinner tonight—what a pity you have another engagement! But wait—I'll telephone and find out if she couldn't see you right away. How long have you before you must dress for your own dinner?"

Actually, I hadn't any time at all, for the tea had been so pleasant I'd lingered far longer than I intended. But that seemed to me more or less immaterial. A moment later, we were in a car dashing through the streets to see Mrs. Sun Yat Sen.

We found that gracious former First Lady of China in her drawing room with several of her stepchildren—some of them older than herself —who were visiting her and for whom she was giving an informal dinner. She was dressed in gray wool and her hair was simply, even severely, arranged; but for all that she looked like a queen stepping down from her throne as she came forward to greet me. Such a woman needed no pageantry to reveal her dignity; it revealed itself; and, robbing that dignity of the slight touch of austerity and sadness it might otherwise have had, a deep dimple dug into one smooth cheek just above the perfect curve of her mouth—a dimple which deepened when she smiled.

"Mrs. Keyes," said Mayling Soong without preamble, "wants to go to

Canton. I had better give her a letter to our brother, don't you think? It might unlock a few doors for her or unwind a little red tape. I am sure he would be glad to help her. I have told her how he is trying to carry on the Doctor's work."

"I shall be very glad," Mrs. Sun replied quietly, "if she goes to Canton."

And we began to discuss plans.

I knew how much this meant, and my excitement increased a hundredfold. For visitors had not always found themselves overwelcome in Canton those past months, and one of the reasons for this, as I also knew, was that they had not always been willing to reserve judgment on what was taking place there or to express it without bias. So I was pleased, indeed, that these women trusted me—the greatest compliment any woman can pay the stranger within her gates—and put out of my mind the disturbing thought that this trust had been lacking in Japan.

Despite the fact that we stayed much longer in Shanghai than most travelers did, we didn't have half the time to do all we wished; and we managed to take only one outside excursion—to Soochow, an ancient city about two hours distant by train (a train with no such concession to an effete civilization as artificial heat, so that we practically had to be dug out with icepicks when we reached our destination). Miss Mayhew was our good angel on this trip, and when we arrived at Soochow, we found Miss Claiborne and Miss Stallings of the Southern Methodist Mission waiting to welcome us, with a houseboat for our use—a squatty little craft propelled by a long pole and with a top like a prairie wagon. It was no more than twelve feet long and six feet wide, but it was divided in two compartments—it is difficult to realize that thousands of Chinese families are born and marry and live and die on just such boats! A protracted stay on one would not have appealed to me greatly, but for a day's outing at "The Venice of the East," it proved an ideal conveyance. We slid along beside the city wall, with its border like a Grecian chain, under the graceful arching bridges, past the leaning tower of China and the "pen and ink" pagodas, the gardens and temples. A day was not nearly long enough to see them all, but even so, we did pack an amazing amount into that one, which began at four in the morning and ended at nine that night. And I never shall forget the touching hospitality of six little school teachers, former pupils of Miss Mayhew, who insisted on giving a feast for her and us at the best restaurant in town, though this must have exhausted their joint salaries for a month at least; or the comfort of eleven o'clock coffee, strong and black and burning hot and smothered with whipped cream, at the home of Mrs. Hern, whose husband was on the faculty of Soochow University, or the warm welcome from thirty-odd American women gathered there that went with it. I enjoyed a rickshaw ride through the crowded narrow streets—so crowded and narrow that nothing except a rickshaw could pass through them—less than the boys, who thought it one of their most delightful experiences, for the filth and noise and confusion and congestion seemed to close in upon me like a nightmare; and in spite of the general picturesqueness and the intriguing shops full of silks and carvings, I was glad when we came out into the open again and I saw, silhouetted black against a dazzling white wall and gorgeous red pillars, a water carrier with his tipping buckets and a train of water buffalo.

But after all, it is not those crowded streets which are the wonder of Soochow. The glory and wonder—at least, as I saw it—was the thousand-handed Goddess of Mercy in the Western Temple, the golden goddess who everlastingly gives, the symbol of womanhood incarnate. We forget that the original meaning of the word "lady" was "giver of bread." As mothers, we have had entrusted to us the most precious of all gifts—the golden gift of life itself to our children. Standing in that ancient temple so far from home, I felt, more than ever before in my life, the compulsion laid upon us that we should not forget to stretch forth generous hands.

Chapter 39

W HEN I left Shanghai, I took with me not only a beautiful little cloisonné incense burner, the gift of that lovely lady Mayling Soong, but also a note she had written her brother Mr. T. V. Soong, Minister of Finance and member of the Executive Committee of the Nationalist (Kuomintang) government of China at Canton.

Dear Brother—

Mrs. Keyes, who is the wife of Senator Keyes, is coming to Canton with her son and Mr. Knowles. . . .

Mrs. Keyes has done a great deal of newspaper work and magazine articles, and she is very much interested in Chinese affairs. She comes to Canton to learn all she can about conditions in the South,—and she brings with her an unprejudiced mind.

I am eager that Mrs. Keyes should see as much as possible while in Canton, and want you to do all you can in explaining how the government is working for Doctor's ideals.

You will find Mrs. Keyes very charming, I am sure, both sister R. and I like her immensely.

As for her two "body-guards," they are like yourself Harvard Men. What more need be said?

With love,
May

In addition, I took a cablegram from Canton Christian College which had reached me a few days earlier, in reply to one of mine. It read:

TRIP TO CANTON PERFECTLY FEASIBLE STOP WELCOME FOR AS LONG AS YOU WILL STAY STOP PRESIDENT HENRY WILL MEET YOUR BOAT HONGKONG AND BRING YOU CANTON NEXT DAY.

Thus armed, I proceeded with placidity. But it was nobody's fault—except Miss Mayling Soong's and President James Henry's—that I did

(382)

so. For if I penetrated to Peking in the face of pleading protest, I went to Canton in the face of downright opposition. Did I want to be carried off by robbers, I was asked, or struck down in the street by the "Reds" or "detained" by a government inimical to foreigners, or *what?* That *what* seemed to accuse me of unreasonableness carried to the nth degree. "I can see nothing," said an eminent journalist who had hitherto been prone to wish me godspeed in my wildest undertakings—and he said it very stiffly indeed—"nothing in the line of duty which calls you to Canton. You will be of much more value to your magazine alive than dead." "After all, you know," a high official remarked whimsically, when he had argued at length and in vain, "Bandits is bandits."

"Yes, I know," I replied stubbornly, "but I want to see Canton for myself and to write about it. And I am going to."

I did. Fortunately, I have never been afraid of bandits—only of snakes, elevators and dentists. I had gone through the Ruhr without a qualm two years earlier, and I had seen the beginning of the Chinese Civil War in Peking and left there on a troop train equally unruffled. The first duty of a reporter is to go where the story is and to stay there until he gets it. Otherwise, he should not attempt to be a reporter and will not last long in that capacity. Wars and rumors of war were still comparatively new to me when I was in China, but they later became a very important part of a pattern. I am glad I have been able to take them as they came.

The trip from Shanghai south to Hongkong was a pleasant one: the sails of the ships grew whiter, the sea grew bluer, the air grew softer, inducing a drowsy sort of feeling. Suddenly I realized this agreeable drifting had brought us to one of the most beautiful harbors in the world—a gentle and generous harbor, with gentle and generous hills sloping down to meet it. There were thickly clustered buildings along the waterfront; then an unbroken rise of green, and above that houses so precariously perched on the heights they gave the impression of chamois ready to leap from crest to crest. It was late afternoon when we first glimpsed that harbor and those hills, all sunny and smooth; then, without warning, the sun dodged behind one of the mountains and spilled its gold until we thought the pot at the end of the rainbow must have emptied, there was such a molten mass of it. Next the harbor and the hills darkened to black velvet and the lights began to come out—crowding around the water's edge, clambering over the mountains like the houses they illumined. And Venus appeared, like the queen of the night she is, and made me think of Helen and Francesca and Juliet and Héloïse and all the other great immortal women the world has known who were primarily lovers; and, a little dim star tagged after her which, for all I know, may have been Cupid. The ship was having hard work docking, so many little ones with fluttering pennants were crowding around her, and I was very glad of it, because it gave an hour and then another to watch undisturbed that miracle of beauty expanding and conquering. . . .

But finally the spell was broken; the ropes were fast and a man with a pleasant ruddy face and twinkling brown eyes was standing beside me, lifting his hat.

"Mrs. Keyes? I am President Henry. Your boat is very late. I've been expecting you all day. Can we plan at once about going to Canton? The riverboat leaves at eight in the morning, and if it's agreeable, I'll meet you at your hotel at seven-thirty and take you over to it."

"Do I need to get a pass or anything?"

"Oh no. Just buy your ticket when you get on board."

"And—is it all right for the boys to come with me?"

It was a moment of great suspense. For I had kept insisting, because of robbers, "Reds" and so on, that it was all right for me to go to Canton—that was only my job—but meanwhile the place for Henry and Larry was in Hongkong. My firmness on this score had brought about the first altercation in months of peaceful companionship. Who was I, they chorused, to keep all the thrills of adventure selfishly to myself? Did I want to deprive them of the romance of robbers and "Reds?" Did I think I had a corner on Canton? In vain I protested that a borrowed boy was a great responsibility and that I might be forgiven a little maternal concern for my own first-born. Denunciations followed, far into the night. Fearing lest the occupants of the next room should complain to the management and we would find ourselves without shelter in a strange city, I finally temporized.

"If President Henry says, when he meets us, that it is all right for you to go, I will consent."

And all that President Henry did was to laugh heartily and say, "Why, of course! We have no Harvard men on the campus, but several from Princeton and Yale. Just the chance, I should say, for some stimulating discussion. . . . Make your baggage as light as possible, if that's convenient. It's apt to be rather a problem. Let me help you to the hotel launch. . . . Well, good-bye until seven-thirty."

It was one in the morning before we viewed with satisfaction, though some weariness, the spectacle of our necessary baggage reduced to three suitcases, a dressing case and a typewriter. It was six when we struggled up again. Two hours later we were drinking coffee in the "main saloon" of the *Fat San,* its engines purring contentedly beneath us. We were on our way up the river to Canton. (At nine, the American Consul arrived at our hotel to tell us we were on no account to go there. He was righteously angry at having been thwarted.)

No one had ever told me of the beauties of the trip—perhaps because in the past, before the "trouble" began, most travelers went back and forth by night. Having seen rural China solely in its more desolate aspects—the wide yellow plains, the deep yellow rivers in the North—I was surprised and delighted to find it could bloom like a garden in Paradise. There were green trees and green hills and green fields about us; jewel-like islands; a blue and placid stream and, over all, a soft warm haze, mellow and caressing. A photograph of the landscape might well have been entitled, "A Picture of Peace."

Stretched out in a long chair to bask and doze, I became aware of a Sikh policeman, turbaned, blue clad, musket in hand, his piercing eyes darting in every direction, as he paced the deck. Presently another appeared and then another until there were six of them patrolling that one small boat; and the entrance to the second class quarters was formed by a row of sharply pointed iron bars, surmounted by barbed wire, and a padlocked iron gate. Noting my slightly startled expression, President Henry nodded at one of the Sikhs and said, "Oh yes, we always travel with a guard nowadays. You see, the bandits used to 'plant' a few of their men in the second cabin, and at a given signal those on shore and those on the ship would join forces. Quite effectually. It's really much better this way."

I agreed.

"There's a boys' school a little above here," he went on, "that had fifty-three of its students kidnapped a few weeks ago. Our launch was held up going from this boat to our pier—the same trip we'll be taking this afternoon—not long after. About eighteen captured, all told. But it's perfectly safe, of course; nothing to get excited over."

I said I was not excited; I hope he believed me.

But, in one sense at least, I was very much excited. For the person who could see Canton for the first time without a thrill would indeed be made of frigid clay. To begin with, you were aware of a sudden thickening of river life—even more congested than in the river at Shanghai; more joyous, too, fluttering pennants, singing its wares, smiling its greetings, with no sign of sullenness or surliness. How could a great group of people living like that be so carefree and so gay and so kind? Often a mother, father and six children were crowded together in a sampan no larger than an ordinary rowboat, and they had no other home; but they seemed happy in that, and washed their rice and their laundry side by side in the same stream; and there was a little stove in the rear, with steam and smoke ascending from it, and a brightly decorated cubby-hole parlor in front, I supposed. And that apparently sufficed.

After the thickening of river life followed the thickening of land life. The scattered villages gave way to brick buildings crowded together—warehouses, factories, foundries, shops. We passed Shameen—the island of the "foreign concession" with its border of banyan trees and its deeply porticoed villas, the broad river on one side, the narrow canal on the other. We passed an American gunboat, a Britisher, a French one; and then the Bund, its bright breadth facing the waterfront, tall department stores, solid banks, wide clubs, packed to a jagged skyline. By this time—for the *Fat San* stopped in midstream after the "trouble"—we had transferred to the launch, flying the Stars and Stripes and painted conspicuously with the words, "Canton Christian College." All sorts of craft lay before us. Many of them were antique dogs of war, their paint peeling, once the pride of the world's great navies and now converted to miscellaneous uses, some of them flying the flag South China had more or less adopted, though it was, strictly speaking, the official emblem of the Chinese navy—red, with a blue sunburst on a white ground in one corner. The salt fleet, consisting of fantastically painted junks two or three deep, stretched the width of the river further up. When we had passed them all and reached quieter waters again, we slid up to the college pier and disembarked. Water buffalo were wallowing in the canal, riverboats choked it, coolies were padding back and forth on the path beside it. At the right was the "matshed" which sheltered the fifty soldiers who had been loaned to the college for its protection, and there too were barbed wire, pickets and padlocks. But beyond was the campus, dotted with green-roofed buildings of rosy brick, intersected by brick walks. Vegetables were growing there, vegetables it was safe for foreigners to eat uncooked, as those grown by Oriental methods were not, and oh how good they tasted! Homely flowers too, sweet peas and cosmos and violets, and here and there, by way of contrast, great exotic poinsettias. There was milk from the dairy of the Agricultural College, which Henry and Larry drank thirstily, for of that also they had been deprived for a long time. We passed a small school, where the children of the coolies were being freely and voluntarily taught by the students, then went to the infirmary, where I dropped in to see eight brand-new babies, who owed their lives to the care they were receiving as, previously, one out of three died from lockjaw within two weeks of birth. Next we came to a field where the younger boys were playing volleyball and to the girls' dormitory, where the coeds—a minority numerically but often a majority scholastically—invited us to drink chrysanthemum tea with them; and so on to the hospitable homes where we were to stay. It was a great pleasure to meet the Chinese members of the staff and the Chinese students; it was no less a pleasure to meet the American staff members, and after so many weeks in hotels and ships good, bad and indifferent, it was a treat to go to bed in a guest room characteristically American—simple, immaculate and comfortable, with magazines lying about, a cross-stitched cover on the bureau and enough hangers in the closet.

"The foreign and Chinese faculty of the college at Canton," said that institution's official booklet, "are working together for a cultural reciprocity between the two great republics of the Pacific. Their work is laying a firm foundation for peace and mutual understanding and is welding the traditional friendship between China and America into a permanent bond."

This task was not an easy one. The college was nondenominational, and nearly two thousand men and women, boys and girls of many different faiths were gathered there in one capacity or another. There were British, Chinese and Americans on the faculty; Chinese as well as Americans, supported the college, not only financially but morally. Both eastern and western methods of education had to be employed—and respected. How well the college was succeeding in its task I had ample opportunity to judge. At a time when a strong anti-Christian feeling was mingled with an antiforeign movement, President Henry, the Canton born son of an American missionary, equally at home in both his native tongues, able, tactful, resourceful, was welcomed everywhere by everyone. None of the college servants had left, though the foreigners in the city and at Shameen had been without them for months as they had either departed voluntarily or been "called out" by the labor unions. In the latter case, servants had been forbidden to return to their employers unless they would agree neither to engage nor discharge any worker without the union's consent.

I would have been perfectly content to remain at the college and rest during my entire visit, it was so peaceful and pleasant there; but that, of course, was not what I had come to Canton to do. So the morning after my arrival, the launch took me back to the city, where I found broad, new, smoothly paved streets, as well as the ancient narrow ones. There were many beggars, some of them writing their sad stories on the sidewalks—occasionally, I was told, in excellent English!—while a throng of the pitying or curious gathered around them. There were a few soldiers, some of them walking about with their fingers, literally, on the trigger; but there were no signs of either disturbance or animosity.

Although all white women had left the city—except a few who still lingered on Shameen and were not permitted to leave it—I went by rickshaw, without attracting so much as an inquisitive or unfriendly glance, to the headquarters of the Kuomintang. According to the official *China Year Book,* this confederation was "the oldest and perhaps the only effective political organization in China," differing from other political groups in that it had "a nationwide membership, a political bureau and a definitely stated program," its leadership being determined by party votes.

Walking down corridors decorated with flowering chrysanthemums in glazed pots, I came to the office of Mrs. Liao, widow of the Provincial Governor, who had been assassinated the previous year, head of the Women's Department and a member of the Provincial Executive Committee. It was a plain room and she was plainly dressed, but it hummed with activity and I was immediately aware that I was in the presence of a woman with great executive ability and driving force. How similar her methods of spreading political gospel were to those used at home: "literature" scattered freely, women speakers sent about, offices kept open at all times and visitors and disciples welcome! In addition, general educational and welfare work was undertaken, so women would be better fitted, mentally and physically, for political understanding and interest. As a chairman or committeewoman, Mrs. Liao would have been a tremendous asset to one of our political parties and would have made herself felt and followed in any part of the Union.

She told me without circumlocution that she regarded her husband's death "as the direct result of foreign imperialism," and questioned me closely as to what the policy of the United States would be toward a free and independent China—questions to which, naturally, I could give no authoritative answers. But I asked her if she would not give me an account of the events leading up to the present "trouble" and she handed me the report of a commission for the investigation of the so-called "Shakee massacre":

> On June 23, 1925, a mass meeting took place to protest the unnecessary killing of Chinese students by British policemen in Shanghai. After the meeting, the crowd . . . comprising first laborers, then farmers and merchants, then student boys and girls and lastly cadets and soldiers, marched . . . along the Bund to Shakee, which is separated by a wide canal from the island of Shameen, the Anglo-French Concession in Canton. As soon as three-quarters of the entire parade and the first part of the student demonstrators had passed the West Bridge of the British Concession, the Britishers on Shameen opened fire, killing fifty-two and wounding one hundred and seventeen Chinese. . . .

I went to see Mr. T. V. Soong and deliver his sister's letter. He was a young man of bounding energy, immense vitality and assertiveness. He was clad in a loose gray flannel suit, very like pajamas in cut but with shorter trousers, and received me in an office clattering with activity; he gave such a vivid account of the demands made by the Finance Division —the state of which, he said, was most satisfactory—upon his time that I felt even a short visit to be an intrusion. The longest and most illuminating talk I had in Canton was with Mr. C. C. Wu, also a member of the Executive Committee of the Kuomintang, as well as Executive Chairman of the Board of Commissioners for Canton—a position very like that of mayor. His father had been Chinese Minister to the United States, Peru and Spain; and a judge in the International Court of Arbitration at the Hague. The equally illustrious son, after being graduated with highest honors from an American grammar and high school, went to the University of London and held the British degree of Barrister-at-Law. Though there was less confusion and bustle in his office than in Mr. Soong's, it was teeming with industry.

"I believe," he said blandly, "that it will be best for us to adjourn to some quieter spot. Will you do me the honor of lunching with me, so we may converse under more auspicious conditions? The pigeons at the Pacific Café have been pronounced the best in the world. I wish to see if you concur in this estimate. Allow me. . . ."

A few minutes later my bodyguard, as everyone insisted on calling Henry and Larry, Mr. Wu and myself were comfortably installed in a sunny private room at the famous restaurant, and we shortly discovered that the pigeons—not to mention the soup, fish, chicken, asparagus and soufflé—were all that the most meticulous epicure could have desired. But even the menu's perfection paled before the charm of Mr. Wu: a conversationalist whose equal I have seldom met and whose superior never, a delightful host, a past master of the English language in its most subtle distinctions, a diplomat who would adorn any court, anywhere. He was dressed in the long flowing coat which is one of the most graceful garments in the world, the flaring linen of snowy undersleeves showing when he raised his arms. His lips, a little thin, a little composed in repose, parted, when he smiled, over teeth of unusual beauty, even for China, where very handsome teeth were the rule rather than the exception. His piercing eyes were liquid and mobile, the rest of his face impassive as a mask. He talked and talked and talked. I can record only fragments of what he said, but those fragments give some idea of the wonderful whole.

"We are accused of being communistic here because we have Russian advisers in our government. It has been for a long time the custom for

China to have foreign advisers. There are many of them in Peking today—who are paid but not used."

"Whereas you use yours but do not pay them?" I could not resist such an opening.

"I am glad you accept the challenge. . . . We have had British advisers, which has not been interpreted to mean we desired to make China a monarchy. Why then should Russian advisers spell Soviet to the outside world?"

"How did it occur to the Kuomintang to have only Russian advisers?"

"It did not 'occur.' We were obliged to have someone with experience to help us, and only the Russians were willing. Besides, their viewpoint was sympathetic. Like us, they have had many wars. Like us, they have been downtrodden. One of the first things we have done with their help has been to reorganize and train our army. This army does not take over property in the villages through which it passes—does that show a communistic spirit? It does not plunder and pillage. It pays its way. It has earned the confidence of the people. Recently, upon entering a village, it asked for food at the first house and was given ricewater of very poor quality. The army drank this with what grace it could and paid for it as if it had been a substantial meal; the next day the entire village was a market at the army's disposal. It is our hope that before too long this army will stamp out banditry. . . .

"The two primary aims of the Kuomintang are the elimination of corruption and the unification of China. In attempting the first, our methods have at times been necessarily—somewhat severe. No matter how many offices a man holds—at present I hold twelve—he may receive compensation for only one. Just lately we learned the secretary of the Military Division—an important post—was receiving several salaries. He is now—ah—being detained. Two prominent magistrates upon the inception of examinations to the judiciary, have—ah—found it convenient to go to Shanghai. . . .

"Anyone may obtain, for twenty cents, a pamphlet outlining the principles of our political faith, so there is no reason why our enemies should misrepresent them. As enumerated by Dr. Sun Yat Sen, they are very like the principles of a government 'of the people, for the people, by the people,' as advanced by Lincoln. In spreading our propaganda, it is less difficult in the South than in the North, as there is much less illiteracy. I think Dr. Henry will bear me out in that. . . ." (He did, as well as in regard to all the statements made about the improvement in the army.)

"In regard to our foreign policy: we are antiforeign in the sense that we do not intend to remain bound forever by unequal treaties. When the nations of the West recognize the principles of customs autonomy and do their share to abolish extrality, we shall believe they are acting in good faith. When the United States ceases to receive dictation from Great Britain, we shall believe her our sincere friend."

I asked Mr. Wu whether or not he believed in the sincerity of the statement made by the Western powers that when China had stamped out illiteracy and established better means of intercommunication—when she had proved herself capable of self-government—they would be willing to revise the treaties.

"I think that is merely an excuse. We cannot educate or build railroads without money, and this money must come, to a large extent, from customs, which we are not yet able to collect."

"Has there been any thought, as there once was in our country, that China might do well to split into a northern and a southern republic?"

"Never. Nor any desire to establish Canton as the national capital as a rival to Peking. We would be willing to move there at any moment it would recognize the principle of a free and unified China. But the government at Peking exists only as a figurehead for the convenience of foreign powers. It would not harbor such a seditious thought." (This was Mr. Wu's opinion, not mine.)

As we regretfully took our leave, Larry remarked that our conversation had been more informative than a year of college history. My only disappointments in my interviews with Cantonese were because, when I expressed a wish to obtain the pamphlet listing Dr. Sun's principles, I was told it was not available in translation; and, every time I suggested meeting Mr. Borodin (designated in the *China Year Book* as "a special representative, being appointed as liaison officer between the Kuomintang and Soviet Russia") or any of the other Russian advisers, so I might talk with them and draw my own conclusions as to the extent of their influence, I was rather vaguely informed, "They are very busy," that they "seldom consent to see foreigners" or something equally ambiguous. This raised a natural doubt in my mind as to whether the *Year Book* did not define Mr. Borodin's position more accurately than the Cantonese with whom I spoke. And kindly as I was treated during my visit, the fact remained that foreigners had not been able to go to Canton without grave risks of discomfort, to put it mildly, and most of them had found it impossible to go at all.

I do not think, however, that it was all the fault of the Chinese that this was so. I was not unmindful of the unfairness, the arrogance and the brutality with which they had long been and still were often treated *in their own land* by Western peoples. In fact, I could not help wondering if the Anglo-Saxon mind did not sometimes become curiously affected in the Orient. I saw a number of unpleasant incidents, for which both Americans and British were responsible, that would certainly cause resentment among any native people; and I could not help feeling it was the attitude which permitted such incidents that had made the Chinese—patient, courteous and cultured—revolt against foreign rule and foreign faiths. But because every question has two sides and because I did not wish to leave Canton without hearing both, I spent some time on Shameen, talking with English and Americans there. It was a dreary place, that "foreign concession," which must in normal times have been very beautiful, with its green spreading banyan trees, its wide walks and its cool, high-pillared, porticoed houses. Entering by the French gate after showing my pass, I threaded my way in and out of barbed wire; leaving by the British gate, I repeated the process. After early evening and before early morning, I could not enter or leave at all, for the gates were closed. Once inside, I went through streets almost deserted and silent as the grave, past shops and houses perforated with bullet holes and high piles of sandbags which barred my way; the courteous clerk who waited on me in the excellent English pharmacy asked me to excuse him from making out my sales slip in full, because a bad shoulder wound still made it difficult for him to write. Another Englishman who had spent forty years in China told me this story:

When it was announced last June that a parade would take place . . . the British Consul at Canton requested that the Cantonese government clear the canal of boats—which could be converted into a temporary bridge—or that the procession should refrain from marching beside the canal, in Shakee. [Shakee was not within the concession, but was strictly Chinese territory, so the Chinese had a right to parade there, though it would seem that the request to clear the canal was entirely reasonable and should have been respected.] He also stated that an attack would be regarded as an unfriendly act, and that firing would be returned. The Cantonese government complains it did not receive this message in time to act upon it; nevertheless, the receipt for the delivery of the letter was returned to the Consul, stamped with the Foreign Office seal at 7:56 A.M. and the parade did not take place until afternoon. The Consul ordered all residents under his jurisdiction to keep off the streets during the parade; soldiers were stationed along the street in Shameen bordering the canal, and facing Shakee, which had been fortified, but the men's arms, though within reach, were not on their persons.

There were several thousand in the parade, with the student group directly in front of the military and, while the former was passing Shameen, two or three shots were fired in its direction from the roof tops above the marchers. These shots were fired by Russians, who undoubtedly intended to create an incident, but who miscalculated their timing; the shots should not have been fired until the students had passed.

Our nationals at once sprang for their arms and fired; and there was a return volley from the military group which was, by then, opposite Shameen. The engagement lasted only about twenty minutes, but several were killed or wounded on both sides; and feeling has run very high ever since—here and in Canton. As you know, all foreign women and as many men as possible left Shameen as rapidly as their consuls could get them away. A few have returned, but not many. As you also know, our Chinese servants left in a body and we have been without them ever since, managing as best we could. We do not go into the city. The Chinese do not come here. It is a dreary life.

There is not the slightest doubt that Soviet Russia is attempting to use Southern China as a base to overrun, eventually, both Japan and India. There have been recent attempts to corrupt the French soldiery of Indo-China. From there, it would be but a step—literally and figuratively—into India.

I left Shameen feeling rather dreary myself; and as I stepped off the bridge, a picket wearing a red armband stopped me and asked me to open the package I was carrying. He spoke politely; but when Dr. Henry, who had kindly acted as my escort, told him in Chinese that I was an American only passing through the city, he still insisted the package must be opened. It contained some cough drops for myself and a box of candy for my hostess, which I had bought at the British pharmacy. A crowd gathered with miraculous celerity and demanded the surrender of these harmless and entirely personal articles. The picket hesitated, prodded the glazed paper on the candy box, shook the cough drops and finally told me I could tie them up again and keep them; by that time I was seeing "red" myself, and if it had been necessary for me to write an account of the experience then and there, I am afraid it would not have been done in a dispassionate spirit.

I was reluctant to go away from that strange place of contrasts—the peaceful Christian College, the bustling Kuomintang, the desolate Shameen. It had taken a peculiar hold on me, and I could understand why Canton was called the city of ginger and jade—ginger so hot and stinging and sweet, jade so cool and smooth and precious. I carried away a bit of both with me—a box of ginger that was given me, a string of jade that I bought myself in a little shop of exquisite neatness and beauty hidden away in a narrow street. That and one where tinted mother-of-pearl was sold were the only two I had time to enter. The shopkeepers were in both cases pathetically grateful for my modest purchases—for the "trouble" had hit trade hard, as it always does—and I hoped some

Chinese baby went to bed that night the better for the bills his father had taken mutely into his delicate hands, as a result of my expenditures.

President Henry very kindly suggested that I should join his staff for a year, and I can think of nothing that would have given me more pleasure. But it was one of those opportunities of which I have not been able to take advantage.

Of Hongkong itself I had only the most fleeting glimpses: that wonderful first view of it at sunset and star rise; an ascent in the "cable-tram" to see the lights of the city and harbor; a drive over the famous "Peak" to beautiful Repulse Bay and tea on the hotel veranda there with a delightful editor whose views were as radical as mine were apt to be conservative; a charming luncheon, at which the American Consul General Mr. Treadway, and a Scotch banker acted as hosts. Then embarkation again, and good-bye to this part of the Orient.

Chapter 40

I STEAMED—physically as well as nautically—into Manila Harbor the morning of December twenty-fourth. The thermometer had sunk to eighty or so, and most of the comments I heard, both aboardship and after landing, were on the chilly quality of the atmosphere; but I must say, as my son John used to do when a very small child, if I told him his conduct was deplorable, "It did not seem that way to me." I stood in the dazzling, moist early-morning sunshine—we had been forcibly awakened hours too soon, according to the time-honored landing-day custom—reflecting that I was very very warm indeed, and that the beauty of the bay had been greatly overstated. Then the Quarantine launch came bobbing alongside the *President Van Buren* and I forgot everything else in the pleasure of seeing in its bow my old friend Mrs. de Veyra, the wife of the former Philippine Commissioner to the United States, with three other ladies. These, I soon learned, were Mrs. Delgado, the wife of a prominent lawyer; Miss Estela Romuáldez, the daughter of Manila's mayor and herself a lawyer of note; and Mrs. Barza, the head of the Manila Y.W.C.A. They had risen at four in order to come and bid me welcome; and they made a lovely sight as they stood there in their blending draperies of black, purple, pink and peach. Practically the first decision I reached about the Philippines was that the women ought never give up their becoming and suitable native costume. The wide outstanding sleeves and the lowcut bodice sloping off the shoulders, finished with a pleated neckerchief, and revealing the lace under-bodice beneath it, were made of gauzy *piñar* cloth; the color and design of this diaphanous bodice were repeated in the material—usually satin or some equally lovely stuff—of which the long, trained skirt, pinned up on one side to reveal the lace-edged petticoat and facilitate walking, was made. This skirt was partially covered, if the wearer came

(395)

from certain provinces, by the *tapis,* or black lace apron. Provincial pride was very strong and Filipinos would tell you they came from Ilo-Ilo or Negros or Batangas in much the same way that Virginians tell you they come from Rappahannock or Albemarle or some other county.

The graceful garments of the Filipino women did not seem to impede their freedom of movement at any time, and when the gangplank was finally lowered, Mrs. de Veyra was the first person who rapidly ascended it, despite the fact that the fiancé of a girl who had come all the way from New York to marry him was also in the launch! Unfortunately, my joy at seeing her was somewhat marred, for it proved impossible to have any coherent conversation with her and her friends, or properly greet a group of hospitable American women waiting for me on the dock, because of a delegation of the most ill-mannered reporters I ever encountered. I was importuned in execrable English and with inescapable persistence to give my views on Philippine independence, the policy of the Governor-General, the scenic and commercial aspects of the islands and other subjects upon which it would be humanly impossible for any traveler to have a definite opinion, especially one who had not even set foot on shore! In the general confusion thus created part of the baggage was lost; and one of the horde even pursued me to my hotel room, unannounced, and thrust a notebook in my face with the demand, "There are just four questions I want you to answer at once. What do you think of. . . ."

He found out in short order what I thought of him, at least; and, following his somewhat precipitate departure, I hurriedly dressed—a process greatly hampered because of the lost baggage—to go to the luncheon which Mrs. Quezon, whose husband was President of the Philippine Senate as well as the leader in the campaign for Philippine independence, was giving in my honor. When I entered her drawing room, thirty or more entrancing ladies—their gauze sleeves reminding me of so many rainbow-winged butterflies—were waiting to greet me. My hostess was in a cloud of rose and gold, and when I heard Mrs. de Veyra address her as Aurora—I could not help commenting that she certainly was Dawn personified! She was a gentle and dignified lady, with composure and cordiality ideally blended in her manner; and the luncheon over which she presided was perfect in both menu and appointments. In the table's center, under a scarlet pendant bell, was a great gilded basket of scarlet poinsettias and white *cadena de amor*—the same flower I had learned to love in Haiti under its French name of *chaine d'amour* and in Panama as coral vine; these flowers trailed the length of the table. There were luscious tropical fruits on ice, *pili* nuts, so rich in oil they burn like tiny tapers if a match is set to them; and, in the middle of the meal, a delicious sweet omelette stuffed with jam, prepared and served after the French fashion. Then, at the end, my hostess presented me with the golden fan she carried, as "a souvenir of our meeting."

There were not more than half a dozen American women at the luncheon, and one of these was the wife of a Filipino senator and I learned that whereas one was careful—if polite—to speak of "Puerto Rican Americans" and "continental Americans" in Puerto Rico and of "territorials" and "mainlanders" in Hawaii, in Manila one said "Americans" and "Filipinos" with decided emphasis; and this emphasis was quite as much desired by one group as the other. Among the Filipino guests were a well-known doctor, an equally well-known lawyer, the President of the Federation of Women's Clubs—of which there were more than four hundred in the islands—the President of the Women's City Club and the heads of several educational institutions. These, as well as the other Filipino ladies, spoke excellent English when addressing me, but I noticed that they invariably spoke in Spanish among themselves. The longer I remained in the Philippines, the more I wondered that English had not made more headway in the quarter century of American insistence that it should be the country's accepted language, gradually supplanting both the Spanish which for hundreds of years had been the language of the cultured classes and the many different native dialects. I was never able to make a single servant or clerk comprehend fully what I said or to fully comprehend what he said to me. Even in the American post office, I labored fruitlessly nearly an hour to make my needs clear before Mrs. de Veyra came to my rescue in Spanish. In some of the schools, I had great difficulty in understanding the teachers and much more in understanding the pupils, mainly because English was usually being taught by those to whom it was not a native tongue and who themselves had been similarly taught, for there were comparatively few American teachers left in the islands. This language difficulty was, in my opinion, one of the very great problems in the Philippines at that time.

When Mrs. Quezon's luncheon was over, Mrs. de Veyra offered to take me for a drive and I accepted gladly, for Henry and Larry had both insisted they must hang up their Christmas socks and, in spite of some sarcastic comments to the effect that I would take adults on my next trip, I wanted to get some candies and "stuffers" for the limp woolly receptacles confidently entrusted to me. This shopping took me to the *Escolta,* Manila's Fifth Avenue, and there I saw for the first time the small, two-wheeled carriages—*calesas*—bobbing along, pulled by men wearing long gauze shirts over their white trousers, their bare feet thrust into sandals of dried grass. We went through the Walled City, which then spoke eloquently of the pomp and power of Spain, though the ancient moat which once surrounded it had been converted to a golf course and the hurry of modern progress had invaded its narrow streets and shaded plazas. Afterward, we drove about the Luneta, the wide grassy expanse which lay between the Manila Hotel and the Army and Navy Club, facing the ocean, and along Dewey Boulevard beside it toward Pasay. The sun splashed into the sea and the lights came out in Cavite, our naval station across the bay, and on the vessels of the Asiatic Fleet at anchor. The Constabulary Band began its evening concert near the monument to Rizal, the Filipino hero who died a martyr to the cause of progress in the days of Spain; and there crept into my veins a sense of the insidious charm of this place with which our destiny had so strangely become interwoven. I had been telling myself complacently that it was not a beautiful city, and then quite suddenly it had taken a clasping hold upon me.

But for the moment it was necessary to shake off the spell and get ready for the next party: the Christmas Eve ball at Tiro al Blanco, the fashionable suburban gun club. Mr. and Mrs. Delgado came for us, and in the streets through which we passed there were many houses in front of which hung a huge paper star, illumined from within, and church doors were standing open. Later we were to leave the ball long enough to visit some of the churches—to see the brilliant facade of St. Augustine's, the wonderful carving at St. Ignatius; to listen to the glorious boyish voices singing *Adeste Fideles* to the strains of a great organ and hear all the city's bells ring at midnight. It was a custom new to me —that of leaving a ball in order to go to church and then returning to the ball and dancing some more—but it seemed to be attended with no irreverence. After all, religion was never meant to be a sad or sober thing or a thing apart from our daily pleasures any more than from our daily griefs.

Tiny multicolored lights hung in long festoons streamed in every direction from Tiro al Blanco as we approached it, and in the garden at the rear a mammoth Christmas tree twinkled, under the full moon, with the same iridescent globes. There was a gift on the tree for every lady present, and being especially favored, I received two—a traveling clock and a bottle of French perfume. Supper—for a thousand—was served at long white-spread tables in a pavilion decorated to represent a scene of ice and snow, with glass icicles hanging from a fluffy cotton ceiling; there was an open-air theater with a performance of a Spanish opera; of course there was dancing, in the ballroom with its painted walls, in the garden with its twinkling tree and its cool fragrance; and there were golden balloons tossed in the air, confetti streaming. Mr. and Mrs. Quezon were there, and so I had my first glimpse of that brilliant and charming man, the President of the Senate. It was too brief to permit any impression beyond that of a very persuasive smile and great elegance of dress and manner. I had heard him described beforehand as one of the best ballroom dancers in the world—an opinion which I speedily shared. Also I had heard him described in terms as black as the ace of spades—at home people were screaming about the "depravity" of the Philippine *"politicos"*—but having lived by that time for twenty-two years in a political atmosphere, I had long since ceased to believe that politicians were ever as bad as they were painted or that any one country had a monopoly on political vice.

It was three-thirty in the morning when we finally started back to our hotel, for Tiro al Blanco, like every other club in Manila I visited, was peculiarly suited to dancing, with a ballroom much airier and cooler than the average stuffy one at home, so it was hard to tear oneself away and few did so until the very early hours. But at last the boys, after many grumbled protests about being dragged off just as things got going, consented to leave and went off to bed while I stayed up to fill the two pathetic socks, suspended from the steel rods of Henry's wardrobe trunk—the nearest approach to a mantel I could find! I finally sank into bed myself, after having been up and doing for twenty-three hours on end, just as the first pale strip of dawn began to show between sea and sky.

Before I went to the Philippines, I was cautioned repeatedly, "Don't judge the people of the islands by those you meet in Manila. Go and see the savage tribes, get into the remote provinces, then you'll realize what the Filipinos really are." Well, I did see some of the savage tribes and some of the provinces and I will admit there was a deep line of demarcation between them and Manila and its inhabitants. But granting this, it seemed to me not undesirable that I should associate, at least for part of my visit, with Filipinos who moved in the best social circles. It seemed to me that many visitors to the islands were so eager to stress the habits of the Igorots and the Moros, so anxious to describe *nipa* huts, that they created the impression there were no Filipinos who possessed any degree of culture and education, despite the fact that among the many universities there one was older than Harvard; while the idea that many Filipinos possessed the finer social graces to a very marked extent never seemed to have been recognized at all. So it was of great satisfaction to me to be able to present the other side of the story and describe the Filipino people at their best and not at their worst—just as I did in every country I visited.

Indeed, I was moved to wonder if much of the strain at that time was not a social quite as much as it was a political problem. In Puerto Rico, which was an insular possession; in Hawaii, which was a territory; in Cuba and Panama, where we had special treaty rights; and in Haiti, where we had that most difficult and delicate of all relationships—one with a military dictatorship—the social relations between the races were pleasant, friendly and constant.[1] In the Philippines, a very different condition prevailed. In writing from China, I remarked that the Anglo-Saxon mind seemed to me to undergo a peculiar psychological transformation in the Orient. I felt this even more keenly in the Philippines. It seemed this transformation must be Anglo-Saxon, for the Spaniards, in spite of their other shortcomings, did not seem to have undergone it, in a social sense. But I met Americans long resident in Manila who told me, with apparent pride, that they had never set foot in a Filipino house. They had missed a great deal, for a high-class Filipino house, with its shell-paned windows, its magnificent furniture carved from native woods, its airy chambers and spacious drawing rooms, all permeated with the twin fragrances of cleanliness and flowers and the subtler perfume of hospitality, is a very lovely spot. I was extremely grateful for the unbounded courtesy and kindness that Americans showed me; but I could not help noticing at how few American homes there were Filipinos among my fellow guests. And I have never believed we can possibly have harmony with any people as long as we maintain an attitude of racial superiority, irrespective of individual character and attainments. When we come to a national realization of this, our foreign—and domestic—problems should be easier to solve.

But the political feeling was also very strong and tense. I was repeatedly warned that the Filipinos would seize every opportunity to make me listen to their propaganda for independence, by Americans who told me that the very idea of independence was ridiculous and that they themselves would be glad to tell me everything I wanted to know and exactly what I ought to write on the subject. I discovered that many of my would-be mentors had scarcely left the islands in over twenty-five years, and I therefore felt their viewpoints might be somewhat restricted —one cannot maintain a proper perspective if he is too close to his

---

[1] Since then I have had occasion to notice, with great regret, the cleavage between the Americans in the Canal Zone and those in the Republic of Panama, which of course is shared and resented by the Panamanians themselves in both localities; but in 1925 this was not evident.

subject; and the world had changed so rapidly in the previous quarter century that what had been true of the Philippines—or any other country, for that matter—in 1900 was not necessarily true in 1925. Moreover, nothing is more damaging to a cause than to tell a writer what he ought to say about it, for he immediately begins to wonder how bad it is, or how insecure, if it requires so much publicity. Consequently, most of the information given me left me in a far from happy state of mind, which I had to strive very hard to keep impartial.

On the other hand, political subjects were tactfully avoided at the Filipino social gatherings I attended and the only two political interviews I had with Filipinos—one with Mr. Sumurong, the minority leader, and one with Mr. Quezon—both took place at my own request and the conversation in the course of them was limited to the questions I asked and the answers they gave. It was not until after I had been talking with Mr. Quezon for over an hour and a half and rose to leave his beautiful study, that he asked, "Are you sure you have made all the political inquiries of me you wish?"

"Yes."

"And you have made up your mind what you are going to write?"

"I think so."

"Then nothing I said could possibly influence you now?"

"I doubt it."

"Then will you accept an invitation to an official dinner? I have not dared ask you before lest someone would say I was trying to color your views; I haven't even dared to pay a social call on you with my wife. But it would give me—and them—great pleasure if I could present some of our distinguished men to you. Will you set an evening?"

So I set an evening and the dinner took place, and to it came the Vice-Governor, every member of the Cabinet, the Speaker of the House of Representatives and several senators and judges. I went back to the hotel after a perfectly marvelous time, which was entirely untinged with politics, and with nothing more incriminating than an enormous bouquet of roses. And I was quite ready to agree with Genevieve Walsh Gudger, who maintained after the two years when Captain Gudger was stationed in the Philippines that the only man she had ever met who had as much magnetism as Key Pittman was Manuel Quezon!

Practically all the political division of feeling centered, of course, on the subject of independence for the Philippines; and since that question was partially settled in 1935 with the inauguration of Quezon as President of the transitional Commonwealth of the Philippines and complete independence came after ten years, the pros and cons of that question no longer affect us in the same measure, for instance, as the question of Communism in China, which is still very much with us. However, it was a burning issue at the end of 1925.

There were many Americans who felt—besides feeling themselves we should remain—that the majority of Filipinos wished this also or that if they did not, they desired independence vaguely, "as if it were some new kind of breakfast food," as I heard one man express it. And it was my opinion—and not an isolated one, I discovered—that if we left, another power much harsher in dealing with subject peoples than ourselves would immediately try to step in—and certainly this proved to be true in 1941. If we had not won the war with Japan, the fate of the Philippines would have been sad, indeed!

However, we were inconsistent when in one breath we exclaimed, "If we go out of the islands, we abandon the unfortunate people to the mercy of the *politicos*," and in the next breath said, "If we go out of the islands, there will be an insurrection by the people and the *politicos* will all be slaughtered!" And I felt there was some justification in President Quezon's exasperated outburst, "If we are wealthy and educated, we are told we want independence solely to further our own selfish ends; if we are poor and ignorant, we are told we cannot possibly know what we want!" Mr. Sumurong's quieter remarks on the same subject were nonetheless poignant, "You have a home, have you not? Children, three of them? If someone—a richer, more beautiful lady with a grander house maybe—said to them, 'Come live with me and be my children; I will do much more for you than your mother can, I will give you a better home, a better education,' do you think your sons would like to go and stay forever with that lady? Don't you know it is their own home and their own mother they love the best? Don't you know it would be so even if you had only a very plain little home to offer them?"

It was very difficult, in the face of such conflicting and apparently equally authoritative opinions, to be sure whether the Filipinos wished us to leave or not. But I became a little distrustful of the insistent declaration that the Philippines were a "sacred trust" and that we must keep them for their own good whether they wished us to or not, followed by the further declaration, "Besides, they have enormous undeveloped resources." They did indeed. They had sugar, pineapples, timber, camphor, practically the entire world's supply of hemp and great potentialities for the growing of rubber, which we used in immense quantities and which we were then finding it very expensive to buy because of the British tariff on and monopoly of rubber. We had a legal right to all these undeveloped resources and they were very desirable; but we greatly weakened our moral case when we tried to couple it with our material and commercial one. We inevitably gave rise to a justifiable doubt as to our singleness of purpose. It would have been better, I thought, to say quite frankly, "Yes, I want this sugar, pineapples, timber, camphor, hemp, rubber and other things. I am a rich nation; I can afford to buy these commodities from any other nation at its own price. But that is not necessary; they are produced in one of my own possessions. Therefore on no account will I allow these possessions to slip through my fingers." That would have been mercenary, but it would at least have been honest; and I think the Filipinos would have respected us more for such a statement than for any we made about a "sacred trust."

Finally, there was the military phase: did we need, for our own protection, an outpost in the Far East? Did we require a foothold in the Orient? I was inclined to think we did and would continue to until there was a great change in world relations. And there was no reason why we should not have it. We maintained a naval station at Guantánamo in Cuba and special treaty rights with that country; but it was an independent republic, just the same. In the larger Philippines we might well have had two or three naval stations and as many military stations; the Filipinos, I was assured, would almost unanimously and gladly have consented to such an arrangement.

My longest trip out of Manila took me to Baguio, the cool mountain resort which was one of the chief prides of the Philippines, where Governor-General and Mrs. Leonard Wood very kindly invited the boys and me to spend New Year's week end with them at Mansion House. We drove for four hours through flat fertile country and then began to climb over a twisting, tortuous road, through tawny, rocky mountains—the kind of precipitous ascent that takes you from Denver up Cripple Creek. A high waterfall which appeared to be entirely wreathed in ivy foamed and fell in the clear green water beneath it; pine trees began to stud the slopes; and we finally came into Baguio, pervaded with freshness and quiet at midafternoon. Near the military reservation of Camp John Hay, with its superb views and its beautiful natural amphitheater, Mansion House stood "tiptoe on a little hill." It was a friendly, simple house encircled with wide piazzas and surrounded by wide lawns and formal gardens. It seemed very strange to me to go practically to the ends of the earth to meet, at last, the man who had been one of the great military and medical heroes of my childhood, and who, not so long before, I had hoped would be the first President from New Hampshire since Franklin Pierce, and to see again the strong and upright woman toward whom I had been so greatly drawn in the one meeting we had had during a conference of the World Services Council at Oyster Bay.

I was sorry to find that as far as the *politicos* were concerned, the Woods did not have a good word to say; and they were particularly bitter—and, I felt, unfair—toward the Quezons, though Aguinaldo was treated with great respect by them. But I realized, after only one or two conversations, the subject was better dropped. New Year's Eve passed quietly, but eleven o'clock on New Year's Day found me at Mrs. Wood's side as she and the General greeted the callers who came from the surrounding country to their official "At Home." In this American house most Filipinos always found a courteous welcome, and many of them were there that day; missionary teachers from the mountain schools, naval and military officers with their wives, casual visitors to the islands, old residents. There were sandwiches, cookies, eggnog and cake on the veranda and a military band on the lawn; and when this party was over, it was time to prepare for the one the following day, which the General gave annually to the "headmen" from the mountain villages for miles around—it took some of them no less than a week to get to Baguio, even riding their sturdy little ponies. The festivities began with a banquet—at ten in the morning—served in the grove below Mansion House, which the guests ate sitting in long silent rows: rice, beef stew, roasted pork and white bread—the greatest luxury of all. Then, preceded by their own musicians, they marched to the lawn of Mansion House and, squatting on the ground in a huge open circle around the General and without speaking a word, they began to smoke the cigarettes and cigars handed them. Some were clad in nothing but a G-string; others had added to this a coat or two around their shoulders; strangely enough, when an Igorot began to dress, he was apt to put on two coats and nothing else. Still others had achieved a hat, a pair of boots, or both; and some were neatly dressed in khaki and white duck. On every side their quiet faces were straining with attention; there was something patriarchal, something touchingly primitive about the scene. The Governor told them how glad he was to see them all and invited them to lay their problems and troubles before him. Gradually they rose to their feet and drew closer; the vexing problems of taxation, of road building, of farming were discussed—patiently and with understanding on the part of the Governor, with ever-increasing eagerness and confidence on the part of the Igorots. When, at last, the long audience was over and they filed down across the fields again, I felt they believed that their difficulties, having been shared, would be lightened. The Igorots apparently loved the Americans and looked to them with confidence for protection; and no one could deny that in dealing with this uncouth, non-Christian tribe, whose code included a strong regard for both truth-fulness and sexual morality, we displayed wisdom and sympathy and they, at any rate, would be sorry to see us withdraw from the islands.

I visited the Igorot market in the center of Baguio with Mrs. Wood early Sunday morning—the most advantageous time—making some modest purchases of basketry and hammered silver and admiring the heavy bracelets of silver and gold—some of them as much as six inches wide—and the gaily colored, beautifully woven materials which many of the women wore. On one of the evenings during our stay, the pupils at the Boys' Agricultural School consented to give a performance of tribal dances for us. A campfire blazed and crackled on one side of a cleared open space ringed with spectators, and in the dip of the distant mountains the late moon rose and hung. Preceded by the beating of tom-toms came the dancers—beautifully built, with bodies like bronze, and naked except for headdresses, ornaments and G-strings, and carry-ing spears and shields. The dances of many tribes were given—the Bontocs, the Lingayenos, the Kalingas, the Ifugaos, the Apayaos—wedding dances, harvest dances, festival dances. A generation before the families from which these boys came had been headhunters who performed these barbaric rites in deadly earnest; now their children, eager for education no less than the Christian tribes—of the thirst for knowledge among the Filipinos there could be no question, and they were willing to make any sacrifice to attain it—were being taught to till, plant and develop the soil at the Agricultural School in a way that would lead them from bitter want to comparative comfort. They were being taught other things as well; I met young Igorots—teachers, nurses, soldiers, a doctor—who ten years before had been savages; little by little the leaven was working, and in the end I thought the bread should be wholesome.

Almost immediately after our return from Baguio, Henry complained of intense fatigue and a terrible headache, and the following day he was obviously in need of a doctor. The physician summoned diagnosed his case as dengue fever—painful but not dangerous. The next few days were very hard for me, as well as for him. A planned trip to the other islands was of course given up, but I felt I must try, as far as possible, to keep several official engagements which had been made for me in Manila. I tried to arrange with Larry to stay with Henry whenever I left the sickroom. Larry meant and tried to be cooperative, but he had be-come greatly attracted to a very pretty American girl who was staying at our hotel with her mother. She was engaged to be married, and a trip around the world had been planned—as so many were in those days—

to divert her mind temporarily from the object of her affections, though she *was* buying her trousseau. It was soon evident that Larry had been able to divert her mind without the slightest effort; and when he came and told me that *he* was engaged to Susan, I was appalled. He had delightful manners and was exceptionally good looking; moreover, he was obviously in "comfortable circumstances" and what is generally known as "a great catch." However, he had been entrusted to me by his parents and I believed he was under age. (I later found I was mistaken about this. I thought he was the same age as Henry; as a matter of fact, he was a year older.) I felt responsible for him and I was by no means sure that Mr. and Mrs. Knowles would approve a match with a girl whom he had met so casually and about whom we knew absolutely nothing.

After a few days, Henry's physician changed his diagnosis; he now pronounced the illness to be not dengue, but catarrhal jaundice. Henry did seem better, and the doctor thought there would be no imprudence in keeping to our schedule and leaving for Singapore, even though the patient had to be taken aboardship on a stretcher.

Chapter 41

OUR Filipino friends tried to make our departure as festive as our arrival had been. A floral wreathed arch embellished with the words "Bon Voyage" surmounted the gangplank where it joined the ship; the Constabulary Band played "Auld Lang Syne," my cabin was filled with gifts; and a gay farewell was waved to us from the pier by the same kindly friends—with some newfound additions—who had waved from the launch on our arrival.

But my calendar tells a different side of the story:

> Jan. 23. All kinds of trouble. Henry put in my stateroom with another man in Larry's. No chance for rest or quiet for writing. Disobliging and insolent steward, incompetent doctor. Henry worse again.
> Jan. 24. Writing and caring for Henry under conditions of dreadful difficulty.
> Jan. 25. Cabled Am. Consul to send doctor and ambulance to meet boat. Found out afterward he resented form of cable. Still working under great difficulties.
> Jan. 26. Landed Singapore 10 A. M. British Customs officer did not recognize special passport. Henry removed on stretcher to Gen. Hospital. Went to see him comfortably installed. Larry and I went to Raffles Hotel, met by Arathoons.

This seems to require some expansion to clarify the situation, and I cannot consult the *Good Housekeeping* "Letters," as I often do, to refresh my memories, because one of Mr. Bigelow's strict rules was that they should contain the briefest mention, if any, of difficulties and depressing episodes. "Nobody wants to hear about those," he maintained. I think that possibly this was one of his (very few!) mistakes, for later a faithful reader complained, "The scene of your articles is always one of unclouded sunshine! Weren't there ever any shadows?" There were, indeed, and this was one of the times when the shadows were very dark. But I actually need nothing to refresh my memory, for my recollection of those dreadful days at sea between Manila and Singapore is just as vivid as if they had occurred last year instead of more than forty years ago. It had been stipulated, before I agreed to go around the world, that I should always be given exclusive occupancy of my cabin, so that I would have the necessary space and privacy for writing; *Good House-keeping* had consented to meet the cost of this, though it meant paying double, as there were no single staterooms, and the Dollar Line had guaranteed it. However, when I reached my cabin, I found that Henry had already been installed there, ostensibly, according to the purser, so that it would be easier for me to take care of him. The purser offered no rebate on the double fare, he had put another man in with Larry, and there was not an empty cabin in the ship. This meant I somehow had to dispose on my bed my reference material, the copybook in which I drafted my articles and the typewriter for the second draft (which had to be mailed in Singapore to meet my deadline) and crouch over the bed as best I could, while working; then I had to pile all these impedimenta beside the bed when I had to get into it myself. Henry's illness by then had taken the form of violent nausea, and every few hours, I had to support him while he vomited. Each attack left him exhausted and drenched with perspiration; his sheets and pillow slips were quickly soaked, and I spread them out, put mine on his bed and lay down myself on the bare mattress; after the next attack I had to use towels for a makeshift, as the sheets had not dried.

If we had been blessed with the same excellent service there had been on the other Dollar ships we had taken, these trying conditions would have been somewhat mitigated; but the first morning out I rang and rang without getting any response, and I soon found this was not a temporary drawback. After telling Henry I would have to leave him for a few minutes to find out what was wrong, I went to the purser's office, which was deserted, and next in search of the chief steward, whom I found in the midst of a heated altercation with another passenger; they were both shouting and swearing, so it was difficult to learn what the matter was, but I did gather that the Chinese crew had mutinied, that if any of us wanted something to eat we would have to go to the galley for it ourselves and that there was no use in trying to appeal to the captain, as everyone who had tried to reach the bridge had been forcibly turned back. At last the angry passenger left, still cursing, and I managed to make myself heard and tried to speak calmly. I didn't mind waiting on myself, I said, if someone would tell me where the supplies were—linen as well as food; and my son was very ill—I must get in touch with the doctor at once. As I spoke, I slipped a ten-dollar bill into the steward's hand.

The result was not very encouraging, but at least I was addressed without oaths or violence. There was only one stewardess aboard, I was informed, and it was not part of her work to carry trays to men—I must know that—and I would have to manage those myself, since the room steward was among the mutineers; there had been some stabbing already, and he couldn't risk stirring up more trouble. As for the doctor, he was a queer bird—"long on hypos."

The doctor in Manila had been one of the quick breezy sort. His habit was to burst suddenly into the sickroom, stare at Henry and shout, "Sleep well? Temperature? Pulse? Vomit?" and, as soon as these questions had been answered and a brief comment made on them, to dart out again. The ship's doctor, on the contrary, seemed to be more or less in a daze, and I could not help fearing that the steward's hint about "hypos" applied not only to the physician's patients but to the physician himself. Quite aside from this, his first words, after making a cursory examination of the sick boy, were far from reassuring; this was not a case of dengue fever or catarrhal jaundice, he insisted; it was a case of malaria. Henry's diet must be changed; he must be given a sedative.

I could not see that his diet would make much difference, since he could not retain a cup of coffee or a drink of water and therefore would simply gag over meat and spinach; as to the sedative, I was suspicious of the need for that too, as he was drowsy all the time except when roused by nausea. But there was no one else to whom I could turn. Despairingly, I watched my son grow steadily worse. Acting for me, Larry cabled the consulate in Singapore, wording the message:

HENRY KEYES SON SENATOR KEYES TRAVELING WITH HIS MOTHER WELL-KNOWN AUTHOR VERY ILL STOP PLEASE HAVE DOCTOR AND AMBULANCE MEET SHIP

I did not see the cable before it went off, and naturally would not have referred to myself as "wellknown"; at the same time, I could understand Larry's wording was chosen for identification and not for ostentation. However, the Consul did not take it that way. He arranged for the doctor and the ambulance, as requested, but he voiced his displeasure at the tone of the message, and echoes of his resentment continued to reach us long afterward.

The doctor who met the ship was a Scot, of very different caliber from the two sorry specimens of the medical profession with whom I

had so far been obliged to deal; and the British Hospital, set high on a
hill overlooking the city, to which we were speedily taken despite the
efforts of customs officials to detain us, was the only one to which I
have ever been, either as a patient or the relative of a patient, for which
I have nothing but praise. In an unbelievably short time Henry was settled in a private room in a long gallery of similar rooms and wards, all
open to a welcome breeze, and a tall, fresh-faced English "Sister" was
at his bedside listening attentively to the doctor who had met us and a
second physician who had been summoned for consultation. I was
shown into a pleasant nearby room and asked to wait until the doctors
could make a report. Presently a Eurasian nurse came in bringing tea
and toast and marmalade. By the time I had consumed this, the nursing
Sister had returned.

"The doctors are not quite ready with their report yet," she said,
"and your son went right to sleep as soon as they left him. I suggest you
go to your hotel now and come back later in the evening."

A San Francisco friend had given me a letter of introduction to Eran
and Ticu Arathoon, who had been educated in her city and whose father was the proprietor of the Raffles Hotel; and these two dark-eyed,
soft-spoken young gentlewomen, Armenian by inheritance and Persian
by birth, almost overwhelmed me with their kindness and understanding
from the moment I met them. They saw me comfortably installed in a
large airy room and later took me, first to the hospital, where I found
Henry resting and indisposed to talk, and then for a drive about the
city. The next day I worked hard on the article, which had missed its
deadline and on which, despite my best efforts, I had not made much
headway aboardship. The calendar reveals that I finished it "late at
night and wrote to Mr. B. [the covering letter] after 1 A.M."; also that
the doctors—with whom I had spoken during my intermittent visits to
the hospital—now thought it would be "all right for me to start for
Java with Larry."

How I could possibly have had the courage to do it, under all the circumstances, or how Henry should have had the will power to insist that
I should, I cannot now understand. But Henry was obviously in good
hands and very cheerful; though his doctors had still not arrived at a
definite diagnosis, they saw nothing critical in his condition; if my stay
in Java was to be protracted, probably he would be able to join me; on
the other hand, if I could complete my work there quickly and return,
perhaps that would be the best solution. . . . Uneasy but allowing myself
to be persuaded there was no real reason why I should be, I sailed late
the following afternoon for Batavia and arrived there thirty-six hours

later, to be met by the American Consul, Mr. Charles Hoover, and a cable from Eran Arathoon:

HENRY WORSE DOCTORS ADVISE YOUR IMMEDIATE RETURN

The local line between Batavia and Singapore had only biweekly sailings, and of course there were no planes. But there was a splendid cruise ship, the *Empress of Scotland,* in the harbor, scheduled to leave for Singapore that very afternoon. We hurried to the Canadian Line office and asked for accommodations—any kind they had or could make available. The agent was extremely sorry; they were not permitted to take local passengers; in fact, there was a five-thousand-dollar fine if they did so; and, besides, it was too late; the gangplanks had already been lifted and the ship had moved away from the dock.

"Then you must stop it," I said, desperately trying to keep my voice steady. "You can reach it by radio. If you explain the situation, I know it will stop. And we can go out to it in a launch. As to the fine— if they insist on having it paid under the circumstances—well, it will be."

The Consul took over where I left off, and however much the one in Singapore may have resented having rank pulled on him, this one did not hesitate to do so. The agent, still unconvinced that it would do any good, consented to radio the ship when he found out that if he did not do so, Mr. Hoover would. We secured a launch and told it to stand by; then we found a vantage point where we could watch the *Empress of Scotland* as she sailed out of the harbor.

She was moving slowly, but she was moving. Minutes passed and she was still moving. After a quarter of an hour, I clenched my teeth so I would not scream, and I must have shut my eyes at the same time, for it was only when Larry grabbed me and shouted, "She's stopped! Do you hear me, she's stopped?" that I knew she really had.

When we reached the top of the emergency ladder that had been lowered for us, we found the cruise director waiting. Nothing could have exceeded his kindness and courtesy; I was given a large pleasant cabin, and a large pleasant stewardess was immediately sent to wait on me, and I was told that a "Sister" was standing by to learn whether I would care to have her and the doctor come to see me. I was grateful for her ministrations; quite aside from the terrible strain I was under, I was finding that the tropics presented weakening physical problems, not unusual for Anglo-Saxon women unaccustomed to the climate. I arranged for the dispatch of several radiograms; other than attending to these, I kept as quiet as possible throughout the voyage back to Singapore. When I reached the hospital, I was told with abrupt kindness that I had better stay there, not only on Henry's account but on my own. I needed no urging. The Arathoons had met me and seen me safely into the hands of the competent English Sister I had met at the hospital before. Then they left me, assuring me I had only to let them know if there were anything they could do for me, and I began my vigil by my desperately sick son.

By this time, Dr. Tull, who was in charge of Henry's case, had diagnosed Henry's illness as spirochetal jaundice, which "bears about as much relation to ordinary jaundice as scarlatina does to scarlet fever." In other words, it was a good deal more serious. Indeed, as I was next told, it had about a thirty percent mortality.

"However, you needn't fear a sudden turn for the worse. If your son's heart doesn't go back on him—and we see no prospect of that—he can hold out a long time. But he may have to fight overwhelming depression —that's one of the most common characteristics of this illness—no desire to struggle as the siege goes on. And we don't know whether he can last long enough to resist starvation."

"Starvation?"

"Yes. That's where the fatal difficulty usually comes. He won't be able to take any nourishment except albumen water for days. Later on, a little fruit juice. Nothing solid for weeks, no fats or stimulants of any kind for weeks after that. He's strong and young; that's in his favor; if he were flabby and elderly, he wouldn't have a chance. So you see, it's a waiting game. I can't tell you how long the wait will be or what its outcome will be. Only that you have to face it. Your son depends on you. I'm counting on you to help us see this through, to give him the will to live he may not have. I think you must make up your mind to an endurance test. That's why I don't want you to use up all your own reserves, but to follow the schedule I'll give you—so much sleep and so much exercise, so much diversion or relaxation or whatever you choose to call it. If you don't, you'll give out. You have no idea what the tropics can do to a woman constituted like you."

The day after this verdict and these instructions were given me, when Larry came to see me, he told me that since we were to be delayed indefinitely in Singapore, Mrs. Smith (not her real name of course), his inamorata's mother, had canceled their passage to Ceylon, and they would be staying in Singapore as long as we did. (The Smiths had also come on from Manila.) This confirmed my unhappy belief that they were afraid Larry might have sober second thoughts about his engagement to a girl he had known only ten days, who was admittedly engaged to someone else when they met but who wanted to take no chances of losing such a good match as Larry obviously was. He was no longer willing to discuss the situation with me, after making his disturbing declaration; and in any case Henry seemed to need me so much that I was unwilling to leave his room a moment more than was absolutely necessary. Desperately, I began to wonder whether I should have to cope, almost simultaneously, with a funeral and a marriage—twelve thousand miles from home. There were only the Arathoons to whom I could appeal for advice and help, since I had received no further word from our Consul, despite the fact that he was aware of my precipitate return from Java, for Larry had taken my article to him and asked if it might be sent, for speed and safety, in the diplomatic pouch. This courtesy was often accorded me and was not declined in this instance, either, but beyond this, it was apparent that as far as an American official in Singapore was concerned, I had nothing to hope for; and though I recognized the exceptional quality of the Arathoons' kindness, I did not know how much they would be authorized to do in a situation like the one I might be facing. A good deal of red tape surrounds both the death and the marriage of an American on foreign soil, which, normally, only our own national officials can untangle; and quite aside from this, no one can offer the moral support and compassion that may be taken for granted from old friends and close relatives in time of need. Still another consideration was our financial status; I had been supplied with enough money for all routine expenses, but I was likely to be faced with costs which were far from routine. As soon as I felt well enough, I took advantage of one of the occasional deep sleeps into which Henry fell and went to the International Bank, where I drew out—as my calendar puts it—"all the money due." What I was going to do when that was gone, I did not know.

Chapter 42

HELP of more than one kind was not long in coming, though not from the sources I had reason to expect. I had become well enough to leave the hospital and no longer had a patient's privileges, so I was now sleeping and eating at the hotel; but I was allowed to spend practically all day with Henry, and one morning when the matron came to pay her daily visit, she asked if we knew anyone at Government House. With some astonishment, we replied that we did not.

"His Excellency's aide-de-camp has telephoned to inquire about our patient's health," insisted the matron. "You must have friends there."

And, as it proved, we did. For later that same day came an imposing-looking letter bearing the seal of the lion and the unicorn encircled by the words "Aide-de-Camp to His Excellency the Governor." It read:

Government House
Singapore

Dear Mrs. Keyes:

Sir Laurence Guillemard has received a cable from his friend Sir Esme Howard, British Ambassador at Washington, stating that you were in Singapore with your son who is lying ill at the General Hospital.

Sir Laurence expects that you are spending most of your time at the hospital, but he would like to know if he can do anything to help you; if so please let me know.

If it is convenient for you he would be very glad if, either now or later, you would come and stay here.

You would be free to look after your son, and to see as much or as little of our Government House life as you might wish.

Yours sincerely,
V. G. Olive, Major
Aide-de-Camp.

One of the cables I had sent from the *Empress of Scotland* had been to Sir Esme Howard, a very good friend of ours; but the most I had expected in the way of a response was the same routine assistance from the local British officials as that which I believed I could count on from the American officials—only to find I had misplaced my confidence. Deeply touched as I was by the kindness that had prompted this invitation, I felt extremely doubtful whether I ought to accept it. Having been the mistress of an official household for some years myself —though a very modest one compared to that of a British Colonial Governor—I knew the demands on its chatelaine were so exacting that others should not be thoughtlessly added by an outsider; I was uncertain whether I had enough self-control and courage to visit anyone right then; and I was unwilling to leave Larry—since the Guillemards were unaware of his existence, he had not been included in the invitation. I finally decided to express my gratitude and my hesitation with equal frankness; and was rewarded by an immediate reply, from Lady Guillemard herself, saying that Major Olive had shown her my letter, and though she understood and appreciated my scruples, she hoped I would allow myself to be persuaded and come to Government House the next day, "bringing Mr. Knowles with you." A car would be available, night and day, to take me to the hospital at any moment.

In the face of such overwhelming hospitality, there was nothing to do but capitulate, and the next day when a hotel servant brought me a neatly typed message reading "Government House car and lorry for Mrs. Henry Wilder Keyes," I followed him. I gazed at the huge truck provided for the luggage with the glad realization that for once in my life I was going to visit someone who did not feel I was bringing too many trunks. Larry and I settled back behind the white-clad, red-capped, red-sashed *syce* driving the limousine, and ten minutes later we turned in the imposing gates of Government Hill, passed the golf course and tennis courts and stopped at the entrance of the great, white-pillared building which we knew must be Government House. Several barefooted servants came forward to meet us, and we found ourselves in a spacious white hall, marble floored, with white marble stairs, carpeted in red velvet and lined with flowering plants, rising to the upper story. We were met by a prim young woman who introduced herself as Lady

Guillemard's secretary and took us to our rooms, which were off a long corridor at the rear of the staircase. A gong, proclaiming that tiffin was only a half hour distant, resounded just as I saw my last piece of baggage conveniently placed. I had nothing to do in the interval, not even to remove my hat, as I had learned that all ladies, including the hostess, wore hats at luncheon; so I employed my time in looking at my new surroundings.

The room was about as large as the ground floor of a fair-sized bungalow and as high as a two-storied house—white walled, green shuttered, with dark polished furniture. In the center stood the most enormous bed I ever saw. A door at one end of the room opened into a bathroom of corresponding proportions; at the other end was an alcove sitting room, containing a chaise longue drawn up beside a table on which were placed a shaded lamp, a bowl of gardenias and a number of books and magazines. A desk, generously equipped with thick, engraved stationery, stood near this table, and there was also a printed pamphlet with the heading:

Government House, Singapore.
General Information.

I found in it a list of the meal hours, the times of Divine Service at the Cathedral, the schedules of mails, railways and ships with various additional information. And soon it was time to go, as I had been told, to the upstairs "veranda," which proved to be a sitting room, not a porch, and there await the ringing of the second gong and the appearance of His Excellency the Governor and Lady Guillemard. When I arrived there, two aides-de-camp, two private secretaries and several other house guests were already assembled; after a few moments, our host and hostess appeared, and we were formally presented to them. This ceremony of assembly and presentation took place before both luncheon and dinner every day, quite as if we had never seen our hosts before, with the variation that on relatively formal occasions the guests met in the drawing room opposite the dining room on the ground floor, then followed an aide-de-camp up the grand staircase, house guests preceding those invited in for the meal only, and all were presented to His Excellency and Lady Guillemard, who awaited them in the ballroom. As invariable as the custom of presentation was the custom of drinking the King's health after dinner. At the end of the meal, the glasses were filled, a hush fell on the murmur of conversation, and His Excellency rose and, lifting his glass, said very solemnly, "The King!" Each guest, with equal solemnity, repeated the words after him before drinking.

No human being who had been invited to such an establishment under the circumstances which led to my presence at Government House could fail to be prepared to like and admire those who had extended the invitation; but discounting all this, I should instantly have liked and admired my host and hostess. Sir Laurence's dignified and slightly formal manner relaxed as he talked, and he revealed powers of penetration and expression, a delightful sense of humor, essential friendliness and interest in people and conditions all over the world. Moreover, for the first time since I could remember, I had the pleasure and stimulation, when sitting beside him at the table, of talking to a man who regarded classical literature as a suitable topic for dinner party conversation and took the initiative of introducing it. As to my hostess, I can say without reservation that she was quite the most charming Englishwoman whom I had ever so far known, with a rare combination of character and intellect and personal loveliness. There was, necessarily, a good deal of formality surrounding the intercourse between the hostess of Government House and her guests; and if I wished to see Lady Guillemard for any reason except at lunch, tea or dinner, I had to send her a note, asking if I might do so, while usually, though not always, she approached me in the same manner. But neither this precaution to insure needed privacy for a busy woman nor the lack of previous acquaintance prevented her constant display of sympathy, solicitude and sweetness. I know that my visit at Government House was one of the greatest official privileges I ever had; but far more than that it was to me a living example of the biblical phrase, "I was a stranger, and you took me in . . . I was sick, and you visited me."

And I had been at Government House only a few days when help came from another unexpected direction The ubiquitous aide-de-camp Major Olive sent a note asking if it would be convenient for me to see him and, when I answered affirmatively, he presented himself at my sitting room with a surprising question.

"Were you expecting a large sum of money from some source?" he inquired.

"I certainly was not," I answered in amazement, all too conscious that I had already withdrawn from the bank every cent due me.

"Well, perhaps you wouldn't call it large, but it's certainly substantial. You don't know anyone who might send you a substantial sum of money?"

Again I was obliged to reply, regretfully, that I did not.

"The manager is very reluctant to pay this sum to you, unless you can give him some idea who sent it to you."

Nearly all the banks in that part of the Orient were controlled by Scots, and their caution increased every year they spent away from home. "Would the manager be willing to divulge the name of the bank the money came from?" I asked hopefully. "That might give me a clue to the sender."

"I'll ask him."

In a few minutes, Major Olive returned with the name of the bank. It was the one on which all my *Good Housekeeping* checks were drawn. "I believe the money was sent by William Frederick Bigelow," I said, drawing a deep breath.

"Right you are. If you like, I'll take you to the bank at once and you can decide yourself whether you consider the amount large or merely substantial."

It was for five thousand—exactly the sum I would have had to pay if the Canadian Pacific had exacted a fine for carrying two local passengers; actually, the company did nothing of the sort, but commended the Captain for his good judgment in knowing when to make an exception to a rule. Though Mr. Bigelow was among the persons to whom I had sent cables, I had not asked for money; I had only said I feared the next article, despite my best efforts, might be delayed because of Henry's illness. Without being told, Mr. Bigelow had realized that only a major catastrophe would have made me say this and that a major catastrophe might well find me short of funds even with my generous travel allowance. He had acted promptly to relieve any possible financial embarrassment and—as far as lay in his power—any personal distress.

My first days at Government House followed a routine pattern: breakfast in my room, a visit to the hospital, a return for lunch and a second visit to the hospital, lasting until it was time to dress for dinner; so I saw very little of the life there except at meals and in the evening. But as Henry improved, I went with Lady Guillemard to the polo games, a great feature of Singapore's social life as they were of Manila's, to the Child Welfare Centers, in which she took an active interest and of which she was President, and to the Y.W.C.A., of which she was also President. Throughout the entire visit, I was able to take part in whatever entertainment had been planned after dinner, as I was never called back to the hospital. Sometimes this was merely a quiet game of bridge, which ended—no matter what stage a game had reached—the instant His Excellency signaled, around eleven, that he was about to retire. One evening it was a musicale with two hundred and fifty guests seated in the glittering ballroom. Once seven high-ranking naval officers from British men-of-war were guests. And once His Excellency and Lady Guillemard gave an audience to some Malay dignitaries on their way to Java. At eleven in the morning, the Governor, his private secretary and an aide-de-camp entered the ballroom and took their places before a formally arranged group of gilded and tapestried sofas and chairs; Lady Guillemard, a private secretary and I were already stationed before a similar group of furniture on the other side of the room. Then the guests arrived, escorted by a second aide-de-camp and their own suite; His Highness the Sultan of Selangor; the Tungku Ampuan of Selangor, his wife; the Raja Muda of Selangor, his son; His Highness the Sultan of Langkat, his son-in-law; and the Raja Permaisuru of Langkat, wife of one sultan and daughter of the other. They were superbly dressed in rich brocades, the men's robes in delicate shades of rose and peach, one of the princesses in black, the other in orange. Both women wore exquisite gauze veils embroidered in gold suspended from their shoulders and the most dazzling jewels I ever saw: huge diamond buttons in the shape of butterflies fastened the bodice of the orange dress; equally large diamond buttons in the shape of stars sparkled on the black one. Besides these buttons, the princesses wore earrings, combs, rings and several necklaces—all of diamonds. I was so overcome by this display that I was thankful the demands made upon me by the audience were slight. The presentations were accompanied by bows, but no curtsys; then the party divided into two groups, as indicated by the carefully prearranged furniture. Thickly sugared coffee and small frosted cakes were followed by ice cream and a large variety of candies —a choice prompted by the Malays' fondness for sweets—and we sat and gazed at each other. The Sultans nibbled their food with delicate enjoyment and smiled, but there was very little conversation, nor did the visitors seem to feel the need of any. I had discovered that Oriental women were not embarrassed by long peaceful silences, and I myself had come to find them soothing in the midst of so much general excitement. When the refreshments were gone, the audience was at an end. That same night, the men dined at Government House and one of them played bridge with such zest that the Governor actually broke his eleven o'clock retirement rule. Their wives did not accompany them—this would have been far too advanced a procedure for Malay custom— though one of them did come with her husband and their nine-year old son—a golden-skinned boy clad in rich raiment—to the polo matches the next day.

My trips to and from the hospital had at first been hurried and my mind had not been on what I was seeing, but gradually the opulent charm of Singapore became too strong for me to ignore. In her broad harbor came and went the ships of every nation and on her broad streets walked the people of every nation, for Singapore was hostess of the world's halfway house! She lay, this capital city of the Straits Settlements, governed by Sir Laurence Guillemard, curving around a blue bay and richly shaded with glossy greens. All her principal buildings were a deep cream color, roofed with crimson or russet, and in their luxuriant setting they looked vital and mellow, not rigid and inanimate, as such edifices are prone to look.

The Chinese wedding or funeral procession, glittering and noisy, was almost as frequent a sight as it was in Shanghai or Peking, for the Singapore population was three-fourths Chinese. During the celebration of the Chinese New Year there was a continuous explosion of fire-crackers, with which the noisiest Fourth of July imaginable could not begin to compare. But, little as I enjoyed the sputtering and flaring of these fireworks reverberating in the path of my car whenever I went out, or the sensation that they were being set off under my bed all night long, the annoyances of these paled completely before the horrors of the Hindu Taipusum, the festival of the god Siva, which also took place during our stay. As penance for crimes, real or imagined, not necessarily their own but of any family member whose sins they wished to expiate, men, women and children paraded through the streets with spikes thrust through lips and tongue, bells fastened to hooks piercing their flesh, nail-studded shoes on their feet. Families and friends accompanied them, chanting as they went their painful way, and often dragging carts behind them to which they were joined by instruments of torture; sometimes they paused in front of houses while the inmates threw water on their bodies and feet. The pilgrimage ended at the main temple, where the means of torture were removed and food was placed in front of them, which they were not allowed to touch until sunset, even though many of them had fasted for days. Their reward, which seemed rather vague and unsubstantial, was supposed to come eventually in the form of mercy from the deity to the offender.

There was a crowded river life, there were open markets and bazaars, and even within the city limits the great evil-smelling rubber factories steamed and groaned; but in the botanical gardens and by the huge reservoirs, where the "traveler's palm" flickered its fringes in the never-failing late afternoon breeze, there was nothing but sweetness, peace and beauty. The suburban streets were lined with deep gardens, and in their depths stood some of the most beautiful homes I had ever seen. And everywhere there were orchids growing, purple orchids that grew higher than my head; I could fill my room with them, whenever I chose, for a few dollars.

I could see all these sights and many more under the sparkling sun by day; and I could see them, just as clearly, under the sparkling moon by night; for never, in all my tropical experience, had I beheld such moonlight as there was in Singapore! And once, when Larry and I were leaving the hospital, we saw a crescent moon lying like a slender, strung bow straight across the sky, which was still rosy with the flush of sunset, and suddenly he caught my arm and whispered, "Look!" In an open grassy space a man, white turbaned, white robed, was sinking on his knees; and having knelt, he bowed reverently to the crescent moon. Something of the feeling that animated that man's spirit must, I think, have entered the soul of every human being who stood beneath the moon of Singapore.

Eran and Ticu Arathoon never let one of those dark days at the hospital go by without some tangible evidence of their thoughtfulness and solicitude; and when Henry was a good deal better and the hotel was again my headquarters, they asked if I would not like to dine one evening at Sea View and dance afterward "at the finest ballroom in the East."

I hesitated. Larry was not included in the invitation, not through any lack of hospitality, but because he had said very plainly that he wished to spend all his evenings in *solitudes à deux* with Susan. But it seemed foolish to feel I must have a "bodyguard" indefinitely, and the party was to include Mr. Arathoon and two young British officers whom I had already met and liked. Then, too, it was a long time since I had danced, and as this was a form of diversion that would appeal to me, I accepted.

I met the Arathoons and their other guests in the lounge of the Raffles Hotel, where so-called "million dollar" cocktails were served us. They were quite potent, and I thought one sufficient for an evening and was startled and a little shocked to see refills being circulated— especially with a long drive ahead and no food in the meanwhile. But nothing occurred to give me as much as a qualm during the drive, though we went at top speed. On arrival at Sea View, where tables were scattered over the white sand in sound of the surf, we found ours was in the very best location and decorated more lavishly than any of the others; and all around the table silver buckets filled with ice formed a glittering array. It was obvious the million dollar cocktails were only curtain raisers.

Sherry, Chablis and Pommard followed each other in swift succession; then came champagne with the *soufflé surprise* and liqueurs after dinner, and though my hostesses and I declined everything but the champagne, our male companions accepted everything that was offered them and emptied their glasses each time these were filled. I dreaded to have the music for dancing begin. I did not see how any of these men could be steady on his feet or in his mind when it was time to go to the pavilion to dance. But when the crucial moment inevitably came, Mr. Arathoon rose and offered me his arm and I had no choice but to take it.

My fears were completely groundless. He was as cold sober as I am at this moment and so were the other two men. The pavilion, open on all four sides, was a perfect place to dance on a warm evening. Between every dance there was a five minute interval, and in every one the gentlemen had a highball. At quarter before twelve, the orchestra played "God Save the King" and the entire company rose. Then we went back to Singapore the long way around, so I could see the moonlight white as snow upon the sands under the coco palms. When we reached the hotel about three in the morning not one of our escorts showed the slightest sign of having had a drink, much less too many drinks.

Singapore did lack newspapers which printed American news—or much of any news at all. On the day we arrived, the front page of the leading local journal was given over to some modest advertisements and an article describing the flora and fauna of Singapore in 1904! I was not able to learn whether or not the Senate had passed the World Court Resolution either through diligent search myself or inquiry at Government House, the International Bank or any other place I could think of; and, though a speech on rubber that Herbert Hoover had made had been the subject of ruthless editorial attack, there was not, apparently, a copy of the speech itself in the city! When I asked a British officer whose official position led me to believe him a source of international information to secure it for me, he asked patiently, "Who is Herbert Hoover anyway? I seem to have heard the name, but can't place him at all. . . ." In a way, it was very wholesome to encounter such blissful ignorance of and indifference to our affairs, since it is one of our national failings to imagine the world is waiting breathlessly to find out what America is going to do next and depending completely on her for pleasure, peace and prosperity. But it would have been comforting to me, halfway around the globe, to pick up an American newspaper.

Apart from this, though all of February and the first days of March were spent in Singapore without any question that there might be a possibility of leaving it, by early March Henry was taking fruit juices freely and eating a little solid food, with a careful elimination of all fats, and going out for short drives, and since neither food nor the drives had any ill effects, the subject of eventual departure naturally arose. But here we ran into an unexpected stumbling-block in Dr. Tull's opinion that Henry should go home by way of the Far East but not return to Harvard for a year. "Surely," the obdurate physician insisted, "he can at once find another nice young fellow who would keep him company for the voyage, and you could find some nice young lady to act as your companion, if you really feel you must go on around the world. Henry should get out of the tropics."

Henry, who had been surprisingly cheerful throughout most of his ordeal, suddenly exploded. If he went home by way of the Far East, he would not be out of the tropics until he got to San Francisco, he pointed out, whereas about the only useful thing the doctor in Manila had told us was that there were in Java mountain resorts, where hotels were combined with sanatoria, at which he could stay and his mother could make her headquarters while taking side trips for her story. He had leave of absence from Harvard to take a trip around the world, which was supposed to be educational, and not for slinking home with some total stranger who probably would not be in the least congenial. Larry Knowles would continue to look after Mother until he could do so himself again. Judging from the examples of stenography part-time secretaries had produced in Singapore, he was extremely doubtful whether his mother would be satisfied with anyone she could find there. And incidentally, Mother had a job and so did he. Our editors had been understanding about the delay in Singapore, but if he turned up in Boston without any more material for the *Globe* and Mother turned up in New York with only half her work done, he hated to think what the financial consequences would be. He hated quitters anyway.

Dr. Tull was so astonished at this outburst that he stared at Henry without making an immediate reply, and I seized the opportunity to take over. I deeply appreciated everything Dr. Tull had done for Henry, but perhaps I could convince him that there *was* another side to the question. Of course Henry's health must be our first consideration, but did the idea of Garoet—I thought that was the name of a highly recommended place in Java—seem to the doctor a menace to this? It was true that I had a position with a good salary and considerable responsibility and I could not jeopardize it, except as a last resort, because I needed the money. Perhaps Dr. Tull would consent to a consultation with Sir David Galloway. His Excellency and Lady Guillemard had thought this might be a wise plan. . . .

An agitated patient was the last thing either Dr. Tull or I wanted, and somehow the situation was smoothed over. Two days later, Sir David Galloway unreservedly recommended the highlands of Java. Two days after that, we were on our way there. Susan and her mother did not accompany us. Lady Guillemard had been most cordial to them all the time Larry and I were at Government House and had included them in the incidental entertainments to which we went later. Whether or not this was the result of an extraordinary degree of intuition, I do not know, but I suspect that it was and that she had found a better way than I had of dealing with my worries about Larry. The Smiths did not "fit in" at Government House—the conversation, protocol and rigidity of routine there were not only strange to them but displeasing to them—whereas Larry had taken to it like a duck to water. When he and Susan parted, it was with the tacit understanding that their tastes were different, and before long the understanding became more definite. The Smiths went out of our lives and later Larry married a delightful girl whom his parents not only approved of but welcomed with enthusiasm.

Chapter 43

THE boys and I embarked on the *Melchior Traub* of the Koninklijke Packetvaart Maatschappji from Singapore to Batavia, Henry still wobbly but happily convalescent and Larry "rarin' to go" after his long and patient wait. We were almost immediately conscious of a change from the atmosphere of a British Crown Colony, for the trim little vessel that bore us swiftly across the equator was stamped from stem to stern with national and colonial characteristics of Insulinde, as the East Indies then belonging to the Netherlands were called. This change was apparent in transitions from a proper regard for cleanliness to almost rabid insistence on scrubbed and scoured spotlessness and from plenty of reasonably good food, with intervals for exercise and diversion between meals, to an almost endless succession of superabundant repasts. Tea was served as soon as we were fairly underway; and, having finished their tea, most of our fellow passengers began on a round of cooling drinks which sustained them until the seven-course dinner to which we were summoned two hours after tea. Breakfast brought coffee and an endless variety of cold meats and cheeses—strangely enough, breakfast was the *only* meal at which cheese appeared—raisin bread, thick porridge served with coconut syrup, tomatoes fried with bacon, and eggs to order. At eleven in the morning came ruby-colored sherbets, surmounted by whipped cream, in tall slim glasses, and at one o'clock, luncheon, which proved a scarcely less extensive feast than dinner.

Of course Henry was on a strict diet; I soon found I could only sample a few of the delicacies offered between and at meals; and even Larry, whose appetite I had hitherto considered insatiable, was speedily defeated in his efforts to compete with the Dutch, who certainly could not be beaten as trenchermen! Nevertheless, so much time was spent at

(425)

table that other events of the voyage were more or less incidental. And a ship which slips across the equator every week does not make much of the occurrence; though the boys and I sat up until eleven in order to know when we "really passed the line," we had little company as we did so.

Any previous opinions that we had hitherto suffered with the heat changed when we reached Batavia. Never before, we unanimously agreed, had we known what heat was or could be—steaming, damp, impenetrable, suffocating. It enveloped us without mercy as we descended from the ship at the man-made port six miles from the city, where we were met by our Vice Consul, Mr. Kuykendahl, who saw us through customs and guided us past clamoring coolies; it followed us along the flat, canal-bordered road dripping with early morning moisture to "Old Batavia" and then to the "New Batavia"—Weltevreden; it jeered at us as we retired "to freshen up a little" in our bedrooms, each behind its own porch-sitting room in the fashion of Javanese hotels—a fashion which seemed delightfully spacious and luxurious until one realized the sitting room excluded both air and light, that there were no electric fans and that electricity was turned off in the daytime. And there was no let-up from it as we ate our first meal ashore. We were still very conscious of the heat as we rose from table, and it came and covered us in place, as it were, of the non-existent upper sheet when we lay down on the huge hard mattresses stretched over springless bedsteads and, shrouded with mosquito netting, endeavored to rest from two until four in the afternoon.

Not that we wished to rest; not that any of us—except the convalescent—needed to rest. But it was the custom of the country to do so, and there were few customs in any country so scrupulously observed. The stores closed, cars ceased to run; the telephone was silent; the servants disappeared. I had heard the sad—and true—story of a writer who once tried to finish an overdue script between those sacred hours and was ejected from his hotel for disturbing the peace; when I dropped my hairbrush and it clattered on the tiled floor, I shuddered lest I should be asked to leave. It was the only time I did shudder in Java.

At four o'clock, unrefreshed and almost desperate with the heat, we rose and faced the problem of bathing before dressing to go to the American Consulate for tea and bridge. Tubs and hot water were both extremely rare in Java; and though at Batavia we each had a private bath, this meant we were each provided with a small cubbyhole in which stood a tank of cold water, carefully constructed so that you could not cheat and get into it; you were supposed to stand beside this and pour the water over yourself with a little bucket. We never discovered a satisfactory solution for soaping ourselves or using a nailbrush under these conditions; and though in time we learned to accept them without shouting our complaints through the partitions at each other, we did not learn to enjoy them.

We finally presented ourselves at the Consulate feeling as if we had been run over by a steam roller but hoping we did not look it. The kindly welcome we received did much to restore our drooping spirits, and Mr. and Mrs. Hoover, our Consul and his wife, strengthened our already strong impression that the United States was, almost without exception, graciously, wisely and worthily represented abroad. The Hoovers had made themselves universally beloved in Java; and though handicapped by inadequate quarters—like so many other American representatives!—dispensed never-failing hospitality in the small house which served as both home and offices and was far less pretentious than most of the foreign consulates in Java.

In spite of the heat and apart from the Hoovers' kindness, we would have been glad to linger in Batavia, for though it lacked the beauty of Singapore, the charm of Manila and the subtle fascination of the Chinese cities, it was far cleaner and better kept, far more prosperous looking than they were; and it still held landmarks of arresting interest, though Old Batavia was almost completely commercialized.

But when the physician who came promptly to see Henry corroborated the advice we had received in Singapore that I should take him without delay to the hills, I immediately hired a car and we set off at dawn, left the city before it was fairly astir and came upon our first stretches of rural Java: corn as tall and vigorous as any in Kansas; fields of glossy tapioca; rice terraces where the first green shoots pierced the wet red soil that shone like lacquer; golden grain already ripe for harvest.

Java was so densely populated though—nearly seven hundred persons to the square mile—that one seldom had the feeling of being really in the country; one little village crowded closely upon another, its houses of plaited bamboo, with great bird cages hanging at almost every entrance, half hidden by the luxuriant growth of foliage; and there was a schoolhouse, a small library and a rural bank in almost every one, for the statement that the Dutch denied all educational and financial opportunities to the Javanese was pure slander. Along the highways, bordered with tall prim trees, the patient tireless people plodded in a constant stream—babies slung across their shoulders in wide *slendangs* (scarves) and the folds of their batik sarongs falling gracefully about them. Many of the girls were very pretty, with large gentle eyes and abundant hair, and the children restored a belief in elves and tiny woodland creatures as they scampered through the villages and trudged beside their elders. They flew gay little kites which we saw stacked in neat piles at the wayside stores; they sat astride the water buffalo—which allowed no white man near them—guiding them, tending them, caressing them, caring for them; they stood poised against the banks of a canal and suddenly plunged; they appeared unexpectedly and mysteriously, in clusters or quite alone, beside a slender tree or from the depths of tangled thickets, far distant from any human habitation or parental guidance, and waited, entirely naked, entirely quiet, entirely unafraid, solemnly staring at the passer-by; and when these small apparitions were seen in the mists of dawn or the glow of dusk, they seemed wrapped with elfin magic.

Noon found us in Bandoeng, a bustling inland city more than two thousand feet above sea level and correspondingly cooler than stifling Batavia. If Bandoeng had never been called the Chicago of Java, I cannot imagine why; the comparison came instantly to my mind. It was pleasant and prosperous and self-important and growing by leaps and bounds; it even aspired to becoming the capital city and had already wrested from Batavia the government headquarters of the army, air force, railway post office, mines and central purchasing department. It had, too, a school system which might have been the pride of any city in the world. I went to a number of these schools and have never seen more beautiful or more nearly perfect equipment.

The first one I visited was the Queen Wilhelmina "particular" school, where I was startled to see, among the flaxen-haired, blue-eyed pupils, a number with skins of dusky cream and soft dark hair. When I asked about this, I was promptly told, "Certainly we have children here who are half Javanese. The issue of mixed marriages are always Dutch in the eyes of the law. They have every recognition. You will find the boys, when they reach maturity, officers in the army, members of the clubs; they and their wives are received in the best society."

As far as I was aware, the Dutch alone gave this official and social recognition in their colonies—indeed, they carried it to the homeland as well—and removed the stigma from the expression "half-caste" in a way which neither the British nor we ourselves did or were willing to do. In writing from the Philippines, I said I believed many of our difficulties there arose from social rather than political causes; and after I had seen the Dutch, also dealing with a Malay race, governing with a much tighter rein than we dreamed of using and yet confronted with fewer problems, this belief was considerably strengthened. Undoubtedly, they owed much of their colonial power to the stand they took in regard to interracial marriages and their offspring. No doubt, they carefully considered this. As the old saying goes, they were hard to beat, and it took a long time to do this.

I returned to Bandoeng more than once and grew to like it increasingly, but my initial visit was a fleeting one, for my first care was naturally to establish the convalescent in the hills above Garoet, which we reached through the rosy mist of one of the most heavenly sunsets I can remember; if the sun splashes into the sea at Manila with a splendid arrogance it displays nowhere else, it spreads a gossamer veil of glory over the mountains of Java at dusk. It is no wonder that Henry, lying on the terrace of the excellent hotel-sanatorium at Ngamplang and gazing peacefully at the shifting panorama of beauty, had already gained greatly before Larry and I left for the first of our jaunts about Java and was immeasurably improved each time we returned to him.

We began our caravaning with hearts lighter than they had been in a long time and feeling nothing could dampen our spirits. But alas! we had reckoned without our car. The venerable vehicle had been hired from a highly recommended firm, which demanded full payment in advance; and though this seemed unusual, we did not attempt to haggle; even our brief sojourn among the Dutch had persuaded us they were invincible in financial matters, as in most others. Our troubles were not long delayed: the aged car refused to climb hills, even in low; the battery died; the gas line ceased to supply nourishment; the springs broke; we spent hours in remote villages and on deserted roads while our patient and gentle *soepir* (chauffeur) tinkered and coaxed and always miraculously triumphed. All this we did soaked to the skin, since the top leaked and the side curtains did not fit. Every day "the rains descended and the floods fell," and every day one more dress was ruined.

The most beautiful country in the world, seen under such conditions, seems less beautiful than it otherwise would, but there was, indeed, endless beauty everywhere. First it was a beauty fertile and developed and controlled; a beauty of irrigation, of bamboo pipes emitting water over paddy and field, of smooth canals and deep reservoirs; of pleasant and prosperous-looking houses grouped around the white factory of a sugar *central,* their flower beds as neat and prim as if they were in Delft or Rotterdam. And then the second day out brought us to more open vistas, hollow and hillside still untouched—luxuriant, deep, mysterious, with strange atmospheric shades of topaz and amethyst floating over them. Great wicker carts painted with gaily colored designs were far more frequent than the familiar two-wheeled carriages, and immense numbers of goats flocked everywhere. We saw fewer people on the highways and they were different: the native girls no longer wore the buttoned muslin jacket that fell to their hips; instead, their only garment was the sarong twisted firmly under the armpits, leaving smooth shoulders bare; sometimes—though not often—it was no higher than the waist. Invariably, the men's torsos were bare and shorts had supplanted their sarongs; wide hats, often painted turquoise blue, or twisted and knotted kerchiefs formed the most characteristic headdress. Their Hindu heritage became more apparent in form, feature and shade, for we were approaching the center of that ancient Hindu Empire which flourished in might and majesty and which left, as monuments to its glory, its wonder temples—after eleven centuries still the most magnificent relics of their kind in the world though, for lack of information about them, they have not been universally acclaimed as such.

The most famous of these was the Borobodur; and it suddenly loomed before us, gray but gleaming in the heat of the Java noon, in plain sight of the road—a gigantic stupa built about a hill. The temple was erected on a broad platform and towered over it in five square terraces, whose alcove chapels—four hundred and thirty-six in all!—held life-size Buddhas seated on lotus-shaped cushions. Surmounting the square terraces were three circular ones, where seventy-two more representations of Buddha were ensconced in latticed niches. Visiting and revisiting it, under the blaze of the noonday sun, in the torrents of afternoon rain, in the cool rosy dusk, the beauty of it, the marvel of it, permeated all my senses. In 1926, there was still no adequate guide to the ruins, and if that lack has since been remedied, this has not been sufficiently publicized—and probably Borobodur will not be visited as frequently as the Pyramids until it is just as easy to do so. A pity, for it is without question one of the world's greatest wonders.

We made the city of Djokjakarta—or Djokja, as it was generally called for short—our headquarters during our explorations of temples, which included several besides Borobodur; and there, more than in any other place, the old Java seemed to live and breathe and have its being. The reins of local government were actually in the hands of the Dutch "Resident" and the Sultan was shorn of his power; but the latter still lived in his vast palace—the Kraton—an enclosure a mile square in the heart of the city, its courtyards peopled with countless retainers, its pavilions, where dancing girls performed, rich with carved teakwood and gleaming with marble and crystal. At Pason Gedeh, about four miles from the city, was the royal mausoleum, its gray marble tombs, each with a canopy of stiff white paper cambric, crowded in a small teakwood temple surrounded by an open cemetery and approached through outer courts with walls and gates of great beauty. The reverent keepers were picturesquely clad figures of great dignity and apparently approved our demeanor, for they led us to an enclosure and showed us the sacred turtle—a great white indolent-looking creature with an evil expression —lolling in a stagnant pool.

Near the Kraton's entrance was a "factory" where beautiful hammered and engraved brass was worked—a series of small thatched huts with a primitive bamboo lathe and laborers squatting on the ground and manipulating crude equipment. Meanwhile, batik was being made within the shelter of the Taman Sari (Water Castle). This marvel of subterranean architecture, designed as a pleasure house by a Portuguese for a Javanese Sultan, stood in ruins; but it had been a veritable Oriental Trianon, and the remains of the guard rooms, the bathing pool of the "first Princess" and the Sultan's chamber—with a stream of water flowing under his bed to cool it!—could still be seen; it was easy to picture the scenes of sensuous splendor once enacted there.

The native markets in Djokja were the most colorful and vital of all we saw; and the native plays were still given there, to the accompaniment of a discordant orchestra composed of crude drums, xylophones and gongs. In the play to which we went the performance was opened by two dancing girls, beautifully formed; long brightly colored scarves floated from their sarongs; their faces were heavily powdered and painted at the sides to simulate additional locks of hair; they moved with a gliding, sinuous rhythm, extremely graceful but far too serpentine for my taste. They were followed by comedians, hideously masked and grotesquely clad; then the handsome hero—he really was handsome —made his appearance and, after vanquishing numerous enemies in mortal combat and overcoming the opposition of his chosen lady's father to his suit, brought the drama to its thrilling climax and eventual happy ending.

Between Bandoeng and Garoet lay some of the most famous tea estates in Java, and I was especially pleased at an invitation to spend a night on one of the plantations. My hostess was a charming Californian married to one of the great Dutch planters. She was truly the chatelaine of the domain, for their plantation had never been taken under the jurisdiction of the Dutch government and the old feudal laws of allegiance to the liege lord still prevailed; the tenants were the planter's vassals and he was magistrate, judge and ruler all in one, and lived in sumptuous state. There were twenty-three servants in the mansion and gardens which surrounded it; a swimming pool, a stable of thoroughbreds, tennis courts, a golf course, a garage full of cars—with any or all of which fortunate guests were free to amuse themselves. Cards which lay on the desk of each perfectly appointed guest room were as expressive of concern for the visitor's comfort and convenience as the pamphlet at Government House in Singapore. The mails, you were informed, left at such and such hours; luncheon, dinner and tea were so and so. "Please fill in the answers to these questions before you go in to dine: Will you breakfast in your room or on the veranda? What time would you like to be called, or will you ring? Do you wish early tea or coffee, and will you have toast or dry biscuits with it?"

But orders that servants should or should not unpack for guests were apparently not covered in any way; our nine-thirty dinner, served with infinite ceremony, was followed by conversation that lasted until one-thirty in the morning; and when I returned, exhausted, to my room, I found that though I was leaving early in the forenoon, every one of my possessions had been removed from my suitcases and dressing bag. The work was magnificently done. All the dresses were on hangers, all the shoes in precise rows, all the underwear piled neatly in bureau drawers. Even the jewel box had been emptied and each brooch and ring placed on a separate piece of cotton, ready for immediate choice. My nightgown lay on the bed, spread invitingly out so I could easily slip into it, but I had no chance to do so. It took me the rest of the night to repack.

Insulinde was ruled by numerous Dutch governors and residents—for the Sultans of Djokja and Solo had only nominal power and the native "regents" in the various cities even less—and, over all, the Dutch Governor General, as direct representative of the Crown, had viceregal power, a salary twice as large as that of the President of the United States and three magnificent palaces for his residences. We were thrilled to receive an invitation from this illustrious personage to spend a week end with him at his country palace at Chimpanas, in the heart of the mountains, but disappointed that the date mentioned was later than that of our intended departure from Java and there seemed no way of altering our plans again, since Henry's illness had already put us far behind schedule. We had to decline. Close on the heels of our written regrets came a second invitation, asking us to lunch at the palace in Buitenzorg instead.

We left Garoet for the last time, met Mrs. Hoover, who was to act as our sponsor, at the hotel in Buitenzorg and received our final instructions for such an important occasion. A message came, saying we were to enter the palace grounds by the central gate, usually kept closed, and we followed directions but allowed time to drive slowly through the botanical garden which encircled the residence like a park. Then we traversed a wide lawn where gentle antelope were grazing and approached the entrance to the palace, which was comparable to those of Europe in size and splendor. Here we were met by Colonel Brewer, the Intendant of the Palace and first aide-de-camp to His Excellency Heer Fock, and Mrs. Brewer, his official hostess. (Though the Governor General, long a widower, had recently remarried, the ceremony had been by proxy and the bride was still in Holland; the wedding had caused much comment in official circles and seemed to smack of medieval times no less than the feudal system of the great tea estates!)

We took our places—ladies on one side, men on the other—in the marble-floored, damask-hung hall, a distant door was opened, and "His Excellency, the Governor-General" was announced. We curtsied and bowed; then, when a genial, unpretentious looking and plainly dressed man approached with a second aide-de-camp and greeted us, we curtsied and bowed again. (Though there were no other indications of ceremony or formality, the same procedure was repeated at the time he took his leave of us in the pleasant chintz-hung sitting room to which we were taken after luncheon.) Presentations over, the Governor-General escorted me into the spacious and almost regal dining room, at one end of which was a fine portrait of Queen Wilhelmina. The delicious meal was simply served; the conversation, in English, was general. We spoke of mutual acquaintances—Governor-General Wood of the Philippines and Johneer de Graeff, then Dutch Minister to the United States, but soon to replace Heer Fock as Governor-General of Insulinde. Comparisons of American, British and Dutch colonial governments were made, as well as of various national and international customs. When we turned to more personal matters, he told me his son, a musician of note who lived in New York, had married a beautiful American girl and spoke with pride and delight of his small grandson.

"An American baby," I said maliciously.

"Certainly not," he replied instantly, "a Dutch baby. The finest in the world."

On land, Insulinde stood for tropics mastered and rendered productive and remunerative and for national characteristics of two alien races kept intact and inviolate; and permeating their life together was an almost unearthly beauty. At sea, a different aspect of the characteristic colonial attitude prevailed, unsentimental and somewhat arbitrary, though sane and sound. The *Indrapoera,* a brand-new motor ship making its first run to Colombo, was as typically Dutch as the *Melchior Traub,* and we had a much longer experience of it.

Breakfast on the bridge was a frequent occurrence, for Captain Boon was the most hospitable master we encountered in the course of our travels. He was also the most inveterate bridge player, except for our

Peking associates, and as deliberate as they were speedy in achieving a rubber. Since by now we had run into a number of local conventions, I decided it might be prudent to inquire if there were any which Captain Boon favored, so that I would have a better chance of conforming to them, especially as I am never at my most alert early in the morning and this was the time he almost invariably preferred for a game. "I play according to the rules of the Knickerbocker Club of New York," Captain Boon informed me, so severely that I knew my question was considered unworthy of any one with pretensions to being a serious bridge player. And this in the middle of the Indian Ocean at eight o'clock in the morning!

Part Eight

Letters From Afar: Suez and West

Chapter 44

I SHALL always think of the sea trip from Colombo to Alexandria as one of the pleasantest I have ever taken. We left in the glow of a sunset under a crescent moon, sailed for days over a glassy sea while the crescent slowly expanded, slipped past islands fringed with twinkling lights at dusk and glaring under the noonday sun as we skirted the coast of Italian Somaliland. When we entered the Red Sea, we found a fresh breeze ruffling its mirrored surface and blowing across the rosy cliffs of Arabia—a breeze so cool that we shortened our afternoon swim and unearthed coats to wrap around us as we watched the afterglow. Sinai was veiled in mist, but I did not share my fellow passengers' disappointment at seeing it thus—for was it not so veiled when Moses spent his wondrous vigil there, with a "thick cloud upon the mount"? And when we came to the place from which we could catch a distant glimpse of "Elim, where there were twelve wells of water and three score and ten palm trees," I wished we might disembark and "encamp there by the waters" as did those weary travelers centuries ago, so verdant and lovely did the still spot seem to me.

The unwritten law that steamships must arrive in port at ungodly hours and unfortunate passengers must be roused at the convenience of inspecting Quarantine officers remained unshattered when we reached Suez. At five o'clock a merciless gong summoned us to "pass the doctors"; having done so, everyone, whether leaving the ship or not, was obliged to have his passport examined and stamped. However, my righteous indignation at all this was not sufficient to keep me from going back to bed and sound sleep—only to be roused again two hours later by Larry with the news that we were entering the canal and I had better hurry on deck.

Once more, I did not leave it all day, not even at mealtime, for the head steward, with unusual thoughtfulness and competence, arranged that both lunch and dinner should be served on the veranda; and I am everlastingly thankful that I was not persuaded to disembark at Suez for Cairo, because in its own way the Suez Canal is no less beautiful than the Panama Canal, and I feel that a trip around the world without the opportunity to make this comparison must lack something very essential. Panama has the great locks and sufficient breadth for two large ships; Suez is at sea level and so narrow at some points that a single vessel churned the sand on both banks in passing and a ship could be delayed for hours when another had the right of way. At Panama, there was verdure, humidity, fertility, lovely misty grays and greens, the tropical jungles closing in at the water's edge; at Suez, there were tawny sands, dryness, barrenness, lovely clear blues and yellows, the limitless undulating desert. Here and there was a tiny clump of palms, a cluster of mud cottages, hobbled camels at rest, donkeys nosing among the scrubby cactus plants, draped figures coming and going; beyond, caravans of laden camels led by other draped figures moved in slow and solemn processional. Evening came and on one side of us hung the round golden sun, on the other the round silver moon, equidistant from the horizon, equally effulgent and huge. Then the sun melted mysteriously away in rosy vapor, and the moon rose higher and higher, and we saw the lights of Port Said glittering in the distance.

We lay at anchor that night with no opportunity to test the veracity of a fellow traveler who had gone out of his way to convince me that Port Said was not only the wickedest but the filthiest city in the world. In the morning, however, we woke to find ourselves drawn up at a spotless waterfront lined with trim buildings on a wide well-paved street, our ship surrounded by boats whose owners clamored to take us ashore. We yielded to one whose business card revealed his name to be Mohamed Mohamed Ayad, while the blue lettering on his white craft proclaimed its as *Jack Dempsey*. From the throng that pounced upon us when we landed, we secured—for twenty-five cents!—the services of a dragoman, which included keeping his colleagues at bay, showing us the sights, directing us to shops and carrying the purchases we made in them, and hiring two carriages, each drawn by white horses—though why Henry, who never can be persuaded to ride on or behind one if he can help it, should have insisted on this touch, I do not know.

Our pleasant impression of the waterfront continued and we enjoyed our wanderings. But most of all we enjoyed sitting in the open air café of the New Bar—in Port Said any and every restaurant was called a bar—drinking Turkish coffee, piping hot, thick and sweet, and watching the world go by. The New Bar was on one corner of a broad intersection and on the opposite corner was the Splendid Bar; and as pedestrians approached, each establishment's mustachioed proprietor rushed forward and importuned them to patronize his; the commotion subsided only when one or the other was victorious and was renewed with the appearance of each potential customer.

This diversion alone would have kept the coffee sipping from becoming monotonous, but there were many others: graceful black-clad women passing by, their limpid eyes soft above transparent veils held in place by golden ornaments; vendors of cooling drinks, brass cymbals in one hand, a brass cup in the other and a huge stick of ice protruding from the container of burnished brass slung across their shoulders; countless hawkers who strove to hang glass beads around our necks and thrust souvenir spoons into our mouths despite our struggles; bootblacks and fortune tellers, each in their own way trying to brighten our existence. The most persistent little magician of all ignored our lack of cordiality and performed his baffling tricks under our very faces, making us laugh in spite of ourselves. "Galli, galli, galli," he called, producing a baby chick from his multicolored vest; the next minute his grubby hand held an egg as large as the tiny bird. "Excuse me, Mr. MacGregor," he said as he apparently plucked an egg from Henry's nose. "Give me a piece of money, Mr. Ferguson," he demanded of Larry. We wondered if all his previous patrons had been Scotch. "No, don't be afraid. You get it back. Put it in your hand. Is it there? Well, now see. Open your hand—all gone! I take it out of your ear. Galli, galli, galli. Thank you very much, Mrs. Campbell."

Replete with coffee, we changed to ice cream, packed smooth and hard in tall silver goblets; and still the gay, shifting panorama continued until the afternoon was nearly gone and we must rejoin the ship. As we drove away in our ancient victorias, our host waved us a fond farewell with a large white napkin—"Good-bye, good-bye! Don't forget the New Bar!" Our dragoman handed over to us the trophies of the day: a round box of Turkish paste; a huge bunch of red roses; a glistening shawl, a pair of tiny tasseled slippers. Mohamed Mohamed Ayad was waiting in the *Jack Dempsey* to return us to the *President Harrison;* and soon we were steaming toward the breakwater, past the statue of De Lesseps, splendid and solitary on the long pier—not the conquered De Lesseps of Panama, but the joyful and triumphant De Lesseps, immortalized in the Suez Canal, in building which he both united and divided the continents of Asia and Africa.

True to form, we arrived in Alexandria at five-thirty in the morning; nevertheless, we missed the nine o'clock train to Cairo, for among the

countries which had so far made landing formalities tedious and difficult, Egypt took the cake. In fact, we encountered so many difficulties
that we ended by feeling thankful that we were able to catch the twelve
o'clock, and not even the first sight of the Nile roused any enthusiasm in
our weary breasts. Fortunately, the trip took only three hours, and once
we were settled in comfortable quarters at an excellent hotel and refreshed by tea, we reminded each other that the moon we had seen,
round and brilliant above the canal two nights earlier, was on the wane
and if we wished to have our first glimpse of the pyramids beneath its
radiance, we should try to do so that evening after dinner. Abdelkarim
Aboud—"contractor for upper and lower Egypt," according to his card
—who had been engaged to guide us was waiting, a snowy turban
wound round his head, a flowing robe of ultramarine sweeping about
him.

The drive out of the city seemed all too short; it was something of a
shock, also, to catch our first sight of the Great Pyramid above the top
of a clanging trolley, to see the well-paved road swing in front of a
large hotel and curve upward almost to the base of the mighty structure.
Then, suddenly, all sense of disappointment was gone; we turned a corner and the desert began to drift across the road; the car would go no
further. We got out, sinking ankle deep in warm sand. The trolley line,
the garish hotel, the glare and noise had miraculously disappeared. Sitting on the slope beside the Sphinx, we could see by the light of that
huge moon and the lesser lights of countless stars the Giza Pyramids—
the three large monuments which were the tombs of kings and the three
small ones which were the tombs of queens—casting their long soft
shadows at our very feet; the "Step Pyramid" and the small perfect
black cones of Memphis and Sakhara rising clear cut in the distance;
the pitched tents of some nomads, the huddled huts of a small lighted
village; the graceful robes of our dragoman, like bright blue sails in the
buoyant breeze, and nothing else but that endless majesty of sand and
sky, that dim divinity of the desert. We must have sat there for hours,
too awed to speak, and still there came no discordant sound to mar that
matchless stillness, that perfect sense of space. At last, obeying tradition, each whispered to the Sphinx the question upon whose answer depended his greatest happiness; and, as ever, the Sphinx did not answer.

We returned again and again to the Pyramids and were delightfully
entertained several times at the "Harvard Camp" near them where the
great archaeologist, Dr. George Andrew Reisner, lived with his wife
and daughter. We were also privileged to see the remarkable discoveries
made in his recent excavations, the results of which were not to be
made public until the following fall, and which vied in significance with

the discoveries at Luxor. Dr. Reisner had the faculty of making ancient history glow with vitality. "The twelve queens of this dynasty, d'you see," he would interrupt himself to say in the midst of a learned discourse, "were beautiful women, all of them. Perfectly charming." And then would follow a minute description of their little vanities and graces. "Rameses the Second," he remarked casually, "used to race his horses right out there. He was a superb horseman himself, d'you see, and had one of the finest stables that ever existed." It almost seemed as if we could hear the hoofbeats through the starlit silence.

It was strangely thrilling to dine there beside the pyramids and the desert in such a peaceful and, at the same time, in such a stimulating way; but there were many other dinners which I enjoyed no less. The time has never come—and probably never will—when I shall cease to enjoy putting on my best clothes and going to a party, simply because it *is* a party! And fortunately, I had been able to replenish my depleted wardrobe, for it was even easier in Cairo than in Shanghai to buy Paris clothes and my first Lucien LeLong dress was purchased in Egypt. Only in Peking had our social calendar been so crowded. For instance, our Consul and Mrs. North Winship entertained constantly and elegantly at luncheon, tea and dinner in their home; the American Minister and Mrs. Williamson Howell gave a dinner at the Mohamed Aly Club, where we dined on the roof above the noise and dust of the city; and there was also the all day fete of the Prince and Princess Lotfallah, held on one of the great Egyptian holidays: a mammoth marquee of multi-colored hand appliqué supported by poles of twisted red and white was set in the midst of a famous rose garden and more than two hundred were served luncheon.

The residential districts of Garden City and Gezirah were adorned with many fine mansions, surrounded by lovely flowers and trees, in the midst of private parks. The broad avenues were bordered with blue jacaranda trees in full bloom, and the wide modern streets were intersected with plazas similar to those in Washington; the narrow ancient streets wound under carved arches between the tiny open shops of tent makers and rug vendors; the Nile, flowing through the midst of it all, was fringed with jaunty houseboats. Aside from its beauty, Cairo teemed with such a variety of sights that it could not fail to charm the stranger within its gates. He could wander through the bazaars or climb to the citadel or enter the courtyard of the Mohamed Aly mosque, where the designs of the stained glass windows were reflected in the priceless carpet and the crystal globes and prisms of myriad lamps gleamed and all was still and spacious and serene. Then he could go out on the parapet and see on one side the quarries from which the stones for the pyramids were taken and, on the other side the whole great city patterned below him, and all about it the endless desert and the endless sky. Or he could find his way to Old Cairo, to see where Moses was discovered in the bulrushes and the still holier place—now sheltered by a Coptic church—where Mary and Joseph and the Young Child took refuge after the Flight. Most of us do not think of Egypt as a Christian country, though there are grounds for the claim that it has the oldest Christian church in the world, which was founded by St. Mark, and that it has given the largest number of martyrs to the faith. The early Coptic Christians were descended directly from the first Egyptian kings, and their own descendants—then numbering about one-tenth of the Egyptian population—were among the finest, the most representative and the most influential of all classes.

The first Egyptian house I entered in Cairo was the beautiful home of such a Christian family—the Khayatts. Habib Khayatt Bey was a member of the Egyptian Senate and his charming wife was one of the country's leading feminists, as was her niece, Mme Fahmy Wissa—also a senator's wife—who was her aunt's house guest at the time of my visit. The educated Christian women of Egypt had discarded the veil about sixty years earlier, and neither Mme Wissa nor Mme Khayatt led a life any more secluded or restricted than mine—indeed, it was most interesting to me, as an American senator's wife, to compare notes with them!

The Egyptian delegates to the International Suffrage Convention in Rome three years earlier had made a profound impression upon me, and therefore I was delighted to see them again. The second Egyptian house to which I was invited was that of Mme Charaoui Pasha, mother-in-law of the current Egyptian Minister to Washington; and she and her niece, Mlle Ceza Nabouroui, editor of the feminist magazine *L'Egyptienne,* who lived with her had been the admired delegates! They were both Moslems and though the Moslem women were slower to discard the veil and receive men than the Christians, the boys were included in my invitation. Our Paris-clad hostesses welcomed us in a drawing room which could easily have been mistaken for a Paris salon and the conversation was carried on entirely in French. The Egyptian ladies I met were almost all beautifully dressed and very beautiful themselves, with clear complexions, soft dark eyes and a very graceful carriage; and Mme. Charaoui Pasha, whose youthful charm made it difficult to believe she had grown children, was one of the loveliest.

Egypt's feminist movement was almost entirely the outgrowth of the national movement for an independent country, since it was not until they had proved their mettle working for liberty with their fathers and brothers, husbands and sons that the women either attempted or asked to obtain other benefits. And my sympathies were stirred and my interest roused by the movement for independence. It was a logical part of the already world wide surging resentment that subject races, many of whom could boast an older civilization than their directors, felt toward the races who sought to govern them in their own lands. We were meeting it in the Philippines; the Dutch were meeting it in Java; the Japanese were meeting it in Korea; the British were meeting it in China and India and Egypt. In China, it had already resulted in civil war, the leadership of Chang Tso Lin in the north and the formation of the Kuomintang by Sun Yat Sen in the south—all of which we had seen with our own eyes.

The British brought forth many of the same arguments we did in the Philippines: they had brought peace and order out of chaos, affording protection to natives and foreigners alike; they had developed natural resources, conserved water; they had provided a stable government, controlled, if not eliminated, corruption in politics. Nor did the similarity end there: they discoursed on the "sacred trust" which the greater power held for the lesser, while the fact was that the cotton grown in Egypt was as necessary to the British as the sugar, pineapples and other commodities of the Philippines were to us. Even as we needed a naval base in the Orient, so did the British need a sure and safe passage to India through the Suez Canal; and its unavailability for international use has meant a great and disastrous change in current history. But the justness of achieving British needs, without regard for the feeling of the "other fellow" in the matter, was sometimes taken for granted in a positively ingenuous manner. For instance, a leading editorial in the *Egyptian Gazette,* a British paper, said in part, "We have before stated . . . that though Egyptians may be concerned with the boundaries of their state, England has the boundaries of her Empire to consider, and the boundaries of the Empire include the connecting links, the lines of communication. These lines cross through Egypt, and we will not allow them either to be broken or to be endangered. Before Egyptian politicians can usefully discuss relations with England, *they must once and for all recognize this right of ours and accept it wholeheartedly, recognizing its full significance.* We are the judges of what our Imperial safety needs on this point, and we do not accept that either Egypt or anybody else should explain to us to what extent these needs may be satisfied."

This was almost equivalent to saying that if Mexico, as well as Canada, happened to belong to the British, we should at once and wholeheartedly recognize their right to occupy the United States indefinitely! Our attitude under such circumstances would hardly have been one of silent submission. In making statements of this kind, Britain has been

her own worst enemy, and though in 1926 her American Colonies—
namely the United States—and Ireland were the only countries under
her control which had successfully rebelled against such expressed policies, they had been at the root of many of her colonial difficulties. She
never believed in the homely adage that more flies are caught with
honey than with vinegar; she poured out the vinegar lavishly and stinted
with the honey. She did not believe in "the right of nations great and
small to choose their own way of life and of obedience"; she believed in
the right of Britannia to rule the waves. Perhaps that is one of the reasons why she has lost it.

But let us be fair; she truly believed this, she did not pretend to believe it. She was so intrinsically honest and sincere that she might well
serve as a model in this regard. She might not have had tact, but she
had integrity; she might not have been generous, but she meant to be
just; she commanded both admiration and respect because, though she
used force to accomplish her ends, she used it wisely and well; her
claim that she could create order out of chaos and afterward maintain
that order was based on solid fact. She believed in decent living, clean
sportsmanship, mental enlightenment and spiritual guidance; and she
lived up to her belief.

When we arrived in Egypt, Henry though thin was in excellent health
again, with no restrictions on either his diet or his activities; his recovery seemed nothing short of miraculous. On the other hand, I myself
was beginning to show the strain of long-continued anxiety, coupled
with a very heavy working schedule to which I had managed to adhere
not only when it was combined with a crowded social calendar but
when I was physically unfit for it. Just before leaving Java, I had fallen
and twisted my ankle so badly that I had to go aboard the *Indrapoera*
on a stretcher—"our fourth embarkation via ambulance," as I noted
somewhat wryly on my calendar—and still I had contrived to get to
those famous bridge breakfasts of the Captain's. I was still experiencing
the not unusual difficulties that many Anglo-Saxon women have with
flooding if they are not accustomed to the tropics and remain in them
too long without a break; and since reaching Cairo, I had suffered a
sharp attack of "gypsy tummy"—also quite usual for the uninitiated.
All this had been troublesome and painful, but it had not been serious;
then I came down with tonsillitis and the doctor who had already treated
me for lesser ailments took what seemed to me a long time over a routine examination and finally said brusquely, "Have you had any trouble
with your heart before?" I must have shown some amazement, for he
added, still brusquely, "Well, you have now. It's functional, not organic.
But I can't advise you too strongly to keep absolutely quiet until I tell

you that you may get up again and then to go pretty slowly for a while after that." (I had almost forgotten about this episode, because for years my doctors have been saying, "You have no business to have such a remarkably good heart, considering how you abuse it." Then I found the entry on my Cairo calendar—at almost the same moment they had changed their tune and were saying the same thing the Cairo doctor had.)

At first I took this enforced physical inactivity very hard; we were already behind schedule on account of Henry's illness, and had been obliged to omit India from our itinerary because he was still not well enough for a long journey or able to face the heat of India's spring and summer. The short voyage to Java and the stay in high and healthful Garoet had provided one solution, but now we had to be back in the United States by the end of September so he could keep his Harvard commitments, and if our stay in Egypt were indefinitely prolonged, that would mean skipping some more countries which Mr. Bigelow was depending on me to visit and describe. In deep discouragement I wrote to my husband, "I have been under such terrific strain that at times I have seemed to feel my whole life crumbling; my boy, my work, everything else. But somehow I have struggled through and the work has gone forward without interruption until now. I have written Mr. B. that if he feels I have not lived up to my contract, I will come back and write about the missing countries some other time."

Fortunately, Mr. B. did not seem to feel that way at all. During a brief visit to New York, Harry called at his office and failed to find him in. He wrote Harry the next day and my husband sent me a copy of the letter, which read, in part, "The letters that Mrs. Keyes are sending back have been immensely satisfactory. I have been surprised at the high standard she has maintained, because Lord knows the trip she undertook was one that might be expected to upset anyone's writing ability. In spite of all her troubles, however, she maintains the even tenor of her work when she gets at the typewriter. If you are not already aware of it, I wish to advise you that you have a most remarkable wife. I do not know of another woman in the world who would or could do what she is doing."

This letter did a great deal to boost my morale, and since my mind was at rest as far as *Good Housekeeping* was concerned and I had not been forbidden to write, as long as I did this lying on a sofa, I took the unfinished scripts of *Queen Anne's Lace* and *The Safe Bridge* from the dispatch case, where they had lain practically untouched ever since I left home, and worked first on one and then on the other until I was able to be up again. This in itself represented a renewal of courage, for I was still without concrete assurance that any publisher would be interested in them and had only my own faith in them to support me.

Chapter 45

W HEN I left home on my trip around the world, I had a very elastic schedule, for to travel with a cast-iron timetable has always seemed to me, like the plague, something to be avoided. Nevertheless, I did have a few definite objectives in mind. I wished, for instance, to be in Peking for the opening of the Customs Conference and in Manila for the Christmas holidays. In each such case I attained my desire. Then another place and date combination began to imprint itself on my consciousness: Jerusalem on Ascension Day. Through the long weeks of delay and anxiety at Singapore, the short weeks of social activities and sightseeing in Java and the first vivid days among the "pleasures and palaces" of Cairo, the thought persisted until it became a definite hope, a definite plan and at last reality.

A train appeared to be our best means of approach. Ours left Cairo at six in the evening, reached Kantara a little after nine and was ferried across the Suez Canal—a proceeding that I felt involved needless delay, for a drawbridge would have shortened the tedious journey by several hours. We tried then to get what rest we could in our dusty and stuffy wagon-lit compartments and—

Waked the next morning to hear church bells ringing and see the soft gray-green of olive trees in the Holy Land.

It was about a two hours' journey from the village of our awakening to Jerusalem, the train winding slowly up a tortuous and barren ascent of rocky hills, unrelieved except for blurred gray-green patches. We passed many flocks of sheep and goats; heavily laden camels and donkeys; men and women with long white scarves floating from their heads, associated in our minds with "Bible pictures" rather than actuality. I was thrilled at the sight of a young woman in blue, so veiled, seated on a donkey and clasping a child in her arms, while a sturdy middle-aged man with a long staff trudged beside her, for this was the road the Holy Family had taken on the Flight into Egypt.

All too soon Jerusalem came in view and we found the American Consul and Mrs. Heizer, to whom we had wired, waiting at the station to meet us and take us at once to the Mount of Olives. Breakfastless—for there was no dining car on our train—we drove through the narrow streets until we gained the wider ones outside the city walls. We passed the Damascus Gate and the former German Hospice which had become the British High Commissioner's residence and came at last to the little domed Chapel of the Ascension, in the midst of a flagged court on the mountain's summit. It was a tiny octagonal building into which scarcely twenty persons could crowd. The services held there every year by the Franciscan Fathers were almost over; but beside the white marble frame surrounding the holy rock two candles burned and the air was sweet with the fragrance of flowers and incense, and pilgrims and priests came and went. We lingered, joining, after our own fashion, in the worship. Then we recrossed the court, climbed the steps of the slender minaret at its entrance and gazed, transfixed, at the scene before us. At our feet was the Holy City, walled, turreted and domed, pale creamy gold against a deep turquoise sky; in the distance the barren hills—"the wilderness of Judea"—were gold tinted, too; further still, the ruins of Jericho were etched; and the Dead Sea sparkled like a huge sapphire cupped in the hollow of the mountains, the slender tree-fringed Jordan flowing into it; more distant yet, along the horizon, lay the gleaming country of Trans-Jordania. Such a panorama, first viewed on such a day, was in itself a miracle—a miracle of earthly beauty transformed to heavenly beauty by the sacred things that have touched it; in its radiance, the miracle of the Risen Christ seemed less a mystery and more a reality than ever before.

The Mount of Olives in the morning, Bethlehem in the afternoon—nothing else would have sufficed that first day. I was very tired and slept for several hours at midday—a rare thing for me—so the cool of evening had already set in when we started for the City of the Star. On the way we passed the so-called Well of the Star; according to tradition, after the shepherds lost sight of their guiding beacon, they found its light reflected therein when they stopped to draw water. We also passed Rachel's tomb, erected at the place she died in giving birth to Benjamin. ("And Rachel died," the ancient story tells us, "and was buried on the way to Ephrath, which is Bethlehem. And Jacob set up a pillar upon her grave; that is the pillar of Rachel's grave until this day." I had been taught to read from the Bible by my maternal grandmother and had been an inveterate Bible reader ever since; and now I began to read even more omnivorously than usual in a Bible bound in olive wood which I purchased in Jerusalem.) The tomb, which was protected by a great dome, was opened only on the eve of the new moon; but we had not known this, so the tiny sickle cutting the luminous sky had no special significance for us beyond its own delicate beauty until we saw that the tomb's narrow entrance was ajar and learned it would not be again for another month. We entered and found candles burning and pilgrims beside the great sarcophagus, pressing their lips to it and reading aloud from the volumes of Holy Writ they carried.

The Well of the Star—the Tomb of Rachel—the Convent of St. Elias, facing the rock where the starving prophet, fleeing Jezebel's wrath, is believed to have rested and received refreshment from the angel before continuing his journey—in the distance the fields of Boaz over which Ruth walked and "gleaned after the reapers"; in the same fields, centuries laters, "Shepherds watched over their flocks by night"—and finally, the serene little hillside village of Bethlehem: a fruitful village, whose very name means "House of Bread"; a comely village, where married women wore tall white coifs and all women dressed in a style of picturesque medieval loveliness and where both men and women lived and moved with a certain grave stateliness, famous throughout the countryside; a happy village, untouched by the tragedy of Jerusalem—a village of the birth of kings, not a city of the death of sufferers—for did not both David and Jesus first see the light of day there? A Christian village in a country of varied faiths, where churches and orphanages and religious institutions seemed actually to outnumber all other buildings and to proclaim the spirit which prompted their construction.

The Basilica of the Nativity was the first of these structures we entered. According to tradition it was the oldest Christian church then still in use, originally built—though it had undergone many changes and alterations in the meantime—by Emperor Constantine in 330 A. D. The nave and aisles were divided by handsome Corinthian columns, and the whole edifice was imposingly simple and spacious. Like the Church of the Holy Sepulchre, it was shared—not, unfortunately, with complete harmony—by different communities: the Latins (Roman Catholics), Greek Orthodox, Abyssinians, Armenians and Coptics, each with their own chapels and appointed hours of service. The feeling between the Latins and Greeks seemed particularly bitter; but however lamentable this might be, none had questioned the authenticity of the site and all agreed as to its sanctity while longing and striving to possess it.

Descending the narrow steps behind the choir, we entered the Grotto of the Nativity. It was very silent there, the stone walls closing in, the soft blackness relieved only by the flickering glow from hanging lamps. A golden star marked the place of the Nativity; an oratory, richly hung, marked the place where the manger stood. The prosperous inn with no room for the tired mother and the humble carpenter because it was full of wealthier guests disappeared into oblivion, the stable cave became a shrine for all the world. And so for the second time that day we paused to worship, and returned to Jerusalem through the quiet dusk at peace with the world.

Jerusalem, inevitably, was a city that aroused many conflicting emotions; and I believe this may have been due less to its own varied attributes than to the conflicting characteristics of those who visited it. I have known trusting, unreasoning souls who, expecting it to be altogether beautiful and perfect, literally a golden city in the midst of a land of milk and honey, have come away from it saddened and disillusioned and who, because of this, have declared their faith "gone forever." I have known enraptured pilgrims who were so filled with thoughts of a holy vision that they saw nothing of a human and mundane reality. After I went there myself, I felt that all such persons—one group no less than the other   were looking about them with eyes that did not see clearly and hearts that did not fully understand and that therefore they missed a very great and rare experience. The Holy Land is holy because holy things have happened there, because holy men—one Holy Man, especially—have lived there, and not because it is ethereal. It is a real land, as real as New Hampshire and Vermont are to me—cold in winter, hot in summer, dry and rainy by turns. It has its beautiful places and its places which are not beautiful at all. Jerusalem, as we saw it, lacked the beauty of open spaces, of green parks and flowing fountains; and though there were pleasant residential sections and many pleasant people living in them, as I was privileged to discover, it seemed a city of churches and mosques and synagogues, of hospices and orphan asylums, rather than a city of homes; the city of prelate and priest, patriarch and pilgrim, rather than the city of family and friend. The sun shone at midday with a harsh glare, and under this, one was made weary walking on the stony pavements and over the tortuous ascents; most of the streets within the walls were too narrow to admit vehicles, and when the wind swept through the passages, the fine dust penetrated every nook and corner and caused acute discomfort. The omnipresent water scarcity was at times a serious consideration, and hotels which met current standards were absolutely nonexistent; the one where we stayed, recommended as the city's best, was by far the poorest we had encountered since leaving the States. (Now, of course, the King David Hotel is one of the best in the world.) I must confess that the drinkable coffee, comfortable beds and intelligent service of Egypt were extremely welcome on our return there, particularly after the terrible desert sandstorm we passed through on the way.

But you could enumerate the city's disadvantages in a sentence. To enumerate its beauties and glories would take volumes. Jerusalem, like Port Said, had been maligned as a place of evil sights and smells, but we found it so clean that there was nothing to offend our senses. It was a city of lovely arches, of graceful columns and carved doorways. There was a picture at every turn: bright pink geraniums hanging in a heavy cluster from a barred window; a slender spire soaring through an oval opening; a pure-white statue of St. Anne with her daughter Mary gleaming through gray stone. And as for stories, every stone seemed to sing with one! The Dome of the Rock, for instance, with its jewel-like windows and rich mosaics and glossy tiles, erected in the ninth century by Moslems and still occupied by them. It was one of their holiest places and was often referred to as "the mosque of Omar." During the Crusades, the Templars used it as a Christian church; the rock was the one upon which Abraham prepared to sacrifice Isaac, where David erected an altar. Moreover, not only was this the site of Solomon's temple, but in its courtyard the columns of Herod's temple still stood. In this very place, the Child Jesus remained, "sitting in the midst of the doctors, both hearing them, and asking them questions"; eighteen years later, He drove out the money changers because they had turned the house of prayer into a den of thieves.

Is there another place which sings so many stories simultaneously?

Very generally, the cleanliness of Jerusalem was credited to the British, who, since the war, had held a mandate over Palestine, previously under the control of Turkey. A British High Commissioner, assisted by an advisory council composed of Christians, Moslems and Jews, acted as the head of the government; and though there had been slight disturbances and the usual grumbling, the dissatisfaction so prevalent in Egypt seemed practically nonexistent, and the majority of inhabitants appeared duly grateful for the benefits that had accrued to them under British rule. The current High Commissioner, Lord Plumer, a former General, was a delightful old gentleman—humorous, able and benign; both he and his wife, who shared her husband's delicacy of wit, were not only greatly admired but much beloved. We lunched pleasantly with them at the hospice-palace and saw the beautiful view from His Excellency's study, the magnificent chapel and Lady Plumer's rare collections of fans and miniatures. The picture that I carried away from Jerusalem of Lady Plumer as she presided at luncheon in a dress of mauve satin and creamy lace flounces was delightful; but so was the one of her, more severely but no less elegantly clad in black satin and black lace, as she came down the aisle beside her husband after morning service at St. George's Cathedral while the congregation respectfully stood, and the one of her at a Boy Scout rally held in the shadow of the same church, when the High Commissioner reviewed the youngsters.

There were others who gave me happy memories to take away from Jerusalem, among them Mrs. Bertha Vester, whose husband was the manager of the American Colony, an institution with religious aims based on non-dogmatic Christianity. The Colony was self-supporting and maintained an orphanage and an industrial school. It was located in an attractive group of buildings originally erected as a residence for a wealthy Moslem, and we had tea there one afternoon in the common room; more delightful still was our visit to the Colony's country house at Ain-Karim, a lovely little village some miles from Jerusalem which is the traditional birthplace of John the Baptist and scene of the Visitation when Mary went to stay with Elizabeth. We stopped at the church— dimly restful and sweet—which commemorates those events before we began the steep and rocky ascent to the Colony's property, but it was on its terrace that the peace and power of the place really began to make themselves felt. Below us lay the vineyards, each with its own little tower, recalling the parable of the "householder which planted a vine- yard and hedged it round about and digged a winepress in it and built a tower." There were hundreds of just such vineyards throughout Pales- tine, but nowhere were they better viewed than at Ain-Karim. On the hills the pointed cypresses sheltered church and convent and dwelling —and there were many, for the feeling of homes seemed to permeate the air. Further off was the gray-green blur of olive trees, the glossy waxed foliage of fig trees. Over all reigned blessed, healing silence, a sense of perfect security and happiness. It was easy to imagine the Mag- nificat with which Mary saluted her cousin in such a setting. "My soul doth magnify the Lord," she exclaimed, "and my spirit hath rejoiced in God my Saviour." We seemed to catch its echo that day.

So the picture of Mrs. Vester, who took us to Ain-Karim, Mrs. Ves- ter with her gentle voice and sweet smile, her dark eyes and fine soft hair, is placed beside that of Lady Plumer in my happy memories. Mrs. Heizer—droll, cordial, thoughtful—is there too. It was she who real- ized the boys would enjoy the Saturday evening dance at the Sport Club, that I would find pleasure in a dinner at which the various Con- suls stationed in Jerusalem were present, and that we would all welcome a quiet game of bridge when the day's sightseeing was over. Her wel- come never failed, so we were at the Consulate daily, sometimes with other guests or playing cards, sometimes listening to Mr. Heizer's wonderful tales of Constantinople and Greece and Bagdad; he had spent thirty years in the Near East, and we never tired of sitting on the magic carpet he spread for us.

It was also a pleasure to have tea at their home with Miss Sophia Berger and Miss Henrietta Szold, for these two friends were leaders in Palestine's Zionist Movement—the organized endeavor to establish a national home there for the Jewish people. These brilliant and remarkable women were also extremely active in Hadassah, the women's Zionist organization with headquarters in America, which was doing philanthropic work in Palestine. It had started fourteen years earlier with less than two hundred members and about five hundred dollars; its membership had grown to sixteen thousand and its assets to nearly five hundred thousand when I was in Palestine. It maintained four hospitals, four infant welfare stations, a nurses' training school, a milk kitchen and numerous other institutions; it distributed luncheons in kindergartens to undernourished children, milk to needy babies and clothing and linen to fourteen hospitals and homes. Christians, Moslems and Jews were all its beneficiaries; I visited several of its centers and had an opportunity to observe how well conducted they were. I also listened attentively to Miss Szold's outline of plans for enriching the impoverished but naturally fertile Palestinian soil, for developing agriculture and industries and utilizing the phosphates of the Dead Sea. All these were afterward done.

Lady Plumer, Mrs. Vester and Miss Berger were all members of the "Council of Nine," elected each year by the Union of Women for Social Work in Palestine, which was made up of forty-five different societies. The Council, upon which the wife of Jerusalem's Governor, the wife of its Attorney-General, and the wife of the Anglican Bishop also served, had an Arab member, as well as several provincial members, and acted, as Mrs. Vester put it, as the "liaison officer between the philanthropies and the government." The government had never refused any request of this Council, and it could point with justifiable pride to its accomplishments, especially in the maintenance of trained midwives, which had helped to reduce infant mortality, and in educational work throughout the provinces.

There were countless interesting excursions from Jerusalem, and best of all, we went to Nazareth—a trip indivisibly connected in my mind with Near East Relief. Mr. Blatchford was in charge of this work in Palestine, and when we were on the housetop of the Austrian Hospice, where he lived, watching the sun go down and the stars come out and listening to the call to prayer from the minarets of eight different mosques, I mentioned my wishes to visit Nazareth and to see something of the Near East activities. He told me one of the most interesting orphanages was there and asked if we would not like to make the trip in his car and visit the home; we gratefully accepted and set out the following morning.

The country was rather bare and rugged—"meager" was the fitting word Mr. Blatchford applied to it—but it was relieved by thriving orchards and glossy vineyards and a profusion of wild flowers: scarlet poppies, yellow cactus blossoms and pastel-tinted hollyhocks, whose name, I learned, dated from the Crusades. "Hock" was Arabic for "mallow," and the Templars called that which they found blooming in Palestine the "holy hocks." By noon we could see snow-crowned Mount Hebron in the distance, rising much as Fujiyama does; nearer to us was Mount Tabor, the site of the Transfiguration, with a shining white church on its summit; beyond the hot and dusty plain we were crossing, Nazareth clung to a hillside, cool and quiet and shaded above the heat. I had not expected to see it so beautiful, for in Bible times it was considered an insignificant place and its inhabitants were regarded as "countrified" by the sophisticated Jerusalemites, nor had it come into greater prominence since. But like Bethlehem and Ain-Karim, Nazareth possessed a hallowed and sweet and peaceful loveliness somehow denied larger and more cosmopolitan places, a quality which is the heritage of quiet villages everywhere. Of course, those of us who have lived much in small secluded spots do not need to be told this, even though it is sometimes difficult to remain undisturbed and content in the face of condescending urban friends who do not know they have missed much which has been vouchsafed to us.

It was two o'clock when we reached Nazareth, so immediately after a tardy lunch at a small German inn there we started over the hills to the Sea of Galilee. The scarlet pomegranate blossoms along our way burst into even greater luxuriance in the orchards of Cana—what gorgeous wedding decorations they would have been, rivaling in splendid color the "best wine kept until the last." Past the village outskirts, we came upon a shepherd and his flock, all obedient but one—a small black lamb that lingered when the others turned from the highway. Patiently the shepherd retrieved the renegade and persuaded him to join his whiter brethren. Finally, from the heights above the valley, we saw the clear brilliant oval of the Sea, its smooth surface unruffled, the mountains beyond it, Tiberias and Capernaum nestling beside it. It was a picture of sapphire and gold, as are most in Palestine—blue sky, blue mountains, luteous villages and hills. It was warm and still, not with the languorous warmth and stillness of the tropics, but with the more vigorous atmosphere of temperate lands—an atmosphere that would stir to effort rather than lull to inertia. And not once in the course of the entire trip had we surveyed a more beautiful view.

There was still time after our return to Nazareth to visit the Virgin's Well and see the women drawing water from it, as they had done for centuries; to see the carpenter shop of the Near East Relief, where boys were taught a useful trade and, glancing up from their work, could see the remains of that other carpenter shop directly opposite them in which long ago another Boy grew strong with the labor that was to fit Him physically to "go about His Father's business." Lastly, we spent an hour in the Church of the Annunciation, sheltering the spot where the Word was made Flesh, and the grotto beneath the church, again, like the one in Bethlehem, was pervaded by soft darkness, penetrated only by the light from suspended golden lamps.

In the grotto hung a painting of the Angel Gabriel, gray clad and bearing lilies; and this painting brings to my mind afresh a sermon I heard while I was in the Holy Land. The subject was doing God's Will; but it was not presented in a very interesting way, so I sat turning the pages of my hymnal, glancing at the stained glass windows and so on. Then, suddenly, the preacher caught my attention.

"Why," he was saying, "can't we bring ourselves to do God's Will as unquestioningly as the angels do? Suppose Gabriel, when he was told to take Mary the message that she was to be the Mother of the Son of God, had said, 'Lord, I don't like that kind of errand. I think she's going to be very much misunderstood in Nazareth. It's going to be a very unpleasant situation. Do give up the idea.' Suppose the angel who was sent to the shepherds had objected, 'I think some other angel could do that better than I can. I don't like or understand shepherds very well. They're dirty people, they sleep with their flocks. In fact, they're not in my class at all.' Suppose the angel who ministered to Our Lord in Gethsemane had remonstrated, 'Oh, I can't bear to see such suffering. It upsets me terribly.' "

A fanciful conception, not based on cold fact? Perhaps. But cold facts can sometimes stand a little warming. At any rate, I never afterward experienced a period of rebellion in which that story did not help me.

We lingered so long in the quiet Church of the Annunciation that there was barely time for a hurried supper before we started for the orphanage, over one of the worst roads I have ever traveled. At our destination we found over a hundred rather shabby and dusty but obviously healthy and happy children housed in a large building formerly used as a stable. There was no heat in their dormitory, even in midwinter when the cold was intense there was only a small oil stove in their school-room, and winter and summer they bathed in a brook! They had bread and tea for breakfast, stew for dinner and bread and fruit for supper. Left homeless in the path of war, they had been gathered in, sheltered, fed and taught. Of course, their shelter and food seemed to me inade-quate, and I vowed then and there never to complain again about being "pestered" for Near East Relief. It took about six dollars a month to maintain a child at the Nazareth Orphanage and the teachers were paid very small salaries. I should not, however, give the idea that the evening was a sad one; quite the contrary. With teachers, the majority of the boys and a few invited guests for an audience, the rest of the boys gave us, between songs by the Glee Club, a dramatic performance based on the story of the prodigal son. All the parts were vividly and understand-ingly rendered, particularly that of the prodigal himself. His discontent in his father's house, his carousing among evil friends—"The prodigal son," read the program, "makes feast in a foreign land with his bad comrades, and he drunks and at last looses everything he has"—and his penitent return were all convincingly portrayed; and the scene where, clad in sheepskin, he sits among weeds, unable even "to eat from the foods of pigs," was made more realistic by off-stage grunts and snorts!

I had almost no disappointments in the Holy Land, but inevitably there were a few, and one of these was in the Church of the Holy Sepulchre. It ought, I think, to be the most beautiful cathedral in the world, but it was architecturally unimposing, badly in need of repair and decorated with indifferent taste. The first time I went there I was accompanied, despite my protests, by a Mohammedan guide whose English was shockingly bad and whose sense of sacredness was entirely lacking. He casually mumbled phrases which should have been pro-nounced with reverence, hastened from chapel to chapel and more than once tossed his fez on an altar before which we stopped. It was also ex-tremely repugnant to me to be asked for money, both by the priest who watched beside the Holy Sepulchre itself and the guard at Calvary. It seemed to me the Church should never have permitted this; though most visitors to the basilica would be more than glad to make an offer-ing, this could be made at the outer door. Feeling that I could not bear to leave Jerusalem with a memory so charged with revulsion, I went a second time with Dr. Mombelli, an Italian-Swiss religious to whom I had been recommended, and I have always regretted this was not my only visit. No fees were solicited in his presence, his quiet knowledge and understanding clarified many troubling questions, and the essential beauty and wonder of the place were finally revealed. Another disappointment, though in a very different way, was Gethsemane. Here a church had been built on the ruins of an old one, recently discovered. It crowded the garden on the hill, formerly spacious, into a corner where a small orchard of olive trees and a few flowers remained. Since every leaf and pebble of the place were already sanctified, it would have seemed sad to sacrifice a single one of them even to build the most beautiful church in the world. To me it was a double tragedy: the gardener-father, working to enlarge and beautify the plot, which had been his care for many years, had himself discovered the old mosaic which had led to the building of the church and the loss of his domain.

As for disillusionment, there was none at all for me in the Holy Land. It seemed a minor matter that a few places we wished to visit were "according to tradition," even though they were slightly less convincing than the great majority which had been approved by every authority. In the record of every people there are such places, and they are permeated with the spirit, if not the letter, of that which we seek. There is no more reason to doubt that Abraham and Moses, Jacob and David, Jesus and Paul were historical characters than there is to doubt that Alexander and Pharoah, Herod and Pilate, Nero and Nebuchadnezzar were historical characters. I had always believed this, but the full force of it was not brought home to me until I went to the Holy Land; then its impact was overwhelming.

There are those of course who are willing to grant that these *were* men of history and try to follow the teachings of Jesus of Nazareth, which were the noblest given the world, but who cannot go beyond that; they cannot believe in what they do not understand—in supernatural things, in miracles. To them, I can perhaps make no adequate reply. I can only say that I myself am profoundly thankful that I have always been able to believe in many things I did not understand, to accept the mysteries of religion as easily as the mysteries of changing seasons, of spring eternally following winter, of human birth and life and death. This faith has always been of tremendous comfort to me, and I am sorry for those who are denied such comfort. I know there are many deeply religious persons who cannot accept the mysteries of religion, and possibly it matters comparatively little, as long as they conscientiously follow the teaching they do acknowledge and if they can only see through a glass darkly. I think, though, that if they could go to the Holy Land, they might see a little more clearly. There was a hymn we sang in Sunday School when I was small, which began:

Lord Jesus, make Thyself to me
A living bright reality.

That is what the Holy Land did for me. It softened the vision of the Sufferer on the Cross and intensified the actuality of the compelling Man Who lived usefully and kindly and wisely in Nazareth and Capernaum and Jerusalem for thirty-three years before He died gloriously on Calvary. And because of this it clarified the vision of the Christ Who ascended to everlasting life from the Mount of Olives, until it was not one of a distant Deity, but one of a near and loving friend, no less God because He was also Man.

Chapter 46

THE boys and I returned to Cairo from Jerusalem by night train, as we had made the trip in the opposite direction, so the journey was unmarked by any outstanding features and the transition was very brief. The Holy Land itself seemed apart, not only in time and place but also in spirit, from all others. It was a blessed interlude, unconnected with the normal sequence of events. We resumed our more usual occupations in more familiar surroundings, refreshed and inspired.

Our last week in Cairo proved an especially agreeable one, full of new expressions of cordiality by our friends there, and on our last day, Mr. Winship took us to the famous health resort Helouan. On the way we drove past the summer palace and fields of glossy, fluffy cotton which bordered the "Great River," through quaint clay villages where swarming children held out their hands for baksheesh; we stopped for tea near one of these villages, at the Diamanti Café, whose little green tables were set behind a high green lattice at the water's edge; and there we watched the sun sink behind the palm trees, flooding field and desert and stream with mellow light. The next morning all our kind friends came to the train to see us off, bearing stuffed dates and flowers and other offerings; and at eleven, when a wicker basket containing steaming tea and thin sandwiches and plum cake miraculously made its appearance in our compartment, we all agreed, as we devoured its welcome contents, that "we can't possibly like Greece as well as this!"

By the time we had finally embarked, however, we had changed our minds. The same formalities which had made our arrival in Egypt a disagreeable experience were repeated upon our departure, and proved no less disagreeable: we joggled over cobblestones to the Quarantine station to be officially declared untainted by noxious diseases; our passports were examined for the seventh time; countless beggars blocked our way, demanding baksheesh and delaying the surrender of our belongings to the ragged porters, who became so agitated they shook their fists in our faces. When the *Famaka* eventually steamed out of the harbor, my chief sensation, besides nervous weariness, was the profound relief that accompanies escape. My relief, unfortunately, was short lived: I was scarcely settled in my steamer chair when the chief steward appeared and said he would like to see my passport and those of the "two young men." With difficulty, I refrained from asking how we had incriminated ourselves since the last examination—as we climbed the gangplank—and fetched them; they were returned just in time to be inspected by the officers who boarded the ship as we approached Piraeus, when we stood in line for an hour before they were delivered to us. They were next demanded as we went down the gangplank and again before we were permitted to leave the customshouse. Later I discovered that Piraeus is a singularly beautiful port, but I was certainly not aware of it on arrival; I was too occupied in displaying my passport. The next day, when I read in a newspaper of a man who had lost his sanity over his difficulties with a passport, I did not doubt the authenticity of the story for a minute!

There is no doubt that Greece is one of the most beautiful countries in the world; and that Athens, blessed with a perfect climate, enriched with peerless historical and artistic treasures, superbly located and surmounted by the Acropolis one of man's noblest architectural achievements—is rightly considered the chief ornament of her classic crown. But one does not immediately fall beneath the spell of her charm—at least I did not. She did not overwhelm me at first glance, but revealed herself slowly. In fact, she seemed determined to put her worst foot forward before she placed her better one firmly on my heart. An excellent road, wide and straight, was "in course of construction" between Piraeus and Athens, but this highway, like most others, was still far from completed and the trip was punctuated by back-breaking jolts. Moreover, as Greek drivers blow their horns constantly, the racket made even the most desultory conversation impossible. This tooting went on all day and practically all night, for the Greeks went to bed very late and rose very early, insisting only upon the noon hours for slumber; and since in addition the streets were narrow and crowded with trolleys, also vociferous, the noise was nerve racking to anyone not used to it. The custom in Greek hotels of not serving dinner during the summer months also presented difficulties; we found one that did, but it turned on the water only three times a week. This arrangement did not commend itself to us very highly, quite aside from sanitary considerations, in a temperature where we needed to bathe twice a day in order to be comfortable. We changed hotels, always more or less of a task, and the second one—the Petit Palais—was excellent, except that it served no dinner unless there was a special party. This practice meant that we must either go to bed dinnerless—which failed to appeal to Henry and Larry—or fare forth, no matter how tired we were, to some distant restaurant, for we were not all constantly guests at some delightful house, as we had been in Peking and Cairo.

Actually, this faring forth acquainted us with many lovely places we might not otherwise have seen—New Phaleron and the Trocadero by the sea, Aephissia in the hill country back of Athens, where many wealthy Athenians had villas—but as dinner was never served earlier than nine and the roads were extremely bad, the effort of securing an evening meal often seemed weary work at the end of a long hard day. And we probably would not have found these pleasant resorts had it not been for the good offices of a remarkable guide named Constantine Bizanis.

I am against guides on general principles, for the stereotyped kind show you what they want you to see—usually with some ulterior motive such as a cut on the price of a meal—and their general attitude is often an outright insult to their customers' intelligence. But many confusing things confronted the newcomer to Greece. All street and shop signs were in Greek script—a tax was imposed on anyone who proclaimed his business in any other tongue—and though I had loved Greek the one year I studied it, all I seemed to remember twenty-seven years later was how many parasangs Xenophon's army had advanced daily and not the characters which revealed this. The money, too, was extremely puzzling: every bill above the value of twenty-five drachmas—roughly thirty cents—had a side clipped off, reducing its actual value by one-fourth. When a courteous, soft spoken, neatly dressed man presented himself to me as Constantine Bizanis and asked for the privilege of serving us, something immediately told me I would be well advised to let him.

I was not mistaken. Every evening after he had taken us, well fed, back to the Petit Palais, he said, "And what time would you like to go out in the morning, Madam?" "Nine-thirty," was my almost invariable answer. (I could take long days then, even after late nights.) "At nine-fifteen, I shall be here," he would respond, and he always was. Never once did he fail us in any way.

The cut that so confused us in the currency had been taken in an effort to replenish a depleted treasury and constituted one of the direct reforms inaugurated by the new dictator, General Theodore Pangalos. It was then a little over a year since this venturesome man had attempted to drive the destinies of Greece before him—destinies which were so tangled that none but a master hand (which his was not) could have unraveled them. Greece, subject for many centuries to Turkey, had become an independent kingdom a hundred years earlier. During World War I her strategic position marked her as a prize to the side which could enlist her help, and her policies were divided: Turkey and Bulgaria were both ancient enemies, and they had thrown their lot with the Central Powers; on the other hand, Queen Sophie was the Kaiser's sister. King Constantine was torn between his regard for his wife's sympathies and the pro-ally attitude of Prime Minister Venizelos. The latter enjoyed a temporary triumph, and as a result, Constantine, Sophie and Crown Prince George were exiled, while the second son, Alexander, was proclaimed king. At first he was somewhat bored by a position he had never expected to attain, he was a sportsman, intensely interested in automobiles, horse racing and hunting; and was perfectly willing to let Venizelos govern Greece and direct her foreign policies. Moreover, no obstacle was suggested to Alexander's marriage to the beautiful young girl with whom he had long been in love—the granddaughter of a Greek general and the daughter of Constantine's aide-de-camp—even though she was not of royal birth. The marriage was a very popular one with the people, and Alexander, a happy man, began to realize the full extent of his opportunities as king.

Had Constantine died before he was exiled, had Alexander lived, had his child been a boy, the story of modern Greece might have been very different, and much happier. But there are no ifs in history, and the tragic death of the young monarch—the result of an infected bite— brought about the return of his father, Constantine; this, combined with other episodes, resulted in Greece's alienation from the Allies, who felt the King could not be trusted; and unhappy Greece went from misfortune to misfortune and from revolution to revolution. When Constantine abdicated a second time, he was succeeded by Prince George, who was shortly exiled in his turn—an exile which still continued in 1926—and Greece became a republic with Admiral Kondouriotis as "Provisional President." Following a coup d'état in June of 1925, General Pangalos assumed virtual dictatorship of Greece and dissolved Parliament, which had still not been reconvened six months later. He next announced that he was assuming increased governmental powers, and soon thereafter Kondouriotis resigned and Pangalos was elected President.

"The war," some clever writer remarked, "was supposed to make the world safe for democracy; instead, it made it safe for dictators." There could be no question that certain world conditions had tended to produce Mussolini in Italy, Primo de Rivera in Spain, Rheza Khan in Persia, Mustapha Kemal in Turkey, Pilsudski in Poland, and Pangalos in Greece and seemed likely to produce a similar national figure in Portugal and possibly even in France. But as far as I was able to judge, the results had been, on the whole, both progressive and beneficial— certainly the improvements in Italy, up to that time, had been nothing short of miraculous!

Though I had listened attentively to the viewpoints expressed by the political opponents of Pangalos, I had gathered he was the most compelling figure of the hour in his country, and personal experience confirmed this impression. He reached home at five one evening after a prolonged absence; at seven I received word he would receive me at nine-thirty the following morning. Having been told that formal dress —morning coats, silk hats, et cetera—was *de rigueur* for Heads of Missions calling upon the President and that it would probably be well if I wore corresponding attire, I arrayed myself accordingly, devoutly hoping my flowered chiffon skirt was long enough to meet the conservative standards of the dictator's well-known decree. I had resigned myself to an extended wait in an antechamber, but as the car in which our Secretary of Legation, Mr. James Denby, and I were riding swung through the palace gates—guarded by sentinels in the picturesque national costume—the President's car drew up at the palace entrance. (He had continued to reside in his own house and went to the palace only to receive visitors and transact official business.) We had barely reached the reception room when the President's aide motioned me toward an inner apartment, and an instant later, without any ceremony whatever, I was shaking hands with General Pangalos.

Like Mussolini, he spoke excellent idiomatic French and apparently ignored the rules he imposed on others, since he was comfortably dressed in a well-tailored light gray suit, a shirt of the blue made fashionable by the then Prince of Wales and a knitted tie of darker blue. He looked tired, but he did not act tired; he plainly revealed that abundant energy which even his enemies admitted was limitless and which constantly spurred him on to fresh fields. He was dark, compact and extremely good looking, and he had dignity and poise as well as force. After remarking briefly that "the unsettled condition of the country had made it absolutely necessary" for him to assume charge of the government, he spoke freely of his work—but more of the progressive aspects such as road building and monetary reforms, than of political issues— and of the refugee problem, which was indeed very great: Greece, with little natural wealth, impoverished by years of war and with a normal population of only five million, had somehow managed to assimilate a

million and a half refugees. He next referred to the long standing rap-
port between his country and the United States, which he hoped might
continue, and of Greece's gratitude to the United States for help,
through Red Cross contributions, with the problem of refugees from
outside Greece itself.

I left the dictator's presence wondering if we, as a nation, had a right
to his gratitude. For thirty-three million dollars, pledged to Greece as a
loan, had then never been paid; and though it was true we had helped
with the refugees for a while, we withdrew this help from all but the
children long before the need for it was past. It was beyond the point to
say Greece was obliged to provide shelter because of her post-war treaties and that the refugees were not our concern; many of them had been
accepted before the treaties were signed; but even dismissing that question, the fact remained that homeless, they found a home with her; hungry, they were fed; sick and in trouble, they were comforted. Above
wars and beyond treaties rings the promise of the Christ to those who
thus minister to those in need; because of this promise, I hoped that
Greece would some day have her reward.

Although I talked with several former Prime Ministers, who were all
leading "strictly private lives" and would have liked to see the end of
the dictatorship, not one was in favor of royalty's return, despite the
fact that the strong Royalist Party numbered about half a million, and
all the royal family was away, except Alexander's young widow. She
lived in Athens with her little girl, not only unmolested but greatly beloved; and I, having heard her beauty and charm highly praised, was
filled with pleasurable anticipation by a cordial invitation from Donna
Julia Brambilla, the American-born wife of the Italian Minister to
Greece, asking me to meet the princess at luncheon. Though the Princess Aspasia was also called the Princess Alexander and even Mme
Manos by uncompromising Republicans, it is by the former name that
I have always thought of her. But it really does not matter very much;
a great lady, whatever you call her, is always a great lady, and when
the Princess Aspasia entered Donna Julia's drawing room, I knew I
was in the presence of a very great lady indeed. She was wearing a
small black hat, a simple black crepe dress with long sleeves, black
suede shoes, black stockings—an unmistakable sign of mourning in
those days when fashion dictated they should not otherwise be worn.
Around her slim throat was a single strand of matched pearls, on one
slim hand an enormous diamond—no other jewels. Under the small hat,
her hair lay in soft curves against her faintly pink cheeks; her perfect
teeth showed very white against the deeper pink of her lips. A beautiful
woman, tender and gentle and cultured, I thought, until I became con-

scious of her eyes—black as her dress and hair, soft as her cheeks and lips, but bright as stars and deep as the sea; then I added, to myself, "a woman who knows how much better it is to have loved and lost, than never to have loved at all." I wished that every woman who had lost the man she loved might have seen what I did: a woman for whom a king had risked his throne, who had lost, through his death, almost all that made life bright and rich and full and who still had the courage and will to face the world with dignity and sweetness and charm.

She kindly asked if the boys and I would go with her to a ruined temple, about two hours' drive from the city, for a picnic supper, but she fixed an evening when we had already invited our Chargé d'Affaires Mr. Herbert Goold and his wife, our Consul General Mr. Arthur Garrels and his wife and Mr. Denby to dine with us. Feeling slightly as if I were committing lèse majesté, I declined, telling her why I was doing so, and asked if she would not come to us instead. She glanced down at her black dress. "I'm in mourning, you know," she said very simply, "but if it is really to be very small and quiet? Yes then, with pleasure. Nine on Thursday?" We drove home with her from the luncheon, and Thursday evening Henry, bursting with pride, took the Princess in to dinner; the maitre d'hotel at the Petit Palais had surpassed himself and the flower-covered table and little feast were all I could have asked.

So General Pangalos was, for me, the personal link with current Greece and Princess Aspasia the personal link with royal Greece; but it was an American who formed the personal link with the Greece which in the 1820's fought the war that made her free and independent. In those days, a young American who had just completed his medical studies and whose imagination had been fired by the verse of Byron decided, like the poet, actively to espouse the cause of Greece. Taking with him provisions, clothing and firearms, he sailed from home, and his grief and disappointment were great when, still at sea, he learned that Byron had died of fever at Missolonghi; and a helmet which the poet had worn became the young doctor's most cherished possession. He remained in Greece until independence was assured, acting as chief doctor in the Greek Navy. He was Samuel Gridley Howe, later the renowned teacher of the blind and husband of Julia Ward Howe, whose fame as an author and one of the earliest suffrage leaders somewhat eclipsed her husband's. He was much older than she and already past middle-age when their gifted children were born. Laura E. Richards, who wrote the well-known *Captain January,* was one of their daughters; and when she and her sister Mrs. Maude Howe Elliott, also a writer of distinction, decided Byron's helmet should be returned to Greece permanently, the latter said she would take it herself! That intrepid lady of seventy-six, as energetic and charming as she was venerable, arrived in Greece about the same time we did and presented the helmet to the Historical and Ethnological Society of Greece during our visit.

The presentation ceremony was an interesting one, and Mrs. Elliott, with all the fire and eloquence that could be expected from the daughter of such parents, delivered the main address. There was no doubt that she had inherited her father's love for Greece, and she put it in tender and glowing form. She quoted, her voice hushed with feeling, from Byron's poetry and from her mother's, she sketched the helmet's history, and then, because as a clever speaker she knew she must draw smiles as well as thrills and tears, she told an amusing story before she said farewell.

"I brought the helmet over in a hat box," she said, "a very large, very modern hat box, and when the customs officer who inspected my baggage saw it, he eyed it suspiciously. 'You must,' he said accusingly, 'be bringing a great many new hats into Greece.' 'Oh no,' I exclaimed quickly, 'I am bringing only one, and it is very old!' "

We went to the Acropolis at high noon, at sunset, and at night when the full moon was shining, climbing its lofty heights with unflagging spirit, resting beside its fluted columns and in the shadow of its facades. We went to one of the Countess Capodistria's famous "Sunday mornings," where all the fashionable Athenians gathered, and where the refreshments consisted of potato chips and *ouzo* and where a bell rang at twelve-thirty to alert the guests it was time to leave! We sat in the garden of the Petit Palais and drank tea with Mr. Kalopothakes of the Foreign Office, who had been at Harvard with my husband and was much more interested in Henry and me when he found we were the son and wife of "the Harry Keyes who was captain of the crew" than he was upon his initial introduction to us as the son and wife of a senator! We were glad he became interested, no matter what the reason, for his English was as perfect as Mr. C. C. Wu's and his skill as a raconteur equally great.

Between these and other events, it seemed we should hardly get outside Athens at all. But one of my letters of introduction had been to Mr. Bert Hodge Hill, who was in charge of American excavations at Corinth; and I determined to find time to go and see him, for I realized that he, better than anyone else, could form for us the personal link with ancient Greece. We finally set out one warm afternoon, rode for miles beside the bluest of blue seas, crossed the Corinth Canal, hewn out of solid rock, drove through luxuriant vineyards and eventually reached the excavations about four. Wonderful work had been done there; and the fountain of Peirene, where the water still flowed as it had for nearly three thousand years, and the market place, still intact, where the town gossips had sat to discuss the marriage of Medea, were among the most thrilling antiquities I had ever seen. The fluted columns of the Temple of Apollo framed a distant mountain, the Acrocorinth, surmounted by fortifications: the remains of the early walls, the gates and battlements dating from crusading days and the time of Venice's supremacy.

The fortifications were in a fine state of preservation, and as we gazed at them, standing in the temple ruins, Dr. Hill remarked casually, "The Acrocorinth doesn't take long to climb and part of the ascent can be made on horseback. The view at the top is really superb, and of course the fortifications—"

"I think we had better climb it," I said immediately.

I met with no very enthusiastic response from Henry and Larry, who wanted their tea, which Dr. Hill had invited us to have at his house—a pink plaster dwelling of two rooms beside the excavations. So I compromised: we would have our tea and *then* we would climb the mountain. I turned a deaf ear to the objection that we could not get back until past dinner time and that Dr. Hill had invited us to that, too.

When we finished tea, our steeds were waiting for us at the gate of the pink house. The saddle destined for me consisted of barrel staves fastened closely together and draped with a bright-colored cloth; on this I sat sideways. (I must confess that my costume—an embroidered white voile dress and a large white hat trimmed with red ribbon—would never have passed muster as approved mountain-climbing apparel.) There was no sign of a bridle, but there was an iron handle at the rear of the saddle and an iron knob in front of it; to these I clung while a little girl led the horse and a man behind urged it forward. Fortunately the horse was sure footed, for the ascent was precipitous and rocky and rolling stones and crumbling earth scattered with every inch we progressed.

A little more than halfway up the incline, my palfrey was guided to a high stone and signs were made to indicate I must alight. My heart sank; I knew I could expect neither sympathy nor succor from either of the boys in their state of hungry resentment. But somehow I struggled along, and in the end, I got my reward for the view from the summit, which we reached just before the light faded, was magnificent. The Grecian sunsets are as different as anything that can be imagined from the vivid riot of color, followed by instant darkness, that marks the splendid tropical sunsets. They are soft and pearly, with shades of moonstone and opal filtering through the velvety atmosphere and lingering past the long twilight far into the night—night with a sky that is not black, but a clear pale blue. They are much less gorgeous, but they are infinitely more restful. And tired as I was, I felt soothed and strengthened as I gazed out over the hills and isles and seas of Greece from that high hill-top at dusk.

I have concluded that archeologists are unusually hospitable persons. I have never forgotten our dinners with Dr. Reisner under the starlit sky on the terrace near the looming pyramids or the dinner Dr. Hill had waiting for us when, having come down from the Acrocorinth in the pitch dark, we reached his little pink house at quarter of eleven. His regular dinner hour was eight-thirty, but neither host nor cook, who acted as table boy as well, seemed at all perturbed because we were so late. We sat at a long narrow table and ate thick brown bread and cheese and honey, soup and stew and Bulgarian cream and cherries; we drank spring water and dark resinated wine. Then, replete and somno-lent, we started back to Athens, reaching there at three in the morning. Fortunately the condition of the road, which bumped us back to con-sciousness every time we dozed, prevented us from missing the scenery on the way: a late moon had risen and in its radiance the solitary sentry at the Corinth Canal stood silhouetted, his bayonet resting over his shoulder; and the sky and sea and hills, which had been so sapphire bright in the sunshine and so pearly in the twilight, sparkled like dia-monds and shone like silver.

If Greece was a difficult country to enter, it was a still more difficult country to leave. We took, or thought we took, every possible precau-tion to safeguard our departure and arrived, with our sixteen pieces of baggage, in ample time before the sailing of the *Famaka*—the same ship in which we had come from Alexandria, which made a regular stop in Greece. We were not allowed to embark, and neither were any other would-be passengers: the Captain had decided that Turkey was about to declare a quarantine against Greece because of a suspected case of plague. What inspired this conclusion, no one knew; there was no official report of such a case. Nor could we understand why the com-pany had not notified us of this decision, made some six hours earlier, as we later discovered; or why, failing this, it would not refund our pas-sage money. But our lack of understanding did not help us—back we had to go to Athens, feeling very sheepish to face again the friends who had bade us farewell with appropriate offerings! The next day we em-barked in an Italian ship, which had no objections whatever to taking passengers; and when we reached Istanbul—or Constantinople, as it was called until 1930—one of the first things we saw was the *Famaka* tied up at the wharf!

The *Famaka,* however, did not monopolize our attention. That had been caught, as we slid over the Sea of Marmora, by the domes and minarets of Istanbul, which formed one of the most exquisite skylines of any city in the world; and its verdure, almost the first we had seen in a city since leaving Ceylon, seemed hardly less lovely than its architecture; even the fact that it was raining hard did not dampen our enthusiasm. But we were not allowed to enjoy this sight in peace very long; the passport officers appeared and all hope of quiet vanished. Two elderly ladies traveling together were told their passports, visaed for Turkey in New York, were valid for only two weeks. Since it was practically impossible to get from America to Turkey in that length of time, much less to visit it, it seemed unlikely that any consul would issue such a visa; but since none of us could decipher Turkish script, the ladies had to accept the official's verdict and sit down and wait when they were told to do so. A young German was the next victim; he had secured his visa from the Turkish consul in Paris, with the assurance it was good for three months, and had come directly there; he felt sure there must be some mistake. Relentlessly he was informed he could not land. Larry, whose visa had been secured in Cairo, got similar treatment; and though Henry and I had been passed without question because of our special passports, we could not desert the other half of the bodyguard. The offending passports were gathered up and taken ashore to be shown the police, while we sat and discussed the apparent lack of cooperation between the home office and the consulates. Two weary hours passed; it began to grow dim and dark. Little boats, in which our baggage had been piled shortly after we had anchored, clustered about our ship. It was evident that not only the clothes we were wearing, but some of those in our luggage would be ruined before we got ashore. At last the passports were returned and stamped in our presence, with no comments on the delay and inconvenience we had been caused, and we were free to go. The men who rowed our rocking boat quarreled all the way, and as I struggled up the slippery steps of the grimy quay, I was knocked backward by one of the shouting, pushing porters, who tried to wrest my handbag from me. There seemed only one ray of light in the general dreariness: the Turkish Minister to Greece, whom I had met at the Countess Capodistria's, had given me a laissez-passer to facilitate our passage through customs. We would not have to face further delay for inspection, but could leave the dingy reeking customshouse at once. It seemed too good to be true.

It was. The inspector read the laissez-passer, looked at our luggage and declared it was so multitudinous and heavy it would have to be opened after all.

Five hours after anchoring, we stood wearily registering at the hotel desk—a registration which consisted not only of names and addresses but also of birth and lineage, profession and avocation, past deeds and future intentions. As the pen dropped from my tired fingers, I turned to the boys with terrible waves of suppressed homesickness fairly choking me.

"I am going to leave this city," I said, "the first thing tomorrow morning. If I have another experience like the one we have just had, the only place for me will be a padded cell!"

The *concierge* heard me and stepped forward.

"You cannot leave tomorrow morning," he proclaimed in broken but determined English. "You must give three days' notice to the police before you can leave the city, five days if a Friday comes in between."

"Then," I said icily, "I'll stay indefinitely in my own room. I've seen all I want to of the Istanbul police."

"You cannot stay indefinitely, madame," the *concierge* rejoined, "unless you take out residence papers. After a fortnight, you must become a Turkish resident. You cannot go and you cannot stay."

So I had no idea what was going to happen to me next. I seemed to be caught both coming and going. But anyhow there I was.

Chapter 47

IT IS perhaps regrettable that first impressions should be so lasting, but it is nevertheless true, especially when one is far from home. After my initial experience in Istanbul, I made a solemn resolve that if ever anyone came to me from abroad in the future, I should do everything I could to make that person's landing and first week in the United States pleasant, no matter how neglectful I was afterward! For I found it almost impossible to overcome the discouragement and homesickness the difficulties of disembarking and getting adjusted in Istanbul aroused. I dreamed of passports, of officials wrapped in red tape, and woke to visions of baggage inspectors burrowing in my trunks. Many of my clothes had, as I feared, been ruined in the course of landing, for the driving rain had penetrated even the heaviest luggage during the three hours it was exposed; taxes of every description and the submission of identification papers at every turn loomed ahead of us. A cable had called Larry home (not that I could blame Turkey for that!) and the knowledge that the lease on my borrowed boy was up, so to speak, did not help raise my spirits. It was understandable that his family wished to see him after a year's absence; but I knew I would miss him terribly. I hoped that some day a son of mine might stand by some other mother as Larry had stood by me during those dark days of Henry's illness and thus vicariously repay that steady faithfulness!

Larry's impending departure had one good effect, however. It roused me to the necessity of making the most of the few remaining days he had, so, shaking off depression, we sallied forth to see the city.

Istanbul, as far as I know, is the only city in the world which is located on two continents; and it has, unquestionably, one of the most superb situations in the world. As you approach it, the Sea of Marmora curves off into the Golden Horn on the left and the Bosphorus on the right. On the curving land between them lay the district called Pera, more or less Europeanized, with its *Grande Rue,* its shops, its hotels and *cafés chantants.* Across the Golden Horn lay the district called Stamboul, and there were the most beautiful mosques, the Seraglio Palace, the Classical Museum, the ancient bazaars. Both these districts were in Europe; while across the Bosphorus, in Asia Minor, were the districts of Scutari and Haida Pasha, where the ancient barracks stood and where one took the train for the interior. One was hardly ever out of sight of the sparkling blue water, ebbing and flowing with a swift tide and current; and the ever-changing and ever-beautiful skyline—turret and tower, dome and wall—combined with this expanse of sapphire to present a glowing panorama from any vantage point. If you went up the Golden Horn to Eheub, ascended the steep hill to the old Turkish cemetery and stopped to rest among the quaint tombstones, it seemed loveliest from there. If you climbed the Byzantine Tower—the Roumeli Hizzar—near Robert College, it seemed loveliest from there. If you wandered through the courtyards of the Seraglio Palace and stopped transfixed before the kiosk of Bagdad—that marvel of azure tiling, mother-of-pearl inlay and brocade stiff with jewels—you thought it was loveliest from there. You thought so in the clear warm light of midday, in the glow of sunset, under the crescent moon and shining star from which Turkey might have copied her flag.

The azure tiles of the kiosk were not the only ones in Istanbul which rendered one almost breathless with their beauty. That rich blue was apparently as greatly favored by the Turks as the Chinese, the art of glazing as highly developed as that of rug making. The combination, seen in many places, reached its highest perfection in the mosque of Sultan Achmed, which to me was the most beautiful of all the mosques. The interior walls and the four splendidly proportioned pillars which support the dome were of those lovely blue tiles; outside six delicate minarets encircled the sacred building like sentinels. The bazaars, also completely roofed in azure, covered thirty-two acres and would have been a delight with their Arabian Nights glow and glitter if it had not been for the swarm of besieging shopkeepers, who actually tugged at my arm in their efforts to persuade me to buy; it was only in a quiet shop outside, where I was taken by Mrs. Julian Gillespie, the wife of the American Trade Commissioner, that I sat peacefully and watched the priceless pageantry of rugs and prints unroll before me. Color, color everywhere, even on the silent stone; at the Classical Museum, blues and reds and golds still lingered in the bas-reliefs adorning the sarcoph-

agus of Alexander the Great, robbing it of the cold whiteness invariably associated with marble that commemorates the noble dead.

Istanbul lacked parks and open spaces, and except for a few villas
and palaces along the Bosphorus, most of the houses were of unpainted
wood, tall and angular; but its steep and narrow cobblestoned streets
were often shaded with fine trees, so there seemed to be an abundance
of vegetation—another glowing color. The sidewalks were so restricted
in breadth that the inhabitants slipped unconcernedly over the curbs
into the street and scattered unhurriedly before honking cars, which observed no speed limits or hard and fast rules of right and left. As in
Egypt, there were beggars everywhere, in striking contrast to Greece
where, despite the prevalent poverty, I did not see one. After the beggars, the *hamars*—the human beasts of burden who carried everything
from a valise to a piano on their backs—were the most familiar figures.
The fez, of course, had been abolished by law and there were very few
veils, with black the predominant color. The quaintest figure I saw was
a Nubian woman who had formerly been a slave in a great family—
coal black, slim and straight as a reed, almost primly dressed, but with
huge gold hoops in her ears. Soldiers and policemen were very trim and
smart; the civilian males were well clad, as were the women, for the
most part. Many still clung to the *bach-ertessi*—the thin scarf twisted
cap-shape about the head—but I think this was mainly because it was
so becoming!

It was easy to observe the beauty of the Turkish ladies—for they *were*
beautiful!—and they danced as the ladies in New York or Shanghai or
Paris danced: maid and matron, the younger generation, the older married set were all dancing. I had expected to find Istanbul foreign and
different, a place apart, as I had found Palestine—though not in the
same way of course. Instead, I found men and women, boys and girls
occupying themselves with interests, vocations and pleasures like those
of their counterparts everywhere else in the world. These simple agreeable indications of our common occupations gave me a new thrill of
world fellowship. I felt it when I went out to dance, whether at the
American Embassy, where we were invited to an especially lovely ball
attended by many Turks, or in a restaurant at Therapia, the Bosphorus
seaside resort to which the Diplomatic Corps transferred their residences
during the summer. I felt it whenever I went out on a Friday, the Moslem Sunday, and saw fathers and mothers picnicking with their children, parties of boys and girls driving on the *Grande Rue* and boating
on the Bosphorus. And I felt it in visiting two of Istanbul's baby clinics.
Mrs. Gillespie, who took a special interest in these centers, asked me if
I would not like to see them, and since child welfare was one of my own

greatest interests, I gladly accepted. We went first to the Stamboul Baby Welfare Clinic of the American Hospital, which was conducted by the American Welfare Committee, and next to the *Goutte de lait*—"drop of milk"—founded under French patronage but then under the direction of a Turkish woman physician, Dr. Safieh Ali; and I saw that the world work of caring for little children went on there as it did in other places, uniting us in the mutual endeavor for health and knowledge.

The religious situation in Turkey was, however, distasteful to me. I was not prejudiced against her because she was a non-Christian country; I have no such feeling about Japan or China or Ceylon, and have earnestly reiterated that we should be not only tolerant and respectful of non-Christian religions but must recognize and acknowledge their beauty and helpfulness before what we consider the superior beauty and helpfulness of our own can be fulfilled. I saw no objection to the opening of a mosque in Paris or to the continued use of a long-established one in London; but even as we should practice toleration, so should we demand it. Turkey was so extremely intolerant as to call the Red Cross the Red Crescent; Japan took no similar action. Turkey forbade any organization to describe itself publicly as Christian; religious instruction was permitted only in private homes or houses of worship— never in any educational connection and only to persons belonging to the teacher's sect. What other non-Christian country went to such lengths? Certainly not China,[1] harshly and often unjustly criticized for her attitude toward Christianity, or any other with which I was familiar. Turks who talked with me on the subject hastened to assure me they had a high reverence for Jesus Christ, that He was, indeed, "one of the Four Great Prophets of their own faith"—a fact of which I was well aware. But it seemed to me that, at the time, they were choosing a strange way to show their reverence.

---

[1] This was true in 1926. Of course, it is no longer true of Communist China.

Chapter 48

I WAS conscious of a feeling similar to the one that always surged through me when I left Washington for Pine Grove Farm as I mounted the gangway of the Italian liner *Brasile* at Istanbul; for after spending fifteen months in countries that were new and strange to me, I was at last going back to one which had been known and dear to me since childhood. It was like returning to old friends from new ones. No matter how wonderful and splendid new friends may be—I have many whom I love dearly—there is a special extra corner in my heart where I keep the thoughts of my old friends; and when I actually see them—at rarer and rarer intervals nowadays—these thoughts are released in a joyful rush that is almost overpowering.

I did not have to wait until I reached Naples to feel I was in Italy. I felt it as soon as I sat down at luncheon to omelette and *risotto* and fresh green salad and found my tablemates very friendly and conversational in assorted languages—none of them speaking a word of English but all unmistakably cordial. I felt it when a sailor who saw me looking helplessly for steamer chairs produced two as if by magic and set them up with a flourish. *"Ecco!"* he exclaimed exuberantly and went off singing, without waiting for a tip. He was *glad* to get the chairs! I saw him frequently after that and he was always singing—as he polished brass, as he sponged woodwork, as he climbed from deck to deck. So were most of the other crew members; so were most of the passengers. They broke into song at the slightest excuse or with no excuse at all; and they danced in the same spirit and with the same frequency. There was perfect order and discipline in that ship, and yet it was riddled with the most infectious gaiety I have ever encountered. The news leaked out that my birthday fell in the course of the voyage, and immediately plans were under way for a fiesta. The head steward produced a magnificent cake surrounded by candles, with American and Italian flags patterned in colored sugar on the frosting and "I whish you a happy berthday" below them. The captain presented me with a bouquet, seated me beside him for dinner and whirled me off at the start of the evening's dancing. One after another, the passengers came to greet me, *"Felicitations, Madame; mille felicitations."* Even the smiling, singing sailor came to wish me joy. For this was Italy, a smiling, singing, friendly nation if there ever was one.

And then we came through a sun-shot, pearly mist to the Bay of Naples. "Italy, thank heaven!" I murmured as we drew near the dock, memories of recent landings that had been neither easy nor pleasant vivid in my mind. There was a large clean concrete wharf, where the *Brasile* could go alongside, and a large clean concrete customshouse, its walls hung with colored posters depicting the charms of Italian cities; so I could feast my eyes on the beauties Italy had in store for me during the brief wait while the baggage was courteously examined. Then we sped through the city, climbing and climbing until we had reached the excellent hotel which was our destination, and Naples and her harbor stretched beneath us in limitless loveliness.

We went to Siena for the *Palio,* the festival first observed in 1656 to honor the *Madonna di Provenzano,* as the Sienese designated the Virgin Mary because of a miraculous apparition near property owned by Provenzano Salvani; then in 1701 a second festival was instituted, honoring her as the city's patroness, the *Madonna dell'Assunta;* ever since, the *Palio* has been run twice yearly—on July second and August sixteenth. It has not changed materially in costumes, characteristics or setting since it took the form of horse racing in the seventeenth century, and around the fringes of the great Piazza del Campo in the heart of a city gay with flags and pennants race horses representing the numerous *contrade,* or wards, into which Siena is divided. Each ward has its insignia—the goose, the snail, the shell, the dragon and so on—and each proudly displayed and raced under banners bearing this. Later, in Venice, came the colorful regatta on the Grand Canal with which the Venice season ends, which we watched from the terrace of the American Consul and Mrs. James Barclay Young. For three hundred years selected gondoliers have raced on this occasion, which is a popular holiday similar to our Labor Day. Italy, with her background of limitless loveliness, keeps such ceremonies of the past forever fresh and beautiful.

But Italy is as young as she is old, as ultramodern as she is venerable and proof of this we saw only twenty minutes away from the Grand Canal at the Lido, which before 1926 had become one of the smartest watering places in the world. Posters in the Near East and other parts of Europe proclaimed it "the land of sunshine and pajamas"; and sure enough, stretched out on the white sand before the cabanas in the brilliant sunshine, were dozens of attractive young men and women in pajamas—gay affairs of satin and brocade, silk and crepe, universally decorative. For the daily swim—which did not occupy very much time —bright and scanty suits were substituted for the pajamas. Beneath the hotel's beautiful dining room of rose brocade and crystal there was a beach restaurant, where the pajama'd ones could go for lunch and tea; and afterward they wandered over to the tennis courts to watch Suzanne Lenglen play her peerless game. When evening came, the pajamas were cast aside for black broadcloth or glittering satin and sequins, and their wearers danced until morning in an elegantly decorated ballroom. For one fete it was flooded with aquamarine light and its walls were hidden by water plants; from the ceiling were suspended translucent denizens of the sea—roseate, violet, topaz. The closing pageant had a pearl for its heroine, a tortoise for a hero and, for good measure, a captured fisherman and dancing sea-anemones!

To its shining shores the Lido drew pleasure seekers, with unlimited wealth and leisure, from almost every country in the world. Many South Americans were there that summer: Argentinians with fabulous fortunes, blasé Brazilians, handsome and elegantly dressed; many, too, from our own part of North America. The King of Roumania's arrival caused a slight stir, but royalty was so constant a visitor that the stir did not last.

Italy's progress, however, showed itself in many other and more significant ways: in ever-increasing freedom from dirt and beggary, in ever-increasing frugality and industry, in prosperous manufactures and the scientific development of its agriculture. In a few short years, Italy had leaped from somewhat negligible international importance to its current place as one of the four great powers of the world. And if it ever can be said that a single human being is largely responsible for the advance of an entire country, this could be said of Mussolini and Italy. Three years earlier, I had written that I thought him the most dynamic man I had ever met and that I believed the material and political improvement in Italy was due almost entirely to his vital force. Now, after circling the globe and having been presented to premiers, presidents and princes of numerous nationalities, many of them compelling figures, I still believed that not one of them could have done for his country what Mussolini had achieved in Italy; and in Greece, Pangalos, who had striven to copy him as a dictator, had been a futile figure in comparison —in fact, the Pangalos regime had just been overthrown by General Kondylis after only eight months of full power, whereas the Mussolini regime had already lasted four years (and would continue to last for another eight without change of policy or prestige). Though some of the measures he had begun to adopt were severe, they were not extreme, and he was not copying anyone or wanting to do so, nor had power become an evil and not a vivifying force. It was not until this happened that tragedy began. Meanwhile, he was still a great and glamorous figure, and my visit with him—it was far more than an interview—was the crowning event of my stay in Italy.

When I had gone to see him before, I had been shaking in my shoes, for it was the first interview of the sort I had ever had; and the fact that he sat firmly entrenched behind an enormous desk at the further end of an enormous room whose entire length I was obliged to traverse did not make the ordeal any easier. I felt as if he were looking me over critically with every step and had not decided, when I reached him, whether he was going to approve of me or not. Even *after* I reached him, as conscious of his powerful personality as if it were an electric current, I felt I had to earn my welcome, and it was not until it was time to leave that I felt reasonably sure I had.

But on this second occasion everything was different. The appointment was set for the very first day of my stay in Rome, and I knew that would not have been the case if I had been remembered unpleasantly. Moreover, Henry had been invited to accompany me—his days of "staying outside with the weapons," as he always described his many weary waits in palace anterooms, were apparently nearing their end. As the door of the huge and beautiful room, with its immense globes and its superb hangings and paintings, swung open, the Prime Minister rose and walked forward to greet us, his white teeth gleaming as he smiled, his hand outstretched!

"Welcome back to Italy! I am very glad to see you again. And so this is your son—well, one of them—and writing, too! Sit down and tell me what you have been doing. Going around the world, I understand!" He indicated a massive carved chair cushioned in brocade. "I want to hear all about it! I am going to interview *you.*"

And he did! With short staccato sentences, he started me off from the beginning of my trip. Whom had I met here? What had I done there? Fearing lest I might presume upon his time, I tried to do a little judicious skipping. He seemed to enjoy my account of seeing Chang Tso Lin—"A small man, you say, slender and small, with slim soft hands like a girl's, and a gentle voice? But a great general." "Yes, indeed,

Monsieur le Président, a very great general. And in Egypt, also, there are two arresting personalities—Zaghloul, the native leader, and Lord Lloyd, the British High Commissioner." "Wait a minute," interrupted Mussolini. "You were in China an instant ago—North China, Mukden. You didn't go directly to Egypt from there! Come now! A great deal of territory lies between. You actually went into Canton? You met all four Soongs, that remarkable man and his three remarkable sisters? I wish to hear about that!"

So I went back. Did I like the Japanese? The Greeks? (Of course, what had happened to Pangalos gave him a special reason for close questioning there.) What about the Turks? Dutch rule in Java? And Quezon, the President of the Philippine Senate—brilliant, eh? Oh, and charming too! Were the women pretty in such and such a place, were the men polite—ah, yes, and did I think them sincere as well? The Holy Land—did I suffer disillusionment? Mussolini turned frequently and in friendly fashion to Henry, asking him where he agreed with me, sympathizing with him for his long illness, confirming the boy's enjoyment in distant places and strange people. At last, step by step, we reached Italy. And still the questions came.

"You find that we continue to make progress? You are in a position to judge now, you still think this is as beautiful as any country in the world?" At that moment, the great man sounded almost like an earnest child saying, "Haven't I a lovely mother? Don't you think there's no one like her?"

It was easy to answer this time. "My stay in Europe is to be very short, *Monsieur le Président,*" I said, "and if I had not felt Italy to be both preeminently beautiful and preeminently important, I should have gone to some other country—there are many where I have not been—instead of coming back here again."

This seemed to satisfy him, and we discussed certain phases of his vast accomplishments. The Lateran Agreement would not be signed for another two years, but groundwork for rapprochement between Vatican and Quirinal was at least laid and the Pontine Marshes were nearly reclaimed and a network of fine roads was started. I inquired for his wife and children and asked him to take Signora Mussolini a gift I had brought her from Japan (a lacquer box, naturally!). With ingenuous interest, he insisted on seeing it then and there, admiring the delicate workmanship and rewrapping it in its folds of silk with his strong and dextrous hands, the hands of a musician—how I should have loved to hear him play that famous violin of his! I am sure I should have enjoyed it as much as I had enjoyed reading his beautiful and simple war diary, written while he was a soldier in the trenches. He promised to deliver the lacquer box when he went to Milan two days later and told me with pardonable paternal pride that his daughter had just won a medal for conspicuous bravery. I had thought her strikingly like her father when I saw her; his story did not alter my impression.

At last, I asked him to tell me something of the recently formed committee on women's dress, of which the Queen was president and Signora Tittoni, the wife of the President of the Senate, one of many distinguished members. It was, I had heard, started at the Premier's instigation.

He laughed. "Don't misunderstand my efforts in that direction," he said. "I haven't attempted to say what the fashions shall be, whether skirts and sleeves shall be long or short and all that. I recognize that fashion is a much greater dictator than I am, and I should never attempt to interfere with it, as General Pangalos did in Greece. I don't care in the least *what* women wear. I only ask that the materials shall be manufactured and the garments made in Italy. Our silks are world famous, and we have excellent dressmakers in Rome—quite as skilled as in Paris, just as Italian cooks are undoubtedly the peers of French chefs. There is not the slightest reason why Italian women should not be stylishly dressed without leaving their own country. Her Majesty the Queen has been good enough to interest herself. I have every expectation and hope that the movement will meet with success."

Now that Rome and Florence both rival Paris seriously in *haute couture,* it is hard to realize that this rivalry was non-existent forty years ago, but it is true, and it is also true that the impetus which brought about the change came from the Chief of State, who had a good many things besides clothes on his mind.

The Premier was in high spirits, punctuating his remarks with frequent laughter and talking in a way as kindly as it was stimulating. Time had wrought some changes in him, and these were all for the better. He wore his well tailored clothes more as if he were comfortable in them and less as if they had been molded to him; his French, which was fluent enough before, was faultless; and his English, practically non-existent before, was fluent. The formality which was slightly defensive, slightly abrupt, had left him; he had added poise to power and friendliness to force. His supreme dignity, his obvious sincerity, his implicit confidence in his own purpose and methods—without which no man or woman can glimpse success, much less attain it—and his overpowering love for Italy and faith in her destiny were as strong as ever. But his strength seemed more mellowed, more vitalized. I did not agree with him. There was no greater dictator in the world than he—not even fashion, which, unlike Pangalos, who had fallen, he had had the wisdom to leave alone!

I doubted that there ever would be.

And having seen him again, I felt that, to a certain degree at least, my world quest was ended. I had come back to Italy after months of wandering, because she was an old friend, and I found I admired her more than ever. And having made this happy discovery, I wanted to go back to the still older friends I had always loved and always shall love best of all. I would get a few new clothes in Paris, so that those friends would not be ashamed of me when they saw me—I had grown very shabby in the course of all my globe trotting!—and while they were being made I would have a brief visit with that other dear friend, France. And then I should be home again.

Part Nine

Home Interlude

Nothing could be more typically French than the boat train that ran between Paris and Cherbourg in those days. The Gare St. Lazare, where we boarded it, seethed with that crowded confusion characteristic of French stations as of no other stations in the world. The luncheon we ate as we sped through the ordered green countryside followed the inevitable French menu—hors d'oeuvres and omelette at the beginning, fruit and cheese at the end and veal somewhere in between! The compartments of six stiff seats upholstered in fawn color; the blue-bloused, vociferous porters who precipitated themselves upon us as the train jolted to its final stop at the gaunt customshouse; the overladen tender to which these same porters hustled us—all these were as French as the tricolor itself! But when we had poured our last clinking franc into the hands that emerged, outstretched and horny, from the blue sleeves; when we had bobbed up and down for two hours on that brilliant, choppy sea; when I had declared, not for the first time, that I would never, *never,* NEVER take a liner again that did not go straight up to a dock—then, suddenly, we were in the United States! The Stars and Stripes were flying stiffly over the *Leviathan,* which we were taking for the second time; the stewardess paid no attention when, from force of habit, I said, *"Entrez!"* as she knocked at the door, and, laughing at myself, I called, "Come in!"

Several senatorial and congressional families were aboard, with all of whom I was on good terms; but I was especially glad to see General and Mrs. John Henry Russell, our High Commissioner in Haiti and his wife, whom I had visited there at the beginning of my world trip. It was great fun to talk over with them what I had been doing in the eighteen months since I had seen them. It meant even more to me to have Mrs.

Russell ask if I had done any work at all on the novel I had told her about.

"Yes," I said hesitantly, "not much, but a little. I was laid up for a while in Cairo and again in Naples. When I couldn't go out and gather material for *Good Housekeeping,* I worked on the novel in bed."

"I'd like to have you read me what you've written, if you have time."

I was immeasurably flattered. It had not occurred to me that she would give a second thought to the hopes I had confided to her, and now she actually wanted to see what form they had taken. Twice I read aloud to Mrs. Russell in the afternoon, and her response was very enthusiastic. Some of her comments gave me courage to go on without any publisher's assurance that the book was or ever would represent an effort that was worth while. "Of course, you can write fiction," Mrs. Russell kept saying. "Just you wait. You'll see I am right." I had a long talk with Mr. William Castle, who had done so much to facilitate my first professional trip to Europe and who was now a fellow passenger, and his continued praise of the "Letters" also meant a great deal; and I was really overwhelmed when Charles Evans Hughes, the former Secretary of State, sought me out and said they were a "very important contribution" to better international understanding. But after all, it was encouragement about the fiction that I needed most.

Howard Chandler Christy, then at the height of his vogue, was among the many celebrities aboard ship, but the two outstanding personalities were certainly Mr. Hughes and Will Rogers. Each in his own way was always remarkable; but a combination of the two, as it came about on this voyage, was prodigious. A disaster of some sort in Florida—I think it was a flood; Henry thinks a hurricane or possibly both—had made a second ship's concert desirable, to supplement the one automatically scheduled for the Seamen's Fund; and Mr. Hughes and Mr. Rogers became joint chairmen of this second benefit. From the moment they agreed to accept these roles, they were in frequent conference, pacing the deck side by side, consulting potential artists for the event and finally presiding over it together. Their appearance on stage at the same time was the occasion of really tumultous applause, even before Will Rogers—who always referred to Mr. Hughes as Charlie and addressed him in the same way—began his wisecracks and the Secretary responded to them, and they reaped a small fortune for the sufferers. And there was a mirth-provoking sequel at the brunch with which we were provided just before landing. Will Rogers rose from his seat, tapped on his glass and asked for his fellow passengers' attention.

"An additional contribution of five thousand dollars reached me this morning," he announced. "It was made anonymously. But I will just say in passing that if any of you buy a chocolate bar and it isn't Hershey's, I hope you choke."

Harry and Mr. Bigelow were both waiting for us at the pier, and each in his own way showed that he was glad to see us; but neither was able to protect me from the customs officer into whose clutches I fell. He exacted duty, without making any allowance for hard wear, on the limp garments bought a year earlier and was quite unmoved by my caustic comments anent the impossibility of taking a trip around the world lasting a year and a half without buying some new clothes to replace those that had disintegrated in the tropics. I had tried—as indeed I always do—to be scrupulously honest in my declaration and had even gone so far as to put the jade necklace bought in Canton in my handbag, so that I could show it easily and quickly. The officer, still pawing over the old dresses, barely glanced at the jade and spoke with scorn. "Them green beads?" he said. "Forget about those." So I returned them to my purse and without further protest paid the duty on the dresses, thereby saving a great deal of money.

That evening Harry, Henry and I went to see the current hit "Sunny," starring Marilyn Miller, then husband and son departed on a midnight train, the former to get back at the first possible moment, as always, to Pine Grove Farm, the latter to register on time at Harvard. I settled in comfortably at the Commodore and stayed over in New York two extra days for various editorial conferences. I had met the associate editor of *The Nation* in the Philippines, and he had asked me if I would write something for that magazine, so I wanted to see him; I had found a letter awaiting me from a prominent publisher, expressing interest in a novel about Washington, and emboldened by Mrs. Russell's praise, I wanted to show him what I had written. But the interview with Mr. Bigelow was the one of primary importance. He had continued to be very pleased with the "Letters" from abroad—in fact, some time in the near future, he would like to discuss the question of where I had better go next; he did not say again that he thought the increased circulation of *Good Housekeeping* was in large measure due to the serial which had appeared simultaneously with the foreign "Letters"; he gave the latter full credit. He would also like to discuss with me the possibility of some more human interest articles. But as far as Washington was concerned, he doubted if he would want any resumption of that as a major subject; he now visualized my chief value to him as a foreign correspondent with the continued rank of associate editor.

I left him feeling that his attitude was understandable and his treatment of me, as always, eminently fair and indeed complimentary; at the same time, I felt slightly deflated. Much as I enjoyed travel, I had been away from home for a long while, and at the moment the last thing I wanted to do was to talk or even think about going abroad again in the foreseeable future; or, actually, going anywhere except to Pine Grove Farm. Congress was not in session and Peter had entered Milton Academy, where Henry had done so well and been so happy; hence there was no longer any question of getting my youngest son back to the Potomac School to begin the fall term. Lukewarm as I had always felt toward the idea of human interest articles, they could be counted on to take care of expenses; moreover, it seemed probable that there would be other sources of revenue from articles indirectly the result of my world trip. I went lightheartedly to the theater again and took the Merchants' Express to Boston: two hundred fifty miles without a jolt or jar, a Pullman as spotless as my mother's paneled parlor at The Oxbow, a delicious dinner; now that I knew what Oriental trains were like, I asked heaven to forgive me for all the harsh things I had said in the past about American trains. Then there was a week end at another good hotel—the Puritan in Boston, as different as possible from the Commodore in size and atmosphere but just as luxurious. Henry met me at the train, and very soon John and Sid, now both at Harvard too, came pelting in from Cambridge and Peter from Milton and Larry from Providence; and we were joined by Molly Gray, Mary's daughter, and the Lamont twins, Mary and Phoebe, who had been part of the spirited group on the trip through the Panama Canal and were now at Wellesley, and we all had dinner and played bridge together. Then, Monday, I went back to Pine Grove Farm. The flag was flying from the tall pole, and the big house had been scoured from cellar to attic, and Cathie had everything I liked best ready for supper—Parker House rolls and broiled chicken and stuffed tomatoes and vanilla ice cream with chocolate sauce —Cathie who had stood so faithfully at the helm of the household all the while I had been gone, thereby making it possible for me to fare forth and see the wonders of the world and, at the same time, to earn the money that meant the needed help to keep that household going. And of course Harry was there, too, quietly glad to have me back again. I was conscious of the deep silence and brooding peace of the countryside descending on a tired mind and body. And when the silence and the peace had done their healing work, there were the old friends —always the best friends—waiting to see me. "Are you going to be busy this afternoon? If you aren't, I thought I'd come over and bring my knitting." . . . "A few of the Old Guard are getting together for a game of bridge this evening; I'll call for you about eight." . . . "Frances, would you feel like doing something for the church supper? Because, if you would . . . oh *thank you!"* And then, presently, guests for supper, with gifts for everybody, a sort of delayed birthday party, and a very happy one, and a week-end visit from a member of the Forestry Department, who was interested in what our six groves could contribute to a program of forestation.

It was my own country, my own state, my own village, my own people, my own house again. It was *home.* In the first joy of being there I wondered how and why I had ever left it. And yet, when I was no longer tired in body and mind, I began to realize that I would want to again, some day.

My first absences were brief. I went frequently to The Oxbow to see my mother, who was not well; and I went to Littleton and Poultney to make long-promised speeches. The drives to these places were beautiful, and there was also a picnic lunch atop Mendon Mountain and a supper at the Woodstock Inn. October, according to my reckoning, is the most beautiful time of year in Vermont and New Hampshire and I was making the most of it. And though I was writing every day, it was with less sense of strain than in a long while. And then, before October was at an end, an unexpected letter suddenly changed the picture. I did not then know that editorial offices are like sieves or I would not have been so surprised. The letter was from Mr. Henry Sell, the new editor of *Delineator* (Mrs. Meloney had left the magazine for another periodical). He had heard rumors that I was entering into an arrangement with *Good Housekeeping* somewhat different from the one I had had in the past. If this were so, would there be any chance that *Delineator* could have the material it had so long wanted from me? At any rate, would I be willing to come to New York, at *Delineator's* expense of course, and talk the matter over?

There could be only one answer to that; with Peter at preparatory school, Henry and John both at Harvard and the law school looming for next year and two more after that, educational expenses would continue to be heavy for some time and I must help with them. On the last day of October I left for New York and, when I started back to Pine Grove Farm on the third of November, I had agreed to write a monthly article about Washington for *Delineator,* beginning with the opening of Congress. *Delineator,* in return, had agreed to pay the highest price I had so far received for articles, to give me a liberal allowance for incidental expenses and to meet the salary of a full-time secretary. I had then managed to get in touch with Miss Shufelt, who had worked for me week ends before I started around the world, and she had consented to give up her current position and come to me when I went back to Washington. Naturally, this meant my financial anxieties were at an end for the present, and it also meant my days at home were numbered. But I continued to make the most of them, in the ways I had always enjoyed the most, and stopped off to see the boys in Boston before I joined Harry in Washington the first of December.

My initial task there was to find a new home for us. At the end of Peter's school year the previous spring, Harry had given up the apartment at Meridian Mansions; it had seemed foolishly extravagant to pay rent for it all the months it would not be needed, and besides, we had outgrown it. I had done all my work at a big desk in a corner of the living room, and since I needed room for files, reference material and so on, had been badly crowded, nor did such office equipment seem suitable in a room that also had to be used for official entertaining; and the presence of a permanent secretary presented another complication in terms of space and suitability. I wanted very much to have a small house, rather than another apartment, and found one I liked very well, which seemed a good buy and which I felt I could afford; unfortunately, Harry took an immediate dislike to it, and I knew there was not the slightest use in pursuing the matter with that disadvantage. But in a surprisingly short time I found quarters we both liked at 1509 Sixteenth Street. There was only one apartment on each floor and light on all four sides; altogether, there were seven large and two small rooms besides the kitchen, and there were three bathrooms. The drawing room and dining room were unusually spacious and well suited for entertaining; they opened into each other, both faced Sixteenth Street and both had fireplaces, as did the first room on the side, which, to begin with, I used as a study. Harry and I took the two connecting bedrooms at the rear, and this still left us space for the Demings and the boys when they came home, not to mention a guest room. We were comfortably installed before the Christmas holidays began and prepared for the usual round of junior gaieties.

The old year ended on a note of well being and festivity: we were settled in a spacious and attractive apartment; Harry was finding more satisfaction in the Senate than he had at first; I had the most glowing prospects for magazine work I had so far achieved; and the boys had had a wonderful vacation and were all doing well at school and college.

Chapter 50

THE new year began on a gloomier note: Cathie was suddenly stricken with appendicitis and taken to Emergency Hospital almost on an hour's notice; for several days her condition was the occasion of considerable anxiety, and her convalescence was very slow; though our janitor's wife, Katie Simmons, consented to pinch-hit for her, domestic cares loomed larger than they had in a long time for me. Then, quite as suddenly as Cathie had been felled by appendicitis, I was rendered helpless with the same terrible pain in my back that had disabled me on the voyage between Panama and California and several times since. Dr. Hardin, who had been our family physician for some time, looked rather grave when he examined me and still more so when he found I had never been X-rayed. That must not be delayed another day, he announced, and neither must consultation with an orthopedic surgeon. And so Dr. Custis Lee Hall, of blessed memory, entered my life, together with a steel harness which I was to wear for the next thirty years —though fortunately I did not know that at the time—to control the damage which had been done by a year and a half of neglect.

Dr. Hall held out no false promises to me; it would take time to get used to the "brace," as he euphemistically called it. I would have to wear it both day and night for a while, and it would be pretty painful until I got used to it. Perhaps I would give up and stay in bed all the time; he would not blame me if I did, though it would make recovery harder in the end.

"What do you want to bet," I asked him, "that after you get this thing adjusted so that joint won't keep slipping out of place, I won't stay in bed a single day?"

He did not believe me, but I was right. I did not stay in bed a whole day after I got used to the "brace" until May, and then it was a grippy cold added to my lame back that landed me there. Meanwhile, I wrote the monthly articles for *Delineator* and did all the things that made them possible—that is, I led an active social life of the type that made news, which was the natural one for a senator's wife. And while I was in bed with the grippy cold a long distance call came from Mr. Meredith, the former Secretary of Agriculture to whose cooperation I owed the material for my first *Good Housekeeping* article. He asked if I would consider undertaking a series of articles for *Better Homes and Gardens,* which was one of several periodicals he owned. If I would, his son-in-law Frederick Owen Bohen would like to meet me in New York the following week to discuss details.

I said I would be there.

I was making a tremendous effort to adjust myself philosophically to my physical limitations, and I was finding it hard going. After all, it was only a little while since I had scrambled to the top of Borobodur and the Acrocorinth, and I had not visualized a time when I would not scorn the handicaps imposed by other monuments and elevations—a few days out of commission now and then were quite a different thing from a prolonged, painful and possibly permanent disability. I had been able to function, both mentally and physically, for long hours on end. I had spent practically the whole night on the Acropolis, when there was a full moon, to keep Henry company while he took the time exposures that resulted in some of his best pictures. I had required no help in the steep ascent, and I was no more tired when we returned to our hotel than he was. Now my days of strenuous climbing and everything that went with it were obviously over, not to mention horseback riding and swimming; probably in time I would be able to dance a little and walk short distances, but there would be no more balls lasting all night or long walks. I had loved all those things, and I was still much too young to even think of giving them up because of age. Although it was actually not for another decade that the world was forced to acknowledge it was now a woman of forty, instead of a woman of thirty, who was or should be at the height of all her powers, the consciousness of this had very generally begun to dawn. I felt bitter and rebellious and defeated.

Then I began to pull myself together. The steel harness, worn under an ordinary foundation garment, did not show; though, for the time being, it was almost impossible for me to go up and down stairs, that made no difference in my daily life, as I lived in a building with an elevator; and, in most of the places to which I went, there were either elevators or dining rooms on the ground floor. When I was invited out to lunch, I inquired about this beforehand, and usually there was some way to manage; actually, I was going out to lunch much less frequently than when I first went to Washington because of my heavier working schedule. When Harry and I went out to dinner, if there was a problem about stairs, he left me near the entrance and went to the drawing room to reconnoiter; by then we knew enough people well so that he did not hesitate to ask a fellow guest to help carry me upstairs, and they made a "chair" with their four hands and did so quite easily. Everyone was very kind and no one made me feel conspicuous.

As far as my writing was concerned, I certainly had no reason to feel bitter or defeated, and the same was true in regard to friends. For instance, the Pittmans indicated during the winter that they hoped Harry and I would come to visit them "at our house on some Sunday when we are always at home." To my great regret, I found it impossible to persuade Harry to go to the Pittmans or anywhere else on Sundays; he left the apartment for his office immediately after his early breakfast and usually did not come home until evening. He was slightly more positive than formerly about invitations to official dinners, when he believed them to be advantageous to my work. I generally went to church in the morning on Sunday and returned to work the rest of the day; if I did not go to church, I went straight from my bed to my desk. By evening I wanted a respite and someone to talk to. The Pittmans' house offered both, and although I did not yet make a regular practice of going there, I went often enough to inaugurate a habit, and our firm friendship changed to a closer one.

Besides this, there was a new friendship closely allied to it, which in a surprising short time, also, began to mean a great deal to me. As I was leaving the gallery after the opening of Congress, I heard someone call, "Hello there! Hold on a minute! I'm glad to see you back." I turned and to my amazement found myself face to face with Senator Gerry of Rhode Island. To the best of my recollection, I had seen him only occasionally at large receptions, when he had seemed detached from his surroundings and completely indifferent to his fellow guests; there had been something almost masklike about his face. Now he was smiling broadly and his hand was outstretched. This was certainly a changed man if I ever saw one, and a sentence in a letter Key Pittman had written me the previous winter flashed through my mind: "Peter Gerry has made a good swap in wives." His first wife, Mathilde Townsend, an heiress, had never been interested in his career or his colleagues, and in her second marriage she was to show the same total indifference to everything which most concerned her husband—doubly unfortunate, since Sumner Welles, who married her after his marriage to Esther Slater ended in divorce, was inevitably destined for a great future. But Edith Stuyvesant Vanderbilt, who had been a tower of strength to George Vanderbilt during his development of Biltmore and had devoted herself wholeheartedly to him during the years of invalidism which preceded his death, now entered into every phase of Peter Gerry's life with intelligence, devotion and zest; and his response to this had been so immediate as to betray how much he must have missed such loving cooperation before. Earlier, Harry had dismissed him as a high-brow millionaire who regarded the Senate as a congenial club. From the moment he hailed me in the Capitol corridor, I found a great deal more to him than that.

It was quite true that Peter Goelet Gerry had been born with a silver spoon in his mouth and a golden bough over his head. The spoon was the product of several substantial and consolidated fortunes; the bough depended from a glittering family tree. Two of his ancestors, Elbridge Gerry and Francis Lewis, were signers of the Declaration of Independence; his father, Elbridge T. Gerry, was one of the founders of the first society for the Prevention of Cruelty to Children and the original instigator of much child welfare legislation. Like the Bayards, the Adamses, the Frelinghuysens and the Roosevelts, both the Gerrys and the Livingstones—the distaff side of the Senator's connections—had served their country capably, conspicuously and continuously. It was almost inevitable that Peter Gerry should seek to continue such a tradition.

After one term in the House of Representatives he had been defeated for re-election, only to turn up triumphantly in the Senate. He was now in his second term, urbane and unruffled. He served on the Naval Affairs Committee, and it was in developing and maintaining an impregnable navy that his chief interest lay. Like Harry, most of his work was done on committees. As a speaker, he was not a spellbinder, though he had manifold conversational gifts, which I became privileged to enjoy, since the Pittmans and the Gerrys were great friends, and I came to see increasingly more of both couples.

I also liked Edith Gerry from the moment I met her, but my real friendship with her began in a rather unusual way. Early in the year, the nominating committee of the Congressional Club asked if I would run for president. I did not see how I could possibly add to my already heavy program, but I had thought that before and had somehow managed to do so; and Harry seemed to feel that my selection was a very distinct compliment, not only to me but indirectly to him. Hesitantly I said I could not face a contest, but if there were no other candidates, I thought it would be possible. I was assured there were none; but a day or two later I heard, quite by chance, that the charming new Mrs. Peter Gerry had been asked to run and was going to!

I suspected that she had been told the same thing I had—that she would be an unopposed candidate. I wrote her a note and asked if she would come to see me; she did so the next day.

My hunch had been correct, though why the committee had told us both the same thing I still cannot imagine. Edith Gerry and I might have begun our acquaintance as rival candidates, both too far committed to withdraw. I instantly told her I would not think of running against her, but that she could count on my support. Though she began by saying she thought she should withdraw also, I begged her not to and she finally agreed. She made by far the most distinguished president the club had during the years I was actively associated with it—Mrs. Towner's presidency had been before my time—and I kept my promise to cooperate by acting as her liaison officer with the press and assuming responsibility for a number of the entertainments. At my suggestion we asked each of the leading women's magazines—*Good Housekeeping, Delineator, Pictorial Review* and *McCall's*—to sponsor programs featuring their best authors. These affairs were a tremendous success, and everyone seemed pleased with the result.

Increasingly it seemed my opinion on foreign affairs was considered worth while. An article entitled "Are We Fair to the Philippines?" had been accepted by *The Nation;* and I had written an article for the National Catholic Welfare Conference News Service called "Catholic Missions in the Orient." My friend Elisabeth Shirley was at that time the official translator of seven or eight languages at the News Service; and she had been so interested in some of my comments on Catholic missions, made in the course of an informal dinner, that she asked me if I would mind incorporating them in a brief article. ("I'm sorry that we don't pay much," she said, "but you could write that article in one evening." "Of course," I replied. "I'd be glad to." So I wrote it in my first free evening, received a check for twenty-five dollars, put it in my savings account and forgot about it—until the following August, when the article was to have significant consequences for me.)

There had been one great disappointment. The prominent publisher had seen nothing worth using in the material Mrs. Russell had liked so much; therefore once again I had been obliged to face the fact that there seemed to be no hope for a Washington novel. On the other hand, Mr. Bigelow, who had been placated by my acquiescence in writing one human interest article—"A Letter to an Invalid"—and who had allowed enough time to elapse before broaching the subject of further journeyings, came to see me late in March. By then I was ready to talk about travel again and even had special suggestions to offer. York

Minster was to celebrate the thousandth anniversary of its founding; shortly thereafter, an Anglo-Catholic Conference was to take place in London and Evelyn Underhill, the great mystic, was to be one of the foremost speakers. Meanwhile, Maude Royden, at a nonsectarian church, was holding services which were attracting wide attention, and Maisie Sheed was braving the crowds at Hyde Park to plead the cause of Catholicism. Austria had a cleric of high degree for a chancellor; a World Conference of Faith and Order was to take place in Lausanne at which almost all major Protestant denominations were to be represented. Would Mr. Bigelow consider a series of articles on religious leaders and religious conferences?

"If you don't like the idea," I concluded, "there are several others I can suggest. But that is really what is in my heart to do this year."

"Then I think you had better do it," he replied.

That was all. No contract, not even any discussion as to costs and timing. This was the way he and I had learned to work together and it was the best way I have ever known. But I had one condition, which I hesitated to mention, though I knew my conscience would not be easy unless I did. Mr. Bigelow was a very strait-laced Methodist, and it would be hard to persuade him that such a series would lose half its value if it did not include the Pope. I said so.

He hesitated, but his sense of news, as well as his sense of fairness, won the day.

"Very well," he conceded, "if you can get a private audience."

I had no idea whether I could or not, and I realized the chances were against it; but I was willing to take the chance.

And now here was this telephone call from Mr. Meredith, suggesting another series of articles. His son-in-law, Frederick Bohen, who was acting as editor-in-chief, had a very decided idea about what he wanted: articles on the homes of prominent American women, homes attractive enough to warrant detailed description, women of unimpeachable character as well as notable attainments. For instance, there must never be any question of a divorced woman. . . .

My heart sank, for I could see two very important deletions if he stuck to that—Mabel Walker Willebrandt, the Assistant Attorney General, and Mary Pickford. But perhaps we could start with someone he would not question and get around to them later. At all events, I agreed to do the series and to have the first three articles in his hands before I left for Europe the end of June.

From the twenty-seventh of May to the eleventh of June, I wrote all day and got the articles finished and was free to enjoy with a united family Class Day at Harvard on the twenty-first and Commencement the twenty-third. Henry received his Bachelor of Arts degree and Harry led the Class of '87, holding its fortieth reunion, to the stadium for the baseball game, in which Harvard won a spectacular victory over Yale.

The next night Henry and I were aboard the *Majestic* bound for London.

Part Ten

Faith and Order

Chapter 51

W E SAILED at the untimely hour of one A.M., so our first drowsi-
ness was punctured by the reverberation of gongs and hoarse
shouts of "All ashore that's going ashore!" We woke on open seas to
the consciousness that, to all intents and purposes, we were already in
England: the struggle for ice water began; the coffee was undrinkable;
and the bath steward pounded at our doors and then lay in wait until we
sleepily stumbled to the tubs he had prepared! Whatever else American
travelers might or might not experience in England or in her ships, they
could be sure of two things: they would always be thirsty and they
would always be clean!

There were over nine hundred first class passengers, and among them
was the Right Reverend William T. Manning, Episcopal Bishop of New
York, who had been invited to deliver the sermon on "City of York
Day" during the Thirteenth Centenary celebration of York Minster's
founding. *Old* York had paid to *New* York a gratifying compliment in
extending this invitation, and as a token of appreciation, the New York
diocese sent a magnificent illuminated parchment upon which its expressions of fellowship were artistically inscribed, which was personally
presented to the Archbishop by Bishop Manning.

The day after our arrival in England, Henry and I reached York late
in the evening, both so tired that we tumbled into bed with scarcely the
formality of a good night. Nothing about the voyage had been restful,
though much had been exhilarating. The dull morning light, seemingly
uncertain whether to presage sunshine or showers, found us struggling
into our Sunday clothes at York, with no running water or adequate
mirrors to aid us with bathing and dressing; and our spirits did not rise
noticeably over bad coffee and cold toast. But once we had left the op-

pressive hotel and entered the walled city, its ancient and mellow charm laid immediate hold upon us. The cathedral spires were constantly in sight as we hurried through the winding cobblestoned streets, and suddenly we turned a corner and saw the magnificent western facade towering before us. The open space in front of it was thronged with people, orderly and restrained as the British crowds always seemed to be and yet surging with suppressed excitement. Those who had tickets were being guided in swiftly moving lines by pleasantly efficient "bobbies." Clutching our precious tickets, we slowly advanced through the minster's central door and halfway up its great nave, where we knelt and felt its splendor surround us—the majesty of its immense proportions, the loftiness of its lantern tower, the magnificence of its stained glass windows, the delicacy of its carved stalls and screens and columns, the simplicity of its altar.

When we rose from our knees, the first of the many processions which preceded the service was moving up the center aisle. In them marched Lord Mayors and Mayors, sheriffs and judges and justices, military and naval officers, troops of soldiers. There were silken robes, some black and full and lustrous, others of fur-trimmed scarlet; there were flowing white wigs, orders and medals and decorations—all the display with which an occasion of this sort could be dignified and which the English know so well how to achieve. When all these personages were seated, there was a brief hush, a stir of anticipation, and then the strains of "God Save the King," as the Princess Mary, her fair loveliness accentuated by the soft blue she wore, appeared with her husband, Viscount Lascelles, at her side. Next, preceded by the vested choir, came the clergy—the Archbishop of York, the Bishops of Whitby, Hull, New York and Western New York and many other prominent ecclesiastics, all in gorgeous robes. The ancient banners which were carried added to the resplendent effect and the procession was rendered the more impressive by the grand old hymn which was its accompaniment:

> *Thy hand, O God, has guided*
> *Thy flock from age to age;*
> *Thy wondrous tale is written*
> *Full clean on every page. . . .*

The music seemed almost celestial in its beauty; and shafts of misty light slanting from high stained-glass windows upon the singers' uplifted faces intensified the impression that we were linked with heavenly choirs. Such a shaft fell, too, upon the pulpit as Bishop Manning ascended its steps, and its radiance never left his countenance during the entire course of his prayers and sermon.

He began by reciting the prayers for the Rulers of England, the church and civil authorities, then chose his text from St. Paul: "Grace to you and peace from God our Father and the Lord Jesus Christ. . . . I thank my God through Jesus Christ for you all, that your faith is spoken of throughout the whole world." He referred briefly to York's notable history, from the Roman occupation to the present, but more especially to the history of York Minster, the site of a church during two-thirds of the Christian era. He next recalled the Archbishop's visit to New York just before our entrance into World War I, and the moving power of the prelate's text on that occasion—"And they beckoned unto their comrades which were in the other ship that they should come and help them." Bishop Manning dwelt on the ties which bound the Church of England to the Episcopal Church in the United States, and then spoke of the desire the Anglican Church was beginning to show for unity with other churches—a desire evidenced by its plans to participate in the World Conference on Faith and Order, soon to take place in Lausanne, to which Trinitarian churches of nearly all denominations in the world were sending delegates in the effort to promote more cooperation and better understanding.

"It is for the Anglican Church to show," he said, "more fully than she has yet done, by the breadth of her standards and by still greater freedom in her worship, that the truths Catholics emphasize and the truths which Protestants emphasize are not contradictory but complementary; that each church needs the other for its own enrichment and completion, and that both are needed for the full power and life of the church. The Anglican Church recognizes and holds the principles for which both the opposing groups contend—authority and liberty, corporate life and individual freedom, sacramental grace and personal experience, the Divine Mission of the Church and the free access of each soul to God. She alone of all churches has been forced to learn this lesson. God had appointed her to the task of reconciliation."

Whether one agreed with it or not, this viewpoint furnished food for thought and had solid basis in fact. For several years before his death, the liberal-minded Cardinal Mercier of Belgium devoted much time and prayer to conversations with the Archbishop and Dean of Canterbury and with Lord Halifax, one of the leading laymen of the Church of England, to whom the Cardinal gave his ring on his deathbed. Though the results of these conversations were not made public, Lord Halifax, speaking before the Anglo-Catholic Congress in London's Albert Hall that summer, stated that he soon hoped to publish them. There is no doubt that nearly forty years before Pope John XXIII gave the first great impetus to ecumenism, Cardinal Mercier and Lord Halifax were striving for it. And the most moving episode of that Congress was the reception given the Greek Metropolitan Strenopoulos Germanos, the ranking representative of the Eastern Church in England. He brought greetings from the members of his faith to those of the Anglican communion and was welcomed by a storm of applause from the twenty thousand delegates so vociferous that it seemed to rock the building.

No one present at that 1927 Congress could possibly have been in any doubt as to the vitality and immensity of the Anglo-Catholic movement. For a week Albert Hall was packed three times a day and at least ten thousand people were unable to gain admission; the enrolled membership dwarfed that of any other religious convention I had ever attended. It included a number of American Episcopalians as well as members of the Church of England from every part of the British Empire; there were bishops on the platform coming literally from Greenland's icy mountains and India's coral strand. All had come for no other purpose than to bear witness to the faith that was in them and to increase that faith. The atmosphere was extremely scholarly, with Oxford, Cambridge and other universities represented among the speakers and leaders; but it was also charged with great devotion.

A series of profound and illuminating addresses approached the same subject from different angles, but I must refer specifically to just one, a speech delivered the first evening of the Congress by Evelyn Underhill.

When she was introduced, the hall resounded with applause and the audience strained forward to catch a glimpse of this small figure in a simple tan dress. She advanced to the microphone—a slim, slightly stooping woman past middle-age, her gray hair bound with a fillet of silver leaves, her dark eyes burning with intensity. Her slow calm manner did not conceal the emotion she felt in delivering her message—the emotion of the true mystic who possesses that blessed quality which has been described as "the intuitive knowledge of God."

> My subject this evening is sacraments and mysticism. . . . By a sacrament, I mean the supernatural given to man through natural means. That is, through consecrating touch, through the hallowing and special use of physical things—oil and water, bread and wine. A sacrament gives us the Invisible Reality in visible ways—it is an outward sign of an inward grace. . . . A mystic is a spiritual realist, a person for whom the Invisible is a matter of more or less firsthand experience. . . .
>
> When we come to look at history—*that remorseless destroyer of religious generalities*—we find that the greatest Christian mystics, from the Fourth Evangelist onward, have also been the greatest sacramen-

tists. . . . Just because of their deeper knowledge of God, their fuller sense of His mysterious richness, the mystics find more and not less reality than others do in His sacramental gifts. . . .

Evelyn Underhill had scarcely finished speaking when I joined a group trying to secure a word with her before she left the platform. If she was astonished by the importunity of a complete stranger with only the most indirect sort of recommendation, she did not show it. But neither did she hold out much hope for an interview.

"I'm leaving London Thursday and my time is so filled until then. Really, I don't see how I could. I'm very sorry—"

She turned away, leaving me the prey to uncertainty; should I have been a little more insistent? On the other hand, I did not like to press her, especially in the face of her weariness. So I went back to the hotel and actually prayed for a chance to talk with her. For never had I heard so beautifully presented the truth of the indivisibility of the spirit and the flesh, of the omnipresence of God and the many ways in which we may feel it. . . . And I knew that if I could see her alone, she could present to me much more.

The jangling telephone jerked me to unwilling consciousness early the next morning. Mrs. Stuart Moore, I was informed, would be glad to see me between five and six at her home in Campden Square Gardens. Would that be convenient? I didn't understand? Oh, perhaps I did not know that Evelyn Underhill, in private life, was Mrs. Stuart Moore?

I took pains to learn not only that but many other things besides before five o'clock: that she was the daughter of a baronet who was also a barrister, and the wife of another barrister; that she had been educated privately and at King's College for Women in London; that she had been a Lecturer on Religion at Oxford; and that she was the author of numerous verses and books on religious subjects. With this much as a conversational background, I started for a part of London I had never visited before. It had, as usual, been raining most of the day, but the rain had stopped and the wistful English sunlight was slanting across the dripping leaves. The taxi stopped and I alighted before a small simple house tucked behind a tiny fragrant garden. An instant later I was ushered into an equally diminutive drawing room overlooking the garden.

There was a soft rustle and my hostess was before me; her dress of garnet-colored silk was made with a long full skirt and a close fitting bodice, and its lace collar was fastened with a delicate, old-fashioned brooch. For a moment it seemed as if I were facing a lovely picture painted long ago; then she spoke and, sitting beside me on the sofa, sent for tea.

As we drank it, I talked—it was very easy to do so. The general subject of our conversation was her address, and there seemed to be no barriers to confidence. We spoke of prayer and faith and guidance, of contemplation and communion. Twice, fearing I was intruding on her valuable time, I offered to leave; twice I was gently bidden to remain. There seemed no limit to the largesse of this spiritual and scholarly woman. I had crossed an ocean hoping to see her; I knew I would cross one gladly, at any time, for the sake of seeing her again.

My next objective was an evening service at the nonsectarian Guildhouse, in Eccleston Square. I was going to hear Maude Royden, the world's most famous woman preacher, and this time I was much better briefed beforehand. She was the daughter of Sir Thomas Royden and had received her education at Oxford, with which she had been associated as a Lecturer in English Literature. She had done settlement work in Liverpool and the country parish of Luffenham and became deeply interested in the women's movement. From 1917 to 1920 she was assistant preacher at the City Temple and helped found the Fellowship Services at Kensington, which were afterward transferred to the Guildhouse. Her gifts as a writer were quite as great as her gifts as a speaker, and her *Prayer As a Force* had given me much food for thought:

> Do not be troubled that your faith is not perfect. There is not an iota of faith that you have ever put in God, in man, in the universe, that has not received its legitimate and exact response. . . .
>
> . . . when you pray for other people you cannot guess in what way you are going to be used by God as His channel; only offer yourself continually for that power to be poured through you. That is the way in which great causes are helped.
>
> We should continually seek to know more and more about God. . . . The difference between faith and superstition is precisely this, that faith depends upon knowledge and superstition on ignorance. . . . Faith is a venture indeed. But its basis is reason. Reason as far as you can. Know all you say. Be honest with your God and with your reason. Then, and only then, take the leap which we call faith. If you do not take the trouble, with the most single-minded and austere determination, to find the right direction, how can you hope to reach the goal? You do not know where you are going! Shut your eyes to knowledge, refuse the light as religious people have a hundred times refused it, and then your faith becomes superstition, and the god you pray to is not there. But if with all your moral sense and intellectual power you seek to know God, your prayer will surely find Him. . . .

As I entered the Guildhouse, an usher came forward and showed me to a seat. I was early, but the building was already crowded with a somewhat heterogeneous gathering, very plainly dressed for the most part. Across the front of the church was a raised platform where a stringed orchestra and a few singers surrounded a piano; above the platform, in an oval niche, was a white pulpit. There was silence, then a stir of expectancy, and suddenly, the pulpit was occupied by a woman in a long black robe, with sheer white collar and cuffs and a small close-fitting black cap on the dark hair which covered her ears and framed her face—a face which was beautiful in its repose but which was soon transfigured to almost unearthly beauty by emotion. She sat so quietly while the orchestra and choir rendered their opening selections that there was a sense of rest merely in watching her. Then she rose and read the first and second lessons—both from the New Testament, one from the Gospels and the other from the Epistles. She asked the congregation to join her in prayer—prayer for homely and tangible needs. Finally, she began to preach.

Her sermon was on pacifism. The conscientious objector in England had been made to suffer for his views in a way scarcely comprehensible to us in the States, and he often needed greater courage to adhere to them than would be required in battle. Maude Royden had herself been a conscientious objector; if she were brave enough, she would always be one. Though I did not agree with her viewpoint, I admired her idealism, and I was enraptured by her personality. The mere cadence of her delicate and dramatic voice had the power to produce tears; her grace of posture and gesture was supreme; regular features, perfect coloring, symmetry—all these her face possessed, and yet these were nearly forgotten in the consciousness of the soul which animated them. Complete sincerity, complete spirituality were depicted; consecration to the cause of man and God; the faith that would move mountains.

All at once, I realized that one of the ushers was speaking to me. "Miss Royden will receive you now," she was saying, "before the second service begins." I had been so transported that I was unaware the first one was over! I rose and followed the girl, Miss Royden's secretary, to the vestry. I had had an earlier appointment, but there was a misunderstanding about the time, so I had waited in vain for nearly an hour that afternoon. I did not regret the delay, however, because it gave me an opportunity to see the people who were seeking out Maude Royden—the physically handicapped, the mentally twisted, sad women, shabby women, angry women. A few were turned away, and none were vouchsafed more than a few minutes; but every one who came out of the office wore a look on her face different from the one with which she entered.

And now Maude Royden was going to see me and I was too dazed to take advantage of it. I found myself in a small warm and friendly study, face to face with the beautiful woman in the black robe, and she had taken my hand and was saying, "I am so sorry there was a mistake about your appointment. It was not your fault; what can I say to make up for your long wait?"

"You have already said it" was all I could manage to answer.

"Will you sit down? And will you forgive me if I have a cup of tea?"

While she poured it, I pulled myself into something like composure, but it was only to discuss details of her work at the Guildhouse and her impending visit to the United States. Of her religion I had no need to question her; of that she had told me, not only by the words of her mouth but by the light of her countenance. . . .

The interview was over. I returned to the hall and waited for the second service to begin. In a moment Maude Royden appeared, suddenly and silently as before. This time, however, she seated herself in a low chair on the platform; her robe flowed about her; her head was bent in soundless petition. When she raised it, her secretary handed her numerous slips of paper; on these were written, anonymously, questions from the congregation, which was still intact, as rapt and devout as during the sermon. Miss Royden read each question in turn, commented on it from her viewpoint and invited discussion. Many questions hinged on different phases of her sermon, but others ranged from the League of Nations to companionate marriage. Through them all she threaded her way with patience, wisdom and understanding, illuminating the way for others. Every man and woman there must have felt she was a friend and that her friendship interpreted the friendship of God.

The work of a third English spiritual leader also made a profound impression on me that summer. Her name was Maisie Ward Sheed. She was as well born and cultured as the others; her father was for many years editor of the Dublin *Review,* and both he and her mother were writers of note and leaders in religious thought. Mrs. Sheed inherited not only literary talent—she had written several books—but a deep interest in religious movements and controversies. When the Catholic Evidence Guild—a society for the explanation of the Roman Catholic faith —started in 1918, she was one of the first two women speakers to appear publicly for it, and she afterward became its general secretary and chairman of its training committee. Her husband, who headed a publishing company, was actively associated with her in the Guild's work, which consisted of presenting the elements of Roman Catholic doctrine; this was done mainly at outdoor meetings, since the Guild felt a larger audience could be reached in this way. The meetings at Hyde Park Corner lasted for eleven consecutive hours on Sundays and for three on weekdays, the speakers changing every hour; and this was only one place, not just in London but throughout England, where such meetings were held. The speakers underwent unbelievable ordeals; they were surrounded by hectoring and aggressive mobs, sometimes insulting, sometimes violent. But they continued to speak patiently, eloquently and simply, giving their message to the few who would listen, in spite of all that was done to prevent them. After I stood for one short afternoon watching the indignities to which these Hyde Park speakers were subjected, I wondered if my faith would bear such a test.

Chapter 52

JOHN and Sid, who had taken a slower ship than ours, soon joined Henry and me and we took a short enjoyable trip out of London. And then suddenly the headlines—"Revolt in Austria"—"Model Apartments Bombed"—"All Borders Closed"—made me insist that Henry go and buy tickets for Vienna without a moment's delay. The next day we were all on the last train that ran from London to Vienna for several weeks.

Despite predictions that we were headed for battle, murder and sudden death, it was a very pleasant journey, and we reached Vienna on schedule time; having arrived there, I wandered about quite as freely as when I went there as a young girl—during the disturbances not a single foreigner was molested or inconvenienced! And, wandering, I found the city as charming as ever: a city of elegance and distinction unsurpassed anywhere in the world; a city of parks and palaces, of insidiously attractive shops, of open-air restaurants set simply on the broad sidewalks or in the midst of gardens. A city of such music as one never heard anywhere else—brilliant, beguiling and hauntingly wistful.

We dined at the Rathskeller or, more fashionably inclined, at the Schloss Café, with scarlet-shaded table candles and the utmost luxury of appointments and service; and being Americans, and fortunate ones at that, we dined at our Legation, where the Minister, Mr. Albert Washburn, and his lovely and charming wife dispensed boundless hospitality. They lived in Vienna's oldest palace, and its rooms were impregnated with history and romance. Poland's King John Sobieski lived there during the Turkish invasion and, after conquering the enemy, he gave a triumphal dinner in the ballroom. Later, the Esterhazy family occupied the palace and in its red drawing room Schubert first rendered his immortal serenade to the beautiful countess. Vaulted underground chambers indicated the presence of an early Christian church beneath the palace, and there was even a traditional ghost protecting buried treasure to make the glamour complete! Many artists had remarked on the friendly atmosphere the old walls had accumulated, which inspired them to do their best work.

Though it had once been "the most brilliant capital in Europe," by 1927 Vienna was a city haunted with tragedy. It was the one metropolis of a poverty stricken republic—an economic dead weight on the rest of the country—for, of Austria's six million citizens, one-third lived in Vienna. Granting that the dogged determination of the new order revealed something far finer than ever existed in the aristocratic but decadent old order, the smothered ashes of empire, redolent of pomp and pageantry forever dead, were not without mourners. This condition in itself emanated grief, but there was another sadder still. Vienna, after World War I, very nearly starved and this is not a figure of speech. "The most brilliant capital in Europe" escaped annihilation by so narrow a margin that it had not yet fully recovered and many survivors of the famine were indelibly marked by what they had suffered. You sometimes succeeded in forgetting this; then, suddenly, you were forcibly reminded of it—by the startled gratitude of a servant whose swift and skillful attentions you sought to recompense, by the musician whose animated expression faded to one of bitter submission, as he put down his violin, by the black-clad noblewoman, who greeted you with the inimitable charm of the *grande noblesse,* but whose outward signs of mourning could not conceal her inner grief. Even in the contented groups of the Rathskeller and Burggarten you caught an undercurrent of feeling so strong, it was hard to believe this had not been put in words. "Yesterday we had no money; tomorrow we may have none, therefore, let us spend what we have today on music that we may be comforted." ... "Yesterday some of us were hungry; tomorrow some of us will be hungry again; let us, therefore, eat, drink and be merry." It was the kind of resignation that produces revolutions.

And so we come to the saddest condition of all—the one which had produced the riots; and which, as described in the American press, caused such concern regarding my visit to Austria. The political situation there was unusual: The *Länder,* or country districts, were almost wholly conservative in both sentiment and government; and the balance of national power was helped by the conservative Nationalists, or Christian Socialists, headed by the Chancellor, Monsignor Ignaz Seipel. Vienna, on the other hand, was Social Democratic—radical in both sentiment and government—and, though Mayor Karl M. Seitz was a strong Socialist, his government had done much for the people's welfare by building model tenements, public baths, schools and playgrounds. Shortly before my visit, a shooting affray had occurred at Shattendorf near the Hungarian border, in which two Socialists had been killed by two Nationalists, and it was alleged that though the latter had pleaded guilty, they had been acquitted. When the verdict was made public, the Socialists in Vienna paraded in protest, and on the morning of the demonstration, the first procession of workers arrived at the Parliament Building about nine o'clock. When they endeavored to enter this and the University, they were held in check by the police but the mob spirit soon asserted itself and the nearby police station was set afire; a few minutes later the rioters had scaled the walls of the Palace of Justice and fired it also. The Mayor's attempts to remonstrate with them were of no avail and irreplaceable records and documents were either burned inside the Palace or in bonfires outside because the fire brigades were unable to approach. A battle ensued in which nearly a hundred were killed, at least five times that number wounded and many more arrested.

That a general strike should follow was inevitable, and by evening, trains and trams had ceased to run, mails and wires were completely tied up, and violent outbreaks were frequent. But the provinces declined to join the turbulent Socialists, and without their cooperation and food supplies, the strike was of short duration. The Chancellor refused to be intimidated by threats to prolong the walk-out, unless he resigned or compromised, and normal conditions of transportation and communication were re-established. Funerals for the riot victims were held without incident and the smoke of battle cleared to reveal Seipel more firmly entrenched than ever, and the majority of the Austrians in agreement with Mr. Coolidge's doctrine that "No one has a right to strike against the public safety, anyhow, anywhere, any time." I reached Vienna in the midst of these events and some of them I saw, others I did not; so I reconstructed them from the best evidence I could obtain.

Ignaz Seipel, born of humble parents, became first a priest and then a college professor. He taught and wrote at the universities of Salzburg and Vienna, and his work *Nation and State* brought him to the attention of Emperor Charles, under whom he served as Minister of Public Welfare and to whom he remained steadfast until the end of the ill-fated empire. In 1922, he became Chancellor of the infant republic, a position which, with slight interruptions, he had held ever since. Because of the consummate skill with which he had worked for the economic and political reconstruction of Austria, he was the undisputed leader of the

Nationalist party; and his triumph over recent events had made him renowned throughout Europe.

On the occasion of my presentation to him, Mrs. Washburn and I were ushered into a formal drawing room in the famous Badehaltz, the severity of its high white paneled walls relieved by gilt tracery, its gilt furniture upholstered in pale green brocade. Next to this salon was the Chancellor's private office, the apartment similarly used by Metternich and known as the "Maria Theresa Room," because of the portrait of the empress which hung on its yellow brocaded walls. Beyond was the famous chamber used during the Congress of Vienna, with its five doors through which the representatives of the participating powers entered simultaneously for their meetings so that none could consult without the others. The Chancellor later took us into these historic state rooms himself, but he welcomed us in the formal drawing room, which he entered from his study—as calm, as erect, as ruddy, as dignified as he was at the opening of Parliament, and dressed in the same black clerical garments.

"It is my great pleasure to meet you, *Gnädige Frau,*" he said, using the salutation which to me is so much more beautiful than that of any with which I am familiar—I always felt I should strive to deserve the title, "gracious lady," whenever I was addressed that way! Then he spoke of my travels and of my writings so kindly that I was embarrassed and quite touched.

And next, "I congratulate you on keeping your appointment with me," he said, "for I am sure you were told in London that it was not safe for you to come, is it not so? And that it was hardly worth while in any case, as I would have been forced to resign before your arrival, and all that? I thought as much. But here you are, and I hope quite comfortable at your hotel and quite free to go about the streets as you observe, and we are very glad to see you."

Of course we spoke of the riots, and the Chancellor did so with great feeling and regret, but refused to concede they were of lasting importance and called attention to the fact that there had not even been a temporary fluctuation in Austrian currency—always a significant indication of a country's stability. But I had not come to talk of riots, but because he was the most famous practicing ecclesiastic of his time who also held a position of extreme political importance and possessed great temporal power—and because I felt such a man would have something to tell which would be invaluable to me personally.

I was neither disappointed nor mistaken. Monsignor Seipel slipped into the subject which I had hoped he might discuss with ease and earnestness.

"You must not suppose," he said, "that there are not many times when I think of my former peaceful life and wish I might return to it. But I know that is a selfish wish and, therefore, I strive to make it a temporary one. For it is here in the Badehaltz, and not in seclusion among my books, that I can best help my country and worship my God. Men—and women—are called upon to serve in different ways, and they must serve where and as they are most needed. Otherwise, they are not true to their religion.

"That my religion has been a source of the greatest strength and comfort to me—that it has been the mainstay of my life, a very present help in all times of trouble, including the crisis through which we have just passed—and the power which has brought me to such success and triumph as I have attained—I do not need to say to you. But this one point I *should* like to stress, *Gnädige Frau: I have never seen the time when my religious life and my political life were incompatible.* Each sustains and illuminates the other; they are complementary; they are, for me, indivisible."

And that was the most important message I took out of Austria.

Chapter 53

L AUSANNE was a happy choice as a meeting place for the World Conference on Faith and Order not only from a viewpoint of convenience but of beauty, as well: the quaint old Swiss city, with its red-
roofed, gray-walled houses, its peaceful parks and fragrant gardens of
flowering hawthorn, has an enviable location, rising as it does in steep
ascent from the Lake of Geneva. "The roofs above the lake, the mountains above the roofs, the clouds above the mountains, the stars above
the clouds, like a staircase upon which my thoughts mount, step by step
and widen at each stage!" exclaimed Victor Hugo many years before
when he visited Lausanne.

The Conference's official invitation was issued to "all Christian Communions throughout the World, both Catholic and Protestant, which
confess our Lord Jesus Christ as God and Saviour." The Roman Catholic Church, though receiving the invitation in a friendly spirit and
promising its prayers, did not feel it could take part in the Conference;
and during it several emphatic and sincere expressions of regret at this
lack of representation were offered. (Two Roman Catholic priests attended the Conference in a journalistic capacity, occupying seats in the
press gallery, and announced their intention of reporting its proceedings
to the proper church authorities, but these clerics declined to have any
official connection with the Conference.)

Practically all the other great Trinitarian Communions sent delegates,
however; eighty-seven different churches from twenty-six countries were
represented, and among the speakers on the second afternoon were two
Germans, a Latvian, a Bulgarian, a Swiss, a Scotsman and an Englishman. Though the majority of the delegates were English speaking, German was mainly used at the sessions I attended, but all statements were

translated into French, as well as those languages, and important reports were later rendered in Greek; and, at the opening service in the Lausanne Cathedral, it was evident that this was, indeed, a *world* conference!

That morning's sermon was preached by the Right Reverend Charles H. Brent, Episcopal Bishop of Western New York, and in it he said:

> It is the call of Christ which arrests us. . . . The general need of unity is set down by Him in a proverbial saying: "Every kingdom divided against itself shall not stand." This is as true today as when it was first uttered. It has been accepted by the world of men as applying to every department of life. . . . In increasingly wide circles men are striving for unity. Lying at the center of all and providing the only enduring cement is religious unity. . . .

Like so many European cathedrals, the one in Lausanne, where the sessions were held, is situated upon a hill, and figuratively as well as literally stands above all lesser buildings. The Conference lasted for three weeks and there were sometimes three sessions a day. One outstanding aspect of them was their atmosphere—the delegates were so faithful in coming, so earnest about the proceedings—that the very air seemed charged with these qualities. Dr. Hertsberg, one of the Norwegian representatives, died shortly after his arrival, but his final act had been the preparation of a message, which was read in its unfinished form to the Conference; and though Bishop Brent was a sick man, he was unflagging in his attendance. The serenity of Dr. William Adams Brown of the Union Theological Seminary in New York; the dignity of the Metropolitan Germanos, Archbishop of Thyateira, whom, like Bishop Manning, I had seen in London; the gentle zeal of Dr. Merle d'Aubigne of France's Reformed Evangelical Church; the enthusiasm of the missionary leaders—all these were remarkable. But considering the divergent views of the numerous delegates, I never would have believed that they could meet day after day, and week after week, without friction and discord. *There was almost none.* Of course there were disagreements— frankly expressed; but coupled with the frankness were tolerance and consideration for the feelings and viewpoints of others. The expression "a spirit of brotherly love" is one about which we are apt to be skeptical; but that spirit was evident throughout the Conference.

A second aspect worthy of mention was the perfection of organization. Often regarded as a purely mechanical thing, not to be associated with things spiritual, it is relegated to the background; but if wheels do not turn smoothly, it is impossible to attain a high spiritual plane in the resultant confusion. The men in charge of the Conference realized this and because of their wisdom, it progressed without delay or mishap.

The short exercises with which the Conference closed were perhaps the most moving of all. Proclaiming his conviction that its success was largely due to the emphasis which had been placed on prayer, Bishop Brent led the final devotions, as all stood in silent petition. Then the immortal passages from the Revelation of St. John the Divine penetrated the stillness:

> And I saw a new Heaven and a new Earth; for the first Heaven and the first Earth were passed away.... And I heard a great voice out of Heaven saying, "Behold the tabernacle of God is with men and He will dwell with them, and they shall be His people, and God Himself shall be with them and be their God."

What, actually, did the Conference accomplish? What was the concrete result of it?

To those who attended it, the "great fact that it actually did happen," to quote the Bishop of Manchester, was almost enough. A few years earlier, it would have been inconceivable to anyone with even the most superficial knowledge of denominational differences that such a religious conference could take place. It would have been equally inconceivable, in the light of World War I, that Frenchmen and Germans, Austrians and Englishmen, Americans and Hungarians and Italians could have attended such a meeting at all, much less done so in a spirit of brotherly love; and therefore it could not have been a *world* conference. So an enormous step forward was taken in world understanding, and not only religious understanding but *all* understanding. If the Conference had done nothing more than meet in the manner it did, it would have been justified, but it went much further. It received *with unanimity* reports on questions so delicate and so debatable that the most optimistic delegate must have been astonished to find how many common professions of faith he shared with his fellow Christians all over the world. I doubt that the average Anglican could have visualized that an interpretation of the Sacraments or Creeds, to which he subscribed, would be equally acceptable to a Lutheran, a Presbyterian and a Friend! *But it proved to be so.* The truth that the things which unite us are far more important than those which divide us was brought home again and again and *had never been so poignantly proven before.* In my mind, that Conference marked the first great step toward ecumenism, though we did not hear much of that word until more than thirty years later.

During the Conference I had an occasional break in the form of a luncheon or dinner, directly or indirectly connected with it. The most important luncheon, as far as future work was concerned, was one with Princess Bandini in Geneva. The original vocation of this remarkable woman had been that of the cloister; but she had reluctantly been forced to seek release from her vows because she did not possess the physical strength to endure the rigid regime and, in the world, had become invaluable to both Quirinal and Vatican and *persona grata* at both and was, at that time, a permanent committee chairman at the Secretariat of the League of Nations. She was also one of eight beautiful sisters, all of whom were deeply religious and all of whom achieved distinction in different ways; eventually, I was privileged to know nearly all of them, as well as their only brother Prince Giustiniani Bandini, and to find a personal welcome at several historic Roman palaces in consequence.

Before 1927, I had known only one sister, Lady Isabella, the wife of Sir Esme Howard, the British Ambassador to the United States who had been of such inestimable help in sending me to the Governor-General and Lady Guillemard in Singapore; but when I was preparing to leave Washington for Europe, Lady Isabella had suggested that I get in touch with Princess Bandini while I was in Lausanne.

I did so and Princess Bandini speedily put me at my ease, telling me almost immediately that her friends called her Donna Cristina and that she would like to have me do so, too. I told her whom I had seen and what I had done so far on my trip, that everything had gone very smoothly and that everything had been approved by my editor. My one difficulty had been in securing his consent to include the Vatican in my series, which I felt would otherwise be incomplete; he was willing to do so under only one condition and I was doubtful whether I could meet it.

"Why, of course you can!" Donna Cristina exclaimed instantly. "Do not give it another thought. How quickly could you leave for Rome?"

"Any time after next week, if I knew in advance when to make reservations."

"I think you are safe in making them right away; but if you prefer, I will send you word shortly."

The message came three days later in the form of a telegram addressed to Donna Cristina, which she sent to me with her card. The wire was from the Vatican and read simply:

YOUR APPLICANT WILL BE RECEIVED UPON ARRIVAL

Three days after that the boys and I boarded a train for Rome.

Chapter 54

OUR train pulled into Rome at eight-thirty the next morning and an hour and a half later, having bathed and breakfasted, I presented myself at the Secretariat of the Vatican, armed with the telegram to Princess Bandini and accompanied by Henry. A pleasant-faced usher spoke to me in excellent English and conducted me across the room to an equally pleasant appearing priest, seated at a large desk, who immediately rose.

"Mrs. Keyes?" he asked cordially. "We were expecting you. Monsignor Caccia, who has charge of audiences, is out at the moment, but I am his secretary. This is your son? He would like, I imagine, to be received also? And is there anyone else traveling with you?"

Almost overcome by so much friendliness, I murmured that there was another son and a young cousin.

"They will be welcome," the secretary assured me. "I understand you are pressed for time and do not wish to remain long in Rome. I am sorry nothing can be arranged for tomorrow, because the President of a Republic is to be received and that will be a lengthy official visit. But certainly by the day after. In any case the invitation will reach you the evening before."

I had expected to wait at least a week, so was dumbfounded at the apology for a twenty-four-hour delay. Also, I had anticipated special directions as to what I should do and say at the audience and, especially, as to what I might write about it afterward, for I had heard that very little latitude in this regard was permitted. So I lingered to receive such instruction and admonition. Neither was forthcoming. The secretary had obviously said all he thought necessary, but much encouraged by his attitude, I inquired if it would be presumptuous to ask a question.

"Certainly not. What would you like to know?"

"I realize that Princess Bandini is a very powerful advocate and I am grateful for her recommendation. But everything has happened so rapidly that I cannot help wondering if there was any other factor. . . ."

He smiled, opened a filing cabinet and extracted a folder. "Actually, you didn't need any recommendation," he said. "If you had applied direct, the answer would have been the same. Even without our complete dossier, this article would have assured you of a welcome." He handed me the folder, and I gazed at a copy of the article I had written for the National Catholic Welfare Conference News Service, at Elisabeth Shirley's request—the article for which I had received twenty-five dollars and had then completely forgotten. It had now proved the Open Sesame for which I had hardly dared to hope! [1]

Expressing my appreciation as best I could, I took my departure, having been in the Secretariat for about five minutes! The following evening, just before dinner, there was a knock at my door and, upon opening this, I was confronted by a smiling messenger who handed me a large limp envelope bearing the seal of the Vatican. Tearing open the envelope, I found that "His Holiness Pope Pius XI will receive Mrs. Frances Parkinson Keyes and three other persons" the next day at a quarter to one. The private audience had been granted, as the secretary had expected, after the lapse of a day!

In the morning, the boys, in full evening dress and very much excited, were waiting when I came out of my room wearing a Drêcoll gown which had been made for the occasion, should it arise—a soft black silk covered with still softer black lace, long sleeved, high necked and reaching to my ankles. It may be hard to visualize such a costume as graceful or becoming, but it really was both and even my critical bodyguard, violently opposed to somber clothing of any sort, agreed that it was "wonderful looking."

A few minutes later our limousine turned behind the semicircle of columns which borders the piazza of St. Peter's and continued beyond the basilica to an inner court. At its entrance were stationed two members of the Swiss guard, in their picturesque costumes of red, blue and yellow, who saluted as we passed. Other guards were waiting at the door where we alighted, one of whom asked to see our invitation; then

---

[1] An author whose judgment I respect feels that no professional writer should consent to write anything for a nominal fee or even at a reduction from the highest price he can command. On this score I have never agreed with him, and the above is a good example of why I do not!

we were motioned toward a staircase, which, as we mounted it, seemed endless. It went on and on and up and up in a succession of low broad stone steps, until at last we came to the cloakroom—that I remembered from my previous visits—in which those to be received in general audience leave their wraps, and where, if anything incorrect is discovered in their apparel, it is rectified. Here, an attendant in crimson brocade livery waved us on to a second, similarly arrayed, who led us across a huge apartment, where clusters of people were already waiting to be received, into a smaller room, and turned us over to a third elegantly attired functionary. This procedure was repeated several times, and in the course of it, to my great uneasiness, our invitation was taken from me. My anxiety increased when we were seated in a room with several other people—an elderly lady with two lovely girls who were dressed in the pure white which is permitted the young and unmarried instead of black; two officers in full dress uniforms; three or four Sisters of Charity—and left there for what seemed an eternity. I was sure I had blundered somewhere, that the audience was not to be a private one after all. . . . And then, just when it seemed I could not endure the suspense another instant, the master of ceremonies, a small stooping man in uniform, appeared with the invitation in his hand and conducted us into still another room, where Monsignor Caccia was waiting.

The room was a handsome one: its walls were covered with crimson brocade and several magnificent pictures hung upon them. At one end was a small throne; on either side were tables of ornate design, one bearing a miniature of St. Cecilia's famous statue, the other a clock of lapis-lazuli. The formality and elegance of these surroundings might have proved overwhelming had it not been for the cordiality and kindness of Monsignor Caccia—a large, well built man, in whose dark face not only intellectuality but humor and more than a little savoir-faire were discernible. There was still a wait ahead of us and during it he talked easily and pleasantly on many subjects, none of them ecclesiastical, and even indulged in several jests that relieved the inevitable tension. We were conscious of the murmur of voices in the adjoining room, and as this ceased, a door was flung open and a tall vigorous-looking man in a brown habit, the zeal of the missionary stamped on his features, strode out and across the room in which we sat. Obviously, he had been reporting on his work in foreign lands, and appreciating the value of such labors, I could not begrudge one instant of the time he had consumed.

The door opened again, less violently this time, and a man dressed in simple white garments stood before us; a man wearing glasses, with an earnest scholarly face, not too grave to be friendly, dignified, impressive, but not unapproachable: His Holiness, Pope Pius XI. We knelt to receive the Papal benediction; but when this had been pronounced, in Latin, a second of general and all-embracing character followed in French: "May God bless and keep you, and all those who are dear to you, also. May He hear your prayers and grant your requests." Then, still speaking in French, he began to talk with us, quietly and naturally. How long had we been in Rome? Were we enjoying it? Where did the boys go to college? And how soon did they have to be back? He understood that I had seen something of missions in the Orient, that I had been interested in them. Would I tell him something further of my impressions? Our replies were no more restricted than were his own words. Like Chancellor Seipel of Austria, he spoke benevolently of my writing and my travels. I felt as if I were speaking with someone I had known a long time. The sense of strangeness and weariness, of bewilderment and anxiety I had experienced earlier left me completely. He seemed to interpret, as I had never heard them interpreted before, the words of Christ, "Come unto me, all *ye* that travail and are heavy laden, and I will refresh you." It is only the very great and the very good who are able so to interpret those words.

Suddenly, dimly, I realized the audience was over. The scholarly, saintly figure, who had been there talking with us so quietly and naturally had blessed us again and passed into another room; the brief general audience had begun. We said farewell to Monsignor Caccia and walked slowly back to the place where the boys had left their tall hats and white gloves. There we found another Vatican official, Monsignor Enrico Pucci, waiting to speak to us.

"I am in charge of the press here," he told us, "and will announce that you have been privately received. I shall report nothing else, however, because I am sure you would like to relate the details yourself."

When I asked if I should submit my article to him, he shook his head. "We have complete confidence in your discretion," he said.

My article was not mentioned again, though Monsignor Pucci dined with us the next evening and the evening before we left Rome, he paid us a farewell visit and brought me a present he said he had been asked to deliver: the Papal Medal of the Good Shepherd. It is, I understand, a very old decoration which always bears the likeness of the current Pope on one side and a representation of Christ as the Good Shepherd on the other; its recipients are honored by the confidence that is placed in them as advocates of world peace.

My treacherous old back, which had not troubled me particularly all summer, gave out suddenly late in the day of the audience and my further activities in Rome were thus greatly curtailed. Both Lady Isabella and Donna Cristina had written their families of my impending visit and Prince Bandini and Countess Colleoni—another of the lovely Bandini sisters—had promptly offered us hospitality. I sent the boys out to do their sightseeing without me—a real disappointment, because there were so many pictures and places I had loved all my life and wanted to see again through their eyes; but I struggled into my clothes long enough to have an afternoon of bridge in the sunny garden of the Giustiniani-Bandini palace and tea with Countess Colleoni at her apartment, with still another sister—Countess Piella—as a fellow guest. History seemed very close when I discovered a copy of the famous Verrocchio statue of Generalissimo Bartolomeo Colleoni which dominates a piazza in Venice among other ancestral treasures in the Countess's drawing room; and her apology for the simplicity of her entertainment—that her husband was an invalid and she had never gone further from him than the next room in two years—showed a touching side of the devotion with which all members of the family seemed endowed.

We started for Paris as soon as I was able to travel and two days after reaching there went on to Rheims, with the hope of seeing another great European ecclesiastic: His Eminence Cardinal Luçon, Dean of all the cardinals of France, now eighty-four years of age, the Archbishop who never left his diocese during the darkest days of the war and who had lived to see his beloved cathedral rise from its ruins. The road from Paris to Rheims was a joyful revelation, a monument to the industry and courage of the French. Where four years earlier there were black and barren fields swept with rusty wire, studded with charred stumps, there were now smooth pastures again, wide acres of grain, cattle and sheep grazing. Where four years earlier there were shattered roofless walls, with only an occasional sign of life, there were now trim villages, lace curtains inside the windows and flower-filled boxes outside. John and Sid, who had never been here before, declared that if they had not known there had been a war, they would have assumed only an occasional fire had taken place.

A short detour took us through Belleau Wood, where the Stars and Stripes flew proudly over the two hundred acres that are American forever and where we found the cemetery green and beautiful.[2] Then, pausing on the outskirts of Rheims, we stopped at the American Hospital for Children which had been presented to the city two years previously as a memorial to the Americans who fought and died in France.

---

[2] The purchase of these acres and the restoration of the village of Belleau Wood, as well as two sister villages, were made possible by the efforts of Mrs. James Carroll Frazer of Washington and the Belleau Wood Memorial Association she founded.

Dr. Marie-Louise Lefort, who had been in charge of the American Temporary Hospital in Rheims during the war and was now director of the new one, welcomed us cordially and showed us over the building, which not only had the most modern equipment but was very attractive because of its frescoed walls, its roof terrace and its garden with a quiet pool. The small patients hailed her joyfully as we approached and it was evident they regarded the doctor with great affection. Americans aware of his generosity could take pride in the fact that John D. Rockefeller, Jr., had made possible the restoration of Rheims cathedral; but many more of us could take *personal* pride in that memorial hospital, because it was made possible by the contributions of France's many American friends, some who gave much, others little, according to their means. The building of that hospital for little children was no less a sacred service than the rebuilding of the cathedral.

Rheims, as we entered it, presented the same changed aspect that the countryside had done. It seemed impossible that this was the place in which, a few short years before, only one house in every thousand had been left intact, only one in every hundred was reparable. Gaily decorated, bustling, crowded, it seemed now not only to hum but to sing. We sought out the tiny Hotel Savoy, which Henry and I remembered as having the best food and the best service we had found anywhere in the world, in spite of its diminutive size and slight shabbiness; and discovered it was now very spruce and smart indeed. We were remembered, too, and were warmly welcomed by the same *maître d'hôtel* who had served us so well before and plans were immediately under way for the preparation of *truite à la meunière, crepes* Suzette and other ambrosial delicacies. Meanwhile, I went upstairs to rest, dispatching Henry with my letter of introduction to the Archbishop's house.

I had scarcely settled myself when my eldest son burst into the room, visibly excited. "Get up and dress quickly!" he exclaimed. "I've seen the old gentleman and he's wonderful and he told me to come and get you at once. *'Allez chercher votre mère,'* he said. Hurry!" As I jumped up and hastily sought the garments I had not anticipated wearing before the next day and therefore had made no effort to unpack, Henry elucidated somewhat. "I had a little trouble finding the house, so I asked a man I met how to get there. 'Do you want to see the Archbishop?' he asked. 'Well, I want to deliver a letter of introduction to him,' I replied. 'You won't need that, he'll be delighted to see you anyway,' my newfound friend informed me, as he took me to the house and, sure enough, the first thing I knew, there I was in the room with Cardinal Luçon! No delay, no formality! He read the letter and asked where you were and when I told him you hoped he might receive you tomorrow, that was when he told me to: '*Allez*' and so forth. Do hurry. He's terrific. Nice white hair, jolly smile, all that sort of thing. Don't you think I can go back with you? John and Sid ought to come, too, on the chance he'll see them . . . he's so darned friendly. Hurry!"

Gathering the rest of the clan together, we started out. The street on which the Archbishop's residence was situated was so narrow our car could not enter it, so we jumped out and slipped and slid over cobbles made treacherous by the pouring rain. A manservant promptly admitted us and ushered us into a drawing room overlooking a garden—a typical French salon of ample proportions, furnished with austere and formal taste. Another door opened almost immediately and a scarlet-robed figure with nobility of face and bearing stood before us—the Cardinal Archbishop himself.

"I am very glad to see you," he said pleasantly, "and glad also that you brought your family with you. Please sit down and we will talk." When I tried to thank him for seeing me so promptly, he interrupted me. "It is the other way around. I thank you for coming, for bringing me another expression of American good will. What do we not owe to America in Rheims! You have not yet seen the cathedral, Madame, but you will tomorrow; it is now open again for the service of God—in fact, it has been since last May. It would not have been possible without help from America—without Mr. Rockefeller's generosity. But it is not only for the restoration of the cathedral that we are in your debt. I shall never forget the American ladies who came during the early days of the war, ladies used to every comfort and luxury who gave them all up to help us. When my poor children—my spiritual children—were driven from their homes, without possessions, without money, without hope, there was the American Relief to help them. We will never forget, here in Rheims; nor can we express sufficiently our gratitude to America."

The Archbishop spoke of the war, without rancor, without heat. "When it broke out, I was not here. I had gone to Rome with Cardinal Mercier. And then I could not get back. The railroad was not running and, though the manager of the line offered to bring me in a special car, the authorities would not permit it. I came at last in a convoy of trucks sent out for the wounded. And my cathedral was already burned—the cathedral that had taken two hundred years to build; the cathedral in which the early Franks received Christian baptism; the cathedral in which the Kings of France were crowned, the cathedral in which Joan of Arc had restored to Charles the Sixth his royal rights. Never have I entered it that I have not thought of that young girl, that simple peasant, untaught, unlettered, who by the grace of God and her faith in Him led an army to victory and saved her native country. I think of her, of what she did in the cathedral of Rheims, and try to be worthy to follow in her footsteps.

"And it was burned, my cathedral. Never had we dreamed that would happen. First, because it was a house of worship, a sanctuary. Second, because it was a historic monument. Third, because it was being used as a hospital. The Red Cross flag flew above it, wounded German prisoners were there, lying upon straw. But it was set on fire, and there was no way of putting out the fire—the enemy had destroyed our waterworks. That they had a right to do—that is war. But not to touch the cathedral! The lead of the famous roof that people came from all over the world to see melted and ignited the straw. All prisoners but one were moved to safety. There were those who said, 'Let them perish, they are our enemies.' But that would have been unworthy of France.

"So I returned from Rome to find my cathedral burned—a sad day, but not the saddest. That was the day it was shelled. My house, too, as well as the others in the city; but that was not as bad as the shelling of God's house. The bombardment lasted for many days—of more than one hundred thousand inhabitants, only fourteen hundred were left in Rheims. But I did not leave; my place was with my cathedral and the remnants of my little flock, for whom I had cared more than fifty years. There were twenty priests in the diocese when war began and not one of them left. I tried to persuade the members of my household to go, but they would not. And every Friday I went to the cathedral and followed the Stations of the Cross.

"At last, by military order, Rheims was completely evacuated; for six months it was a deserted city, but at the end of that time, I managed to return; meanwhile, I found shelter in a nearby village that was in my diocese. When the armistice was signed, I obtained a permit to visit my scattered flock. And, Madame, before I found a single one, I went for a distance of seventy miles, without encountering one living thing—not a chicken, not a cat or a dog, not a sheep or a horse or a cow. Needless to say, no man, woman or child. Such desolation.

"But through the goodness of God and the help of our friends, better days have come to us at last. The cathedral was opened again on the sixtieth anniversary of my ordination—let me give you a booklet describing the ceremony; it will be a souvenir of this visit which has given me so much pleasure."

It was hard to realize, when we stepped out into the rain-darkened street again, that our visit had lasted nearly two hours, for during it we had been transported far beyond the limits of time and space, and the Archbishop of Rheims had taught us a great lesson—of the beauty of bravery, of steadfastness, of the faith that moves mountains.

Part Eleven

American Chronicle Resumed

Chapter 55

THE greater part of my voyage home was spent in my own comfortable cabin, writing—and writing—and writing. A ship was still almost the only place where I was sure of being uninterrupted and undisturbed while putting on paper, when they were fresh in my mind, records of my impressions and experiences. Still more, it was the place where I was able to catch up with personal correspondence. And the formidable pile of envelopes labeled "Unanswered Letters," which confronted me when I embarked, was only a slim bundle on my desk as I packed before disembarking.

It was just as well that I landed with a clean slate as far as *Good Housekeeping* articles were concerned, for after a day's respite in Providence with Larry and his family I went to New York for a series of editorial conferences every day and excellent plays every evening. It is only fair to say that owing to the fringe benefits connected with the conferences—luncheons which I ate with relish at the best restaurants and gifts of current bestsellers which I read with avidity—I did not find them a great hardship. Then, after a scant two weeks at Pine Grove Farm, I started for the Midwest, accompanied by Miss Shufelt, who had rejoined me when I was in New York. Mr. Meredith had been most insistent that I must *visit* the homes of the prominent women about whom I was to write for *Better Homes and Gardens;* and this trip was designed to include Judge Florence Allen's in Columbus, Emily Newell Blair's in Joplin and Mrs. Medill McCormick's in Chicago, as well as the Merediths' in Des Moines, where we were pampered house guests for several days. The elegance which had distinguished their way of living in Washington was even more marked when they were in their own large house (the only one, I believe, at which I have ever stayed where

(527)

every guest room had its own sitting room). But my bad back once more landed me in bed for nearly a week before I left home, and as I literally got out of bed to make the trip, it was a good deal of an endurance test, even without the speech before the New York Federation of Women's Clubs in Syracuse which climaxed it.

Next came brief family visits in and around Boston: with my mother in Andover; with my dear aunt Fannie in Winchester; with the boys, two of them now in Cambridge and one at Milton, who came to the Puritan and brought their friends. These sojourns should have marked intervals of quiet pleasure, but I was too tired to really enjoy them; and after that I was back in Washington, where I followed the now more or less established pattern of working hours combined with and interrupted by a heavy social schedule. The brief notations on my calendar tell the story: "Received with Mrs. Dawes." . . . "Our dinner for the Szes." . . . "Dinner with the Gerrys." . . . "Dinner with Associate Justice and Mrs. Stone." . . . "Gave luncheon to twenty-two in honor of Mme Matsadaira." . . . "Worked on *Delineator* article all day." . . . "In bed most of day but went on writing."

A badly infected finger added to my miserable (and apparently inescapable) back trouble, though I managed to get to Manchester, New Hampshire, and make a long-promised speech before the Women's Republican Institute—this time with a distinctly political purpose, as Harry's colleague Senator George Moses was being tentatively groomed as a vice-presidential candidate and it would have been difficult to explain my failure to appear. I also went to Albany, since Oscar Graeve—Sell's successor as editor of *Delineator*—was just as eager as Mr. Meredith to have me visit on their home territory the persons about whom I wrote and there was no doubt that Alfred E. Smith would again be the Democratic presidential candidate. I was very cordially received at the gubernatorial mansion, and luncheon with Mrs. Smith and several younger members of the family passed off pleasantly; but the Governor did not present himself until midafternoon and everything about my talk with him seemed fated to go wrong—not only the interview itself, but the unsatisfactory arrangements that had been made for it. I returned to Washington deeply discouraged. I did not see how I could honestly write a favorable article, and *Delineator,* like *Good Housekeeping,* was adamant in its attitude about excluding anything unpleasant. In desperation I told Key Pittman and Peter Gerry exactly what had happened and begged for their advice and cooperation.

They were both committed to Smith's candidacy and both as truly in favor of it as I was against it; at the same time, they saw and understood my feeling in the matter, though insisting it was largely the result of mismanagement. Evidently this at least was quite generally recognized, for Mrs. Belle Israels Moskowitz, Vice Chairman of the National Democratic Committee, who naturally was active in the campaign, wrote Mr. Graeve demanding to see a copy of the article before it was published—a demand which he courteously refused, saying that this was against the magazine's policy, which was quite true. Next, to my great surprise, I received a letter from Mrs. Franklin D. Roosevelt, whom I had not seen since 1920, asking me to dine and go to the theater with her the next time I was in New York. As she was also working actively for Smith, I could not help feeling, much as I liked her, that there was an ulterior purpose in this sudden show of hospitality, and with great regret I declined. Somehow the article was written, but it certainly was one of those which was achieved through blood and tears. Looking back on it, I think gratefully of Vice President Dawes's cryptic remark that, "Mrs. Keyes never says anything disagreeable about anyone; but there are some very conspicuous silences!"

There were, indeed, some very conspicuous silences in the article I wrote about that day in Albany, but either Mr. Smith's supporters were less perceptive than Mr. Dawes or they decided these did not matter, since I had said such nice things about the luncheon. I was finding it increasingly difficult, however, to keep up with every phase of my current existence, though apparently Mr. Bigelow was the only person besides Dr. Hardin who realized how near the breaking point I was. The former had come to see me about another assignment abroad—one that would be as lengthy and as ambitious as my 'round the world trip—and had tentatively settled on a tour of "All the Americas"; but, even before he heard Dr. Hardin's opinion of my condition, he voiced one of his own.

"I've never seen you look so badly," he announced with his usual abruptness. "Hasn't your doctor told you to slow down?"

"Something of the sort. This miserable finger won't heal and it's very painful—I shouldn't let it get me down; but he keeps talking about going to Bermuda and relaxing."

"That sounds like an excellent idea. Couldn't you go during Peter's spring vacation and take him? As guests of *Good Housekeeping,* of course. We've got big things ahead of us and you won't be up to them if you go on this way."

Now that three of my grandchildren have seized upon Bermuda as the only place they would even consider for a honeymoon, I feel guiltier than ever that I did not enjoy it. No automobiles were allowed on the island, and twelve miles was considered the maximum drive a pair of horses, hired at our very expensive hotel, could undertake. Even going at a moderate pace, such a distance did not take long to cover, and there did not seem to be much to do the rest of the day, as I could not go swimming because of my bad back and Peter would not go alone. I had once been a very good swimmer and I looked back with delight on the swimming I had done at Lake Tarleton; but I had never enjoyed idling away endless hours on a beach, and though I encouraged Peter to do so, there seemed to be no children in the hotel with whom he could make friends. Actually, the majority of guests we saw seemed to have come mainly to escape Prohibition, and I was three times obliged to have our dining room table changed owing to the uproarious behavior and unrestrained language of those occupying adjacent tables. The American Consul and his wife duly invited us to a cocktail party, which, under the circumstances, was the last sort of entertainment likely to appeal to me, and there were no other social diversions offered. I made allowances for the fact that there was inevitably a great difference in being a guest at Puerto Rico's *La Fortaleza* and a stranger in a Bermuda hotel; but the only real thrill which the stay in the islands gave me came from the fields of Easter lilies, which were beautiful beyond description; and I constantly kept thinking how much the trip was costing and how good Mr. Bigelow was to have given it to me and how ungrateful I was not to get more out of it. And he did not even want me to write about it, so I could not show my appreciation that way (though I did write about it later for the English *Good Housekeeping*).

Though I covered the 1928 National Republican Convention at Kansas City as conscientiously as I could, its issues do not remain as vivid as they should in my memory. What I do remember with vividness is Kansas City's enthusiastic estimate of itself. Having found my way into the "Heart of America"—so described on the badges of its welcoming committee—I discovered this heart to be throbbing with kindness and expanded with cordiality. The man from Missouri is credited with a desire to be "shown"; but the stranger within his gates realized that, this time, the native was doing the showing himself! For the Kansas City man glowed with pride in his home, and he spared no effort to convince his visitor this pride was pardonable. The night before the Big Show began, there was a Procession of Flambeaux which as far outrivaled the torchlight parades of my youth as car headlights outshine a bayberry candle. Witnessed by a surging crowd of over two hundred thousand, the cavalcade progressed, ten thousand strong, with banners, bands and floats. And at the end was the Hoover band wagon, huge and scarlet, proclaiming the triumph to come. . . .

But the Democratic Convention in Houston I remember for all sorts of reasons.

Miss Shufelt had returned to her former position for the summer, and with the end of the spring semester at the Harvard Law School Henry rejoined me as my secretary during his vacation. He could not reach Kansas City until the Convention was almost over, but it was just as well, for he was no more enthusiastic about Kansas City than I was. I was very glad to have him with me again, and we had a good trip from there to Houston on the famous "Katy" Railroad. The Pittmans had insistently suggested that we should go to Texas with them in their car, but I had thought this impractical for several reasons; and as it turned out, Senator Pittman was selected as Chairman of the Platform and Resolutions Committee and had to remain in the East working on the platform too late for them to drive, so we met in Houston.

Though I had known Senator Pittman would do everything he could to help me during the Convention, I was not prepared for quite as warm a welcome as Henry and I received. Both Pittmans and both Gerrys met us at the train, and as they took us to our hotel, we learned the Gerrys had rented a spacious house for the week (though they did not tell us so, the modest cost of this was five thousand dollars) and they expected us to dine with them that night—they had brought their servants with them—and spend as much time there as we would like from then on. This proved to be a godsend, for it was always cool and quiet and Henry had a daily swim in the pool while I enjoyed the seclusion of the house itself.

As we quickly discovered, Houston, like Kansas City, was not one of those cities which took conventions nonchalantly, displaying indifference to the strangers who came and went. Festooned bunting fluttered in the breeze; electric signs blazed their words of welcome; brass bands blared "Dixie"; pictures of vice-presidential hopefuls plastered every available corner and corridor; sidewalks and streets, lobbies and elevators seethed to the suffocation point, not only with conscientious reception and information committees, distracted police, darting taxi drivers, screaming newsboys, delegates and near-delegates, reporters and near-reporters—all of whom had or felt they had some logical reason to fight for a foothold—but also with bustling children, bewildered middle-aged ladies, belligerent elderly gentlemen, rangers, ranchers and members of various fraternal organizations, whose lack of official connection and whose danger of being trampled underfoot in no way lessened their unalloyed joy of participation in the fray.

Badges, credentials, ribbons and emblems adorned ample breasts; dress became increasingly casual; delegates left coats behind in hotel bedrooms which had been submissively accepted as "desirable reservations" designed to accommodate "three or four persons each." But single occupancy was permitted—at a price. My room was equipped with a three-quarter bed close to the window, with barely room to walk sideways without hitting the dressing table, and Henry's—connecting with mine through a bathroom—was exactly like it. Straw hats were pushed back from perspiring brows, hard-bitten cigars were clamped in the corners of determined mouths. Elevator service was so undependable that even Will Rogers betrayed his annoyance, and one distracted guest, who had waited three hours to be conveyed to the floor where his "desirable reservation" was located, finally fired four shots straight through the elevator door. A telegraph operator was not only bewildered but insulted when a delegate tried to send a wire to the Virgin Islands; she had never heard of them and could not be convinced they existed. The situation was not helped when an amused bystander murmured they were directly opposite the Isle of Man.

Henry's recollections of our first dinner at the Gerrys' are not quite the same as mine, and I have found them doubly interesting on this account. "I think the Senators were Pittman, Gerry, Harrison and Wagner," he says. "The wives of some were there, but I forget which, except that I am rather clear that Mrs. Pittman was not present. These men planned the program—and the action!—of the entire Convention at that dinner. This was during the early days of the use of radio in political campaigns and I had kept quiet most of the time, but got into the swing of the thing and suggested swapping one of the afternoon agendas for the evening one for better radio audience appeal, and it was done. I thought and still think it was a great compliment to us that we not only were invited, but were trusted to use some discretion without being specifically pledged not to reveal obviously confidential matter."

He doesn't mention Senator Robinson of Arkansas, who was to serve as the Convention's Permanent Chairman, but he certainly was there, and so was Mrs. Pittman.

I was thankful for the diversion of the Gerrys' dinner and, like Henry, touched by the confidence in my discretion (though less surprised than he was, because by then I had had so many examples of it, none of which I had abused), and the following morning it was with a real glow of gratitude for the intrinsic and dependable kindness of human nature that I finally reached Convention Hall.

It was a low-lying structure in cream and green tints, with flags flying jauntily around it; its interior was no less attractive and though it was actually much larger than Madison Square Garden, it was so well proportioned that one was hardly aware of its vastness.

"For heaven's sake, don't describe this as a colorful scene," Senator

Gerry whispered to me as we surveyed our surroundings, "because that is so obviously the thing to say about it!"

"Of course I won't," I whispered back indignantly, though that was what I had been planning to do. "From here, it looks like the squares of a patchwork quilt—green and red and blue and yellow, with the state standards for white."

"I see what you mean," interrupted Mrs. Pittman, who happened to be there for that session. "I think it is even more like a garden. Can't you visualize those standards lettered 'Marigolds,' 'Cinnamon Pinks,' 'Roses,' and 'Petunias,' instead of 'Rhode Island,' 'Nebraska,' 'South Dakota' and 'Canal Zone?' "

I found the comparison completely delightful and was glad that I did, for there was little else in the first sessions of the Convention to hold my interest or excite my admiration. The meetings were all late in starting; the limited repertoire of the three bands grew almost unbearable when rendered twenty or thirty times the same day; and the proceedings themselves lacked form and vigor. When Mr. Claude E. Bowers, the temporary chairman, was introduced, there was a pleased stir of anticipation, especially among those who had heard his splendid Jackson Day address the previous winter; but as the New York *Times* said editorially, "It was the most shrill 'key-note' ever sounded. . . . He drew upon every known, or unknown, source of attack and invective. It was one long arraignment of the Republican Party, couched in the kind of rolling rhetoric and alliterative abuse which, perhaps, he learned in his youth."

But the Permanent Chairman of the Convention, Senator Robinson of Arkansas, took over his duties the following day, and from the moment he began to preside, the Convention took form and substance and gained strength under his steady stalwart leadership.

At a national convention the platform is usually presented to the delegates for consideration before the names of presidential candidates are placed in nomination, but at Houston the order was reversed. The paramount necessity was to draw up a platform with supreme care, and an immense amount of time was inevitably consumed in doing this; so the nominating speeches began at the second evening session. On the first roll call Alabama yielded to Georgia, then Arizona yielded to New York, and, supported by strong and affectionate arms, Franklin Roosevelt appeared at the rostrum. The spectacle of this man crippled in his very prime but rising indomitably above the handicap in body no less than in mind and spirit was infinitely moving, infinitely inspiring. Honorably bearing an honorable name, trained in statesmanship by both tradition and experience, cultured, courageous, compelling, Franklin Roosevelt had devoted himself for years to the cause of his chosen leader. It was not the least of the tributes paid Governor Smith that many persons of this caliber had rallied to his support. As with Mrs. Roosevelt I had not seen Roosevelt since he was Assistant Secretary of the Navy and popularly known as "the Adonis of the Little Cabinet"; now in Houston, I chanced to meet him in an upper corridor of the hotel when he was being wheeled from one room to another. His color was as fresh, his smile as beguiling as ever; it was his charm and vitality, not his disablement, with which you were instantly struck; and though the thought did not take conscious form until some time afterward, I believe it was in that moment of chance meeting that I first realized that physical disabilities might be a handicap but never a preventive in doing one's destined work. And though the speech he made when he reached the lectern in Houston is not as well known as the "Happy Warrior" speech made in New York four years earlier or the first inaugural address in which he convinced us that the only thing we had to fear was fear itself, it still seems to me one of the greatest speeches I have ever heard:

> What sort of a president do we need today? A man, I take it, who has four great characteristics, every one of them essential to the office. First of all, leadership. . . . Next, experience. . . . Then, honesty. . . . Last, and in this time most vital, that rare ability to make popular government function as it was intended to. . . .
>
> It is possible, with only these qualifications, for a man to be a reasonably efficient president, but there is one thing more needed to make him a great president. It is that quality . . . of sympathetic understanding of the human heart, of real interest in one's fellow men. . . .
>
> America needs not only an administrator but a leader—a pathfinder. . . . We offer one who has the will to win—who not only deserves success but commands it. Victory is his habit—the happy warrior—Alfred E. Smith!

Like a storm at sea, the response to Roosevelt's speech surged over Convention Hall, only to be followed by a period of comparative apathy as other speeches continued far into that night and all through the next day.

Meanwhile, the sessions of the Platform and Resolutions Committee went on for thirty-six hours straight, with Senator Pittman presiding almost continuously; and, though he did not once appear at the Convention during that period, the power of his personality seemed to penetrate the hall for, to a large degree, the fate of the platform, as well as the party, lay in the Chairman's hands.

At last, Senator Pittman sauntered up the steps to the speaker's stand, took his place at the microphone and began to speak; by the time the weary delegates realized their platform was being presented to them, he had relegated the reading of it to the official secretary and seated himself in the nearest chair. Then suddenly the gathering was galvanized into alert attention.

"Speaking for the National Democracy," proclaimed the secretary, "this Convention pledges the party and its nominees to an honest effort to enforce the Eighteenth Amendment and all other provisions of the Federal Constitution and all laws enacted pursuant thereto."

In turn, Governor Dan Moody of Texas, Governor Albert C. Ritchie of Maryland and Senator Carter Glass—all fervent drys—approached the microphone; when each had spoken, the sudden realization that there was to be no discord, no dissension, swept the hall; all differences had been settled in committee; the platform was about to be adopted— it *had* been adopted!

Like everyone else, I was overwhelmed by what this realization meant—that Smith would be nominated on the first ballot. And then I was aware that Key was standing behind me with his hand on my shoulder.

"It's all over but the shouting," he said. "Shall we leave before that ends?"

I rose and permitted myself to be guided through the throng of reporters and down the center aisle to the exit, where Henry joined us. When we reached the hotel I asked Key if this meant he would be asked again to run for Vice President.

"Yes."

"And you will?"

"No, I'm going to stay just where I am. Robinson wants it. He can have it."

There did not seem to be anything more that needed saying. Key turned and left us, and the next day Henry and I left for Los Angeles. Everything was, indeed, all over but the shouting.

Chapter 56

The Ambassador
Los Angeles
July 5, 1928

My dear Key:

I am sending you herewith, according to my promise, a carbon copy of my article on the National Democratic Convention, together with a copy of my letter concerning it to the editor of *Delineator*. I hope very much you will think the typescript worthy of going forward without changes; but as you will see I have asked that any changes you may suggest should be respected. Naturally, I depend upon you not to tamper with any compliments or the opposite I have paid anybody, since those are personal opinions! But any inaccuracies regarding proceedings or platform, you are at liberty to correct.

With love to Mimosa, and kind regards to yourself,

Very sincerely yours,
Frances Parkinson Keyes

POSTAL TELEGRAPH—COMMERCIAL CABLES

WASHINGTON, D. C.—JULY 6, P. M.

MRS. FRANCES PARKINSON KEYES, AMBASSADOR HOTEL, LOS ANGELES
LEAVING AT FOUR TO JOIN GOVERNOR SMITH AND BE HIS GUEST AT ALBANY
UNTIL WEDNESDAY WHEN WE ATTEND MEETING OF NATIONAL COMMITTEE
STOP HAVE RECEIVED CONGRATULATORY LETTERS FROM ALL OVER COUN-
TRY STOP SENATOR UNDERWOOD WRITES QUOTE OF COURSE GOVERNOR
SMITH NOMINATION WAS FORESHADOWED BEFORE THE CONVENTION MET
BUT TO BRING IT OFF ON THE FIRST BALLOT WITHOUT BAD FEELING OR
RANCOR ON THE PART OF HIS OPPONENTS WAS A HAPPENING THAT COULD
HARDLY BE EXPECTED IN ADVANCE OF THE MEETING OF THE CONVENTION
AND OF COURSE WILL PROVE A GREAT ASSET TO THE PARTY STOP BUT

YOUR MASTER STROKE WAS TO REPORT A PROHIBITION PLANK THAT MET WITH THE APPROVAL OF THE EXTREME PROHIBITIONISTS AND YET LEFT GOVERNOR SMITH FREE TO EXPRESS HIS OWN POSITION TO THE AMERICAN PEOPLE WITHOUT EMBARRASSMENT A REAL ACCOMPLISHMENT STOP YOU DESERVE TO BE DECORATED UNQUOTE STOP EVERYONE WHO MET YOU AT CONVENTION LOVES YOU BESIDES THOSE WHO MET YOU BEFORE STOP RE-GARDS TO HENRY AND LOVE FROM MRS. PITTMAN AND MYSELF—KEY PITTMAN

WESTERN UNION TELEGRAM

NEW YORK, N. Y.—JULY 11, 1928

FRANCES PARKINSON KEYES, AMBASSADOR HOTEL, LOS ANGELES, CAL.
GOVERNOR [SMITH] ANXIOUS TO MEET YOU WITH ME STOP YOUR STORY WONDERFUL IN SPITE OF INACCURACIES CONCERNING ME THEY ARE SO PLEASING I AM SENDING ON ARTICLE JUST AS WRITTEN STOP WILL BE AT WARWICK HOTEL FIFTY-FOURTH AND SIX AVENUE UNTIL FRIDAY STOP LOVE—KEY

WESTERN UNION TELEGRAM

LOS ANGELES, CAL.—JULY 11, 1928

HON. KEY PITTMAN, WARWICK HOTEL, 54TH ST AND 6TH AVE., NEW YORK
BOTH YOUR WIRES HAVE REACHED ME SAFELY STOP SO GLAD YOU LIKE ARTICLE AND THAT YOUR SERVICES ARE RECEIVING SUCH WELL MERITED AND GENERAL RECOGNITION STOP HAVE HAD SUCCESSFUL AND DELIGHTFUL VISIT HERE AND HAVE BEEN DEEPLY TOUCHED BY KINDNESS SHOWN ME BY ALL MY MOTION PICTURE FRIENDS WHO HAVE WELCOMED ME WARMLY AND ACCORDED ME EVERY COURTESY AND CONFIDENCE STOP HENRY AND I LEAVE TOMORROW THURSDAY TO SPEND WEEK END WITH FAMOUS WRITER KATHLEEN NORRIS AT SARATOGA CALIFORNIA WHERE WIRE WILL REACH ME STOP EXPECT TO START FOR NORTH HAVERHILL EARLY NEXT WEEK BY MOST DIRECT ROUTE AVAILABLE STOP IF YOU WILL LET ME KNOW WHEN THE GOVERNOR WOULD LIKE TO RECEIVE ME WITH YOU GIVING IF POSSI-BLE CHOICE OF DATES I WILL ENDEAVOR TO MEET HIS CONVENIENCE AND YOURS STOP KIND REGARDS—FRANCES PARKINSON KEYES

WESTERN UNION TELEGRAM

NEW YORK, N. Y.—JULY 14, 1928

FRANCES PARKINSON KEYES, C/O NORRIS, SARATOGA, CAL.
THE OFTENER I READ YOUR ARTICLE THE MORE I WONDER STOP IT IS THE MOST VIVID DESCRIPTION OF CONVENTION EVER WRITTEN STOP YOUR DE-SCRIPTION OF ROOSEVELT BROUGHT TEARS TO MY EYES STOP EXCITED BY GRATITUDE AND IT IS AWFUL HARD NOT TO SHOW ARTICLE TO GOVERNOR STOP I HAVE JUST FINISHED VISITING SEVERAL DAYS WITH HIM AT ALBANY STOP HIS HOME LIFE IS BEAUTIFUL STOP ALL THE FAMILY WERE THERE WITH THEIR DESCENDANTS STOP THEY TOOK ME IN AS ONE OF THE FAMILY STOP NOT A MISTAKE HAS YET BEEN MADE NOT EVEN SOUTHERN STATES

COULD DEFEAT HIM STOP WE WILL ARRANGE A MEETING AND NOTIFY HIM
STOP LOVE FROM BOTH OF US—KEY PITTMAN

Pine Grove Farm
North Haverhill
August 2, 1928

Dearest Mimosa,

My secretary has a "lady friend" visiting him, so I am trying to make his labors as light as possible and, consequently, I am going to beg you to forgive a letter in my own bad typewriting, since as you— and many others!—have reminded me, my handwriting is even worse!

Your sweet letter of July ninth reached me at Saratoga, California. . . . I have been busy getting straightened out and settled after my long absence and, as yet, have had no time to rest at all. Harry has not been well, and with all three boys home, the housekeeping has been strenuous. I have bought the boys a car of their own—a Pontiac— which they are enjoying hugely, and which I think will also simplify my own problem of getting about.

There is nothing essential at present to call me to Washington and, unless something arises, I shall not come, my time here is so very short at best. Thank you, however, a thousand times, for asking me to come and visit you in case I did do so. You know without my telling you how much I should enjoy that. But we will, I hope, have many good visits beside your open fire next winter.

With my best love, as always,
Frances Parkinson Keyes

United States Senate
Washington

August 21, 1928

Mrs. Frances Parkinson Keyes
North Haverhill, New Hampshire
Dear Frances:

Mrs. Pittman got a sweet letter from you the other day announcing that you had returned to your home.

I wish the public already knew what a wonderful article you have written about the Houston Convention. It seems so long to wait for it to come out. Of course, it will be very effective when it is read. . . .

My own campaign is annoying me considerably. The situation does not look so good in Nevada. My detention here in the East has prevented organization in the state. . . .

I had hoped that Governor Smith would have some time for our joint conference, but he has been too busy preparing for his acceptance speech and meeting leading politicians to find any time such as I sought.

Mrs. Pittman and I will leave on the morning of the twenty-third for

Nevada. All I can do is to look forward to our return to Washington next fall. We have missed you greatly since we left Houston. We cannot express our appreciation for your friendship and for the many kindnesses you have shown us.

Give my regards to Senator Keyes and your sons, and with love from Mrs. Pittman and myself, I am

Sincerely,
Key Pittman

Pine Grove Farm
North Haverhill
September 6, 1928

Dear Key:

Thank you for your letter of August twenty-first.

I am sorry that the national campaign has made such heavy demands upon you that your personal affairs have, perforce, been neglected because of them. Nevertheless, I . . . have followed your activities in the New York *Times* with pride and pleasure. And I cannot help feeling that you are so firmly entrenched in the confidence and affection of your constituents that you will not suffer anything as a result of your unselfish work. I shall be much interested in hearing how your own campaign is progressing, however, and I hope you will let me know.

Please do not feel distressed because Governor Smith "did not choose" to see me again. I felt all the time that he might not, and only offered to go to Albany again, as I am sure you realized perfectly, because I was sincerely anxious to revise my first impressions of him. As a writer, I have left no stone unturned which would permit me to present public questions and public characters impartially to my readers, uninfluenced by my own personal feeling, and I did not wish to do so in this case.

I am not sure whether I told Mimosa in writing her that Harry has been laid up all summer. He went on a fishing trip in New Brunswick in June, and injured his leg very badly, so that he has had to go about on crutches, and only recently has been promoted to a cane. In addition to this, he has had the grippe, and so has my faithful maid Cathie; while I am just struggling to my feet after being confined to my bed with a very painful abscess in my ear. All this combined with other complications, including the fact that we have had a great deal of company, has meant that I have not as yet had much rest, but I have managed to turn out the usual amount of work, and am not behind with my writing; so that I have not that terrible sense of pressure that nearly overwhelmed me last winter.

With all good wishes for your success in November, and my love to Mimosa, I am always, with kind regards,

Faithfully yours,
Frances Parkinson Keyes

When I wrote Mimosa Pittman on August second that I was looking forward to a little respite, I anticipated a period of comparative quiet. However, it was not until the twenty-first of September that the boys finally left, triumphantly driving their car, which they had christened "Ponti," and most of the next two days I spent drafting what was eventually to form the nucleus of *Honor Bright*. I finished typing it on Sunday and, with Harry much better at last, was just getting settled at my desk early Monday morning when the telephone rang. It was Mr. Bigelow, speaking in that bright cheerful tone which editors always seem to adopt when they have something in mind that is going to be far from acceptable to an unfortunate author.

"Mrs. Keyes? Mrs. Walbridge, the President of the Legion Auxiliary, is here in my office. She says she and the President of the Legion are agreed you are the *only* person from *Good Housekeeping* they want to cover the Convention which is to begin in San Antonio October eighth, and I *agree* with her. Why don't you start right away and go by boat? You always enjoy an ocean voyage and I'll arrange for passage on the *Henry Mallory* for Galveston, leaving Saturday. I assume you'll arrive here in time for a conference beforehand—say Thursday. Get hold of Miss Shufelt and take her with you if it will simplify matters. I'm looking forward to seeing you and to a very fine article. Good-bye, good-bye."

I tried to break in and tell him I had vowed, when I left Houston after the Democratic Convention, I would never return to Texas as long as I lived, that I simply could not face the noise, the confusion, the lack of rudimentary comfort and convenience in a hotel during a convention. But we were disconnected before I could voice my protests, so I contacted Miss Shufelt, put my desk in order and went downstairs to pack.

Edith Gerry came to see me off, bringing a lavish bon voyage basket, which provided practically all the nourishment of which my secretary and I partook aboardship, for the food was abominable. Our quarters, though spacious, were far from any plumbing, and on the whole, the voyage was pretty uncomfortable. But I finished the first draft of *Queen Anne's Lace* and did a good deal of reading and dictating.

And then San Antonio was completely different from Houston as far as the hotel and everything else was concerned. It is, without any doubt, one of the most charming and distinctive cities in the United States. There, unmistakably, one is on the soil over which Spain's gold and crimson banner once floated; in the old cathedral of San Fernando the notices are in Spanish as well as in English; the palace of the Spanish governors still reveals in its noble doorway remnants of past majesty. There also is the Alamo where the cornerstone of Texan independence was laid—gray and peaceful now, with bright flowers in its gardens and fruitful pecan trees along its walks. The visitor to San Antonio is indeed made aware at every turn that it is a city of history. Five other flags have been raised over it since that gold and crimson banner was first planted there—the flags of France, of Mexico and of the Texan Republic, the Stars and Bars of the Confederacy and now the Stars and Stripes. There Robert E. Lee reached the great decision which made him the leader of "The Lost Cause"; there Theodore Roosevelt organized the Rough Riders; there John J. Pershing was called from his post at Fort Sam Houston to take command of the American Expeditionary Forces. How could any city have provided a more suitable setting for a gathering of the American Legion?

But it was not only from the historical point of view that San Antonio seemed so fitting. Its beauty, its spaciousness, its cosmopolitan progressiveness all contributed; it was in holiday attire to greet the Legionnaires, with bells ringing, lights twinkling, flags fluttering; and its proverbial hospitality was breaking even its own exalted records. This all-embracing hospitality supplied, among other blessings, a "sponsor" for every special guest; and under the kindly wing of my own, Mrs. Ralph Durkee, I was escorted from my room to her car, and guided swiftly to platforms, parties and meetings, thus escaping the confusion, the delays and bewilderment which can be so disturbing to the newcomer in a strange city.

And I had the honor of being one of three ladies chosen for presentation to the Convention from the platform. We were escorted to the opening meeting in San Antonio's magnificent auditorium and introduced by Commander Edward Spafford to the vast assembly of six thousand, seen dimly, rising row upon row beyond the blazing lights—that multitude of Legionnaires who served "in peace as in war," who were dedicated to the task of "visiting the fatherless and widows in their affliction" and of trying to pave the way to a permanent and stable peace.

As I acknowledged my own presentation, I remembered others made to other persons—to kings and queens, to princes and premiers—and realized this was the greatest and most thrilling presentation of all. I never shall forget the applause that went up from that great body of men when my name was mentioned, for I had no idea there were so many who had read and liked what I had written, and it certainly served as an incentive to spur me on to further effort.

The joyous mood of the Legionnaires was at all times reflected in the hearty welcome they extended each and every guest. They paid a rousing tribute to Major George Scapini, a blind French veteran; they rose as one man to greet General Pershing with a resounding roar; they accorded Field Marshal Lord Allenby, often described as "the last of the Crusaders," a moving ovation.

But as I have reviewed the account of the Legion Convention which I wrote at that time, I have not been able to do so without overwhelming sadness. Every one of the speakers who talked about paving the way for a permanent and stable peace was honestly under the impression that he had helped to do so and that the comrades he had lost had not died in vain. And yet within less than twenty years we were involved in another war much more dreadful and far reaching than the one in which these men had fought, as they firmly believed, "to end all wars." And for more than ten long years we have been engaged in another of which the end, as I write, is not yet in sight. It is probably just as well that no one at San Antonio was gifted with prophetic vision in the autumn of 1928. With it, there would have been far less rejoicing.

Chapter 57

THE autumn after my return from San Antonio, as I review it, seems more like a mad scramble from one place to another and from one experience to another than like an organized life. Within a month I made speeches in five different cities—Shreveport, Boston, Keene, Salem and Bridgeport; I wrote regularly for three magazines and irregularly on the fictional stories which I hoped would some day become novels; I moved my household from Pine Grove Farm to Washington for the winter; and I spent several days in New York, where my time was divided, as usual, between editorial luncheon conferences and dinners with theater afterward. And that fall was notable for a new idea which I presented to Mr. Graeve and another which Mr. Bigelow presented to me.

So far I had managed without undue difficulty to handle the Washington material and the foreign material simultaneously and not have either seem dated, and also to do a good deal of incidental traveling throughout the United States in connection with speeches and the articles for *Better Homes and Gardens*. But with the prospect of an eighteen months' absence from the continent while working on the "All America Series," I knew such a program would become impossible. When I told Mr. Graeve this, he seemed so genuinely upset at the thought of losing me as a contributor to *Delineator* that I made a bold suggestion.

"I've been working for years on a novel with a Washington setting," I told him. "I've just finished drafting it. Why don't you use that as a serial, instead of nonfiction articles? I mean, for the present. When I come back from South America, I can write articles again, if you want me to."

He was not particularly enthusiastic. My first two novels had not been failures—indeed, both had been modest successes—but neither had they achieved conspicuous acclaim, and *Delineator* needed a "name" on its serials; mine did not measure up to their requirements for fiction. If I would only give up that "All America Series," he would make it worth while in other ways. . . .

I finally convinced him that I could not do this, and would not even if I could, and rather grudgingly he told me to send him the script of the Washington novel.

Mr. Bigelow had something entirely different on his mind. Although he had said so firmly that he had dismissed Washington from his curriculum as far as I was concerned, he was still hankering after it and he had thought of a new approach. Someone had reminded him—though actually he had known this for a long time—that Mrs. John B. Henderson, the aged and eccentric but lively chatelaine of Henderson Castle who had been my next-door neighbor as long as I stayed at Meridian Mansions and who had been favorably disposed toward me from the moment of my arrival in Washington, should, as the widow of a prominent senator and a long-time resident of Washington, have a worthwhile story to tell. Mr. Bigelow asked me if I would try to win her consent to doing this, with me as her interpreter, and offered a very substantial sum for the work, which he wanted finished before I left for my "All America Series."

As soon as I was back in Washington in mid-November I approached her, and she readily agreed to cooperate. She felt the most effective way to work would be by lunching together twice a week and talking while we ate the strictly vegetarian meal which she provided and by my remaining as long afterward as she felt like rambling over her reminiscences. Consequently my schedule, already overcrowded, was jammed. As always, when the three boys came home for their holidays, their pursuits and pleasures were given precedence over everything else and there were the usual staggering number of tea dances, debutante parties and balls to wedge in. Moreover, this year Henry had a house guest, who was very important to him, so I went on an extensive shopping tour with her, as she was afraid—with reason—that she did not have everything she would need to wear; and a luncheon in her honor demanded my immediate and careful attention to hospitality in order that she might meet the girls who would contribute to her general welcome. There were the usual official dinners to attend besides a luncheon in honor of the Cuban Ambassadress and dinners in honor of the Brazilian Ambassador, the Japanese Ambassador and Mme Debuchi and the Spanish Ambassador and Mme Padilla that were also on my own calendar for entertaining—the first two with eighteen guests, the last with fifty; and I resumed my days "At Home" with a reception which Mimosa Pittman and I gave together at my apartment.

But far more important for me than any of these functions was the letter received from Oscar Graeve on the twenty-ninth of January, telling me that they—that is, the editor-in-chief and associate editors of *Delineator*—had all read my novel about Washington, *Queen Anne's Lace,* and were unanimously in favor of using it as a serial in the magazine. Just as I had gone years before to spend prayerful hours of thanksgiving in a grove at the Farm because the acceptance of my first story marked a poignant turning point in my life, I now went to St. Matthew's, the nearest church that was open, to offer thanks. I stayed there a long time and when I reached home telephoned my great news to Harry. He did not seem to be unduly impressed with it, and our conversation ended with his brief statement that he would not be home to dinner because there was a night session of the Senate. I knew this meant that Key would probably not be going home either, so I telephoned Mimosa and asked if I might come out to supper. She responded warmly and the evening climaxed a wonderful day. The air was heavy, for a storm was imminent, and presently there was a roar of thunder and a crackle of lightning. Then we realized something near us had been struck, that the electricity had gone off. As we grew accustomed to the enveloping darkness, we could see the gleaming eyes of the police dogs, who were crouched on the hearth beside us. Nothing else. No sight, no sound. There was a strange tenseness in the atmosphere, and I strove to ease it.

"Tell me about your trip down the Yukon, Peg, when you went to marry Key. You never have, you know, in detail."

She began quietly, telling me what I myself will try to tell in substance, though I cannot clothe the story with the poignant beauty of her words. They had started out with four dog-sleds, one for her, one for her brother, two for the guides and provisions. It took them more than three months to make the two-thousand-mile trip. They traveled during the day and made camp at night on the ice, except occasionally when they had the good luck to find a trapper's cabin. When that happened, they always found a fire laid, ready to light; and when they left, they laid one for the next comer—that was the unwritten law of the North. They had plenty of provisions—bacon, beans, dried fish, tea. There were some days when she was not well enough to travel, and then just lay still and her brother sat beside her and smoked; but on the whole she stood the journey very well, and they were not often delayed. They got through all right before the ice broke. And anyway, what did a few hardships matter? The point was that she reached Nome, that she married Key. . . .

While Peg was talking, the lights began to come on with that creep-
ing slowness which characterizes the return of current after a storm.
The one under which she was sitting was a tall lamp with a soft yellow
shade, and gradually its effulgence encircled her bronze hair like a halo;
then the radiance spread until it encompassed her face and figure. If I
were asked to specify the most dramatic moment of my Washington
years, I would not need to grope for an answer. I should say, without
hesitation, it was the night when Mimosa Pittman told me the most
splendid love story I have ever heard and I saw her enveloped in light
as the glowing words came from her lips.

Key himself gave still another slant to the story when he could be
persuaded to dwell on it, which was infrequently. "I had no place to
take her except an abandoned jail," he would say humorously. "It had
been outgrown as the town became larger and livelier. You should have
seen it! It was made of corrugated iron. But we had a good time in it,
just the same." His eyes would wander around the paneled redwood
walls of "Ridgelands," the spacious property on Foxhall Road they had
acquired several years earlier when they decided to move from their
Sixteenth Street house. His voice would soften as he conjured up the vision of that corrugated jail. "Yes, we were very happy. But sometimes I
had to leave her, and distances are immense in Alaska and means of
transportation were pretty limited in those days. I went forty miles on
snowshoes once because I had a feeling she wasn't well. And she
wasn't. She was very ill. So we left Alaska in order that she could have
better care. We went to Nevada and I practiced law and developed my
mining interests. And after a while, I got absorbed in politics. You
know all the rest—"

I did not know all of it, of course, but I knew a good deal of it, because I saw so much of it first hand. As I have said, that wintry afternoon in 1922, when I assisted at an official reception at the Pittmans'
and guided guests through a doorway on the stairs, marked the beginning of a new era in friendship. It was not long afterward that I began
to go with casual frequency to Ridgelands for formal dinners and informal breakfasts, eaten under the shade of the trees or beside the warm
hearthstone. Now, every Sunday afternoon, as soon as my work was
done—Sunday being, unfortunately, my hardest writing day—I started
almost automatically for Ridgelands, sure that I would find a bright fire
and a warm welcome awaiting me. Sometimes Key and Peg were out
when I arrived, but sooner or later they came in, and then there was
supper by candlelight and afterward one of those long quiet talks in the
course of which vital elements of true comradeship are found and
merged.

Chapter 58

H AVING lived the greater part of my life within fifty miles of the Canadian border, it would have been a simple matter to cross it at
most any time, but I had never done so; then, in the busiest part of the
busiest Washington season I had known, I went to Ottawa in February
to attend the opening of the Dominion Parliament and the very formal
festivities connected with it, because that seemed the best moment for
story purposes as far as my "All America Series" was concerned. I unpacked the white tulle veil and three white feathers which I had worn
on the "grand and glorious" occasion at Buckingham Palace and purchased an ermine coat and a blue velvet dress with pearl embroidery
and a court train; then, accompanied by my "family treasure" Cathie,
who was almost as excited as I was, I finally went to Canada—and had
a lovely time.

Soon after my return came the inauguration of President Hoover,
which left me uninspired; there were no outstanding speeches or even
outstanding passages in speeches, and there were no seemingly symbolic
shafts of light to illuminate his grim countenance as there had been to
brighten Harding's handsome face at his. As for the new Vice President, "good old Charlie Curtis," the limelight was on his sister Mrs.
Gann rather than on him. He was a widower and had "appointed" her
his hostess—an appointment without official sanction, for a sister is not
automatically raised to her brother's rank as a wife is to her husband's.
Therefore the contention that Mrs. Gann was now the Second Lady of
the Land roused much opposition, the opposing forces led by Alice
Roosevelt Longworth, whose husband Nicholas was the Speaker of the
House. The Dean of the Diplomatic Corps, Sir Esme Howard, was
called upon to render a decision and ruled, somewhat reluctantly, in

(547)

favor of Mrs. Gann. This tempest in a teapot raged with almost unbelievable fury and did not abate until some time after the inauguration.

Harry and I gave a dinner of one hundred in compliment to the New Hampshire delegates to the inauguration the night before it—in a private suite at the Willard, since we naturally could not handle so many guests for a meal in the apartment, though it was astonishing how many we did manage to accommodate—and on the night of the inauguration itself we gave a dinner in honor of the Cuban Ambassador and Mme Ferrara and took all our guests to the Inaugural Ball, for which we had a box. Henry had been able to get away from Harvard for a long week end and shared in these festivities, as well as a dinner at the Pittmans the previous Friday. I recorded on my calendar, "I had a good visit with him" that day and on the following Tuesday that I had "a complete breakdown at parting from him."

At the time I was very troubled about several aspects of the Washington scene, glamorous though it appeared, as far as it affected me personally, and I felt the sooner I left it, the better it would be, not only for me but for several other persons. Consequently I was glad, rather than otherwise, that the date of departure for an indefinite absence was drawing very close. My problems were personal, rather than professional, and so private in character that my eldest son was the only one in whom I confided, either then or later.

Tedious and tiring as I was finding my conferences with Mrs. Henderson, I regarded these as a financial bonanza, of which I was in great need. With one son in the law school, one at college and one at preparatory school, educational expenses were heavy; and though my allowance for entertaining connected with my work was generous, rent, wages and clothes still presented major items for me, since the senatorial salary did not go very far when it came to maintaining a legal residence in New Hampshire and headquarters in Washington. To be sure, finances were no longer my chief worry; I could handle those all right if nothing interfered with my earning powers; but I had reckoned that the money for the Henderson memoirs would put me a little ahead of the game and give me a breathing space, and I philosophically endured the long, dull conferences, the almost uneatable luncheons and the time lost from other activities because of this undertaking on that account.

Then, like a bolt from the blue, came a letter from Mr. Bigelow, saying he was disappointed in the material. What he wanted, as I was well aware, were reminiscences about the political situation after the repeal of the Missouri Compromise and Mrs. Henderson's early experiences in Washington as a senator's wife. What Mrs. Henderson wanted was an outlet for her enthusiastic views on vegetarianism and Prohibition. I had done my level best to steer her away from these subjects toward those which had more historical value, and sometimes I had briefly succeeded; but by and large the undertaking had been a failure. Probably I had become overconfident because for a long while everything else I had attempted had been successful; but it simply had not occurred to me that Mr. Bigelow would cancel a definite order without even giving me a second chance to make good. It was a deeply embarrassing experience to go to the old lady, who had always been very kind to me, and tell her that the material she had highly approved was unacceptable to an editor. I dreaded it and, as usual, when confronted with something disagreeable which must be done, did not try to postpone it, but put it behind me as quickly as possible. To this day, I remember with gratitude the understanding and courtesy with which Mrs. Henderson received my faltering recital. She instantly recognized my unhappiness and made that, not the affront to her, a very real concern. She had enjoyed having me with her so frequently, she said, and we must go on seeing each other often, as soon as I returned from South America. As far as the magazine was concerned, the more she looked it over, the more she was relieved to find she would not figure in its pages; it carried countless recipes and advertisements in which meat was the main feature!

Naturally, I did not report this reaction to Mr. Bigelow; I only said that Mrs. Henderson had been very considerate of my feelings and let it go at that. Possibly it occurred to him that he had not been, for he suddenly asked for a human interest article, giving me only two days in which to write it, and after I had somehow managed to do this, wired his enthusiastic approval and sent a check which he hoped would make up for what I had lost on the Henderson material. Of course it did not, but it was what is called in the North Country a tidy sum; and a letter I received from Harry, who was briefly in New Hampshire when the blow fell, did still more to mitigate the situation:

> I feel so sorry for you about the Henderson matter for I can imagine your disappointment. Just try to think of all the things you have succeeded in. A 100% record is almost too much to expect. You have accomplished great things and I have always been proud of you and I know you will do *more* great things.

To the best of my recollection, this was only the second time Harry had ever told me he was proud of me (the first having been when John was born and I endured forty-eight hours of labor without complaining), and for him to do so was certainly welcome. Meanwhile, Mr. Bigelow's plans for the "All American Series" trip were becoming more and more grandiose and it would have been very poor policy on my part to show resentment over a closed issue. With Canada satisfactorily behind me, it was now decided that I should go first to Portugal and Spain, the mother countries of those I should be visiting in South America, and that I should attend the opening of the Ibero-American Exposition in Seville, where they would be represented.

It was a very ambitious project and one which had already required long and careful planning; and thanks to a strange omission in such planning on the part of Congress, I was able to develop a related project of my own, which worked out to perfection. Congress had voted one hundred thousand dollars for an exhibit from the Women's and Children's Bureaus of the Department of Labor at the Exposition; but, more or less characteristically, it had neglected to appropriate funds to transport it to Spain. I was on excellent terms with Secretary of Labor Davis, so I telephoned and asked for an appointment, which he quickly gave me. Then I made my bold suggestion: I told him I was going to Seville to write about the Exposition and was entitled to take a secretary with me, at *Good Housekeeping's* expense. If he could see his way clear to giving Miss Elisabeth Shirley, who in 1927 had accepted a position in the Children's Bureau, a two months' leave of absence—she was a very good friend of mine and we would work well together—we could take the exhibit over as part of our baggage.

He listened pleasantly but noncommittally and said he would think it over. I had learned from my experience with Evelyn Underhill in London that the best results could be obtained by lack of insistence and, after a chat about this and that, took my departure. When I reached home, the telephone was ringing and the Secretary was on the line.

"Sister Keyes," he said brightly. (He belonged to the Loyal Order of Moose which always used the terms "Brother" and "Sister" in addressing fellow members, and had carried the practice over into official life.) "I've decided not to think the matter over. If I did, I'd probably remember some old law that forbids doing what you want, and it's a good idea. What's your friend's name again? Elisabeth Shirley? Two months —maybe we'd better make it three.... All right. Glad to have seen you. Good-bye, good-bye."

On the strength of this telephone call I asked Elisabeth to dine with me and discuss a matter of "great importance" to us both. She came willingly and agreeably in response to this summons, but without the slightest idea of what I had in mind. Henry was no longer available as a traveling secretary, since he was working with the Legal Aid Society in Boston during his summer vacation; but John was scheduled to be graduated from Harvard in June, and though there could have been no question of taking him away for a year in the middle of his college course, his father and I had decided he was entitled to the same amount of educational travel his elder brother had had and that I was justified in wanting to have one of our sons with me. John had faithfully studied shorthand all the previous summer and had done very well with it. There was still a certain amount of uneasiness in our minds about some of his other studies and no definite assurance that he would get his degree in June; but we had agreed to take that risk; and prior to my brainstorm about Elisabeth Shirley, I had been prepared to get along alone until John could join me; now I must break the news to her in the hope that she would be as pleased with it as I was.

I am thankful to say that she was delighted, and in the few remaining weeks before our departure for Spain preparations for this and farewell parties were predominant. We finally left Washington on a night train —"dead tired after many delays and inconveniences"—on April sixteenth, allowing ourselves a day to spare for financial arrangements, shopping and so on before the last full day when a large luncheon at the Good Housekeeping Institute, with Mr. Bigelow as host, and a large dinner at the Biltmore, with the Pittmans as hosts, would represent about all we could undertake. We had decided, in anticipation of these events, to go to bed after our shopping was done and our last-minute arrangements were made; however, we had reckoned without the Brazilian Ambassador, who had been among those to entertain in our honor before we left Washington and who had telephoned the Brazilian Consul General in New York to show us every courtesy while we were there. This meant another dinner on the seventeenth, to which we dragged ourselves without due gratitude for such hospitality because we were almost frantic with fatigue. We did our best to conceal this and apparently succeeded only too well; for as we rose to take our leave, the Consul General protested vehemently and reproachfully.

"Why, the night is yet young!" he exclaimed. "I had arranged that we should go on to Radio City. There is a splendid show and I have the very best seats reserved. Surely you won't disappoint me now!"

We did not see how we could, and Elisabeth and I finally returned to our hotel so exhausted that we hardly spoke to each other before we tumbled into bed. There was not much left of the night which the Consul General had considered so young; and when I eventually roused myself the following day, I was far from being in a party-going mood, with two still ahead of me. Moreover, the morning, instead of bringing Harry in person, brought me a letter from him which, kindly and affectionate as it was, spelled further disappointment and explanations which would be hard to make, for he naturally had been included in both Mr. Bigelow's and the Pittmans' invitations.

Dearest—

I deeply appreciate your "little note" which I found on my pillow last night. It was sweet of you. To honor you I would gladly contribute at least my presence, but to join in "farewell festivity" I simply can not do it. I am awfully sorry. Apparently I am constituted so that such occasions are not to me festivities. No matter how hard I might try my presence would be a wet blanket. I always dread farewells and shrink from them and I do so now. I of course deeply appreciate the kindness of your friends and their good wishes. I wish I could trust myself to participate on such occasions as you will have tomorrow, but I *can't*. I hope you will understand me, and I believe you will.

I have today wired you and Mr. Bigelow that I cannot be in New York Thursday. I still hope to see you at the foot of 31st Street Friday noon.

If I have "found myself" in the Senate I want you to know that you greatly helped me. You have been a *brick* and I am utterly at a loss to know how to express to you my feelings. You have done wonders and I have always been proud of your accomplishments. I believe you are to add to your position attained in the literary field. My future is political and that is always uncertain, but I shall try my best to be re-elected in spite of one great handicap.

I shall do my best to care for our three fine boys up to July 1st; when John, I hope, will sail to join you and when Henry and Peter will still be with me. By this I do not mean to give the impression that I shall not always, so far as I can, care for them. I have and shall.

I do wish you were not going.

As ever,

Harry

P.S. I shall try to keep the home fires burning.

This letter, with its unmistakable note of yearning, which had not been shown or expressed in a long while, was of course emotionally disturbing. It was too late now to make any changes in the program for which I was under contract, and Harry was as well aware of this as I was; moreover, dependent as he was on me for financial cooperation, it would have been a fearful blow to have this withdrawn, especially after the Henderson fiasco; but I could not help wishing we could have had a confidential talk, which might have made us both feel better, before plans for another long separation had been made. Now, since he would come only to the pier, where a dozen or so others would be on hand to wish Elisabeth and me bon voyage, we would not have a chance for even a few words in private.

While I was turning this over in my mind, not without considerable distress, the telephone rang and I found that Oscar Graeve was on the line.

"By the way," he said, as if this thought had just struck him, "you haven't told us who's going to publish *Queen Anne's Lace*—in book form, I mean. We should be getting in touch with them right away."

"But I haven't any idea who's going to publish it in book form," I said, almost in a wail. "You've never brought that up. I thought you'd be the one to make the necessary arrangements for that."

"No, no! That's the *author's* job and we can't use a story for a serial that isn't sure of book publication. It wouldn't look well. You will have to do something about that right away."

I glanced at my watch and answered in some desperation. "Look here, Oscar, you know I'm sailing in the morning and I haven't a free minute today. I can't start scouting around for a publisher. But I can suggest something that might help. Several years ago Horace Liveright assured me that if I ever wrote a novel about Washington which told the other side of his horrible *Revelry,* he'd like very much to see it. That's *Queen Anne's Lace,* all right. Send it to him. I'm sorry but I simply have to ring off. I'm already late for luncheon at the Institute."

The luncheon went off well, and at it Mr. Bigelow, obviously without any such intention, provided me with a source of amusement which acted as a release from tension. He announced that since I had attained the status of Associate Editor, he felt I should have *Good Housekeeping* stationery to use on my trip, with my name added to the usual letterhead. He had therefore ordered two kinds for me, a ream of each, with matching envelopes, which would be delivered to me on shipboard: the usual commercial size and, also, notepaper size, which I might find more convenient, even for professional correspondence, if transportation of baggage became a problem. Somehow, Elizabeth and I immediately visualized overladen donkeys struggling under the weight of *Good Housekeeping* stationery as they made the difficult ascent of the Andes. We avoided looking at each other and hoped our broad smiles would be interpreted as appreciation for the compliments which Key was paying us, with apparent spontaneity, in a carefully prepared speech, of which I still have the copy he sent me that same afternoon together with one of the most useful bon voyage presents I ever received: a Mark Cross dispatch case with a sesame lock, which the Pittmans had had made especially for me. They had had the same experience with searched baggage in Japan that I had and felt confident they had found a way to circumvent this for me in the future.

Despite the brief release from tension, the day seemed destined to be one of turmoil. At the last minute the Pittmans had invited a distinguished journalist who was a complete stranger to me to fill in for Harry at their dinner; and this gentleman insisted not only on acting as my escort but on coming for me early enough to get an interview for publication the next day. Then he decided he needed still more material and insisted on another conference after the dinner. Elisabeth was having difficulties of her own with a persistent visitor, who was not too happy about the prospect of her prolonged absence or, more especially, the possibility that in the course of it she might meet someone who would change her long and stubborn refusal to consider matrimony. We were both at our wits' end, though for entirely different reasons, trying to deal with so many importunities, and the next morning was equally hectic. Genevieve Gudger and other friends from Washington had come to see us off, and Harry, as I had foreseen, arrived only when our suite was filled with well-wishers. More and more boxes of flowers and baskets of fruit kept arriving. When the reams of *Good Housekeeping* paper, with matching envelopes, and a huge open carton of books very casually tied with string were delivered, the last inch of standing room was exhausted and the state of confusion reached its climax.

I was glad when it was over, for I had reached the point where, instead of dreading farewells, I wanted them behind me; and I did not find Mr. Bigelow's final admonitions particularly amusing, though they were pleasantly meant. Jesting was definitely not his forte.

"Well, good-bye," he said for the third or fourth time. "I have tried to give you all the latitude you need about itineraries, expenditures and so on; and of course you can always cable. I can't think of anything you'd need to consult me about though, unless someone should invite you to take a side trip to Antarctica. In that case, I'd want to know."

"I can't think of anything, either," I replied, "and if that happens, I *will* cable. I know I'm safe in promising that."

I have made few promises that I lived to regret as much as I did that one.

The *Providence* docked long enough in Boston the following afternoon for another farewell party. My mother, my three sons, several cousins and numerous friends came to see me off, so again the suite was crowded and there was no chance for private conversation. But somehow the occasion seemed much gayer and less of an ordeal than the similar leave-taking in New York, perhaps because so many of the well-wishers were young and in high spirits generally. And we were hardly out to sea for good when I received a radio message calculated to raise my own:

> DELIGHTED TO PUBLISH QUEEN ANNE'S LACE STOP WITH WHOM
> SHALL I NEGOTIATE—HORACE LIVERIGHT

With my reply, Henry became my lawyer and another new era began for us both.

When the *Providence* stopped at Ponta Delgado in the Azores my primary preoccupation was the necessity of discovering some sort of container in which the *Good Housekeeping* stationery and reading material could be carried ashore without danger of scattering it indiscriminately over the wharf in Lisbon. Evidently, the inhabitants of Ponta Delgado were not much given to travel and neither was it a popular tourist center; so Elisabeth and I had quite a search for a shop that sold baggage, and our best find was a receptacle which we christened "the immigrant's trunk" and with which we were not particularly proud to be seen. However, it served its purpose and became such a standing joke that we ended by regarding it with a certain amount of affection.

In our original plans Lisbon had figured largely as a port of disembarkation before proceeding to Spain; but a postponement of the Ibero-American Exposition's official opening permitted us to see a good deal of that lovely city towering like Rome and Richmond on seven hills, and of rural Portugal. Then it was on to Seville and the Exposition planned to "mark the resumption by Spain of its position as a world power in commerce" that Elisabeth and I had crossed the ocean especially to see. King Alfonso XIII opened the Exposition, and both the King and the Queen visited the exhibit from the Children's Bureau that Elisabeth had planned and assembled. The Queen read Herbert Hoover's "Child's Bill of Rights" and examined models representing a juvenile court, a child-health conference, a playground, the care of dependent children and the study of child hygiene. The King seemed entranced by the large mechanical book, its pages turned by electricity, which told the story of "John, a typical American boy," and the conditions which would surround him when he left school and went to work. The visit was a prolonged one, and as they finally prepared to leave, it was with words of warmest commendation. They both thanked us and the Queen added, "It has all been most interesting and the work you are doing for children in the United States is most remarkable." (Medals of gold were awarded both to Elisabeth personally and to the Children's Bureau for this exhibit. It was displayed again by the Child Welfare Commission of South Dakota at the State Fair at Huron and also at Boston, under the auspices of the American Legion, and was eventually purchased for permanent exhibition by the Pernambuco Legion for the Prevention of Infant Mortality in Brazil.)

Elisabeth and I had barely recovered from the excitement of the Exposition's opening when Captain Sidney Morgan, who was in charge of the Department of Commerce's exhibit, appeared at our hotel and made a charming suggestion.

"Before I left the United States," he said, "several automobile companies offered cars to be used in connection with the activities of our officials here. . . . I think it especially desirable that distinguished visitors to the Exposition should not only see as much of Seville as possible, but as much of Spain as possible. You and Miss Shirley are distinguished visitors. How would you like to use one of these cars for a trip through Andalucía?"

And so we enjoyed a beautiful tour through that most fruitful part of Spain, a region lush with productiveness, as well as visits to the cities of Ronda, Granada and Córdoba in the course of it. Then we took a train from Seville to Barcelona, where I had the audience with Alfonso XIII which I wrote about previously.[1] And almost before we knew it, the time had come to sail—from Barcelona in the small Spanish ship *Juan Sebastián Elcano*—for Venezuela.

---

[1] Chapter 27.

Part Twelve

From a South American Journal

Somehow the first sight of a new continent is always stirring and inspiring. But the first sight of South America—we wakened to see the sun rising over the mountains which like somber sentinels guard its northern coast—was so strangely beautiful and impressive that it was almost overpowering. The tawny hills, partially covered with cool brilliant green, plunged straight into the sea and seemed an impenetrable barrier. Small white-walled, red-roofed buildings which clung to them emphasized the magnificence of the mountains. The ancient stone fortress towering over the harbor at La Guaira strengthened the conviction that we had reached the shores of an impregnable nation. When this panorama was turned to splendor by the dawn, it seemed to symbolize the spirit of an enchanted and unfathomable land.

The magic vision was too powerful to be dispelled even by the comparative insignificance of the town of La Guaira itself; and since Quarantine and customs officials were agreeable and considerate, the process of landing was not the grueling one it is in some places. The American Chargé d'Affaires, Mr. Cornelius Engert, was kind enough to meet us, and, reassured as to the whereabouts and safety of our belongings, we began the ascent to Caracas, the capital city, more than three thousand feet above sea level.

Concerning the road which leads to it and which since has been greatly improved, we had been regaled with accounts scarcely less blood curdling than others we had heard about a recent revolution. It was, we had been assured, one of the most dangerous highways in the world because of its twists and turns and its precipitous character; and crosses along the way—so the story continued—"marked the spot" where travelers had been hurled to their death. There was indeed one such cross, but there seemed no reason for it, presupposing the average degree of common sense on the part of a motorist. And all preconceived ideas as to the dangers of driving having been so promptly shattered, I was not surprised to learn that the revolution—such as it was!—had already ended. The government forces had never been stronger than they were at the time of our visit.

My initial impressions of Caracas were not wholly favorable, for the city presented its least attractive side first, though I discovered many lovelier aspects later on. There were a few green plazas, each containing a central statue of some national hero; but there were almost no flowers in evidence, except in these squares and in the markets. I had the feeling of being in a wholly alien land, more alien than any I had ever visited, though this is hard to explain, since there was no sensation of hostility; on the contrary, there was kindliness and courtesy on every side. Perhaps the feeling arose from the fact that Venezuela had not yet had time to express her own individuality in architecture and custom and that she had turned her back rather definitely upon the architecture and custom she inherited. The absence of Spanish atmosphere was surprising in light of the fact that it was not until 1822 that Venezuela achieved her independence. The links which bound her to the mother country seem to have been much more slender than those forged elsewhere—even in Puerto Rico, for instance, I was much more conscious of them. The first time a Venezuelan lady told me that she had spent four years in Europe but had never visited Spain, I was astonished; but by the time three of them had told me the same thing, I had ceased to feel surprise. Paris, not Madrid, was their mecca.

A stay in Caracas begins with a visit to the "Bolívar House" quite as logically as a stay in Washington begins with a visit to Mount Vernon. For Simón Bolívar, the "Liberator," was the father of his native country—as well as the four other "Bolivarian Republics" of Colombia, Ecuador, Peru and Bolivia, to which he gave his name—quite as definitely as George Washington is the Father of the United States; and both came from families of wealth and distinction and have had their birthplaces preserved as national monuments. The exterior of Bolívar's was unimposing, like that of many Venezuelan houses; but once inside the entrance, we found one splendid and dignified room opening into another about patios of unusual beauty. Pomegranates were blooming in one of these patios; in another, there were two royal palms side by side, a symbol that the family was of royal blood—a proud custom of colonial days. The room in which Bolívar was born is directly off the main salon—for it was the custom of the nobility to deck their handsome four-posters with priceless counterpanes and leave the bedroom doors open so that all their guests might see them! The walls of the largest room were just then being decorated with paintings of incidents in Bolívar's life by Tito Salas, one of Venezuela's leading painters, and we found him working in the courtyard with the royal palms, his canvas stretched out in their shade.

Bolívar's beloved bride, whom he married in Madrid when they were both in their teens—the loveliest picture in the Bolívar house was one depicting this wedding—died ten months later in Caracas of yellow fever, and therefore, though he had a mistress, Manuela Saenz, who followed him faithfully from one country to another in the course of his conquests, this Father of his Country, like our own, left no direct descendants. But when Elisabeth and I were in Venezuela, one grand-niece, Señorita Antonia Estella Clemente Camacho y Bolívar, then nearly ninety years old, still survived him. She sent word that she would like to meet us, and when we called, we found a slim, erect little old lady clad in lace-trimmed white cashmere waiting in a pleasant drawing room, beneath a portrait of her famous ancestor, to receive us. She was entirely conversant with questions of the day and proud of the fact that she wrote a daily article for one of the leading Caracas papers. She showed us the medals which had been conferred upon her, among them the celebrated "Order of the Liberator," then recently bestowed upon Lindbergh; and she served us delicious refreshments which, she informed us, had been sent by the Minister of War when he heard of our impending visit.

Doña Antonia linked the history of Venezuela with its present for us in an unforgettable way and made our other visits seem more significant. We went to the Capitol, an imposing building whose court was filled with vivid tropical flowers and luxuriant trees; to its gold and deep rose "Salon Eliptico," where official receptions were held, and to the Senate and Chamber of Deputies, where constitutional amendments were passed with great dispatch. The sessions on the day we were there lasted a scant fifteen minutes, but a good deal was apparently accomplished, and to anyone who has waited in our Senate for endless hours for something to happen, Venezuelan legislation had much to recommend it! Mr. Engert accompanied us to the striking Miraflores Palace for an extremely ceremonious audience with the new President, Señor Juan Bautista Pérez, and Prime Minister and Señora Arcaya invited us to a large reception where we were privileged to meet their friends and see their beautiful house in the attractive suburb of Paraiso: the drawing room with crystal chandeliers and rose brocade, the dining room in which sixty guests could be seated for dinner, the library with its fifteen thousand volumes.

In the course of conversation at the Arcayas', the Prime Minister murmured that he would like to give me some sort of souvenir of my stay in Venezuela and asked if I was interested in any definite type of collection. Feeling that this was a safe answer, I replied that Governor Towner of Puerto Rico had suggested a few years earlier that I should collect fans and had indeed started a collection for me. Since then, I had added to it in Spain. Señor Arcaya said rather doubtfully that he did not think there were any especially typical of Venezuela [1] and he would think of something else. I was afraid I had unintentionally suggested something more valuable than he had in mind and was a little worried—quite unnecessarily, as it turned out!

Although Elisabeth and I were having practically no meals there except breakfast, we were staying at a hotel which was not sufficiently up-to-date to abandon the type of doors which were typical of the country at that time. I have heard them called Dutch doors though I never saw anything like them in Holland. They were pairs of swinging doors with open spaces above and below them, and fastened with a sliding bolt. When one of the hotel servants—nearly all of them male and colored—needed or wanted to enter the room, he simply reached over the top, slid the bolt and came in. The only warning the occupant had was the sight of a long black arm suddenly appearing in the open space above the doors. No matter how watchful you tried to be, you were often caught unprepared for visitors. Shortly after our evening at the Arcayas, an arm appeared one morning while I was still in bed, and a white-clad figure with a beaming face then entered the open doorway.

"Señora," the man said proudly, "you have a present from His Excellency, the Prime Minister."

"That's very kind of him," I said, drawing the bedclothes more closely around me. "Please bring it in."

"Señora, I cannot bring it in. It is in the patio resting on the shoulders of four strong men."

I called to Elisabeth, who was in the adjoining room and who was already dressed. She accompanied the servant to the patio, and presently I heard an exclamation which seemed to denote both amazement and amusement; then she returned almost beside herself with laughter.

"The Prime Minister has sent you a dug-out canoe—a very rare primitive type. It is a noteworthy gift!"

It was indeed. We succeeded in getting the hotel to store it for us temporarily and then Mr. Engert arranged to have it sent duty free to

---

[1] In this he was mistaken; I later had one given me made of feathers, which is a great ornament to my collection.

Harry, since we could not possibly add it to the impedimenta with which we were already burdened—we were having enough difficulty with the immigrant's trunk. The canoe arrived safely at the Senate Office Building, freight collect to the tune of thirty dollars, and there it created quite a stir, though I cannot say that it was very warmly welcomed. Then it was sent to Pine Grove Farm where, the last I heard, it was still reposing in the barn.

It was also in Paraiso that boundless hospitality was extended to us by Mr. Engert and his wife Sara. At their home there I met not only the Americans stationed in Caracas in official capacities but those who had gone there for commercial reasons, Venezuela's oil fields having attracted many of our countrymen. I met, too, a number of delightful Venezuelans and most of the Diplomatic Corps and their wives and carried away pleasant memories of them all, but particularly of Signora Cavicchioni, the mother of the Italian Minister, who acted as his hostess since he was not married. This intrepid little old lady, who spoke every known language and smiled placidly on the world, which she regarded with a twinkle in her eye, was a Venetian by birth and a Bolognese by later associations, but had accompanied her son to all his posts— including Afghanistan!—and her animated accounts of her experiences added a rare and stimulating spice to dinner party conversation.

But no visitor to a foreign country should see only its capital area, and Elisabeth and I were glad that our wanderings took us outside, especially to Maracay, to keep an appointment with the preeminent figure of that "one-man" country, a millionaire soldier and statesman whose name was on everyone's lips on practically every occasion. A quarter of a century earlier Juan Vicente Gómez, who was born in a little town near the Colombian frontier and grew up without "advantages" of any sort, had become President of Venezuela, having already shown great gifts as a financier and a leader. He acquired vast tracts of land and achieved a distinguished military career before entering politics, in which he proved his extraordinary ability as a chief executive from the first. Under his rule the unsettled, undeveloped and debt-ridden country became solvent, then prosperous. Loans were repaid, roads built, industries established, oil fields opened, civil disturbances quelled, international relations strengthened; and the credit was due to "the General," who was also the President. Then, in April of 1929—just two months prior to my visit—he electrified the country by turning his office over to the Supreme Court, which elected one of its members, Juan Bautista Pérez, Provisional President. A few weeks later General Gómez was re-elected President at a joint session of Congress—under the Venezuelan constitution the Chief Executive is chosen by this body and not by the people at large. He declined to accept, but he agreed to become Commander-in-Chief of the Army and to assist Congress in selecting his successor to the presidency; and a constitutional amendment creating the office of Commander-in-Chief was proclaimed on the twenty-ninth of May; on the thirtieth, Congress unanimously elected Pérez Constitutional President of the Republic and Gómez Commander-in-Chief of the Army, with equal powers regarding all important prerogatives.

Our route to Maracay led over a mountain range, but because of our early start and perfect roads facilitating rapid travel, midday found us at San Juan de los Morros, the last town to the south before the beginning of an impenetrable forest which stretches to the Orinoco. Famous sulphur springs are located there, and the gaunt rugged peaks from which the locality takes its name rise around them in haggard splendor. We lunched in full view of them with Mr. and Mrs. Dolge, the "veterans" of the American colony, who had lived in Venezuela for more than thirty years and had just built a house outside the town on a grant of land given them by "the General." And at our host's suggestion, we decided to follow the southern shore of the Lake of Valencia, taking the route over which the great German scientist Friedrich Humboldt journeyed when he visited Venezuela as the guest of the Spanish government at the end of the eighteenth century.

It was a memorable experience. After a few miles we swerved from the main arteries of travel and found ourselves in almost undiscovered country. The superb trees took on new magnificence as we wound through them. Occasionally we came to a tiny village where naked children darted from thatched mud huts followed by a flurry of chickens and, at a more leisurely pace, the family pig, and once in a while we passed a not overly dressed bronzed giant, gleaming machete in hand; but for the most part there was no sign of even the most primitive human habitation, no sign of human life. When, from a cleft in the foliage, we saw the Lake of Valencia at the foot of a great hill, it lay like a huge opal in the midst of virgin forest under a pure translucent sky. Not a ripple moved the water's shining surface, not a breath stirred the branches of the trees, not a sound disquieted the air.

We had meant to spend some time in visiting Valencia, the ancient capital where the final battle for Venezuela's independence was fought and won in 1824; but it was so late when we reached there that we pushed on to Maracay, only to find that the caretakers in the diplomatic "guest house" where "the General's" visitors were lodged had gone to bed, assuming that our plans had changed and that we would not arrive until morning. Reluctantly we waked them and, having secured shelter, sank wearily to bed, our bodies numb with fatigue, our minds chaotic with new strange impressions.

As I came halfway to my senses the next morning, I had a creepy sensation that someone was fumbling at the "Dutch door" and then that a ghostly figure was advancing toward my bed. Stifling a scream, I sat up as the mosquito netting enclosing the bed was untucked and a black hand thrust at me a paper, which I vaguely realized must be a telegram. Surely nothing but a death in the immediate family could have necessitated such a message, I told myself as I broke the seal; Mr. Engert's office must have forwarded a cable from Caracas because of some great emergency. The light was dim, for dawn was only just breaking; but I made out the message: JOHN GOT HIS DEGREE LOVE—HARRY.

Of course I was tremendously relieved that the question which had still been unsettled when I left home had been satisfactorily resolved: John had improved his grades and would be able to join me in Brazil, where Elisabeth would leave me. He would have his year of wonderful travel as my secretary, just as Henry had done, and I would have the best of companionship in my work. But it took a few minutes to pull myself together, and when Elisabeth burst into my room with the blithe exclamation, "I have news for thee," I felt her levity to be ill timed.

From the farther side of the screen in front of my door—the only concession to privacy—Mr. Engert explained the reason for her intrusion: I must be up and doing without delay if I wished to see "the General." He was not in Maracay after all, but in Ocumare de la Costa, where he had been detained. His secretary had telephoned to say that he would be glad to receive us there instead, and would place one of his cars at our disposal for the trip. It would be a hard journey in some ways, over another mountain range and down to the sea again, but we would pass through beautiful forests and would have further glimpses of the lake, from the north side this time.

Exhausted as I still was, I could not forego such a prospect, and within an hour we were on the road again—a road which almost immediately took us into deep, luxuriant tropical jungle, beyond which stretched groves of cocoa trees, their great red and yellow pods clinging to their graceful branches. The cocoa trees, shaded with rubber, grew on the banks of a pleasant little stream fringed with feathery bamboo; and as we drove beside this, we became increasingly conscious of the presence of soldiers guarding the road—an unmistakable sign that we were approaching our destination. At last we reached the sea, and as we stopped beside a simple wooden pavilion on the shore, a scholarly-looking, pleasant-faced man came forward to greet us and help us from the car.

This was Dr. Requena, "the General's" private secretary; a person of great importance and influence in Venezuela. Welcoming us in English, he led us toward the pavilion; an instant later an elderly man who had been standing on the beach turned and came in our direction. He was wearing riding boots, a sun helmet, a linen uniform and brown suede gloves; dark eyes gleamed through his steel-rimmed glasses, his mouth was almost concealed by an iron-gray moustache; he gave an impression of vigor; his carriage was erect, his manner alert. This was "the General," the power and personality by which Venezuela moved and breathed and had its being.

He seemed in good spirits and hailed Mr. Engert with something that was certainly cordiality and seemed very like affection; then he turned, smiling broadly, to Elisabeth and me. He talked rapidly, asking questions in quick succession and chuckling a little between them. What did we think of his roads? Pretty fine, weren't they? And the mountains— were they not beautiful? So we had lunched with the Dolges? And did we think Venezuela an interesting country? Splendid! How long were we going to remain? Too bad it wasn't longer. But he was glad we had come to Ocumare de la Costa to visit him; he had especially wished us to see this part of the country. He supposed we had risen early to make the trip, but doubtless we always rose early in the morning. (I sincerely hoped my expression would not betray me at this point. My conscience smote me and I quailed, for not much escaped those shrewd searching eyes.) He himself had risen early all his life. He was up at five and had most of the day's business dispatched before breakfast at eight. Now then—Dr. Requena would take us to his house for lunch before we went on our way. He shook hands all around, said *adiós* and started off across the sand. The simple audience was over and "the General" had certainly not given the impression of a man worried about revolutions or anything else.

Our luncheon was delicious—*sancocho de pescado,* a chowder of fish, plantain and potato; small corn cakes called *arepas* which accompanied it; meat and mangoes, which brought the meal to a close. Best of all, hot chocolate was served instead of after-dinner coffee—the fresh product of the cocoa bean, made without cream and with the natural oil still in it, a drink far superior to any chocolate I have ever tasted. But delectable as this luncheon was and delightful as our host proved to be, I did some solid thinking during the course of it and still more during the long drive back to Caracas.

In the crystallization of these reflections lay the substance of my impression of Venezuela. With its tremendous resources still undeveloped, and in many instances still undiscovered, with vast tracts still uninhabited, with its cities confined to its coast and civilization stretching not far beyond, it was already one of the most interesting and significant countries in the world and one which had risen to that position within the span of a man's life and under his guidance. The country was not a paradise; the man was not superhuman. As a nation we are prone to criticize, and we could, if we chose, find fault with both—to our disadvantage rather than theirs. But by the recognition of their intrinsic greatness, by the establishment of mutual accord, I felt we had as much to gain as we had to give.

Chapter 60

M Y FIRST view of the famous harbor and the city of Rio de Janeiro was somewhat disappointing, partly because—as usual—we had been roused at five to make a landing which did not take place until eleven and partly because the seasons had reversed when we crossed the equator and both the port and its encircling hills were obscured by the clouds and mist so prevalent on midwinter mornings in Brazil. But by noon clouds and mist had rolled away and the superb landlocked harbor was revealed in all its glory, islands studding its water, beaches curving about it, mountains towering above it; and at night I was enthralled at the sequences of sparkling lights which outlined the waterfront, as if all the glittering topazes of opulent Brazil had been joined to form a regal necklace for this queenly city to wear. But I saw Rio at various hours and from almost every angle, and each time I discovered gorgeous new aspects of it. I thought I had seen it in its most transcendent loveliness late one afternoon as the sun plunged suddenly into the sea and the mellow amber light of day turned swiftly to fiery rose and the stars began to pierce this glowing color. Beneath lay the harbor, fifteen miles long and seven miles wide; the city, sixty miles square, its buildings white as mansions of Paradise; beyond both, the hills, some soft with lush tropical green, others starkly gray and gaunt; Corcovado, with its lofty statue of Christ; the Organ Mountains, whose five "Fingers of God" point everlastingly to heaven. Nothing, I thought as I stood looking out at this panorama from "Sugar Loaf," could surpass or even equal it in natural beauty. But when I saw Rio from other heights —from Tijuca, where the "Chinese View" is spread forth in spectacular splendor; from Corcovado itself, standing beside the majestic figure of the Redeemer, the most strikingly situated religious monument on this hemisphere—I realized that "Sugar Loaf" had given me only a fore-taste of future delights. As my visit lengthened into weeks, I found that each day revealed some wonder hitherto undiscovered.

The older streets of Rio are narrow and dark and twisting; but in spite of its age, in spite of the ancient viaduct transecting a busy up-to-date quarter and the venerable carved and gilded chapel of São Bento set high upon a hill, in spite of occasional glimpses of old tiles and grillework and courtyards and other reminders of antiquity, Rio presented itself essentially as a modern city. The main artery running through its heart was broad and straight, its fine length shaded with splendid trees, its sidewalks paved in elaborate patterns of black and white mosaic. For the most part the private houses, somewhat ornate but distinctly pleasing in design, were set at a comfortable distance from each other and surrounded by gardens. In those which we were privileged to visit, we saw striking collections of antique jacaranda furniture and tooled silver arranged with the utmost taste and discrimination, and besides those omnipresent private gardens there were the great public ones: the Botanical Garden with its famous vistas of hundred-foot palms and its six thousand varieties of tropical plants and the *Quinta de Bõa Vista,* once the Emperor's private pleasure park. Everywhere there was the sense of spaciousness, of cleanliness, of verdure, of stimulating air and bright sunshine. As for the people of Rio, Elisabeth remarked, quite early in our visit, that she had never been in a city where all the inhabitants seemed to be going about their business so constantly and yet so quietly. Everyone seemed to be occupied. And yet there were no signs of haste, impatience or rudeness. Pedestrians were scrupulously polite to each other, even at the most crowded hours of the day; and an entente cordiale had apparently been established between those who drove cars and those who walked! And Rio was not one of those Latin cities where it was unsafe or unpleasant for women to go about alone.

To our surprise we found the Brazilians are extremely fond of sports, soccer being a great favorite; and a game we attended between a Brazilian and a visiting Hungarian team—begun at ten in the evening and played at the Flumenensia Club before thirty thousand enthusiastic fans —proved the occasion for such a discharge of firearms and such a display of fireworks that the excitement incident to the average football game paled before it. The weekly races at the spectacular Jockey Club provided another popular pastime, and much of Rio's social life centered around that and "the other Jockey Club," as it was somewhat confusingly called, on the Avenida Rio Branco and the two beautifully situated country clubs of Gavea and Ipanema. A good deal of informal entertaining was done at these and other clubs; but whether we were entertained formally or informally, at a private house or a club, we felt especially fortunate when typically Brazilian foods were served. First on the list of these logically comes *canja,* the soup which is a meal in itself, thick with rice and cubes of chicken, steaming hot, savory. Next are shrimps, made into muffin-like patties and called *empadinhas de camarão* or served with *chu-chu,* the delicate green vegetable of which we have no equivalent. We did not see at "company" meals the hearty *feifcada* of beans and beef, mingled with rice in a rich thick sauce; but coconut in some form invariably formed the dessert, and a *manjar de coco*—coconut shape—served with a rich sweet sauce made from fresh guavas was delectable.

It was a pleasure to renew acquaintance with Doña Berta Lutz, who had been an outstanding figure at the Convention of the League of Women Voters in Baltimore a few years earlier and was now President of the Brazilian Federation of Feminine Progress. Thanks to her brilliant and untiring leadership, women already had the vote in eight Brazilian states. The advancement of the feminist movement in a Latin country which was as surprising, in a different way, as the Brazilian enthusiasm for sports, owed much of its impetus to Doña Berta and the able and faithful Vice President of the Federation, Doña Jeronyma Mesquita. The latter, a member of an old and conservative family, had exhibited great courage in her espousal of many progressive measures. These ladies were responsible, both directly and indirectly, for much of the hospitality shown us, including a copious and delicious meal we enjoyed with Count and Countess Pereira Carneiro at their villa in Nictheroy, across the bay from Rio. Our trip there was made in a private launch. Then we took a series of elevators to the top of the cliff, upon which the house was set and drank our tea on a veranda overlooking our hosts's great salt storehouses and drydock below us and that ever-changing panorama of harbor and city and mountains beyond.

Count Pereira Carneiro, the owner of one of Brazil's greatest newspapers, was also one of her greatest industrialists; and, aware that he and his wife had built and developed a "model village" for their employes, I asked if we might not see this before we returned to town. The project to which we were promptly driven was breathtaking in its peace and loveliness; it was the original conception of the "spotless town" come true. The Count said the Countess was responsible for its existence, while she insisted the credit was his; anyway, there it was! Entering an arched gateway, on either side of which were neat shops whose goods were sold at cost, we came to a tiny square with a beautiful chapel and a small schoolhouse. Beyond, lining a trim, tree-bordered street, were attractive stucco cottages, each with a terrace and garden. We circled about, admiring it all and mentally contrasting it with the squalid slums in which many American laborers lived; but it was the schoolhouse to which we were irresistibly drawn. Accompanied by its teacher, who taught not only the boys and girls but their parents—there were night classes for adults desiring instruction—we inspected it with mounting enthusiasm. Immaculate, attractive and perfectly equipped, it offered free education to all children between five and fifteen whose parents were employed at Nictheroy by the Count; and students who showed some special bent or talent were given an opportunity to develop this. Childless themselves, the Pereira Carneiros provided countless children with the advantages they could not bestow upon sons and daughters of their own. No better news from abroad has reached me lately than the information that after all these years the Countess is still continuing this fine work, even though she must now do it without the husband who was in every way her helpmeet.

Rudolph Schoenfeld, Chargé d'Affaires at our embassy, began his good offices by facilitating our passage through customs and continued them by being most hospitable for the length of our stay. His courtesies —luncheon at the Jockey Club, a drive outside of Rio, and so on— marked the beginning of a friendship which still endures, and shortly after our arrival in Rio we made another acquaintance which proved to be even more far-reaching in its consequences. At the time, Captain John M. Enochs was acting head of the American Naval Mission, which enjoyed as much prestige as the embassy on the social scene and was equally hospitable. "Elisabeth and I dined with Captain Enochs." "Went to Sugar Loaf with Captain Enochs." "Soccer game in evening with Captain Enochs," my calendar reminds me. We had become so accustomed to such attentions in Rio that we did not take them very seriously, and in ninety-nine cases out of a hundred there was no reason why we should have. Not until the very day of Elisabeth's return to Washington did I realize that this was the hundredth case! The Captain had long been considered a highly eligible but completely confirmed bachelor, and Elisabeth had discouraged and dismissed every promising suitor; but when she bade him good-bye, I immediately suspected that for a gentlewoman of her natural reserve, her manner of leave-taking meant more than an effusion of appreciation. He insisted later on that he by no means felt sure of her then; but he well might have, for it had been a mutual case of love at first sight. Though she did go back to the United States and resume her position at the Children's Bureau, this was a mere prelude to her return to Brazil and the bridegroom who was eagerly awaiting her. Their wedding took place in the American Embassy, and the marriage was a happy one. Though I was an inadvertent matchmaker, I was certainly a most successful one.

Personally, I owe a great deal to Captain Enochs. He asked if I would not like to see the beautiful harbor of Rio from the air—if I would, he would arrange to have me take a short flight in a naval plane. As such a privilege was something not usually afforded a civilian, especially a female civilian, I accepted with alacrity. I had never flown, but it did not occur to me to be frightened, either before the flight or when I discovered that the plane had an open cockpit and its pilot delighted in stunt flying. When the adventure was over and I was back on solid ground again, I realized that henceforth flying would never be an intimidating experience for me, and this was just as well: my second flight, also in an open cockpit, was over the Chaco, the huge jungle which formed the disputed territory between Paraguay and Bolivia; my third one, again in an open cockpit, was over the Andes. Two years later, my son John and I went from Beirut to Isfahan and back by freight plane, and this was more spacious, but hardly less hazardous: such passengers as were accepted sat on wooden benches around an open space about the size of a card table. I was pretty well shaken up by the time I got back from that trip and it took me a long while to recover physically. But I can truthfully say that I was never frightened, and I lay this largely to my initiation which was due to Captain Enochs.

Before Elisabeth was obliged to leave, my son John and his friend Russell Thayer arrived to continue the journey southward with me, so when I set sail for Uruguay, it was in their buoyant company.

The short voyage was so pleasant that it seemed all too brief, but after reaching our destination, it was impossible to feel other than happy that the trip had ended. For Montevideo, Uruguay's capital, was a city that produced an immediate sense of well-being and imparted an immediate sense of content. It was not a large or magnificent city, compared to Rio, but why compare it with any other when it had so delightful an individuality of its own? It was a city of progress and prosperity, of kindliness and welcome, of comfort and composure. Something of the rolling countryside's peace and plenty seemed to have penetrated its limits; the soft gray and violet tones of Uruguay's beautiful agates and amethysts seemed reflected in its wide, well-ordered streets; its gardens were fresh and fragrant with roses; and around it curved the shining silver of its broad Rio de la Plata and its splendid beaches of Pocitos and Carrasco, enjoyed not only by Uruguayans, but by Brazilians and Argentinians as well. Its sights included the old Spanish Government

House on the Plaza Constitución; the colonnades of the Plaza Independencia; and the statue of the *gaucho*—the dashing horseman of the silver stirrups and spurs and knife, of flowing poncho and wide sombrero and sheepskin saddle, who personified both romance and progress in Uruguay. His successors could still be seen at the Tablada, the open market outside the city where cattle and sheep, shipped by train or driven in from the country, were sold for the great freezing plants. Brilliant figures they were, those Uruguayan horsemen, the tawny yellow, the dazzling white, the scarlet, the azure of their graceful garments shining in the sun as they rounded up the cattle; and on the *estancias*—the great estates with their avenues of eucalyptus trees, their rambling white houses with bright caged birds singing on the verandas, their acres and acres of orchard and tilled ground and pasture—the herds and the herdsmen were still the center of attraction.

Well worth journeying far to find, all this and much besides; nevertheless, one's first sensation was not a desire for sightseeing, but a longing to settle down and respond to the cordiality and spontaneity with which one was received; to learn to understand and speak the language; and to learn to know the people, in whom the inherent courtesy and culture of the Spaniard was blended with the vigor and progressiveness of a younger nation. Climatically, Uruguay is greatly blessed; its winters, while never severe, are cool enough to refresh and invigorate; its summers are bland without being tropical. And the combination affects not only its productiveness—it is as generally fertile as it is generally level—but the character of its population.

Montevideo proved to be essentially a city of homes, with the family as the supreme and final unit. But the patriarchal form of existence which was so prevalent there was not the type which excluded outsiders; on the contrary, it welcomed them with the utmost cordiality. Before we had been in Montevideo twenty-four hours, we had been invited to tea in one of its typical and charming homes, and we afterward saw many of them. A large number of the finest residences were in the business section, as is often the case in European capitals, and the Uruguayans had adapted the patio to the requirements of their customs and climate with skill and taste. They had, in most cases, covered it with glass and added a fireplace, transforming it from an open court to a living room. From it other apartments led: a drawing room, for instance, with formal brocade furniture and often a priceless collection of antique fans; a library lined to the ceiling with books; a dining room where distinctive delicacies were offered to visitors—small hot croquettes speared on toothpicks and *dulce de leche,* made by boiling milk and sugar together. But it was the converted patio which was really the center of family life.

It was here that a woman of ripening years gathered her sons and daughters, her grandsons and granddaughters, their fiancés and friends about her. There did not seem to be the slightest sign of condescension on the part of the older ones toward the younger, nor did the presence of their elders seem to hamper the enjoyment of the boys and girls. They pulled up the rugs and danced the tango, or clustered in groups to sing wistful haunting folksongs to the accompaniment of a guitar; or stood about and badgered each other after the fashion of youth. I was already familiar with the Spanish saying, "If there is anyone in a household who has more authority than the mother, it is the grandmother." Now, privileged to be included in such gatherings, I wondered how we ever acquired the idea in the United States that there was necessarily a gulf between the generations, that they interfered with each other's enjoyment instead of enhancing it.

It was a damp chilly evening when the boys and I boarded one of the immaculate and attractive river steamers which plied nightly between Montevideo and Buenos Aires. The *mucamo*—whom we could not resist calling the moo-cow-moo—placed my heavy hand baggage in my cabin without a murmur; but it was with difficulty that we induced him to give the boys a suitcase apiece, the necessity for pajamas and toothbrushes leaving him quite unmoved. Having finally convinced him, we next had to persuade him that extra blankets would be acceptable; vigorously protesting, he led me the length of the corridor, triumphantly showed me a small stove and assured me this *estufa* emanated unlimited heat! But eventually we prevailed and all necessities, as we understood them, were duly secured; and we went up on deck to watch the disappearing lights of the city before we piled our coats on top of the begrudged blankets and crept beneath them.

At six-thirty the next morning we were on deck again, refreshed with sleep and *café con leche* and gazing with bewilderment at the crowded stream and congested wharf. Never since I went up the Yangtze to Shanghai had I seen a river so teeming with every imaginable kind of craft, from every quarter of the globe. A score of nations were represented by the flags flying on the hundreds of ships which churned their way through the Rio de la Plata or lay at anchor by its wharves, and as our own boat nosed into her berth, it did not have an inch to spare. But the docking was swift and skillful, as was our passage through customs.

Buenos Aires, that splendid and sophisticated capital of Argentina, one of the largest cities in South America and perhaps the proudest, was only a way station for us, however, since our real visit there was to come after our voyage over inland waters was finished.

In leaving Buenos Aires we had expected to go by boat to Concordia, a thriving town on the Rio Uruguay, and then by rail to Posadas, the capital of Argentina's Misiones District, where we would board the river steamer that plied along the Upper Paraná. But we were forced to change our plans at the last moment and take the quicker and shorter route by train from Buenos Aires to Posadas. And as is often the case, our slight disappointment met with immediate compensation: we found that at Zarate, about sixty miles north of Buenos Aires, our train would be placed on a ferry and we would spend five hours on the delta of the Paraná. This passage proved to be one of complete and quiet pleasure, beginning about seven and ending at midnight. The country through which we passed was almost uninhabited; only twice did a gliding beacon reveal the presence of another ship; and not more than three or four times did we see a twinkling light on land. The deepening dusk covered the placid water with soft blackness; then the succeeding starlight flooded it with silver, enhancing the luminous crescent moon; currents of fresh fragrance rose from the trees beside the shore.

Thirty hours later, somewhat travel stained and weary, we found ourselves on the station platform at Posadas; and the thin coffee and thick bread of which we partook on our way to the wharf failed to raise our spirits. The wharf itself, where unshaven men with pajama jackets over their trousers were pursuing and killing rats and where unkempt women, their hair arranged in long funnels at the back of their heads, were smoking cigars, proved even more depressing. In fact, truth compels me to confess that as we boarded a steamer along with a cow, a turkey, a number of hens, a large quantity of corrugated iron and what seemed like a superfluity of other passengers, I would gladly have retreated to Buenos Aires if either of my companions had encouraged my dejection. Wisely, they did nothing of the sort; and before the day was over, I was thankful they had not. For as we chugged along between riverbanks fringed with feathery bamboo, the sense of glorious adventure, of which fatigue, ptomaine poisoning and a bad cold had temporarily deprived me, revived. The absence of hot water for bathing, ice water for drinking, adequate plumbing, deck chairs, stewardesses and so on faded to comparative unimportance; so did heat, dirt, overcrowding and innumerable stinging, biting and crawling creatures of every description. Our fellow passengers—from every quarter of the globe and speaking every imaginable language—proved interesting and congenial. Though I was slightly startled the first time one of them suddenly pulled out a revolver and shot an alligator on the bank, I soon began to regard such episodes as very much in order and hardly worth a second thought; and a little further on, I watched the pursuit and capture of a deer by a native without a qualm. The open slaughter of the ill-fated cow, which proved to be our source of meat and not milk, as we had supposed, was more upsetting. Considerable excitement was occasioned when the members of a relief party, dispatched to rescue a struggling figure discerned in the water after dark, found they had gone to the aid of a mountain lion!

Otherwise, the voyage proceeded calmly; each night, a deep enveloping fog forced us to lie to until morning; each day, the steamer's dilapidated rowboat was dispatched at frequent intervals to meet a similar craft sent out from shore, thus facilitating embarkations and debarkations without undue ceremony or delay at the various ports we passed —at which we conjectured whether the assembled crowd represented the town's entire population or merely the immediate families of our arriving and departing passengers! We did not pull up alongside until we reached the German settlement of El Dorado, where Dr. Hector Barreiro, the Governor of Misiones, and his staff, who had been our most illustrious fellow passengers, left us. They were welcomed by the local officials and Prince Louis Ferdinand, son of Germany's former Crown Prince, who was visiting there in the course of a world trip. It seemed uncanny to find in that distant territorial village the young man who might have ruled a great empire if history had not decreed otherwise.

It was six in the evening some days after our departure from Posadas when we reached Puerto Aguirre, our own debarkation point. Our baggage was dumped unceremoniously on the sandbank, the steamer tooted its shrill whistle, and we were alone. Two or three lights blinked uncertainly in the distance, but there was no sign of the waiting cars we had expected. However, the scene was so unspeakably lovely as to obliterate all uneasy thoughts. The river's smooth coils were stained to crimson by the reflection of the spreading sunset; high above us, the moon loomed —a smooth golden oval. The stillness and sweetness which mark the merging of day into night cast a spell of enchantment over the landscape, and with this spell strong upon us, we found our way up the shore. The promised cars, concealed by a bend in the road, had not failed us, and with us and our belongings safely aboard, they plunged into the woods. Every now and then a rabbit scuttled across our road; every now and then there was a whirr of unseen wings. But through the maze and tangle of tree and vine and shrub there was no other sound until, an hour later, the sound of the Falls of Iguazú—the "Great Waters" of the Guarani Indians—met our ears. Only a murmur at first, it became a tumult and a roar. For moments before we could see the falls, they seemed to rush toward us through the magic of their music. Then suddenly the forest cleared, the lights of a low-built hotel gleamed on one side of us, and on the other, under that oval moon, fell the pearly torrent of the great cascades, their base hidden in tropical verdure, their summit seeming to touch the heavens.

Perhaps the Victoria Falls in Africa may equal these in majesty; this I do not know. But that they or any other natural wonder of the world can surpass the Falls of Iguazú in grandeur is unimaginable. They are higher than Niagara by thirty or forty feet and half again as wide. But it is not their magnitude alone that makes them so superb. It is also their setting, which is so glorious in itself, and their disposition in this setting. They are not all massed together; the Two Sisters, the Bossetti Falls and the Falls of San Martín lie at one end of the great island-dotted delta of the Iguazú River; farther up are the Three Musketeers, reached only by a long circuitous route; and farther still, approached through the gorge of the "Devil's Throat," is the greatest group of all —Pueyrredon, Mitre, Rivadavia, Belgrano, Unión and Floriances.

It was in going to these, the morning after our arrival, that we had one of our most thrilling adventures. The first evening we had contented ourselves with a superficial inspection of the Two Sisters, Bossetti and San Martín by moonlight; but later I confronted "La Señora," the capable and decided manager of the hotel, with a degree of determination equal to her own. Yes, I was aware that the river was in flood, that no *turista* had been permitted to visit the Garganta del Diablo in three weeks. But I was not a *turista*. I was an *escritora,* and it was unthinkable that an *escritora* should travel thousands of miles for the express purpose of thrusting her head into the jaws of the devil, so to speak, and then fail to do so. The argument lasted so long that, when all the lights were turned out, according to a custom of which I was unaware, promptly at eleven, I was in the midst of my nightly ablutions and had to grope my way from the bathroom to my bedroom. But the next morning, in spite of the boys' glee at my predicament, I had my reward: I learned that La Señora had arranged to have us start for the Garganta del Diablo promptly at nine.

About that hour, we climbed into a vehicle which in some previous incarnation might have been classified as a truck and began our jolting way through the forest over something that bore not even a slight resemblance to a road, though it rejoiced in the musical name of the Camino del Monte. Ferns and palms, begonias and orchids bloomed about us; birds of gorgeous plumage rose and dipped overhead; butterflies with brilliant wings floated by. And when we reached the *embarcadero* and found our guides and boat had not yet arrived, our husky truck driver produced a net and pursued those drifting bits of color with the zeal of a true naturalist!

There is of course a serpent in every Paradise and we had almost been devoured by a variety of insects when our swarthy smiling guides and their craft finally glided into sight, nor had the attack abated by the time we reached midstream. But by then we were so excited we had forgotten them. The crude boat rocked uncertainly over the swollen river; frequently the swift current caught us and we lurched downstream; then we were swept back again by the sure strokes of the oars. Twisting, turning, plunging, we came to a small stony island, where a path had been beaten between crevices and bushes; leaving our boat behind us, we threaded our way to a ledge where another boat was tied. A second passage began, more wildly thrilling than the first; as the heavy water spread over the sides of the boat, it quivered and tilted; then it leaped forward again toward another island, porous with rivulets. Here there was not even a path, only stepping stones and an occasional rough board. But slipping, sliding, stretching, making a chain with our hands, bracing our feet against rocks, we climbed toward the sound of the rushing water which we knew must lie only around the next corner or the next. Then, standing level with their summit, we saw them— streaming and foaming to limitless depths below us, banded in crystalline bubbles, snowy white and tawny yellow, they gushed and fell and sprang, sunlight slanting across the spray, mist rising from them and birds flying through the mist; relentless, stupendous, transcendently beautiful, a culmination of divine and everlasting power made manifest through the might and majesty of nature.

In going from Posadas to Ascunción in those days, you did not decide which train was most convenient for you and secure upon it the type of reservation most pleasing to you—and of course there were no commercial airlines. You rose at three-forty-five in the morning to take *the* train, which ran twice a week; and unless there happened to be a free *camerote* in the *dormitorio* which came from Buenos Aires, you sat upright on a very uncompromising sort of a seat while the train loped along like a rocking horse. The train was not due in the capital city of Paraguay until seven-thirty in the evening; and if you reached there— as we did—at ten-thirty instead, you were considered virtually on time. It was not an easy journey; but it took us past a landscape of elusive charm to an ancient and appealing inland city completely different from the teeming ports. The jouncing train carried us across wide fertile plains where herds of vigorous cattle grazed, past deep marshes where the song of strange birds sounded like castanets, through thick bright forests inviolate in their promise of future wealth, parallel to distant purple hills framing a sunset sky of burnished copper. Mammoth ant-hills rose like beehives in the pastures; narrow strips of lace-edged linen fluttered from wayside crosses; barefoot women with shawls around their shoulders walked slowly along; grisly old men with pipes and ponchos jogged by on diminutive donkeys; small stoical children clad in a single abbreviated garment stood and stared; the soft guttural tones of Guarani began to reach our ears as often as the familiar musical Spanish. Then, as we approached Asunción, the moon above softened with its radiance the high walls encircling homes and gardens, brightened the cobblestoned streets, turned to gold the iron grillework of long low windows; and if I had not already succumbed to the charm of Paraguay, I should have done so in that first moonlit revelation of the city.

Nor did the next morning bring a sense of disillusionment. On the contrary, the spell was stronger than ever. A fortunate chance had taken us to a rambling old hotel built in a succession of units about informal patios, where the wide paved verandas proved to be only one of many charms. Others were the pomarosa trees with powder-puff blossoms at the entrance; the puppies who gamboled about a drab hound, a plump black cat and a quivering white rabbit; the grape arbor dappling the tiles with soft light and shade; the orchard fragrant with the scent of oranges and limes and mangoes; the open laundry where the graceful barefooted women plunged their washing in deep clean water and spread it out to dry; the baby daughter of the *mozo,* gold rings in her tiny lobes, her black eyes dancing as she toddled between kitchen and office; the fair grave children of the German proprietor; the patient and hopeful *vendadoras* who waited with their yards and yards of fairy-fine *nanduty,* the native lace, inspired by a spider web; the lovely mysterious lady, her full-flounced pink dress dipping to the ground, a high pink comb thrust above her braids, who swiftly appeared before us there and just as swiftly vanished.

If I had been free to stay indefinitely in that enchanting city, I think I might have been able to interpret Asunción as it should be interpreted; as it is, I can give only glimpses of its character and its charm. I went, for instance, to the Botanical Garden through streets decorated with tiny triangles of multicolored paper arranged in festoons because it was someone's *fiesta.* I learned that the white-clad policemen spoke only Guarani, whereas those dressed in blue spoke Spanish as well, just as the bilingual Bishop, Monsignor Bogarin, insisted his clergy should do. I went to the other end of town, past the open *tiendas* with their billowing curtains and the oxcarts peddling water from door to door, and through the finest residential quarter to the Recoleta Cemetery, where the crumbling tombs of centuries ago were mingled with the austere new ones, and all were bright with flowers. I had hardly learned that when there was a funeral in a family of modest means, the hearse was attached to the rear of the trolley car which regularly passed the cemetery and thus conveyed there when I saw this for myself! I went to the cathedral sacristy to see the heavy Spanish silver. I went to the waterfront warehouse where the fragrant leaves of the wild yerba maté were pulverized and packed in heavy burlap bags. By then, I had learned to drink maté—hot or cold, with or without sugar and lemon; indeed, this great staple of Paraguay, of which millions of pounds were exported every year, had become a favorite beverage which I enjoyed as much as tea. And what leisurely untroubled days those were, divided between the sunny courtyard with its pomarosas and its puppies and the wide cobbled streets that led so picturesquely to the churches, the homes and gardens of Asunción!

Chapter 61

I HAVE little use for the traveler who, though unhampered by financial considerations, takes a tramp steamer the same day a *Leviathan* is sailing; or stays at a squalid little foreign inn when there is a fine hotel directly across the street—and then laments that there are no good accommodations to be had outside the United States! I despise persons like these for their hypocrisy. And I despise quite as much—for their bad sportsmanship—the persons who do not make the best of disagreeable conditions when these cannot be helped.

But I frankly envy those who wholeheartedly and joyously prefer discomforts, who tell you—and mean it—that the more they have to rough it, the happier they are! For though I have never yet hesitated to visit any place I wanted or needed to do, for fear of being uncomfortable, no matter what kind of conveyance I had to take to get there or what kind of accommodations I found after my arrival, and though I have enjoyed many places in spite of their lack of essential comforts, I must confess that I prefer space to crowding, cleanliness to dirt, warmth to cold, good food to bad and plumbing to pitchers! I shall be thankful to my dying day that I went to see the cataracts of Iguazú, but my aversion to cabbage soup, boiled brains, bad water, flies, fleas and other incidentals of the trip increased rather than diminished as it drew near its end; and when I at last saw, around a curve of the Paraná River, the city of "goodly airs" looming before me, my flagging spirits rose to such a pitch that it was hard to refrain from hailing it with a paean of thanksgiving!

But Buenos Aires inspires this feeling for many other reasons than because it offers every conceivable luxury, refinement and distraction that the most exacting, fastidious and pleasure-loving traveler could demand; for many other reasons than because of its enormous size and the omnipresent evidences of power and progress with which it pulses. Besides all this, there is a joyous quality about it, of which one is conscious from afar and which floods every fiber of one's being on closer acquaintance. It has in it something of golden mellow Tokay wine, of amber, of Venetian velvet, of Indian summer, of love that comes late and lasts long. There may be crowded and ugly districts in it—I cannot say, for I never saw any, but only spaciousness and beauty and magnificence. There may be inclement and chilly weather—I cannot say, for I never saw any, but only sunshine and warmth and that wonderful clear sparkling air to which the city owes its name. From the moment I landed to the moment I left, I was filled with a stimulating *joie de vivre.*

We were met at the wharf by that same Dr. Vance Murray of the United States Public Health Service who, four years earlier when he was stationed in Japan, had met Henry and me when our ship reached Yokohama. Perhaps more than any other one person, Dr. Murray had taught us to know Japan and love it, for he was much besides a skilled physician and conscientious public servant. He had that rare "gift of tongues" which enabled him to learn almost any language in an unbelievably short time, and the still rarer gift which enabled him to conform rapidly to the customs of any country, share its viewpoint, enjoy its pleasures and understand its psychology, free from antagonisms, unerring in judgment, sympathetic in spirit. And now, fortunately indeed, John and Russ and I were to have him as our "guide, philosopher and friend" in our exploration of Buenos Aires.

We darted about in a small unpretentious car, and in an amazingly short time several of the city's landmarks became familiar: the Casa Rosada on the Plaza Mayor, which was the President's official residence and headquarters for several government departments; the wide Balneario curving about the silver waterfront; the Tigre, that beautiful suburban island which was always a kaleidoscopic scene of color and motion. We sat in the Plaza Once beneath the wide-spreading Ombu, that tree of both good and evil omen famous in song and fable of the country; we lingered in the dim cathedral before the tomb of San Martín, the country's liberator; we wandered through the chapel-bordered walks of Recoleta, the cemetery with hundreds of mausoleums and not a single grave in the heart of the city. And we visited the Immigrants' Hotel, in which the humble traveler could find abundant welcome—food and lodging furnished free for five days; a dining room and laundry, immaculate dormitories, spotless bathrooms, a model hospital and a great sunny plaza in which to sit. Four thousand persons could be, and frequently were, housed there at one time, for Argentina placed no restrictions upon the number of Caucasian settlers she gladly received. They brought in their belongings duty free, and at the end of five days were furnished free transportation to any part of the Republic in which they wished to settle. If there had been time and opportunity for me to see nothing else in Buenos Aires, I would have felt amply repaid by the hours I spent at this institution; the warm sweet bread fresh from the great ovens, which I ate slowly and thoughtfully, seemed to have in it a quality of nourishment for the soul no less than the body, because of the feeling with which it was dispensed.

The Immigrants' Hotel was one of the most interesting establishments in Buenos Aires and another was the Sociedad de Beneficencia—the Benevolent Society—with which I became acquainted through Mrs. Robert Woods Bliss, the wife of the American Ambassador, to whom I was indebted for many other privileges and pleasures. The Beneficencia had the status of a sub-department of the government—a rare position for a charitable organization and for one, moreover, which was under feminine direction and management! It is not often that I feel impelled to devote a large part of my time in any one city to visiting institutions and organizations; but at that period not many of the cities I had visited seemed to have so many which commanded attention and admiration. After I had been to the Immigrants' Hotel, the office of the Beneficencia and the Casa de Huerfanos—the Orphans' Home—I was only too eager to follow Mrs. Bliss's suggestion that I should also become acquainted with the Amigos del Arte—the Friends of Art—whose original object had been to foster the work of Argentine artists and protect them from extortionate picture dealers. Founded by a small group of interested people without any special grant, the Amigos del Arte had grown in less than six years to a position of importance and influence and extended its activities in many directions.

I had been warned so often by presumably reliable persons before I went to Buenos Aires that I would "never see the inside of an Argentine house" that I was prepared to face a long succession of hotel meals with what philosophy I could. But within a few hours of our arrival the boys and I were invited out to lunch the following day, and very shortly my engagement calendar resembled my Washington one at the height of the season! My letters went unanswered, my mending undone, and often my clothes were not picked up, for I changed them too rapidly to put them away; and meanwhile, I saw the inside of so many Argentine houses that it is difficult to describe them adequately. They were very beautiful, and I doubt if there was any world capital where there was more elegance of living than in Buenos Aires at that time. Draperies, rugs, tapestries, brocades, silver, porcelains, crystals, paintings, marble, objets d'art, carved and polished woods were assembled in settings of spaciousness and grandeur. Not in every house, of course, but in a very great proportion of them. You drew up before a magnificent marble edifice and leaped to the conclusion that your taxi driver had brought you by mistake to a museum, only to discover it was the residence of the family with whom you were to take tea. Or your hostess admitted, very casually, in reply to your admiring question, that the two masterpieces above the sofa—always the place of honor for a guest in a South American house—were both Murillos.

But there was nothing solemn or stiff about all this richness of possession; the damask sofa where you had taken your appointed place was deep and soft and comfortable; the needlepoint chairs were disposed in companionable clusters; there were vases of flowers and family pictures scattered about, and often there were toys as well. For here, as in Uruguay, the patriarchal form of existence was predominant, and you joined a family group more often than you "assisted" at an official function. There was usually a baby in the house, and occasionally several, for some of the married daughters almost invariably continued to live at home, and they and their husbands always seemed to be in complete harmony with their parents, their sisters, their brothers and all the corresponding in-laws, as well as the friends of all those persons. In one household where we lunched, there were eleven members of the immediate family at the table, not including a bride and groom who returned from their honeymoon just in time to join us for dessert and several children upstairs who were too young to appear at meals! Another house, to which we went more than once, harbored four generations, and the great-grandmother, a sprightly old lady of eighty-six, was more or less occupied on the occasion of our first visit with preparations for a dance in honor of her twenty-year-old-great-granddaughter which was to take place there the following evening!

I thought the atmosphere of Buenos Aires delightful, its public parks and buildings majestic, its institutions inspiring and its people cultured, charming and wholly hospitable. I thrilled like a girl over the roses that were sent me by the square yard—where, except in Argentina, would they have been given in so lavish a fashion? I felt entirely at home in the Senate Chamber, where a battle was being waged over the seating of a member, and I exulted at the invitation to visit the Senate cloakroom, a sanctum sanctorum I never expected to penetrate in any country. I admired the headquarters of *La Prensa,* at that period the finest newspaper building in the world and one which contained a public library; a conservatory where music was taught free of charge; and a handsome assembly room—a copy of Versailles's Hall of Nations—in which, also free of charge, weekly addresses were given by famous lecturers; and a free clinic. Indeed, I cannot recall that I have ever visited a city where my impressions were more generally favorable or favorable for a greater variety of reasons. So there was something personal in my regret that though Argentines *as individuals* often reciprocated the admiration and affection they inspired in us as individuals, there was in Argentina *as a nation* greater and more widespread feeling of suspicion and antagonism toward the United States as a nation than in any other Latin American country I had visited. And because this feeling was so self evident, I ventured at one of those hospitable Argentine homes, where the hostess and I were the only women present, to inquire the reasons for this from the other guests—men of learning and experience occupying positions of responsibility and importance and all firm friends of the United States.

Greatly as I respected the sincerity and earnestness of their replies, when I analyzed them, I did not find the enlightenment I had sought. Resentment against the Monroe Doctrine; distrust of "imperialism"; fundamental differences between Latin and Anglo Saxon civilizations; the assumption of superiority by North Americans; misconceptions in each country concerning the true character of the other; insidious and indirect European propaganda against the United States, largely prompted by economic rivalry rather than actual hostility; commercial reactions and political capital; indigenous jealousy toward a country which had preceded it in securing recognition as a world power—all these were advanced as probable contributing causes for contention.

No doubt they were; nevertheless, the same obstacles exist in other places with less regrettable results.

If it had been possible to embark whenever we felt inclined for our next port, I think the boys and I would have been tempted to remain in Buenos Aires almost indefinitely; but boats bound for the Straits of Magellan stopped at the Falkland Islands only biannually and I was especially anxious to go there, for I had long been intrigued by the position of the Falklands, both politically and geographically; so we had no choice but to leave Buenos Aires the second week of October. We sailed in a staunch British steamer that had seen many years of service, and there was a quick change in atmosphere from one that was thoroughly Latin to one that was thoroughly Anglo-Saxon. Argentina has always disputed Great Britain's possession of the Falklands—which the former insists on calling the Islas Malvinas—and official recriminations have been a matter of yearly procedure; and still Great Britain has managed to cling to them and administer them as a crown colony.[1] There are in all about two hundred islands, only two of any size—East and West Falkland—and most of them uninhabited. The two large islands are about three hundred miles east of the Straits and their dependencies are scattered down into Antarctica.[2] Even at their best, these islands are rocky, bleak, windswept and drenched by chill rains, and a people less tenacious than the British might have been persuaded to let them go rather than bother with such an isolated and unpromising possession. But that has never been their way, and as sheep thrive in the northerly islands and oil is obtained from whales and seals in the waters surrounding the southerly ones, they have continued to represent a sound investment as well as an example of tenacity.

Sir Esme Howard had given me a letter of introduction to the Colonial Governor, Captain Arnold Hodson, who was a good friend of his, and I felt reasonably sure of a welcome at Port Stanley, on East Falkland, though I did not foresee one quite as hospitable as it proved; and while awaiting with no impatience the results of this letter which I had sent ahead, I derived great enjoyment from the voyage in the little steamer. Our first day out was one of drifting fog and gray skies and a smooth but sullen sea; then came high-crested waves breaking with boisterous impact against the ship, and that clean hard blue of sky and ocean which is no less deep than the azure of tropical heavens and waters, but which is as cold and clear as the other is warm and glowing, and which betokens the approach to frigid zones. The "roaring forties" greeted us with tumultuous clarity, and through the crisp frosty atmosphere came another greeting, a wireless message from Port Stanley:

HIS EXCELLENCY WILL BE DELIGHTED IF YOU WILL STOP WITH HIM
AT GOVERNMENT HOUSE DURING STAY PLEASE REPLY SECRETARY

And we gratefully radioed our acceptance to this invitation.

Though we were on deck early the morning of arrival at Port Stanley, our ship had already anchored in the crowded little landlocked harbor and the town lay before us—a cluster of unpretentious red-roofed houses, made of stone or corrugated iron, clinging to bleak and stony ground. Beyond it on every side were rocky hillocks and pastureland, dun colored and gray except where touched to rare brightness by the gold of flowering gorse. There was not a tree in sight, and a filmy fog veiled a landscape which even under glowing sunshine would have

---

[1] In 1968, officials of the islands declared their opposition to being ceded to Argentina.

[2] In 1962, the territory south of 60° south latitude was made a separate colony and named British Antarctic Territory.

lacked variety and verdure. But the effect was of solitude and strength rather than of monotony and sadness—there was something poignantly peaceful about it—and as we looked at it and waited for the launch to take us ashore, we agreed that we were glad we had come.

Mr. Hugh Thomas, the editor of the *Daily Penguin,* appeared and introduced himself, saying he had been sent to fetch us and hoped we would not mind walking, as there was only one car on the island. So we set off down the road bordering the waterfront, past the town hall containing the museum and library and post office, past the trim houses. We turned in, after ten minutes or so, at a white gate, and there, immediately before us, lay Government House, not a huge viceregal palace like the one in Ottawa; not a dazzling white marble mansion like the one in Singapore, but a comfortable unostentatious English home of medium size, built partly of brick and partly of wood in rambling and informal fashion, with daisies pushing through the windswept lawn and daffodils crowding beneath the shelter of the eaves.

Mr. Thomas opened the front door and led us down a hall to the drawing room, where a glowing peat fire burned under a white mantel, chairs and sofas covered with bright chintz were agreeably arranged, tigerskins were scattered over an Oriental rug, engravings of British royalty hung on the walls and there were flowers, books and small silver ornaments everywhere—a room of comfort, cheerfulness and quiet charm. Toward us came a tall slender man in tweeds, with a dark vibrant face and a beautifully modeled head: His Excellency Captain Arnold Hodson, a famous big game hunter, a versatile and accomplished writer, an officer in World War I, for thirteen years a Consul in Abyssinia and now Governor of the Falklands and their dependencies—South Georgia, the South Shetlands, the South Orkneys, the South Sandwich and other islands, a territory sparsely inhabited, mostly by Scots, but covering three million square miles.

He was sorry, the Governor told us, that his wife was not there to welcome us, but she was in Scotland; he would show us to our rooms, and would we tell him what time we would like our baths? It was necessary to plan because of the rather limited hot water supply; and the water was not dirty—it was dark in color because it flowed through peat bogs, but it was very soft and refreshing. Luncheon would be at one, tea at four—if that would be convenient—and dinner at half-past eight, with additional guests, among them the captain of the whaling fleet that had just come in. Would we like to see something of the town during the afternoon and go to the penguin rookery the next morning?

Fine. . . . And in the evening there would be a dance at the town hall in honor of our ship's arrival.

Port Stanley is a compact and self-reliant little town and we enjoyed our walk through its windy streets and returned from it hungry and invigorated. In a very different way, I found the expedition to see the penguins equally agreeable and it still remains unique in my experience. Almost every place I have visited has some sights similar in a general way to those of every other—monuments, parks, celebrities past or present or both. But only in the Falkland Islands were flightless aquatic birds a leading feature of interest. We crossed the harbor to Sparrow Cove by launch and then walked over rough spongy ground and fragrant peat bogs almost to Rabbit Cove, a considerable distance. It was hard going and slow, but it brought us to the secluded rookery, where over two thousand of those strange birds with futile finlike wings and shell-like tails made their home. Their nests of coarsely woven twigs lay close together and in each were two eggs, for it was nearly time for the baby penguins to hatch, after which they would be guarded by their mothers until they ceased to be small puffs of gray down and had grown sleek black and white feathers. Then they would join that peculiar parade that solemnly marched every morning to the sea for fish, making a path like a sheep track as it went; and every afternoon they would solemnly return, two by two, replete and satisfied. Strangely human they looked, as if they had just dressed for dinner in black broadcloth and spotless white linen; a little self-important, as if their elegance had been recently achieved; a little proud and pompous. And they made weird sounds; they gargled and screamed and hissed; they were parvenu birds who studied the fashions before they studied voice culture; and yet, they had a remote and inborn dignity.

On the other hand, far from being exotic in atmosphere, the dance at the town hall was so like those of the old days in Newbury and Haverhill that it made me homesick. We met a number of pleasant people, most of whom had come in from their sheep ranches on horseback or by small local boats, for there were no roads outside of Port Stanley. I could not help noticing that the girls and women were wearing dresses that were both fresh and fashionable, and I wondered if much of this finery had not arrived in the same ship we had.

Dinner was outstanding for different and very special reasons: because it was the first time at a British house that I had heard the President of the United States toasted with the same solemnity as the King of England; and because I received, in earnest, the one invitation which, in jest, I had promised not to accept without consultation with my editor. It seemed the captain of the whaling fleet, who was the owner's son, had been a reader of mine for some time; if we would care to, he would be very pleased to have us go to Antarctica with him. It would mean roughing it, but I could have a cabin of sorts to myself and the boys could bunk with the crew. He thought the experience might appeal to me— as far as he knew, I would be the first woman to have such a trip and he did not know when he could offer me another. . . .

By the time he had got this far both boys were beside me, excitedly urging me to accept and I was hesitating, miserably conscious that almost my last words to Mr. Bigelow had been a promise not to leave my established route without consulting him.

"Could you wait until I could cable New York and get a cabled reply?" I asked, clinging to the hope that the answer would be yes. The pleasant young Norwegian shook his head.

"Unfortunately, no. We must start at daybreak. But you can send a cable saying you have gone."

No one will ever know what it cost me not to do exactly that, and my consciousness of what I had missed is keen to this day, despite the fact that I keep advising other travelers not to dwell on what they have missed seeing and doing—as they are so apt to do—but on what they have seen and done. And certainly I had seen and done a great deal more in the Falkland Islands than I had had any right to expect. And as I walked for the last time down the fenced walk of Government House, it was not of this disappointment, nor of the political disputes between Argentina and Great Britain, that I thought. It was of some lines in one of Rupert Brooke's sonnets:

> *If I should die, think only this of me,*
> *That there's some corner in a foreign field*
> *That is forever England. . . .*

Not in death, but in life, that corner of a foreign land seemed to me inherently of England—less the England that had power to win battles and tenacity to cling to disputed territory than the England which stamped the sterling strength of her character on the remote and barren shores; the England whose spirit no climate could dampen or congeal, that no loneliness could appall and no hardships terrify; the England of pioneers and settlers and homebuilders; the England of culture and intelligence, of sensitiveness and courage; the England of clean and simple living, of fresh flowers and bright chintzes and warm fires. The England we were proud to call our mother.

Chapter 62

I<small>N HIS</small> excellent biograph *Magellan,* Arthur Sturges Hildebrand tells us:

> The navigation of the Straits was a marvelous achievement. Indeed, Magellan's Strait is the end of the earth. No portion of the world frequented by man has worse weather; there is no fine season, and summer and winter alike, snow, hail, rain, and wind are absent only for very brief periods; every feature which can add difficulty and danger to navigation is here present in a superlative degree. Bold coasts . . . passage so narrow that a lee shore is never more than five miles away . . . water so deep that it is impossible to anchor, except too close to shore for safety . . . sudden and violent squalls in which no ship is manageable . . . an atmosphere too thick for visibility; submerged rocks and heavy overfalls and whirlpool currents. . . .

Fortunately for us, the Straits were in one of their infrequent moods of benignity the night we entered them; and when we anchored the next morning at Magallanes—not only Chile's southernmost port but the southernmost city in the world—it was bright and clear and the nearby range of snow-capped mountains rose unclouded about us, the cone of Sarmiento sloping in sparkling whiteness. A bitter wind whipped the cold blue of the breakwater into angry futile waves, however, and our progress in an open launch to an uncovered pier proved a chilling experience; and it was not until ten hours after our arrival that we succeeded in wresting so much as a handbag from the customs authorities. But when we found refuge in a comfortable hotel, one of the pleasantest I have known anywhere in the world, our spirits began to rise and we discovered immediate and continuous enjoyment in store for us in this small city which, originally founded as a convict settlement, had changed both its character and its name and become the thriving and cosmopolitan port for the great sheep-raising region of Patagonia.[1]

A fine bronze statue of Magellan dominated the main plaza, where the cathedral and the Provincial Governor's residence were located side by side. At right angles to these were the beautiful houses of the "first families"—the Brauns, the Menendezes, the Contes—who were closely allied both by marriage and the industries they had founded: steamboat lines, mercantile establishments, sheep raising, freezing plants and many others. Beyond the plaza, the neat, bare cobblestoned streets, without lawns or trees, were unimpressive. Most of the houses were of corrugated iron and low built. Here and there was a fine residence surrounded by greenhouses and gardens, the barracks and the zoological garden were superbly located above the city, and there was a unique and highly interesting museum.

But it was indoors rather than outdoors, and in private rather than public places, that the greatest amount of enjoyment was to be found in Magallanes. There were several excellent clubs, which served as a meeting place for the masculine contingent before the late dinner hour; at the same time of day their mothers, wives, sisters and daughters were usually found having tea at the Governor's, at the Consulates and in the homes of the first families. And there were more formal entertainments as well. I went to a delightful dinner at a beautiful house owned by an English family—over a fifth of the developed land in Patagonia belonged to Britishers and ninety percent of the great *estancias* were administered by them; and Governor and Señora de Chaparro invited us to one of the most elaborate and elegant luncheons I have ever attended.

The Argentine Consul, Señor Mango, and his wife were also fellow guests at the Chaparro luncheon, and as we went on afterward to the races, Señor Mango outlined his plans for a trip to Gallegos, which would take the boys and me across the tip of the mainland and into Argentina. Don Julio Berdera, Governor of the Argentine Province of Santa Cruz, had already sent his car to Magallanes, so there was no reason why we should not start out the following morning, if agreeable to me. We would break our journey at the great *estancia* of San Gregorio, belonging to the Menendez-Behety family; and young Don Francisco Campos Menendez would accompany us.

I had hardly assimilated the details of these pleasing plans when an extremely attractive young man in uniform joined us and was presented

---

[1] The port originally called Punta Arenas—sandy point—had changed its name to Magallanes in honor of the Straits' discoverer, but has now reverted to the former name.

to me as our prospective host and began to talk with us in faultless English. He had no trace of accent, and his command of idiom and vocabulary was comprehensive and graceful. He had just been graduated from Oxford with a degree in Economics and had returned to Chile for his year of obligatory military service. He had secured three days' leave to accompany us to San Gregorio; and much as he regretted that his parents were away just then, he hoped our first visit to a Patagonian *estancia* might still be marked with some elements of comfort and pleasure. It was the first time his family had had the privilege of welcoming North Americans at their farm. Should he join us at nine the following day?

Midmorning found us well on our journey, but the excellent road which skirted the sea for a short distance beyond Magallanes ended all too soon in the "track" across the plains, and though we were assured this was in "fine condition," the deep ruts and wide holes sent us bouncing from one end of the car to the other. Fortunately, however, from the first moment that I glimpsed the endless expanse of the tableland known as the *pampa,* I loved it in all its aspects. Little abrupt hills rose and fell; seagulls drifting inland from the Straits dipped and rose with undulating grace; wild geese strutted solemnly away from our intruding presence, not in swarming flocks, but in isolated couples, for this was "the season of the nests." All about us were sheep: young sheep, middle-aged sheep, old sheep, ewes which had apparently put the levity of youth behind them, lambs whose one concern was to frisk—twin lambs often and sometimes even triplets, friskier still! Always they stared at us before they moved; then clumsily—or fleetly—they turned and fled. But no matter how many fled, more remained. There were over two million sheep in Patagonia and it seemed as if we saw most of them as we drove along; and seeing them, it was hard to realize that less than fifty years earlier, Julius Beerbohm recorded that he once beheld "four or five sheep grazing, with which, judging by their splendid condition, the pasturage of Patagonia evidently agreed!" Later he lamented that southern Patagonia seemed "destined to remain almost entirely unpopulated and uncultivated until the end of time!" The development of that great region, previously regarded as worthless desert, has taken place within our own day.

One sheep required about two acres and a half for pasturage and a flock of twenty thousand sheep was considered small; so the size of the *estancias* was immense and the stretches of rolling plain over which we rode, without glimpsing any sign of human habitation, were long and wide. It was afternoon before we caught sight of the great freezing plant where, during the season, thousands of shorn sheep are "treated" each day and the meat, hides, tallow and casings prepared for export. Wool was sorted in a separate shed. The resident manager's spacious house stood close beside the plant; nearby were the houses of other staff members, the workmen's quarters and the offices; just beyond were the San Gregorio stables, the stud, the dairy, the library, the blacksmith shop; more staff houses, more workmen's quarters, more offices—as complete and large a unit as many villages in the United States.

We were to visit all the component parts of the unit, but at the moment we turned up the long broad driveway to the "big house" which, built of concrete and surrounded by a windbreak of tall white wooden fences, loomed solidly before us. Tennis courts, conservatories and gardens encircled it; a profusion of plants bloomed brightly in its glass-enclosed entrance; beyond the wide hall with its spreading staircase, a fire burned cheerfully before a table set for lunch—a meal which we approached in a state of great hunger, since we were very late for it. We rose in a condition of total repletion, for which delicious roast lamb and the *empanadas a la criolla*—individual mince pies, eaten as a meat course, though sprinkled with sugar and containing chopped egg and olives as well as beef and raisins—were largely responsible, though several other hearty dishes also contributed!

As for "roughing it on a Patagonian sheep farm," truth compels me to admit that the only discomfort I underwent was from the cold—for though San Gregorio was equipped with steam heat, the Chileans prefer to keep their houses much cooler than we do. Aside from this, there was considerable luxury and manifold diversion. My bedroom was beautifully furnished in mahogany and flowered chintz and had an adjoining bathroom. There were five similar guest rooms; and there were two dining rooms, two drawing rooms and spacious service quarters. During the day we could ride or hunt or devote ourselves to leisurely and prolonged inspection of the huge plant; in the evening there was music, for another guest was a skilled pianist; there was dancing—the Chilean *Cuequa,* the Argentine *Pericón*—and there was bridge of a very scientific and sophisticated order. Don Francisco proved a charming host; other visitors came and went, drifting in for meals or the night; and the long table in the larger dining room was still uncrowded when fourteen of us sat at it for dinner. The old Spanish welcome *"Esta es su casa"*—"This is your house"—was nowhere more literally interpreted than in Patagonia. Every traveler had to go long distances through uninhabited regions, over rough "tracks" and against bitter winds, whatever his destination; and there was usually no inn available when hunger assailed him or night overtook him. But he could count on food and shelter at any *estancia* where he chanced to stop, whether a magnificent establishment like San Gregorio or a very humble one; in either case there was never any question about the "convenience" of having company. It was always convenient; it was the custom of the country.

It was with real regret that we said good-bye to Don Francisco and left the *estancia;* but once on the "track" again, we found the open country even more interesting than between Magallanes and San Gregorio. There were still the sheep, the geese and the gulls; but there were countless hares as well, scurrying across our path; there were vultures and the bleached skeletons of animals—grim evidence that these birds of prey had not gone hungry; there were dapper, dust-colored wild ostriches; there were guanacos, those curious tawny mammals of Patagonia with "the head of a camel, the body of a deer, the wool of a sheep, and the neigh of a horse," whose ultimate destiny was to provide rugs of extraordinary warmth, thickness and luxuriance! We reached the Argentine frontier late in the afternoon. As we approached Gallegos, the roadside was strewn with lumps of solidified lava from the extinct volcanoes we passed; then, after we had crossed the river from which the town takes its name and entered the port itself, we had the unique experience of finding that in this remote part of the world we were to stay at a freezing plant owned and operated by a North American company! Since Governor Berdera's family was away, he kindly suggested as he welcomed us that we might prefer to make our headquarters with fellow countrymen, though he had reserved the privilege of arranging the program for our visit. Accordingly, we soon found ourselves settled in the guest quarters of the comfortable housekeeping apartment provided for the plant's administrative staff.

I was too exhausted that night to do anything but crawl under the guanaco rug spread over my bed and sink to oblivion, not to emerge until lunch time the next day. Later, I enjoyed a pleasant tea at the plant; the private viewing of a film showing scenes in southern Argentina and a delightful dinner of sixty, at which the Governor was host, that climaxed our entertainment.

Early the next morning we were on our way again, straight across country, with Ultima Esperanza our objective—that beautiful Chilean region traversed by the tip of the Andes which owes its name and its discovery to a thrilling adventure! A band of pioneers from Gallegos found it impossible to travel overland—there were not even "tracks" at that time—to a part of the country they believed to be both fertile and lovely, so they attempted to reach it by the roundabout route of the Straits and the Chilean fjords—the so-called "canals"—a confusing term, since they are of natural formation. The explorers were suddenly sucked into the rapid current of a narrow channel. Realizing it was impossible to steer their boat to safety, they cried out that their last hope —*su ultima esperanza*—was in discovering a safe harbor ahead. Miraculously, it seemed, they were swiftly swept into just such a port—one of ineffable beauty and peace; while beyond lay the promised land, which surpassed their every dream.

We crossed the wide rough *pampa* of Las Leoneras, passing salt swamps lying lightly on the tufted grass, moving toward a mirage which spread a shallow shimmer of blue along the horizon. Las Orquetas had been recommended as the logical *estancia* at which to break our journey; reaching it at lunch time, we feasted on *cazuela*—rich Chilean soup thick with chunks of chicken and corn-on-the-cob—and numerous other delicacies. Afterward we visited the pet pumas and foxes and the plaintive pedigreed lambs. *"Tienen todos nombres"*—"They all have names"—the manager told us, affectionately calling a ewe to prove she recognized her own; then, sensing our deep interest in everything around us, he took us from room to room in the comfortable though unpretentious house. We left him with his pets gathered about him, waving farewell, as we drove off again.

For seemingly endless miles, there was no change of scenery; then, late in the afternoon, we suddenly came upon masses of trees, the first we had seen in days, which looked as if they were covered with hoarfrost, they gleamed with such sparkling brightness in the sunshine. It was a surprise to discover the trees were actually completely bare and that it was their dead gray trunks and branches that shone with such ghostly radiance. But beyond these arboreal specters lay verdure; and in the distance, above the slopes and domes of lesser mountains, the trenchant peaks of Paine pointed toward the sky. These peaks were unassailable and there was something awful and remote about their majesty; their magnitude was overpowering, a grandeur unconfined and ungoverned, passing the limits both of physical boundaries and human comprehension. There were no trim patterns of convention there, no smug and petty barriers; there was only vastness and glory and a sense of God. We had come to the place of last hope—the *ultima esperanza* of the pioneer—lying between the relentless sea and the insurmountable hills.

We spent the night at the *Estancia* Cerro Castillo in sight of all this splendor, but we wanted to get closer to it still; so once more we started out early in the morning, taking the "track" to *Estancia* Cerro Guido, the last possible shelter we could seek. The late October days were very long and it was light by four in the morning and still light after eight at night, and we had thought beforehand we should be able to penetrate as near to Paine as possible and still return to sleep at Cerro Castillo. But as we slowly progressed through scenery increasingly superb, we became more and more conscious that so superficial an impression would never satisfy us. So when we reached our intended destination and our cordial hosts, Herr Richard Lauezzari and his wife, suggested that we should prolong our visit with them and push up the Rio Paine to the Laguna Amarga, we did not hesitate a single second. What if we did not have a comb or a toothbrush among us? What if our carefully planned schedule was shot to pieces? Immaterial, in the face of those beckoning mountains.

Our decision resulted in absolute joy. With the Lauezzaris to guide and keep us company, we made our way beside the winding river, past the bland, expansive Laguna Sarmiento and into the hollow among the hills where the Laguna Amarga—the bitter lake—lies like a glittering emerald set in jade and jasper. The air was crystalline; a spring of icy water bubbled at our feet; a flock of fiery-rose flamingoes floated like flowers on the lake's surface. There was complete tranquillity. Suddenly on the mountainside the wind swirled the smooth snow in puffs and spirals and cascades down the blurred slopes. The storm, however, was only transitory. All the time the sun shone above and below it; and after it was over came the peace of evening, illuminated by a glow which spread from sky to summit and from hill to valley.

We returned late to Cerro Guido filled with supreme contentment, and I was still conscious of it as I drifted off to sleep (in a borrowed nightgown) in a huge bed under the softest, wooliest, whitest sheepskin in the world, in front of an open fire that spread its generous warmth all around me. The next day we came back to the *pampa* and spent the night at Penitente, where our hostess was a wonderful Scotswoman who had settled in Patagonia forty years earlier as a bride, whose six sons had been born there and who seemed to personify the spirit of the pioneer mother. I wanted to stay and listen to the wonderful stories I knew she could tell me, but this time there was no chance of prolonging my visit, unless I were willing to give up going to Tierra del Fuego, which I had traveled eight thousand miles to see. So we pushed on and began our preparations for our next adventurous voyage.

These preparations proved more difficult to perfect than we had foreseen. The "Land of Fire" appears to be very close to the mainland, but this is because of the extraordinary clarity of the atmosphere; actually, they are separated by a channel about as wide as the one between Calais and Dover. This is, of course, no great distance—twenty miles more or less. But there was no cable connection; there were no regularly scheduled boats, and in bad weather there were none at all because the waters were so treacherous; and there were no means of transportation available for hire on the island. Would-be visitors had to secure a car in Magallanes, wait watchfully for some kind of craft that would consent to convey them and their automobile across the Straits and then depend upon the hospitality of the region for sustenance and shelter, without previous warning of their arrival!

One boat, sailing with an hour's notice, escaped our vigilance; another delayed its departure from day to day until we wisely decided to put no faith in it at all. But finally and triumphantly we saw the sedan we had borrowed hoisted on board a diminutive and dirty vessel called the *Minerva*. Our car used up most of the deck space, and since what was left was exceedingly filthy, we climbed into the sedan and—so to speak—crossed the Straits by automobile!

Sheltered from the bitter wind and yet situated in the bow, we had an unobstructed view. The sky, partially veiled by soft massed clouds, revealed, as these shifted and lifted, the deep rich tones of the "Patagonian blue" which is unlike any blue elsewhere in the world; the swelling water shone like quicksilver; and between sky and sea flew and floated those mysterious birds of poetry and fable called albatross. It seemed as if we ourselves had embarked in a painted ship upon a painted ocean, so great was our feeling of unreality; and even after we had safely landed at Porvenir and begun to climb the snow-capped range immediately behind it, this sense of unreality persisted. A weird, wild forest that lay midway across the island culminated among strange stark trees beyond which were scattered lakes and isolated boulders carved into fantastic shapes by the wind; there were endless plains and impenetrable mountains; there was always solitude. The sounds which stirred It did not seem to come from the wind alone, though this shrieked or sang according to its mood; the silence which enfolded it when the wind sighed and was still had not the quality of emptiness.

We saw in this "Land of Fire"—literally—hundreds of thousands of grazing sheep, but we had grown less continually aware of these than when we began our Patagonian wanderings. Again we met with hospitable *estancias*—San Sebastián, Rio Grande, Coleta Josefina—where we broke our journey and rested and were nourished; but they were far apart—San Sebastián alone had an area sixty-six miles square—and our stops were fewer and shorter than they had been earlier. Our days in the open began as soon as it was light and ended after dark, for we carried food with us and ate as we went along. We did not know where the "track" lay and sometimes we lost it; and with each succeeding day, the sense of complete detachment from the world, from its cares, its complexities, its problems, its pettiness, deepened and increased.

Suddenly, inevitably, this blessed sense of detachment came to an end. We had returned to San Sebastián a second time—to its simple little white house with a hawthorn hedge and fostered flowers—unpacked our modest belongings and settled ourselves for a quiet hour beside a blazing fire before dinner and a good night's rest when a message came that a boat was sailing from Porvenir for Magallanes the following day; after that, there was no telling when there would be another—probably not for weeks. Mournfully, we repacked, hastily we dined; then, setting off in the darkness, we drove until nearly midnight. At seven the next morning, we were on our way again; at noon the car was hoisted to the deck of a boat even smaller and dirtier than the *Minerva;* by night, we were back again in Magallanes, and beside the other vessels anchored at the breakwater was a ship which was to take us up the western coast. . . .

I was obliged to go away; but I took with me a "vision of a new heaven and a new earth." This was not just because I had journeyed through a land different from any I had ever visited before—vast, untrammeled; a country which was sparsely settled but sent its exports into every corner of the globe. It was not just because I had penetrated to remote, almost inaccessible places of unviolated beauty. It was rather because I had seen the spirit as well as the substance of Patagonia—the spirit which had transfigured a desolate wilderness, which had interpreted the meaning of hospitality in its most literal and lovely sense, which had entered into the souls of human beings and made them brave and strong and free. The men and women who discovered the unexpected richness of this region did not drain it and then desert it. They explored it, settled it, developed it and made it their home, putting back into it more than they took out, tendering it, as its due, the best that was in them; and those who came after them followed in their footsteps and fulfilled their ideals. There was no feeling that talents and learning, culture and accomplishments, were wasted on the *pampa* and among the mountains; the young economist with his Oxford degree and the skilled musician under whose fingers rippled immortal melodies both offered their gifts in the same spirit of service to the land with which the shepherd guarded his sheep and the gardener nourished his flowers. This spirit I saw, and as long as I live, I shall never forget it.

Chapter 63

I T WAS noon when our trim little boat pulled away from Magallanes, so our progress through the most magnificent part of the Straits was made by daylight. A bluish haze softened the atmosphere and seemed to unite earth and ocean. Tierra del Fuego was on one side of us; on the other, the extremity of the mainland narrowed to a steep snowy point high above the turbulent water. In the distance a glacier sparkled, partially concealed by twin mountain peaks; immediately ahead the converging shores appeared about to close completely in upon us as we swung round one precipitous promontory only to be confronted with another. At each corner we turned, it seemed the heights and depths of grandeur and solemnity must have been reached; but the next one always revealed some new beauty.

Darkness shut in upon us before we left the Straits and entered the "canals," taking the "inside passage," nearly a thousand miles in length, which lies between the mainland of Chile and the line of almost countless islands strung along the southern part of her coast. This passage was not navigable by large vessels because of its nearly impenetrable narrowness in many sections; and it strewed difficulties, not to say dangers, in the path of any craft that ventured through it: swift and sudden currents, strong winds, thick fogs, heavy rains and hidden rocks. But it also offered a voyage of unrivaled and unblemished loveliness. There was the same variety of scene as in the Straits, the same spectacle of surprise at every turn; but the splendor was softened and subdued, the colors were warmer, the outlines gentler. There were snow-capped mountains, not rising sheer from the water, but above hills covered with verdant woods; there were glittering glaciers secluded in deep ravines and winding inlets. Islands, richly green and smaller than those which guard the coastline, studded the inland bays; waterfalls fluttered like silver ribbons over shining rocks.

For three days we wound our way in and out of the canals without seeing any sign of human habitation except one crude thatched hut, or any sign of human life except three Indians in a canoe. Then, coming into more open waters, we began to toss about on the Golfo de Peñas, which the boys promptly and rightly nicknamed the Painful Gulf! For sixteen long miserable hours existence was made wretched; but after that we came into the sheltered fjords again and steamed quietly along the eastern side of the island of Chiloé. There were still woods about us, but these alternated with fields and pastures. Sheep and cows grazed near an isolated group of humble farm buildings; a white church spire rose above a cluster of small white houses. We were back in pastoral country again, country Arcadian in its simplicity but beautiful with the verdure which clothed it and the peace which enveloped it. We all felt so irresistibly attracted to it that we were glad to find our boat was to make an unexpected stop at Castro and we would have time to go ashore. We ascended the steep street which led to the picturesque plaza and bought some rugs and blankets of handwoven wool colored with vegetable dye. Everywhere we found the same tranquillity, unspoiled by contact with a harsher and more hurried world beyond.

The *Alfonso* was one of the best boats in which it has ever been my good fortune to travel, anywhere in the world; and as we approached Puerto Montt, where we intended to disembark, our spirits sank at the thought of leaving the soft beds, delicious food, deep baths and perfect service of our *vapor* for the primitive conditions we had been assured existed in the Chilean Lake district. In fact, they sank so low, as far as Russ was concerned, that he decided to stay with the boat as far as it went and then join forces with us again in Santiago; John and I bade him a temporary but mournful farewell and went ashore.

At first, we were sure we had made a mistake. The harbor of Puerto Montt was said to be beautiful, but the morning was misty and the port's charms were veiled. Although we had come from one Chilean city directly to another, we were obliged to pass through customs, at the usual depressing hour, before crossing an uninspiring plaza to our grimy hotel. My room did not bear the slightest resemblance to the *camarote de lujo* I had so regretfully vacated, and though there was an adjacent bathroom, which I was expected to share with John, it had no door. I asked for the *patrón* and called his attention to this omission.

"Have you ever been to Biarritz?" he inquired.

I failed to see that this was germane to the subject, but admitted that I never had, adding I should like very much to do so however.

"Well," said the *patrón* triumphantly, "when you do, you will see that none of the bathrooms has doors. It is no longer the fashion."

I changed my mind about wishing to visit Biarritz and my disinclination to remain where I was increased by leaps and bounds.

"I think my son and I had better go over to Puerto Varas," I said. "Then we will be in good time for the next boat crossing Lake Llanquihué."

"A boat left yesterday and there will not be another for three days."

"It might be possible to hire one," I ventured.

"No, Señora, there would be no *combinación*. In order to get from Puerto Varas to Peulla it is necessary to have a *combinación*."

I had no idea what he meant, since the word signified nothing to me but an undergarment popular in the days of my youth. I decided not to press the point and held firmly to my purpose of departure, despite continued assurances as to the nonexistence of a boat and the undesirability of accommodations in Puerto Varas. The drive between the two ports consumed about an hour and the landscape was peculiarly pleasing in the early spring weather of mid-November. Gorse spread its golden glory in every direction; apple blossoms and lilacs bloomed in profusion; the scarlet of wild plum flowers painted the hillsides with flame. Many of the weatherbeaten cottages along the way were so reminiscent of New England that the dark-skinned natives trudging or riding past, their short striped ponchos stained a beautiful brown with vegetable dye, seemed strangely far from their element, until I realized *I* was the one far from home.

At the rambling hotel, which faced both placid Lake Llanquihué and the snow-capped mountains, we found the boat had left but that the manager could secure a *vapor especial* to take us across to Ensenada. Though this would not connect with the regular automobile that carried passengers to Petrolhué on Lake Todos los Santos, some arrangement could doubtless be made. So after an excellent dinner and a very comfortable night—we never did encounter the "primitive conditions" of which we had been warned—we embarked for Ensenada and lunched at its estimable German hotel before boarding the bus—known locally as a gondola!—for the shores of Todos los Santos. There a most attractive little steamer, the *Esmeralda,* awaited us.

The sky shone with sapphire brilliance; the jade-green water reflected the luxuriant foliage; the mountains seemed molded of smooth, glittering white marble; the trip down the lake to Peulla was one of indescribable beauty. John insists that this lake and its encircling mountains—Osorno, Puntiagudo, Casa Blanca, Tronodor and the others—afford the most magnificent spectacle we saw in our travels through Latin lands. I hesitate to indulge in such a superlative—remembering the splendors of the Bay of Rio, the cataracts of Iguazú, Ultima Esperanza and the Straits of Magellan; nevertheless, I feel that no traveler who passes it by can claim complete acquaintance with South America's natural wonders. The lake owes its name to the date of its discovery centuries ago —All the Saints, a title which seems singularly appropriate, for in its solitude and stillness an enfolding sanctity can be felt.

The beauty of Santiago had not the inescapable quality of Rio's; on the contrary, the bustling business section provided no outlook that could not be found in similar districts anywhere. Beyond these the Cerro Santa Lucia, the heart-shaped hill in the capital city's center, with its terraced garden, was slightly rococo in its prettiness; there were almost too many cliffs, grottoes, pavilions, rustic seats, hanging balconies, shrubs and overflowing urns. But the hill was a pleasant place for all of that, and from this vantage point one could see the Central Market and the Vega Market, congested with delicious fruits and vegetables and meats; the Public Library where the priceless archives of the Conquistadores were preserved; the Congreso Nacional; the two great cemeteries with avenues and fountains, trees and flowers, all permeated with the brilliant sunshine.

But alas! we were obliged to descend and return to the crowded, noisy, nondescript part of the city where our hotel was located—not to sleep, for sleep was impossible in the midst of an uproar which never ceased, but at least to go to bed. As the night wore on, the tooting of horns, blaring of whistles and clanking of cars increased. Since all hotels were situated in the same quarter, there was no point in moving to another; but at the end of a week I hopelessly exclaimed that unless we could find a house on a quiet street for a temporary home, I would have to leave Santiago.

Hopelessness in any form is one of the most ridiculous and unnecessary of human failings. The morning after I made my rash declaration, the young and charming wife of our Naval Attaché was announced and wasted no time in stating the object of her visit. "I heard you say yesterday at tea that you would like a house," she said. "I have come to offer you mine."

"Thank you so much," I replied, trying to emulate her brevity. "When could I move in?"

"Oh, immediately. My husband is leaving on an official trip for southern Chile and I want to go with him. I could leave everything for you—silver, linen and so on. And there are three maids: Alejandrina the cook, Abelina the waitress and Otilla the chambermaid. Of course, none of them speaks a word of anything but Spanish, but they are efficient. I am sorry I can't suggest that you take over our chauffeur too, but he has been promised a vacation while we are gone."

The arrangement was completed, as far as I was concerned, before my visitor had finished speaking; and it was cemented with the first glimpse I had of the *casita:* a house of gray stone and stucco, its narrow balconies tiled in black and white, with wrought-iron grillework shielding its arched windows; a demure house on a cobblestoned street; a house whose paneled door opened to reveal a stone staircase lighted by a hanging lantern and curving upward to a hall, a small salon decorated with the formal and elegant restraint of the best Latin traditions and a writing room furnished mainly with a large desk. Beyond, a living room with a large fireplace, a comfortable sofa and chairs, convenient tables and shaded lamps; this led to the dining room and its immense carved sideboard and highbacked chairs upholstered in brocade. Above were three small bedrooms and two large dressing rooms, all amply furnished, and two bathrooms. Below, in the basement, were the quarters of the three maids. There was no dumbwaiter, there was not a ray of natural light in the kitchen or any visible means of ventilation; there was no laundry, no tub or shower for the maids, only three slitlike bedrooms with the barest necessities. I was appalled at the lack of comfort under which they labored and became even more so when I learned the Chilean domestic was always obliged to furnish her own room and even supply the bed linen and towels she used, but my sympathy was wasted, for I found that my "retinue" of three were highly contented with both quarters and wages!

Having taken possession, I began my housekeeping with zest. Alejandrina needed neither suggestions nor guidance; upon my arrival, she asked how many different dishes I wished for each meal; after our first consultation, she presented herself about three times a week to report she was out of money; replenished, she sallied forth and purchased provender, which she converted into most tempting and delicious repasts. Once I decided to go to the Central Market with her; the result was that I spent more in one morning than she ever spent in a week; so after that I limited myself to the Flower Market.

I think I could have been contented to remain indefinitely within the four walls of my *casita* or at least to venture no further from it than the Flower Market; but it was essential to go out enough not only to establish and maintain the usual social contacts but also to do the necessary family shopping—one of the hardest things to achieve in Santiago. You could buy all sorts of exquisite luxuries at a very moderate figure; antiques were beautiful enough to undermine the sternest sense of economy. But I spent days in search of a carpet sweeper and finally found it in a grocery store! It took weeks to locate unfringed towels and white handkerchiefs. I therefore welcomed with more cordiality than I would have believed possible beforehand an applicant for the position of chauffeur. He was immaculate in appearance and respectful in bearing; a short test drive revealed he knew the city like a book; and when we returned to the *casita* he stood, cap in hand, awaiting my verdict with a wistful expression that was very appealing. Not since Ko, the Peking coolie who patiently waited until I conquered my prejudices against rickshaws, had I felt so helpless in the face of a request for employment.

"What is your name?" I asked weakly.

"It is Manuel. I will be here at nine to begin work."

"I never go out at that hour," I protested. "I study Spanish."

"It is evident," replied Manuel with adroit flattery. "But perhaps the young *caballeros* may wish to go out."

"They also study Spanish," I informed him. But further argument was useless and Manuel joined our "retinue"—a most happy addition. He was always prompt, always polite, always reliable and resourceful; and it was to him we owed the crowning adventure of our Chilean spring.

We had approached Chile with two primary purposes: to go through the Straits of Magellan and to go to the Christ of the Andes, that colossal statue made from the melted bullets of two disbanded armies and placed as a symbol of everlasting peace between Chile and Argentina, long bitter enemies, on the mountain pass which forms part of their boundary. The first purpose had been achieved under conditions that surpassed our every expectations; the second seemed impossible under any conditions whatever. The Trans-Andean train ran only three times a week; and there was no inn at Caracoles, the last stop before the train entered the tunnel for Argentina, above which wound the tortuous road to the Christ. Juncal, the station before Caracoles, was devoid of accommodations; and the village of Rio Blanco, where there was a shelter of sorts, was too far away to serve as a practical starting point for the climb, even if we could have been assured of securing mules or a car there—and we could obtain no such assurance. Indeed, the only assurance we did secure was that the roads were very rough, that swollen mountain streams were rushing over them, that drifts of snow were blocking them—in short, that they were impassable and would remain so indefinitely. We waited for weeks in the tenuous hope that later in the spring conditions might be better, a hope killed by a severe and un-seasonable snowstorm. The lovely lady who had lent us her *casita* wrote to say she hoped it might be convenient to give up the house soon; Russell Thayer received a cable calling him home earlier than he had expected to go. Emergency measures were indicated and I appealed to the person I thought would be most helpful.

"Manuel," I said one night, "I want to go to the *Christus.*"

"*Como no?*"—"Why not?"—he responded cheerfully, as usual.

"Have you ever been there?"

"No, Señorita. But I can find the way."

It is unnecessary to dwell at length on the discomforts of the journey which followed. Twice we forded deep streams from which the bridges had been swept away; a hundred times at least we backed and turned and backed and turned again in order to negotiate a sharp bend in the road—usually unfenced; we wedged our way through snowdrifts that towered above us and hemmed us in; we were so badly burned—sun and wind and high altitude combined to produce the effect of fire—that our hands were bandaged for a week afterward, our faces swollen and distorted almost past recognition, and we suffered from high fever. But such episodes fade from memory when I remember how we picnicked on the site of the famous battle of Chacapucho; how we suddenly caught sight of Aconcagua—the highest peak in this hemisphere, the highest in the world after Everest—rising clear and unclouded above four tiers of lesser mountains; how we sped through the town of Los Andes, where the walls seemed to merge into houses and the houses into walls; how we passed the "Soldier's Leap," a tawny rocky gorge through which foaming waters rushed and roared sixty feet below the road, and the Lake of the Inca, cold and clear beneath the sharp and savage peaks around it; how the yellows and pinks of the Andean flowers blended with the purple and gray on the hillside to which they clung and the mountains folded into each other in long triangles of deep mysterious blue and glittering white; how we went on and on and up and up, thousands and thousands and thousands of feet, until it seemed we could go no further; and how suddenly, at the sharpest and highest curve of all, Manuel took both hands from the wheel and exclaimed, *"There is the* Christus! *I told you we would get here,* Señorita, *and we have!"*

Directly in front of us, surrounded by eternal snows, surmounting the perilous pass of Uspallata, rose the benign and beautiful figure of the Christ of the Andes. It faces north, in order that it may overlook both the countries it blesses with uplifted hand; the attitude is all-encompassing, the expression all-forgiving; and placed in this sublime and significant position, it seemed, literally as well as figuratively, to stand on the summit of the world in revelation and redemption and resurrection. Beside it, I felt uplifted as with the presence and power of a Risen Lord; coming away from it, I carried with me something of the inspiration it gives to all the world.

Chapter 64

THERE was real grief in our hearts when John and I finally said good-bye to our little gray *casita* and stowed ourselves and our baggage in Manuel's car for the last time to make our mournful way from Santiago to the coast. We spent a night in Viña del Mar; embarked the next day from nearby Valparaiso; and sailed northward to the nitrate port of Tocopilla, where a cordial welcome awaited us in a comfortable guest house.

Probably because we were totally unprepared for the charms of Tocopilla, our enjoyment of them was all the greater. We found it fascinating to watch the bags of nitrate transferred in swinging nets from the freight cars, which had brought them from the inland *oficinas,* to the lighters, which carried them to waiting ships at the roadstead; to wind our way beside the ocean, among the mounds and caves where priceless Indian relics had been unearthed; to visit the model village which challenged comparison with the one at Nictheroy and in which the natural rocky contours formed a setting for delightful gardens and a grottolike shrine of exquisite delicacy and loveliness; and we left all these attractions regretfully, to strike out by car across the desert wastes to the nitrate *oficina* of María Elena.

At first our route was bordered by curious rectangular formations of creamy rock, towering on either side; then we came out on the high plateau of the *pampa—pampa* far more desolate, far more barren than any we had seen, and bearing gruesome names—The *Pampa* of the Dead Ox—the Dead Indian—the Dead Chinaman—indeed, death seemed inevitably associated with the place. There was not a blade of grass, a bush, a brook, to relieve its aridity; and it stretched, in unbroken desolation, to the equally bald hills which edged the horizon. But eventually we passed the guard of *carbineros* stationed at the settlement's outskirts; were warmly welcomed at the general office; and guided to the pleasant cottage that was to serve as our home during our stay.

With this agreeable setting as a base, we inspected the *oficina* at our leisure. The nitrate was extracted by a process of "surface" mining: the uppermost layer of barren ground was first stripped off with dragline elevators; then the ore itself, which had been blasted into lumps, was picked up by electric shovels and hauled in open freight cars from the pits to the plant. There it was dumped into a huge crusher and then conveyed through three more sets of crushers, the lumps becoming smaller with each stage; next it was deposited in huge vats and a hot solution circulated through it to dissolve the nitrate. As soon as the solution became charged with nitrate, it was refrigerated, which caused part of the nitrate to crystallize. When this had been dried, it was carried to the "graining plant," melted and shaped into small hollow pellets—the most convenient form for fertilizer—and bagged for shipment.

Our interest was challenged not only by the plant operations, but by the triumphant achievement of establishing, developing and beautifying a community of ten thousand people in a wilderness. Every tree, shrub and flower in María Elena had been planted in earth brought there from outside—for, until the nitrate had been separated from the soil and processed, it acted as a destructive and not a constructive force. In its natural state, the ground produces no vegetation; and the gardens were irrigated with distilled water brought from a great distance, for there is no natural rainfall. Yet there was hardly a house without its complement of shrubs and vines and flowers; there were schools, clubs, tennis courts, swimming pools, golf courses, football fields, shops, a theater, a hospital and a church; and the humblest workman was provided with the same sanitary living conditions, the same assurance of medical attention, the same opportunities for education and diversion as any member of the administrative staff. A spirit of cooperation and good will pervaded the "camp"; and the social life was permeated with a genuine spirit of hospitality. So, as before, our anticipation of a new and agreeable experience to come was tempered by the regret of leaving people who had entertained us so cordially. But the open road never has failed to lure me on and, as we struck out across the wilderness again, mounting higher and higher as we went, it was with the sensation of glorious adventure which seldom deserts me. We crossed one stream, the Loa, the only flowing water within two hundred miles, its lush riverbed a striking contrast to its bleak surroundings. As we neared the *cumbre* of the mountain range, over which we passed, crimson flowers bloomed along the way; and the rich vivid colors, indicating the prevalence of copper in the surrounding peaks, began to glow against the cloudless sky. After we had crossed the summit of the *cordillera,* we seemed to glide straight into the "camp" of Chuquicamata, where the largest single deposit of copper-bearing ore in the world was found. Like the nitrate, this lies above the surface and the mining operations could be viewed with comfort and ease.

We spent three pleasant days at Chuquicamata; then drove to Calama, where we caught the train that was to take us from Chile to Bolivia. The journey was rich in new impressions and crowded with color; the desert wastes were succeeded by a greener and more glowing country, the dusty plains slid away behind us and snowy slopes began to rise before us. Caravans of mincing llamas wound their slow and solemn way along the scattered villages of mud huts and cavelike stone hovels built against the hillsides. Indians clad in gay ponchos and slit trousers or voluminous multicolored skirts and bright fringed shawls, according to their sex, squatted impassively on the ground or wandered with no evident purpose. Some of the women carried spindles and spun as they walked; many wore striped blankets bundled on their backs—a blanket which contained anything from provender and firewood to babies, and often all three; most of them sported varnished white hats perched precariously above their dark braids, but which miraculously never seemed to blow off. The gorgeous tones of rose, orange, emerald and azure which were mingled without apparent premeditation in complex designs made these costumes inescapably effective, and the countryside enlivened by them took on aspects of brilliance imparted by no other national costume I have ever seen.

It was midafternoon when we left Calama, ten in the evening when we reached the frontier into Bolivia; and about three the next day we suddenly saw a deep circular hollow at the right of the plateau we were crossing. Its shape, coloring and seeming smoothness were reminiscent of a huge bowl of blue and brown agate; at its base, rectangles of crimson, bands of green and stripes of gray glittered in the crystalline light. It was a strange and startling sight and for a moment we were too stupefied to realize we were looking down on La Paz; even when we did so, we could not imagine how we were to reach it, since it seemed completely enclosed and encircled. But the train slid slowly along a track which twisted and turned and doubled upon itself, descending as it went; the agate bowl was transformed into a curved valley guarded by towering hills; the red rectangles revealed as the roofs of houses; the green bands as avenues of trees, the gray stripes as narrow sheltered streets. We had reached our journey's end.

At the risk of being bromidic, I am mentioning that La Paz, with its elevation of twelve thousand feet, is the highest capital in the world, because this altitude is responsible not only for many of the city's characteristics—its remoteness, its intangibility, its individuality, its climatic conditions, its charm—but for the manner in which acquaintance with it must be made. In the rarefied atmosphere, it is impossible to hurry, especially over almost perpendicular cobblestoned streets. Even if one escapes the dreaded mountain sickness—the *soroche*—the slightest attempt to hasten brings one to a breathless standstill. Consequently, one saunters and thus makes acquaintance with the shops, which seem only slits in the thick walls, where curiously wrought silver, richly twilled silks and soft furs are sold; with the exquisitely carved facades of the cathedral and the Church of San Francisco and the equally exquisite doorways of the colonial mansions and their blossoming patios.

La Paz revealed itself in many ways: its color of costume and flower; its dignity and seclusion; its wealth of antiquity; its glorious setting; its courtesy of life. It was a city reserved but hospitable and we were received with infinite kindness in more than one lovely old house. The streets, thronged with Indians and *Cholas,* gave little idea of the life led by those cultured and aristocratic families of Spanish descent; it was necessary to penetrate beyond paved patios and stone stairways and flowering gardens to discover how delightful this was. All the Bolivians we met possessed that talent in dress, that charm and composure in manner, that ability to speak several languages fluently so often the heritage of Latin gentlewomen. Their jewels, worn with selective good taste, were beautiful; in two of the houses we visited there were magnificent antiques, which included pottery of the pre-Inca and Inca period, woven and embroidered materials, silver, paintings, porcelain and ivory. The dominance of the family as a unit, the compactness of the social circle was quite as noticeable here as elsewhere in South America, but nowhere was it pervaded with more graciousness toward the outsider.

Agreeable as was every aspect of Bolivian life with which we came in contact, there was a strong undercurrent of national feeling centering on the long unsettled boundary contention between Paraguay and Bolivia which made itself constantly felt; in fact, the situation assumed aspects of tenseness the day after our arrival in La Paz when Bolivian planes were dispatched to the Chaco. But it was not this undercurrent of which we were most vitally conscious, but of the spirit of celebration throughout the city, for it was filled with the crowds that had come for the *Fiesta de las Alacitas*—the Festival of Little Things—and for three days the central square and all the streets converging upon it were congested with booths, stands and tables; with wares hung upon the walls or spread upon the pavements: pottery, copper vessels, silver, jewelry;

furs, rugs, blankets; toys, trinkets and talismans; in short, all the products of the country which, though isolated, impoverished, sparsely settled, overlooked by the average tourist and disregarded by the superficial student, had nevertheless struggled forward, maintaining an intense individualism and a profound and loyal nationalism, while preserving and developing those unique and exquisite arts which were its priceless heritage, both from the Incas, who were its first leaders, and from the Conquistadores who brought from Spain the essentials of the culture and beauty of that magic land.

Among the pleasant acquaintances John and I had made in Santiago were Mr. L. S. Blaisdell, the general manager of the Southern Railway of Peru, and his pretty Peruvian wife, who were on their way to La Paz via Chile and Argentina; and shortly after our own arrival in the Bolivian capital, they reached there, too, and promptly called upon us. As we sat comparing experiences since our previous meeting, Mr. Blaisdell made a delightful suggestion.

"How would you like to leave here Thursday in a special car," he asked, "stop off for an hour or so to see the pre-Inca ruins at Tiahuanaco, go on to Guaqui and take a boat there for a two days' cruise on Lake Titicaca, visiting the shrine of Copacabana and the Island of the Sun? The regular route—from Guaqui on the Bolivian side across to Puno on the Peruvian side— bypasses these and I think you might find them interesting. From Puno you could take another special car to Chuquibambilla, where the Government Experimental Farm is situated, and spend the week end there. Mrs. Blaisdell and I are tied up for the next few days and can't go with you, but could meet you at Chuquibambilla and take you on to Cuzco with us. If this appeals to you, I'll make the necessary arrangements; all you need to do is turn up at the station Thursday morning."

John and I had intended to remain longer in La Paz, but the opportunity to see unfrequented and alluring places was too rare to resist, so at the appointed time we boarded the special car and began the beautiful curving ascent to Alto La Paz; sped swiftly over the mesa beyond and arrived some three hours later at the picturesque village of Tiahuanaco and its remarkable relics of the pre-Inca period. The arches, the doorways, the walls, the flights of steps, the figures of human beings and animals, many of them enormous and covering an immense area, are constructed of stone unlike any in the vicinity. There is no key to the designs with which they are ornamented; the carving on the rectangular images is inexplicable. In grandeur and isolation they guard the secret of their significance; and it is unfortunate that they cannot be viewed in silence and solemnity, for they are tremendously impressive. But innumerable ragged urchins, all afflicted with terrible head colds and all apparently unacquainted with a handkerchief or its uses, swarmed around us, whining unintelligibly and proffering miniature idols, patently of recent manufacture, for sale. Driven almost to desperation by their importunities, we retreated to the sanctuary of the special car and continued our contemplation of the ruins from its windows.

It was early afternoon when we pulled into Guaqui, where awaiting us lay the *Yavari,* the sturdy little vessel which had been constructed in Scotland nearly sixty years before; brought in separate parts over two oceans; carried piecemeal on the backs of Indians, llamas and mules from coast to *cordillera;* and finally reassembled for service on the highest navigable body of water in the world! We were warmly welcomed by its jovial captain who, though a native of Peru, spoke English with the brogue which was a legacy from his Irish father! We ascended to the open deck and settled ourselves for uninterrupted observance of Lake Titicaca's wonders.

Unfortunately, she was in one of her sterner moods: the lofty white mountains that towered around her were concealed by grim gray clouds and her ruffled waters reflected their somber color; a chilly breeze blew relentlessly and, before long, we were driven inside to the salon which was not much warmer than the deck. In South America you were supposed to take your weather as you found it: fuel was so scarce as to be exorbitantly expensive and artificial heat of any sort was extremely rare, even in the localities which are always cool and usually cold. So, climbing into my narrow bunk with my coat on over my dressing gown, I embraced my hot-water bottle and drifted off to sleep, praying I might dream of Ceylon, Java, Singapore and Texas, repenting sincerely any invidious comments I had ever made about their climatic conditions!

We were to dock in Copacabana at six the next morning, so we dressed and breakfasted in the dark and were rewarded by seeing the sun rise above the domes and towers of that famous shrine. It was still very early when we started up the rough winding way that led to the village and the church. Picturesquely lovely as they must be at any period, they were doubly so at that particular time, just before the great feast of the Candelaria, when the vanguard of the ten thousand Indians who come to celebrate the festival had begun to arrive and the streets and plaza were thronged with life and color. The three massive stone crosses, erected by the early Spaniards and enclosed in a lofty pillared cupola, rose dark and strong before the church, above the surge of brilliant ponchos, bright petticoats, gay headgear and painted candles. As we entered the dim nave, a Franciscan came forward and greeted us.

Services, he said, were about to begin in the chapel beyond. Perhaps we would like to attend? We followed him, glimpsing as we went the beautiful cloisters built by the Augustinians nearly three centuries before; then, mounting ancient steps of stone, we entered the sanctuary—the *camarín*—where, above the altar, stood the small, richly robed statue of Our Lady of Copacabana, carved by an Inca, Francisco Tito Yupanqui, in 1583 and represented as a woman of his own race.

The golden crown surrounded by a golden halo which the Virgin wore, the silver crescent moon on which she stood, the multicolored jewels with which her garments were adorned, glittered and sparkled in the candlelight. Mass was celebrated by Indian priests, their dark faces gleaming above lace-edged surplices; and all about knelt Indian worshipers, the orange, the purple, the blue, the green, the crimson of their clothing glowing against the somber pavement. As the ceremony drew near its close, an Indian choir at the rear of the chapel began to sing to the accompaniment of a small organ—plaintive, piercing music, less harsh than haunting.

It was only a short distance across the water to our next destination which, in that amazing period of civilization which preceded the advent of the Spanish conquerors, was the scene of Inca dominion and Inca worship—the Island of the Sun, where the green and fertile ground rises from a curved shore with many small calm bays and some precipitous slopes to a steep ridge which crowns the land. The crumbling palace of the great chieftains stood in a desolate deserted spot, above a bare and rocky section of the coast. But over a verdant arbor which shielded an ancient stone seat, a terraced garden rose on either side of a large flight of stone steps shaded by bending boughs; beside this dappled stairway, water descended from the carved stone fountain which surmounted it in a clear and slender stream that flowed into the lake. Intermingled with the pansies, sweetpeas and forget-me-nots, the marigolds, roses and petunias, the crimson sprays of the *Flor del Inca* spread its vivid glory. That royal flower of an exterminated monarchy had survived its annihilation, and the other blossoms were pale and commonplace in comparison; there was something mocking in the quality of its permanence, so splendid and so supreme.

We landed at three separate places on the Island of the Sun and penetrated to the points of its greatest beauty; then we headed toward Puno. The somber weather of the afternoon before had been succeeded by a day of mingled shower and sunshine, with wonderful effects of light and shade, which ranged from gray and deep purple, through cold glittering greens and blues, to pale tints of pearl and violet. The lake lay like a great quiet pool of moonstone beneath an opalescent sky; then suddenly it rippled and changed, glowing as deeply mellow as amber reflecting beams of topaz. This golden transparency was the briefest and most beautiful; it came only in flashes and dark against it rose the wings of the water fowl—gulls, wild ducks and cormorants—dipping and soaring in graceful flight, and the sails of the tiny craft in which the native fishermen glided across the water.

After another early disembarkation, we were soon speeding northward in Peru, leaving the lake behind us and entering agricultural country. At Juliaca, the first important town at which we stopped, a radical change in costume was evident. The multitudinous petticoats still prevailed. (The *India* who is true to tradition buys a new one each year and, though one sometimes falls to pieces of old age, it is never voluntarily discarded; and, even if the petticoat perishes, the waistband is retained as evidence that it existed!) These skirts, however, were not silken, as they often were in La Paz, but of heavy woolen fabrics; and the jaunty white hat of Bolivia was supplanted by a much wider one of black felt, gaily ornamented with braid and edged, on either side, with small flapping curtains. This astounding headgear is shifted so that its wearer is always shielded from the sun's rays; thus protected and equipped with the inevitable spindle and almost equally inevitable baby, the *India* seems more quaintly pleasing than the male, though he, too, is an object of interest when he saunters by, strumming on a guitar or carrying the silver-crowned staff which proclaims him the *alcalde* of his village.

Midmorning found us alighting—fourteen thousand feet above sea level—at the Chuquibambilla station; directly opposite were the rose-colored buildings of the Government Experimental Farm—the *Granja Modela*—where we were to be the guests of its director Colonel Stordy. He escorted us to a rambling old house, erected around a succession of patios which, with remarkable skill, ingenuity and perseverance, he and his family had remodeled, adapted to the essentials of comfort and invested with particular attractiveness. There was no central heating, but every room had a corner fireplace where warm flames rose from the smouldering lumps of dried dung which were used for fuel. There was no plumbing, but water for bathing was heated by a great tubular stove which stood in one of the rear patios, and carried to a deep tub in an adjacent room. The adobe walls, inside and out, had been tinted in pleasing colors; there were bright Indian blankets, woven in as many shades as Joseph's coat; thick soft rugs of vicuña and llama scattered about and gay chintz hangings everywhere. The dining room cabinets were filled with beautiful old Peruvian silver; in the living room were the great brass trays and heavy, studded brass chests the Stordys had brought with them from Africa, where the Colonel had been employed by the British government. There was early-morning tea brought to your bedside; there was rich pure milk at any hour; there were tropical fruits and vegetables brought up from the warm valley, fish from Lake Titicaca, eggs, butter, cheese and poultry from the farm itself, as well as the most wonderful mushrooms that ever grew—succulent and spicy and hot. There was an Indian woman who acted indiscriminately as ladies' maid and watchful housekeeper; a swift-footed *mozo,* a tireless cook and a humble barefooted rather ragged servitor who built the fires and heated the water and performed endless other tasks. In short, there was all the charm of setting, all the comfort of equipment, all the excellence of service, all the culture of living with which the British, perhaps better than any other people, know how to surround themselves no matter where they go or what they do.

Slightly more than a decade earlier, General Archibald Cooper, the Lima representative of the Peruvian Railroad, concluded "that the immense Andean tablelands traversed by the Peruvian Railway could maintain a much greater number of sheep and other stock than they had hitherto done." He presented his idea to Señor Leguía, then President of Peru, who quickly visualized its potentialities and asked him to recommend an expert to take charge of scientific experiment and development. General Cooper, who was familiar with Colonel Stordy's East African service, suggested him; an official invitation was extended and accepted, and the Government Farm established. The expansion and success of the project proved a national asset of prime importance. The *Granja,* eighteen thousand acres in extent, afforded grazing land for fourteen thousand sheep, besides several hundred head of cattle, llamas, alpacas, and vicuña; and the productiveness of those sheep, both from the point of view of wool and weight, had been increased to four times that of the average native stock!

The time we had spent on the sheep-raising *estancias* of Patagonia and Tierra del Fuego rendered our visit with the Stordys doubly interesting by comparison; and it would have been delightful to prolong our stay, but the private car reappeared, bringing not only the Blaisdells, but Mr. Robertson—the secretary of the British Legation in La Paz— and Mrs. Robertson, who were to go on to Cuzco as our fellow guests.

In this congenial company we proceeded on our journey—a journey which seemed more enchanting with every speeding moment. After an hour of climbing, we reached La Raya, fourteen thousand five hundred feet above sea level. From the sloping Vilcanota glaciers above us an icy stream descended and spread in clear deep pools on either side of the track, drenching the verdant watercress and smooth brown stones beneath; from these pools, which marked the Andean divide, the waters flowed south to Lake Titicaca and north to the Amazon and on to the Atlantic. Through this lofty pass, between still loftier mountains, led the track from Cuzco to the southern boundary of the Inca Empire; over it marched the Spanish Conquistadores and—two centuries later —the armies of the War of Independence; while, as a trade route, its importance dated back to earliest times.

Gradually the descent from this magnificent summit began; we stopped at Aguas Calientes, where mineral springs steamed and bubbled; at Sicuani, where soft furs and silver pins shaped like condors were temptingly displayed; at Chectuyoc where, outside a modern woolen mill, scores of *Indias* with their primitive spindles defied the march of progress. The adobe villages were closer and closer together; the cultivation of the land became more intensive. Aside from the half dozen small volcanoes clustered near Sicuani, the landscape was one of infinite peace and tranquillity; it was hard to visualize it as the scene of conquest, cruelty, oppression, destruction, bloodshed and suffering. The widening valley became increasingly greener and lovelier; the very air seemed charged with a still remoteness and, as evening closed down and a soft silvery rain slanted against the gathering darkness, we glided gently into Cuzco, the sacred city of the Inca.

Nowhere are the Conquistadores revealed more relentlessly as destructionists before they were builders; and the civilization they demolished was one of the most remarkable which ever flowered on earth. The magnificent walls, whose stones, perfectly fitted together without cement, often have as many as twelve angles; the immense aqueduct in three tiers of arches, which supplied the water for a city of two hundred thousand, as well as irrigation for the surrounding country; the subterranean tunnels and mountain baths; the fortress of Sacsahuaman, surmounted with the Inca Throne; the remains of the Emperor's Palace in the Lomellini gardens; the gold and silver ornaments, the painted pottery—all these and other relics, mutilated but enduring, bear tragic testimony to the art of the annihilated race. If the Spaniards had helped them develop their domain, what a nation might have sprung from a union of the two empires! But, though the Conquistadores destroyed where they might have created, they did superimpose their own faith, their own culture, and their own sovereignty upon those they had destroyed. They used the Temple of the Sun as their foundation when they erected the Convent Church of Santo Domingo; and other monuments they left are compellingly splendid: the cathedral is a superb building, its central choir exquisitely carved, its high altar of solid silver; while the pictures and woodwork with which it is adorned and its jeweled monstrance have the beauty of true art, as well as great antiquity. The facades of the *Compañía* and adjacent University—founded in 1692; the pulpit of San Blas, a miracle of wood carving; the majestic doorways; paintings, fabrics, silver and furniture—all surpassed anything of the sort we had seen in South America and bore comparison with anything we had seen in Spain itself.

The comfortable *coche* finally carried us away from Cuzco, this time directly to Arequipa, which was the Blaisdells' home city; so we lost them as traveling companions, but not as hosts, for they entertained us delightfully in their attractive house. The journey—as usual—had begun and ended early in the morning and our acquaintance with Peru's second largest city commenced in broad daylight, with its attractions and advantages spread lavishly before us. Though it is higher than Mt. Washington, above it tower the guardian mountains of Chachani, El Misti and Picchupicchu. It is intersected by the gushing Chile River and around it are green fields and pleasing pastureland. Flowers, fruit and foliage abound, for Arequipa is singularly blessed climatically; the days are brilliant and balmy, the nights clear and cool; and both are permeated with tranquillity and light. There was little variety and activity in the streets; many of the houses and some of the churches were painted a bright clear blue, a dark deep rose, or a rich soft yellow, and this was most effective; but there was no riot of color in costume, no variety and expansiveness of custom, as there had been in La Paz and Cuzco. Women of every degree wore black gowns and black mantillas; and life proceeded at a leisurely pace; the dreamiest, drowsiest city I had ever entered before seemed to me a merry-go-round of movement compared to Arequipa!

Fortunately, there was not much sightseeing to be done, though we were advised—and rightly—to visit both the cathedral and the *Compañía;* but in almost the same breath, we were informed that the two unique features of Arequipa—and those of which it was most proud—were the sunsets and the *Quinta* Bates.

Nowhere in the world, except in Java, have I seen such sunsets. The clouds covering the guardian mountains suddenly part and lie in soft ethereal masses above and below them, while their snowy peaks rise rosy and glittering between those wreaths of azure. Then the color ascends; the lower clouds grow gray; the mountains take on a new and dazzling whiteness; and the clouds beyond turn to glowing pink. Not only the whole horizon, but the whole heaven is transfigured.

These sunsets with their lavish glory can be seen from any part of the city; but there is no better place from which to appreciate them than the smooth flat roof of the *Quinta* Bates, where a latticed sitting room, furnished in chintz and wicker, made an ideal outlook. We generally had tea there and waited quietly afterward for the scene of splendor which we knew would soon be spread before us. So, simultaneously, we enjoyed both of Arequipa's unique offerings.

In South American parlance, a *quinta* is simply a house with ample grounds and the *Quinta* Bates, built of deep old rose stucco, with wide paved steps leading up to it and a wide paved veranda, set in the midst of one of those spacious gardens so characteristic of Arequipa, answered this description; inside, it was a pleasant, comfortable place, well supplied with reading material, easy chairs and other homely comforts, but quite without pretentious luxuries. In the twenty-four years since it had opened its doors, every visitor to Arequipa for whom Mrs. Bates could make room had sought and found shelter there. As a young matron, *Tia* Bates—as she was known to the entire continent—living in a Bolivian mining camp, took in two or three paying guests to augment her modest income—a venture so successful that it led to the establishment of the *Quinta* in Arequipa. Again and again, I heard her described as "the best-loved woman on the West Coast" and still feel, if I had found nothing else on top of the world, it would have been worth going there to find the *Quinta* Bates.

Chapter 65

A T THIS stage of my travels, flying still seemed like an adventure and
I was both surprised and pleased to learn there was a regular plane
service between Arequipa and Lima, which meant we could make the
trip in five hours by air, whereas it would take ten times as long by
train or ship. The brevity of the flight made the contrast between the
cities seem all the greater: Arequipa, perennially slumberous and serene; Lima, spirited and sparkling, but reaching the height of its exuberance in its celebration of Carnival, which begins the Saturday before
Mardi Gras.

This was the day of our arrival and we were immediately caught up
in the merrymaking. This was incessant and before the climax came we
had begun to feel the strain, but the Limenians became more and more
ebullient. The sidewalks of the Paseo Colón were packed with the ex-
pectant populace; the official pavilion at one end of it was hardly less
crowded; but the avenue itself had been completely cleared. Then there
was a flash of brilliant color, of metal glittering in the sun, of gleaming
helmets, of fluttering pennants as a troop of cavalry clattered past; directly behind them, in an open landau drawn by four bay horses, rode
the slim, smiling President Augusto Leguía.

Bowing in every direction, he ran up the steps of the pavilion. A
band blared forth its clamorous music and the Carnival floats began
their progress up the avenue, pausing to receive and return the President's salute. There was a battleship, a pirate ship; a whole menagerie,
including a white winged horse and an elephant so solid and substantial
that any loyal Republican would have coveted it. But it was the King of
Beasts the Queen had chosen to honor: colored paper ribbons fell in
such profusion from her throne high above his crouching form that he

was blanketed in their billows. Threading her way through those clinging strands, the Queen ascended to the pavilion and the President led
her to a seat beside his. She looked like a medieval bride in her white
satin gown and headdress of pearls; and certainly her attendants in their
pastel raiment could have taken their places in a troubadour's "Court of
Love." The party, which was already high-spirited, became more frolic-
some still with the arrival of those young and lovely visitors. The air
was filled with the sweet spray from the *chisguetes*—those small atom-
izers of ether and perfume, which sting and startle and stimulate; but it
was permeated with something even stronger and more subtle: the ani-
mating, effervescent spirit of Carnival in Lima.

The sightseer, eager to discover the ancient wonders of "the most
glorious work of Pizarro's creation," needed to search in the heart of
Lima and—having found them—be prepared to meet with disappointment and disillusionment in some instances. The beautiful carved stalls
of the cathedral choir had been brightly varnished; the even more beautiful ceiling of the Senate Chamber garishly painted. Still worse, the
charming pleasure palace of La Périchole, the sweetheart of the last
Viceroy, was being used for a barracks, with horses stabled in the basement, which a riverbed had been diverted to encircle because a lovely
woman wished to be lulled to sleep by the sound of running water!
Many magnificent buildings had been mutilated or completely destroyed; and it seemed strange that the Limenians, who take enormous
pride in the glorious past of their city, should have permitted these des-
ecrations.

But, in spite of such artistic sacrilege, there were still many lingering
evidences of unspoiled architectural beauty. A special example was the
Torre-Tagle Palace, for centuries the home of the family by that name,
and a center of the most elegant and cultured social life of the city; and
now the Ministry of Foreign Affairs. Nowhere else in the city do those
shuttered, rectangular balconies of dark carved wood, so typically and
uniquely Limenian, disclose such delicate craftsmanship; nowhere else
are the sculptured ceilings, the tiled floors, the broad staircases and galleries, the superb suites of apartments, so imposing and stately. Late in the
day when everything is quiet, the house seems peopled from the past:
the *tapadas*—those lovely Limenian ladies who draped their black *man-
tas* about their heads in such a way as to leave one eye exposed, and
held those half-concealing, half-revealing draperies against their breasts
with a bejeweled hand; the Archbishop in his scarlet and purple; the
Viceroy in his velvet and lace; the courtiers and Conquistadores, the
Jesuits—across the patio, up the tiled steps, through the galleries, in

and out of the balconies, they come and go, filling them with the vibrant life, the vivid color of the Carnival city as it must have been centuries ago.

There were two other ancient buildings in the city which seemed to me scarcely less lovely and interesting, even though less imposing, than the Torre-Tagle. One of these was the palace of the Paz-Soldan family, with its exquisite private chapel, carved and gilded; the "earthquake arches" solidly built of stone between adjoining rooms; the deep, shuttered shelves—also placed between rooms—where lamps were set, frugally illuminating both apartments at once; the dark wooden bars, not unlike corkscrews in shape, on the tall windows, so characteristic of Lima, but reminiscent of our own Victorian "spool" furniture; the "summer" dining room, cool, huge, open to the pleasant flickering breezes. The other ancient building, or, rather, group of buildings, was now called the *Santuario* of Santa Rosa, but had once been the home of that remarkable girl, who dedicated herself to the service of humanity and of God, and became this hemisphere's first saint. Limenians couple her name with that of Maggie Conroy as the two greatest women Peru has produced, and though it may seem a far cry to compare a sixteenth-century saint with a twentieth-century woman of the world, the contrast is not really too great when we remember that the latter has earned the title of Joan of Arc of Peru through her manifold services to her country. She was an outstanding delegate at the Baltimore Pan-American Conference, and among her various talents is that of a noteworthy gift for languages and, at that period, she found time to give private instruction in these. Immediately after our arrival in Lima, I asked her if she would accept me as a pupil, for I was still working hard to improve my Spanish. She did more than this; she accepted me as a friend and introduced me to many persons who already had the privilege of her friendship. Among the closest to her was Alice Kurusu, the American wife of the Japanese Minister to Peru. I went frequently to the Legation, which was not only one of the most elegant in Lima, but very naturally pro-American in character, and I found both husband and wife charming and distinguished. Years later, when the Japanese attacked Pearl Harbor at the very moment that Saburo Kurusu was in Washington on a special mission, it seemed incredible that he should have been an accomplice in such treachery; and, to this day, Maggie firmly believes that he was not even aware of what was about to happen. I sincerely hope that she is right and someday his name may be cleared.

When my daily lessons were over, Maggie and I went to tea at the country club; to the dedication of the new Beneficencia in Magdalena

—seven buildings consecrated to the care of children; and to the lovely and hospitable house of Admiral and Mrs. William Pye, set in the midst of an olive grove planted by Pizarro. . . .

There was no sense, in Lima, of either haste or friction; and the warm tranquil days slid past filled—but not crowded—with pleasures, with impressions which proved rich and lasting, rather than transitory and stimulating. How peaceful it was in the ancient convent garden of the Sacred Heart where all the flowers—one of the nuns told us—"turn toward the Virgin's Shrine"—what poetry lay hidden in her words of simple and unquestioning faith. How the learning and wisdom of the ages seemed to fill the colonnaded courtyards of San Marcos University —the oldest university on our hemisphere, for it was founded in 1551, nearly a century before Harvard or William and Mary came into existence! What priceless archeological specimens of a buried and remote civilization have been assembled in the Inca Museum. How vital seems the personality of "The Liberator," the first President of independent Peru, when visualized through the relics and records of the *Museo Bolivariano*.

I sat up very late the night I left Lima; as usual, I had been out to dinner, and a dinner which began at nine was considered early there. I had been sitting on a wide paved terrace, facing a beautiful garden at the back of a beautiful house with my hosts and some of my fellow guests, listening to the strains of Inca music from the opera *Ollantay,* which other guests were playing for us—on a violin and on the piano at the end of the entrance hall, under the somber, ancient portrait of one of the Conquistadores; but from outside, it sounded like the call of the *quenas*—the Inca flutes which still echo over the Cuzco hills. There was nothing on the terrace to destroy the illusion—no noise, no motion, no light except that from the dim lantern above the garden gate, and the two little flickering lamps at either side of the sacred image on the wall. There were so many delightful dinners in Lima—at the different legations—in the American houses—in Peruvian homes—but none more significant and more lovely than this. And since it was time for me to go away from the Carnival city, I was glad I could leave it, as I entered it, feeling it was filled with music!

Chapter 66

EVERYONE I met who had been to Ecuador seemed enchanted with it and I had no reason to suppose I would not find it equally delightful. Consequently, when John and I sailed away from Peru, past the venerable fort of San Felipe at Callao, it was not in one of the express ships which would carry us directly to the Panama Canal, but in a freighter bound for the country that takes its name from the equatorial line which bisects it. The voyage was a pleasant one; the air mild and hazy; and through the mist a low blue coast range was visible, for we were never far from shore. Just out of Callao, the translucent water was russet-tinged with the myriads of huge, amber-colored jellyfish which floated through it; and when we ceased to see these, the ocean was still peopled with playful porpoises and gleaming malignant sharks. We were almost sorry when we entered the wide, turbulent Guayas River—strangely reminiscent of the stream which flows from Canton down to the sea—and realized our indolent cruise was almost over.

Guayaquil, Ecuador's principal port, is about thirty miles upstream and we saw nothing particularly imposing about the Malecón, though it was broad, well paved and well planted. Most of the best society, foreign and native, resided in large airy apartments above commercial establishments and there were few outstanding dwellings. It must be confessed that John and I found our hotel less than luxurious, though we did derive a great deal of amusement from the archaic, ponderous and extraordinary plumbing of our quarters and from the necessity of moving our baggage around whenever it rained—all too frequently—because streams of water poured through the high, decorated ceilings and gathered in pools on the unpolished, unpainted wooden floors. As the walls, for the sake of better ventilation, were open at the top, the conversations and occupations of guests in adjacent rooms were audibly pursued. But it was all highly entertaining and the service was friendly and faithful; the luscious tropical fruits and vegetables were succulent and sustaining; and we found the brief time we were there agreeably employed: we went to a festive reception aboard the British cruiser *Despatch;* and a dinner at the American Consulate. We had tea with the Director of Customs and Mrs. Reddy and tasted for the first time ice cream made from *naranjillas*—a delicacy I recommend highly. All too soon, we had to leave and, ferrying the river at Durán, took the early morning train for Riobamba.

It was not an easy trip; the train had no dining car or plumbing and stopped so frequently and so long that an enormous amount of time was consumed in covering very little ground; nevertheless, the journey was not a dull one. Regarded simply as an engineering feat, the line was extraordinary: after crossing about fifty miles of delta, it ascended—in the next fifty miles—over ten thousand feet; and the double zigzag of the "Devil's Nose" afforded a thrill to the most jaded traveler. Besides the opportunity to marvel at this skillful construction was that of beholding greater physical contrasts than were to be found in any other excursion of equal length. The fields of sugar cane on the lowlands merged almost without warning into tropical forests; while above and beyond lay some of the highest snow-topped mountains in the Andean range. The weather, steamingly hot in Guayaquil, had moderated perceptibly before Huigra—the stopping place for lunch—was reached; by the time the little engine puffed wearily into Riobamba at seven in the evening, the passengers had all wrapped themselves in their coats before descending, stiff and shivering, into the chilly damp night air.

There were then no night trains in Ecuador, but it was possible to continue on to Quito the next day if one felt inclined to rise a second morning at five and spend twelve more hours in a train. Neither John nor I did, however; and fortunately it was not necessary, for, between Riobamba and Ecuador's capital, there was a splendid road. So we stopped over for thirty-six hours and then continued by automobile, branching off the main road to take the one which led straight to the edge of the vast region of the Oriente, which was still almost unpenetrated by civilization. The highway was bordered with the glossy *capulí* trees which bear the wild cherry of which the Indians are so fond, and the spiky *cabonya* plant, which furnished them hemp, sweets and a lather-forming juice used for soap. Hovering clouds shadowed the latter part of our journey and we were unable to see the mountains which, when unobscured, render the approach to Quito and its situation so magnificent. Though we had been warned that the evenings were cold, the extreme crispness of the atmosphere struck us with surprise, for it is hard to realize that a city located almost directly on the magic circle—usually associated with intense heat—can have so bracing a temperature. There is little change of season; there is an almost daily shower of brief duration; aside from this, the sun shines with constant and invigorating warmth. Since the houses were entirely unheated, as elsewhere in South America, the newcomer was apt to feel more comfortable outdoors than in, but, at the same time, find it difficult to get much strenuous exercise because of the altitude; but it did not take us long to get acclimated and the climate is an unusually healthful one.

In Quito, as in Cuzco, there was a highly developed Indian civilization before the coming of the Spaniards; and in the early colonial days a degree of culture and a consciousness of art found expression in a remarkable school of painting and sculpture, as well as in the erection of buildings of lasting loveliness. The plazas, even on a continent that has concentrated on making these attractive, are unusually picturesque and impressive; in the one on which the Church of San Francisco is located, the first wheat planted in the new world was grown. Quito's churches exceed in beauty of architecture and adornment any that I have seen on this hemisphere; while the *Compañía*—a miracle of color and carving—exceeds any of its size I have seen in the world. The thoroughfares were, for the most part, steep and narrow and twisting, bordered with houses which gave little indication of either their size or splendor until one had entered them.

Ecuador, like Peru, has a saintly patroness and there are many points of likeness between Rosa of Lima and Mariana of Quito. Both were born of gentle parents, late in the sixteenth century, and both from infancy showed that they had great spiritual gifts; both loved their gardens and seldom strayed from the enclosures which these formed. Neither entered a convent as a nun, though Rosa sought refuge in the peace and seclusion of one, as a guest, the latter part of her life, while Mariana secured it in a large quiet room at the top of her parents' home. Both encouraged the poor and afflicted to come to them and Mariana showed great talent in teaching little children; in a way, they were the first welfare workers—as we understand the term today—on this hemisphere. Both spent a great deal of time in prayer and practiced great austerity, but the rigidity on which they insisted in their own lives was lacking in the tenderness with which they treated others. Their saintly characters were recognized during their lifetimes and their memories are held in the greatest reverence. Mariana's family home is now a Carmelite convent, which it is possible to visit, except of course for the cloister; and nearly everyone who goes there feels the imprint she has

left and a better understanding of her era than is possible without following the story of her life.

The Ecuadorians are among the most hospitable of the South American people; and the very day after our arrival in Quito, John and I
began to enjoy evidence of this hospitality when an invitation to attend
a Quitenian wedding was delivered to us. Promptly at the appointed
hour, we started for the bride's house, a fine colonial mansion in the
city's center, built and originally occupied by Ecuador's first President.
The narrow street in front of the house was so crowded with onlookers
that it was almost impossible to pass; and on the door hung an immense
star of white roses. Inside the entrance, on either side of the stairway
and scattered about the galleries and drawing rooms, were more of the
same flowers, for in Ecuador it is customary for every wedding guest to
send white roses to the bride. These were arranged in stars—crescents
—fans; birds—balls; there was even a huge clock with its hands pointing to the hour of five!

The typical marriage ceremony in Quito is divided in several parts: a
general meeting at the home of the bride; a departure for the church, to
which the guests go in couples (a wedding was the only occasion when a
young man was permitted to escort a young girl unchaperoned); attendance at the religious ceremony, and a return to the house for the reception and supper.

As the guests were assembling, the bride's mother, the groom's
parents and the groom moved about among them quite informally;
eventually the bride made her appearance, seated herself on a sofa and
chatted with her immediate relatives and the members of the bridal
party. The company at large, however, did not approach her, but reserved the expression of their good wishes until after the ceremony.

After about an hour, the signal for departure came and the guests
started for the Church of Santo Domingo two by two, each man escorting a lady exactly as if he were taking her in to dinner. The plaza in
front of the church was just as crowded as the street in front of the
house had been. All the seats had been removed from the body of the
church and the guests, directed by two Dominicans, took their place in
two long lines, extending from altar to entrance; the officiating clergy
waited in the chancel; and, as the organ began to play, the bridal party
appeared, the bride on the arm of the groom's father, the groom with
the bride's mother, the bridesmaids and flower girls following. . . .

The return to the house was made in the same manner that the progress to the church had been accomplished; and after the usual felicitations had been extended and the gifts inspected, the guests moved to
rooms at the rear of the patio where tables had been laid with individ-

ual service for each one. The excellent and substantial repast which was served was eaten standing; but each person stood comfortably in his or her appointed place and there was none of the confusion of the average buffet supper about it; after it was over, there was quiet and general departure without formal leave-taking.

I have written of this marriage celebration partly because it differed so greatly in detail from a wedding in the United States and partly because it seemed so intrinsically dignified and, at the same time, so delightful from start to finish. I also confess that the custom of spending the honeymoon in the quiet seclusion of some *quinta* or hacienda, instead of traveling frantically about, has, in my opinion, much to commend it. This couple spent their honeymoon at a hacienda very close to one John and I visited, through the kindness of the great Mena family; and from our own experience at Tampillo Alto we were able to form an opinion of how ideally suited an Ecuadorian country place would prove for retirement and rest. The house, built of pale blue stucco, with a tiled roof and frescoes along the outer walls, was long and rambling with deep galleries, a private chapel and a great bell which hung above stone steps leading from one balcony to another; it contained twenty rooms on each floor and a splendid staircase. But attractive as was the house itself, the garden was even lovelier. Here cascades fell in smooth broad sheets over a background of lilies, gleaming white through the translucency; here little placid curving streams widened gradually into quiet pools where ducks and turtles swam indolently about; here violets and orchids, forget-me-nots and roses hung in clusters over the terraces. And, as the house and garden had for a setting a sloping verdant valley, and for a background remote and lofty mountains, the beauty of the situation was as great as the charm of the hacienda.

There were five brothers in the Mena family, all equally hospitable, and it was to one of them, Eduardo—who had married an American —that we owed our trip far out on the new highway leading to the Colombian frontier; while another brother Alberto introduced us to Quitenian painting, of which he had a fine collection. There was such a genuine kindness toward foreigners in Quito, such an evident desire to share the natural and artistic beauties which abounded there, that there was no sense of being a stranger in a strange land; and this kindly attitude was not confined to any one class or condition. You met with it in your room boy; you also met with it in the President of the Republic.

That remarkable man, Isidro Ayora, was of partly Indian stock and rightly proud of the fact. He had never been especially interested in politics; he was a physician who had supplemented his Ecuadorian medical training with years of study in Germany and was regarded as Quito's outstanding doctor. He founded the Red Cross in Ecuador; he headed a renowned private clinic; he was the instigator of many hygienic reforms. When a group of prominent men, with the essential cooperation of the army, looked for an honest man, who was also capable and free from political affiliations, their choice fell upon Dr. Ayora, who, even after becoming President, continued to practice medicine; and he was still doing so and still engaged in many other activities when I last saw him in 1960.

I first met and talked with him in his own house, adjoining the clinic, and not in the palace which was his official residence, for his wife was not strong and they were living very quietly. But they were punctilious about participating in official functions of real importance and I met them several times after this audience and my favorable early impressions were confirmed and strengthened.

For the first time since Ecuador had declared its independence, a Spanish naval training ship—named, oddly enough, the *Juan Sebastián Elcano*—was making an official visit there; and, with the arrival of the Admiral and his staff in Quito, a round of celebrations began. There were parades and processions, dinners and dances. The Minister of Spain and his wife—the Count and Countess of Villamediana—gave a splendid reception at the Spanish Legation; while the leading newspaper featured a large picture of King Alfonso with the statement:

> We decorate this page with the photograph of the Spanish Monarch as a tribute of admiration and respect to the Mother Country, in the person of our distinguished visitors, the sailors of the training ship, *Juan Sebastián Elcano.*

The paper also carried a long editorial entitled, *Enter, Spanish sailors, you have arrived at your own house;* and which concluded:

> Never was Spain greater than when, conflict over, it knows that the peoples of America were calling it Mother; and never were the American peoples prouder than when it was granted that we should declare ourselves the sons of Spain. You are at home, Spanish sailors. You have returned to the hearthstone which is forever yours. Enter, enter! toward you, brothers, we cherish only love.

With Lisbon as a port of entrance, I began my joyous journey through Latin lands in Spain—where the Mother Country was welcoming home, at the beautiful and symbolic exposition of Seville, all those nations which owed their life and being to her. Therefore, it seemed to me a peculiarly significant and happy coincidence that I ended it in Ecuador—"daughter in her mother's house, but mistress in her own"

—just at the time when, with filial respect and affection, she was receiving a parental visit!

Colombia had, of course, been in our original itinerary, designed to include every country in South America. But shortly before we left Lima, we learned that our very good friend Dr. Enrique Olaya Herrera, who had been for eight years Colombian Minister to the United States, had been elected President and I received a letter from him, asking if I would not delay my visit until he had taken office. I gladly availed myself of this suggestion for, by awaiting the Herreras' return to Colombia before making an extended visit there myself, I knew that the pleasures of my stay would be immensely enhanced. I could not help being sorry that Bogotá should be the one capital in South America which I did not visit; but looked forward to going there on my next joyous journey which, at the time, it seemed probable I would make in that direction. I was mistaken and, unfortunately, have never yet gone there, though I have been five times to Peru, three to Ecuador and twice to Venezuela and Chile. I did, however, make a landing in Colombia, even if only of a few hours. For the ship in which we re-embarked at Guayaquil stopped at the prosperous port of Buenaventura and our Vice Consul Mr. Daniels invited me to attend the inauguration of a new electric plant—the first to serve the general public there. It was raining hard and the only way to reach the plant was in a small launch, but we were soon chugging across a moistly pretty harbor, overhung with the tangled tropical verdure which also overspread the shore and swept into the water. It was a lovely sight, all gray and green and peaceful. The Mayor and numerous other officials were present in full force at the exercises and the parish priest made the main speech of the occasion. With an ardor and an eloquence that were most inspiring, he spoke of the human need for both material and spiritual light, and of the way in which each could magnify the other. Literally and loftily, he interpreted the words that have echoed down through the ages: "I am the Light of the world; he that followeth Me shall not walk in darkness." Never have I heard them rendered with such a significant loveliness before.

We dined with Mr. Daniels and saw such sights as the town afforded. It was not until after a stop of thirty-six hours—during the course of which coffee had been steadily loaded—that our cargo was complete and we steamed away toward Panama. We reached Balboa early in the morning and found Admiral Blakely, then Commandant of the Fifteenth Naval District, and Mr. Lawrence Higgins, one of the Secretaries of the American Legation, waiting to welcome us. The Admiral proposed that we should take a look at the new cruiser *Pensacola* and when this highly interesting visit was over, we went shopping—those fascinating Panama shops!—with Mrs. Higgins, and lunched delightfully at the Legation with the American Minister and Mrs. Davis. Our ship, meanwhile, had continued on to Colón, prior to sailing northward at midnight; but we were not disturbed because, having already been through the Canal by ship, and having crossed the Isthmus by both train and "scooter"—for months I had been planning that *this* time I was going to fly!

The flight was a fitting climax for all our wanderings. We took off rather slowly, skimming over the water for some moments before we began to rise; then we soared smoothly and surely into the air. The Canal lay beneath us like a silver chain cast carelessly down on green velvet—on which bits of white thistledown had blown. It was as delicate and as exquisite as that. And it was brief, like the blowing and breaking of an iridescent bubble—another delicate and exquisite thing. As if the unseen hand of a lovely lady had quickly gathered up the chain and replaced it around her throat, as if she had swept aside the thistledown and folded away the velvet, they vanished from our sight. The sibilant sound of waves came swiftly to our ears.

The flight was over and so, except for the final voyage from Panama to New York, which was devoted to long hours of work, was my joyous journey through Latin lands.

Chapter 67

THE homecoming was joyous, too. Harry and Henry both met us at
the pier and—largely due to the gracious and tactful manner with
which the former dealt with the customs officials—we passed through
them with more speed and ease than ever before. That evening we all
went to the theater together and, though I was obliged to stay in New
York for editorial conferences after Harry had returned to Washington
and Henry to Cambridge, I had the strong feeling that we were on our
way to becoming a united family again and was very happy about it.

The conferences were harmonious and I had another very definite
cause for rejoicing in finding that my work had been considered so satisfactory by the editors of both *Good Housekeeping* and *Delineator;*
while a very substantial factor in my satisfaction lay in my bank balance. A great many beautiful dolls and fans, succeeding those presented
me in Puerto Rico and Panama, had been given me and I had increased
their number by occasional purchases, so that I now had the nucleus of
two interesting collections; and I had also made acquisitions of lasting
value in the way of Peruvian silver and beautiful old carved furniture
from Cuzco. I had bought new clothes as and when I needed them and I
still had managed to save ten thousand dollars from my earnings. I had
been too far from the seat of the trouble to have the market crash of '29
make much impression, for, in those days, the newspapers in Latin
America carried little or no news from the United States; and none of
my correspondents had harassed me with information which they felt
would upset me, without justification. Of course, the day was not far
distant when I realized that this was mistaken kindness on their part,
but for the time being I had the rare experience of eating my cake and
having it, too; and the first reminder that this is never possible for long

came not from financial worries, for a change, but from an entirely different and unforeseen source of trouble.

It was, I suppose, largely due to this general feeling of satisfaction that I disregarded the fact that my eyes were bothering me. I had been conscious of intermittent dimness or blurred vision in the course of the voyage north, but had laid it to the poor light in my cabin and thought that, as soon as I had a good desk lamp again, I would see as well as ever. But it was not only at sea that the lighting had been poor; it had been inadequate even in the best hotels at which we had stopped and I had, nevertheless, held fast to my purpose of studying Spanish six hours out of twenty-four, even if I began at midnight after a day in which hours of writing had been wedged in between hours of sightseeing and social diversion, ending with the typically late dinner party. It was not until I had been home for several weeks that I realized I was still not seeing any better, despite a good desk lamp, and went to consult an oculist about my intermittent loss of sight.

He examined my eyes and then asked how much I had been using them and under what conditions. When I told him he inquired sternly what I expected: why should I suppose that the eye muscles, when abused, should not rebel like any other muscles of the body when overstrained? There was nothing the matter with the eyes themselves, so the present condition—sometimes called technical blindness—could probably be cured in time with care and patience; meanwhile, it was serious.

Is there any word more dreadful to a writer than blindness? Indeed, it is a dreadful word to anyone. I listened attentively to the prescribed treatment, which would effectually put an end to long working hours, no matter how good the light might be; then I went out of the office to the street and stumbled because I could not see, but this was not strange, for I was unable to hold back my tears. In any case, I was in no condition to walk home. Directly across the street was St. Matthew's Church—now the cathedral—and the doors, after the custom of Catholic churches, stood wide open. I took refuge in the church, still sobbing, but I was completely calm when I came out and, from that moment, I never doubted that my eyes would recover. It was a long, hard, tedious struggle, but I followed the treatment and in less than a year I no longer had to consider how much I would use my eyes; at eighty-four, I am still in that fortunate state.

Aside from the anxiety about my sight, the months of May and June, both spent in Washington, were much the same as the months before my long absence: I worked as many hours as I dared, stopping to rest with compresses, alternately hot and cold, on my eyes every four hours;

I saw the people who had become my best friends—the Pittmans, the Kendricks, the Gudgers and Senator Walsh—and many others and went, as usual, to innumerable luncheons, receptions and dinners, none of which I recorded or remember as especially outstanding, except a reception at the Cuban Embassy, magnificent in itself, where I saw practically everyone I knew and where everyone seemed so glad to see me back that I found it very heartwarming; a reception at the National Geographic for Admiral Byrd, who had captured the admiration of the American people on his return from his Antarctic expedition, accompanied by every one of the men who had originally embarked on this venture with him; and a dinner honoring the President-elect of Brazil at the Pan-American Union on a beautiful night when the galleries and garden were open and illuminated, as well as the great ballroom, and the perfect weather made it possible to enjoy them all.

On the first of July, I left for home and, after a brief stop in New York and occasional short trips, either for pleasure or for speech-making, spent the rest of the summer and the larger part of the autumn uneventfully at Pine Grove Farm. I worked steadily and with an able assistant—Lisle Cobb, who managed to come to me most days for at least a few hours and helped tremendously, especially with the typing of correspondence; and I had a great deal of company, as the boys had now reached the stage when they all wanted to have house guests; and election year automatically meant a certain amount of political entertaining. Harry, who was up for re-election, was unopposed for the nomination, but the election was much closer than the previous ones had been and there were some anxious hours, particularly the evening of November third, when it looked as if he had lost. Indeed, it was not until two in the morning of the fourth that we were sure he had come through and, though I worked as usual the next day, I was too tired to accomplish much and finally tumbled into bed and slept for nine hours straight.

Now that the question as to whether or not we were to remain in Washington for another six years was settled, we began preparations for a step we had been considering for some time: moving from our second Sixteenth Street apartment which, like the first, we had outgrown because my work required more and more room, to a house in Georgetown spacious enough for all our needs. I had seen several, with any one of which I would have been satisfied, but it took time to find one that Harry liked, too, and this had finally been done. Before the end of the year, we moved to 3053 P Street. Meanwhile, our household staff had been enlarged to include a wonderful, middle-aged woman named Clara Wilson, a Missourian by birth, but who had already worked in

Washington for several years and whose talents as a cook were matched by several other excellent qualities and attainments. She came, on trial, for six months and remained until her retirement twenty-six years later! Her character, her presence and her accomplishments combined to lighten household labors for both Cathie and myself; and I had several reasons to be encouraged about my writing, besides the boost it gave my bank account; *Delineator* bought all but one of the poems I had written in South America and presented them very attractively; *Queen Anne's Lace,* though it did not make a national best-seller list, did surprisingly well in several big centers. ("In a bad year, the book goes steadily forward," Julian Messner, my editor at Liveright, wrote me when it very quickly went into a third printing, each larger than its predecessor, with a fourth already planned within a few months of its publication.) And Liveright was more than disposed to follow up its success, not only by publishing the South American articles in book form, but also publishing *Lady Blanche Farm,* which had been turned down by so many publishers since it was written ten years earlier that I had almost decided never to submit it to another. Its eventual reception taught me a very valuable lesson, namely, if the author himself honestly has faith in a story, sooner or later he will find that others have, too. The following spring, I went to Ottawa and learned from my friend Margaret Lawrence, who was also a writer, that the *Canadian Home Journal* was in desperate straits for a serial. The author who had begun the one they expected to run had died before it was finished; its editor had asked Miss Lawrence to inquire whether I might possibly have anything available. I had with me a copy of *Lady Blanche,* in which I was making a few minor changes and, conscientiously telling her how many times it had been turned down before it was accepted, I handed it over. Within twenty-four hours, I had a telephone message from Mr. Dawson voicing enthusiastic acceptance that I realized might be largely due to desperation, considering his plight; but, when the fan mail began to come in, first on the book and then on the serial, and the story stayed in print year after year, I felt my faith had been justified. When it was chosen ten years later still as the book which my English publishers preferred above everything else I had so far written, for distribution in a special edition among the armed forces, I knew it had more than justified itself.

Chapter 68

I RETURNED from Canada well pleased about my serial, to find awaiting me a letter from Theodore Roosevelt, Jr., who had succeeded
Judge Towner as Governor of Puerto Rico. It read:

My dear Mrs. Keyes:

Mrs. Roosevelt and I were speaking about you the other day and it
occurred to both of us that you might like to visit us and get first-hand
information on the Puerto Rican situation. Our problems and our possibilities should be known by the women of the continental United
States, and I think you could put these effectively before them. Furthermore, I think you would enjoy meeting our people and seeing the
Island. Not only are present-day questions interesting and vital, but we
have here as beautiful relics of Colonial Spain as exist anywhere in the
world. I hope that you will come and come soon.

This letter came as a complete surprise. At that time, I had met the
Theodore Roosevelts only at a few formal functions and had no reason
to suppose they were especially interested in me, either personally or
professionally. They were a very attractive couple and I had been hoping for a chance to know them better, but no such opportunity had so
far arisen. Mrs. Roosevelt was a golden-haired beauty and it was easy
to understand why she had been considered the best-looking and most
popular of the year's debutantes when she came out; since then, she had
logically been likened to Mrs. Coolidge in her charm and tactfulness.
Much of her girlhood had been spent abroad and she had grown up bilingual; she was accomplished as a musician and as a needlewoman and
had been decorated by a grateful government for her war work in
France. Theodore Roosevelt, Jr., had, inevitably, been overshadowed by
his father's fame and, in one sense, his name had been a handicap,

rather than an advantage, since it inescapably invited comparison. He was a slim, dark-haired, dynamic man, with a shining face, whose eyes were piercing as well as kindly, and whose geniality of manner was coupled with so much vitality and driving power that these immediately made themselves felt even by a relative stranger. I was greatly complimented by the invitation, but hesitated to accept it. In the first place, I had been traveling intensively for a year and was hardly settled in the Georgetown house I had sought so long and worked so hard to get; just then, I wanted to remain there more than I wanted to do anything else. Besides, Puerto Rico had given me my first dazzled impression of tropical charm and I have always believed an attempt to recapture a delightful experience is dangerous. In this case, it might be doubly so, since the auspices under which I would make the proposed visit would, necessarily, offer a great contrast to those under which I had stayed at *La Fortaleza* before. It was one thing to work intensively as the house guest of old friends and quite another to do so with celebrities I hardly knew. In hoping for a chance to know the Roosevelts better, I had not dreamed of such proffered hospitality.

But, while I was turning all this over in my mind, I inadvertently glanced at the picture I had brought home from Puerto Rico seven years earlier: the western gallery of *La Fortaleza* with the setting sun streaming through the stained glass on the black and white marble flooring, which had originally formed the ballast of the treasure ships from Spain. I looked at this picture often and always with renewed fascination; it was symbolic of the glory and strength of Spain and it conjured pleasant memories not only of Government House itself, standing four square about its great patio and rising straight from the sea wall, but also of the entire "rich port" which it guards and crowns. On that particular occasion, as I turned from it, my eyes fell again on the signature of the letter which lay before me. It would be "embroidering the obvious," as Justice Holmes so delightfully expressed it, to enlarge on all that the name of Theodore Roosevelt brings to mind. After gazing at it for a few moments and dismissing from *my* mind the dozen cogent reasons why I should not leave home, I began my preparations for departure.

A fortnight later, I shook myself reluctantly but resolutely from slumber one hot still morning just before dawn, dressed hurriedly and went on deck. The sturdy little ship which had rolled out of New York four days earlier was rounding the promontory surmounted by the splendid and impregnable fortress at *El Morro*. The gray sky, after turning to ashes of roses, suddenly glowed pink above a harbor of ethereal loveliness, fringed with tropical verdure and circled with azure-colored hills. I had reached the port of San Juan and, far from feeling disillusionment, it seemed to me more beautiful than ever.

I was still standing on deck, enthralled, when one of the ship's men approached me, accompanied by a charming Italian lady, who must have told me her name at the time, but which I never heard again, for she was invariably addressed merely as Signorina. She had originally come to the Roosevelts as a governess for their youngest son shortly after World War I—in which numerous decorations had been bestowed upon her for distinguished services—and had remained with the family ever since as an invaluable member of their household staff. She had been designated to welcome me and see me safely to my room, which I was delighted to find was the same one I had occupied before; and, when she said she would send a maid to help me unpack and I ventured to ask if it would be Magdalena, she looked surprised and replied, certainly, if that would be my choice; she had thought of giving me one who was younger and more accomplished, but was sure Magdalena would be glad I had remembered her. Then she left, saying she would return to take me down to luncheon.

Magdalena did seem very glad to see me and I found her quite capable of doing everything I needed done hours before it was time to go down for luncheon, so I had what was (for me!) the rare experience of reading quietly all the morning. Signorina reappeared and escorted me down the beautiful curved staircase and ushered me into the great *sala,* which I recalled as the scene of many pleasant gatherings, but which had been embellished with an exquisite chandelier of antique glass, given to the Roosevelts by members of the Spanish *casino,* the addition of long gilt-framed Louis XVI mirrors and tapestry-covered gilt furniture. At the door of this room we were met by Miss Hensey, the Governor's energetic little secretary, who weighed ninety-five pounds and did as much work in a day as the average person does in a week. Shepherded by her and Signorina, I was introduced to other guests as they arrived—about twenty in all—and took the place assigned to me in the circle which had been formed and completed. Then, on the stroke of twelve-thirty, the door of the adjacent office was thrown open, Governor and Mrs. Roosevelt entered the drawing room together and greeted each of the assembled company in turn. As soon as they had made the rounds, Mrs. Roosevelt said, very pleasantly, "Shall we go in to luncheon?" and the move to the dining room was made in the same orderly fashion as the reception.

I had been totally unprepared for so much formality, for, though I had become acquainted with such procedures in the residences of English colonial governors I had visited, where they seemed a logical part of the picture, I had never been in any American establishment where there was quite so much ceremony. But I quickly understood that, with the amount of entertaining the Roosevelts did and the manifold activities of their lives otherwise, this arrangement for greeting their guests saved a great deal of strain on the Governor and his wife. Though I missed something of spontaneity in my welcome on arrival, I never felt it afterward; and the hours spent in the dining room soon became the most exhilarating of my visit, for, as a conversationalist, I have never seen the Governor surpassed and very seldom have I seen him equaled. His magnetism and force made themselves felt immediately, but he seemed so hurried and harried by something stronger than he was that the pressure was evident and contagious; and, as he seated himself at table, he was apt, momentarily, to appear slightly abstracted. He often had not yet wrenched his mind free from the problems with which he had been wrestling since early morning; and though he insisted he was never tired, there were brief periods when he seemed engulfed by fatigue. But the vigorous animation which was so integral a part of his personality was never long dormant. His abstraction evaporated with a velocity that was startling. He began to talk on all imaginable subjects, and some that were unimaginable, with penetration, comprehension, uncanny vision and an all-pervading sense of humor. It was evident that he had read as omnivorously as he had hunted and that he had taken his studies and his sports in much the same spirit. His voice was extraordinary and his range of expression limitless. His memory was prodigious —he forgot neither episodes nor impressions nor individuals nor statistics. As a raconteur he was peerless. He could and did tell the best stories, and the largest number of them, on the greatest variety of subjects, of any human being I have ever met. He broke into verse as naturally, as easily and as frequently as a Neapolitan bursts into song, and he talked "shop" with the same gusto that he declaimed hexameters. In fact, the luncheon and dinner guests were often invited with the double purpose of affording Governor Roosevelt not only valuable social contacts, but also the opportunity to confer with his co-workers on the problems that faced them. There was not a single person at his table, no matter how large a group was gathered there, whom he did not include in his questions, his observations, his attention. He listened with the same intensity and the same enthusiasm with which he talked. Meanwhile, he consumed, heartily and rather hastily, generous helpings of simple and solid fare and drank water from the silver mug which he had used since babyhood. As the meal drew near its close, he fumbled for a package of cigarettes and began to smoke in a leisurely fashion as he poured out one cup of coffee after another from the silver pot that was placed at his elbow and that he drained to the last drop before he left the table.

Permeated though it was with intensity, this was his one period of comparative relaxation and he lingered over it. The minute that he rose from the table, he returned to his desk in the private office adjoining the state dining room and flanked on the farther side by the general *secretaria,* which was once the viceregal throne room and which, despite the utilitarian purpose for which it had been adapted, still retained much of its formal beauty. Directly after luncheon, there would be a long Spanish lesson, for he had put intensive effort into the mastery of that language and only those who have striven—through blood and tears—to acquire the knowledge of a strange tongue at middle age can guess or gauge the determination and application which such an endeavor demands. After the lesson was over, he continued to "celebrate conferences" with political leaders and countless others until five o'clock. Then, accompanied by Mrs. Roosevelt, he would go to the country club and exercise strenuously—usually by playing tennis—for two hours, returning to *La Fortaleza* just in time for a seven-thirty dinner; and, as soon as it was over, even though there were guests, he went back to the office again, to dictate to the indefatigable Miss Hensey the letters for which there had been no time earlier in the day. *La Fortaleza* was steeped in stillness before he stopped. All the lights had been turned out except those he burned. Only long after everyone else had gone to sleep would he call it a day and go to his room, to gallop through a book or so—which he would practically know by heart the next morning—before the thought of slumber crossed his mind.

There was practically no variation to this program. No social invitations of any sort were accepted. No hours were spent at ease around a tea or bridge table. There were no holidays—not even any half holidays —on the Governor's calendar. His only outings were those which took the form of unannounced visits to farm schools, to milk stations, to social-service centers, to hospitals. He went to every part of the island and, wherever he went, he carried with him a sense of abounding energy, penetrative interest and intelligent observation, the will and the power to serve. Wherever he went, crowds collected which hailed him —and which he hailed—with enthusiasm. But such visits as these were not diversions; they were, as he saw them, obligations. It was the omnipresent sense of Puerto Rico's crying need that drove him so hard, that created the impression he was hurried and harried by something stronger than he was, that made the pressure under which he worked so evident and so contagious, and confirmed the impression that he was consecrating all that he had and all that he was to the island.

According to a contemporary press report,

> Within less than ten weeks [after his inauguration] Governor Roosevelt had visited most of the island's seventy-seven towns. This is more than some of the governors had done in as many years. He had seen all classes and all conditions. Both Mrs. Roosevelt and the Governor have visited systematically some of the very poorest homes in the city slums and rural *barrios*. Both are studying the job that lies ahead of them. They are making teamwork of it. To *La Fortaleza*, they have invited high and low alike.

There is a comfortable theory, held—I may say in passing, only by those who never tried to master it—that Spanish is an easy language. To be sure, it is not very hard to learn to ask for the necessities of life in it—or in any other language, for that matter. But its grammar is extremely complicated, the number of synonyms which it contains is staggering, and it is riddled with colloquialisms. To speak it fluently and idiomatically after a few weeks of unguided study is an achievement of which few persons can boast, and Theodore Roosevelt would have been the last to do so. Indeed, he related with relish that, during his early experimental stages, he referred to himself as the mother of four children and to the Chief of the Bureau of Insular Affairs as a tapeworm, instead of a bachelor! But he was the first American Governor of Puerto Rico who had even attempted to speak Spanish and that, in itself, counted for much; his proficiency, which was remarkable, was based in no slight measure on his willingness to "barge in" and do the best he could from the beginning. He made part of his inaugural address to the people of the island in their mother tongue; and his wife welcomed the guests to the inaugural reception in the same language; and when, with an earnestness and a thoroughness and a devotion unsurpassed in the record of American administration, Theodore Roosevelt began his executive duties, Eleanor Roosevelt undertook the task that awaited her as the chatelaine of *La Fortaleza* in a spirit comparable to his.

She kept much the same office hours as her husband and had a schedule almost as strenuous as his. Since her own skill as a needlewoman had raised this to the rank of an art, it was natural that she should recognize a similar talent in others and strive to organize the underprivileged women of Puerto Rico, who possessed the same gift and needed to make it profitable. Very few of us who casually bought Puerto Rican embroidery at that time realized that, in many cases, the women who had slaved over it were receiving less than a dollar a week in wages. If we had, it is to be hoped none of us tried to beat down their prices when we visited the island, or at bargain sales in our cities. Few of us realized, either, that with the increased volume of this work, combined with the starvation wages, the superior quality we once took for granted had greatly deteriorated. It was to combat both these conditions that the Needlework Relief Fund was organized.

In spite of her skill with the needle, neither Mrs. Roosevelt nor any of the women who joined in her undertaking had the slightest knowledge of industry or market conditions. They had no capital with which to start their venture and money had to be advanced to buy materials and meet the first payrolls. Outlets for the finished product had to be found; the relative salability of different articles investigated. None of these obstacles daunted Mrs. Roosevelt in the least. She threw herself wholeheartedly into the project, paring her social schedule to the minimum, in order to leave time free for philanthropy. She borrowed the necessary funds to meet the first essential expenditures. Then, laden with suitcases full of samples, she embarked for New York and spent days going from one shop to another soliciting orders.

Miss Mildred Hayes, who headed the needlework department in the Episcopal Mission at Mayagüez, joined the organization and assisted Mrs. Roosevelt in the supervision, manufacture and plans for expansion. A huge vaulted room, with whitewashed walls and grilled windows in the old *manicomio*—which, at one and the same time during the Spanish regime, served as prison, hospital, lunatic asylum and a home for foundlings!—was secured for the central *taller* or factory. Here the orders were received; all the materials cut and stamped, and a model made for each design to be executed. Then the work was dispatched to the units which functioned in connection with the central office. At the time of my visit, six such units were operating on the island, each in the charge of a competent woman who supervised the needlework and was responsible for it; there were several other potential units which were to come into definite existence as soon as the number of orders justified their establishment. Meanwhile, early and late, day in and day out, week in and week out, Mrs. Roosevelt was at the *taller,* planning, directing, working. . . .

Shortly after my arrival, the Governor spent an hour or so with me reviewing the material he felt it most important to emphasize in my article, and, later, two mornings were spent in the same way. When everything seemed to be organized to our mutual satisfaction, I told him it had been a disappointment, during the course of my stay with the

Towners, not to visit Santo Domingo and the Virgin Islands and that I hoped I could do so before I returned home. He immediately replied, "I'll wire Watson—Major T. E. Watson of the United States Marines. He went to Santo Domingo as Food Administrator, at President Trujillo's request, just after the hurricane and has stayed on as 'Unofficial Advisor.' He and Trujillo have been friends for a long while—Watson even lives in a bungalow on the palace grounds. His wife is just as nice as she can be and they'll meet you and see that you do a lot in a day. You can take a night boat from here that gets to Santo Domingo City the next morning and come back the next night."

"What about the Virgin Islands?" I called after the Governor's retreating figure, as he dashed off to arrange for the dispatch of the wire to Major Watson.

"Oh, I'll wire Governor Pearson, too. You can charter a plane from Pan-American Airways to take you over and bring you back the same night."

The doctrine of the "strenuous life" is contagious. At five in the evening, I was headed out of San Juan harbor aboard the *Coamo;* and the next morning, while I was gazing out of my porthole at the magnificent ruins of the castle from which Diego Columbus—Christopher's son and Second Admiral and Viceroy of the Indies—had ruled the New World, word was brought me that Major and Mrs. Watson were waiting in the foyer.

Hastening from my cabin to join them, I was greeted by a cordial little lady in a brown dress and an alert-looking officer in uniform, who expressed himself in brief staccato sentences. They led the way to a tender, which carried us swiftly over the choppy blue water, past the crumbling castle and to the arched gate of the oldest city on the Western Hemisphere, where the University of Santo Tomás de Aquino was founded; where the first Royal Court of Justice in America was established; where, in the Gothic cathedral, lies the pioneer whose discoveries changed the history of the world; and where in 1930, a cyclone threatened annihilation, but where in the midst of its wreckage the Dominicans had gone about their reconstruction with tireless industry and unswerving perseverance.

Their efforts were evident everywhere and I was amazed to see all that had been accomplished, as we drove in the Watsons' car past the Palace of Government—in colonial days, the residence of the Governors General; through the tortuous narrow streets and along the Avenida Independencia.

It was just after nine when we drew up at the Watsons' back door, which they always used because it was much more convenient. The screen had barely slammed behind us when Mrs. Watson asked, "Haven't you a cousin here? An assistant manager of the National City Bank?"

"I certainly have," I rejoined, horrified at my forgetfulness of Cousin Joe Wheeler, even though I had known only a day or two ahead that I was going to Santo Domingo. "I must get in touch with him right away."

"That's easily arranged," Mrs. Watson told me. "I think I'll give a party. It's my birthday. I'll write a note—beginning 'My dear friend'— and under that list the guests I want to come. Then Arthur [one of her efficient servitors] can take it around; each lady can put a mark against her name to show whether she can come or not. I'll ask your cousin's wife, Mary, and Mrs. Curtis the wife of the American Minister and the wife of the Collector of Customs and . . . there, while Arthur delivers the invitation, we'll walk up and see Señora Trujillo."

"Just go right over?" I asked.

"Oh, yes. She's expecting us and, afterward, she's going to take us to the cathedral in her car."

I have made presidential visits under many different circumstances, but this was the first one I had made simply by walking out the back door, crossing a lawn and climbing the front steps of the *Residencia,* while the sentries stationed there smiled and motioned us on.

We went through an attractive hall and up a carpeted stairway to a family sitting room where a sweet-faced, graceful lady came forward and kissed Mrs. Watson before turning to shake hands with me and ask if we would not like to go out on the veranda where we could get the breeze. When we were comfortably settled, she talked with us, part of the time in Spanish and part of the time in English; there was a feeling of pleasantness and peacefulness in just being with her. She moved only once during the next half hour and that was when a tall distinguished-looking man stepped out onto the veranda. Then she rose and said, "This is my husband, Señora. He is very busy this morning, but he would like to greet you."

So that is the way I met the President of the Dominican Republic and Señora Trujillo.

After a while, Señora Trujillo asked if we would not like to drive in to the city to see the cathedral and, when we reached it, we circled the building, so I could view it from every side, as well as the splendid statue of Christopher Colombus in the plaza before it. Inside, it was cool and dark and lovely, and we saw the Murillo and the copy of *La Señora de la Antigua* at Seville and the monument of marble and bronze which is a symbol to all the world. We waited while the verger arranged the treasure, which I had heard was extraordinary—that one of Benvenuto Cellini's masterpieces was among it, in addition to other examples of the silversmith's art. Having seen the treasure of the cathedrals in Toledo and Seville and Milan and Cologne, I was not prepared to be overwhelmed by the treasure in the Cathedral of Santo Domingo. But I was. The monstrances, the chalices and all the other holy vessels were miracles of workmanship and beauty. The jewels of the Madonna were incomparable—the crown of emeralds, the pearls, the huge irregular rough-cut diamonds, the rubies, the sapphires. Spread out in all its gorgeousness, it covered the top of the mammoth *amario* which stretched across the length of the sacristy, in glittering, multicolored splendor. It fascinated me; I did not want to leave.

Ever since Governor Towner started my collection, it had been my custom to acquire, if possible, an antique fan in each country I visited. When we left the cathedral, I asked if we could look for a fan. Though we combed the shops in which such a souvenir could logically be found, we could not discover one anywhere, but our search was, in a measure, rewarded, for we did find a lovely old necklace, unadorned with gems, but curiously and artistically wrought of gold. Since I have always preferred to buy one really choice thing, rather than a large number of articles, I was perfectly satisfied with the necklace as the one memento of my visit and returned happily to the Watsons' to prepare for the birthday party. It was a delightful one—delightful because the table looked so pretty; delightful because the food was so superlatively good; delightful because the guests were all so friendly and congenial. Mary Wheeler was much nicer to me than I deserved under the circumstances and invited the Watsons and me to come to tea after we had been to the Fort of San Jerónimo.

It is a ruin in a million—with a history, of course. It was built in 1628 as an advance defense for the city of Santo Domingo and is located three kilometers from it on the Sanchez Highway. During the English invasion of 1655, the castle was a main factor in the defeat of the British forces and it was also of great service during the War of the Spanish Reconquest against the French.

Then came tea with Joe and Mary before they and the Watsons escorted me to the tender which was waiting to transport me back to the *Coamo*. I hated the thought of leaving because I was fascinated with Santo Domingo and I doubt if I could have torn myself away if I hadn't kept thinking about the plane which was due to take off at nine the next morning, taking Mrs. Roosevelt and me to the Virgin Islands.

She was waiting for me on the pier, wearing one of those sleeveless cotton dresses and one of those small straw hats which formed her usual daytime attire and which enhanced the natural charm, freshness and youthfulness of her appearance. She had to wait a long time, for Quarantine and customs inspection took forever, even if you had been away from Puerto Rico only thirty-six hours and were bursting with health and had made no purchases. At last I was able to join her and we wound through the narrow streets to the airfield, settled ourselves in our plane, which scuttled over the stubbly ground prior to taking off over the harbor, and soaring above the coast and the sea before circling another harbor that looked like a miniature Bay of Rio—the same glorious coloring; the same irregular coastline; the same effect of scattered islets and guarding promontories; it was like looking through the wrong end of a telescope, but as we fluttered down to our mooring, I found the telescope had been rightly held and we had come to rest in a port so indigenously and uniquely beautiful there was no need to compare it with any other, not even Rio de Janeiro.

To one familiar with the French and Spanish West Indies and who expects to find Latin characteristics outstanding in St. Thomas, even the first short drive through its streets is a revelation, for there is, naturally, no trace of Latin influence. We should have realized this, but, like most visitors, had done too little thinking beforehand. Even the streets, which still bore their Danish names, looked as if they had just been scrubbed; the heavy cyclone shutters on the square-set, solid houses bespoke careful Nordic forethought. The United States had purchased the Virgin Islands from Denmark in 1917 and it was surprising how faint had been the imprint, how thin the overlay of our nationality since then. For all its tropical setting, for all its American administration, it was a colony characteristic of Denmark and all that Denmark represented.

This feeling was so immediate and so strong that it had crystallized before the drive between the waterfront and Government House was over; and the appearance of Government House strengthened it: the great drawing room with its walls of brown and yellow—colors practical rather than pretty—and its crystal chandeliers, the beauty of their prisms marred by opaque globular shades; the dining room designed to hold a long and "groaning" board; the vast bedrooms, austerely neat and white—all these bespoke a habit of living as alien to ours as any somber Spanish splendor, and as inexterminable.

Our smiling and benign host, Governor Paul M. Pearson, had a notable record as an author, an educator—he had been president of Swarthmore—and a lecturer, though his fame has been eclipsed by the great success of his son Drew as a columnist. The Governor's manner was one of expansive candor and good will and he invited confidence and friendliness; he was, indeed, a Friend, and his faith was a matter of both conviction and practice. After he and his niece, who acted as his hostess, had made Mrs. Roosevelt and me wholeheartedly welcome, we sat down to a luncheon substantial and delicious enough to serve as a worthy successor to the "groaning" board of the Danes. The meal began with a "Quaker Grace" with which I was wholly unfamiliar and, for a moment, I was startled when the gentleman on each side of me reached for my hand and took it in his. I glanced across the table to Mrs. Roosevelt and saw that she, too, seemed surprised. But the still, linked circle produced a feeling of poignant significance and there was no need of words with it and a sensation of more than human contact in its solemnity.

After a most enjoyable luncheon, I went out and spent the afternoon enjoyably also, buying basketry and perfumes and trying to buy antiques, which is almost as much fun as really doing so. I visited the settlement of the "Chas-Chas"—the French fisherfolk who, for centuries, have lived a life apart from all the islanders. I viewed the Caribbean and the Atlantic simultaneously from the eminence of "Fairchild Place" and wished I could sit for weeks and do nothing else. I went to "Bluebeard's Tower" and the "Old Fort" and the old cemetery and the Moravian church and then I rejoined Mrs. Roosevelt; we said good-bye to our kind hosts and, surrounded by my precious packages, settled ourselves again in the waiting plane which, within an hour, had taken us back to *La Fortaleza*.

The next day I devoted to local sightseeing, which culminated in a moonlight visit to Morro Castle. Then, on Good Friday, after Signorina and I had viewed the processions—much more elaborate than those which had so intrigued me in San Germán—the Roosevelts joined us for a farewell picnic supper by the sea.

The following night, I was on board the freighter *Barbara* bound for home again. Though we ran into very rough weather, I did not let this keep me from writing during the day and playing bridge at night. As soon as we had docked in Philadelphia, I caught the first train I could for New York, where I spent the next two days in conferences with publishers and the evenings at the theater.

I reached Washington late Sunday, just in time to dress to go out for dinner, "and awfully glad to be back." Between then and the nineteenth of June, when Peter and I sailed for Europe, I was to leave home only three times: to speak at a "Pan-American Dinner" in Baltimore, to attend a business meeting of the Kenmore Association in Fredericksburg, and to visit Ottawa in connection with an article I was writing. In the meantime, though I was caught up in the usual round of luncheons, teas and dinners, I found I was spending more and more time at my desk, and realized this was the way it would have to be from now on.

Afterword

Afterword

F RANCES PARKINSON KEYES'S script ended here.
After serving three terms in the Senate, her husband retired in 1937, and died at Pine Grove Farm the next year. Mrs. Keyes continued to maintain her legal residence there, but following her mother's death in 1939, spent more and more time at The Oxbow, which had been willed to her for life.

Peter, like his brothers, was also graduated from Harvard and, after his marriage to Louise McNeil of Chestnut Hill in 1937, began teaching at the Westminster School in Simsbury, Connecticut. Henry, a Boston lawyer, married Betty Louise Main in Denver just before his father's death. John, the only one of the brothers to serve in our forces during World War II, was married, at London, to Alice Curley of Scranton in August, 1945; they were both lieutenants, he in the navy and she in the army.

The 1930's were no easier for Frances Parkinson Keyes than they were for many others. Fortunately, she was accustomed to earning money, but her writing was not as productive of income as she often could have wished. She ended her career as an associate editor of *Good Housekeeping* in 1935 and, in 1937, became editor of the *D.A.R. Magazine,* which she renamed *The National Historical Magazine,* and transformed into an embryonic *American Heritage*. This effort to broaden the magazine's scope did not find favor with ladies whose photographs, depicting them with be-ribboned, be-badged and be-corsaged bosoms dedicating an interminable succession of plaques, were no longer a feature; while Mrs. Keyes, on her part, became disenchanted with a budget which was less than the allowance for official flowers and did not provide for legal fees to collect overdue advertising charges. In vain, she pleaded with the society to pay secretarial salaries commensurate with those then current in Washington. The climax came when Marian Anderson's scheduled concert at Constitution Hall—owned by the Daughters of the American Revolution—was canceled. The latter may not have been to blame, but Mrs. Keyes thought they could and should have insisted that the concert take place there. She resigned as editor of the magazine and, with much regret, as a member of the organization. This incident is here recounted in detail because something of a mystery has been made of it before.

During her editorships, Mrs. Keyes had continued to write fiction, and the typescript of *Senator Marlowe's Daughter* had been delivered, and payments for subsidiary rights received by Horace Liveright, when the firm went into bankruptcy. Henry's mother summoned him to New York and together they took legal steps which failed to rescue the funds but did, pursuant to the original contract, retrieve the script. Julian Messner, who had been the Liveright editor working most closely with Mrs. Keyes, decided to found his own publishing house and *Senator Marlowe's Daughter* was the first book brought out by the new company. With it began a happy and profitable association which continued until his death in 1948, and was prolonged by his businesslike and astute widow. For many years, contracts contained little more than royalty schedules, standard clauses and essential dates for script deliveries and publication. Beginning in 1936, with *Honor Bright,* one best seller after another rolled from the pencil of Frances Parkinson Keyes and the presses devoted to Julian Messner, Inc. Problems were solved and differences of opinion reconciled over a good dinner in New York or Washington, or wherever Mrs. Keyes happened to be.

She reached a good many places. One of her bewildered schoolfriends invariably greeted Mrs. Keyes's son at church with the query: "Where is your mother now?"

She went to France to gather material for *Written in Heaven, Bernadette, Came a Cavalier* and *Steamboat Gothic;* to Germany for *The Great Tradition;* to Spain for *The Land of Stones and Saints, Station Wagon in Spain, The Third Mystic of Avila* and *I, the King.* She traveled to Greece and Jerusalem for *St. Anne: Grandmother of Our Saviour;* to Mexico for *The Grace of Guadalupe* and to Italy for *Mother Cabrini* and *Three Ways of Love.* She went to Ecuador and Peru for *The Rose and the Lily* and *The Explorer;* to England for *The Royal Box* and to Ireland for *The Heritage.*

Once she returned to the milieu of her school days to write fiction with a purpose. Cleveland Amory's *Proper Bostonians* and Marquand's perceptive *Late George Apley* had emphasized and perpetuated the

Yankee protestant, Ivy League tradition of Boston at the very time when Frances Parkinson Keyes thought recognition of others was long overdue and that Boston might have a future. Over a period of more than two years, with the assistance of Lee Barker of Doubleday, Charles Moorfield Storey, Esq., of Boston, the late Hermann B. Deutsch of the New Orleans *Item,* and her son Henry, a general plan was put together. During the summer of 1950 the book itself was written under severe pressure, in a suite at the Ritz-Carlton, where Henry joined his mother to help with local detail, legal background, and occasional tentative text of trials in court. In this novel, as in all her books, Frances Parkinson Keyes insisted on accuracy in every respect. If a character drove along a one-way street, he went in the right direction. If he took a streetcar, its route was correct. If he had a zoning problem, the applicable law was searched as for a client.

Joy Street was finished that fall while the first part was already being set for book and serial publication in both the United States and England. Later in the year, while lunching with Henry in Boston, Douglas Jerrold, Director of Eyre & Spottiswoode, Mrs. Keyes's British publishers, divulged that the sale of serial rights had been a near thing.

In consternation, Henry replied, "But I thought the first ten per cent came in."

"Oh, they're on now, but they were very nearly off. When they had only the first half of the script, they telephoned me and said, 'We have a question and must have the answer today, though we doubt whether we could obtain one today.' "

"Well," I said, "what is it?"

" 'We must know whether or not Mrs. Keyes's heroine was seduced.' "

"I can assure you," I told him, "that no matter how precarious her position may appear, in no circumstances is Mrs. Keyes's heroine ever seduced."

There was a change in this respect in Mrs. Keyes's later books! However, McGraw-Hill posed no similar questions and did not need to.

Perhaps the most important change in Mrs. Keyes's own life, next to her "gradual growth to Catholicism," as she preferred to describe it— she disliked the word "conversion"—was her move to Louisiana. She had first met Clarence Hewes, whose family lived in Jeanerette, Louisiana, in Peking, and when they renewed their acquaintance in Washington, where he had established his headquarters, he urged her to use his native state for her next *mise en scène. Crescent Carnival* was the result. This book was so successful that she developed a rhythm of alternating books about Louisiana with those in other settings, spending the late winter in New Orleans, the summer in Europe, and the latter part of the year in New England or South America. Hermann Deutsch was of great assistance to her, both in authenticating Louisiana backgrounds and as a genuinely severe, honest and constructive critic. He was especially helpful in plotting *Dinner at Antoine's.*

In 1942, Frances Parkinson Keyes rented a badly deteriorated Southern mansion near Baton Rouge on the River Road, and produced the book by that name. She kindly restored the property to its former beauty, knowing the investment would revert to the owner, but not that her expenditures would be questioned by the Internal Revenue Service. She bought, remodeled, lived in and later sold a house in the heart of Louisiana's rice country, the locale of *Blue Camellia,* which the Crowley *Daily Signal* praised as the most authentic book on the region.

Mrs. Keyes gradually developed a more permanent center in the New Orleans French Quarter at Beauregard House, which had been built by the maternal grandfather of the chess genius Paul Morphy, who, logically, became the leading character of *The Chess Players.* The house also provided the major setting for *Madame Castel's Lodger,* in which another famous Creole was the hero: General Pierre Gustave Toutant Beauregard, who resided in the mansion after the Civil War; and held the final review of his troops from its front gallery.

The property which, in addition to the main house, includes a rear patio, renovated slave quarters and a side garden, was eventually acquired by The Keyes Foundation, a charitable trust established by Mrs. Keyes in 1948 to help potential writers and to preserve structures of historical and architectural merit.

It was with great difficulty that Mrs. Keyes managed to return to New Orleans for the 1969–1970 winter. For many years, because of a back injury in the twenties, she had worn a steel brace; she was a victim of diverticulitis and suffered increasing pain from arthritis. She walked with two aluminum canes as best she could, with obvious strain on her breathing and heart rate. Determined, after a winter at patio level, to conquer at least one flight of stairs, she struggled, with assistance, to the dining room in the main house on successive days in April. She never could again. Writing less and less, dressing less and less, eating less and less, she died listening to the gentle flow of water in the fountain which had been brought all the way from Wells River, Vermont, at her instigation.

After a funeral mass in which her sons participated, she was buried beside her husband in the Keyes's lot adjoining the cemetery in Newbury, Vermont.

Frances Parkinson Keyes was survived by her three sons, ten grandchildren, two great-grandsons—and her books.

HENRY W. KEYES

Pine Grove Farm
September 3, 1971